P9-DMI-502

Microeconomics

Robert S. Pindyck
Massachusetts Institute of Technology

Daniel L. Rubinfeld
University of California, Berkeley

Microeconomics

Macmillan Publishing Company
New York

Collier Macmillan Publishers
London

To Our Daughters,

Maya, Talia, and Shira ▪ Sarah and Rachel

Copyright © 1989, Macmillan Publishing Company, a division of Macmillan, Inc.

Printed in the United States of America

All rights reserved. No part of this book may be reproduced or
transmitted in any form or by any means, electronic or mechanical,
including photocopying, recording, or any information storage and
retrieval system, without permission in writing from the publisher.

Macmillan Publishing Company
866 Third Avenue, New York, New York 10022

Collier Macmillan Canada, Inc.

Library of Congress Cataloging in Publication Data

Pindyck, Robert S.
  Microeconomics.

  Includes index.
  1. Microeconomics. I. Rubinfeld, Daniel L. II. Title.
HB172.P53   1989   338.5   88-1365
ISBN 0-02-395810-3

Printing: 1 2 3 4 5 6 7 8   Year: 9 0 1 2 3 4 5 6 7 8

Contents

*Sections marked with an asterisk are more demanding and can easily be omitted.

PART III MARKET STRUCTURE AND COMPETITIVE STRATEGY

PART IV INFORMATION, MARKET FAILURE, AND THE ROLE OF GOVERNMENT

LIST OF EXAMPLES

Preface

For students who care about how the world works, microeconomics is one of the most relevant and interesting subjects they study. A good grasp of microeconomics is vital for managerial decision making, for designing and understanding public policy, and more generally for appreciating how a modern economy functions.

We wrote this book, *Microeconomics,* because we believe that students need to be exposed to the new topics that have come to have a central role in microeconomics over the past few years—topics such as game theory and competitive strategy, the roles of uncertainty and information, and the analysis of pricing by firms with market power. We also felt that students need to be shown how microeconomics can be used as a tool for decision making. Microeconomics is an exciting and dynamic subject but students need to be given an appreciation of its relevance and usefulness. They want and need a good understanding of how microeconomics can actually be used outside the classroom.

To respond to these needs our book provides a fresh treatment of microeconomic theory, that stresses its relevance and application to both managerial and public-policy decision making. This applied emphasis is accomplished by including more than eighty extended examples that cover such topics as the analysis of demand, cost, and market efficiency, the design of pricing strategies, investment and production decisions, and public policy analysis. Because of the importance that we attach to these examples, they are included in the flow of the text, rather than being ''boxed'' or screened. (A list of the examples is included in the table of contents on pages xiv–xvi.)

The coverage in *Microeconomics* incorporates the dramatic changes that have occurred in the field in recent years. There is growing interest in game theory and the strategic interactions of firms (Chapters 12 and 13), in the role and implications of uncertainty and asymmetric information (Chapters 5 and 17), and in the pricing strategies of firms with market power (Chapters 10 and 11). These topics, which are missing or barely covered in most books, receive prominent attention here.

Because the coverage in *Microeconomics* is comprehensive and up-to-date, coverage does not mean that it is "advanced" or difficult. We have worked hard to make the exposition clear and accessible, as well as lively and engaging. We believe that the study of microeconomics should be enjoyable as well as stimulating. We hope that our book reflects this. Except for appendices and footnotes, *Microeconomics* uses no calculus. As a result, it should be suitable for students with a broad range of backgrounds. (Those sections that are more demanding are marked with an asterisk and can be easily omitted.)

Alternative Course Designs

Microeconomics offers instructors substantial flexibility in course design. For a one-quarter or one-semester course stressing the basic "core" material, we would suggest using the following chapters and sections of chapters: 1, 2, 3, 4.1-4.4, 6.1-6.5, 7.1-7.4, 8, 9.1-9.4, 10.1-10.4, 11.1-11.3, 12.1-12.2, 12.5-12.6, 14, 15.1-15.4, 18.1-18.2, and 18.5. A somewhat more ambitious course might also include parts of Chapters 5 and 16, and additional sections in Chapters 6, 7, 9, 10, and 12. To emphasize uncertainty and market failure, an instructor should also include substantial parts of chapters 5 and 17.

Depending on one's interests and the goals of the course, other sections could be added or used to replace the materials listed above. A course that emphasized modern pricing theory and business strategy would include all of Chapters 10, 11, 12, and 13, and the remaining sections of Chapter 15. A course in managerial economics might also include the Appendices to Chapters 4, 7, and 11, as well as the Appendix on regression analysis at the end of the book. A course that emphasized welfare economics and public policy should include Chapter 16 and additional sections of Chapter 18.

Supplementary Materials

We are fortunate to be able to offer instructional aids of exceptionally high quality. The Instructor's Manual, written by Geoffrey Rothwell of Stanford University, provides the answers to all of the Questions for Review and the Exercises that appear at the end of the chapters, as well as a summary of the key points in each chapter and a series of teaching suggestions. It is available from the publisher on request, as is a separate Test Bank. The Study Guide, by Richard Eastin of the University of Southern California, provides a wide variety of review materials and exercises for students. The study guide can be purchased separately. Finally, Arthur Lewbel of Brandeis University has developed an innovative software package that extends many of the examples, and reinforces an understanding of the concepts and their application by allowing the student to easily work through a number of simulation exercises. This software is also available for separate purchase.

Acknowledgments

Since this text has been the outgrowth of years of experience in the classroom, we owe a debt of gratitude to our students and to the colleagues with whom we often discuss microeconomics and its presentation. We have also had the help of capable research assistants, including Walter Athier, Phillip Gibbs, Kathy O'Regan, Karen Randig, and Subi Rangan. Kathy Hill helped with the art, while Assunta Kent, Mary Knott and Dawn Elliott Linahan provided secretarial assistance.

Writing this book has been a painstaking and enjoyable process. At each stage we received exceptionally fine guidance from teachers of microeconomics throughout the country. A first draft of several chapters and a detailed outline were extensively reviewed and edited. Then, a completed first draft was edited, reviewed,and discussed at a two-day focus group meeting in New York. This provided us with the opportunity to get ideas from instructors from a wide variety of backgrounds and perspectives. We would like to take this opportunity to thank the following members of the focus groups for advice and criticism: Carl Davidson of Michigan State University, Richard Eastin of the University of Southern California, Judith Roberts of Cal State Long Beach, and Charles Strein of the University of Northern Iowa.

The focus group meeting led naturally to a new and improved draft that was further reviewed and edited. We would like to thank all those who reviewed the manuscript at each stage of it's evolution:

Ted Amato, University of North Carolina, Charlotte
John J. Antel, University of Houston
Kerry Back, Northwestern University
Jeremy Bulow, Stanford University
Larry A. Chenault, Miami University
Jacques Cremer, VPI and State University
Carl Davidson, Michigan State University
Arthur T. Denzau, Washington University
Richard V. Eastin, University of Southern California
Harish C. Gupta, University of Nebraska, Lincoln
Jonathan H. Hamilton, University of Florida, Gainesville
George Heitman, Pennsylvania State University
George E. Hoffer, Virginia Commonwealth University
Robert Inman, University of Pennsylvania
B. Patrick Joyce, Michigan Technological University
Leonard Lardaro, University of Rhode Island
Peter Linneman, University of Pennsylvania
R. Ashley Lyman, University of Idaho
Wesley A. Magat, Duke University
Anthony M. Marino, University of Southern Florida
Michael J. Moore, Duke University

Daniel Orr, VPI and State University
Judith Roberts, Cal State Long Beach
Garth Saloner, Massachusetts Institute of Technology
Edward L. Sattler, Bradley University
Charles T. Strein, University of Northern Iowa
Michael Wasylenko, Syracuse University
Lawrence J. White, NYU

Apart from the formal review process, we are especially grateful to Ernst Berndt, Frank Fabozzi, Joseph Farrell, Robert Inman and Jeffrey Perloff, who were kind enough to provide comments, criticisms, and suggestions as our manuscript developed.

Finally, we wish to express our sincere thanks for the extraordinary effort those at Macmillan made in the development of our book. Bonnie Lieberman provided spiritual guidance and encouragement for the entire project; Ken MacLeod kept the progress of all aspects of the book on an even keel; Gerald Lombardi provided masterful editorial assistance and advice throughout the book's development; and John Molyneux ably oversaw the book's production.

Introduction: Microeconomics and Markets

Part I surveys the scope of microeconomics and introduces basic concepts and tools. Chapter 1 discusses the range of problems that microeconomics addresses, and the kinds of answers it can provide. It also explains the meaning of a market, and discusses the measurement of price.

Chapter 2 covers one of the most important tools of microeconomics: supply-demand analysis. We explain how a competitive market works, and how supply and demand determine the prices and quantities of goods. We also show how supply-demand analysis can be used to determine the effects of changing market conditions, including government intervention.

CHAPTER 1

Preliminaries

Economics is divided into two main branches: microeconomics and macroeconomics. Microeconomics deals with the behavior of individual economic units. These units include consumers, workers, investors, owners of land, business firms—in fact, any individual or entity that plays a role in the functioning of our economy.[1] Microeconomics explains how and why these units make economic decisions. For example, it explains how consumers make purchasing decisions and how their choices are affected by changing prices and incomes. It also explains how firms decide how many workers to hire and how workers decide where to work and how much work to do.

Another important concern of microeconomics is how economic units interact to form larger units—markets and industries. Microeconomics helps us to understand, for example, why the American automobile industry developed the way it did and how producers and consumers interact in the market for automobiles. It explains how automobile prices are determined, how much automobile companies invest in new factories, and how many cars are produced each year. By studying the behavior and interaction of individual firms and consumers, microeconomics reveals how industries and markets operate and evolve, why they differ from one another, and how they are affected by government policies and global economic conditions.

By contrast, macroeconomics, the other major branch of economics, deals with aggregate economic quantities, such as the level and growth rate of national output, interest rates, unemployment, and inflation. But the boundary between microeconomics and macroeconomics has become less and less distinct in recent years. The reason is that macroeconomics also involves the analysis of markets—the aggregate markets for goods and services, for labor, and for

---

[1]The prefix *micro-* is derived from the Greek word meaning "small." However, many of the individual economic units that we will study are small only in relation to the U.S. economy as a whole. For example, the annual sales of General Motors, IBM, or Exxon are larger than the gross national products of many countries.

corporate bonds, for example. To understand how these aggregate markets operate, one must first understand the behavior of the firms, consumers, workers, and investors who make up these markets. Thus, macroeconomists have become increasingly concerned with the microeconomic foundations of aggregate economic phenomena, and much of macroeconomics is actually an extension of microeconomic analysis.

1.1 The Use and Limitations of Microeconomic Theory

Like any science, economics is concerned with the *explanation* and *prediction* of observed phenomena. Why, for example, do firms tend to hire or lay off workers when the prices of raw materials needed in the production process change? How many workers are likely to be hired or laid off by a firm or an industry if the price of raw materials increases by, say, 10 percent?

In economics, as in other sciences, explanation and prediction are based on *theories*. Theories are developed to explain observed phenomena in terms of a set of basic rules and assumptions. The theory of the firm, for example, begins with a simple assumption—firms try to maximize their profits. The theory uses this assumption to explain how firms choose the amounts of labor, capital, and raw materials that they use for production, as well as the amount of output they produce. It also explains how these choices depend on the *prices* of inputs such as labor, capital, and raw materials, as well as the price the firm can receive for its output.

Economic theories are also the basis for making predictions. Thus, the theory of the firm tells us whether a firm's output level will increase or decrease in response to an increase in wage rates or a decrease in the price of raw materials. With the application of statistical and econometric techniques, theories can be used to construct *models*, from which quantitative predictions can be made. A model is a mathematical representation, based on economic theory, of a firm, a market, or some other entity. For example, we might develop a model of a particular firm and use it to predict by *how much* the firm's output level will change as a result of, say, a 10 percent drop in the price of raw materials.[2]

No theory, whether it be in economics, physics, or any other science, is perfectly correct. The usefulness and validity of a theory depend on whether it succeeds in explaining and predicting the set of phenomena that it is intended to explain and predict. Consistent with this goal, theories are continually tested against observation. As a result of this testing, theories are often modified or

---

[2]Statistics and econometrics also let us measure the *accuracy* of our predictions. For example, suppose we predict that a 10 percent drop in the price of raw materials will lead to a 5 percent increase in output. Are we sure that the increase in output will be exactly 5 percent, or might it be between 3 and 7 percent? Quantifying the accuracy of a prediction can be as important as the prediction itself.

refined and occasionally even discarded. The process of testing and refining theories is central to the development of economics as a science.

When evaluating a theory, it is important to keep in mind that it is invariably imperfect. This is the case in every branch of science. For example, in physics, Boyle's law relates the volume, temperature, and pressure of a gas.[3] The law is based on the assumption that individual molecules of a gas behave as though they were tiny, elastic billiard balls. Physicists today know that gas molecules do not, in fact, always behave like billiard balls, and partly because of this, Boyle's law breaks down under extremes of pressure and temperature. Nonetheless, under most conditions it does an excellent job of predicting how the temperature of a gas will change when the pressure and volume change, and it is therefore an essential tool for engineers and scientists.

The situation is much the same in economics. For example, firms do not maximize their profits all the time. Perhaps because of this, the theory of the firm has had only limited success in explaining certain aspects of firms' behavior, such as the timing of capital investment decisions. Nonetheless, the theory does explain a broad range of phenomena regarding the behavior, growth, and evolution of firms and industries, and it is an important tool for managers and policymakers.[4]

EXAMPLE 1.1   UNEMPLOYMENT AND THE LABOR FORCE PARTICIPATION OF WOMEN[5]

Women's participation in the labor force has increased rapidly since World War II, from 31.4 percent in 1950 to 54.5 percent by 1985. (A person participates in the labor force by either working or looking for work.) There are a number of economic reasons for this important change, but the question that concerns us is, *How should we expect the labor force participation rate of married women to change in response to changes in the unemployment rate?* (The unemployment rate is the number of unemployed people divided by the number of people in the labor force.)

People who are unemployed or who have dropped out of the labor force because they could not find suitable work are a cause for concern in our society.

---

[3]Robert Boyle (1627–1691) was a British chemist and physicist who discovered experimentally that pressure (P), volume (V), and temperature (T) were related in the following way: $PV = RT$, where R is a constant. Later, physicists derived this relationship as a consequence of the kinetic theory of gases, which describes the movement of gas molecules in statistical terms.

[4]A recent study shows that the managers of large American corporations are increasingly familiar with microeconomic concepts. See Giuseppe A. Forgionne, "Economic Tools Used by Management in Large American Operated Corporations," *Business Economics*, 19 (April 1984): 5–17.

[5]This example is based on an inspirational Princeton University lecture by William G. Bowen, as reported in "Economics 101 . . ." *Princeton Alumni Weekly*, November 19, 1963.

When the unemployment rate decreases, it is thus important to know whether it is the result of economic policies that reduce the number of people who are unemployed or because people have become frustrated and dropped out of the labor force by stopping their job search. Microeconomics lets us structure this problem in terms of two conflicting theories that can be empirically tested.

According to the *additional-worker theory*, a higher unemployment rate will lead to a *higher* labor force participation rate for married women because previously unemployed wives are forced to enter the labor force to support their families when husbands are unemployed. This theory suggests that a wife's decision to seek employment depends on total family income, not simply on the income she expects to earn. If high unemployment means less work for a husband, the likelihood that his wife will enter the labor force will increase.

By contrast, the *discouraged-worker theory* says that a higher unemployment rate will lead to a *lower* labor force participation rate for married women because people who might otherwise look for work will become discouraged and drop out of the labor force. This theory suggests that the most important determinant of a wife's decision to seek work is the tightness of the labor market, not her potential income. The tighter the market, the less likely she will make the effort.

Which of these two theories is correct? One way to find out is to examine data that relate the labor force participation rate for married women to the overall unemployment rate for different cities in the United States. A careful examination of the data for large cities shows that higher unemployment rates are associated with lower labor force participation rates. Specifically, for every 1 percent increase in the overall unemployment rate, the labor force participation rate of married women falls by 1.4 percent. Thus, the data support the discouraged-worker hypothesis and reject the additional-worker hypothesis.

But can we be certain that the second theory is right and the first wrong? After all, this negative relationship between the labor force participation rate and the unemployment rate might not hold for other cities or for other times. Or other unknown variables might explain the labor force participation rate of married women. The answer is that we can never prove that an economic theory is correct. We can either find more evidence to support the theory or we can use microeconomics to develop a more plausible theory, as we do, for example, in our analysis of the supply of labor in Chapter 14. In the case of married women, the evidence is quite strong—the discouraged-worker hypothesis has been supported by other, more sophisticated statistical analyses.[6]

[6]These analyses covered other time periods and included other variables. See William G. Bowen and T. Aldrich Finegan, *The Economics of Labor Force Participation* (Princeton, N.J.: Princeton University Press, 1969).

1.2   Positive Versus Normative Analysis

Microeconomics deals with both *positive* and *normative* questions. Positive questions have to do with explanation and prediction, normative questions with what ought to be. Suppose the U.S. government imposes a quota on the import of foreign cars. What will happen to the price of cars and to their production and sales? What impact will this have on American consumers? On workers in the automobile industry? These questions are all in the realm of positive analysis. Positive analysis is central to microeconomics. As we explained above, theories are developed to explain phenomena, are tested against observations, and are used to construct models from which predictions are made.

The use of economic theory for prediction is important both for the managers of firms and for public policy. Suppose a major new federal gasoline tax is under consideration. The tax would affect the price of gasoline, consumers' preferences for small versus large cars, the amount of driving that people do, and so on. To plan sensibly, oil companies, automobile companies, producers of automobile parts, and firms in the tourist industry would all want to know how large the various effects of this tax will be. Government policymakers also would need quantitative estimates of the effects of the tax. They would want to determine the costs imposed on consumers (perhaps broken down by income categories); the effects on profits in the oil, automobile, and tourist industries; and the amount of tax revenue likely to be collected each year.

Sometimes we want to go beyond explanation and prediction to ask questions such as "What is best?" This involves *normative* analysis, which is also important both for managers of firms and for designers of new public policies. Again, consider a new tax on gasoline. Automobile companies would want to determine the best (profit-maximizing) mix of large and small cars to produce once the tax is in place, or how much money should be invested to make cars more fuel-efficient. For policymakers, the primary issue is likely to be whether this tax is in the public interest. The same policy objectives (say, an increase in tax revenues and a decrease in our dependence on imported oil) might be met more cheaply with a different kind of tax, such as a tariff on imported oil.

Normative analysis is not only concerned with alternative policy options; it also involves the design of particular policy choices. For example, once it is decided that a gasoline tax is desirable, the issue becomes how large it should be. Balancing costs and benefits, we then ask what is the optimal size of a gasoline tax?

Normative analysis is often supplemented by value judgments. For example, a comparison between a gasoline tax and an oil import tariff might conclude that the gasoline tax is easier to administer but has a greater impact on lower-income consumers. At that point society must make a value judgment, weighing equity against economic efficiency.[7] When value judgments are involved, microeconomics cannot tell us what the best policy is. However, it can clarify the trade-offs and thereby help to illuminate and sharpen the debate.

1.3 Why Study Microeconomics?

We think that after reading this book, you will have no doubt about the importance and broad applicability of microeconomics. In fact, one of our major goals is to show you how to apply microeconomic principles to actual decision-making problems. Nonetheless, some extra motivation early on never hurts. Here are two examples that show the use of microeconomics in practice and also provide a preview of the book.

Corporate Decision Making: Ford Introduces the Taurus

In late 1985 Ford introduced the Taurus—a newly designed, aerodynamically styled front-wheel drive automobile. The car was a huge success and helped Ford almost to double its profits by 1987. The design and efficient production of this car involved some impressive engineering advances, but it also involved a lot of economics.

First, Ford had to think carefully about how well its new design would be accepted by the public. How would consumers be swayed by the styling and performance of the car? How strong would demand be initially, how fast would it grow, and how would demand depend on the price Ford charged? Understanding consumer preferences and trade-offs and predicting demand and its responsiveness to price were essential parts of the Taurus program. (We discuss consumer preferences and demand in Chapters 3, 4, and 5.)

Next, Ford had to be concerned with the cost of the car. How high would production costs be, and how would this depend on the number of cars Ford produced each year? How would costs be affected by union wage negotiations or by the prices of steel and other raw materials? How much and how fast would costs decline as managers and workers gained experience with the production process? And to maximize profits, how many cars should Ford plan to produce each year? (We will discuss production and cost in Chapters 6 and 7 and the profit-maximizing choice of output in Chapter 8.)

Ford also had to design a pricing strategy for the car and consider how its competitors would react to this strategy. For example, should Ford charge a low price for the basic stripped-down version of the car but high prices for individual

---

[7]Most of the value judgments involving economic policy decisions boil down to just this trade-off—equity versus economic efficiency. This conflict and its implications are discussed clearly and in depth in Arthur M. Okun, *Equality and Efficiency, The Big Tradeoff,* (Washington, D.C.: Brookings Institution, 1975).

options such as air conditioning and power steering? Or would it be more profitable to make these options "standard" items and charge a high price for the whole package? Whatever prices Ford chose, how were its competitors likely to react? Would GM and Chrysler try to undercut Ford by lowering prices? Might Ford be able to deter GM and Chrysler from lowering prices by threatening to respond with its own price cuts? (We will discuss pricing in Chapters 10 and 11 and competitive strategy in Chapters 12 and 13.)

The Taurus program required a large investment in new capital equipment, and Ford had to consider the risks involved and the possible outcomes. Some of this risk was due to uncertainty over the future price of gasoline (higher gasoline prices would shift demand to smaller cars), and some was due to uncertainty over the wages that Ford would have to pay its workers. What would happen if world oil prices doubled or tripled again, or if the government imposed a new tax on gasoline? How much bargaining power would the unions have, and how might this affect wage rates? How should Ford take these uncertainties into account when making its investment decisions? (Commodity markets and the effects of taxes are discussed in Chapters 2 and 9. Labor markets and union power are discussed in Chapter 14. Investment decisions and the role of uncertainty are discussed in Chapters 5 and 15.)

Ford also had to worry about organizational problems. Ford is an integrated firm—separate divisions produce engines and parts, then assemble finished cars. How should the managers of the different divisions be rewarded? What price should the assembly division be charged for engines it receives from another division? Should all the parts be obtained from the upstream divisions, or should some of them be purchased from outside firms? (We discuss internal pricing and organizational incentives for the integrated firm in Chapters 11 and 17.)

Finally, Ford had to think about its relationship to the government and the effects of regulatory policies. For example, the Taurus had to meet federal emission standards, and production line operations had to comply with health and safety regulations. How were these regulations and standards likely to change over time? How would they affect the company's costs and profits? (We discuss the role of government in limiting pollution and promoting health and safety in Chapter 18.)

Public Policy Design: Automobile Emission Standards

In 1970, the federal Clean Air Act imposed strict tail-pipe emission standards on new automobiles. These standards have become increasingly stringent, so that if the program reaches its desired goal in the 1990s, the 1970 levels of nitrogen oxides, hydrocarbons, and carbon monoxide emitted by automobiles will be reduced roughly 90 percent.

The design of a program like the Clean Air Act involves a careful analysis of the ecological and health effects of auto emissions. But it also involves a good deal of economics. First, the government has to evaluate the monetary impact of the program on consumers. The emission standards affect both the cost of purchasing a car (catalytic converters would be necessary, which would raise the cost of cars) and the cost of operating it (gas mileage would be lower and the catalytic converters would have to be repaired and maintained). Consumers ultimately bear much of this added cost, so it is important to know how it affects their standards of living. This requires an analysis of consumer preferences and demand. For example, would consumers drive less and spend more of their income on other goods? If so, would they be nearly as well off? (Consumer preferences and demand are discussed in Chapters 3 and 4.)

To answer these questions, the government needs to determine how the standards would affect the cost of producing cars. Might automobile producers use other materials to produce cars, so that cost increases would be small? (Production and cost are discussed in Chapters 6 and 7.) Then the government needs to know how the changes in production costs affect the level of production and the prices of new automobiles—are the additional costs absorbed or passed on to consumers in the form of higher prices? (Output determination is discussed in Chapter 8, and pricing in Chapters 10 through 13.)

Finally, the government needs to ask why the problems related to air pollution are not solved by our market-oriented economy. The answer is that much of the cost of air pollution is external to the firm. If firms do not find it in their self-interest to deal with auto emissions adequately, then what is the most appropriate way to alter their incentives? Should standards be set, or is it more economical to impose air pollution fees? How do we decide what people will pay to clean up the environment when there is no explicit market for clean air? Is the political process likely to solve these problems? The ultimate question is whether the auto emissions control program makes sense on a cost-benefit basis. Are the aesthetic, health, and other benefits of clean air worth the higher cost of automobiles? (These problems are discussed in Chapter 18.)

These are just two examples of how microeconomics can be applied; you will see more applications throughout this book. Many of these applications deal with markets and prices. These two words are a part of our everyday language, but it is important to be clear about what they mean in microeconomics.

1.4 Markets and Prices

We can divide individual economic units into two broad groups according to function—*buyers* and *sellers*. Buyers include consumers, who purchase goods and services, and firms, which buy labor, capital, and raw materials, which they use to produce goods and services. Sellers include firms, which sell their goods and services; workers who sell their labor services; and resource owners, who rent land or sell mineral resources to firms. Clearly, most people and most firms act as both buyers and sellers, but we will find it helpful to think of them as simply buyers when they are buying something, and sellers when they are selling something.

Together, buyers and sellers interact to form *markets*. *A market is a collection of buyers and sellers that interact, resulting in the possibility for exchange*. Note that a market includes more than an industry. An *industry* is a collection of firms that sell the same or closely related products. In effect, an industry is the supply side of the market.

Markets are at the center of economic activity, and many of the most interesting questions and issues in economics concern how markets work. For example, why do only a few firms compete with one another in some markets, while in other markets a great many firms compete? Are consumers necessarily better off if there are many firms? Is so, should the government intervene in markets with only a few firms? Why have prices in some markets risen or fallen rapidly, while in other markets prices have hardly changed at all? And which markets offer the best opportunities for an entrepreneur thinking of going into business?

Competitive Versus Noncompetitive Markets

In this book we study the behavior of both competitive and noncompetitive markets. A *prefectly competitive market* has many buyers and sellers, so that no single buyer or seller has a significant impact on price. Most agricultural markets are close to being perfectly competitive. For example, thousands of farmers produce wheat, which thousands of buyers purchase to produce flour and other foods. As a result, no single farmer and no single buyer can significantly affect the price of wheat.

Many other markets are competitive enough to be treated as if they were perfectly competitive. The world market for copper, for example, contains a few dozen major producers. That is enough for the impact on price to be small or unnoticeable if any one producer goes out of business. The same is true for many other mineral and natural resource markets, such as those for coal, iron, tin, or lumber.

Other markets containing only several producers may still be treated as competitive for purposes of analysis. For example, the airline industry in the United States contains several dozen firms, but most routes are served by only a few firms. Nonetheless, competition among those firms is often (but not always!) fierce enough, so that for some purposes (but not others) the market can be treated as competitive.[8] Finally, some markets contain many producers but are *noncompetitive*; that is, individual firms can affect the price of the product. The world oil market is one example; since the early 1970s, the market has been

---

[8] We will examine the U.S. airline industry in a series of examples throughout the book.

dominated by the OPEC cartel. (A *cartel* is a group of producers that act collectively.)

Real Versus Nominal Prices

Markets permit transactions between buyers and sellers: Quantities of a good are sold at specific prices. In a competitive market, a single price, which we refer to as the *market price*, usually prevails. Of course, the market price of a good can change over time, perhaps rapidly. The stock market, for example, is highly competitive—there are typically many buyers and sellers for any one stock. As anyone who has invested in the stock market knows, the price of any particular stock fluctuates from minute to minute and can rise or fall substantially during a single day. Similarly, the prices of such commodities as wheat, soybeans, coffee, oil, gold, silver, or lumber can also rise or fall dramatically in a day or a week.

We often want to compare the price of a good today with what it was in the past. Or we may ask how much higher or lower the price of a good is likely to be in the future. To make such a comparison meaningful, we need to measure prices relative to the overall price level. In absolute terms, the price of a dozen eggs is many times higher today than it was 50 years ago, but relative to prices overall, it is actually lower. Therefore, we must be careful to correct for inflation when comparing prices across time. This means measuring prices in *real* rather than *nominal* terms.

The *nominal price* of a good (sometimes called its "current dollar" price) is just its absolute price. For example, the nominal price of a gallon of gasoline was about 50 cents in 1972, about $1.50 in 1982, and about $1.00 in 1987. These are the prices you would have seen at gas stations in those years. The *real price* of a good (sometimes called its "constant dollar" price) is the price relative to an aggregate measure of prices, such as the Consumer Price Index (CPI). The CPI is calculated by the U.S. Bureau of Labor Statistics, which records how the cost of a large market basket of goods changes over time for a large sample of consumers.

After correcting for inflation, was gasoline more expensive in 1987 than in 1972? To find out, let's calculate the 1987 price of gasoline in terms of 1972 dollars. The CPI was 125.3 in 1972 and rose to about 337 in 1987.[9] (There was considerable inflation in the United States during the 1970s and early 1980s.) In 1972 dollars the price of gasoline was therefore

$$\frac{125.3}{337} \times \$1.00 = \$0.37$$

---

[9]Two good sources of data on the national economy are the *Economic Report of the President* and the *Statistical Abstract of the United States*. Both are published annually and are available from the U.S. Government Printing Office.

In real terms, the price of gasoline was lower in 1987 than it was in 1972. Put another way, the nominal price of gasoline went up by 100 percent, but the CPI went up by 169 percent, so that relative to inflation, gasoline prices fell.

In most of this book, we will usually be concerned with real, rather than nominal, prices because consumer choices involve an analysis of how one price compares with another. These relative prices can most easily be evaluated if there is a common basis of comparison. Stating all prices in real terms achieves this objective. Thus, even though we will often measure prices in dollars (or other currencies), we will be thinking in terms of the real purchasing power of those dollars.

EXAMPLE 1.2   THE PRICE OF EGGS AND THE PRICE OF A COLLEGE EDUCATION

In 1970 Grade A eggs cost about $0.61 a dozen. In the same year, the average cost of a college education in a private, four-year college was about $2,530.[10] By 1985 the price of eggs had risen to $0.80 a dozen, and the average price of a college education was $8,156. In real terms, were eggs more expensive in 1987 than in 1972? Had a college education become more expensive?

Table 1.1 shows the nominal price of eggs, the nominal cost of a college education, and the CPI for 1970–1985. (The CPI is based on 1967 = 100.) Also shown are the *real* prices of eggs and a college education, in 1970 dollars, calculated as follows:

$$\text{Real price of eggs in 1975} = \frac{\text{CPI}_{1970}}{\text{CPI}_{1975}} \times \text{nominal price of eggs in 1975,}$$

$$\text{Real price of eggs in 1980} = \frac{\text{CPI}_{1970}}{\text{CPI}_{1980}} \times \text{nominal price of eggs in 1980,}$$

and so forth.

TABLE 1.1 The Real Prices of Eggs and a College Education

	1970	1975	1980	1985
Nominal Prices				
Grade A Eggs	$0.61	$0.77	$0.84	$0.80
College Education	$2530	$3403	$4912	$8156
Consumer Price Index	116.3	161.2	246.8	322.2
Real Prices				
Grade A Eggs	$0.61	$0.55	$0.40	$0.29
College Education	$2530	$2455	$2315	$2944

[10]The data are from the *Statistical Abstract of the United States,* 1987, Tables No. 247 and 782.

The table shows clearly that the real cost of a college education rose (by 16 percent) during this period, while the real cost of eggs fell (by 53 percent). It is these relative changes in the prices of eggs and college that are important for the choices that consumers must make, not the fact that both eggs and college cost more in dollars today than they did in 1970.

Summary

1. Microeconomics is concerned with the decisions made by small economic units—consumers, workers, investors, owners of resources, and business firms. It is also concerned with the interaction of consumers and firms to form markets and industries.

2. Microeconomics relies heavily on the use of theory, which can (by simplification) help to explain how economic units behave and predict what that behavior will be in the future. Models are mathematical representations of theory that can help in this explanation and prediction process.

3. Microeconomics is concerned with positive questions that have to do with the explanation and prediction of phenomena. But microeconomics is also important for normative analysis, in which we ask what choices are best—for a firm or for society as a whole. Normative analyses must often be combined with individual value judgments, because issues of equity and fairness as well as economic efficiency may be involved.

4. A *market* refers to a collection of buyers and sellers who interact and the possibility for sales and purchases that results. Microeconomics involves the study of both perfectly competitive markets in which no single buyer or seller has an impact on price and noncompetitive markets in which individual entities can affect price.

5. To eliminate the effects of inflation, we measure real (or constant dollar) prices, rather than nominal (or current dollar) prices. Real prices use an aggregate price index such as the CPI to correct for inflation.

Questions for Review

1. What is the difference between a market and an industry? Are there interactions among firms in different industries that you might describe as taking place within a single market?

2. It is often said that a good theory is one that can in principle be refuted by an empirical, data-oriented study. Explain why a theory that cannot be evaluated empirically is not a good theory.

3. In Example 1.1, both the additional-worker and the discouraged-worker theories are economic in nature, because they reflect the responses of married women to the economic conditions that their husbands face in the market. Could it be that both theories are correct, but the additional-worker theory applies to certain households, and the discouraged-worker theory to others? If so, how might you figure out which theory applies to whom?

4. Which of the following two statements involves positive economic analysis and which normative? How do the two kinds of analysis differ?

a. Gasoline rationing (allocating to each individual a maximum amount of gasoline that can be purchased each year) is a poor social policy because it interferes with the workings of the competitive market system.

b. Gasoline rationing is a policy under which more people are made worse off than are made better off.

5. In Example 1.2, what economic forces explain why the real price of eggs has fallen, but the real price of a college education has increased? How do you think these changes have affected consumer choices?

6. Suppose that the Japanese yen grows in value in relation to the U.S. dollar. Explain why this simultaneously increases the real price of Japanese cars for U.S. consumers and lowers the real price of U.S. automobiles for Japanese consumers.

CHAPTER 2

The Basics of Supply and Demand

One of the best ways to appreciate the relevance of economics is to begin with the basics of supply and demand. Supply-demand analysis is a fundamental and powerful tool that can be applied to a wide variety of interesting and important problems. To name a few: understanding and predicting how changing world economic conditions affect market price and production; evaluating the impact of government price controls, minimum wages, price supports, and production incentives; and determining how taxes, subsidies, tariffs, and import quotas affect consumers and producers.

We begin with a review of how supply and demand curves are used to describe the market mechanism. Without government intervention (e.g., through the imposition of price controls or some other regulatory policy), supply and demand will come into equilibrium to determine the market price of a good and the total quantity produced. What that price and quantity will be depends on the particular characteristics of supply and demand. And how price and quantity vary over time depends on how supply and demand respond to other economic variables, such as aggregate economic activity, labor costs, etc., which are themselves changing.

We will therefore discuss the characteristics of supply and demand and how those characteristics may differ from one market to another. Then we can begin to use supply and demand curves to understand a variety of phenomena—why the prices of some basic commodities have fallen steadily over a long period, while the prices of others have experienced sharp gyrations; why shortages occur in certain markets; and why announcements about plans for future government policies or predictions about future economic conditions can affect markets well before those policies or conditions become reality.

Besides understanding *qualitatively* how market price and quantity are determined and how they can vary over time, it is also important to learn how they can be analyzed *quantitatively*. We will see how simple "back of the envelope" calculations (and sometimes more detailed calculations) can be used to analyze and predict evolving market conditions, and how markets respond both to domestic and international macroeconomic fluctuations and to the effects of government interventions. We will try to convey this understanding through simple examples and by urging you to work through some exercises at the end of the chapter.

2.1   The Market Mechanism

Let us begin with a brief review of the basic supply-demand diagram as shown in Figure 2.1. The vertical axis shows the price of a good, P, measured in dollars per unit. This is the price that sellers receive for a given quantity supplied and that buyers will pay for a given quantity demanded. The horizontal axis shows the total quantity demanded and supplied, Q, measured in number of units per period.

The *supply curve S* tells us how much producers are willing to sell for each price that they receive in the market. The curve slopes upward because the higher the price, the more firms are usually able and willing to produce and sell. For example, a higher price may enable existing firms to expand their annual rate of production in the short run by hiring extra workers or by having existing workers work overtime (at greater cost to the firm), and in the long run by increasing the size of their plants. A higher price may also attract into the market new firms that face higher costs because of their inexperience and that

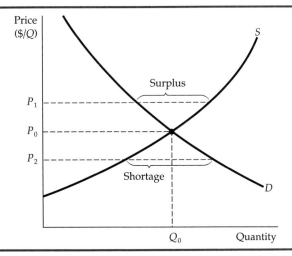

FIGURE 2.1   Supply and Demand.   The market clears at price P_0 and quantity Q_0. At the higher price P_1 a surplus develops, so price falls. At the lower price P_2 there is a shortage, so price is bid up.

therefore would have found entry into the market uneconomical at a lower price.

The *demand curve D* tells us how much consumers are willing to buy for each price per unit that they must pay. It slopes downward because consumers are usually ready to buy more if the price is lower. For example, a lower price may encourage consumers who have already been buying the good to consume a larger quantity, and it may enable other consumers who previously might not have been able to afford the good to begin buying it.

The two curves intersect at the *equilibrium*, or *market-clearing*, price and quantity. At this price P_0 the quantity supplied and the quantity demanded are just equal (Q_0). The *market mechanism* is the tendency in a free market for the price to change until the market clears (i.e., until the quantity supplied and the quantity demanded are equal). At this point there is neither shortage nor excess supply, so there is also no pressure for the price to change further. Supply and demand might not *always* be in equilibrium, and some markets might not clear quickly when conditions change suddenly, but the *tendency* is for markets to clear.

To understand why markets tend to clear, suppose the price were initially above the market clearing level, say, P_1 in Figure 2.1. Then producers would try to produce and sell more than consumers were willing to buy. A surplus would accumulate, and to sell this surplus or at least prevent it from growing, producers would begin to lower their prices. Eventually price would fall, quantity demanded would increase, and quantity supplied would decrease until the equilibrium price P_0 was reached.

The opposite would happen if the price were initially below P_0, say, at P_2. A shortage would develop because consumers would be unable to purchase all they would like at this price. This would put upward pressure on price as consumers tried to outbid one another for existing supplies and producers reacted by increasing price and expanding output. Again, the price would eventually reach P_0.

When we draw and use supply and demand curves, we are assuming that at any given price, a given quantity will be produced and sold. This makes sense only if a market is at least roughly *competitive*. By this we mean that both sellers and buyers should have little *market power* (i.e., little ability *individually* to affect the market price). Suppose instead that supply were controlled by a single producer—a monopolist. In this case there would no longer be a simple one-to-one relationship between price and quantity supplied. The reason is that a monopolist's behavior depends on the shape and position of the demand curve. If the demand curve shifted in a particular way, it might be in the monopolist's interest to keep the quantity fixed but change the price, or keep the price fixed and change the quantity. (How and why this could occur is explained in Chapter 10.) So as we draw supply and demand curves and move them around, we implicitly assume that we are referring to a competitive market.

2.2   Shifts in Supply and Demand

Supply and demand curves tell us how much competitive producers and con-sumers are willing to sell and buy as functions of the price they receive and pay. But supply and demand are also determined by other variables besides price. For example, the quantity that producers are willing to sell depends not only on the price they receive, but also on their production costs, including wages, interest charges, and costs of raw materials. And in addition to price, quantity demanded depends on the total disposable income available to con-sumers, and perhaps on other variables as well. Later we will want to determine how changes in economic conditions or tax or regulatory policy affect market prices and quantities. To do this, we must understand how supply and demand curves shift in response to changes in such variables as wage rates, capital costs, and income.

Let's begin with the supply curve S in Figure 2.2. This curve shows how much producers are willing to sell as a function of market price. For example, at a price P_1, the quantity produced and sold would be Q_1. Now suppose the costs of raw materials *fall*. How does this affect supply?

Lower raw materials costs, and for that matter lower costs of any kind, make production more profitable, encouraging existing firms to expand production and enabling new firms to enter the market and produce. So if the market price stayed constant at P_1, we would expect to observe a greater supply of output

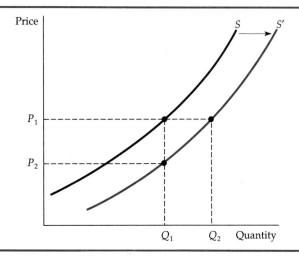

FIGURE 2.2   Shift in Supply. If production costs fall, firms can produce the same quantity at a lower price or a larger quantity at the same price. Supply curve shifts to the right.

than before. In Figure 2.2 this is shown as an increase from Q_1 to Q_2. Output increases no matter what the market price happens to be, *so the entire supply curve shifts to the right*, which is shown in the figure as a shift from S to S'.

Another way of looking at the effect of lower raw materials costs is to imagine that the quantity produced stays fixed at Q_1 and consider what price firms would require to produce this quantity. Because their costs are lower, the price they would require would also be lower—P_2 in Figure 2.2. This will be the case no matter what quantity is produced. Again, we see in the figure that the supply curve must shift to the right.

Of course, neither price nor quantity will always remain fixed when costs fall. Usually both will change as the new supply curve comes into equilibrium with the demand curve. This is illustrated in Figure 2.3, where the supply curve has shifted from S to S' as it did in Figure 2.2 As a result, the market price drops (from P_1 to P_3), and the total quantity produced increases (from Q_1 to Q_3). This is just what we would expect: Lower costs result in lower prices and increased sales. (And indeed, gradual decreases in costs resulting from technological progress and better management are an important driving force behind economic growth.)

Now let's turn to Figure 2.4 and the demand curve labeled D. How would an *increase in disposable income* affect demand?

With greater disposable income, consumers can spend more money on any good, and some consumers will do so for most goods. If the market price were held constant at P_1, we would therefore expect to see an increase in quantity demanded, say, from Q_1 to Q_2. This would happen no matter what the market

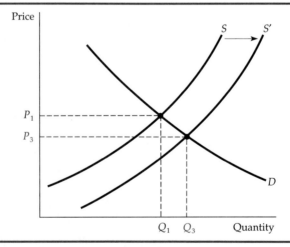

FIGURE 2.3 New Equilibrium Following Shift in Supply. When the supply curve shifts to the right, the market clears at a lower price P_2 and a larger quantity Q_2.

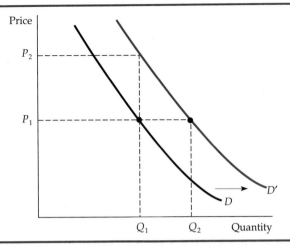

FIGURE 2.4   Shift in Demand.   The demand for a product depends on its price but may also depend on other variables, such as income, the weather, and the prices of other goods. For most products, demand increases when income rises. A higher income level shifts the demand curve to the right.

price was, so that the result would be a *shift to the right of the entire demand curve*. In the figure, this is shown as a shift from D to D'. Alternatively, we can ask what price consumers would pay to purchase a given quantity Q_1. With greater disposable income, they should be willing to pay a higher price, say, P_2 instead of P_1 in Figure 2.4. Again, *the demand curve will shift to the right*.

In general, neither price nor quantity remains constant when disposable income increases. A new price and quantity result after demand comes into equilibrium with supply. As shown in Figure 2.5, we would expect to see consumers pay a higher price P_3 and firms produce a greater quantity Q_3 as a result of an increase in disposable income.

Changes in the prices of related goods also affect demand. For example, copper and aluminum are substitute goods. Because one can often be substituted for the other in industrial use, the demand for copper will increase if the price of aluminum increases. Automobiles and gasoline, on the other hand, are complementary goods (i.e., they tend to be used together). Therefore a decrease in the price of gasoline increases the demand for automobiles. So the shift to the right of the demand curve in Figure 2.5 could also have resulted from an increase in the price of a substitute good or from a decrease in the price of a complementary good.

In most markets both the demand and supply curves shift from time to time. Consumers' disposable incomes change as the economy grows (or, during economic recessions, contracts). The demands for some goods shift with the sea-

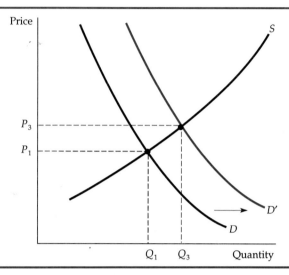

FIGURE 2.5   New Equilibrium Following Shift in Demand.   When the demand curve shifts to the right, the market clears at a higher price P_2 and a larger quantity Q_2.

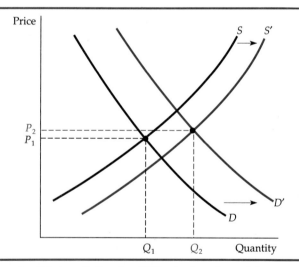

FIGURE 2.6   New Equilibrium Following Shifts in Supply and Demand.   Supply and demand curves shift over time as market conditions change. In this example, rightward shifts of the supply and demand curves lead to slightly higher price and a much larger quantity. In general, changes in price and quantity depend on the amount by which each curve shifts and the shape of each curve.

sons (e.g., fuels, bathing suits, umbrellas), with changes in the prices of related goods (an increase in oil prices increases the demand for natural gas), or simply with changing tastes. Similarly wage rates, capital costs, and the prices of raw materials also change from time to time, which shifts supply.

Supply and demand curves can be used to trace the effects of these changes. In Figure 2.6, for example, shifts to the right of both supply and demand result in a slightly higher price (from P_1 to P_2) and a much larger quantity (from Q_1 to Q_2). In general, price and quantity will change depending both on how much the supply and demand curves shift and on the shapes of those curves. To predict the sizes and directions of such changes, we must be able to quantitatively characterize the dependence of supply and demand on price and other variables. We will turn to this in the next section.

EXAMPLE 2.1 THE LONG-RUN BEHAVIOR OF MINERAL PRICES

The early 1970s was a period of "consciousness raising" about the earth's natural resources. Groups like the Club of Rome predicted that our energy and mineral resources would soon be depleted, so that prices would skyrocket and end economic growth.[1] But these predictions ignored basic microeconomics. The earth does indeed have only a finite amount of minerals such as copper, iron, and coal. Yet during the past century, the prices of these and most other minerals have declined or remained roughly constant relative to overall prices. For example, Figure 2.7 shows the price of iron in real terms (adjusted for inflation), together with iron consumption for 1880 to 1985. (Both are shown as an index, with 1880 = 1.) Despite short-term variations in price, no significant long-term increase has occurred, even though annual consumption is now about 20 times greater than in 1880. Similar patterns hold for other mineral resources, such as copper, oil, and coal.[2]

The demands for these resources grew along with the world economy. (These shifts in the demand curve are illustrated in Figure 2.8.) But as demand grew, production costs fell. This was due first to the discovery of new and bigger deposits, which were cheaper to mine, and then to technical progress and the economic advantage of mining and refining on a large scale. As a result, the

---

[1]See, for example, Dennis Meadows et al., *The Limits to Growth* (New York: Potomac Associates, 1972). This book and others like it struck a resonant chord in the public consciousness. Unfortunately these studies ignored such basic economic phenomena as cost reduction resulting from technical progress, experience, and economies of scale, and substitution of alternative resources (including nondepletable ones) in response to higher prices. For a discussion of these issues, see Julian L. Simon, *The Ultimate Resource* (Princeton, N.J.: Princeton University Press, 1981).

[2]The data in Figure 2.7 are from Robert S. Manthy, *Natural Resource Commodities—A Century of Statistics* (Baltimore: Johns Hopkins University Press, 1978), supplemented after 1973 with data from the U.S. Bureau of Mines.

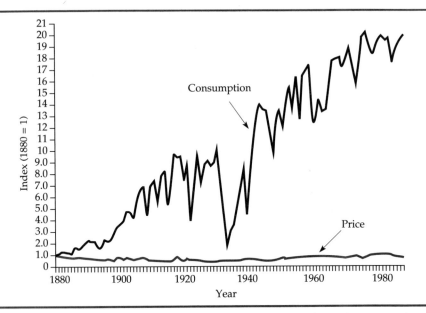

FIGURE 2.7 Consumption and Price of Iron, 1880–1985. Annual consumption has increased about twentyfold, but the real (inflation-adjusted) price has not changed much.

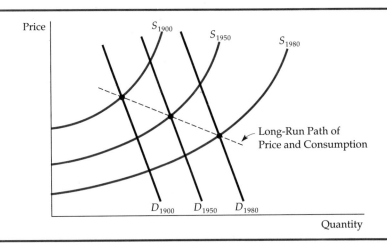

FIGURE 2.8 Long-Run Movements of Supply and Demand for Mineral Resources. Demand for most resources has increased dramatically over the past century, but prices have fallen or risen only slightly in real (inflation-adjusted) terms because cost reductions have shifted the supply curve to the right just as dramatically.

supply curve shifted to the right over time. Over the long term, these shifts in the supply curve were greater than the shifts in the demand curve, so that price often fell, as shown in Figure 2.8.

This is not to say that the prices of copper, iron, and coal will decline or remain constant forever—these resources are *finite*. But it is likely that as their prices begin to rise, consumption will shift at least in part to substitute materials. For example, copper has already been replaced in many applications by aluminum, and more recently in electronic applications by fiber optics. (See Example 2.5 for a more detailed discussion of copper prices.)

EXAMPLE 2.2   THE MARKET FOR WHEAT

Wheat is an important agricultural commodity, and the market for it has been studied extensively by agricultural economists. During the 1980s, important changes in the wheat market have occurred that have had major implications for American farmers and for U.S. agricultural policy. To understand what has happened, let us examine the behavior of supply and demand.

From statistical studies, we know that for 1981 the supply curve for wheat was approximately as follows[3]:

$$Supply: \qquad Q_S = 1800 + 240P$$

where price is measured in dollars per bushel and quantities are in millions of bushels per year. These studies also indicate that in 1981 the demand curve for wheat was

$$Demand: \qquad Q_D = 3550 - 266P$$

By setting supply equal to demand, we can determine the market-clearing price of wheat for 1981:

$$Q_S = Q_D$$

$$1800 + 240P = 3550 - 266P$$

$$506P = 1750$$

$$P = \$3.46 \text{ per bushel}$$

The demand for wheat has two components—domestic demand (i.e., demand by U.S. consumers) and export demand (i.e., demand by foreign con-

---

[3]For a survey of statistical studies of the demand and supply of wheat and an analysis of evolving market conditions, see Larry Salathe and Sudchada Langley, "An Empirical Analysis of Alternative Export Subsidy Programs for U.S. Wheat," *Agricultural Economics Research* 38, No. 1 (winter 1986). The supply and demand curves in this example are based on the studies they survey.

sumers). By the mid-1980s the domestic demand for wheat had risen only slightly (due to modest increases in population and income), but export demand had fallen sharply and appeared likely to continue to fall. Export demand had dropped for several reasons. First and foremost was the success of the Green Revolution in agriculture—developing countries like India that had been large importers of wheat became increasingly self-sufficient. On top of this, the increase in the value of the dollar against other currencies made U.S. wheat more expensive abroad. Finally, European countries adopted protectionist policies that subsidized their own production and imposed tariff barriers against imported wheat. In 1985, for example, the demand curve for wheat was

Demand: $\qquad Q_D = 2580 - 194P$

(The supply curve remained more or less the same as in 1981.)

Now we can again equate supply and demand and determine the market-clearing price for 1985:

$$1800 + 240P = 2580 - 194P$$

$$P = \$1.80 \text{ per bushel}$$

We see, then, that the major shift in export demand led to a sharp drop in the market-clearing price of wheat—from \$3.46 in 1981 to \$1.80 in 1985.

Was the price of wheat actually \$3.46 in 1981, and did it actually fall to \$1.80 in 1985? No—consumers paid about \$3.70 in 1981 and about \$3.20 in 1985. Furthermore, in both years American farmers received more than \$4 for each bushel they produced. Why? Because the U.S. government props up the price of wheat and pays subsidies to farmers. We will see exactly how this is done and evaluate the costs and benefits for consumers, farmers, and the federal budget in Chapter 9.

2.3 Elasticities of Supply and Demand

We have seen that the demand for a good depends on its price, as well as on consumer income and on the prices of other goods. Similarly, supply depends on price, as well as on variables that affect production cost. For example, if the price of coffee increases, the quantity demanded will fall and the quantity supplied will rise. Often, however, we want to know *how much* supply or demand will rise or fall. How sensitive is the demand for coffee to its price? If price increases by 10 percent, how much will demand change? How much will demand change if income rises by 5 percent? We use *elasticities* to answer questions like these.

An elasticity is a measure of the sensitivity of one variable to another. Specifically, it is a number that tells us *the percentage change that will occur in one variable in response to a 1 percent change in another variable.* An important example is the *price elasticity of demand,* which measures the sensitivity of quantity demanded to price changes. It tells us what the percentage change in the quantity demanded for a good will be following a 1 percent increase in the price of that good.

Let's look at this in a little more detail. Denoting quantity and price by Q and P, we write the price elasticity of demand as

$$E_p = (\%\Delta Q)/(\%\Delta P)$$

where "$\%\Delta Q$" simply means "percentage change in Q" and $\%\Delta P$ means "percentage change in P."[4] But the percentage change in a variable is just the absolute change in the variable divided by the original level of the variable. (If the Consumer Price Index were 200 at the beginning of the year and increased to 204 by the end of the year, the percentage change—or annual rate of inflation— would be 4/200 = .02, or 2 percent.) So we can also write the price elasticity of demand as[5]

$$E_p = \frac{\Delta Q/Q}{\Delta P/P} = \frac{P}{Q}\frac{\Delta Q}{\Delta P} \tag{2.1}$$

The price elasticity of demand is usually a negative number. When the price of a good increases, the quantity demanded usually falls, so $\Delta Q/\Delta P$ (the change in quantity for a change in price) is negative, and therefore E_p is negative.

Equation (2.1) says that the price elasticity of demand is the change in quantity associated with a change in price ($\Delta Q/\Delta P$) times the ratio of price to quantity (P/Q). But as we move down the demand curve, $\Delta Q/\Delta P$ may change, and the price and quantity will always change. Therefore, the price elasticity of demand must be measured *at a particular point on the demand curve* and will generally change as we move along the curve.

This is easiest to see for a *linear* demand curve, that is, a demand curve of the form

$$Q = a - bP$$

For this curve, $\Delta Q/\Delta P$ is constant and equal to $-b$ (a ΔP of 1 results in a ΔQ of $-b$). However, the curve does *not* have a constant elasticity. Observe from Figure 2.9 that as we move down the curve, the ratio P/Q falls, and therefore the elasticity decreases in magnitude. Near the intersection of the curve with the price axis, Q is very small, so $E_p = -b(P/Q)$ is large in magnitude. When $P = a/2b$ and $Q = a/2$, $E_p = -b(a/2b)(2/a) = -b/b = -1$. And at the intersection with the quantity axis, $P = 0$ so $E_p = 0$.

Because we draw demand (and supply) curves with price on the vertical axis and quantity on the horizontal axis, $\Delta Q/\Delta P = (1/\text{slope of curve})$. As a result,

---

[4]The symbol Δ is the Greek capital letter delta; it means "the change in." So ΔX means "the change in the variable X," say, from one year to the next.

[5]In terms of infinitesimal changes (letting the ΔP become very small), $E_p = (P/Q)(dQ/dP)$.

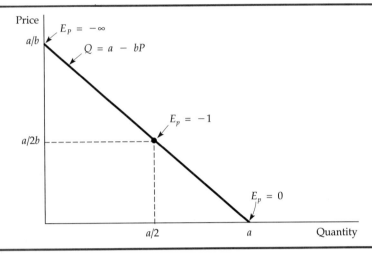

FIGURE 2.9 Linear Demand Curve. The price elasticity of demand depends not only on the slope of the demand curve, but also on the price and quantity. The elasticity therefore varies along the curve as price and quantity change. Slope is constant for this linear demand curve. Near the top of the curve, price is high and quantity is small, so the elasticity is large. The elasticity becomes smaller as we move down the curve.

for any price and quantity combination, the steeper the slope of the curve, the less elastic demand is. Figures 2.10a and b show two special cases. Figure 2.10a shows a demand curve that is *infinitely elastic*. There is only a single price P^* at which consumers will buy the good; for even the smallest increase in price above this level, quantity demanded drops to zero, and for any decrease in price, quantity demanded increases without limit. The demand curve in Figure 2.10b, on the other hand, is *completely inelastic*. Consumers will buy a fixed quantity Q^*, no matter what the price.

We will also be interested in elasticities of demand with respect to other variables besides price. For example, demands for most goods usually rise when aggregate income rises. The *income elasticity of demand* is the percentage change in the quantity demanded Q resulting from a 1 percent increase in income I:

$$E_I = \frac{\Delta Q/Q}{\Delta I/I} = \frac{I}{Q}\frac{\Delta Q}{\Delta I} \tag{2.2}$$

The demands for some goods are also affected by the prices of other goods. For example, because butter and margarine can easily be substituted for each other, the demand for each depends on the price of the other. A *cross-price elasticity of demand* refers to the percentage change in the quantity demanded for a good that results from a 1 percent increase in the price of another good.

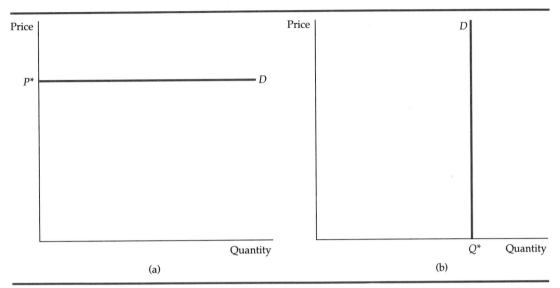

FIGURE 2.10a Infinitely Elastic Demand. For a horizontal demand curve, $\Delta Q/\Delta P$ is infinite. (A tiny change in price leads to an enormous change in demand.) The elasticity of demand is therefore infinite.

FIGURE 2.10b Completely Inelastic Demand. For a vertical demand curve, $\Delta Q/\Delta P$ is zero. The quantity demanded is the same no matter what the price, so the elasticity of demand is zero.

So the elasticity of demand for butter with respect to the price of margarine would be written as

$$E_{P_m} = \frac{\Delta Q_b/Q_b}{\Delta P_m/P_m} = \frac{P_m}{Q_b}\frac{\Delta Q_b}{\Delta P_m} \tag{2.3}$$

where Q_b is the quantity of butter and P_m is the price of margarine.

In this example of butter and margarine, the cross-price elasticities will be positive because the goods are *substitutes*—they compete in the market, so a rise in the price of margarine, which makes butter cheaper relative to margarine than it was before, leads to an increase in the demand for butter. (The demand curve for butter will shift to the right, so its price will rise.) But this is not always the case. Some goods are *complements*; they tend to be used together, so that an increase in the price of one tends to push down the consumption of the other. Gasoline and motor oil are an example. If the price of gasoline goes up, the quantity of gasoline demanded falls—motorists will drive less. But the demand for motor oil also falls. (The entire demand curve for motor oil shifts to the left.) Thus, the cross-price elasticity of motor oil with respect to gasoline is negative.

Elasticities of supply are defined in a similar manner. The *price elasticity of supply* is the percentage change in the quantity supplied resulting from a 1 percent increase in price. This elasticity is usually positive because a higher price gives producers an incentive to increase output.

We can also refer to elasticities of supply with respect to such variables as interest rates, wage rates, and the prices of raw materials and other intermediate goods used to manufacture the product in question. For example, for most manufactured goods, the elasticities of supply with respect to the prices of raw materials are negative. An increase in the price of a raw material input means higher costs for the firm, so other things being equal, the quantity supplied will fall.

2.4 Short-Run Versus Long-Run Elasticities

When analyzing demand and supply, it is important to distinguish between the short run and the long run. In other words, if we ask how much demand or supply changes in response to a change in price, we must be clear about *how much time is allowed to pass before measuring the changes in the quantity demanded or supplied*. If we allow only a short time to pass, say, one year or less, then we are dealing with short-run demand or supply. In general, short-run demand and supply curves look very different from their long-run counterparts.

Demand

For many goods, demand is much more price elastic in the long run than in the short run. One reason is that people take time to change their consumption habits. For example, even if the price of coffee rises sharply, the quantity demanded will fall only gradually as consumers slowly begin to drink less of it. Another reason is that the demand for a good might be linked to the stock of another good, which changes only slowly over time. For example, the demand for gasoline is much more elastic in the long run than in the short run. A sharply higher price of gasoline reduces the quantity demanded in the short run by causing motorists to drive less, but it has its greatest impact on demand by inducing consumers to buy smaller and more fuel-efficient cars. But the stock of cars changes only slowly, so that the quantity of gasoline demanded falls only slowly. (We hope this is more obvious to you than it was to the OPEC cartel.) Figure 2.11a illustrates short-run and long-run demand curves for goods such as these.

On the other hand, for some goods just the opposite is true—demand is more elastic in the short run than in the long run. These goods (automobiles, refrigerators, televisions, or the capital equipment purchased by industry) are *durable*, so that the total stock of each good owned by consumers is large relative to the annual production. As a result, a small change in the total stock that consumers want to hold can result in a large percentage change in the level of

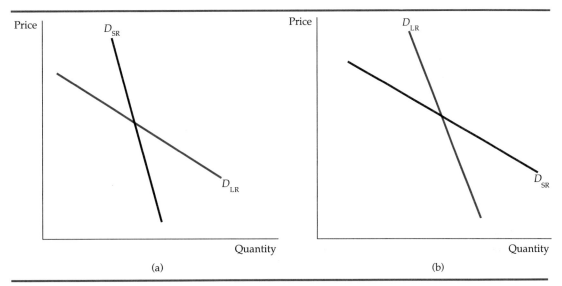

FIGURE 2.11a Gasoline: Short-Run and Long-Run Demand Curves. In the short run an increase in price has only a small effect on the demand for gasoline. Motorists may drive less, but they will not change the kind of car they are driving overnight. In the longer run, however, they will shift to smaller and more fuel-efficient cars, so the effect of the price increase will be larger. Demand is therefore more elastic in the long run than in the short run.

FIGURE 2.11b Automobiles: Short-Run and Long-Run Demand Curves. The opposite is true for automobile demand. If price increases, consumers initially defer buying a new car, so that annual demand falls sharply. In the longer run, however, old cars wear out and must be replaced, so that annual demand picks up. Demand is therefore less elastic in the long run than in the short run.

purchases. Suppose, for example, that price goes up 10 percent, causing the total stock of the good consumers want to hold to drop 5 percent. Initially, this will cause purchases to drop much more than 5 percent. But eventually, as the stock depreciates (and units must be replaced), demand will increase again, so that in the long run the total stock of the good owned by consumers will be about 5 percent less than before the price increase.

Automobiles provide an example. (Annual U.S. demand—new car purchases—is about 7 to 10 million, but the stock of cars is around 70 million.) If the price of automobiles rises, many people will delay buying new cars, and the quantity demanded will fall sharply (even though the total stock of cars that consumers want to hold falls only a small amount). But eventually, old cars wear out and have to be replaced, so demand picks up again. As a result, the long-run change in the quantity demanded is much smaller than the short-run change. Figure 2.11b illustrates demand curves for a durable good like auto-mobiles.

Income elasticities also differ from the short run to the long run. For most goods and services—foods, beverages, fuel, entertainment, etc.—the income elasticity of demand is larger in the long run than in the short run. For example, consider the behavior of gasoline consumption during a period of strong economic growth when aggregate income rises by 10 percent. Eventually people will increase their gasoline consumption—they can afford to take more trips and perhaps own a larger car. But this change in consumption takes time, and initially demand increases only a small amount. Thus, the long-run elasticity will be larger than the short-run elasticity.

For a durable good the opposite is true. Again, take automobiles as an example. If aggregate income rises by 10 percent, the stock of cars that consumers will want to hold will also rise, say, by 5 percent. But this means a much larger increase in *current purchases* of cars. (If the stock is 70 million, a 5 percent increase

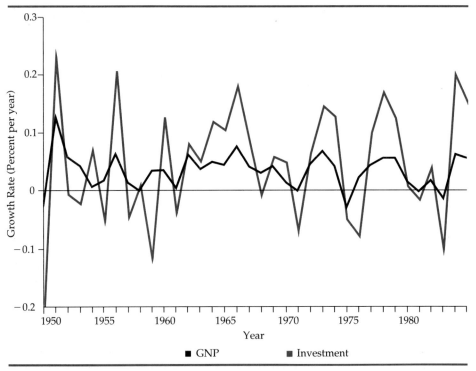

FIGURE 2.12 GNP and Investment in Durable Equipment. Annual growth rates are compared for GNP and investment in durable equipment. The short-run GNP elasticity of demand is larger than the long-run elasticity for long-lived capital equipment, so changes in investment in equipment magnify changes in GNP. Hence, capital goods industries are considered "cyclical."

is 3.5 million, which might be about 50 percent of normal demand in a single year.) Eventually consumers succeed in building up the stock of cars, after which new purchases are largely to replace old cars. (These new purchases will still be greater than before because with a larger stock of cars outstanding, more cars need to be replaced each year.) Clearly, the short-run income elasticity of demand will be much larger than the long-run elasticity.

Because the demands for durable goods fluctuate so sharply in response to short-run changes in income, the industries that produce these goods are very vulnerable to changing macroeconomic conditions, and in particular to the business cycle—recessions and booms. Hence, these industries are often called *cyclical* industries—their sales tend to magnify cyclical changes in gross national product (GNP) and national income.

Figures 2.12 and 2.13 illustrate this. Figure 2.12 plots two variables over time,

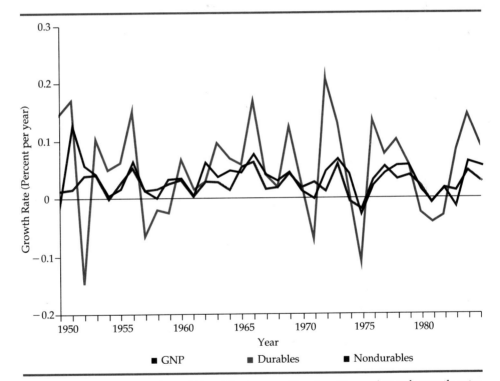

FIGURE 2.13 Consumption of Durables versus Nondurables. Annual growth rates are compared for GNP, consumer expenditures on durable goods (automobiles, appliances, furniture, etc.), and consumer expenditure on nondurable goods (food, clothing, services, etc.). The stock of durables is large compared with annual demand, so short-run demand elasticities are larger than long-run elasticities. Like capital equipment, industries that produce consumer durables are "cyclical" (i.e., changes in GNP are magnified). This is not true for nondurables.

the annual real (inflation-adjusted) rate of growth of GNP, and the annual real rate of growth of investment in producers' durable equipment (i.e., heavy equipment purchased by manufacturing industries). Note that the durable equipment series follows the same pattern as the GNP series, but the changes in GNP are magnified. For example, in 1961–1966 GNP grew by at least 4 percent each year. Purchases of durable equipment also grew but by much more (over 10 percent in 1962–1965). On the other hand, during the recessions of 1974–1975 and 1982 purchases of durable equipment fell by much more than GNP.

Figure 2.13 also shows the real rate of growth of GNP, and in addition, the annual real rates of growth of spending by consumers on durable goods (automobiles, applicances, etc.), and on nondurable goods (food, fuel, clothing, etc.). Note that both consumption series follow GNP, but only the durable goods series tends to magnify the changes in GNP. Changes in consumption of nondurables are roughly the same as changes in GNP, but changes in consumption of durables are usually several times larger. It should be clear from this why companies such as General Motors and General Electric are considered "cyclical"—sales of cars and electrical appliances are strongly affected by changing macroeconomic conditions.

EXAMPLE 2.3   THE DEMANDS FOR GASOLINE AND AUTOMOBILES

Gasoline and automobiles exemplify some of the different characteristics of demand discussed above. They are complementary goods—an increase in the price of one tends to reduce the demand for the other. And their respective dynamic behaviors (long-run versus short-run elasticities) are just the opposite from each other—for gasoline the long-run price and income elasticities are larger than the short-run elasticities, and for automobiles the reverse is true.

There have been a number of statistical studies of the demands for gasoline and automobiles. Here we report estimates of price and income elasticities from two studies that emphasize the dynamic response of demand.[6] Table 2.1 shows price and income elasticities of demand for gasoline in the United States for the short run, the long run, and just about everything in between.

Note the large differences between the long-run and the short-run elasticities. Following the sharp increases that occurred in the price of gasoline with the rise of the OPEC cartel in 1974, many people (including executives in the automobile and oil industries) claimed that the demand for gasoline would not change much—that demand was not very elastic. Indeed, for the first year after

---

[6]The study of gasoline demand is in Robert S. Pindyck, *The Structure of World Energy Demand* (Cambridge, Mass.: MIT Press, 1979). The estimates of automobile demand elasticities are based on the article by Saul H. Hymans, "Consumer Durable Spending: Explanation and Prediction," *Brookings Papers on Economic Activity* 1(1971): 173–199.

TABLE 2.1 Demand for Gasoline

Elasticity	Years Following Price or Income Change					
	1	2	3	5	10	20
Price	−0.11	−0.22	−0.32	−0.49	−0.82	−1.17
Income	0.07	0.13	0.20	0.32	0.54	0.78

the price rise, they were right—the quantity demanded did not change much. But demand did eventually change. It just took time for people to alter their driving habits and to replace large cars with smaller and more fuel-efficient ones. This response continued after the second sharp increase in oil prices that occurred in 1979–1980. It is partly because of this that OPEC could not maintain oil prices above $30 per barrel, and prices fell.

Table 2.2 shows price and income elasticities of demand for automobiles. Note that the short-run elasticities are much larger than the long-run elasticities. It should be clear from the income elasticities why the automobile industry is so highly cyclical. For example, GNP fell by nearly 3 percent in real (inflation-adjusted) terms during the 1982 recession, but automobile sales fell by about 8 percent in real terms.[7] Auto sales recovered, however, during 1983–1984.

TABLE 2.2 Demand for Automobiles

Elasticity	Years Following Price or Income Change					
	1	2	3	5	10	20
Price	−1.20	−0.93	−0.75	−0.55	−0.42	−0.40
Income	3.00	2.33	1.88	1.38	1.02	1.00

Supply

Elasticities of supply also differ from the long run to the short run. For most products, long-run supply is much more price elastic than short-run supply because firms face *capacity constraints* in the short run and need time to expand

[7]This includes imports, which were capturing a growing share of the U.S. market. Domestic auto sales fell by even more.

their capacity by building new production facilities and hiring workers to staff them. This is not to say that supply will not increase in the short run if price goes up sharply. Even in the short run, firms can increase output by using their existing facilities more hours per week, paying workers to work overtime, and hiring some new workers immediately. But firms will be able to expand output much more given the time to expand their facilities and hire a larger permanent work force.

For some goods and services, short-run supply is completely inelastic. Rental housing in most cities is an example. In the very short run, because there is only a fixed number of rental units, an increase in demand only pushes rents up. In the longer run, and without rent controls, higher rents provide an incentive to renovate existing buildings and construct new ones, so that the quantity supplied increases.

For most goods, however, firms can find ways to increase output even in the

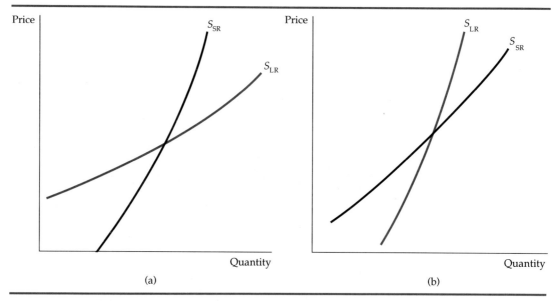

FIGURE 2.14a   Primary Copper: Short-Run and Long-Run Supply Curves.   Like most goods, supply is more elastic in the long run. If price increases, firms would like to produce more but are limited by capacity constraints in the short run. In the longer run they can add to capacity and produce more.

FIGURE 2.14b   Secondary Copper: Short-Run and Long-Run Supply Curves.   If price increases, there is a greater incentive to convert scrap copper into new supply, so initially secondary supply (i.e., supply from scrap) increases sharply. But later, as the stock of scrap falls, secondary supply contracts. Secondary supply is therefore less elastic in the long run than in the short run.

TABLE 2.3 Supply of Copper

Price Elasticity of:	Short-run	Long-run
Primary supply	0.20	1.60
Secondary supply	0.43	0.31
Total supply	0.25	1.50

short run, if the price incentive is strong enough. The problem is that because of the constraints that firms face, it is costly to increase supply rapidly, so that it may require a large price increase to elicit a small short-run increase in supply. We discuss these characteristics of supply in more detail in Chapter 8, but for now it should be clear why for many goods, short-run and long-run supply curves resemble those in Figure 2.14a. (The figure refers to the supply of primary [newly mined] copper, which we will say more about in a moment, but it could also apply to many other goods.)

For some goods, supply is more elastic in the short run than in the long run. Such goods are durable and can be recycled as part of supply if price goes up. An example is the *secondary supply* of many metals (i.e., the supply from *scrap metal*, which is regularly melted down and refabricated). When the price of copper goes up, it increases the incentive to convert scrap copper into new supply, so that initially secondary supply increases sharply. But eventually the stock of good-quality scrap will fall, making the melting, purifying, and refabricating more costly, so that secondary supply will contract. Thus the long-run price elasticity of secondary supply will be smaller than the short-run elasticity.

Figures 2.14a and 2.14b show short-run and long-run supply curves for primary (production from the mining and smelting of ore) and secondary copper production. Table 2.3 shows estimates of the elasticities for each component of supply, and then for total supply, based on a weighted average of the component elasticities.[8] Because secondary supply is only about 20 percent of total supply, the price elasticity of total supply is larger in the long run than in the short run.

EXAMPLE 2.4   THE WEATHER IN BRAZIL AND THE PRICE OF COFFEE IN NEW YORK

Brazil is occasionally hit with subfreezing weather that destroys or damages many of its coffee trees. Because Brazil produces much of the world's coffee, the result is a decrease in the supply of coffee and a sharp run-up in its price.

---

[8]These estimates were obtained by aggregating the regional estimates reported in Franklin M. Fisher, Paul H. Cootner, and Martin N. Baily, "An Econometric Model of the World Copper Industry," *Bell Journal of Economics* 3 (Autumn 1972): 568–609.

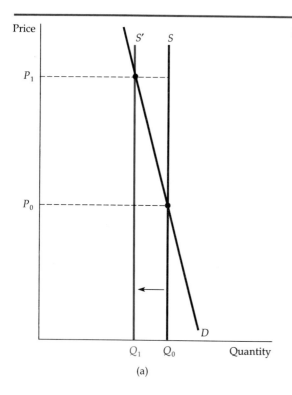

(a)

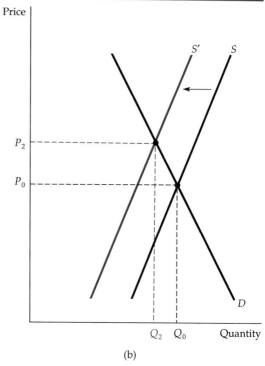

(b)

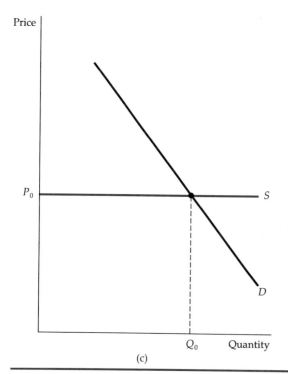

(c)

FIGURES 2.15a, b, and c   Supply and Demand for Coffee.   (a) A freeze in Brazil causes the supply curve to shift to the left. In the short run, supply is completely inelastic; only a fixed number of coffee beans can be harvested. Demand is also relatively inelastic; consumers change their habits only slowly. As a result, the initial effect of the freeze is a sharp increase in price, from P_0 to P_1. (b) In the intermediate run, supply and demand are both more elastic, so price falls partway back, to P_2. (c) In the long run supply is extremely elastic; new coffee trees will have had time to mature, so the effect of the freeze will have disappeared. Price returns to P_0.

A dramatic example of this occurred in July 1975, when a frost destroyed most of Brazil's 1976–1977 coffee crop. (Remember that it is winter in Brazil when it is summer in the northern hemisphere.) The spot price of a pound of coffee in New York went from 68 cents in 1975 to $1.23 in 1976, and then to $2.70 in 1977.

The run-up in price following a freeze is usually short-lived, however. Within a year price begins to fall, and within three or four years it returns to its pre-freeze level. For example, in 1978 the price of coffee in New York fell to $1.48 per pound, and by 1983 it had fallen in real (inflation-adjusted) terms to within a few cents of its prefreeze 1975 price.[9]

The behavior of coffee prices indicates that both demand and supply (especially supply) are much more elastic in the long run than in the short run. Figures 2.15a, 2.15b, and 2.15c show this situation. Note that in the very short run (within one or two months after a freeze), supply is completely inelastic; there are simply a fixed number of coffee beans, some of which have been damaged by the frost. Demand is also relatively inelastic. As a result of the frost, the supply curve shifts to the left, and price increases sharply, from P_0 to P_1.

In the intermediate run, say, one year after the freeze, both supply and demand are more elastic, supply because existing trees can be harvested more intensively (with some decrease in quality), and demand because consumers have had time to change their buying habits. The intermediate-run supply curve also shifts to the left, but price has come down from P_1 to P_2. The quantity supplied has also increased somewhat from the short run, from Q_1 to Q_2. In the long run, price returns to its normal level; coffee growers have had time to replace the trees damaged by the freeze. The long-run supply curve, then, simply reflects the cost of producing coffee, including the costs of land, of planting and caring for the trees, and of a competitive rate of profit.

2.5 Understanding and Predicting the Effects of Changing Market Conditions

We have discussed the meaning and characteristics of supply and demand, but our treatment has been largely qualitative. To use supply and demand curves to analyze and predict the effects of changing market conditions, we must begin to attach numbers to them. For example, to see how a 50 percent reduction in the supply of Brazilian coffee may affect the world price of coffee, we need to

[9]During 1980, however, prices temporarily went just above $2.00 per pound as a result of export quotas imposed under the International Coffee Agreement (ICA). The ICA is essentially a cartel agreement implemented by the coffee-producing countries in 1968. It has been largely ineffective and in most years has had little impact on price. We will discuss cartel pricing in detail in Chapter 12.

write down actual supply and demand curves and then calculate how those curves will shift, and how price will then change.

In this section we will see how to do simple "back of the envelope" calculations with linear supply and demand curves. Although they are often an approximation to more complex curves, we use linear curves because they are the easiest to work with. It may come as a surprise, but one can do some informative economic analyses on the back of a small envelope with a pencil and a pocket calculator.

First, we must learn how to "fit" linear demand and supply curves to market data. (By this we do not mean statistical fitting in the sense of linear regression or other statistical techniques, which we discuss later in the book.) Suppose we have two sets of numbers for a particular market: (i) The price and quantity that generally prevail in the market (i.e., the price and quantity that prevail "on average," or when the market is in equilibrium, or when market conditions are "normal"). We call these numbers the equilibrium price and quantity, and we denote them by P^* and Q^*. (ii) The price elasticities of supply and demand for the market (at or near the equilibrium), which we denote by E_S and E_D, as before.

These numbers might come from a statistical study done by someone else; they might be numbers that we simply think are reasonable; or they might be numbers that we want to try out on a "what if" basis. What we want to do is *write down the supply and demand curves that fit (i.e., are consistent with) these numbers.* Then we can determine numerically how a change in a variable such as GNP, the price of another good, or some cost of production will cause supply or demand to shift and thereby affect the market price and quantity.

Let's begin with the linear curves shown in Figure 2.16. We can write these curves algebraically as

$$\textit{Supply:} \qquad Q = a_0 + a_1 P \qquad\qquad (2.4a)$$

$$\textit{Demand:} \qquad Q = b_0 - b_1 P \qquad\qquad (2.4b)$$

The problem is to choose numbers for the constants a_0, a_1, b_0 and b_1. This is done, for supply and for demand, in a two-step procedure:

Step One: Recall that each price elasticity, whether of supply or demand, can be written as

$$E = (P/Q)(\Delta Q/\Delta P)$$

where $\Delta Q/\Delta P$ is the change in quantity demanded or supplied resulting from a small change in price. For linear curves, $\Delta Q/\Delta P$ is constant. From equations (2.4a) and (2.4b), we see that $\Delta Q/\Delta P = a_1$ for supply, and $\Delta Q/\Delta P = -b_1$ for demand. Now, let's substitute these values for $\Delta Q/\Delta P$ into the elasticity formula:

$$\textit{Supply:} \qquad E_S = a_1(P^*/Q^*) \qquad\qquad (2.5a)$$

$$\textit{Demand:} \qquad E_D = -b_1(P^*/Q^*) \qquad\qquad (2.5b)$$

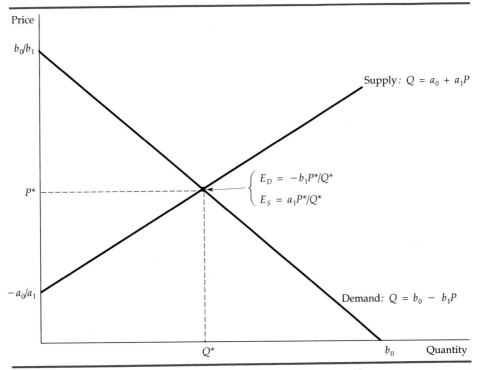

FIGURE 2.16 Fitting Linear Supply and Demand Curves to Data. Linear supply and demand curves provide a convenient tool for analysis. Given data for the equilibrium price and quantity P^* and Q^*, and estimates of the elasticities of demand and supply E_D and E_S, we can calculate the parameters a_0 and a_1 for the supply curve, and b_0 and b_1 for the demand curve. The curves can then be used to analyze the behavior of the market quantitatively.

where P^* and Q^* are the equilibrium price and quantity for which we have data and to which the curves will be fit. Because we have numbers for E_S, E_D, P^*, and Q^*, we can substitute these numbers in equations (2.5a) and (2.5b) and solve for a_1 and b_1.

Step Two: Since we now know a_1 and b_1, we can substitute these numbers, as well as P^* and Q^*, into equations (2.4a) and (2.4b) and solve for the remaining constants a_0 and b_0. For example, we can rewrite equation (2.4a) as

$$a_0 = Q^* - a_1 P^*$$

and then use our data for Q^* and P^*, together with the number we calculated in Step One for a_1, to obtain a_0.

Let's do this for a specific example—long-run supply and demand for the world copper market. The relevant numbers for this market are as follows[10]: quantity $Q^* = 7.5$ million metric tons per year (mmt/yr); price $P^* = 75$ cents per pound; elasticity of supply $E_S = 1.6$; elasticity of demand $E_D = -0.8$. (The price of copper has fluctuated during the past decade between 50 cents and more than $1.20, but 75 cents is a reasonable average price for 1980–1986.)

We begin with the supply curve equation (2.4a) and use our two-step procedure to calculate numbers for a_0 and a_1. The long-run price elasticity of supply is 1.6, $P^* = .75$, and $Q^* = 7.5$.

Step One: Substitute these numbers in equation (2.5a) to determine a_1:

$$1.6 = a_1(0.75/7.5) = 0.1a_1,$$

so that $a_1 = 1.6/0.1 = 16$.

Step Two: Substitute this number for a_1, together with the numbers for P^* and Q^*, into equation (2.4a) to determine a_0:

$$7.5 = a_0 + (16)(0.75) = a_0 + 12,$$

so that $a_0 = 7.5 - 12 = -4.5$. We now know a_0 and a_1, so we can write our supply curve:

Supply: $\qquad Q = -4.5 + 16P$

We can now follow the same steps for the demand curve equation (2.4b). An estimate for the long-run elasticity of demand is -0.8. First, substitute this number, and the values for P^* and Q^*, in equation (2.5b) to determine b_1:

$$-0.8 = -b_1(0.75/7.5) = -0.1b_1$$

so that $b_1 = 0.8/0.1 = 8$. Second, substitute this value for b_1 and the values for P^* and Q^* in equation (2.4b) to determine b_0:

$$7.5 = b_0 - (8)(0.75) = b_0 - 6,$$

so that $b_0 = 7.5 + 6 = 13.5$. Thus, our demand curve is

Demand: $\qquad Q = 13.5 - 8P$

To check that we have not made a mistake, set supply equal to demand and calculate the equilibrium price that results:

$$\text{Supply} = -4.5 + 16P = 13.5 - 8P = \text{Demand}$$

$$16P + 8P = 13.5 + 4.5,$$

or $P = 18/24 = 0.75$, which is indeed the equilibrium price that we began with.

We have written supply and demand so that they depend only on price, but they could easily depend on other variables as well. For example, demand might

---

[10]The supply elasticity is for total supply, as shown in Table 2.3. The demand elasticity is a regionally aggregated number based on Fisher, Cootner, and Baily, "An Econometric Model." Quantities refer to the non-Communist world market.

depend on income as well as price. We would then write demand as

$$Q = b_0 - b_1 P + b_2 I \qquad (2.6)$$

where I is an index of aggregate income or GNP. (For example, I might equal 1.0 in a base year and then rise or fall to reflect percentage increases or decreases in aggregate income.)

For our copper market example, a reasonable estimate for the long-run income elasticity of demand is 1.3. For the linear demand curve (2.6), we can then calculate b_2 by using the formula for the income elasticity of demand: $E = (I/Q)(\Delta Q/\Delta I)$. Taking the base value of I as 1.0, we have

$$1.3 = (1.0/7.5)(b_2)$$

so $b_2 = (1.3)(7.5)/(1.0) = 9.75$. Finally, substituting the values $b_1 = 8$, $b_2 = 9.75$, $P^* = 0.75$, and $Q^* = 7.5$ into (2.6), we can calculate that b_0 must equal 3.75.

We have seen how to fit linear supply and demand curves to data. Now, to see how these curves can be used to analyze markets, look at Example 2.5 on the behavior of copper prices and Example 2.6 on the world oil market.

EXAMPLE 2.5   DECLINING DEMAND AND THE FALL IN COPPER PRICES

After reaching a level of about $1.00 per pound in 1980, the price of copper fell sharply to about 60 cents/lb. in 1986. In real (inflation-adjusted) terms, this price was even lower than during the Great Depression 50 years earlier. Figure 2.17 shows the behavior of copper prices in 1965–1986 in both real and nominal terms.

The worldwide recessions of 1980 and 1982 contributed to the decline of copper prices; as mentioned above, the income elasticity of copper demand is about 1.3. But copper demand did not pick up as the industrial economies recovered during the mid-1980s. Instead, the 1980s saw the beginning of a deep decline in the demand for copper.

This decline occurred for two reasons. First, a large part of copper consumption is for the construction of equipment for electric power generation and transmission. But by the late 1970s, the growth rate of electric power generation had fallen dramatically in most industrialized countries. (For example, in the United States the growth rate fell from over 6 percent per annum in the 1960s and early 1970s to less than 2 percent in the late 1970s and 1980s.) This meant a big drop in what had been a major source of copper demand. Second, in the 1980s other materials, such as aluminum and fiber optics, were increasingly substituted for copper.

How will a decline in copper demand affect price? This is a question of considerable concern to firms in the copper industry, many of which have shut down or face the prospect of shutting down because of low prices. We can use

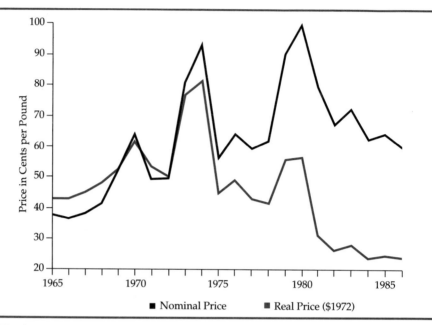

FIGURE 2.17 Copper Prices, 1965–1986. Copper prices are shown in both nominal (no adjustment for inflation) and real (inflation-adjusted) terms. In real terms copper prices have declined steeply since the early 1970s because the demand for copper has fallen.

the linear supply and demand curves that we just derived to address this question. Let us calculate the effect on price of a 20 percent decline in demand. Since we are not concerned here with the effects of GNP growth, we can leave the income term b_2I out of demand.

We want to shift the demand curve to the left by 20 percent. In other words, we want the quantity demanded to be 80 percent of what it would be otherwise for every value of price. For our linear demand curve, we simply multiply the right-hand side by 0.8:

$$Q = (0.8)(13.5 - 8P) = 10.8 - 6.4P$$

Supply is again $Q = -4.5 + 16P$. Now we can equate supply and demand and solve for price:

$$16P + 6.4P = 10.8 + 4.5$$

or $P = 15.3/22.4 = 68.30$ cents/lb. A decline in demand of 20 percent therefore implies a drop in price of roughly 7 cents per pound, or 10 percent.

EXAMPLE 2.6   THE WORLD OIL MARKET ON THE BACK OF AN ENVELOPE

Since 1974, the world oil market has been dominated by the OPEC cartel. By collectively restraining output, OPEC succeeded in pushing world oil prices well above what they would have been in a competitive market. OPEC producers could do this because they accounted for a large fraction of world oil production (about two-thirds in 1974).

We will examine OPEC's pricing strategy in more detail in Chapter 12 as part of our analysis of cartels and the behavior of cartelized markets. But for now, let's see how simple linear supply and demand curves (and the back of a small envelope) can be used to predict what should happen, in the short and longer run, following a cutback in production by OPEC.

Because this example is set in 1973–1974, all prices are measured in 1974 dollars (which, because of inflation, were worth much more than the dollars of today). Here are some rough figures: 1973 world price = \$4/barrel, world demand and total supply = 18 billion barrels/year (bb/yr), 1973 OPEC supply = 12 bb/yr. and competitive (non-OPEC) supply = 6 bb/yr. And here are some price elasticity estimates consistent with linear supply and demand curves[11]:

	Short-run	Long-run
World Demand:	−0.05	−0.40
Competitive Supply:	0.10	0.40

You should verify that these numbers imply the following for demand and competitive supply *in the short run*:

$$\text{Short-run Demand:} \qquad D = 18.9 - 0.225P$$

$$\text{Short-run Competitive Supply:} \quad S_C = 5.4 + 0.15P$$

Of course, *total* supply is competitive supply *plus* OPEC supply, which we take as constant at 12 bb/yr. Adding this 12 bb/yr to the competitive supply curve above, we obtain the following for total short-run supply:

$$\text{Short-run Total Supply:} \quad S_T = 17.4 + 0.15P$$

You should check that demand and total supply are equal at a price of \$4/barrel. You should also verify that the corresponding demand and supply curves

[11]Note that these elasticities are larger when price is higher. For the sources of these numbers and a more detailed discussion of OPEC oil pricing, see R. S. Pindyck, "Gains to Producers from the Cartelization of Exhaustible Resources," *Review of Economics and Statistics* 60 (May 1978): 238–251, and James M. Griffin and David J. Teece, *OPEC Behavior and World Oil Prices* (London: Allen & Unwin, 1982).

for the *long run* are

$$\text{Long-run Demand:} \qquad D = 25.2 - 1.8P$$

$$\text{Long-run Competitive Supply:} \quad S_C = 3.6 + 0.6P$$

$$\text{Long-run Total Supply:} \qquad S_T = 15.6 + 0.6P$$

Again, you can check that supply and demand equate at a price of $4.

Now let's calculate what should happen if OPEC cuts production by one-third, or 4 bb/yr. For the *short-run*, just subtract 4 from total supply:

$$\text{Short-run Demand:} \qquad D = 18.9 - 0.225P$$

$$\text{Short-run Total Supply:} \quad S_T = 13.4 + 0.15P$$

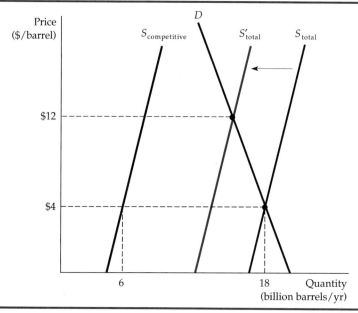

FIGURE 2.18 Oil Market Following OPEC Production Cut. Total supply is the sum of competitive (non-OPEC) supply and the 12 billion barrels per year of OPEC supply. These are short-run supply and demand curves. If OPEC reduces its production, the supply curve will shift to the left. In the short run, price will increase sharply.

By equating this total supply with demand, we can see that in the short run, the price should rise to $12/barrel, which in fact it did. Figure 2.18 illustrates the shift in supply and its effect on price. The initial equilibrium is at the intersection of S_{total} and D. After the drop in OPEC production, the equilibrium occurs where S'_{total} and D cross.

In the *long run*, however, things will be different. Because both demand and competitive supply are more elastic in the long run, a one-third cut in production by OPEC will no longer support a $12 price. By subtracting 4 from the long-run total supply function and equating with long-run demand, we can see that the price will be only $5.25. This is $1.25 above the old $4 price but much lower than $12.

We would therefore expect to see a sharp increase in price, followed by a gradual decline, as demand falls and competitive supply rises in response to price. And this is what did occur, at least until 1979. But during 1979–1980 the price of oil again rose dramatically. What happened? The Iranian Revolution and the outbreak of the Iran-Iraq war. By cutting about 1.5 bb/yr from Iranian production and nearly 1 bb/yr from Iraqi production, the revolution and war allowed oil prices to continue to increase, and consequently they were a blessing for the other members of OPEC.

Yet even though the Iran-Iraq war dragged on, by 1986 oil prices had fallen much closer to competitive levels. This was largely due to the long-run response of demand and competitive supply. As demand fell and competitive supply expanded, OPEC's share of the world market fell to about one-third, as compared with almost two-thirds in 1973.

2.6 Effects of Government Intervention—Price Controls

In the United States and most other industrial countries, markets are rarely free of government intervention. Besides imposing taxes and granting subsidies, governments often regulate markets (even competitive markets) in a variety of ways. Here we will see how to use supply and demand curves to analyze the effects of one common form of government intervention: price controls. Later, in Chapter 9, we will examine the effects of price controls and other forms of government intervention and regulation in more detail.

Figure 2.19 illustrates the effects of price controls, where P_0 and Q_0 are the equilibrium price and quantity (i.e., the price and quantity that would prevail without government regulation). The government, however, has decided that P_0 is too high and has mandated that the price can be no higher than a maximum allowable *ceiling price*, which we denote by P_{max}. What is the result? Because the price is lower, producers (particularly those with higher costs) will produce less, and supply will be Q_1. Consumers, on the other hand, will demand more at this low price; they would like to purchase the quantity Q_2. So demand exceeds supply and a shortage develops, known as *excess demand*. The amount of this excess demand is $Q_2 - Q_1$.

This excess demand sometimes takes the form of queues, as when drivers lined up to buy gasoline during the winter of 1974 and the summer of 1979. (In both instances, the gasoline lines were the result of price controls; the government prevented domestic oil and gasoline prices from rising along with world oil prices.) Sometimes it takes the form of curtailments and supply rationing, as with natural gas price controls and the resulting gas shortages of the mid-1970s, when industrial consumers of gas had their supplies cut off, forcing factories to close. And sometimes it spills over to other markets, where it artificially increases demand. For example, in the 1960s natural gas price controls had not yet caused curtailments, but potential new buyers could not hook into the pipeline system and were forced to use oil instead.

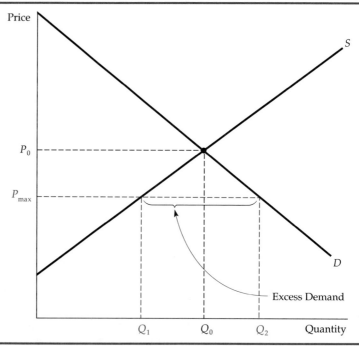

FIGURE 2.19 Effects of Price Controls. Without price controls the market clears at the equilibrium price and quantity P_0 and Q_0. If price is regulated to be no higher than P_{max}, supply falls to Q_1, demand increases to Q_2, and a shortage (excess demand) develops.

Some people gain and some lose from price controls. As Figure 2.19 suggests, producers lose—they receive lower prices and some leave the industry. Some but not all consumers gain. Consumers who can purchase the good at a lower price are clearly better off, but those who have been "rationed out" and cannot buy the good at all are worse off. How large are the gains to the winners, how large are the losses to the losers, and do the total gains exceed the total losses? To answer these questions we need a method to measure the gains and losses from price controls. We will discuss such a method in Chapter 9.

EXAMPLE 2.7 PRICE CONTROLS AND THE NATURAL GAS SHORTAGE

Since 1954, the federal government has regulated the wellhead price of natural gas.[12] Initially the controls were not binding; the ceiling prices were above those that cleared the market. But about 1962, these ceiling prices did become binding, and excess demand for natural gas developed and slowly began to grow. In the 1970s, this excess demand, spurred by higher oil prices, became severe and led to widespread curtailments. Ceiling prices were far below those that would have prevailed in a free market.

To analyze the impact of these price controls, we will take 1975 as a case in point. Based on econometric studies of natural gas markets and the behavior of those markets as controls were gradually lifted during the 1980s, the following data describe the market in 1975.[13] The free market price of natural gas would have been about $2.00 per mcf (thousand cubic feet), and production and consumption would have been about 20 Tcf (trillion cubic feet). The average price of oil (including both imports and domestic production), which affects both supply and demand for natural gas, was about $8/barrel.

A reasonable estimate for the price elasticity of supply is 0.2. Higher oil prices also lead to more natural gas production because oil and gas are often discovered and produced together; an estimate of the cross-price elasticity of supply is 0.1. As for demand, the price elasticity is about −0.5, and the cross-price elasticity

---

[12]This regulation began with the Supreme Court's 1954 decision requiring the then Federal Power Commission to regulate wellhead prices on natural gas sold to interstate pipeline companies. This decision resulted from an appeal in a case brought by the attorney general of Wisconsin against the Phillips Petroleum Company. Phillips' prices had been increasing, and it was alleged that this hurt Wisconsin consumers. For a detailed discussion of natural gas regulation and its effects, see Paul W. MacAvoy and Robert S. Pindyck, *The Economics of the Natural Gas Shortage* (Amsterdam: North-Holland, 1975), and Arlon R. Tussing and Connie C. Barlow, *The Natural Gas Industry*, (Cambridge: Ballinger, 1984).

[13]For a more detailed analysis see MacAvoy and Pindyck, op. cit., and R. S. Pindyck, "Higher Energy Prices and the Supply of Natural Gas," *Energy Systems and Policy* 2 (1978): 177–209.

with respect to oil price is about 1.5. You should verify that the following linear supply and demand curves fit these numbers:

$$Supply: \quad Q = 14 + 2P_G + .25P_O$$

$$Demand: Q = -5P_G + 3.75P_O$$

where Q is the quantity of natural gas (in Tcf), P_G is the price of natural gas (in dollars per mcf), and P_O is the price of oil (in dollars per barrel). You should also verify, by equating supply and demand and substituting $8 for P_O, that these supply and demand curves imply an equilibrium free market price of $2.00 for natural gas.

The regulated price of gas in 1975 was about $1.00 per mcf.[14] Substituting this price for P_G in the supply function gives a quantity supplied (Q_1 in Figure 2.19) of 18 Tcf. Substituting for P_G in the demand function gives a demand (Q_2 in Figure 2.19) of 25 Tcf. Price controls thus created an excess demand of $25 - 18 = 7$ Tcf, which ultimately manifested itself in the form of widespread curtailments.

Price regulation was a major component of U.S. energy policy during the 1960s and 1970s, and it continued to influence the evolution of natural gas markets in the 1980s. In Example 9.1 of Chapter 9, we will show how to measure the gains and losses that result from natural gas price controls.

Summary

1. Supply-demand analysis is one of the basic tools of microeconomics. In competitive markets, supply and demand curves tell us how much will be produced by firms and how much will be demanded by consumers as a function of price.

2. The market mechanism is the tendency for supply and demand to equilibrate (i.e., for price to move to the market-clearing level), so that there is neither excess demand nor excess supply.

3. Elasticities describe the responsiveness of supply and demand to changes in price, income, or other variables. For example, the price elasticity of demand measures the percentage change in the quantity demanded resulting from a 1 percent increase in price.

[14]In fact, natural gas ceiling prices have varied across the country among gases of different vintages (that is, gas produced under old versus new contracts), between intra- and interstate gas, and especially, following the Natural Gas Policy Act of 1978, among gases of different regulatory classifications.

4. Elasticities pertain to a time frame, and for most goods it is important to distinguish between short-run and long-run elasticities.

5. If we can estimate, at least roughly, the supply and demand curves for a particular market, we can calculate the market-clearing price by equating supply and demand. Also, if we know how supply and demand depend on other economic variables, such as income or the prices of other goods, we can calculate how the market-clearing price and quantity will change as these other variables change. This is a means of explaining or predicting market behavior.

6. Simple numerical analyses can often be done by fitting linear supply and demand curves to data on price and quantity and to estimates of elasticities. For many markets such data and estimates are available, and simple "back of the envelope" calculations can help us understand the characteristics and behavior of the market.

Review Questions

1. Suppose that unusually hot weather causes the demand curve for ice cream to shift to the right. Explain why the price of ice cream will rise to a new market-clearing level.

2. Use supply and demand curves to illustrate how each of the following events would affect the price of butter and the quantity of butter bought and sold: (a) an increase in the price of margarine; (b) an increase in the price of milk; (c) a decrease in average income levels.

3. Suppose a 3 percent increase in the price of corn flakes causes a 6 percent decline in the quantity demanded. What is the elasticity of demand for corn flakes?

4. Why do long-run elasticities of demand differ from short-run elasticities? Would you expect the price elasticity of demand for paper towels to be larger in the short run or in the long run? Why? What about the price elasticity of demand for televisions?

5. Explain why for many goods, the long-run price elasticity of supply is larger than the short-run elasticity.

6. Suppose the government regulates the prices of beef and chicken and sets them below their market-clearing levels. Explain why shortages of these goods will develop and what factors will determine the sizes of the shortages. What will happen to the price of pork? Explain briefly.

7. In a discussion of tuition rates, a university official argues that the demand for admission is completely price inelastic. As evidence she cites the fact that the university has doubled its tuition (in real terms) over the past 15 years, but the number or quality of students applying has not decreased. Would you accept this argument? Explain briefly.

Exercises

1. Much of the demand for U.S. agricultural output has come from other countries. The export component of demand has fallen, however, and U.S. farmers are concerned that it will continue to shrink. Suppose the export demand for wheat falls by 40 percent.

a. Use the supply and demand curves of Example 2.2 to determine how this would affect the free market price of wheat in the United States.

b. Now suppose the U.S. government wants to buy enough wheat each year to raise the price to $3.00 per bushel. Without export demand, how much wheat would the government have to buy each year? How much would this cost the government?

2. The rent control agency of New York City has found that aggregate demand is $Q_D = 100 - 5P$, with quantity measured in tens of thousands of apartments, and price, the average monthly rental rate, measured in hundreds of dollars. The agency also noted that the increase in Q at lower P results from more three-person families coming into the city from Long Island and demanding apartments. The city's board of realtors acknowledges that this is a good demand estimate and has shown that supply is $Q_S = 50 + 5P$.

a. If both the rent control agency and the board of realtors are right about demand and supply, what is the free market price? What is the change in city population if the rent control agency sets a maximum average monthly rental of $100, and all those who cannot find an apartment leave the city?

b. Suppose the agency bows to the wishes of the board of realtors and sets a rental of $900 per month on all apartments to allow landlords a "fair" rate of return. If 50 percent of any long-run increases in apartment offerings comes from new construction, how many apartments are constructed?

3. Refer to Example 2.2 on the market for wheat. Suppose that in 1985 the Soviet Union had bought an additional 200 million bushels of U.S. wheat. Calculate what the free market price of wheat would have been and what quantity would have been produced and sold by U.S. farmers.

4. In Example 2.5 we examined the effect of a 20 percent decline in copper demand on the price of copper, using the linear supply and demand curves developed in Section 2.5. Suppose the long-run price elasticity of copper demand were -0.4 instead of -0.8.

a. Assuming, as before, that the equilibrium price and quantity are $P^* = 75$ cents per pound and $Q^* = 7.5$ million metric tons per year, derive the linear demand curve consistent with this smaller elasticity.

b. Using this demand curve, recalculate the effect of a 20 percent decline in copper demand on the price of copper.

5. Example 2.6 analyzes the world oil market. Using the data given in that example,

a. Show that the short-run demand and competitive supply curves are indeed given by

$$D = 18.9 - 0.225P$$

$$S_C = 5.4 + 0.15P$$

b. Show that the long-run demand and competitive supply curves are indeed given by

$$D = 25.2 - 1.8P$$

$$S_C = 3.6 + 0.6P$$

c. Use this model to calculate what would happen to the price of oil in the short run *and* the long run if OPEC were to cut its production by 6 bb/yr.

6. Refer to Example 2.7, which analyzes the effects of price controls on natural gas.
a. Using the data presented in the example, show that the following supply and demand curves indeed describe the market in 1975:

Supply:	$Q = 14 + 2P_G + 0.25P_O$
Demand:	$Q = -5P_G + 3.75P_O$

where P_G and P_O are the prices of natural gas and oil, respectively. Also, verify that if the price of oil is $8, these curves imply a free market price of $2.00 for natural gas.
b. Suppose the regulated price of gas in 1975 had been $1.50 per mcf, instead of $1.00. How much excess demand would there have been?
c. Suppose that the market for natural gas had *not* been regulated. If the price of oil had increased from $8 to $16, what would have happened to the free market price of natural gas?

Handwritten work:

$$S: \quad Q = 14 + 2\overset{a_1}{P_G} + .25\overset{a_2}{P_O} \quad \Big\} \quad \begin{matrix} P_G^* = \$2 & E_S^G = .2 \\ Q_G^* = 20T & E_P < -.5 \\ P_O^* = \$8 & E_S^{60} = .1 \\ & E_{G0}^P = 1.5 \end{matrix}$$

$$D: \quad Q = -5\overset{b_1}{P_G} + 3.75\overset{b_2}{P_O}$$

a_0 a_1 $a_2 = 1$

$b_0 = 0$ b_1 b_2

$$E_S = \frac{\Delta Q}{\Delta P} \cdot \frac{P}{Q} \qquad E_P = \frac{\Delta Q}{\Delta P} \cdot \frac{P}{Q}$$

$$.2 = a_1 \left(\frac{2}{20}\right) \qquad -.5 = -b_1 \left(\frac{2}{20}\right)$$

$$.2 = a_1 \left(\frac{1}{10}\right) \qquad -.5 = -b_1 \left(\frac{1}{10}\right)$$

$$2 = a_1 \qquad -5 = -b_1$$

$$b_1 = 5$$

$$E_S^{60} = \frac{\Delta Q_S^G}{\Delta P_O} \cdot \frac{P_O}{Q_S^G}$$

$$.1 = a_2 \left(\frac{8}{20}\right)$$

$$.1 = a_2 \left(\frac{2}{5}\right)$$

$$\left(\frac{1}{10}\right)\left(\frac{2}{5}\right) = \frac{1}{4} = .25 = a_2$$

$$\therefore \quad 20 = a_0 + 2(2) + .25(8)$$

$$20 = a_0 + 4 + 2$$

$$14 = a_0$$

cont →

$$E_{GO}^{P} = \frac{\Delta Q_D^G}{\Delta P_U} \cdot \frac{P_0}{Q_D^G}$$

$$1.5 = b_2 \left(\frac{8}{20}\right)$$

$$1.5 = b_2 \left(\frac{2}{5}\right)$$

$$\left(\frac{3}{2}\right)\left(\frac{5}{2}\right) = b_2 = \frac{3}{5}$$

$$\frac{15}{4} = b_2 = 3.75$$

$$Q = b_2 - 5P_G + 3.75P$$

$$20 = b_0 - 5(2) + 3.75(8)$$

$$20 = b_0 - 10 + 30$$

$$0 = b_0$$

$$Q_S = Q_D$$

$$14 + 2P_G + \frac{1}{4}(8) = -5P_G + \frac{15}{4}(8)$$

$$2P_G + 16 = -5P_G + 30 \qquad \left(\text{END A}\right)$$

$$7P_G = 14$$

$$P_G = 2$$

(b)

$\$ 2.00$
1.50

20 22.5

$$Q = -5\left(\frac{3}{2}\right) + \frac{15}{4}(8)$$

$$Q = -\frac{15}{2} + 30 = 22\frac{1}{2}$$

$$S = 14 + 2(1.5) + .25(8)$$

$$S = 14 + 3 + 2$$

$$S = 19$$

EXCESS DEMAND $3\frac{1}{2}T$

(c) $Q_D = Q_S$

$$14 + 2P_G + \frac{1}{4}(16) = -5P_G + \frac{15}{4}(16)$$

$$14 + 2P_G + 4 = -5P_G + 40$$

$$18 + 2P_G = -5P_G + 60$$

$$7P_G = 42$$

$$P_G = 6$$

PART II

Producers, Consumers, and Competitive Markets

Part II presents the theoretical core of microeconomics.

Chapters 3 and 4 explain the principles underlying consumer demand. We see how consumers make consumption decisions, how their preferences and budget constraints determine their demands for various goods, and why different goods have different demand characteristics. Chapter 5 contains somewhat more advanced material that shows how to analyze consumer choice under uncertainty. We explain why people usually dislike risky situations, and show how they can reduce risk, and choose among risky alternatives.

Chapters 6 and 7 develop the theory of the firm. We see how firms combine inputs, such as capital, labor, and raw materials, to produce goods and services, in a way that minimizes the costs of production. We also see how a firm's costs depend on its rate of production and on its production experience. Chapter 8 then shows how firms choose their profit-maximizing rate of production. We also see how the production decisions of individual firms combine to determine the competitive market supply curve and its characteristics.

Chapter 9 applies supply and demand curves to the analysis of competitive markets. Government policies such as price controls, quotas, taxes, and subsidies, can have wide-ranging effects on consumers and producers. We explain how supply–demand analysis can be used to evaluate them.

CHAPTER 3

Consumer Behavior

In 1962, Pillsbury Co. acquired a company that produced a new premium ice cream in Woodbridge, New Jersey. The ice cream was marketed under the name of Haagen-Dazs. The inclusion of more cream and eggs made the ice cream richer and more flavorful than most other brands, and the Scandinavian-sounding name suggested that it was a quality product worth a higher price. But before Haagen-Dazs could be extensively marketed, the company had to resolve an important problem—*how high a price should it charge?* No matter how good the ice cream was, its profitability would be affected considerably by the company's pricing decision. Knowing that consumers would pay more for a premium ice cream was not enough; at issue was *how much more.* Pillsbury therefore had to conduct a careful analysis of consumer preferences to determine the demand for ice cream and its dependence on both price and quality.

In the early 1960s, reports showing the extent to which the poor were underfed and malnourished aroused public concern. In response, Congress passed the Food Stamp Act of 1964, which directed the federal government to fund a program in which households with sufficiently low incomes would receive coupons that could be exchanged for food. But a problem arose in the design and evaluation of this program. To what extent would food stamps provide people with more food, as opposed to simply subsidizing food that they would have bought anyway? In other words, would the program turn out to be little more than an income supplement that would be spent largely on nonfood items, instead of a solution to the nutritional problems of the poor? Once again, an analysis of consumer behavior was needed. In this case, the government had to determine how spending on food, as opposed to other goods, is affected by changing income levels and prices.

These two problems—one involving corporate policy and the other public policy—exemplify the importance of the economic theory of consumer behavior and the kinds of issues it can help resolve. In this chapter and the next, we will see how consumers allocate their incomes and how this determines the demands for various goods and services. This, in turn, will help us understand how changes in income and prices affect demands and why the demands for some products are more sensitive than others to price and income changes.

Consumer behavior is best understood in three steps. The first step is to examine *consumer preferences*. Specifically, we need a practical means of describing how people might prefer one good to another. Second, we must account for the fact that consumers face *budget constraints*—they have only limited incomes to allocate among consumption items. Depending on the prices of different goods, their incomes impose limits on the combinations of goods that consumers can buy. The third step is to put consumer preferences and budget constraints together to determine *consumer choices*. In other words, given their preferences and limited incomes, what combinations of goods will consumers choose to buy to maximize their satisfaction? We will go through each of these steps in turn.

3.1 Consumer Preferences

Given the vast number of goods and services that our industrial economy provides for purchase and given the wide diversity of personal tastes, how can we describe consumer preferences in a coherent way? A good way to begin is to think of preferences in terms of comparisons of market baskets. A *market basket* is just a collection of one or more commodities. For example, it might contain the various food items in a bag of groceries or the combination of food, clothing, and fuel that a consumer buys each month.

Because people in fact purchase combinations of goods, we can ask whether one market basket is preferred to another. Table 3.1 shows several market baskets consisting of various amounts of food and clothing purchased monthly. For example, market basket A consists of 20 units of food and 30 units of clothing, basket B consists of 10 units of food and 55 units of clothing, and so on. By asking consumers to compare these different baskets, we can describe their preferences for food and clothing.

TABLE 3.1 Alternative Market Baskets		
Market Basket	Units of Food	Units of Clothing
A	20	30
B	10	55
C	40	20
D	30	45
E	10	20
F	10	45

Some Basic Assumptions

The theory of consumer behavior begins with three basic assumptions regarding people's preferences for one market basket versus another. These assumptions hold for most people in most situations.

The first assumption is that preferences are *complete*, which means that consumers can compare and rank all market baskets. In other words, for any two market baskets *A* and *B*, a consumer will prefer *A* to *B*, will prefer *B* to *A*, or will be indifferent between the two. (By "indifferent" we mean that a person is equally happy with either basket.) Note that these preferences ignore costs. A consumer might prefer a steak to a hamburger but buy the hamburger because it is cheaper.

The second important assumption is that preferences are *transitive*. Transitivity means that if a consumer prefers market basket *A* to market basket *B*, and prefers *B* to *C*, then the consumer also prefers *A* to *C*. For example, if a Rolls Royce is preferred to a Cadillac and a Cadillac is preferred to a Chevrolet, then a Rolls Royce is also preferred to a Chevrolet. This transitivity assumption ensures that the consumer's preferences are rational in the sense of being consistent.

The third assumption is that all goods are "good" (i.e., desirable), so that leaving costs aside, *consumers always prefer more of any good to less*. This assumption is made for pedagogic reasons; it simplifies the graphical analysis. Of course, some goods such as air pollution may be undesirable, and consumers will avoid them whenever possible. We ignore these undesirable goods in the context of consumer choice, because most consumers would not choose to purchase them. We will, however, discuss them later in the book.

These three assumptions form the basis of our model of consumer theory. They don't explain consumers' preferences—they only describe them. However, as we will see, an interesting, rich variety of descriptions are possible.

Indifference Curves

We can show a consumer's preferences graphically with the use of *indifference curves. An indifference curve represents all combinations of market baskets that provide the same level of satisfaction to a person.* That person is therefore indifferent among the market baskets represented by the points on the curve.

Given the three assumptions about preferences discussed above, we know that a consumer can always indicate a preference for one market basket over another or indifference between the two. This information can then be used to rank all possible consumption choices. To see this in graphic form, we assume there are only two goods, food F and clothing C, available for consumption. In this case, market baskets describe combinations of food and clothing that a person might wish to consume. Table 3.1 provides some examples of market baskets containing various amounts of food and clothing.

Figure 3.1 shows the same market baskets that are in Table 3.1. The horizontal axis measures the number of units of food purchased each month, and the vertical axis measures the number of units of clothing. Market basket *A*, with 20 units of food and 30 units of clothing, is preferred to market basket *E*, because *A* contains more food *and* more clothing (recall our third assumption that more is better than less). Similarly, market basket *D*, which contains still more food and more clothing, is preferred to *A*. In fact, we can easily compare all market baskets in the shaded areas (such as *D* and *E*) to *A*, because they contain either more or less of both food and clothing. However, comparisons of market basket *A* with market baskets *B* and *C* are not possible without more information about

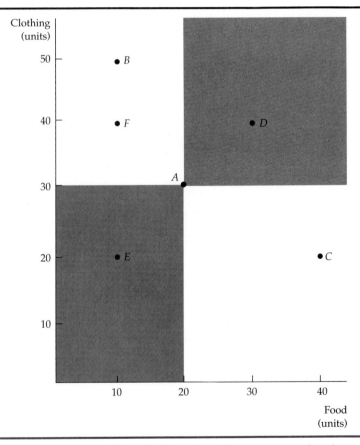

FIGURE 3.1   Describing Individual Preferences.   Because more of each good is preferred to less, some comparisons between market baskets can be made. Market basket *A* is clearly preferred to market basket *E*, while *D* is clearly preferred to *A*. However, *A* cannot be compared with either *B* or *C* without additional information.

the consumer's ranking, because B contains more clothing but less food, and C contains more food but less clothing than A.

This additional information is provided in Figure 3.2, which shows an indifference curve, labeled U_1, that passes through points A, B, and C. This curve indicates that the consumer is indifferent among these three market baskets. It tells us that the consumer feels neither better nor worse off in giving up 10 units of food to obtain 20 units of clothing in moving from market basket A to B. Likewise, the consumer is indifferent between points A and C (i.e., will give up 10 units of clothing to obtain 20 units of food).

Note that the indifference curve in Figure 3.2 slopes downward from left to right. To understand why this must be the case, suppose instead that the indifference curve sloped upward at A through D. This would violate the assumption that more of any commodity is preferred to less. Since market basket D has more of both food and clothing than market basket A, it must be preferred

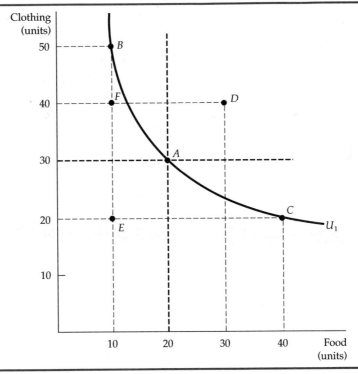

FIGURE 3.2   An Indifference Curve.   A person's indifference curve U_1 shows all market baskets that generate the same level of satisfaction as does market basket A. The person prefers market basket D, which lies above U_1, to A but prefers A to market basket F, which lies below U_1.

to A and therefore cannot be on the same indifference curve as A. In fact, note that any market basket lying above and to the right of indifference curve U_1 in Figure 3.2 is preferred to any market basket on U_1.

To describe a person's preferences for all combinations of food and clothing, we can graph a set of indifference curves that we call an *indifference map*. Each indifference curve shows the market baskets among which the person is indifferent. Figure 3.3 shows three indifference curves that form part of an indifference map. Indifference curve U_3 generates the highest level of satisfaction, followed by indifference curves U_2 and U_1.

Indifference curves cannot intersect. To see why, let's assume the contrary and see why it violates our assumptions about consumer behavior. To do this, examine Figure 3.4. The figure shows two indifference curves, U_1 and U_2, which intersect at A. Since A and B are both on indifference curve U_1, the consumer must be indifferent between the two market baskets. Both A and C lie on indifference curve U_2, so the consumer must be indifferent between both these market baskets. As a result, the consumer must also be indifferent between B and C. But this can't be true, because market basket B must be preferred to C as it contains more of both food and clothing than C. The assumption that indifference curves intersect thus contradicts our assumption that more is preferred to less.

Of course, there are an infinite number of nonintersecting indifference curves, one for every possible level of satisfaction. In fact, each point on the

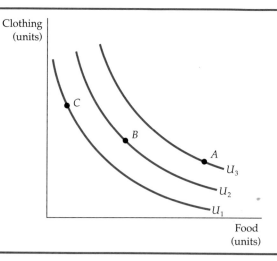

FIGURE 3.3 An Indifference Map. An indifference map is a set of indifference curves that describes a person's preferences. Market basket A on the highest of the three indifference curves is preferred to market basket B, which in turn is preferred to market basket C on the lowest indifference curve.

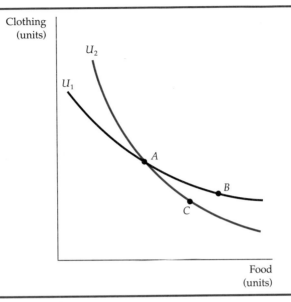

FIGURE 3.4   Indifference Curves Cannot Cross.   If indifference curves U_1 and U_2 intersected, one of the assumptions of consumer theory would be violated. In this diagram, the consumer is indifferent among market baskets A, B, and C, yet B is preferred to C, because B has more of both goods.

graph (representing a market basket) has an indifference curve passing through it. We have shown only three indifference curves in Figure 3.3 to simplify the presentation. These three curves provide an *ordinal ranking* of market baskets. An ordinal ranking places market baskets in the order of most preferred to least preferred, but it does not tell us by *how much* one market basket is preferred to another. For example, we know that consumption of any basket on U_3, such as A, is preferred to consumption of any basket on U_2, such as B, but we don't know by how much. The amount by which A is preferred to B (and B to C) is not revealed by the indifference map. We cannot, for example, say that consumers on U_2 are twice as happy as they might be on U_1. Fortunately, this ordinal ranking is sufficient to help us explain how most individual decisions are made. In the few instances where it is not, we will describe an alternative approach to describing preferences.

The Marginal Rate of Substitution

People face trade-offs when choosing between two or among three or more goods, and indifference curves can help to make those trade-offs clear. The indifference curve in Figure 3.5 illustrates this. Starting at market basket A and

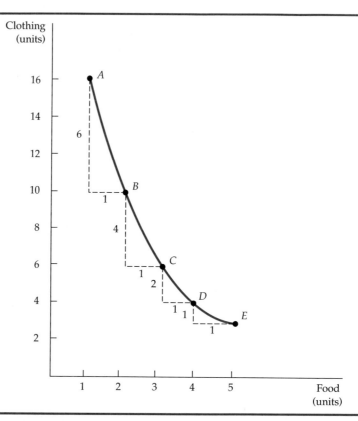

FIGURE 3.5 The Marginal Rate of Substitution. The slope of an indifference curve measures the consumer's marginal rate of substitution between two goods. In the figure, the marginal rate of substitution $-\Delta C/\Delta F$ falls from 6 to 4 to 2 to 1. When the marginal rate of substitution diminishes along an indifference curve, preferences are convex.

moving to market basket B, we see that the consumer is willing to give up six units of clothing to obtain one unit of food. However, moving from B to C, he is willing to give up only four units of clothing to obtain an additional unit of food, and in moving from C to D, he will give up two units of clothing to obtain one unit of food. The more clothing and the less food a person consumes, the more clothing she will give up to obtain more food. Similarly, the more food that a person possesses, the less clothing she is willing to give up to obtain more food. This pattern reflects the fact that most consumers derive less and less additional satisfaction as they consume more and more of any good. In general, the amount of additional satisfaction a consumer gets from consuming more of an item decreases as the total consumption of the item rises. Thus, indifference curves are *convex* in shape (i.e., bowed inward). With convex indifference curves, the consumer prefers a balanced market basket to market baskets that contain all of one good and none of the other.

To quantify the amount of one good a consumer will give up to obtain more of another good, we use a measure called the *marginal rate of substitution*. The *marginal rate of substitution* (MRS) of food F for clothing C is the maximum amount of clothing that a person is willing to give up to obtain one additional unit of food. To be consistent throughout the book, we will describe the MRS in terms of the amount of the good drawn on the vertical axis that must be given up to obtain one unit of the good drawn on the horizontal axis. Thus, if we denote the change in clothing by ΔC and the change in food by ΔF, the marginal rate of substitution can be written as $-\Delta C/\Delta F$. The negative sign is included to allow the marginal rate of substitution to be a positive number (ΔC is always negative). As a result, the marginal rate of substitution at any point is equal in absolute value to the slope of the indifference curve at that point. The only difference is that the slope is negative, reflecting a trade-off between consumption of the two goods, whereas the MRS is chosen to be positive as a matter of convenience.[1]

To see why indifference curves must be convex, consider how the marginal rate of substitution varies as we move along an indifference curve. Starting with market basket A in Figure 3.5 and moving to market basket B, we note that the MRS of clothing C for food F is $-\Delta C/\Delta F = -(-6)/1 = 6$. However, when starting at market basket B and moving from B to C, the MRS falls to 4. Beginning at market basket C and moving from C to D, the MRS equals 2, and beginning at market basket D and moving from D to E, the MRS equals 1. We see, then, that as food consumption increases, the slope of the indifference curve falls, so the MRS falls. Thus, a *diminishing marginal rate of substitution* (i.e., convex indifference curves) is an important characteristic of consumer preferences.[2]

The shapes of indifference curves can imply different degrees of willingness to substitute one good for another. Consider, for example, Philip's and Jane's preferences for juice and soft drinks in Figure 3.6. In 3.6a Philip's indifference curves show a relatively low (although still decreasing) marginal rate of substitution of soft drinks for juice; for any amount of juice he consumes, Philip will give up very little juice to obtain another soft drink. Clearly, Philip has a strong preference for juice that is not affected much by his soft drink consumption.

---

[1] A minor discrepancy arises when the MRS is calculated on the basis of discrete changes in Y and X. $\Delta Y/\Delta X$ measured over an arc of a curve is slightly different from the value of the slope of a line at a point. We are assuming that this difference is small. When we deal with infinitesimal changes, the MRS is measured by the magnitude of the slope of the line tangent to the indifference curve.

[2] With nonconvex preferences, the MRS increases as the amount of the good measured on the horizontal axis (X) increases along any indifference curve. This unlikely possibility might arise if one or both goods are addictive. The willingness to substitute an addictive drug for other goods might increase as the use of the addictive drug increased.

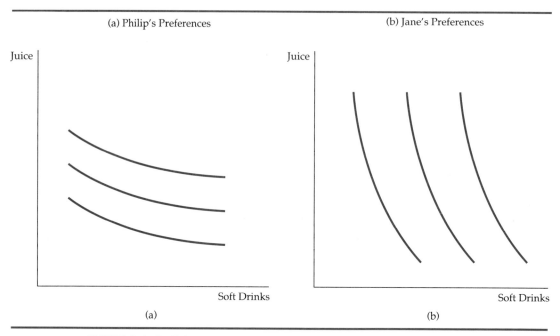

FIGURE 3.6 Individual Differences in Preferences. People have different preferences, which appear as different indifference maps. Here Philip strongly prefers juice, whereas Jane prefers soft drinks.

Jane's preferences are shown in Figure 3.6b. She has a high marginal rate of substitution of soft drinks for juice; her preference for soft drinks is much stronger than for juice. If Jane did not care about juice at all, her indifference curves would be vertical straight lines. Likewise, if Philip were neutral toward soft drinks, then his indifference curves would be horizontal straight lines.

EXAMPLE 3.1   DESIGNING A NEW AUTOMOBILE

Suppose you are an executive in an automobile company who must plan new model cars that will be introduced in the next few years. If you commissioned a marketing study, one of the things you would learn is that two of the most important attributes of a car are its styling and its performance (e.g., acceleration and handling). You know that both styling and performance are desirable attributes; the better the styling and the better the performance, the greater the demand for the car. However, it costs money to add style and performance to your new car. How much of each attribute should you offer?

The answer to this question depends in part on the costs of production, but it also depends on consumer preferences for automobile attributes. In planning

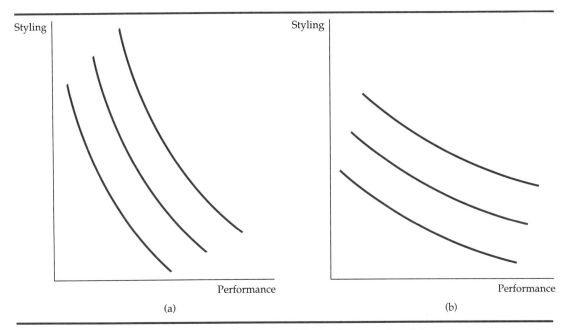

Styling

Performance

(a)

Styling

Performance

(b)

FIGURE 3.7 Preferences for Automobile Attributes. People's preferences concerning the attributes of an automobile can be described using indifference curves. Each indifference curve describes the combinations of performance and styling that give the same satisfaction. Because some attribute combinations cost less than others, an automobile company can use this preference information to cut budgetary costs and to design new automobiles.

the new model, it is crucial to understand what those preferences are. One way to do this is to conduct a study in which people are interviewed and given a choice of several levels of styling (from simple and relatively uncomfortable to sophisticated and plush) and several levels of performance. By designing the study properly, one can ascertain which of the two attributes is preferred, and more importantly, to what extent the person being interviewed is willing to trade off one attribute to get more of the other.[3]

Suppose most people share the preferences shown in Figure 3.7a. They tend to prefer performance to styling in the sense that they are willing to give up quite a bit of styling to get better car performance. Compare this with Figure 3.7b, which shows the preferences of a much smaller segment of the population.

[3]Many businesses carry out marketing studies, and business schools teach marketing research. Much of this research effort is presented in the leading marketing journals, including the *Journal of Marketing* and the *Journal of Marketing Research*. Or see Joel Evans and Barry Berman, *Marketing* (New York: Macmillan, 1987).

These people tend to prefer styling to performance and are willing to put up with bad mileage to get a more stylish car.

With detailed knowledge about the costs of providing each attribute, a good manager can choose exactly what model to put on the market next year. This is the type of exercise that Lee Iacocca performed at the Ford Motor Company in 1964. Iacocca believed the market needed a car that would spark the interest of those younger Americans who were growing more affluent and independent.[4] Iacocca took the idea for the design of such a car from his co-worker Donald Frey and helped to sell it to Ford and to the consuming public. Frey and Iacocca designed a car that had style and could be produced more cheaply than other stylish cars such as General Motors' Corvette. The result was the Ford Mustang, one of the major car marketing successes of all time. In its first year of production, over 418,000 Mustangs were sold; this generated hundreds of millions of dollars in profit for Ford.

3.2 Budget Constraints

An indifference map describes a person's preferences concerning various combinations of goods and services. But preferences do not explain all of consumer behavior. Individual choices are also affected by *budget constraints*, which limit people's ability to consume in light of the prices they must pay for various goods and services.

The Budget Line

To understand how a budget constraint limits a person's choices, let's consider a situation in which a woman has a fixed amount of income, I, that can be spent on two goods, food and clothing. Let F be the amount of food (good F) purchased, and C the amount of clothing (good C). Finally, we will represent the price of the two goods as P_F and P_C. Then $P_F F$ (i.e., price of food times the quantity) is the amount of money spent on food, and $P_C C$ is the amount of money spent on clothing.

The *budget line* indicates all combinations of F and C for which total money spent is equal to income. Since there are only two goods, the woman will spend her entire income on food and clothing. As a result, the combinations of food and clothing that she can buy will all lie on this line:[5]

$$P_F F + P_C C = I \tag{3.1}$$

[4]This characterization is based on David Halberstam, *The Reckoning* (New York: William Morrow, 1986), chapter 20.

[5]The assumption that all income is spent on the two goods is not as restrictive as it seems, because money not spent (savings) can be considered to be a good as well. In this case, income would be allocated between current consumption (spending) and future consumption (saving).

To take an example, let's say that the woman has a weekly income of $40, the price of food is $1.00 per unit, and the price of clothing is $2.00 per unit. Table 3.2 shows the various combinations of food and clothing that she can purchase each week with her $40. If all her budget were allocated toward clothing, the most that she could purchase would be 20 units (at a price of $2.00 per unit), as represented by market basket A. If she spent all her budget on food, she could buy a total of 40 units (at $1 per unit), as given by market basket E. Market baskets B, C, and D show three additional ways in which $40 could be spent on food and clothing.

Figure 3.8 shows the budget line associated with market baskets A through E given in Table 3.2. Because giving up a unit of clothing saves $2.00 and buying a unit of food costs $1.00, the amount of clothing given up for food along the budget line must be the same everywhere. As a result, the budget line is a straight line from point A to point E. In this particular case, the budget line is given by the equation $F + 2C = \$40$.

The intercept of the budget line is represented by market basket A. As she moves along the line from market basket A to market basket E, the woman spends less on clothing and more on food. It is easy to see that the extra clothing that must be given up to consume an additional unit of food is given by the ratio of the price of food to the price of clothing ($1/$2 = 1/2). Since clothing costs $2.00 per unit, while food is only $1.00 per unit, ½ a unit of clothing must be given up to get 1 unit of food. In Figure 3.8 the slope of the line $\Delta C/\Delta F = -\frac{1}{2}$ measures the relative cost of food and clothing.

In terms of equation (3.1), we can see how much of C must be given up to consume more of F by dividing both sides of the equation by P_C and then solving for C:

$$C = (I/P_C) - (P_F/P_C)F \tag{3.2}$$

Equation (3.2) is the equation for a straight line; it has a vertical intercept of I/P_C and a slope of $-(P_F/P_C)$.

The slope of the budget line $-(P_F/P_C)$ is the negative of the ratio of the prices of the two goods. The magnitude of the slope tells us the rate at which the two goods can be substituted for each other without changing the total amount of money spent. The vertical intercept (I/P_C) represents the maximum amount of

TABLE 3.2 Market Baskets and the Budget Line

Market Basket	Food(F)	Clothing(C)	Total Spending
A	0	20	$40
B	10	15	$40
C	20	10	$40
D	30	5	$40
E	40	0	$40

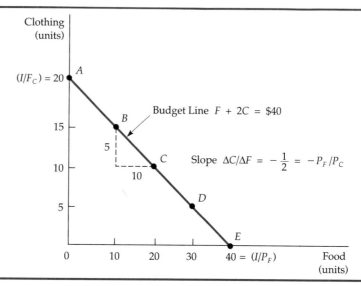

FIGURE 3.8 A Budget Line. The consumer's budget line describes the combinations of goods that can be purchased given the consumer's income and the prices of the goods. Line AE shows the budget associated with an income of $40, a price of food of $P_F = \$1$ per unit, and a price of clothing of $P_C = \$2$ per unit. The slope of the budget line is $-P_F/P_C$.

C that can be purchased with income I. Finally, the horizontal intercept (I/P_F) tells us how many units of F could be purchased if all income were spent on F.

The Effects of Changes in Income and Prices

We have seen that the budget line depends on income and on the prices of the goods P_F and P_C. Prices and income often change, however. Let's see what such changes do to the budget line.

Income Changes What happens to the budget line when income changes? From the equation for the straight line, we can see that a change in income alters the vertical intercept of the budget line but does not change the slope (because the price of neither good changed). Figure 3.9 shows that if income is doubled (from $40 to $80), the budget line shifts outward (from budget line L_1 to budget line L_2). Note, however, that L_2 remains parallel to L_1. If she desires, the woman could now double her purchases of both food and clothing. Likewise, if her income is cut in half (from $40 to $20), the budget line shifts inward, from L_1 to L_3.

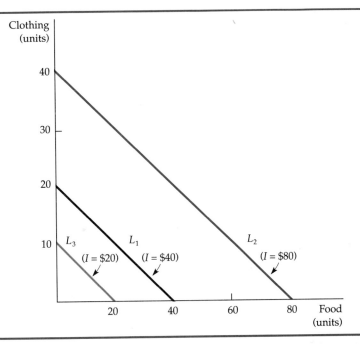

FIGURE 3.9 Effects of a Change in Income on the Budget Line. A change in income (with prices unchanged) causes the budget line to shift parallel to the original line (L_1). When the income of $40 (on L_1) is increased to $80, the budget line shifts outward to L_2. However, when the income falls to $20, the line shifts inward to L_3.

Price Changes What happens to the budget line if the price of one good changes but the price of the other good does not? We can use the equation $C = (I/P_C) - (P_F/P_C)F$ to describe the effects of a change in the price of food on the budget line. Suppose the price of food F falls by half, from $1.00 to $0.50. Then the vertical intercept of the budget line remains unchanged, but the slope changes from $-P_F/P_C = \$1/\$2 = -\frac{1}{2}$ to $-\$0.50/\$2 = -\frac{1}{4}$. In Figure 3.10, we obtain the new budget line L_2 by rotating the original budget line L_1 outward, pivoting from the C-intercept. This rotation makes sense intuitively because a person who consumes only C (clothing) and not F (food) is not affected by the price change. However, a man who purchases a substantial amount of food has greatly increased his purchasing power. In fact, the maximum amount of food that he can purchase has doubled in response to the decline in the price of food.

On the other hand, when the price of food doubles from $1 to $2, the budget line rotates inward to line L_3, because the person's purchasing power has diminished. Once again, a person who consumed only clothing would be unaffected by the price increase in food.

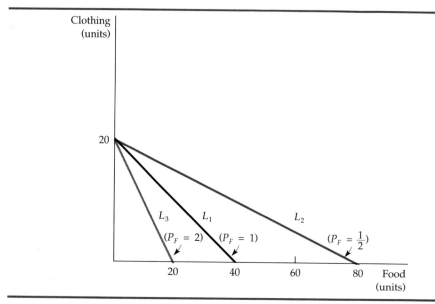

FIGURE 3.10 Effects of a Change in Price on the Budget Line. A change in the price of one good (with income unchanged) causes the budget line to rotate about one intercept. When the price of food falls from \$1.00 to \$0.50, the budget line rotates outward from L_1 to L_2. However, when the price increases from \$1.00 to \$2.00, the line rotates inward to L_3.

What happens if both the price of food and the price of clothing change, but in a way that leaves the *ratio* of the two prices unchanged? Because the slope of the budget line is equal to the ratio of the two prices, the slope will remain the same. The slope of the budget line must shift so that the new line is parallel to the old one. For example, if the prices of both goods fall by half, then the slope of the budget line does not change, but both intercepts double, and the budget line is shifted outward.

This tells us something about the determinants of a person's *purchasing power*—her ability to buy goods. Purchasing power is determined not only by income, but also by prices. For example, a person's purchasing power can double either because her income doubles *or* because the prices of all goods that she buys fall by half.

As a final example, consider what happens if everything doubles—the prices of both food and clothing *and* the consumer's income. (This can happen in an inflationary economy.) Because both prices have doubled, the ratio of the prices has not changed and, therefore, neither has the slope of the budget line. Because the price of clothing has doubled as has income, the maximum amount of clothing that can be purchased (represented by the intercept of the budget line) is unchanged. The same is true for food. Therefore, an inflation in which all prices and income levels rise proportionately will have no effect on the consumer's budget line or purchasing power.

3.3 Consumer Choice

Having examined preferences and budget constraints, we can now show how individual consumers choose how much of each good to buy. We assume that consumers make this choice in a rational way. By this we mean that they choose goods to *maximize the satisfaction they can achieve, given the limited budget available to them.*

The maximizing market basket must satisfy two conditions. First, *it must be located on the budget line.* To see why, note that any market basket to the left of and below the budget line leaves some income unallocated, which if spent could increase the consumer's satisfaction. Of course, consumers can—and sometimes do—save some of their incomes for future consumption. But this means that the choice is not just between food and clothing, but between food or clothing now, or food and clothing in the future. At this point we will keep things simple by assuming that all income is spent now. Then, note that any market basket to the right of and above the budget line cannot be purchased with available income. Thus, the only possible choice is a market basket on the budget line.

The second condition is that *the maximizing market basket must give the consumer the most preferred combination of goods and services.* These two conditions reduce the problem of maximizing consumer satisfaction to one of picking an appropriate point on the budget line.

In our food and clothing example, as with any two goods, we can graphically illustrate the solution to the consumer's choice problem. Figure 3.11 shows how the problem is solved. Here, three indifference curves describe a man's preferences for food and clothing. Remember that of the three curves, the outermost curve U_3 yields the greatest amount of satisfaction, the curve U_2 yields the next greatest amount, and the curve U_1 yields the least.

First, note that point B on indifference curve U_1 is not the most preferred choice, because a reallocation of income in which more is spent on food and less on clothing can increase the consumer's satisfaction. In particular, by moving to point A, the consumer spends the same amount of money and achieves the increased level of satisfaction associated with indifference curve U_2. Second, note that market baskets to the right and above indifference curve U_2, like the market basket associated with C on indifference curve U_3, achieve a higher level of satisfaction but cannot be purchased with the available income. Therefore, A maximizes the consumer's satisfaction.

We see from this that the market basket that maximizes satisfaction must lie on the highest indifference curve that touches the budget line. Point A is the point of tangency between indifference curve U_2 and the budget line. At A the

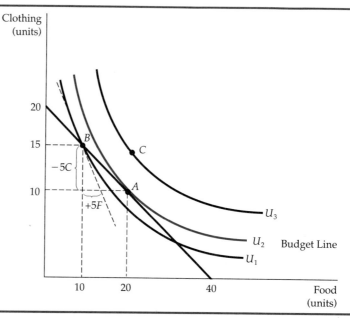

FIGURE 3.11 Maximizing Consumer Satisfaction. When the budget line and the indifference map are combined, consumers maximize their satisfaction by choosing A. At this point the budget line and indifference curve U_2 are tangent, and no higher level of satisfaction can be attained. At A, the point of maximization, the marginal rate of substitution between the two goods equals the price ratio. At B, however, the marginal rate of substitution (1) is greater than the price ratio (1/2), and maximization does not occur.

slope of the budget line is exactly equal to the slope of the indifference curve. Because the MRS is the negative of the slope of the indifference curve, we can say that satisfaction is maximized (given the budget constraint) at the point where

$$MRS = P_F/P_C \tag{3.3}$$

This is an important result: Satisfaction is maximized when *the marginal rate of substitution (of* F *for* C*) is equal to the ratio of the prices (of* F *to* C*).* Thus, the consumer can obtain maximum satisfaction by adjusting his consumption of goods F and C so that the MRS equals the price ratio. In other words, the rate at which the consumer is willing to substitute food for clothing is equal to the market rate at which he can substitute.

The condition given in equation (3.3) is an example of the kinds of optimization conditions that arise in economics. In this instance, maximization is achieved when the *marginal benefit*, that is, the benefit associated with the consumption of one additional unit of food, is equal to the *marginal cost*. The marginal benefit is measured by the MRS. At point A it equals ½ (at this point on the budget line $P_F = 1$ and $P_C = 2$), which implies that the consumer is willing to give up ½ unit of clothing to obtain 1 unit of food. At the same point, the marginal cost is measured by the value of the slope of the budget line; it also equals ½, because the cost of getting one unit of food is to give up ½ unit of clothing.

If the MRS is less or greater than the price ratio, maximization has not been achieved. For example, compare point B in Figure 3.11 to point A. At point B, the consumer is purchasing 10 units of food and 15 units of clothing. The price ratio (or marginal cost) is equal to ½, because food costs $1.00 and clothing costs $2.00. However, the MRS (or marginal benefit) is greater than ½. (It is approximately equal to 1.) As a result, the consumer is willing to substitute one unit of food for one unit of clothing without loss of satisfaction. Because food is cheaper than clothing, it is in his interest to buy more food and less clothing. If the consumer purchases one less unit of clothing, for example, that $2.00 can be allocated to two units of food, when only one unit is needed to maintain his level of satisfaction.[6]

The reallocation of the budget continues in this manner (moving along the budget line), until we reach point A, because at A the price ratio of ½ just equals the MRS of ½, which implies that the consumer is willing to trade one unit of clothing for two units of food. Only when the condition MRS $= ½ = P_F/P_C$ holds is he maximizing his satisfaction.

EXAMPLE 3.2   THE DECISION MAKING OF A LOCAL PUBLIC OFFICIAL

Grant programs from the federal government to state and local governments serve many purposes. One program might seek to stimulate spending for primary and secondary schooling, another to redistribute income from relatively wealthy states and localities to those that are relatively poor, and a third to ensure that individual governments provide minimum service levels to their constituents.

Which kinds of grant programs are best suited to achieve these different objectives? The answer depends on the incentive effects that each program generates; by changing the constraints that local public officials face, a grant program can alter the official's decision about how much the local government should spend. Let's look at two types of grant programs and see how they evoke different responses from public officials.

---

[6]The result that the MRS equals the price ratio is deceptively powerful. Imagine two different consumers who have just purchased various quantities of food and clothing. Without looking at their purchases, you can tell both persons (if they are maximizing) the exact value of their MRS (by looking at the prices of the two goods). What you cannot tell, however, is the quantity of each good purchased because that is determined by their individual preferences or tastes. If the two consumers have different tastes, they will consume different quantities of food and clothing, even though each MRS is the same.

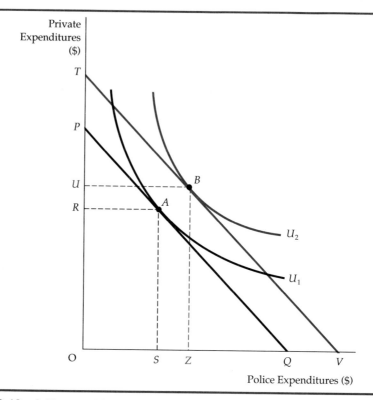

FIGURE 3.12   A Nonmatching Grant.   A nonmatching grant from the federal government to a local government acts just like an increase in income in the traditional consumer analysis. The local government official moves from A to B, thereby allocating a portion of the grant to public expenditures and a portion to lower taxes and therefore to an increase in private expenditures.

Suppose that a public official is in charge of the police budget, which is paid for by local taxes. Her preferences reflect what she believes should be allocated for police spending and what she feels citizens would prefer to have available for private consumption. Before the introduction of the grant program, the city's budget line is PQ in Figure 3.12. This budget line represents the *total* amount of resources available for public police spending (shown on the horizontal axis) and private spending (shown on the vertical axis).[7] The preference-maximizing market basket A on indifference curve U_1 shows that OR is spent on private expenditures, and OS is spent on police expenditures. Since public expenditures are paid for by local taxes, these private expenditures represent after-tax spending.

[7]This sum would approximately equal the per capita income of the jurisdiction (say, $10,000) times the number of taxpayers (say, 50,000).

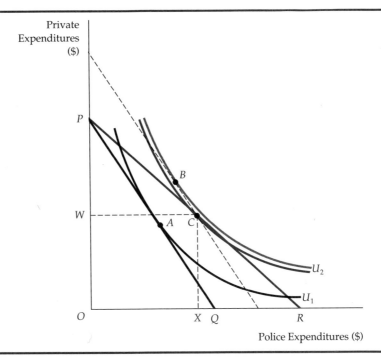

FIGURE 3.13 A Matching Grant. A matching grant from the federal government to a local government acts just like a price decrease in the traditional consumer analysis. The local government official moves from *A* to *B*, allocating a portion of the grant to public expenditures and a portion to private expenditures. Relatively more money, however, is spent on public expenditures than would be spent if there were a nonmatching grant (and the consumer chose *C*) that involved the same government expenditure.

The first type of grant program, a *nonmatching grant*, is simply a check to the local government that can be spent without restriction. An unconditional grant of this sort expands the community budget line outward from *PQ* to *TV*, where *PT = QV* is the dollar amount of the grant. The response to this influx of dollars is to move to a higher indifference curve by selecting market basket *B*, with more of both goods (*OU* of private expenditures and *OZ* of police expenditures). But more private expenditures means that some of the money for police that came previously from taxes now comes from government grants.

The second type of grant is the *matching grant*. Matching funds are offered as a form of subsidy to local spending. For example, the federal government might offer to pay $1.00 for every $2.00 that the local government raises to pay for police. As a result, a matching grant lowers the relative cost of the publicly provided good. In terms of Figure 3.13, the matching grant rotates the budget line outward from *PQ* to *PR*. If no local money is spent on police, the budget line is unchanged. However, if the public official decides to spend money on the public sector, the public budget increases.

In response to the matching grant, the official chooses market basket C rather than A. This move involves an increase in both police and private expenditures. At C, a total of OX dollars are allocated to police and OW to private expenditures.

The spending effects of a matching grant are different from the effects of a nonmatching grant. With the matching grant the public official chooses to move from A to C rather than A to B. The diagram shows that the matching grant leads to greater police spending than does the nonmatching grant when the two grant programs involve the identical government expenditure.[8]

A Corner Solution

Consumers do not always balance their consumption. Occasionally, they consume in extremes, at least within categories of goods. For example, some people spend no money on travel and entertainment. The indifference curve analysis can be used to show conditions under which consumers choose not to consume a particular good.

In Figure 3.14, faced with budget line AB, a man chooses to purchase only food and no clothing. This is called a *corner solution* because when one of the goods is not consumed the consumption bundle appears at the corner of the graph that describes the person's budget line. At B, which is the point of maximum satisfaction, the marginal rate of substitution of food for clothing is greater than the slope of the budget line, which suggests that if the consumer had more clothing to give up, he would gladly trade it for additional food. In fact, the marginal rate of substitution is greater than the price ratio no matter how much food the man consumes. Or to put it differently, the marginal benefit associated with the additional consumption of food is greater than the marginal cost.

When a corner solution arises, the consumer's MRS does not equal the price ratio.[9] The marginal benefit–marginal cost condition that we described in the previous section holds only when some amounts of all goods are consumed.

An important lesson from our corner solution analysis is that predictions about how much of a product consumers will purchase when faced with changing economic conditions depend on the nature of consumer preferences for that product and related products and on the slope of the consumer's budget line.

---

[8]Note also that the matching grant achieves a slightly lower level of satisfaction than the nonmatching grant. The intuition is that the nonmatching grant leaves the public official free to spend the grant any way she wishes, but the matching grant "distorts" the official's choice toward police spending and away from private spending.

[9]It is possible, but unlikely, that a corner solution will be reached at which the MRS is equal to the price ratio. We have omitted this from the text to simplify the discussion.

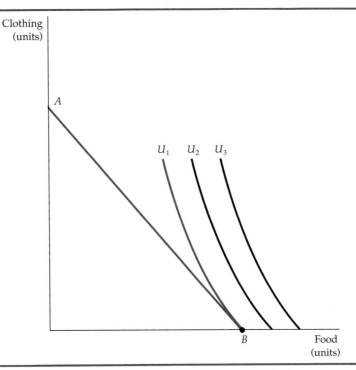

FIGURE 3.14   A Corner Solution.   When the consumer's marginal rate of substitution is greater than the price ratio for all levels of consumption, then a corner solution arises. The consumer maximizes satisfaction by consuming only one of the two goods. Given budget line AB, the highest level of satisfaction is achieved at B on indifference curve U_2, and only food is consumed.

If the MRS of food for clothing is substantially greater than the price ratio, as in Figure 3.14, then a small decrease in the price of clothing will not alter the consumer's choice—he will still choose to consume only food. But if the price of clothing falls far enough, the consumer could very quickly choose to consume a great deal of clothing.

EXAMPLE 3.3   A COLLEGE TRUST FUND

Jane Doe's parents have provided a trust fund for her college education. Jane, who is 18, can receive the entire trust fund on the condition that it be spent only on education. The trust fund is a welcome gift to Jane but perhaps not as welcome as an unrestricted trust would be. To see this consider Figure 3.15, in which dollars per year spent on education are shown on the horizontal axis, and dollars spent on other forms of consumption on the vertical axis.

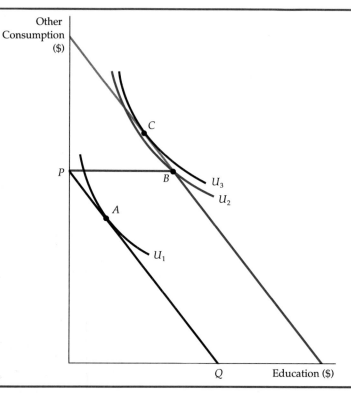

FIGURE 3.15 A College Trust Fund. A student is given a college trust fund that must be spent on education. The student moves from A to B, a corner solution. If, however, the trust fund could be spent on other consumption as well as education, the student would be better off at C.

The budget line that Jane faces before the awarding of the trust is given by line PQ. The trust fund expands the budget line outward so long as the full amount of the fund, shown by distance PB, is spent on education. By accepting the trust fund and going to college, Jane increases her utility, moving from A on indifference curve U_1 to B on indifference curve U_2.

Note that B represents a corner solution, because Jane's marginal rate of substitution of other consumption for education is lower than the relative price of other consumption. Jane would prefer to spend a portion of the trust fund on other goods as well as education. Without the restriction on the trust fund, she would move to C on indifference curve U_3, decreasing her spending on education (perhaps going to a junior college rather than a four-year college) but increasing her spending on items that she enjoys more than education.

From the point of view of the trust recipient, a restriction of the kind described generally makes the benefit of the trust smaller as compared with an unrestricted trust. Trusts of this kind are popular, however, because they allow parents to control their children's expenditures in ways that they believe are in the children's long-run best interests.

3.4 The Concept of Utility

Indifference curve analysis allows us to describe consumer preferences graphically and builds on the assumption that consumers can rank alternatives. But consumer preferences can also be described using the concepts of utility and marginal utility. We will describe how each of these concepts is defined and then relate each to the indifference curve analysis.

Utility and Satisfaction

Utility is the level of satisfaction that a person gets from consuming a good or undertaking an activity. Utility has an important psychological component, because people obtain utility by getting things that give them pleasure and by avoiding things that give them pain. In economic analysis, however, utility is most often used to summarize the preference ranking of market baskets. If buying three books makes a person happier than the purchase of one shirt, then we say that the books give that person more utility than the shirt.

A *utility function* is obtained by attaching a number to each market basket, so that if market basket A is preferred to market basket B, the number will be higher for A than for B. For example, market basket A on the highest of three indifference curves U_3 might have a utility level of 3, while market basket B on the second-highest indifference curve U_2 might have a utility level of 2, and market basket C, on the lowest indifference curve U_1, a utility level of 1. Thus, the utility function provides the same information about preferences that an indifference map does. Both utility functions and indifference maps order consumer choices in terms of levels of satisfaction.

The utility function is more easily applied to the analysis of choices involving three or more goods simply because it is difficult to graph indifference curves in this case. But it is important to be careful about how a utility function is used. When economists first studied utility, they hoped that individuals' preferences could be easily quantified or measured in terms of basic units and, therefore, could provide a *cardinal* ranking of alternatives. Today, however, we know that the particular unit of measurement of utility is unimportant. For example, the levels of utility associated with the three market baskets A, B, and C might be 4, 2, and 1, or they might be 3, 2, and 1. Because most choices can be explained simply by the *ordinal* ranking of utility levels, the indicators 4, 2, and 1 provide the same information as the indicators 3, 2, and 1. What is important is the *relative* rankings that are given when a particular set of numbers is chosen.

We use information about the choices that people make to infer their preferences and tastes. For example, if a man chooses to buy three units of food and two of clothing with a $50.00 check instead of two units of food and three of clothing, then we can infer that he prefers the first choice to the second. But we do not use information about choices to tell us by *how much* one market basket is preferred to another.

Bearing in mind that we are using the ordinal properties of the utility function, we now look carefully at a particular utility function. The function $u(F,C) = FC$ tells us that the level of satisfaction associated with the consumption of F units of the first good and C units of the second good is the product of F and C. Figure 3.16 shows some of the indifference curves associated with this function. The graph was drawn by choosing one particular market basket, say, $F = 5$ and $C = 5$, which generates a utility level of 25. Then the indifference

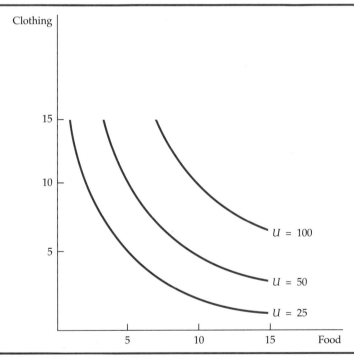

FIGURE 3.16 Utility Functions and Indifference Curves. A utility function can be represented by a series of indifference curves, to each of which is attached a numerical indicator. The figure shows three indifference curves, with utility levels of 25, 50, and 100.

curve was drawn by finding all market baskets for which $FC = 25$ (e.g., $F = 10$, $C = 2.5$; $F = 2.5$, $C = 10$). The second indifference curve drawn contains all market baskets for which $FC = 50$, and the third all baskets such that $FC = 100$.

The important point is that the actual numbers attached to the indifference curves are for convenience only. Suppose the utility function were changed to $u(F,C) = 4FC$. Consider any market basket that previously generated a utility level of 25, say, $F = 5$ and $C = 5$. Now the level of utility has increased by a factor of 4 to 100. Thus, the indifference curve labeled 25 looks the same, but it should now be labeled 100 rather than 25. In fact, the only difference between the indifference curves associated with the utility function $4FC$ and the utility function FC is that the indifference curves are numbered 100, 200, and 400, rather than 25, 50, and 100. Most often when we do use utility functions, we care about their ordinal rather than cardinal properties. On the few occasions when we do plan to use the stronger assumption that utility has cardinal meaning, we will let you know.

EXAMPLE 3.4   GASOLINE RATIONING

In the winter of 1974 and the summer of 1979, the government imposed price controls on gasoline, and many gas stations had to reduce their prices substantially (world oil prices rose but controls kept domestic prices low). As a result, motorists wanted to buy more gasoline than was available at the lower controlled prices, and gasoline was rationed without the use of the price system. Nonprice rationing provides an alternative to the market that some people would consider fair. Under one form of rationing everyone has an equal chance to purchase a rationed good, whereas under a market system those with higher incomes can outbid those with lower incomes to obtain goods that are in scarce supply.

In this case gasoline was allocated by long lines at the gas pumps: Those who were willing to give up their time waiting got the gas they wanted, while others did not. By guaranteeing every person access to a minimum amount of gasoline, rationing can provide some people with access to a product that they could not otherwise afford. Unfortunately, the rationing process hurts others by limiting the amount of gasoline that they can buy.[10]

We can see this clearly in Figure 3.17, which applies to a woman with an annual income of $20,000. The horizontal axis shows her annual consumption

---

[10]For a more elaborate and extensive discussion of gasoline rationing, see H. E. Frech III and William C. Lee, "The Welfare Cost of Rationing-By-Queuing Across Markets: Theory and Estimates from the U.S. Gasoline Crises," *Quarterly Journal of Economics* (1987): 97–108. Other, more general examples of rationing appear in Martin L. Weitzman, "Is the Price System or Rationing More Effective in Getting a Commodity to Those Who Need it Most," *Bell Journal*, 8 (Autumn 1977): 517–525.

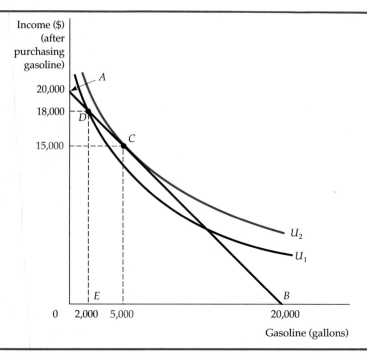

FIGURE 3.17 Inefficiency in Gasoline Rationing. When a good is rationed, that is, when less of the good is available than consumers would like to buy, consumers may suffer a loss in satisfaction. Without gasoline rationing, the consumer is at C on indifference curve U_2, consuming 5000 gallons of gasoline. However, with a limit of 2000 gallons of gasoline under rationing, the consumer moves to D and falls to a lower indifference curve U_1.

of gasoline, and the vertical axis shows her remaining income after purchasing gasoline. Suppose the controlled gasoline price is $1.00 per gallon. Because her income is $20,000, she is limited to the points on budget line AB, which has a slope of -1. At $1.00 per gallon, the woman might wish to buy 5000 gallons of gasoline per year and spend $15,000 on other goods, represented by C. At this point, she has maximized her utility (by being on the highest possible indifference curve U_2), given her budget constraint of $20,000.

Because of rationing, the woman can purchase only 2000 gallons of gasoline. As a result she no longer faces budget line AB, but rather ADE. The budget line is no longer a straight line because purchases above 2000 gallons are not possible. The figure shows that her choice to consume at D involves a lower level of utility U_1 than would be achieved without rationing, U_2, because she is consuming less gasoline and more of other goods than she would otherwise like.[11]

Marginal Utility

There are occasions when we might find it valuable to use some of the cardinal properties of utility functions. One situation occurs when people face risky choices that involve comparisons of utility at two different points in time. Another occurs when we wish to analyze the costs and benefits of public projects, which involves comparisons of utility among individuals. This section explains the concept of marginal utility and shows one example of how our previous analysis of consumer choice can be recast using the concepts of total and marginal utility. Other examples are given in Chapters 5 and 16.

To begin, let's distinguish between the total utility obtained by consumption and the satisfaction obtained from the last item consumed. *Marginal utility* (MU) measures the additional satisfaction obtained from consuming an additional amount of a good. For example, the marginal utility associated with a consumption increase from 0 to 10 units of food might be 9; from 10 to 20 it might be 7; and from 20 to 30 might be 5.

These numbers are consistent with the principle of *diminishing marginal utility:* As more and more of a good is consumed, the process of consumption will (at some point) yield smaller and smaller additions to utility. Imagine, for example, the consumption of television—marginal utility might fall after the second or third hour (and could become negative after the fourth or fifth).

We can relate the concept of marginal utility to the consumer's utility maximization problem in the following way. Consider a small movement down and along an indifference curve. We know that the additional consumption of F, ΔF, will generate additional or marginal utility MU_F for each unit. This results in a total increase in utility of $MU_F \Delta F$. At the same time, the loss of consumption of C, ΔC, will lower utility per unit by MU_C, resulting in a total loss of $MU_C \Delta C$.

Since all points on an indifference curve generate the same level of utility, the total gain in utility associated with the increase in F must balance the loss

---

[11]If we knew the exact form of her utility function, we could calculate her utility loss associated with the rationing process. If, for example, her utility function $u(X,Y)$ were equal to $(X^{.25})(Y^{.75})$, then without rationing, the level of utility achieved is $U_2 = (5000^{.25})(15{,}000^{.75})$, which equals 11,398. With rationing, utility falls to $U_1 = (2000^{.25})(18{,}000^{.75})$, which equals 9064. The utility loss of 2334 is difficult to interpret. However, we know that the loss is substantial because this woman would need an additonal \$2350 to be as well off under a rationing scheme as when the market is uncontrolled. (With rationing the woman spends \$2000 on gasoline and has \$18,000 to spend on other goods. The \$2350 was obtained as the solution of the equation $(2000^{.25})[(18{,}000 + x)^{.75}] = 11{,}398$. Graphically, this solution is given by the length of the vertical line segment from D in Figure 3.17 to indifference curve U_2.

due to the lower consumption of C. Formally,

$$0 = MU_F(\Delta F) + MU_C(\Delta C)$$

Now we can rearrange this equation so that

$$-(\Delta C/\Delta F) = MU_F/MU_C$$

But since $-(\Delta C/\Delta F)$ is the marginal rate of substitution of F for C, MRS, it follows by substitution that

$$MRS = MU_F/MU_C \tag{3.4}$$

Equation (3.4) tells us that the marginal rate of substitution is the ratio of the marginal utility of F to the marginal utility of C. As the consumer gives up more and more of C to obtain more of F, the marginal utility of F falls and the marginal utility of C increases.

We saw earlier in this chapter that when consumers maximize their satisfaction, the marginal rate of substitution of F for C is equal to the ratio of the prices of the two goods:

$$MRS = P_F/P_C \tag{3.5}$$

Since the MRS is also equal to the ratio of the marginal utilities of consuming F and C (from equation (3.4)), it follows that

$$MU_F/MU_C = P_F/P_C$$

or

$$MU_F/P_F = MU_C/P_C \tag{3.6}$$

Equation (3.6) tells us that utility maximization is achieved when the budget is allocated so that *the marginal utility per dollar of expenditure is the same for each good.* To see why this must hold, note that if a person gets more utility from spending an additional dollar on food than a dollar on clothing, her utility will be increased by spending more on food. So long as the marginal utility of spending more on food and less on clothing continues, she should shift her budget toward food and away from clothing. Eventually, the marginal utility of food will decrease (because there is diminishing marginal utility in consumption) and the marginal utility of clothing will increase (for the same reason). Only when the consumer has equalized the marginal utility per dollar of expenditure across all goods will she have maximized utility. This *equal marginal principle* is an important principle of maximization in microeconomics. It will reappear in different forms throughout our analysis of consumer and producer behavior.

Summary

1. The theory of consumer choice is built on the assumption that people behave rationally in an attempt to maximize the satisfaction that they can obtain by purchasing a particular combination of goods and services.

2. Consumer choice can be viewed in two related parts: the study of the consumer's preferences, and the analysis of the budget line, which constrains the choices a person can make.

3. Consumers make their choices by comparing market baskets or bundles of commodities. Their preferences are assumed to be complete (they can compare all possible market baskets) and transitive (if they prefer market basket A to B, and B to C, then they prefer A to C). In addition, we have assumed that more of each good is always preferred to less.

4. Indifference curves, which represent all combinations of goods and services that give the same level of satisfaction, are downward-sloping and cannot intersect one another.

5. Consumer preferences can be completely described by a set of indifference curves, or indifference map. This indifference map provides an ordinal ranking of all choices that the consumer might make.

6. The marginal rate of substitution of F for C is the maximum amount of C that a person is willing to give up to obtain one additional unit of F. The marginal rate of substitution diminishes as we move down along an indifference curve. This diminishing marginal rate of substitution is alternatively described as a case of convex preferences.

7. Budget lines represent all combinations of goods for which consumers expend all their income. Budget lines shift outward in response to an increase in consumer income, but they pivot and rotate about a fixed point (on the vertical axis) when the price of one good (on the horizontal axis) changes but income and the price of the other good do not.

8. Consumers maximize the satisfaction they can achieve, given the limited budget available to them. When a consumer maximizes satisfaction by consuming some of each of two goods, the marginal rate of substitution is equal to the ratio of the prices of the two goods being purchased.

9. Utility maximization can sometimes be achieved at a corner solution in which one good is not consumed. In that case the condition that the marginal rate of substitution is equal to the ratio of the prices does not hold.

10. The theory of the consumer can be presented using either an indifference curve approach, which uses the ordinal properties of utility (that is, which allows for the ranking of alternatives), or a utility function approach. A utility function is obtained by attaching a utility indicator or number to each market basket; if market basket A is preferred to market basket B, A generates more utility than B.

11. When risky choices are analyzed or when comparisons must be made among individuals, the cardinal properties of the utility can be important. The utility function that we will

study is consistent with the principle of diminishing marginal utility: As more and more of a good is consumed, the consumer obtains smaller and smaller increments to utility.

12. When the utility function approach is used and both goods are consumed, utility maximization occurs when the ratio of the marginal utilities of the two goods (which is the marginal rate of substitution) is equal to the ratio of the prices.

Questions for Review

1. What does the term *transitivity of preferences* mean? Can you think of an example in which preferences are not transitive?

2. Suppose that a set of indifference curves were not negatively sloped. What could you say about the desirability of the two goods?

3. Explain why two indifference curves cannot intersect.

4. Draw a set of indifference curves for which the marginal rate of substitution is constant. Draw two budget lines with different slopes and show what the utility-maximizing choice will be in each case. What conclusions can you draw from this exercise?

5. Explain why a person's marginal rate of substitution between two goods must equal the ratio of the price of the goods for the person to achieve maximum satisfaction.

6. Explain why consumers are likely to be made worse off when a product that they consume is rationed.

7. Describe the equal marginal principle. Explain why this principle may not hold if increasing marginal utility is associated with the consumption of one or both goods.

8. What is the difference between ordinal utility and cardinal utility? Explain why the assumption of cardinal utility is not needed in order to rank consumer choices.

Exercises

1. Suppose Jones and Smith have decided to allocate $1000 per year on liquid refreshment in the form of alcoholic or nonalcoholic drinks. Jones and Smith differ substantially in their preferences for these two forms of refreshment. Jones prefers alcoholic to nonalcoholic drinks, while Smith prefers the nonalcoholic option.
    a. Draw a set of indifference curves for Jones and a second set for Smith.
    b. Discuss why the two sets of curves are different from each other using the concept of marginal rate of substitution.
    c. If both Smith and Jones pay the same prices for their refreshments, will their marginal rates of substitution of alcoholic for nonalcoholic drinks be the same or different? Explain.

2. The price of records is $8 and the price of tapes is $10. Philip has a budget of $80 and has already purchased 4 records. As a result, he has $48 more to spend on additional records and tapes. Draw his budget line. If his remaining expenditure is made on 1 record and 4 tapes, show Philip's consumption choice on the budget line.

3. Suppose Bill views butter and margarine as perfectly substitutable for each other in any of their uses.
 a. Draw a set of indifference curves that describes Bill's preferences for butter and margarine.
 b. Are these indifference curves convex? Why?
 c. If butter costs $2/package, while margarine is only $1, and Bill has a $20 budget to spend for the month, which butter-margarine market basket will he choose? Can you show this graphically?

4. In this chapter consumer preferences for various commodities did not change during the analysis. Yet in some situations preferences do change as consumption occurs. Discuss why and how preferences might change over time with consumption of the following commodities:
 a. cigarettes
 b. dinner for the first time at a restaurant with a special cuisine.

5. Anne is a frequent flyer whose fares are reduced (through coupon giveaways) by 25 percent after she flies 25,000 miles a year, and then by 50 percent after she flies 50,000 miles. Can you graph the budget line that Anne faces in making her flight plans for the year?

6. The utility that Jane receives by consuming food F and clothing C is given by $u(F,C) = FC$.
 a. Draw the indifference curve associated with a utility level of 12, and the indifference curve associated with a utility level of 24. Are the indifference curves convex?
 b. Suppose that food costs $1 a unit, clothing costs $3 a unit, and Jane has $12 to spend on food and clothing. Graph the budget line that she faces.
 c. What is the utility-maximizing choice of food and clothing? (Suggestion: Solve the problem graphically.)
 d. What is the marginal rate of substitution of food for clothing when utility is maximized?
 e. Suppose that Jane decided to buy 3 units of food and 3 units of clothing with her $12 budget. Would her marginal rate of substitution of food for clothing be greater or less than 3? Explain.

CHAPTER 4

Individual and Market Demand

Chapter 3 laid the foundation for the theory of consumer demand. We discussed the nature of consumers' preferences and saw how, given a budget constraint, consumers choose a consumption basket that maximizes their satisfaction. From here it's a short step to analyzing demand itself and how the demand for a good depends on its price, the prices of other goods, and income.

We begin by examining the demands of individual consumers. Since we know how changes in price and income affect a person's budget line, we can determine how they affect consumption choice. In this way we can also determine a person's demand curve for a good. Next, we will see how individual demand curves can be aggregated to determine the market demand curve. We will also study the characteristics of demand and see why the demands for some kinds of goods differ considerably from the demands for others. In addition, we will show how demand curves can be used to measure the benefits that people receive when they consume a product, above and beyond the expenditure they make. Finally, we will briefly describe some of the methods that can be used to obtain useful empirical information about demand.

4.1 Individual Demand

This section shows how the demand curve of an individual consumer follows from the consumption choices that a person makes when faced with a budget constraint. To illustrate the concepts with graphs, we will limit the available goods to food and clothing, as in Chapter 3.

Price Changes

We begin by examining how a person's consumption of food and clothing changes when the price of food changes. Figures 4.1a and 4.1b show the con-

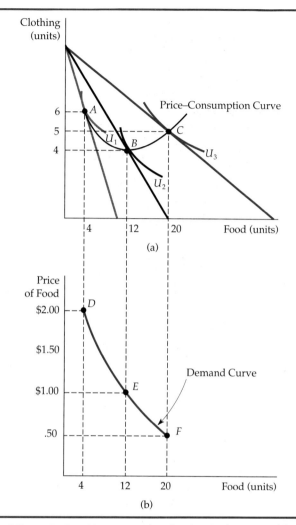

FIGURE 4.1 The Effect of Price Changes.   A reduction in the price of food, with income and the price of clothing fixed, causes this consumer to alter her choice of market basket. In part (a) the market baskets that maximize consumer satisfaction for various prices of food (point A, $2; B, $1; C, $0.50) trace out the price-consumption curve. Part (b) gives the demand curve, which relates the price of food to the quantity of food demanded. (Points D, E, and F correspond to points A, B, and C, respectively.)

sumption choices that one would make when allocating a fixed amount of income between the two goods as the price of food changes.

Initially, the price of food is $1.00, the price of clothing is $2.00, and the consumer's income is $20.00. The utility-maximizing consumption choice is at point B in Figure 4.1a. Here, the consumer buys 12 units of food and 4 units of clothing, which achieves the level of utility associated with indifference curve U_2.

Now look at Figure 4.1b, which shows the relationship between the price of food and the quantity demanded. The horizontal axis measures the quantity of food consumed, just as in Figure 4.1a, but the vertical axis now measures the price of food. Point E in Figure 4.1b corresponds to point B in Figure 4.1a. At E the price of food is $1.00, and the consumer purchases 12 units of food.

Now suppose the price of food increases to $2.00. As we saw in Chapter 3, the budget line in Figure 4.1a rotates inward about the vertical intercept, becoming twice as steep as before. The higher relative price of food has increased the magnitude of the slope of the budget line. The consumer now achieves maximum utility at A, which is on a lower indifference curve U_1. (Because the price of food has risen, the consumer's purchasing power, and hence attainable utility, has fallen.) At A, the consumer chooses 4 units of food and 6 units of clothing. In Figure 4.1b, this modified consumption choice is at D, which shows that at a price of $2.00, 4 units of food are demanded. Finally, what will happen if the price of food *decreases* to $0.50? Now the budget line rotates outward, so the consumer can achieve the higher level of utility associated with indifference curve U_3 in Figure 4.1a by selecting C, with 20 units of food and 5 units of clothing. Point F in Figure 4.1b shows the price of $0.50 and the quantity demanded of 20 units of food.

The Demand Curve

The exercise can be continued to include all possible changes in the price of food. In Figure 4.1a, the *price-consumption curve* traces the utility-maximizing combinations of food and clothing associated with each and every price of food. Note that as the price of food falls, attainable utility increases and the consumer buys more food. This pattern of increasing consumption of a good in response to a decrease in price holds in almost all demand situations. But what happens to the consumption of clothing as the price of food falls? As Figure 4.1a shows, the consumption of clothing may either increase or decrease. Both food *and* clothing consumption can increase because the decrease in the price of food has increased the consumer's ability to purchase both goods.

The *demand curve* shown in Figure 4.1b tells us the quantity of food that the consumer will buy as a function of the price of food. The demand curve has two important properties. First, the level of utility that can be attained changes as we move along the curve. The lower the price of the product, the higher the level of utility. (Note from Figure 4.1a that a higher indifference curve is reached as the price falls.)

Second, at every point on the demand curve, the consumer is maximizing utility by satisfying the condition that the marginal rate of substitution of clothing for food equals the ratio of the prices of food and clothing. As the price of food falls, the price ratio and the marginal rate of substitution also fall. In Figure 4.1 the price ratio falls from 1 ($2/$2) at D (because the curve U_1 is tangent to a budget line with a slope of -1 at B) to 1/2 ($1/$2) at E, to 1/4 ($0.50/$2) at F. Because the consumer is maximizing utility, the marginal rate of substitution of clothing for food decreases as we move down the demand curve. This makes good intuitive sense, because it tells us that the relative value of food falls as the consumer buys more of it.

The fact that the marginal rate of substitution varies along the individual's demand curve tells us something about the benefits that consumers enjoy from consuming a good or service. Suppose we were to ask a consumer how much she would be willing to pay for (i.e., value) an additional unit of food when she is currently consuming 4 units of it. Point D on the demand curve in Figure 4.1b provides the answer to that question: $2.00. Why? As we pointed out above, since the marginal rate of substitution of clothing for food is 1 at D, one additional unit of food is worth one additional unit of clothing. But a unit of clothing costs $2.00, which is, therefore, the value (or marginal benefit) obtained by consuming an additional unit of food. Thus, as we move down the demand curve in Figure 4.1b, the marginal rate of substitution falls, and the value that the consumer places on an additional unit of food falls from $2.00 to $1.00 to $0.50.

Income Changes

We have seen what happens to the consumption of food and clothing when the price of food changes. Now let's see what happens when income changes.

The effects of a change in income can be analyzed in much the same way as a price change. Figure 4.2a shows the consumption choices that a consumer would make when allocating a fixed income to food and clothing, when the price of food is $1.00 and the price of clothing is $2.00. Initially the consumer's income is $10.00. The utility-maximizing consumption choice is then at A, at which he buys 4 units of food and 3 units of clothing.

This choice of 4 units of food is also shown in Figure 4.2b as D on demand curve D_1. Demand curve D_1 is the curve that would be traced out if we held income fixed at $10.00 *but varied the price of food*. Because we are holding the price of food constant, we will observe only a single point D on this demand curve.

What happens if the consumer's income is increased to $20.00? His budget line then shifts outward parallel to the original budget line, allowing him to attain the utility level associated with indifference curve U_2. His optimal consumption choice is now at B, where he buys 10 units of food and 5 units of clothing. In Figure 4.2b, his consumption of food is shown as E on demand curve D_2. (D_2 is the demand curve that would be traced out if we held income

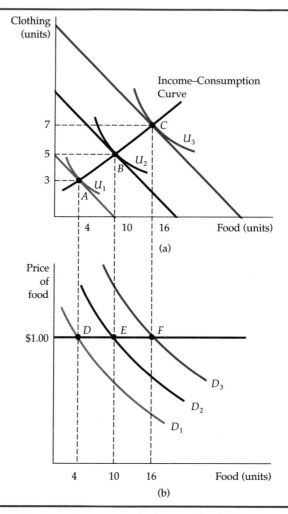

FIGURE 4.2 Effect of Income Changes. An increase in their income, with the prices of all goods fixed, causes consumers to alter their choice of market basket. In part (a) the market baskets that maximize consumer satisfaction for various incomes (point A, $10; B, $20; C, $30) trace out the income-consumption curve. The shift to the right of the demand curve in response to the increases in income is shown in part (b). (Points D, E, and F correspond to points A, B, and C, respectively.)

fixed at $20.00 but varied the price of food.) Finally, note that if his income increases to $30.00, he chooses C, with a market basket containing 16 units of food (and 7 units of clothing), represented by F in Figure 4.2b.

This exercise could be continued to include all possible changes in income.

In Figure 4.2a, the *income-consumption curve* traces out the utility-maximizing combinations of food and clothing associated with each and every income level. This income-consumption curve moves from lower left to upper right because the consumption of both food and clothing increase as income increases. Previously, we saw that a change in the price of a good corresponded to a movement along a demand curve. Here, the story is different. Because each demand curve is measured for a particular level of income, any change in income must lead to a shift in the demand curve itself. Thus, A on the income-consumption curve in Figure 4.2a corresponds to D on demand curve D_1 in Figure 4.2b, and B corresponds to E on a different demand curve D_2. The upward-sloping income consumption curve implies that an increase in income causes a shift to the right in the demand curve, in this case from D_1 to D_2 to D_3.

When the income-consumption curve has a positive slope, the quantity demanded increases with income and the income elasticity of demand is positive. The greater the shifts to the right of the demand curve, the larger the income elasticity. In this case the goods are described as *normal*: Consumers want to buy more of them as their income increases. In some cases, quantity demanded *falls* as income increases, and the income elasticity of demand is negative. We then describe the good as *inferior*. The term *inferior* is not pejorative—it simply means that consumption falls when income rises. For example, hamburger may be an inferior good, because people whose income is increasing may want to buy less hamburger and more steak.

Figure 4.3 shows the income-consumption curve for an inferior good. For relatively low levels of income, both hamburger and steak are normal goods. However, as income rises, the income-consumption curve bends backward (from point B to C). This occurs because hamburger has become an inferior good—its consumption has fallen as income has increased.

4.2 Income and Substitution Effects

A fall in the price of a good has two effects. First, consumers enjoy an increase in real purchasing power; they are better off because they can buy the same amount of the good for less money and thus have money left over for additional purchases. Second, they will consume more of the good that has become cheaper, and less of those goods that are now relatively more expensive. These two effects normally occur simultaneously, but it will be useful to distinguish between them in our analysis. The specifics are illustrated in Figure 4.4, where the initial budget line is RS and there are only two goods, food and clothing. Here, the consumer maximizes utility by choosing the market basket at A, thereby obtaining the level of utility associated with the indifference curve U_1.

Now, let's see what happens if the price of food falls, causing the budget

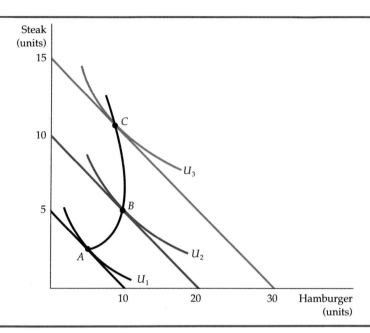

FIGURE 4.3   Effect of Income Changes—An Inferior Good.   An increase in a person's income may lead to less consumption of one of the two goods being purchased. In the figure, hamburger is a normal good between A and B, but becomes an inferior good when the income-consumption curve bends backward between B and C.

line to rotate outward to line RT. The consumer now chooses the market basket at B on indifference curve U_2. Thus, the reduction in the price of food allows the consumer to increase her level of satisfaction—her purchasing power, or *real income*, has increased. The total change in the consumption of food caused by the lower price is given by F_1F_2. Initially, the consumer purchased OF_1 units of food, but after the price change, food consumption has increased to OF_2. Line segment F_1F_2, therefore, represents the increase in desired food purchases. What has happened to the consumption of clothing? It has fallen from OC_1 to OC_2, a drop represented by line segment C_1C_2. Remember, food is now relatively inexpensive while clothing is now relatively costly.

The drop in price has a substitution effect and an income effect. The *substitution effect* is the change in food consumption associated with a change in the price of food, *with the level of satisfaction (or real income) held constant*. The substitution effect captures the change in food consumption that occurs as a result of the price change that makes food relatively cheaper than clothing. This substitution is marked by a movement along an indifference curve. In Figure 4.4, the substitution effect can be measured by drawing a budget line parallel to the new budget line RT (reflecting the lower relative price of food) but that is just

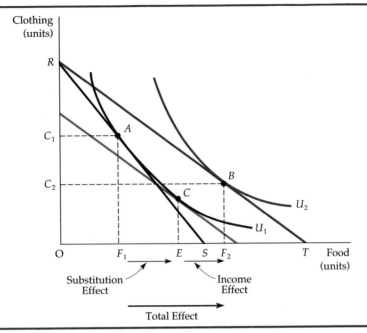

FIGURE 4.4 Income and Substitution Effects—Normal Good. A decrease in the price of food has an income effect and a substitution effect. The consumer is initially at A on budget line RS. When the price of food falls, consumption increases by F_1F_2 as the consumer moves to B. The substitution effect, F_1E (associated with a move from A to C) changes the relative prices of food and clothing but keeps real income (satisfaction) constant. The income effect EF_2 (associated with a move from C to B) keeps relative prices constant but increases real income. Food is a normal good, because the income effect EF_2 is positive.

tangent to the original indifference curve U_1 (holding the level of satisfaction constant). Given that budget line, the consumer chooses market basket C and consumes OE units of food. The line segment F_1E thus represents the substitution effect.

Figure 4.4 makes it clear that when the price of food declines, the substitution effect always leads to an increase in the quantity of food demanded. The explanation lies in our assumption that preferences are convex. With indifference curves such as those shown in the figure, the point that maximizes satisfaction on the new budget line RT must lie below and to the right of the original point of tangency.

Now consider the *income effect* (i.e., the change in food consumption brought about by the increase in purchasing power, with the price of food held constant). In Figure 4.4, the income effect occurs when the dotted budget line passing through C shifts outward to budget line RT. The consumer chooses market

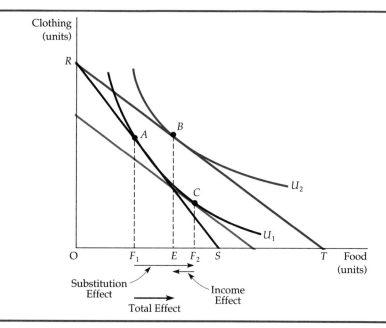

FIGURE 4.5   Income and Substitution Effects—Inferior Good.   The effect of a decrease in the price of food is again broken down into a substitution effect F_1F_2 and an income effect EF_2. In this case, food is an inferior good, because the income effect is negative. However, the substitution effect is larger than the income effect, so the decrease in the price of food leads to an increase in the quantity of food demanded.

basket B rather than market basket C on indifference curve U_2 (because the lower price of food has increased the consumer's level of utility). The increase in food consumption from OE to OF_2 is the measure of the income effect, which is positive, because food is a normal good. Because it reflects a movement from one indifference curve to another, the income effect measures the change in the consumer's real purchasing power.

When a good is inferior, the income effect is negative—as income rises, consumption falls. Figure 4.5 shows income and substitution effects for an inferior good. The negative income effect is measured by line segment F_2E. Even with inferior goods, the income effect is rarely large enough to outweigh the substitution effect. As a result, when the price of an inferior good falls, its consumption almost always increases.

The income effect may theoretically be large enough to cause the demand curve for a good to slope upward. We call such a good a *Giffen good*, and

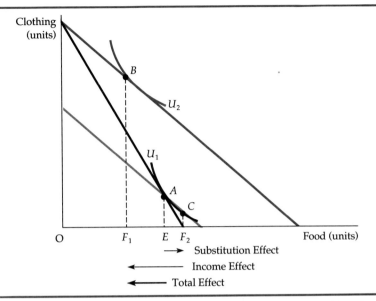

FIGURE 4.6 Upward-Sloping Demand Curve: The Giffen Good. When food is an inferior good, and the income effect is large enough to dominate the substitution effect, the demand curve will be upward-sloping. The consumer is initially at point A. But after the price of food falls, the consumer moves to B and consumes less food. The income effect F_2F_1 is larger than the substitution effect EF_2, so that the decrease in the price of food leads to a lower quantity of food demanded.

Figure 4.6 shows the income and substitution effects.[1] Initially, the consumer is at A, consuming relatively little clothing and much food. Now the price of food declines. The decline in the price of food frees enough income, so that the consumer desires to buy more clothing and fewer units of food, as illustrated by B. Perhaps the better-dressed consumer is likely to receive more dinner invitations and have less need to cook at home.

Although theoretically intriguing, the Giffen good case is rarely of practical interest. It necessitates a large negative income effect. But the income effect is usually small—it is important only when the good under consideration makes up a substantial portion of the consumer's budget. And large income effects are often associated with normal rather than inferior goods (e.g., for housing, food, or transportation).

[1]Alfred Marshall first described the case of the upward-sloping demand curve and gave credit for the idea to economist Robert Giffen. See Alfred Marshall, *Principles of Economics*, 8th ed. (New York: Macmillan, 1949), p. 132.

EXAMPLE 4.1 THE EFFECTS OF A GASOLINE TAX

Ever since the Arab oil crisis of 1973, the U.S. government has considered substantially increasing the tax on gasoline. Because the object of this tax would be to discourage the consumption of gasoline rather than raise revenue, the government has also considered ways of passing the resulting income back to consumers. One popular suggestion was a rebate program in which the tax revenues would be returned to households on an equal per capita basis. Is this a good idea?

Let's calculate the effect of such a program over five years. The relevant price elasticity of demand is about −0.5.[2] Suppose that a low-income consumer uses about 1200 gallons of gasoline a year, that gasoline costs $1.00 per gallon, and that the consumer's annual income is $9000.

Figure 4.7 shows the effect of the gasoline tax. (The graph has not been drawn to scale, so the effects we are discussing can be seen more clearly.) The original budget line is *AB*, and the consumer maximizes utility (on indifference curve U_2) by consuming the market basket at *C*, buying 1200 gallons of gasoline and spending $7800 on other goods. If the tax is 50 cents per gallon, price will increase by 50 percent, shifting the new budget line to *AD*. (Recall that when price changes and income stays fixed, the budget line rotates around a pivotal point on the unchanged axis.) With our price elasticity of −0.5, consumption will decline 25 percent from 1200 to 900 gallons, as shown by the utility-maximizing point *E* on indifference curve U_1 (because for every 1 percent increase in the price of gasoline, demand drops by 1/2 percent).

The rebate program, however, partially counters this effect. Suppose that the tax revenue per person is about $450 (900 gallons times 50 cents/gallon), so that each consumer receives a $450 rebate. How does this increased income affect gasoline consumption? The effect can be shown graphically by shifting the budget line upward by $450 to line *FG*, which is parallel to *AD*. How much gasoline does our consumer buy now? In Chapter 2 we saw that the income elasticity of demand for gasoline is approximately 0.3. Because the $450 represents a 5 percent increase in income ($450/$9000 = 0.05), we would expect the rebate to increase consumption by 1.5 percent (0.3 times 5 percent) of 900 gallons, or 13.5 gallons. The new utility-maximizing consumption choice at *H* illustrates this. Despite the rebate program, the tax would reduce gasoline consumption by 286.5 gallons, from 1200 to 913.5. Because the income elasticity of demand for gasoline is relatively low, the income effect of the rebate program is dominated by the substitution effect, and the program would reduce consumption.

Figure 4.7 reveals that a gasoline tax program with a rebate makes the average low-income consumer slightly worse off, because *H* lies just below indifference

---

[2]We saw in Chapter 2 that the price elasticity of demand for gasoline varied substantially from the short run to the long run, ranging from −0.11 in the short run to −1.17 in the long run.

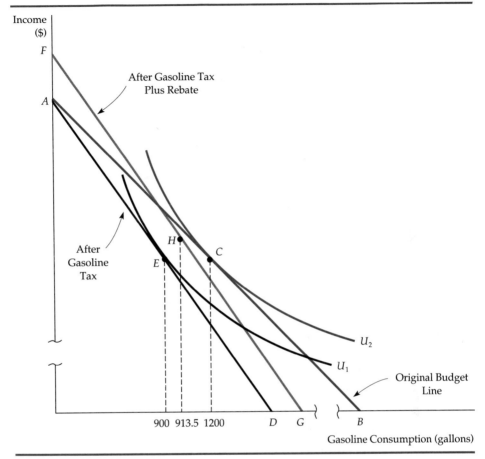

FIGURE 4.7   Effect of a Gasoline Tax with a Rebate.   A gasoline tax is imposed when the consumer is initially buying 1200 gallons of gasoline at point *C*. After the tax the budget line shifts from *AB* to *AD* and the consumer maximizes his preferences by choosing *E*, with a gasoline consumption of 900 gallons. However, when the proceeds of the tax are rebated to the consumer, his consumption increases somewhat to 913.5 gallons at *H*. Despite the rebate program, the consumer's gasoline consumption has fallen, as has his level of satisfaction.

curve U_2.[3] Why introduce such a program? Those who have supported gasoline taxes have argued that they promote national security (they encourage conservation and therefore reduce dependence on foreign oil) and help weaken OPEC.

[3]Of course, some consumers (those who spend little on gasoline) will be better off after receiving the rebate, while others (those who spend a lot on gasoline) will be worse off.

4.3 Market Demand

We have been talking largely about the demand curve for an individual consumer. But where do *market demand* curves come from? In this section we show how market demand curves can be derived as the sum of the individual demand curves of all consumers in a particular market.

From Individual to Market Demand

To keep things simple, let's assume that only three consumers (A,B, and C) are in the market for food. Table 4.1 tabulates several points on each of the three demand curves for these consumers. The market demand column (5) is determined by adding columns (2), (3), and (4) to determine the total quantity demanded by consumers at every price. For example, when the price of the good is equal to $3, the quantity demanded by the market is equal to 2 + 6 + 10, or 18.

Figure 4.8 describes these same three consumers' demand curves for food. In the graph, the market demand curve is the *horizontal summation* of the demands of each of the consumers (labeled D_A, D_B, and D_C). We sum horizontally by asking what is the total amount that the three consumers will demand at a given price. This sum can be determined by moving horizontally across the graph at that particular price level. For example, when the price of the good is equal to $4, the quantity demanded by the market (11 units) is the sum of the quantity demanded by A (no units), by B (4 units), and by C (7 units). Because all the individual demand curves slope downward, the market demand curve will also slope downward. However, the market demand curve need not be a straight line, even though each of the individual demand curves is. In our example, the market demand curve is *kinked* because some consumers wish to make no purchases at prices other consumers find inviting (those above $4).

Two points should be noted. First, the market demand curve will shift to the right as more consumers enter the market. Second, factors that influence the demands of many consumers will also affect the market demand. Suppose, for

TABLE 4.1 Determining the Market Demand Curve				
Price ($)	Individual A (units)	Individual B (units)	Individual C (units)	Market (units)
1	6	10	16	32
2	4	8	13	25
3	2	6	10	18
4	0	4	7	11
5	0	2	4	6

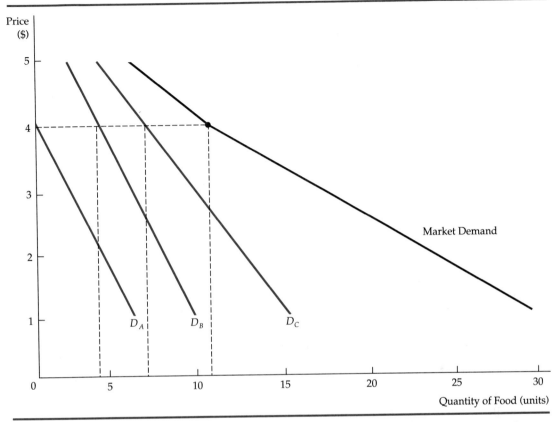

FIGURE 4.8 Summing to Obtain a Market Demand Curve. The market demand curve is obtained by summing the consumers' demand curves D_A, D_B, and D_C. At each price, the quantity of food demanded by the market is the sum of the quantity demanded of each consumer. For example, at a price of $4, the quantity demanded by the market (11 units) is the sum of the quantity demanded by A (no units), by B (4 units), and by C (7 units).

example, that most consumers in a particular market earn more income, and as a result increase their demands for food. Because each consumer's demand curve shifts to the right, so will the market demand curve.

The aggregation of individual demands into market demands is not just a theoretical exercise. It becomes important in practice when market demands are built up from the demands of different demographic groups or from consumers located in different areas. For example, we might obtain information about the demand for home computers by adding independently obtained information about the demands of (i) households with children, (ii) households without children, and (iii) single individuals. Or we might obtain the U.S. demand for natural gas by aggregating the demands for natural gas of the major regions (East, South, Midwest, Mountain, and West, for example).

The Price Elasticity of Demand

We saw in Chapter 2 that the price elasticity of demand measures the sensitivity of demand to changes in the price of a product. In fact, price elasticity can be used to describe either individual or market demand curves. Denoting the quantity of a good by Q and its price by P, we define the price elasticity as

$$E_P = \frac{\Delta Q/Q}{\Delta P/P} = \frac{\Delta Q/\Delta P}{Q/P} \tag{4.1}$$

When the price elasticity is greater than 1 in magnitude, we say that demand is *price elastic*, because the percentage decline in quantity demanded is greater than the percentage increase in price. If the price elasticity is less than 1 in magnitude, demand is said to be *price inelastic*. In general, the elasticity of demand for a good depends on the availability of other goods that can be substituted for it. When there are close substitutes, a price increase will cause the consumer to buy less of the good and more of the substitute. Demand will then be highly price elastic. When there are no close substitutes, demand will tend to be price inelastic.

The elasticity of demand has implications for the total amount of money that a consumer spends on a product. When demand is inelastic, the quantity demanded is relatively unresponsive to changes in price. As a result, the total expenditure on the product increases when the price increases. Suppose, for example, that a family currently uses 1000 gallons of gasoline a year when the price is $1.00 per gallon. Suppose, in addition, that the family's price elasticity of demand for gasoline is −0.5. Then if the price of gasoline increases to $1.10 (a 10 percent increase), the consumption of gasoline falls to 950 gallons (a 5 percent decrease). Total expenditures on gasoline, however, will increase from $1000 (1000 gallons × $1.00 per gallon) to $1045 (950 gallons × $1.10 per gallon).

However, when demand is elastic, the total expenditure on the product decreases as the price goes up. Suppose that a family buys 100 pounds of chicken a year, at a price of $2.00 per pound, and that the price elasticity of demand for chicken is −1.5. Then if the price of chicken increases to $2.20 (a 10 percent increase), the family's consumption of chicken falls to 85 pounds a year (a 15 percent decrease). Total expenditures on chicken will fall as well, from $200 (100 pounds × $2.00 per pound) to $187 (85 pounds × $2.20 per pound).

The intermediate case in which total expenditure remains the same after a price change is the *unit elastic* case. In this situation, a price increase leads to a decrease in quantity demanded, which is just sufficient to leave the total consumer expenditure unchanged.

Table 4.2 shows all three cases that describe the relationship between price

TABLE 4.2 Price Elasticity and Consumer Expenditures

Demand	If Price Increases, Expenditures	If Price Decreases, Expenditures
Inelastic	Increase	Decrease
Unit elastic	Are unchanged	Are unchanged
Elastic	Decrease	Increase

elasticity and consumer expenditures. It might be useful to review the table from the point of view of the seller of the good rather than the purchaser. When demand is inelastic, a price increase leads only to a small decrease in quantity demanded, so that the total revenue received by the seller increases. But when demand is elastic, a price increase leads to a large decline in quantity demanded, and total revenues received fall.

Point and Arc Elasticities of Demand

The calculations of price elasticity for a straight-line demand curve that we did in Chapter 2 were straightforward because (1) we calculated a *point elasticity*, which is an elasticity measured at one particular point on the demand curves, and (2) $\Delta Q/\Delta P$ is constant everywhere along the demand curve. When the demand curve is not a straight line, however, calculating a demand elasticity can be confusing. Suppose, for example, that we are concerned with a portion of a demand curve in which the price of a product increases from $10 to $11, while the quantity demanded falls from 100 to 95. How should we calculate the price elasticity of demand? We can calculate that $\Delta Q = -5$, and $\Delta P = 1$, but what values do we use for P and Q in the formula $E_P = (\Delta Q/\Delta P)(P/Q)$?

If we use the lower price of $10, we find that $E_P = (-5)(^{10}/_{100}) = -0.50$. However, if we use the higher price, the price elasticity is given by $E_P = (-5)(^{11}/_{95}) = -0.58$. The difference between the two elasticities is not large, but it is discomforting to have two choices, neither of which is obviously preferable to the other. To solve this problem when we are dealing with relatively large price changes, we use the *arc elasticity* of demand, which is given by

$$E_P = (\Delta Q/\Delta P)(P'/Q')$$

where P' is the *average* of the two prices and Q' is the *average* of the two quantities.

In our example, the average price is $10.50 and the average quantity is, 97.5, so the price elasticity calculated from the arc elasticity formula is $E_P = (-5)(^{10.5}/_{97.5}) = -0.54$. The arc elasticity will always lie somewhere (but not necessarily halfway) between the two point elasticities calculated at the lower and the higher prices.

EXAMPLE 4.2 THE AGGREGATE DEMAND FOR WHEAT

In Chapter 2 (Example 2.2) we discussed the two components of the demand for wheat—domestic demand (by U.S. consumers) and export demand (by foreign consumers). Let us see how the world demand for wheat in 1981 can be obtained by aggregating the domestic and foreign demands. The domestic demand for wheat is given by the equation $Q_{DD} = 1000 - 46P$, where Q_{DD} is the number of bushels (in millions) demanded domestically, and P is the price in dollars per bushel. Export demand is given by $Q_{DE} = 2550 - 220P$, where Q_{DE} is the number of bushels (in millions) demanded from abroad. As shown in Figure 4.9, the domestic demand for wheat, given by AB, is relatively price inelastic. In fact, statistical studies have shown that the price elasticity of domestic demand is about -0.2. However, export demand, given by CD, is more price elastic, with an elasticity of demand of -0.4 to -0.5. Export demand is more elastic than domestic demand because many poorer countries that import U.S. wheat turn to other grains and foodstuffs if wheat prices rise.[4]

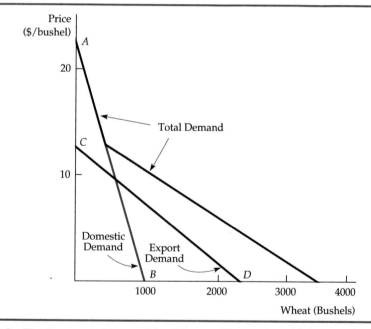

FIGURE 4.9 The Aggregate Demand for Wheat. The total world demand for wheat is the horizontal sum of the domestic demand AB and the export demand CD. Even though each individual demand curve is linear, the market demand curve is kinked, reflecting that there is no export demand when the price of wheat is greater than $12 per bushel.

[4]For a survey of statistical studies of demand and supply elasticities and an analysis of the U.S. wheat market, see Larry Salathe and Sudchada Langley, "An Empirical Analysis of Alternative Export Subsidy Programs for U.S. Wheat," *Agricultural Economics Research* 38, No. 1 (winter 1986).

To obtain the world demand for wheat, we simply add the two wheat demands horizontally. To do this, we set the left-hand side of each demand equation equal to the quantity of wheat (the variable on the horizontal axis). Then we add the right-hand side of the equations. Therefore, $Q_D = Q_{DD} + Q_{DE} = (1000 - 46P) + (2550 - 220P) = 3550 - 266P$.

At all prices above C, there is no export demand, so world demand and domestic demand are identical. However, below C, there is both domestic and export demand. As a result demand is obtained by adding the quantity demanded of domestic wheat and export wheat at each price level. As the figure shows, the world demand for wheat is kinked. The kink occurs at the price level above which there is no export demand.

EXAMPLE 4.3 THE DEMAND FOR HOUSING

The demand for housing may differ substantially depending on the age and family status of the household making a purchasing decision. One approach to housing demand is to relate the number of rooms per house for each household (the quantity demanded) to an estimate of the price of an additional room in a house and to the household's family income.[5] (Prices of rooms vary across the United States because of differences in construction costs.) Table 4.3 lists some of the price and income elasticities obtained for demographic groups.

In general, the elasticities show that the size of houses that consumers demand (as measured by the number of rooms) is relatively insensitive to differences in either income or price. However, differences among subgroups of the population are important. For example, married families with young heads of households have a price elasticity of -0.221, substantially greater than married households with older household heads. Presumably, families are more price

TABLE 4.3 Price and Income Elasticities of the Demand for Rooms

Group	Price Elasticity	Income Elasticity
Single individuals	−0.139	0.186
Married, Head of household age less than 30, 1 child	−0.221	0.069
Married, Head age 30–39, 2 or more children	0	0.113
Married, Head age 50 or older, 1 child	−0.084	0.180

[5]See Mahlon Strazheim, *An Econometric Analysis of the Urban Housing Market* (New York: National Bureau of Economic Research, 1975), chapter 4.

sensitive when buying houses when the parents and their children are younger and the parents may plan on having more children. Among married households, the income elasticity of demand for rooms also increases with age, perhaps because older households have more income to spend and additional rooms are a luxury rather than a necessity.

Price and income elasticities of demand for housing can also vary depending on where people live.[6] Demand in the central cities was substantially more price elastic than the suburban elasticities. Income elasticities, however, increase as one moves farther from the central city. Thus, poorer (on average) central city residents (who live where the price of land is relatively high) are more price sensitive in their housing choices than their wealthier suburban counterparts. Not surprisingly, the suburban residents have higher income elasticities because of their wealth and because larger, more varied housing can be built in their areas.

4.4 Consumer Surplus

Consumers buy goods because the purchase makes them better off. *Consumer surplus* measures how much better off individuals are in the aggregate. Because different consumers value consumption of particular goods differently, the maximum amount they are willing to pay for those goods also differs. Consumer surplus is a measure of the maximum amount that a consumer of a good would pay for its purchase minus the actual payments that she makes. Specifically, *consumer surplus is the difference between what a consumer is willing to pay for a good and what she actually pays when buying it.* Suppose, for example, that a man would have been willing to pay $3 per pound for beef, even though he had to pay only $2 per pound. The $1 per pound that he saved is his consumer surplus.[7] When we add the consumer surpluses of all consumers who buy a good, we obtain a measure of the aggregate consumer surplus.

Consumer surplus can be calculated most easily by the use of the demand curve. We can show the relationship between demand and consumer surplus by examining the individual demand curve for food shown in Figure 4.10.[8]

---

[6]See the study by Allen C. Goodman and Masahiro Kawai, "Functional Form, Sample Selection, and Housing Demand," *Journal of Urban Economics* 20 (Sept. 1986): 155–167.

[7]The fact that consumer surplus can be measured in dollars involves an implicit assumption about the shape of consumers' indifference curves—that a consumer's marginal utility associated with increases in income remains constant within the range of income in question. For many economic analyses this is a reasonable assumption, although it might be suspect when large changes in income are involved. See Robert D. Willig, "Consumer Surplus Without Apology," *American Economic Review* 65 (1976): 589–597.

[8]The following discussion applies to an individual demand curve, but a similar argument would also apply to a market demand curve.

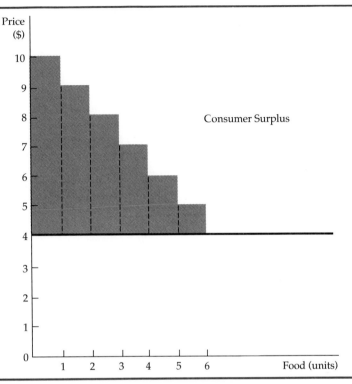

FIGURE 4.10 Consumer Surplus. Consumer surplus represents the total benefit associated with the consumption of a product, after the total cost has been paid. In this figure the consumer surplus associated with the consumption of 6 pounds of food (purchased at $4 per pound) is given by the shaded area.

Drawing the demand curve to look more like a stepladder than a straight line allows us to measure the value that this consumer obtains when he buys the food, which is assumed to come in packages of one pound.

When deciding how much food to purchase, the consumer might perform the following calculation. Since the price of food is $4 per pound, the first pound of food costs $4 but is worth $10. This $10 valuation is obtained by using the demand curve to find the maximum amount that the consumer will pay to buy each additional unit of the product ($10 is the maximum this consumer will pay to buy the first pound of food). The food is worth purchasing because it generates $6 of excess or surplus value above and beyond the cost of the purchase.

The second pound of food is also worth purchasing, because it generates an excess value or surplus of $5 ($9 − $4). The third pound of food also generates a surplus of $4. However, the fourth pound generates a surplus of only $3, the fifth pound a surplus of $2, and the sixth pound a surplus of just $1. Accordingly, the consumer is indifferent about purchasing the seventh pound of food (since it generates zero surplus) and prefers not to buy any more food than that, as the value of each additional unit is less than its cost.

In Figure 4.10 consumer surplus is obtained by adding the excess values or surpluses for all units purchased. In this case,

$$\text{Consumer surplus} = \$6 + \$5 + \$4 + \$3 + \$2 + \$1 = \$21.$$

In a more general case, the stepladder demand curve can be easily transformed into a straight-line demand curve by making the units of the good smaller and smaller. In Figure 4.11, the stepladder is drawn when the units of food become 1/2 pound, rather than 1 pound, and the stepladder begins to approximate the straight-line demand curve. We tend to use such demand curves as approximations and correspondingly use the triangle in Figure 4.11

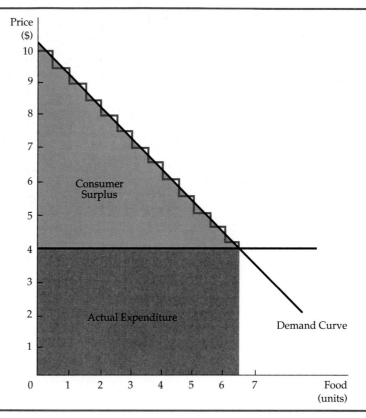

FIGURE 4.11 Consumer Surplus Generalized. When the units of consumption of a good (here, food) are small, the consumer surplus can be measured by the area under the demand curve and above the line representing the purchase price of the good. In the figure the consumer surplus is given by the shaded triangle.

to measure consumer surplus. When the demand curve is not a straight line, the consumer surplus is measured by the area below the demand curve and above the price line.[9] When we wish to calculate the aggregate consumer surplus in a market, we simply calculate the area below the market demand curve and above the price line.

Consumer surplus has important applications in economics. When added over many individuals, consumer surplus measures the aggregate benefit (net of costs) that consumers obtain from buying goods in a market. When we combine consumer surplus with the aggregate profits that producers obtain, we can evaluate the costs and benefits of alternative market structures and of public policies that alter the behavior of consumers and firms in those markets.

EXAMPLE 4.4 VALUING CLEAN AIR

Air is free in the sense that one need not pay to breathe it. Yet the absence of a market for air may help explain why the air quality in some cities has been deteriorating for decades. In 1970 Congress amended the Clean Air Act to tighten automobile emissions controls. Were these controls worth it? Were the benefits of cleaning up the air sufficient to outweigh the costs that would be imposed directly on car producers and indirectly on car buyers?

To answer this question, Congress asked the National Academy of Sciences to evaluate these emissions controls in a cost-benefit study. The benefits portion of that study examined how much people value clean air, using empirically determined estimates of the demand for clean air.

Although there is no explicit market for clean air, people do pay more to buy houses where the air is clean than they pay to buy comparable houses in areas with dirtier air. This information was the basis for an empirical determination of the demand for clean air.[10] Detailed data for house prices among neighborhoods in Boston and Los Angeles were compared with the levels of various air pollutants, while the effects of other variables that might affect house value were taken into account statistically. The study determined a demand curve for clean air that looked approximately like that shown in Figure 4.12.

The horizontal axis measures the amount of *air pollution reduction*, and the vertical axis measures the increased value of a home associated with those

---

[9]In the demand curve drawn in Figure 4.11, the consumer surplus is $21 ⅛, a close approximation to the $21 previously determined. The demand curve is assumed to involve a maximum price of $10.50 and a quantity sold of 6½. In this case, the triangle has a base of 6½, a height of $6.50, and an area of $21⅛.

[10]The results are summarized in Daniel L. Rubinfeld, "Market Approaches to the Measurement of the Benefits of Air Pollution Abatement," in A. Friedlaender, ed., *The Benefits and Costs of Cleaning the Air* (Cambridge: M.I.T. Press, 1976).

pollution reductions. For example, consider the demand for cleaner air of a homeowner in a city in which the air is rather dirty, as exemplified by a level of nitrogen oxides (NOX) of ten parts per hundred million (pphm). If the family were required to pay $1000 for each 1 pphm reduction in air pollution, it would choose A on the demand curve to obtain a pollution reduction of 5 pphm.

How much is a 50 percent, or 5 pphm, reduction in pollution worth to the typical family just described? We can measure this value by calculating the consumer surplus associated with reducing air pollution. Since the price for this reduction is $1000 per unit, the family would pay $5000. However, the family values all but the last unit of reduction by more than $1000. As a result, the shaded area in Figure 4.12 gives the value of the cleanup (above and beyond the payment). Since the demand curve is a straight line, the surplus can be calculated from the area of the triangle whose height is $1000 ($2000 − $1000)

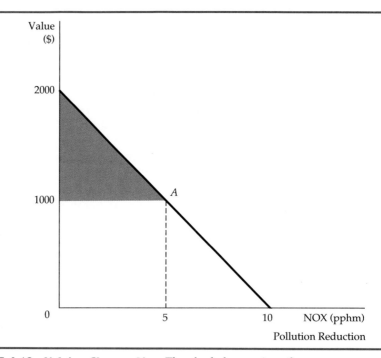

FIGURE 4.12 Valuing Cleaner Air. The shaded area gives the consumer surplus generated when air pollution is reduced by 5 parts per hundred million of nitrogen oxide at a cost of $1000 per part reduced. The consumer surplus is created because most consumers are willing to pay more than $1000 for each part per million of nitrogen oxide reduction.

and whose base is 5 pphm. Therefore, the value to the household of the pollution reduction is $2500.

A complete benefit-cost analysis would use a measure of the total benefit of the cleanup (the benefit per household times the number of households). This could be compared with the total cost of the cleanup to determine whether such a project were worthwhile.

4.5 Network Externalities

So far our discussion has assumed that people's demands for a good are independent of one another. In other words, Tom's demand for coffee depends on Tom's tastes, his income, the price of coffee, and perhaps the price of tea, but it doesn't depend on Dick's or Harry's demands for coffee. This assumption enabled us to obtain the market demand curve by simply summing individuals' demands.

For some goods, however, a person's demand also depends on the demands of *other* people. In particular, a person's demand may be affected by the number of other people who have purchased the good. If this is the case, there is a *network externality*. Network externalities can be positive or negative. A *positive* network externality exists if the quantity of a good that typical consumers purchase increases their quantity demanded in response to the growth in purchases of other consumers. If the opposite is true, there is a *negative* network externality.

One example of a positive network externality is the *bandwagon effect*.[11] This refers to the desire to be in style, to have a good because almost everyone else has it, or to indulge in a fad. The bandwagon effect often arises with children's toys (Barbie Dolls, for example). Creating this effect is a major objective in marketing and advertising these toys. Building a bandwagon effect is also often the key to success in selling clothing.

The bandwagon effect is illustrated in Figure 4.13, where the horizontal axis measures the sales of some fashionable good in thousands per month. Suppose consumers think that only 20,000 people have purchased the good. This is a small number relative to the U.S. population, so consumers would have little motivation to buy the good to be in style. Some consumers may still buy it (depending on its price), but only for its intrinsic value. In this case, demand is given by the curve D_{20}.

---

[11]The bandwagon effect and the snob effect (discussed below) were introduced by Harvey Liebenstein, "Bandwagon, Snob, and Veblen Effects in the Theory of Consumers' Demand," *Quarterly Journal of Economics* 62 (Feb. 1948): 165–201.

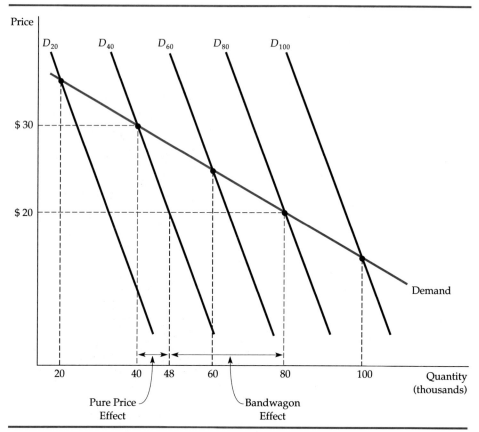

FIGURE 4.13   Positive Network Externality: Bandwagon Effect.   A bandwagon effect is an example of a positive network externality, in which the quantity of a good that an individual demands grows in response to the growth of purchase of other individuals. Here the demand for a good shifts to the right from D_{40} to D_{80} due to the bandwagon effect as the price of the product falls from $30 to $20.

Suppose instead consumers think that 40,000 people have purchased the good. Now they find the good more attractive and want to buy more. The demand curve is D_{40}, which is to the right of D_{20}. Similarly, if consumers thought that 60,000 people had bought the good, the demand curve would be D_{60}, and so on. The more people consumers believe have bought the good, the farther to the right is the demand curve.

Ultimately, consumers would get a good sense of how many people *have* purchased the good. This number would, of course, depend on its price. In

Figure 4.13, for example, if the price were \$30, 40,000 people would buy the good, so the relevant demand curve would be D_{40}. Or if the price were \$20, 80,000 people would buy the good, and the relevant demand curve would be D_{80}. *The market demand curve is therefore found by joining the points on the curves* D_{20}, D_{40}, D_{60}, *and so on that correspond to the quantities 20,000, 40,000, 60,000. etc.*

The market demand curve is relatively elastic compared with the curves D_{20}, etc. To see why the bandwagon effect leads to a more elastic demand curve, consider the effect of a drop in price from \$30 to \$20, with a demand curve of D_{40}. If there were no bandwagon effect, demand would increase from 40,000 to only 48,000. But as more people buy the good, it becomes stylish to own it, and the bandwagon effect increases quantity demanded further, to 80,000. So the bandwagon effect increases the response of demand to price changes (i.e., makes demand more elastic). As we'll see later, this result has important implications for firms' pricing strategies.

The bandwagon effect is associated with fads and stylishness, but a positive network externality can arise for other reasons. The intrinsic value of some goods to their owners is greater the greater the number of other people who own the goods. Compact disc (CD) players are an example. If I am the only person to own a CD player, it will not be economical for companies to manufacture compact discs, and without the discs, the player will be of little value to me. The more people who own CD players, the more discs will be manufactured, and the greater will be the value of the player to me. The same is true for personal computers; the more people that own them, the more software will be written, and thus the more useful the computer will be to me. So CD players and personal computers are also goods whose demands we describe in Figure 4.13.

Network externalities are sometimes negative. Consider the *snob effect*, which refers to the desire to own exclusive or unique goods. The quantity demanded of a snob good is higher the *fewer* the people who own it. Rare works of art, specially designed sports cars, and made-to-order clothing are snob goods. Here, the value I get from a painting or sports car is in part the prestige, status, and exclusivity resulting from the fact that very few other people own one like it.

Figure 4.14 illustrates the snob effect. D_2 is the demand curve that would apply if consumers believed only 2000 people owned the good. If people believe that 4000 people own the good, it is less exclusive and its snob value is reduced. Quantity demanded will therefore be lower; the curve D_4 applies. Similarly, if people believe that 6000 people own the good, demand is even smaller, and D_6 applies. Eventually consumers learn how widely owned the good actually is, so the market demand curve is found by joining the points on the curves D_2, D_4, D_6, etc., that actually correspond to the quantities 2000, 4000, 6000, etc.

The snob effect makes market demand less elastic. To see why, suppose the

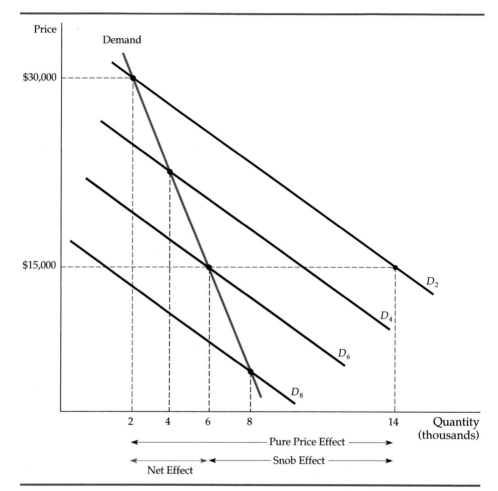

FIGURE 4.14   Negative Network Externality: Snob Effect.   A snob effect is an example of a negative network externality, in which the quantity of a good that an individual demands falls in response to the growth of purchases of other individuals. Here the demand for a good shifts to the left from D_2 to D_6 as the price of the product falls from $30,000 to $15,000.

price were initially $30,000, with 2000 people purchasing the good, and was then lowered to $15,000. If there were no snob effect, the quantity purchased would increase to 14,000 (along curve D_2). But as a snob good, its value is greatly reduced if more people own it. The snob effect dampens the increase in quantity demanded, cutting it by 8000 units, so the net increase in sales is only to 6000 units. For many goods, marketing and advertising are geared to creating a snob effect. This means that demand will be less elastic—a result that has important implications for pricing.

Negative network externalities can arise for other reasons. The value I obtain from a lift ticket at a ski resort is lower the more people there are who have bought tickets, because I prefer short lines and fewer skiers on the slopes. And likewise for entry to an amusement park, skating rink, or beach.[12]

EXAMPLE 4.5 NETWORK EXTERNALITIES AND THE DEMAND FOR COMPUTERS

The 1950s and 1960s saw phenomenal growth in the demand for mainframe computers. From 1954 to 1965, for example, annual revenues from the leasing of mainframes increased at the extraordinary rate of 78 percent per year, while prices declined by 20 percent per year. Prices were falling, and the quality of computers was increasing dramatically, but the elasticity of demand would have to have been quite large to account for this kind of growth. IBM, among other computer manufacturers, wanted to know what was going on.

An econometric study by Gregory Chow, then working at IBM, helped provide some answers.[13] Chow found that the demand for computers follows a "saturation curve"—a dynamic process where at first demand is small and grows slowly, but then grows rapidly, until finally nearly everyone likely to buy a computer has done so, and the market is saturated. The rapid growth occurs because of a positive network externality. As more and more organizations own computers, more and better software is written, and more people are trained to use computers, so that the value of having a computer increases. This causes demand to increase, which results in still more software and better trained users, and so on.

This network externality was an important part of the demand for computers. Chow found that it could account for close to half the rapid growth of rentals in 1954–1965. Reductions in the inflation-adjusted price (he found a price elasticity of demand for computers of -1.44.) and major increases in the power and quality of computers, which also made them much more useful and effective, accounted for the other half. About 15 years later, this same kind of network externality helped to fuel a rapid rate of growth in the demand for personal computers.

---

[12]Tastes differ. Some people associate a *positive* network externality with skiing or a day on the beach; they enjoy crowds and might find the mountain or beach lonely without them.

[13]See Gregory Chow, "Technological Change and the Demand for Computers," *American Economic Review* 57 No. 5 (Dec. 1967): 1117–1130.

*4.6 Empirical Estimation of Demand

Later in this book, we will see how demand information is used as an input to firms' economic decision making. For example, General Motors needs to understand automobile demand to decide whether to offer rebates or below-market-interest-rate loans for new cars. Knowledge about demand is also important for public policy decisions. For example, understanding the demand for oil can help Congress decide whether to pass an oil import tax. Here, we briefly examine some of the tools for evaluating and forecasting demand. The more basic statistical tools needed to estimate demand curves and demand elasticities are described in the Appendix to the book.

Interview and Experimental Approaches to Demand Determination

The most direct way to obtain information about demand is through *interviews* in which consumers are asked about how much of a product they might be willing to buy at a given price. Direct approaches such as these, however, are unlikely to succeed because people may lack information or interest, or may want to mislead the interviewer. Therefore, market researchers have designed more successful indirect interview approaches. Consumers might be asked, for example, what their current consumption behavior is and how they would respond if a certain product were available at a 10 percent discount. Or interviewees might be asked how they would expect others to behave. Although indirect survey approaches to demand estimation can be fruitful, the difficulties of the interview approach have forced economists and marketing specialists to look to alternative methods.

In *direct marketing experiments* actual sales offers are posed to potential customers. An airline, for example, might offer a reduced price on certain flights for six months, partly to learn how this price change affects demand for its flights and how other firms will respond.

Direct experiments are real, not hypothetical, but substantial problems remain. The wrong experiment can be costly, and even if profits and sales rise, the firm cannot be sure that the increase was the result of the experimental change, because other factors probably changed at the same time. Also the response to experiments—which consumers often recognize as short-lived—may differ from the response to a permanent change. Finally, a firm can afford to try only a limited number of experiments.

The Statistical Approach to Demand Estimation

Firms often rely on market data based on actual studies of demand. Properly applied, the statistical approach to demand estimation can enable one to sort out the effects of variables such as price and income on the quantity of a product demanded, from other variables such as the price of other products and the weather. In this section we outline some of the conceptual issues involved in the statistical approach.

The data in Table 4.4 describe the quantity of raspberries sold in a market once each year. Information about the market demand for raspberries might be valuable to an organization representing growers; it would allow them to predict sales on the basis of their own estimates of price and other demand-determining variables. To focus our attention on demand, let's suppose that the quantity of raspberries produced is sensitive to weather conditions but not the current price in the market (because farmers make their planting decisions based on last year's price).

The price and quantity data from Table 4.4 are graphed in Figure 4.15. If one believed that price alone determined demand, it would be plausible to describe the demand for the product by drawing a straight line (or other appropriate curve), $Q = a - bP$, which "fit" the points as shown by demand curve D. We cannot discuss the process of curve-fitting here, but we do so in the Appendix to the book.

Does curve D (which is given by the equation $Q = 28.7 - 0.98P$), really represent the demand for the product? The answer is yes, but only if there are not important factors other than product price that affect demand. But in Table 4.4 we have included data for one omitted variable—the average income of purchasers of the product. Note that income has increased twice during the study, suggesting that the demand for agricultural products has shifted twice. Thus, demand curves d_1, d_2, and d_3 in Figure 4.15 give a more likely description of demand. This demand relationship would be described algebraically as

$$Q = a - bP + cI.$$

The income term in the demand equation allows the demand curve to shift in a parallel fashion as income changes. (The demand relationship is given by $Q = 5.07 - 0.40P + 0.94I$.)

TABLE 4.4 Demand Data

Year	Quantity(Q)	Price(P)	Income(I)
1980	4	24	10
1981	7	20	10
1982	8	17	10
1983	13	17	17
1984	16	10	17
1985	15	15	17
1986	19	12	20
1987	20	9	20
1988	22	5	20

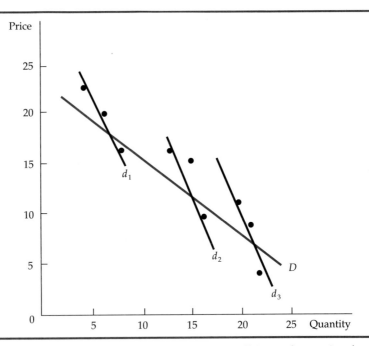

FIGURE 4.15 Determining Demand Relationships. Price and quantity data can be used to determine the form of a demand relationship. But the same data could describe a single demand curve D, or three demand curves d_1, d_2, and d_3, which shift over time.

The Form of the Demand Relationship

The demand relationships that we have discussed are both straight lines, so that the effect of a change in price on quantity demanded is a constant, independent of the price level. However, with a straight-line demand relationship, the price elasticity of demand varies with the price level. From the demand equation $Q = a - bP$, for example, the price elasticity of demand E_P can be determined as follows:

$$E_P = (\Delta Q/\Delta P)(P/Q) = -b(P/Q) \tag{4.4}$$

Equation (4.4) shows that the price elasticity of demand increases in magnitude as the price of the product increases (and the quantity demanded falls).

There is no reason to expect elasticities of demand to be constant. Nevertheless, we often find the *isoelastic demand* curve, in which the price elasticity and the income elasticity are constant, useful to work with. When written in its *log-linear form*, it appears as follows:

$$\log (Q) = a - b \log (P) + c \log (I) \tag{4.5}$$

log( ) is the logarithmic function, I is income, and a, b, and c are the constants in the demand equation. The appeal of the log-linear demand relationship is that the slope of the line $-b$ is the price elasticity of demand, and the constant c is the income elasticity.[14] Using the data in Table 4.4, for example, we obtained the regression line $\log (Q) = -0.81 - 0.24 \log (P) + 1.46 \log (I)$.[15] This relationship tells us that the price elasticity of demand for raspberries is -0.24 (that is, demand is inelastic), and the income elasticity is 1.46.

The constant elasticity form can also be useful for distinguishing between goods that are complements and goods that are substitutes. Suppose that P_2 represents the price of a second good, which is believed to be related to the product we are studying. Then, we can write the demand function in the following form:

$$\log (Q) = a - b \log (P) + b_2 \log (P_2)$$

When b_2, the cross-price elasticity, is positive, the two goods are substitutes, and when b_2 is negative the two goods are complements.[16]

Summary

1. Individual consumers' demand curves for a commodity can be derived from information about their tastes for all goods and services and from their budget constraints.

2. The effect of a price change on the quantity demanded of a good can be broken into two parts—a substitution effect, in which satisfaction remains constant but the price changes, and an income effect, in which the price remains constant but utility changes. Because the income effect can be positive or negative, a price change can have a small or a large effect on quantity demanded. In one unusual but interesting case (that of a Giffen good), the quantity demanded may move in the same direction as the price change (leading to an upward-sloping individual demand curve).

3. The market demand curve is the horizontal summation of the individual demand curves of all consumers in the market for the good. The market demand curve can be very

---

[14]The logarithmic function has the property that $\Delta(\log (Q)) = \Delta Q/Q$ for any change in $\log (Q)$. Similarly, $\Delta(\log (P)) = \Delta P/P$ for any change in $\log (P)$. It follows that $\Delta(\log (Q)) = \Delta Q/Q = -b[\Delta(\log (P))] = -b(\Delta P/P)$. Therefore, $(\Delta Q/Q)/(\Delta P/P) = -b$, which is the price elasticity of demand. By a similar argument, the income elasticity of demand c is given by $(\Delta Q/Q)/(\Delta I/I)$. The same argument follows for infinitesimal changes, because $d[\log (Q)] = (1/Q) dQ$.

[15]When reporting price and income elasticities of demand, we usually follow one of two procedures. Either we obtain their elasticities from constant elasticity demand equations, or we use other demand relationships and evaluate the price and elasticities when each of the variables to be considered is calculated at the mean of the data set. In the equation $Q = a - bP$, for example, we would calculate the price elasticity using the mean price P''' and the mean quantity sold Q''', so that $E_P = b(P'''/Q''')$.

[16]It is important to allow for income differences when looking at whether goods are substitutes or complements, because the coefficient on the P_2 variable could change when income is added to the equation.

useful when we wish to calculate how much people value the consumption of particular goods and services.

4. Demand is price inelastic when a 1 percent increase in price leads to a less than 1 percent decrease in quantity demanded, so that the consumer's expenditure increases. Demand is price elastic when a 1 percent increase in price leads to a more than 1 percent decrease in quantity demanded, so that the consumer's expenditure decreases. Demand is unit elastic when a 1 percent increase in price leads to a 1 percent decrease in quantity demanded.

5. The concept of *consumer surplus* can be useful in determining the benefits that people receive from the consumption of a product. Consumer surplus is the difference between what a consumer is willing to pay for a good and what he actually pays when buying it.

6. There is a network externality when one person's demand is affected by the purchasing decisions of other consumers. One example of a positive network externality, the bandwagon effect, occurs when a typical consumer's quantity demanded increases because she considers it stylish to buy a product that others have purchased. An example of a negative network externality, the snob effect, occurs when the quantity demanded increases the fewer the other people who own the good.

7. A number of methods can be used to obtain information about consumer demand. These include interview and experimental approaches, direct marketing experiments, and the more indirect statistical approach. The statistical approach can be very powerful in its application, but it is necessary to determine the appropriate variables that affect demand before the statistical work is done.

Questions for Review

1. How is an individual demand curve different from a market demand curve? Which curve is likely to be more price elastic?

2. Is the demand for a particular brand of a product, such as Head skis, likely to be more price elastic or price inelastic than the demand for the aggregate of all brands, such as downhill skis? Explain.

3. Tickets to a rock concert sell for $10. But at that price the demand is substantially greater than the available number of tickets. Is the value or marginal benefit of an additional ticket greater than, less than, or equal to $10? How might you determine that value?

4. Suppose a person allocates a given budget between two goods, food and clothing. If food is an inferior good, can you tell whether clothing is inferior or normal? Explain.

5. Which of the following combinations of goods are complements and which are substitutes? Discuss.
   a. a mathematics class and an economics class
   b. tennis balls and a tennis racket

c. steak and lobster

d. a plane trip and a train trip to the same destination

e. bacon and eggs

6. Which of the following events would cause a movement along the demand curve for U.S.-produced clothing, and which would cause a shift in the demand curve?

a. the removal of quotas on the importation of foreign clothes

b. an increase in the income of U.S. citizens

c. a cut in the industry's costs of producing domestic clothes, which is passed into the market in the form of lower clothing prices

7. For which of the following goods is a price increase likely to lead to a substantial income (as well as substitution) effect?

a. salt

b. housing

c. theater tickets

d. food

8. Among the following three groups, which is likely to have the most and which the least price-elastic demand for membership in the Association of Business Economists?

a. students

b. junior executives

c. senior executives

Exercises

1. Suppose the income elasticity of demand for food is 0.5, and the price elasticity of demand is -1.0. Suppose also that a woman spends $10,000 a year on food, and that the price of food is $2, and that her income is $25,000.

a. If a $2 sales tax on food were to cause the price of food to double, what would happen to her consumption of food?

b. Suppose that she is given a tax rebate of $5000 to ease the effect of the sales tax. What would her consumption of food be now?

c. Is she better or worse off when given a rebate equal to the sales tax payments? Discuss.

2. Suppose you are in charge of a toll bridge that is essentially cost free. The demand for bridge crossings Q is given by $P = 12 - 2Q$.

a. Draw the demand curve for bridge crossings.

b. How many people would cross the bridge if there were no toll?

c. What is the loss of consumer surplus associated with the charge of a bridge toll of $6?

3. The ACME corporation determines that at current prices the demand for its computer chips has a price elasticity of -2 in the short run, while the price elasticity for its disk drives is -1.

a. If the corporation decides to raise the price of both products by 10 percent, what will happen to its sales? to its sales revenue?

b. Can you tell from the available information which product will generate the most revenue for the firm? If yes, why? If not, what additional information would you need?

4. You are managing a city budget in which monies are spent on schools and public safety. You are about to receive aid from the federal government to support a special antidrug law enforcement program. Two programs that might be available are (1) a $100,000 grant that must be spent on law enforcement; (2) a 50 percent matching grant, in which each dollar of local spending on law enforcement is matched by a dollar of federal money. The federal matching program limits its payment to each city to a maximum of $100,000.

a. Explain why the two programs are likely to have different effects on the city's choice of spending on schools and safety.

b. Which program would you (the manager) choose if you wish to maximize the satisfaction of the citizens in your jurisdiction?

APPENDIX TO CHAPTER 4

Demand Theory—
An Algebraic Treatment

This appendix presents an algebraic treatment of the basics of demand theory. Our goal is to provide a short overview of the theory of demand for students who have some familiarity with the calculus in general. To do this, we will explain and then apply the concept of constrained optimization.

Utility Maximization

Demand theory is based on the premise that consumers maximize utility subject to a budget constraint. Utility is assumed to be an increasing function of the quantities of goods consumed, but marginal utility is assumed to decrease with consumption. The consumer's optimization problem when there are two goods, X and Y, may then be written as

$$\text{Maximize } U(X,Y) \tag{A4.1}$$

subject to the constraint that all income is spent on the two goods:

$$P_X X + P_Y Y = I \tag{A4.2}$$

Here, $U(\ )$ is the utility function, X and Y are the quantities of the two goods that the consumer purchases, P_X and P_Y are the prices of the goods, and I is income.[1]

To determine the individual consumer's demand for the two goods, we choose those values of X and Y that maximize (A4.1) subject to (A4.2). When we know the particular form of the utility function, we can solve to find the consumer's demand for X and Y directly. However, even if we write the utility function in its general form $U(X,Y)$, the technique of constrained optimization can be used to describe the conditions that must hold if the consumer is maximizing utility.

---

[1]To simplify the mathematics, we assume that the utility function is continuous (with continuous derivatives) and that goods are infinitely divisible.

The Method of Lagrange Multipliers

To solve the constrained optimization problem given by equations (A4.1) and (A4.2), we use the method of Lagrange multipliers, which works as follows. We first write the "Lagrangian" for the problem. To do this, rewrite the constraint (A4.2) as $P_X X + P_Y Y - I = 0$. The Lagrangian is then

$$\Phi = U(X,Y) - \lambda(P_X X + P_Y Y - I) \tag{A4.3}$$

The parameter λ is called the *Lagrange multiplier*; we will discuss its interpretation shortly.

If we choose values of X and Y that satisfy the budget constraint, then the second term in equation (A4.3) will be zero, and maximizing Φ will be equivalent to maximizing $U(X,Y)$. By differentiating Φ with respect to X, Y, and λ and then equating the derivatives to zero, we obtain the necessary conditions for a maximum[2]:

$$MU_X(X,Y) - \lambda P_X = 0$$

$$MU_Y(X,Y) - \lambda P_Y = 0 \tag{A4.4}$$

$$P_X X + P_Y Y - I = 0$$

Here, MU is short for marginal utility (i.e., $MU_X(X,Y) = \partial U(X,Y)/\partial X$, the change in utility from a small increase in the consumption of good X).

The third condition is the original budget constraint. The first two conditions of (A4.4) tell us that each good will be consumed up to the point at which the marginal utility from consumption is a multiple (λ) of the price of the good. To see the implication of this, we combine the first two conditions to obtain

$$\lambda = [MU_X(X,Y)/P_X] = [MU_Y(X,Y)/P_Y] \tag{A4.5}$$

In other words, the marginal utility of each good divided by its price is the same. To be optimizing, *the consumer must be getting the same utility from the last dollar spent by consuming either* X *or* Y. If this were not the case, consuming more of one good and less of the other would increase utility.

Marginal Rate of Substitution

To characterize the individual's optimum in more detail, we can rewrite the information in (A4.4) to obtain

$$MU_X(X,Y)/MU_Y(X,Y) = P_X/P_Y \tag{A4.6}$$

---

[2]These conditions are necessary for an "interior" solution in which the consumer consumes positive amounts of both goods. However, the solution could be a "corner" solution in which all of one good and none of the other is consumed.

We can use this equation to see the link between utility functions and indifference curves. An indifference curve represents all market baskets that give the consumer the same level of utility. If U^* is a fixed utility level, then the indifference curve that corresponds to that utility level is given by

$$U(X,Y) = U^*$$

As the market baskets are changed by adding X and subtracting Y, the total change in utility must equal zero. Therefore

$$MU_X(X,Y)\, dX + MU_Y(X,Y)\, dY = dU = 0 \qquad (A4.7)$$

It follows by rearrangement that

$$-dY/dX = MU_X(X,Y)/MU_Y(X,Y) = MRS_{XY} \qquad (A4.8)$$

where MRS_{XY} represents the individual's marginal rate of substitution of X for Y. Because the left-hand side of (A4.8) represents the negative of the slope of the indifference curve, it follows that at the point of tangency the individual's marginal rate of substitution (which trades off goods while keeping utility constant) is equal to the individual's ratio of marginal utilities, which in turn is equal to the ratio of the prices of the two goods, from (A4.6).[3]

When the individual indifference curves are convex, the tangency of the indifference curve to the budget line solves the consumer's optimization problem. This was illustrated by Figure 3.11 in Chapter 3.

An Example

In general, the three equations in (A4.4) can be solved to determine the three unknowns X, Y, and λ as a function of the two prices and income. Substitution for λ then allows us to solve for the demands for each of the two goods in terms of income and the prices of the two commodities. This can be most easily seen in terms of an example.

A frequently used utility function is the Cobb-Douglas utility function, which can be represented in two forms:

$$U(X,Y) = a\log(X) + (1-a)\log(Y)$$

and

$$U(X,Y) = X^a Y^{1-a}$$

---

[3]We are implicitly assuming that the "second-order conditions" for a utility maximum hold, so that the consumer is maximizing rather than minimizing utility. The convexity condition is all that is required for the second-order conditions to be satisfied. In mathematical terms, the condition is that $d(MRS)/dX < 0$, or that $d^2Y/dX^2 > 0$, where $-dY/dX$ is the slope of the indifference curve. It is important to note that diminishing marginal utility is not a sufficient assumption to ensure that indifference curves are convex.

The two forms are equivalent for the purposes of demand theory because they both yield the identical demand functions for goods X and Y. We will derive the demand functions for the first form and leave the second as an exercise for the student.

To find the demand functions for X and Y, given the usual budget constraint, we first write the Lagrangian:

$$\Phi = a\log(X) + (1-a)\log(Y) - \lambda(P_X X + P_Y Y - I)$$

Now differentiating with respect to X, Y, and λ, and setting the derivatives equal to zero, we obtain

$$\partial\Phi/\partial X = a/X - \lambda P_X = 0$$

$$\partial\Phi/\partial Y = (1-a)/Y - \lambda P_Y = 0$$

$$\partial\Phi/\partial\lambda = P_X X + P_Y Y - I = 0$$

The first two conditions imply that

$$P_X X = a/\lambda \tag{A4.9}$$

$$P_Y Y = (1-a)/\lambda \tag{A4.10}$$

Combining these with the last condition (the budget constraint) tells us that $\lambda = 1/I$. Now we can substitute this expression for λ back into (A4.9) and (A4.10) to obtain the demand functions:

$$X = (a/P_X)I$$

$$Y = [(1-a)/P_Y]I$$

In this example the demand for each good depends only on the price of that good and on income, not on the price of the other good. Thus, the cross-price elasticity of demand is 0.

Marginal Utility of Income

Whatever the form of the utility function, the Lagrange multiplier λ represents the extra utility generated when the budget constraint is relaxed—in this case by adding one dollar to the budget. To see this, we differentiate (A4.1) totally with respect to I:

$$dU/dI = MU_X(X,Y)(dX/dI) + MU_Y(X,Y)(dY/dI) \tag{A4.11}$$

Because any increment in income must be divided between the two goods, it follows that

$$dI = P_X \, dX + P_Y \, dY \tag{A4.12}$$

Substituting from (A4.5) into (A4.11), we get

$$dU/dI = \lambda P_X(dX/dI) + \lambda P_Y(dY/dI) = \lambda(P_X\,dX + P_Y\,dY)/dI \quad \text{(A4.13)}$$

and substituting (A4.12) into (A4.13), we get

$$dU/dI = (\lambda P_X\,dX + \lambda P_Y\,dY)/(P_X\,dX + P_Y\,dY) = \lambda \quad \text{(A4.14)}$$

Going back to our original analysis of the conditions for utility maximization, we see from equation (A4.5) that maximization requires that the utility obtained from the consumption of every good, per dollar spent on that good, be equal to the marginal utility of an additional dollar of income. If this were not the case, the consumer could increase her utility by spending more on the good with the higher ratio of marginal utility to price, and less on the other good.

To clarify some of the results that we have discussed, it will be helpful to reconsider the earlier Cobb-Douglas utility function example. In the Cobb-Douglas example, we saw that when $U = a\log(X) + (1-a)\log Y$, the demand functions were $X = (a/P_X)I$, and $Y = [(1-a)/P_Y]I$, and the Lagrange multiplier was $\lambda = 1/I$. Now we can see how the Lagrange multiplier can be interpreted when specific values have been chosen for each of the parameters in the problem. Let $a = 1/2$, $P_X = \$1.00$, $P_Y = \$2.00$ and $I = \$100$. Then the choices that maximize utility are $X = 50$ and $Y = 25$. Also note that $\lambda = 1/100$. The Lagrange multiplier tells us that if an additional dollar of income were available to the consumer, the level of utility achieved would increase by $1/100$. This is relatively easy to check. With an income of \$101, the maximizing choices of the two goods are $X = 50.5$ and $Y = 25.25$. A bit of arithmetic tells us that the original level of utility is 3.565, and the new level of utility is 3.575. As we can see, the additional dollar of income has indeed increased utility by .01, or 1/100.

Duality in Consumer Theory

One important feature of consumer theory is the *dual* nature of the consumer's decision. The optimum choice of X and Y can be analyzed not only as the problem of choosing the highest indifference curve (the maximum value of $U(\ )$) that touches the budget line, but also as the problem of choosing the lowest budget line (the minimum budget expenditure) that touches a given indifference curve. To see this, consider the following dual consumer optimization problem, the problem of minimizing the cost of achieving a particular level of utility:

$$\text{Minimize } P_X X + P_Y Y$$

subject to the constraint that

$$U(X,Y) = U^*$$

The corresponding Lagrangian is given by

$$\Phi = P_X X + P_Y Y - \mu(U(X,Y) - U^*) \quad \text{(A4.15)}$$

where μ is the Lagrange multiplier. Differentiating Φ with respect to X, Y, and μ, and setting the derivatives equal to zero, we find the following necessary conditions for expenditure minimization:

$$P_X - \mu MU_X(X,Y) = 0$$
$$P_Y - \mu MU_Y(X,Y) = 0$$

(A4.16)

and

$$U(X,Y) = U^*$$

By solving the first two equations, we see that

$$\mu = [P_X/MU_X(X,Y)] = [P_Y/MU_Y(X,Y)] = 1/\lambda$$

Because it is also true that $MU_X(X,Y)/MU_Y(X,Y) = MRS_{XY} = P_X/P_Y$, the cost-minimizing choice of X and Y must occur at the point of tangency of the budget line and the indifference curve that generates utility U^*. Because this is the same point that maximized utility in our original problem, the dual expenditure minimization problem yields the same demand functions that are obtained from the direct utility maximization problem.

To see how the dual approach works, let's reconsider the Cobb-Douglas example once more. The algebra is somewhat easier to follow if we used the exponential form of the Cobb-Douglas utility function, $U(X,Y) = X^a Y^{1-a}$, and we will do so here. In this case, the Lagrangian is given by

$$\Phi = P_X X + P_Y Y - \mu[X^a Y^{1-a} - U^*]$$

Differentiating with respect to X, Y, and μ and equating to zero, we obtain

$$P_X = \mu a U^*/X$$
$$P_Y = \mu(1-a)U^*/Y.$$

Multiplying the first equation by X and the second by Y and adding, we get

$$P_X X + P_Y Y = \mu U^*$$

If we let I be the cost-minimizing expenditure (the individual must spend all of his income to get utility level U^* or U^* would not have maximized utility in the original problem), then it follows that $\mu = I/U^*$. Substituting in the equations above, we obtain

$$X = aI/P_X \text{ and } Y = (1-a)I/P_Y$$

These are the same demand functions that we obtained before.

Income and Substitution Effects

The demand function tells us how any individual's utility-maximizing choices respond to changes in income and in the prices of goods. It is important, however, to distinguish that portion of any price change that involves the movement along an indifference curve and that portion that involves a movement to a different indifference curve (and therefore a change in purchasing power). To do this, we consider what happens to the demand for good X when the price of X changes. The change in demand can be divided into a substitution effect (the change in quantity demanded when the level of utility is fixed) and an income effect (the change in the quantity demanded with the level of utility changing but the relative price of good X unchanged). We denote the change in X that results from a unit change in the price of X by $\partial X/\partial P_X|_{u=u^*}$ using a partial derivative, since the price of the other good and income are unchanged. Thus

$$\partial X/\partial P_X = \partial X/\partial P_X|_{u=u^*} + (\partial X/\partial I)(\partial I/\partial P_X) \qquad (A4.17)$$

The first term on the right-hand side of equation (A4.17) is the substitution effect (because utility is fixed), and the second term is the income effect (because income increases).

From the consumer's budget constraint, $I = P_X X + P_Y Y$, we know by differentiation that

$$\partial I/\partial P_X = X \qquad (A4.18)$$

Suppose for the moment that the consumer owned goods X and Y. Then equation (A4.18) would tell us that when the price of good X increases by \$1, the amount of income the consumer can obtain by selling the good increases by \$$X$. In our theory of the consumer, however, the consumer does not own the good. As a result, equation (A4.18) tells us how much additional income the consumer would need to leave him as well off after the price change as before. For this reason, it is customary to write the income effect as negative (reflecting a loss of purchasing power) rather than positive. Equation (A4.17) then appears as follows:

$$\partial X/\partial P_X = \partial X/\partial P_X|_{u=u^*} - X(\partial X/\partial I) \qquad (A4.19)$$

In this new form, called the *Slutsky equation*, the first term represents the substitution effect, the change in demand for good X obtained by keeping utility fixed. The second term is the income effect, the change in purchasing power resulting from the price change times the change in demand resulting from that change in purchasing power.

Exercises

1. Which of the following utility functions are consistent with convex indifference curves, and which are not?
  a. $U(X,Y) = 2X + 5Y$
  b. $U(X,Y) = (XY)^{.5}$
  c. $U(X,Y) = $ Min (X,Y), where Min is the minimum of the two values of X and Y.

2. Show that the two utility functions given below generate the identical demand functions for goods X and Y:

  a. $U(X,Y) = \log (X) + \log (Y)$
  b. $U(X,Y) = (XY)^{.5}$

3. Assume that a utility function is given by Min (X,Y), as in Exericse 1c. What is the Slutsky equation that decomposes the change in the demand for X in response to a change in its price? What is the income effect? What is the substitution effect?

CHAPTER 5

Choice Under Uncertainty

So far we have assumed that prices, incomes, and other variables are known with certainty. However, many of the choices that people make involve considerable uncertainty. For example, most people borrow to finance large purchases, such as a house or a college education, and plan to pay for the purchase out of future income. But for most of us, future incomes are uncertain. Our earnings can go up or down; we can be promoted, demoted, or even lose our jobs. Or if we delay buying a house or investing in a college education, we risk having its price rise in real terms, making it harder to afford in the future. How should we take these uncertainties into account when making major consumption or investment decisions?

Sometimes we must choose how much risk to bear. What, for example, should you do with your savings? Should you invest your money in something safe, like a savings account, or something riskier but potentially more lucrative, like the stock market? Another example is the choice of a job or even career. Is it better to work for a large, stable company where job security is good but the chances for advancement are limited, or to join (or form) a new venture, which offers less job security but more opportunity for advancement?

To answer questions such as these, we must first be able to quantify risk so we can compare the riskiness of alternative choices. We therefore begin this chapter by discussing measures of risk. Afterwards, we will examine people's attitudes (i.e., preferences) toward risk. (Most people find risk undesirable, but some people find it more undesirable than others.) Next, we will see how people can deal with risk. In some situations, risk can be reduced—by diversification, by buying insurance, or by investing in additional information. In other situations (e.g., when investing in stocks or bonds) people must choose the amount of risk they will bear.

5.1 Describing Risk

To describe risk quantitatively, we need to know all the possible outcomes of a particular action and the likelihood that each outcome will occur.[1] Suppose, for example, that you are considering whether to invest in a company that is exploring for offshore oil. If the exploration effort is successful, the company's stock will increase from $30 to $40 a share; if not, it will fall to $20 a share. Thus, there are two possible future outcomes, a $40 per share price and a $20 per share price.

Probability

Probability refers to the likelihood than an outcome will occur. In our example, the probability that the oil exploration project is successful might be ¼, and the probability that it is unsuccessful ¾. Probability is a difficult concept to formalize because its interpretation can depend on the nature of the uncertain events and on the beliefs of the people involved in them. One *objective* interpretation of probability relies on the frequency with which certain events tend to occur. Suppose we know that of the last 100 offshore oil explorations 25 have succeeded and 75 have failed. Then the probability of success of ¼ is objective, because it is based directly on the frequency of similar experiences.

But what if there are no similar past experiences to help measure probability? In these cases objective measures of probability cannot be deduced, and a more *subjective* measure is needed. Subjective probability is the perception that an outcome will occur. This perception may be based on a person's judgment or experience, but not necessarily on the frequency with which a particular outcome has actually occurred in the past. When probabilities are subjectively determined, different people may attach different probabilities to different outcomes and thereby make different choices.[2] For example, if the search for oil were to take place in an area where no previous searches had ever occurred, I might attach a higher subjective probability than you to the chance that the project will succeed because I have known more about the project, or because I have a better understanding of the oil business and can therefore make better use of the information. Either different information or different abilities to

---

[1]Some people distinguish between uncertainty and risk along the lines suggested by the economist Frank Knight some sixty years ago. *Uncertainty* can refer to situations in which many outcomes are possible but the likelihoods of the various outcomes are unknown. *Risk* then refers to situations in which we can list all possible outcomes, and we know the likelihood that each outcome occurs. We will always refer to risky situations but will simplify the discussion by using uncertainty and risk interchangeably.

[2]In any case, the probable outcomes must be *mutually exclusive,* in the sense that one and only one actual outcome will occur in the future. As a result, the probabilities associated with each possible outcome will sum to one.

process the same information can explain why subjective probabilities vary among individuals.

Whatever the interpretation of probability, it is used in calculating two important measures that help us describe and compare risky choices. One measure tells us the *average value* and the other the *variability* of the possible outcomes.

Expected Value

The *expected value* (or expectation) associated with an uncertain situation is a weighted average of all possible outcomes, with the probabilities of each outcome used as weights. The expected value measures the *central tendency*, i.e., the outcome that we would expect on average. Our offshore oil exploration example has two possible outcomes: success yields a value of $40 per share, while failure yields a value of $20 per share. Denoting "probability of" by Pr, the expected value in this case is given by

$$\text{Expected Value} = \text{Pr(Success)}(\$40/\text{share}) + \text{Pr(Failure)}(\$20/\text{share})$$

$$= (\tfrac{1}{4})(\$40/\text{share}) + (\tfrac{3}{4})(\$20/\text{share}) = \$25/\text{share}$$

More generally, if there are two possible outcomes having values X_1 and X_2, and the probabilities of each outcome are given by π_1 and π_2, then the expected value $E(X)$ is

$$E(X) = \pi_1 X_1 + \pi_2 X_2 \tag{5.1}$$

Variability

Suppose you are choosing between two part-time sales jobs that have the same expected income ($1500). The first job is based entirely on commission—the income earned depends on how much you sell. The second job is salaried. There are two equally likely incomes under the first job—$2000 for a good sales effort and $1000 for one that is only modestly successful. The second job pays $1510 most of the time, but you would earn $510 in severance pay if the company should go out of business. Table 5.1 summarizes these possible outcomes and their probabilities.

Note that the two jobs have the same expected income because .5($2000) +

TABLE 5.1 Income from Sales Jobs

	Outcome 1		Outcome 2	
	Probability	Income ($)	Probability	Income ($)
Job 1: commission	.5	2000	.5	1000
Job 2: fixed salary	.99	1510	.01	510

TABLE 5.2 Deviations from Expected Income ($)

	Outcome 1	Deviation	Outcome 2	Deviation
Job 1	2000	500	1000	500
Job 2	1510	10	510	990

.5($1000) = .99 ($1510) + .01 ($510) = $1500. But the variability of the possible outcomes is different for the two jobs. This variability can be usefully analyzed by a measure that presumes that large differences (whether positive or negative) between actual outcomes and the expected outcome, called *deviations*, signal greater risk. Table 5.2 gives the deviations of actual incomes from the expected income for the example of the two sales jobs.

In the first commission job, the average deviation is $500, which is obtained by weighting each deviation by the probability that each outcome occurs. Thus,

$$\text{Average Deviation} = .5(\$500) + .5(\$500) = \$500$$

For the second fixed salary job, the average deviation is calculated as follows:

$$\text{Average Deviation} = .99(\$10) + .01(\$990) = \$19.80$$

The first job is thus substantially more risky than the second, because its average deviation of $500 is much greater than the average deviation of $19.80 for the second job.

In practice one usually encounters two closely related but slightly different measures of variability. The *variance* is the average of the *squares* of the deviations of the values associated with each outcome from its expected value. The *standard deviation* is the square root of the variance. Table 5.3 gives the relevant calculations for our example.

The average of the squared deviations under Job 1 is given by

$$\text{Variance} = .5(\$250,000) + .5(\$250,000) = \$250,000.$$

The standard deviation is therefore equal to the square root of $250,000, or $500. Similarly, the average of the squared deviations under Job 2 is given by

$$\text{Variance} = .99(\$100) + .01(\$980,100) = \$9,900.$$

TABLE 5.3 Calculating Variance ($)

	Outcome 1	Deviation Squared	Outcome 2	Deviation Squared
Job 1	2000	250,000	1000	250,000
Job 2	1510	100	510	980,100

The standard deviation is the square root of $9,900, or $99.50. Whether we use variance or standard deviation to measure risk (it's really a matter of convenience—both provide the same ranking of risky choices), the second job is substantially less risky than the first. Both the variance and the standard deviation of the incomes earned are lower.

In general, when there are two outcomes with values X_1 and X_2, each occurring with probability π_1 and π_2 and $E(X)$ is the expected value of the outcomes, the variance is given by[3]

$$\sigma^2 = \pi_1[(X_1 - E(X))^2] + \pi_2[(X_2 - E(X))^2] \tag{5.2}$$

The standard deviation, which is the square root of the variance, is written as σ.

The concept of variance applies equally well when there are many alternative outcomes rather than just two. Suppose, for example, that the first job yields incomes ranging from $1000 to $2000 in increments of $100 that are all equally likely. The second job yields incomes from $1300 to $1700 (again in increments of $100) that are also all equally likely. Figure 5.1 shows the alternatives graphically.

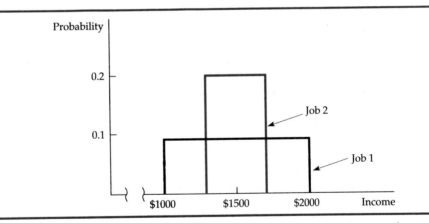

FIGURE 5.1 Variance—Equal Probability Outcomes.   The distribution of outcomes associated with Job 1 has a greater spread and a greater variance than the distribution of outcomes associated with Job 2. Both distributions are flat because all outcomes are equally likely.

[3]Equivalently, $\sigma^2 = E\{[X - E(X)]^2\}$.

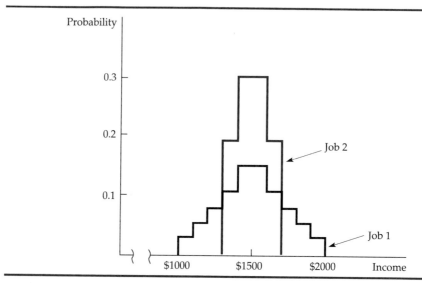

FIGURE 5.2 Variance—Unequal Probability Outcomes. The distribution of outcomes associated with Job 1 has a greater spread and a greater variance than the distribution of outcomes associated with Job 2. Both distributions are peaked because the extreme outcomes are less likely than those near the middle of the distribution.

You can see from Figure 5.1 that the first job is riskier than the second. The "spread" of possible outcomes for the first job is much greater than the spread of outcomes for the second. And the variance of the outcomes associated with the first job is greater than the variance associated with the second.

In this particular example, all outcomes are equally likely, so the curves describing the outcomes under each job are flat. But in many cases, some outcomes are more likely than others. Figure 5.2 shows a situation in which the more extreme outcomes are the least likely. Again, the salary from Job 1 has a greater variance. From this point on we will use the variance of outcomes to measure the variability of risky situations.

Decision Making

Suppose you are choosing between the two sales jobs described in our original example. Which job would you take? If you dislike risk, you will take the second job. It offers the same expected income as the first but with less risk. But suppose we add $100 to each of the outcomes in the first job, so that the expected value increases from $1500 to $1600. Table 5.4 gives the new earning outcomes and the squared deviations.

TABLE 5.4 Incomes from Sales Jobs—Modified ($)

	Outcome 1	Deviation Squared	Outcome 2	Deviation Squared
Job 1	2100	250,000	1100	250,000
Job 2	1510	100	510	980,100

The jobs can then be described as follows:

Job 1:   Expected Value = $1600   Variance = $250,000

Job 2:   Expected Value = $1500   Variance = $9,900

Job 1 offers a higher expected value but is substantially riskier than the Job 2. Which job is preferred depends on you. An aggressive entrepreneur may opt for the higher expected income and higher variance, but a more conservative person might opt for the second. To see how people might decide between incomes that differ in both expected value and in riskiness, we need to develop our theory of consumer choice.

5.2 Attitudes Toward Risk

We used a job example to describe how people might evaluate risky outcomes, but the principles apply equally well to other choices. In this section we concentrate on consumer choices generally, and on the utility that consumers obtain from choosing among risky alternatives. To simplify things, we'll consider the consumption of a single commodity—the consumer's income, or more appropriately, the market basket that income can purchase. We assume that all consumers know all probabilities.

Figure 5.3a shows how we can describe a woman's attitudes toward risk. The curve OB, which gives her utility function, tells us the level of utility (on the vertical axis) that she can attain for each level of income (measured in thousands of dollars on the horizontal axis). The level of utility increases from 10 to 16 to 18 as income increases from $10,000 to $20,000 to $30,000. But note that marginal utility is diminishing, falling from 10 when income increases from 0 to $10,000, to 6 when income increases from $10,000 to $20,000, to 2 when income increases from $20,000 to $30,000.

Now suppose she has an income of $15,000 and is considering a new but risky sales job that will either double her income to $30,000 or cause it to fall to $10,000. Each possibility has a probability of .5. As Figure 5.3a shows, the utility level associated with an income of $10,000 is 10 (at point A), and the utility associated with a level of income of $30,000 is 18 (at B). The risky job must be compared with the current job, for which the utility is 13 (at C).

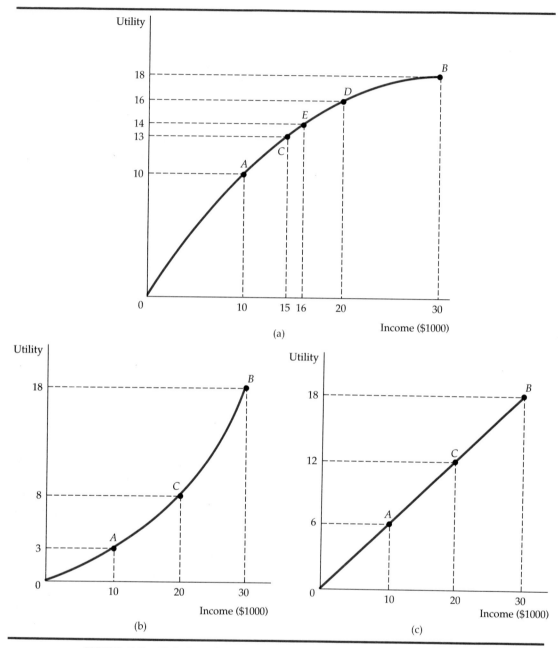

FIGURE 5.3   Risk Aversion.   People may differ in their preferences toward risk. In Figure 5.1a a consumer's marginal utility diminishes as income increases. The consumer is risk averse, because she would prefer a certain income of $20,000 (with a utility of 16) to a gamble with a .5 probability of $10,000 and a .5 probability of $30,000 (and expected utility of 14). In Figure 5.1b the consumer is risk loving, because she would prefer the same gamble (with expected utility of 10.5) to the certain income (with a utility of 8). Finally, in Figure 5.1c the consumer is risk neutral and is indifferent between certain events and uncertain events with the same expected income.

To evaluate the new job, she can calculate the expected value of the resulting income. Because we are measuring value in terms of the woman's utility, we must calculate the *expected utility* she can obtain. The expected utility is the sum of the utilities associated with all possible outcomes, weighted by the probability that each outcome will occur. In this case, expected utility is

$$E(u) = (\tfrac{1}{2})u(\$10,000) + (\tfrac{1}{2})u(\$30,000) = 0.5(10) + 0.5(18) = 14.$$

The new risky job is thus preferred to the original job because the expected utility of 14 is greater than the original utility of 13.

The old job involved no risk—it guaranteed an income of $15,000 and a utility level of 13. The new job is risky, but it offers the prospect of both a higher expected income ($20,000) and, more important, a higher expected utility. If the woman wished to increase her expected utility, she would take the risky job.

Different Attitudes Toward Risk

People differ in their willingness to bear risk. Some are risk averse, some are risk loving, and some are risk neutral. A person who prefers a certain given income to a risky job with the same expected income is described as being *risk averse*. (Such a person has a diminishing marginal utility of income.) Risk aversion is the most common attitude toward risk. To see that most people are risk averse most of the time, note the vast number of risks that people insure against. Most people not only buy life insurance, health insurance, and car insurance, but also seek occupations with relatively stable wages.

Figure 5.3a applies to a woman who is risk averse. Suppose she can have a certain income of $20,000, or a job yielding an income of $30,000 with probability .5 and an income of $10,000 with probability .5 (so that the expected income is $20,000). As we saw, the expected utility of the uncertain income is 14, an average of the utility at point A (10) and the utility at B (18), and is shown by E. Now we can compare the expected utility associated with the risky job to the utility generated if $20,000 were earned without risk. This utility level, 16, is given by D in Figure 5.3a. It is clearly greater than the expected utility associated with the risky job.

A person who is *risk neutral* is indifferent between earning a certain income and an uncertain one, as long as the uncertain income is the same as the expected income. In Figure 5.3c the utility associated with a job generating an income of either $10,000 or $30,000 with equal probability is 12, as is the utility of receiving a certain income of $20,000.[4]

---

[4]When people are risk neutral, the marginal utility of income is constant, so the income they earn can be used as an indicator of well-being. A government policy that doubled peoples' incomes would then also double their utility. At the same time, government policies that alter the risks that people face, without changing their expected incomes, would not affect their well-being. Risk neutrality allows one to avoid the complications that might be associated with the effects of governmental actions on the riskiness of outcomes.

Figure 5.3b shows the third possibility—*risk loving*. In this case the expected utility of an uncertain income that can be $10,000 with probability .5 or $30,000 with probability .5 is *higher* than the utility associated with a certain income of $20,000. Numerically,

$$E(u) = .5u(\$10,000) + .5u(\$30,000) = .5(3) + .5(18) = 10.5 > u(\$20,000) = 8$$

The primary evidence for risk loving is that many people enjoy gambling. Some criminologists might also describe certain criminals as risk lovers, especially when a robbery is committed that has a relatively high prospect of apprehension and punishment. These special cases aside, very few people are risk loving, at least with respect to major purchases or large amounts of income or wealth.[5]

The *risk premium* is the amount of money that a risk-averse person would pay to avoid taking a risk. The magnitude of the risk premium depends in general on the risky alternatives that the person faces. In the analysis underlying Figure 5.3a, for example, the risk premium is equal to $4000. To calculate this number in our example, recall that an expected utility of 14 is achieved by a woman who is going to take a risky job with an expected income of $20,000. But the utility level of 14 can also be achieved if she has an income of $16,000 with certainty. Thus, $4000 is the amount of income ($20,000 minus $16,000) she would give up to leave her indifferent between the risky job and the safe one.

How risk averse a person is depends on the nature of the risk involved and on the person's income. Generally, risk-averse people prefer risks involving a smaller variability of outcomes. We saw that when there are two outcomes, an income of $10,000 and an income of $30,000, the risk premium is $4000. Now consider a second risky job, involving a .5 probability of receiving an income of $40,000 and a utility level of 20 and a .5 probability of getting an income of $0. The expected value of this alternative is also $20,000, but the expected utility is only 10:

$$\text{Expected utility} = .5u(\$0) + .5u(\$40,000) = 0 + .5(19) = 10$$

Since the utility associated with having a certain income of $20,000 is 16, the woman loses 6 units of utility if she is required to accept the job. The risk premium in this case is equal to $10,000, because the utility of a certain income of $10,000 is 10. She can afford to give up $10,000 of her $20,000 expected income to have the certain income of $10,000 and will have the same level of expected utility. Thus the greater the variability, the more a person is willing to pay to avoid the risky situation.

---

[5]People may be averse to some risks and act like risk lovers with respect to others. This issue was treated by Milton Friedman and L. J. Savage in ''The Utility Analysis of Choices Involving Risk,'' *Journal of Political Economy* (1948): 279–304.

EXAMPLE 5.1   BUSINESS EXECUTIVES AND THE CHOICE OF RISK

When business executives are presented with several alternative strategies, some risky, some safe, which do they choose? In one study 464 business executives were asked to respond to a questionnaire that described risky situations that the executive might face as the vice-president of a hypothetical company.[6] In the in-basket were four risky items, each of which had a given probability of a favorable and an unfavorable outcome. The outcomes and probabilities were chosen so that each item had the same expected value. In increasing order of the risk involved (as measured by the difference between the favorable and unfavorable outcomes), the four items were (1) a lawsuit involving a patent violation, (2) a customer threat concerning the supplying of a competitor, (3) a union dispute, and (4) a joint venture with a competitor. The executives were asked a series of questions to learn how much they were willing to take or avoid risks. Thus, in some situations executives could opt to delay a choice, to collect information, to bargain, or to delegate a decision, so as to avoid taking risks or to modify the risks that they would take later.

The study found that executives vary substantially in their preferences toward risk. Roughly 20 percent of those answering indicated that they were relatively neutral toward risk, while 40 percent opted for the more risky alternatives, and 20 percent were clearly risk averse (20 percent did not respond). More important, executives (including those who chose risky alternatives) made substantial efforts to reduce or eliminate risk, usually by delaying decisions and by collecting more information.

In general, risk can arise when the expected gain is either positive (e.g., a chance for a large reward versus a small one) or negative (e.g., a chance for a large loss or for no loss). The study found that executives differ in their preferences toward risk, depending on whether the risk involved gains or losses. In general, those executives who liked risky situations did so when losses were involved. (Perhaps they were willing to gamble against a large loss in the hope of breaking even.) However, when the risks involved gains, the same executives were more conservative, opting for the less risky alternatives.[7]

---

[6]This example is based on Kenneth R. MacCrimmon and Donald A. Wehrung, "The Risk In-Basket," *Journal of Business* 57 (1984): 367–387.

[7]Once we develop a deeper understanding of people's attitudes toward risk, we can explain why some people occasionally appear irrational—they treat the risk of a small gain in income very differently from the risk of a small loss, for example. Prospect theory, developed by psychologists Daniel Kahneman and Amos Tversky, helps to explain this phenomenon. See, for example their "Rational Choice and the Framing of Decisions," *Journal of Business* 59 (1986): S251–S278, and "Prospect Theory: An Analysis of Decision under Risk," *Econometrica* 47 (1979): 263–292.

EXAMPLE 5.2   DETERRING CRIME

Fines may deter certain types of crimes, such as speeding, double-parking, tax evasion, and air polluting better than incarceration.[8] The party choosing to violate the law in these ways has good information and can reasonably be assumed to be behaving in a rational manner.

Other things being equal, the greater the fine, the more the potential criminal will be discouraged from engaging in the crime. If it were costless to catch criminals and if the crime imposed a calculable cost of $1000 on society, we might choose to catch all violators and impose a fine of $1000 on each. That would discourage people from engaging in the activity, if the benefit of the activity to them were less than the fine.

In practice, however, it is very costly to catch lawbreakers. Therefore, we save on administrative costs by imposing relatively high fines but allocating resources, so that the probability of a violator's being apprehended is substantially less than one. Thus the size of the fine that needs to be imposed to discourage criminal behavior depends on the risk preferences of the potential violators. In general, the more risk averse a person is, the smaller the fine that must be imposed to discourage him or her, as the following example demonstrates.

Suppose that a city wants to deter people from double-parking. By double-parking, a typical resident saves $5.00 in terms of his own time available to engage in activities that are more pleasant than searching for a parking space. If the driver is risk neutral and if it were costless to catch violators, a fine of just over $5.00, say, $5.01, would need to be assessed every time he double-parked. This would ensure that the net benefit of double-parking to the driver (the $5.00 benefit less the $5.01 fine) would be less than zero, so that he would choose to obey the law. In fact, all potential violators whose benefit was less than or equal to $5.00 would be discouraged, while a few whose benefit was greater than $5.00 would violate the law (they might have to double-park in an emergency).

Heavy monitoring is expensive but fortunately may not be necessary. The same deterrence effect can be obtained by assessing a fine of $50.00 and catching only one in ten violators (or perhaps a fine of $500 with a one in one-hundred chance of being caught). In each case the expected penalty is $5.00 ([$50.00][.1] or [$500.00][.01]). A policy of high fine and low probability of catching a violator is likely to save substantial enforcement costs.

---

[8]This discussion builds indirectly on Gary S. Becker, "Crime and Punishment: An Economic Approach," *Journal of Political Economy* (March/April, 1968), pp. 169–217. See also, Mitchell Polinsky and Steven Shavell, "The Optimal Tradeoff Between the Probability and the Magnitude of Fines," *American Economic Review*, 69 (December, 1979), pp. 880–891.

The fines to be assessed need not be large. If drivers were substantially risk averse, a much lower fine could be used, because they would be willing to forgo the activity in part because of the risk associated with the enforcement process. In the previous example, a $25 fine with a .1 probability of catching the violator might discourage most people from violating the law.

5.3 Reducing Risk

Sometimes consumers choose risky alternatives that suggest risk-loving rather than risk-averse behavior, as the recent growth in state lotteries shows. Nonetheless, in the face of a broad variety of risky situations, consumers are generally risk averse. In this section we describe three ways to reduce risks: diversification, the purchase of insurance, and obtaining more information about choices and outcomes.

Diversification

Suppose that you are risk averse and wish to avoid uncertain outcomes as much as possible. You plan to take a part-time job selling appliances on a commission basis. You have a choice as to how to spend your time—you can sell only air conditioners or only heaters, or you can spend half your time selling each. Of course, you can't be sure how hot or cold the weather will be next year. How should you apportion your time to minimize the risk involved in the sales job?

The answer is that risk can be minimized by *diversification*—by allocating your time toward selling two different products (whose sales are not closely related), rather than a single product. Suppose, for example, that there is a fifty-fifty chance that it will be a relatively hot year, and a fifty-fifty chance that it will be relatively cold. Table 5.5 gives the earnings that you can make selling air conditioners and heaters.

TABLE 5.5 Income from Sales of Equipment

	Hot Weather	Cold Weather
Air conditioner sales	$10,000	$ 4,000
Heater sales	$ 4,000	$10,000

If you decide to sell only air conditioners or only heaters, your actual income will be either $4,000 or $10,000 but your expected income will be $7,000 [.5($10,000) + .5($4,000)]. But suppose you diversify by dividing your time evenly between selling air conditioners and heaters. Then your income will certainly be $7,000, whatever the weather conditions. If the weather is hot, you will earn $5,000 from air conditioner sales and $2,000 from heater sales; if it is cold, you will earn $2,000 from air conditioner sales and $5,000 from heater sales. In either case, by diversifying you assure yourself of a certain income and eliminate all risk.

Diversification is not always this easy. We have chosen an example in which heater and air conditioner sales were inversely related—whenever the sales of one were strong, the sales of the other were weak. But the principle of diversification has a general application. As long as you can allocate your effort or your investment funds toward a variety of activities whose outcomes are not closely related, you can eliminate some risk.

Insurance

We have seen that risk-averse people will be willing to give up income to avoid risk. In fact, if the cost of insurance is equal to the expected loss (i.e., the insurance is actuarially fair—a policy with an expected loss of $1,000 will cost $1,000), risk-averse people will want to buy enough insurance to allow them to fully recover for any financial losses they might suffer (i.e., people will fully insure against monetary losses).

The reasoning is implicit in our discussion of risk aversion. Buying insurance assures a person of having the same income whether or not there is a loss. Because the insurance cost is equal to the expected loss, this certain income is equal to the expected income from the risky situation. For a risk-averse consumer, the guarantee of the same income whatever the outcome generates more utility than would be the case if that person had a high income when there was no loss and a low income when a loss occurred.

To clarify this argument, suppose a homeowner faces a 10 percent probability that his house will be burglarized and he will suffer a $10,000 loss. Let's assume he has $50,000 worth of property. Table 5.6 shows his wealth with two possibilities—to insure or not to insure.

TABLE 5.6

Insurance	Burglary ($p = .1$)	No Burglary ($p = .9$)	Expected Wealth
No	$40,000	$50,000	$49,000
Yes	$49,000	$49,000	$49,000

The decision to purchase insurance does not alter his expected wealth. It does, however, smooth it out over both possible outcomes. This is what generates a higher level of expected utility for the homeowner. Why? We know that the marginal utility in both no-loss and loss states is the same for the man who buys insurance (because his wealth is the same). But when there is no insurance, the marginal utility in the event of a loss is higher than if no loss occurs (recall that with risk aversion there is diminishing marginal utility). Therefore, a transfer of wealth from the no-loss to the loss state must increase total utility. And this transfer of wealth is exactly what the purchase of insurance accomplishes.

Consumers usually buy insurance from companies that specialize in selling it. In general, insurance companies are profit-maximizing firms that offer insurance policies because they know that when they pool risk, they face relatively little risk. The ability to avoid risk by operating on a large scale is based on the *law of large numbers*, which tells us that although single events may be random and largely unpredictable, the average outcome of many similar events can be predicted. For example, I may not be able to predict whether a coin toss will come out heads or tails, but I know that when many coins are flipped, approximately half will turn up heads and half tails. Similarly, if I am selling automobile insurance, I cannot predict whether a particular driver will have an accident, but I can be reasonably sure, judging from past experience, about how many accidents a large group of drivers will have.

By operating on a sufficiently large scale, insurance companies can assure themselves that over a large enough number of events, the total premiums paid in will be equal to the total amount of money paid out. To return to our burglary example, a man knows that there is a 10 percent probability that his house will be burgled; if it is he will suffer a $10,000 loss. Prior to facing this risk, he calculates the expected loss to be $1,000 ($.10 \times $10,000$), but there is substantial risk involved, since there is a 10 percent probability of a large loss. Now suppose 100 people are similarly situated and all of them buy burglary insurance from an insurance company. Because they are all similarly situated, the insurance company charges each of them a premium of $1,000 for the insurance. This $1,000 premium generates an insurance fund of $100,000 from which losses can be paid. The insurance company can rely on the law of large numbers. In this case the law tells us that the expected loss over the 100 individuals is likely to be very close to $1,000 each. Therefore, the total payout will be close to $100,000, and the company need not worry about losing more than that.

Insurance companies typically charge premiums above the expected loss because they need to cover their administrative costs. As a result, many people choose to self-insure rather than buy from an insurance company. One way to avoid risk is to self-insure by diversifying. For example, self-insurance against the risks associated with investing usually takes the form of diversifying one's portfolio, say, by buying a mutual fund. Self-insurance against other risks can be achieved by spending money. For example, a person can self-insure against the risk of loss by putting money into a fund to cover future loss. Or one may self-insure against the loss of future earnings by putting funds into an individual retirement account (IRA).

EXAMPLE 5.3 THE VALUE OF A HOME IN A RISKY HOUSING MARKET

Suppose a family is buying its first home. The family knows (from their realtor or lawyer) that to close the sale of the house they will need a deed that gives them the clear "title" to (ownership of) the house. Without such a clear title, there is always a chance (sometimes greater than one might think) that the seller of the house is not its true owner. Of course, the seller could be a crook but is more likely to be unaware of the exact nature of his or her ownership rights. For example, the owner may have borrowed heavily, using the house as "collateral" for the loan. Or the property might carry with it a legal require- ment (a covenant) that limits the use to which it may be put.

Suppose the family is willing to pay $150,000 for the house but believes there is a one in ten chance that careful research will show that the current seller does not own all the property. The property would then be worth only $50,000. If there were no insurance available, a risk-neutral family would bid at most $140,000 for the property (.9[$150,000] + .1[$50,000]). However, a family that expects to tie up most of their assets in their house would most likely be risk averse and would therefore bid substantially less to buy the house, say, $120,000.

In situations such as this, it is clearly in the interest of the seller to assure the buyer that there is no risk of a lack of full ownership. The seller does this by purchasing "title insurance." The title insurance company researches the history of the property, checks to see whether any legal liabilities are attached ot it, and generally assures itself that there is no ownership problem. The in- surance company then agrees to bear any remaining risk that might exist.[9]

Because the title insurance company is a specialist in such insurance and can collect the relevant information relatively easily, the cost of such title insurance is often less than the expected value of the loss involved. A fee of $1,000 for title insurance is not unusual, and the expected loss can be substantially higher. Clearly, it is in the interest of the sellers of homes to provide such insurance, because all but the most risk-loving buyers will pay substantially more for the house when it is insured than when it is not. In fact, most states require sellers to provide title insurance before the sale can be complete.

---

[9]Because such risks are also of concern to mortgage lenders, banks and other such lenders often require new buyers to have title insurance before they will issue a mortgage.

The Value of Information

The decisions that consumers make when outcomes are uncertain are based on limited information. If more information were available, consumers could make better predictions and reduce risk. Because information is a valuable commodity, people will pay for it. The *value of complete information* is the difference between the expected value of a choice when there is complete information and the expected value when information is imperfect.

To see how valuable information can be, suppose you are a store manager and must decide how many suits to order for the fall season. If you order 100 suits, your cost is $180 per suit, but if you order only 50 suits, your cost increases to $200. You know you will be selling the suits for $300 each, but you are not sure what total sales will be. All suits not sold can be returned, but for only half of what you paid for them. Without additional information, you will act on your belief that there is a .5 probability that 100 suits will be sold and a .5 probability that sales will be 50. Table 5.7 gives the profit that you would earn in each of the two cases.

Without additional information, you would choose to buy 100 suits if you were risk neutral, taking the chance that your profit might be either $12,000 or $1,500. But if you were risk averse, you might buy 50 suits because then you would know for sure that your income would be $5,000.

To calculate the value of complete information, we assume that with such information you can make the correct suit order whatever the sales might be. If, for example, sales were going to be 50 and you ordered 50 suits, your profit would be $5,000. If, on the other hand, sales were going to be 100 and you ordered 100 suits, your profit would be $12,000. Since both these outcomes are equally likely, your expected profit under conditions of certainty would be $8,500. The value of information is computed as

Expected value under conditions of certainty:	$8,500
Less: Expected value with uncertainty (buy 100 suits):	$-\$6,750$
Value of complete information	$1,750

Thus, it is worth paying up to $1,750 to obtain an accurate prediction of sales. Even though forecasting is inevitably imperfect, it may be worth investing in a marketing study that provides a better forecast of next year's sales.

TABLE 5.7 Profits from Sales of Suits

	Sales of 50	Sales of 100	Expected Profit
1. Buy 50 suits	$5,000	$5,000	$5,000
2. Buy 100 suits	$1,500	$12,000	$6,750

EXAMPLE 5.4 THE VALUE OF INFORMATION IN THE DAIRY INDUSTRY

Historically, the U.S. dairy industry has allocated its advertising expenditures more or less uniformly throughout the year.[10] But per capita consumption of milk declined by 24 percent between 1955 and 1980, and this stirred milk producers to look for a new sales strategy to encourage milk consumption. One strategy would be to increase advertising expenditures and to continue to advertise at a uniform rate throughout the year. A second strategy is to invest in market research to obtain more information about the seasonal demand for milk, and then reallocate expenditures, so that advertising is most intense when the demand for milk is greatest.

Research into milk demand shows that sales follow a strong pattern, with demand the greatest during the spring and lowest during summer and early fall. The price elasticity of milk demand is negative but small and the income elasticity positive and large. Most important is that milk advertising has the most effect on sales when consumers have the strongest preference for milk (March, April, and May), and the least when preferences are weakest (August, September, and October).

In this case, the cost of obtaining the seasonal information about milk demand is relatively low, and the value of the information is quite substantial. To estimate this value we can compare the actual sales of milk during 1972–1980 with what the sales would have been had the advertising expenditures been made in proportion to the strength of the seasonal demand. In the latter case 30 percent of the advertising budget would be allocated in the first quarter of the year, and only 20 percent in the third quarter.

When these calculations were made for the New York metropolitan area, it was found that the value of information—the value of the additional milk sales—was $4,046,557, which translates into a 9 percent increase in the profit to producers.

*5.4 The Demand for Risky Assets

Not Responsible For

Most people are risk averse. Given a choice, they prefer a fixed monthly income to one that is as large on average but that fluctuates randomly from month to month. Yet many of these same people will invest all or part of their savings in stocks, bonds, and other assets that carry some risk. Why do risk-averse people invest in the stock market, and thereby risk losing part or all of their

---

[10]This example is based on Henry Kinnucan and Olan D. Forker, "Seasonality in the Consumer Response to Milk Advertising with Implications for Milk Promotion Policy," *American Journal of Agricultural Economics* 68 (1986): 562–571.

investment?[11] How do people decide how much risk to bear when making investments and planning for the future? To answer these questions, we need to examine the demand for risky assets.

Assets

An *asset* is something that provides a monetary flow to its owner. For example, each apartment in an apartment building can be rented out, providing a flow of rental income to the owner of the building. Another example is a savings account in a bank that pays interest (usually every day, every month, or every three months). Typically, these interest payments are reinvested in the account.

The monetary flow that one receives from owning an asset can take the form of an explicit payment, such as the rental income from an apartment building: every month the landlord receives rent checks from the tenants. Another explicit payment is the dividend on shares of common stock; every three months the owner of a share of General Motors stock receives a quarterly dividend payment.

But sometimes the monetary flow from ownership of an asset is implicit; it takes the form of an increase or decrease in the price or value of the asset. (An increase in the value of an asset is a *capital gain,* a decrease a *capital loss.*) For example, as the population of a city grows, the value of an apartment building may increase. The owner of the building will then earn a capital gain beyond the rental income he or she receives. Although the capital gain is *unrealized* until the building is sold because no money is actually received until then, there is an implicit monetary flow because the building *could* be sold at any time. The monetary flow from owning General Motors stock is also partly implicit. The price of the stock changes from day to day, and each time it does, the owner of the stock gains or loses.

A *risky asset* pays a monetary flow that is at least in part random. In other words, the monetary flow is not known with certainty in advance. A share of General Motors stock is an obvious example of a risky asset—one cannot know whether the price of the stock will rise or fall over time, and one cannot even be sure that the company will continue to pay the same (or any) dividend per share. But although people often associate risk with the stock market, most other assets are also risky.

The apartment building is one example of this. One cannot know how much land values will rise or fall, whether the building will be fully rented all the time, or even whether the tenants will pay their rent promptly. Corporate bonds are another example—the corporation that issued the bonds could go bankrupt and fail to pay bond owners their interest and principal. Even long-term U.S.

---

[11]Most Americans have at least some money invested in stocks or other risky assets, but often the investment is made indirectly. For example, many people who hold full-time jobs have shares in a pension fund, funded in part by their own salary contributions, and in part by contributions made by their employers. Usually these pension funds, or at least part of them, are invested in the stock market.

government bonds (i.e., bonds that mature in 10 or 20 years) are risky. Although it is highly unlikely that the federal government will go bankrupt, the rate of inflation could unexpectedly increase and make future interest payments and the eventual repayment of principal worth less in real terms, and thereby reduce the value of the bonds.

In contrast to a risky asset, we call an asset *riskless* (or risk free) if it pays a monetary flow that is known with certainty. Short-term U.S. government bonds—called Treasury bills—are a riskless, or almost riskless, asset. Because these bonds mature in a few months, there is very little risk from an unexpected increase in the rate of inflation. And one can be reasonably confident that the U.S. government will not default on the bond (i.e., refuse to pay back the holder when the bond comes due). Other examples of riskless or almost riskless assets include passbook savings accounts in a bank and short-term certificates of deposit.

Asset Returns

People buy and hold assets because of the monetary flows they provide. To compare assets with each other, it helps to think of this monetary flow relative to the asset's price or value. The *return* on an asset is the total monetary flow it yields as a fraction of its price. For example, a bond worth $1000 today that pays out $100 this year (and every year) has a return of 10 percent.[12] If an apartment building was worth $10 million last year, increased in value to $11 million this year, and also provided a net (of expenses) rental income of $0.5 million, it would have yielded a return of 15 percent over the past year. Or if a share of General Motors stock had been worth $80 at the beginning of the year, fell to $72 by the end of the year, and paid a dividend of $4, it would have yielded a return of −5 percent (the dividend yield of 5 percent less the capital loss of 10 percent).

When people invest their savings in stocks, bonds, land, or other assets, they usually hope to earn a return that exceeds the rate of inflation, so that by delaying consumption, they can buy more in the future than they could by spending all their income now. As a result, we often express the return on an asset in real (inflation-adjusted) terms. The *real return* on an asset is its simple (or nominal) return *less* the rate of inflation. For example, if the annual rate of inflation had been 5 percent, the bond, the apartment building, and the share of GM stock described above would have yielded real returns of 5 percent, 10 percent, and −10 percent, respectively.

Since most assets are risky, an investor cannot know in advance what returns

─────────

[12]The price of a bond often changes during a year. If the bond appreciated (depreciated) in value during the year, its return would be greater than (less than) 10 percent. Also, the definition of return given above should not be confused with the "internal rate of return" sometimes used to compare monetary flows occurring over some time. We discuss other return measures in Chapter 15, when we deal with present discounted values.

TABLE 5.8 Investments—Risk and Return (1926–1981)

	Real Rate of Return (%)	Risk (standard deviation, %)
Common stocks	8.3	21.9
Long-term corporate bonds	0.9	8.2
U.S. Treasury bills	0.1	4.4

they will yield over the coming year. For example, the apartment building might have depreciated in value instead of appreciating, and the price of GM stock might have risen instead of falling. However, we can still compare assets by looking at their *expected returns*. The expected return on an asset is just the expected value of its return (i.e., the return that it should earn on average). In some years the *actual* return that an asset earns may be much higher than its expected return, and in some years much lower, but over a long period the average return should be close to the expected return.

Different assets have different expected returns. For example, Table 5.8 shows that the expected real return on a U.S. Treasury bill has been less than 1 percent, while the real return for a representative stock on the New York Stock Exchange has been 8.3 percent.[13] Given this difference in expected return, why would anyone buy a Treasury bill when the expected return on stocks is so much higher? The answer is that the demand for an asset depends not just on its expected return, but also on its *risk*. Although stocks have a higher expected return than Treasury bills, they also carry more risk. One measure of risk, the standard deviation of the real return, is equal to 21.9 percent for common stocks, but only 8.2 percent for corporate bonds, and 4.4 percent for U.S. Treasury bills. Clearly, the higher the return on investment, the greater the risk involved. As a result, a risk-averse investor must balance expected return against risk. We examine this trade-off in more detail below.

The Trade-off Between Risk and Return

Suppose a woman has to invest her savings in two assets—Treasury bills, which are almost risk free, and a representative group of stocks.[14] She has to decide how much of her savings to invest in each of these two assets—she might invest only in Treasury bills, only in stocks, or in some combination of the two. As

[13]The expected real return for the New York Stock Exchange Index, an average of all stocks traded on the exchange, is about 8 percent. For some stocks the expected return is higher, and for some it is lower.

[14]The easiest way to invest in a representative group of stocks is to buy shares in a *mutual fund*. A mutual fund invests in many stocks, so that by buying the fund, one effectively buys a portfolio of many stocks.

we will see, this is analogous to the consumer's problem of allocating a budget between purchases of food and clothing.

Denote the risk-free return on the Treasury bill by R_f.[15] Also, let the expected return from investing in the stock market be R_m, and the *actual* return be r_m. The actual return is risky. At the time of the investment decision, we know the set of possible outcomes and the likelihood of each, but we do not know what particular outcome will occur. The risky asset will have a higher expected return than the risk-free asset ($R_m > R_f$). Otherwise, risk-averse investors would buy only Treasury bills and no stocks would be sold.

To answer our initial question about how much money the investor should put in each asset, let's set b equal to the fraction of her savings placed in the stock market, and (1 − b) the fraction used to purchase Treasury bills. The expected return on her total portfolio, R_p, is a weighted average of the expected return on the two assets:[16]

$$R_p = bR_m + (1 - b)R_f \tag{5.3}$$

Suppose, for example, that Treasury bills pay 6 percent, the stock market 8 percent, and b = ½. Then R_p = 7 percent. How risky is this portfolio? One measure of its riskiness is the variance of the portfolio's return. Let's describe the variance of the risky stock market investment by σ_m^2 and the standard deviation by σ_m. With some algebra, we can show that the standard deviation of the portfolio (with one risky and one risk-free asset) is the fraction of the portfolio invested in the risky asset times the standard deviation of that asset[17]:

$$\sigma_p = b\sigma_m \tag{5.4}$$

The Investor's Choice Problem

We have still not determined how this investor should choose this fraction b. To do this, we must first show that she faces a risk-return trade-off analogous to the budget line of a consumer. To see what this trade-off is, note that equation (5.3) for the expected return on the portfolio can be rewritten as

$$R_p = R_f + b(R_m - R_f)$$

---

[15]Because the return is risk free, the expected and actual returns are the same.

[16]The expected value of the sum of two variables is the sum of the expected values, and the expected value of a nonrandom variable (e.g., R_f) is just that variable. So $R_p = E[br_m] + E[(1 - b)R_f] = bE[r_m] + (1 - b)R_f = bR_m + (1 - b)R_f$.

[17]To see why this is true algebraically, recall from Section 5.1 that we can write the variance as $\sigma_p^2 = E[br_m + (1 - b)R_f - R_p]^2$. Substituting equation (5.3) for the expected return on the portfolio, R_p, we have

$$\sigma_p^2 = E[br_m + (1 - b)R_f - bR_m - (1 - b)R_f]^2 = E[b(r_m - R_m)]^2 = b^2\sigma_m^2.$$

Because the standard deviation of a random variable is the square root of its variance, $\sigma_p = b\sigma_m$.

Now, from equation (5.4) we see that $b = \sigma_p/\sigma_m$, so that

$$R_p = R_f + \frac{(R_m - R_f)}{\sigma_m}\,\sigma_p \qquad\qquad (5.5)$$

This equation is a *budget line* because it describes the trade-off between risk and return. Note that it is the equation for a straight line; R_m, R_f, and σ_m are constants, so the slope $(R_m - R_f)/\sigma_m$ is a constant, as is the intercept R_f. The equation says that *the expected return on the portfolio R_p increases as the standard deviation of that return σ_p increases.* We call the slope of this budget line $(R_m - R_f)/\sigma_m$ the *price of risk* because it tells us how much extra risk an investor must incur to enjoy a higher expected return.

The budget line is drawn in Figure 5.4. As the figure shows, if the investor wants no risk, she can invest all her funds in Treasury bills ($b = 0$), and earn an expected return R_f. To receive a higher expected return, she must incur some risk. For example, she could invest all her funds in stocks ($b = 1$), and earn an expected return R_m, but incur a standard deviation σ_m. Or she might invest some fraction of her funds in each type of asset, earn an expected return somewhere between R_f and R_m, and face a standard deviation less than σ_m but greater than zero.

Figure 5.4 also shows the solution to the investor's problem. Three indifference curves are drawn in the figure. Each curve describes combinations of risk and return that leave the investor equally satisfied. (The curves are upward-sloping because risk is undesirable, so with a greater amount of risk, it takes a greater expected return to make the investor equally well-off.) The curve U_1 yields the greatest amount of satisfaction, and U_3 the least amount. (For a given amount of risk, the investor earns a higher expected return on U_1 than on U_2, and a higher expected return on U_2 than on U_3.) Of the three indifference curves, the investor would prefer to be on U_1, but this is infeasible because it does not touch the budget line. Curve U_3 is feasible, but the investor can do better. Like the consumer choosing quantities of food and clothing, our investor does best by choosing a combination of risk and return at the point where an indifference curve (in this case U_2) is tangent to the budget line. At that point, the investor's return has an expected value R^* and a standard deviation σ^*.

People differ in their attitudes toward risk. This is illustrated in Figure 5.5, which shows how two different investors choose their portfolios. Investor A is very risk averse. His indifference curve U_A is tangent to the budget line at a point of low risk, so he will invest almost all his funds in Treasury bills and earn an expected return R_A just slightly larger than the risk-free return R_f. Investor B is less risk averse. She will invest most of her funds in stocks, and the return on her portfolio will have a higher expected value R_B but also a higher standard deviation σ_B.

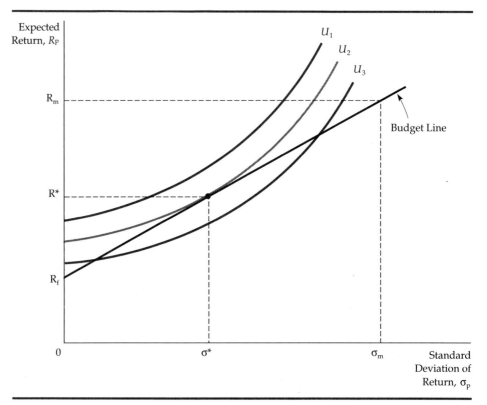

FIGURE 5.4 Choosing Between Risk and Return. An investor is dividing her funds between two assets, Treasury bills, which are risk free, and stocks. The budget line describes the trade-off between the expected return and the riskiness of that return, as measured by its standard deviation. The slope of the budget line is $(R_m - R_f)/\sigma_m$, which is the price of risk. Three indifference curves are shown; each curve shows combinations of risk and return that leave an investor equally satisfied. The curves are upward-sloping because a risk-averse investor will require a higher expected return if she is to bear a greater amount of risk. The utility-maximizing investment portfolio is at the point where indifference curve U_2 is tangent to the budget line.

In Chapters 3 and 4, we simplified the problem of consumer choice by assuming the consumer had only two goods to choose from, food and clothing. In the same spirit, we have simplified the investor's choice between only Treasury bills and stocks. However, the basic principles would be the same if we had more assets (e.g., corporate bonds, land, different types of stocks, etc.).

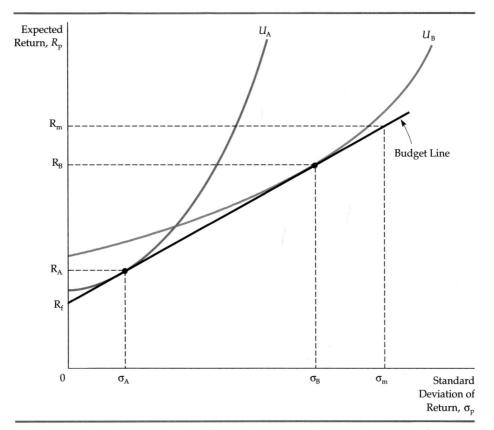

FIGURE 5.5 The Choices of Two Different Investors. Investor A is very risk averse. His portfolio will consist mostly of the risk-free asset, so his expected return R_A will be only slightly greater than the risk-free return, but the standard deviation of his return σ_A will be small. Investor B is less risk averse. She will invest a large fraction of her funds in stocks. The expected return on her portfolio R_B will. be larger, but the return will also be riskier.

Every investor faces a trade-off between risk and return.[18] How much extra risk an investor is willing be bear to earn a higher expected return depends on how risk averse that investor is. Less risk-averse investors tend to include a larger fraction of risky assets in their portfolios.

[18]Although we have not discussed this point, what matters is ''systematic'' or nondiversifiable risk, since investors can eliminate ''nonsystematic'' risk by holding a well-diversified portfolio (e.g., via a mutual fund). We will discuss systematic versus nonsystematic risk in Chapter 15. For a more detailed treatment, see a standard text on finance. A good one is Richard Brealey and Stewart Myers, *Principles of Corporate Finance* (New York: McGraw-Hill, 1985).

EXAMPLE 5.5   THE AGGREGATE DEMAND FOR COMMON STOCKS

Investors buy common stocks because these stocks pay returns in the form of dividends and capital gains. As we have seen, these returns are risky compared with those on an asset such as a Treasury bill. But on average the return on common stocks is higher than the return on Treasury bills, so investors are compensated for the additional risk.

The price of any particular common stock must be just high enough so that the dividend rate (the annual dividends divided by the price) plus the expected rate of capital gain—the total return—just compensates investors for the risk they bear by holding the stock. If the price were any lower than this, rational investors would rush to buy the stock because it would dominate other investment opportunities. (For example, it would offer a higher expected return than other stocks with the same amount of risk.) If the price were any higher than this, rational investors would rush to dump the stock because it would be dominated by other investment opportunities. As a result, the demand curve for a common stock is almost *infinitely elastic*; whatever supply is available will be demanded at a single price.

That price, however, will fluctuate over time as investors' expectations about the company change. For example, if the company develops a promising new product that is indicative of higher profits in the future, the price will rise, so that the expected return from holding the stock is again commensurate with the risk. Or if events unfold that make the stock seem riskier, the price will fall, so that the expected return is higher and commensurate with this greater risk. So this horizontal demand curve will move up and down in response to changes in expected profitability, risk, and other variables.

The demand for common stocks *in the aggregate* is likewise extremely elastic, and moves up and down in response to changes in aggregate corporate profitability, risk, and other economic variables that influence investors' demand for stocks versus other assets. As an approximation, we can write this demand as

$$P = a_1 + a_2(PRO - PRO_a) + a_3(R - R_a) + a_4(RISK - RISK_a)$$

where P is an aggregate stock price index (such as the New York Stock Exchange Index in logarithmic form), PRO is the current rate of profitability, R is the current interest rate on bonds, and RISK is the variance of returns. The subscript "a" on the variables PRO, R, and RISK means the average value of a variable. So $PRO - PRO_a$ is the amount by which current profitability differs from its average value.

Statistical estimates of equations like this tell something about what the elasticities of demand are with respect to the variables PRO, R, and RISK. One set of estimates indicates that a_2 is about 2, a_3 is about -1, and a_4 is about -2.[19] The average pretax profit rate PRO_a in the United States is about 0.11, so this says that if the current rate rises to 0.12, it would increase the price of common stock by $2(0.01) = 0.02$, or 2 percent. (The increase isn't larger because investors, from experience, would expect the higher rate of profitability to be only temporary.) On the other hand, the average annual variance of common stock returns $RISK_a$ is about 0.04 or 4 percent, so that an increase in the current variance to 0.05 would depress stock prices by about 2 percent.

Summary

1. Consumers and managers frequently make decisions in which there is uncertainty about the future. This uncertainty is characterized by the term risk, when each of the possible outcomes and its probability of occurrence is known.

2. Consumers and investors are concerned about the expected value and the variability of uncertain outcomes. The expected value is a measure of the central tendency of the value of the risky outcomes. The variability is frequently measured by the variance of outcomes, which is the average of the squares of the deviations of each possible outcome from its expected value.

3. Facing uncertain choices, consumers maximize their expected utility, an average of the utility associated with each outcome, with the associated probabilities serving as weights.

4. A person who would prefer a certain return of a given amount to a risky investment whose return is the same amount is risk averse. The maximum amount of money that a risk-averse person would pay to avoid taking a risk is the risk premium.

5. A person who is indifferent between a risky investment and the certain receipt of the expected return on that investment is risk neutral.

6. A risk-loving consumer would prefer a risky investment with a given expected return to the certain receipt of that expected sum.

7. Risk can be reduced by a) diversification, b) purchasing insurance, and c) obtaining additional information.

8. The *law of large numbers* enables insurance companies to provide actuarially fair insurance for which the premium paid is equal to the expected value of the loss being insured against.

[19]These estimates are from R. S. Pindyck, "Risk Aversion and the Determinants of Stock Market Behavior," *Review of Economics and Statistics* (May 1988). A related study is by Nai-Fu Chen, Richard Roll, and Stephen A. Ross, "Economic Forces and the Stock Market," *Journal of Business* (July 1986).

9. Consumer theory can be applied to the decision to invest in risky assets. The budget line reflects the price of risk, while consumers' indifference curves reflect their attitudes toward risk.

Questions for Review

1. What does it mean to say that a person is risk averse? Why are some people likely to be risk averse, while others are risk lovers?

2. Why is the variance a better measure of variability than the range?

3. What does it mean for consumers to be expected utility maximizers? Can you think of a case in which a person might not maximize expected utility?

4. Why does a person want to fully insure against uncertain situations when insurance is actuarially fair?

5. Why is an insurance company likely to behave *as if* it is risk neutral, even if its managers are risk-averse individuals?

6. When is it worth paying to obtain more information to reduce uncertainty?

7. How does the diversification of an investor's portfolio avoid risk?

8. Why do some investors put a large portion of their portfolios into risky assets, while others invest largely in risk-free alternatives?

Exercises

1. Suppose you have invested in a new computer company whose profitability depends on a) whether the U.S. Congress passes a tariff that raises the cost of Japanese computers, and b) whether the U.S. economy grows slowly or fast. What are the four mutually exclusive states of the world that you should be concerned about?

2. Suppose an investor is concerned about a business choice in which there are three prospects, whose probability and returns are given below:

Probability	Return
0.2	$100
0.4	50
0.4	− 25

What is the expected value of the uncertain investment? What is the variance?

3. Draw a utility function over income $u(I)$ that has the property that a man is a risk lover when his income is low but a risk averter when his income is high. Can you explain why such a utility function might reasonably describe a person's tastes? (Note: Such a utility function was discussed by Friedman and Savage in "The Utility Analysis of Choices Involving Risk," *Journal of Political Economy* 56 [1948].)

4. A city is considering how much to spend monitoring parking meters. The following information is available to the city manager:

    i. Hiring each meter-monitor costs $10,000 per year.

    ii. With one monitoring person hired, the probability of a driver getting a ticket each time he or she parks illegally is equal to .25.

    iii. With two monitors hired, the probability of getting a ticket is .5, with three monitors the probability is .75, and with four the probability is equal to 1.

    iv. The current fine for overtime parking with two metering persons hired is $20.

a. Assume first that all drivers are risk neutral. What parking fine would you levy and how many metering monitors would you hire (1, 2, 3, or 4) to achieve the current level of deterrence against illegal parking at the minimum cost?

b. Now assume that drivers are substantially risk averse. How would your answer to *a.* change?

c. (For discussion) What if drivers could insure themselves against the risk of parking fines? Would it make good public policy to allow such insurance to be available?

CHAPTER 6

Production

In the last three chapters we focused on the demand side of the market—the preferences and behavior of consumers. Now we turn to the supply side and examine the behavior of producers. We will see how firms can organize their production efficiently and how their costs of production change as input prices and the level of output change. We will also see that there are some strong similarities between the optimizing decisions of firms and those of consumers—understanding consumer behavior will help us understand producer behavior.

The theory of production and cost is central to the economic management of the firm. Just consider some of the problems that a company like General Motors faces regularly. How much assembly-line machinery and how much labor should it use in its new automobile plants? If it wants to increase production, should it hire more workers, or should it also construct new plants? Does it make more sense for one automobile plant to produce different models, or should each model be manufactured in a separate plant? What should GM expect its costs to be during the coming year, and how are these costs likely to change over time and be affected by the level of production? These questions apply not only to business firms, but also to other producers of goods and services, such as governments and nonprofit agencies.

In this chapter we study the firm's production technology—the physical relationship that describes how inputs (such as labor and capital) are transformed into outputs (such as cars and televisions). We do this in several steps. First, we show how the production technology can be represented in the form of a production function—a compact description that facilitates the analysis. Then, we use the production function to show how the firm's output changes when first one and then all the inputs are varied. We will be particularly concerned with the scale or size of the firm's operation. Are there technological advantages that make the firm more productive as its size increases?

We will also examine production by a multiproduct firm. For example, we will see how the manager of a firm that produces two different products can allocate scarce inputs to maximize the output of both products. Finally, we will see how to obtain and use empirical information about a firm's production process, including the presence of cost advantages resulting from producing a large output.

6.1 The Technology of Production

Production is what firms do. Firms turn *inputs*, which are also called *factors of production*, into *outputs*. For example, a bakery uses such inputs as the labor of its workers, raw materials like flour and sugar, and the capital invested in its ovens, mixers, and other equipment to produce outputs such as bread, cakes, and pastries.

We can divide inputs into the broad categories of labor, materials, and capital, each of which includes more narrow subdivisions. Thus, labor inputs include skilled workers (carpenters, engineers) and unskilled workers (agricultural workers), as well as the entrepreneurial efforts of the firm's managers. Materials include steel, plastics, electricity, water, and any other goods that the firm buys and transforms into a final product. Capital includes buildings, equipment, and inventories.

The relationship between the inputs to the production process and the resulting output is described by a production function. A *production function* indicates the maximum output Q that a firm can produce for every specified combination of inputs. For simplicity, we assume that there are two inputs, labor L and capital K. We can then write the production function as

$$Q = F(K,L) \tag{6.1}$$

This equation states that the quantity of output depends on the quantitites of the two inputs, capital and labor. For example, the production function might describe the maximum number of personal computers that can be produced in a given year with existing computer chip technology, a given plant size, and a specific amount of assembly-line labor. Or the production function could describe the maximum crop that a farmer can obtain under a given set of weather conditons with a specific amount of farm machinery and workers. Thus, the production function reflects that inputs can be combined to produce a given output in many ways. For example, wine can be produced in a labor-intensive way by people stomping the grapes, or in a capital-intensive way by machines squeezing the grapes. Note that equation (6.1) applies to a *given technology* (i.e., a given state of knowledge about the various methods that might be used to transform inputs into outputs). As the technology becomes more advanced, a firm can obtain more output for a given set of inputs.

The phrase "maximum output" in the definition of a production function is important. Production functions do not allow for wasteful or inefficient production processes—they presume that firms are *technically efficient*, that is, that firms can use each combination of inputs as effectively as possible. Because production functions involve attaining a maximum output for a given set of inputs, inputs will never be used if they decrease output. This presumption that production is always technically efficient need not always hold, but it is reasonable to expect that profit-seeking firms will not waste resources.

For most of our discussion, we assume that firms produce a single, clearly defined output. Only near the end of the chapter do we briefly consider the nature of the production process when inputs can be used to produce two or more distinct but related outputs.

6.2 Isoquants

Let's begin by considering the firm's production technology when it can vary both of its two inputs, labor and capital. Suppose that food (the output) is produced by using labor and capital. Table 6.1 tabulates the maximum output achievable for various combinations of inputs.

Labor inputs are listed across the top row, capital inputs down the column on the left. Each entry in the table is the maximum output that can be produced with each combination of labor and capital inputs. (For example, 2 units of capital and 4 units of labor yield 85 units of food.) Reading along each row we see that total output increases as labor inputs are increased, with capital inputs fixed. Reading down each column, we see that total product also increases as capital inputs are increased, with labor inputs fixed.

The information contained in Table 6.1 can also be represented graphically using isoquants. An *isoquant* is a curve that shows *all the combinations of inputs that yield the same total output*. Figure 6.1 shows three production isoquants. (Each axis in the figure measures the amount of inputs for a particular period.) They are determined directly from Table 6.1 but have been drawn as smooth curves to allow for the use of fractional amounts of inputs. For example, isoquant Q_1 measures all combinations of inputs that combine to yield 55 units of output. Two of these points, A and D, correspond to Table 6.1, and the remainder of

TABLE 6.1 Production with Two Variable Inputs					
	Labor Input				
Capital Input	1	2	3	4	5
1	20	40	55	65	75
2	40	60	75	85	90
3	55	75	90	100	105
4	65	85	100	110	115
5	75	90	105	115	120

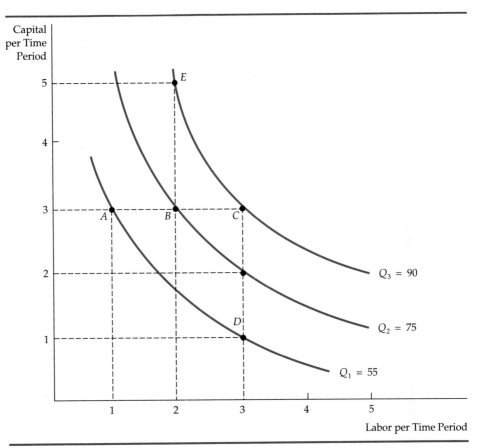

FIGURE 6.1 **Production with Two Variable Inputs.** Production isoquants show the various combination of inputs necessary for the firm to produce a given output. A set of isoquants, or isoquant map, describes the firm's production function. Output increases as one moves from isoquant Q_1 (55 units) to isoquant Q_2 (75 units) and to isoquant Q_3 (90 units).

the curve portrays the typical shape of an isoquant. At A, 1 unit of labor and 3 units of capital yield 55 units of output; whereas at D, the same output is produced from 3 units of labor and 1 unit of capital. Isoquant Q_2 measures all combinations of inputs that yield 75 units of output and corresponds to the four combinations of labor and capital underlined in the table. Isoquant Q_2 lies above and to the right of Q_1 because it takes more of either labor or capital or both to obtain a higher level of output.

Isoquants are similar to the indifference curves that we used to study consumer theory. Where indifference curves order levels of satisfaction from low to high, isoquants order levels of output. However, unlike indifference curves, each isoquant is associated with a *specific level of output*. By contrast, the numerical labels attached to indifference curves are meaningful only in an ordinal way—higher levels of utility are associated with higher indifference curves, but we cannot measure a specific level of utility the way we can measure a specific level of output with an isoquant.

An *isoquant map* is a set of isoquants each of which shows the maximum output that can be achieved for any set of inputs. An isoquant map is an alternative way of describing a production function, just as an indifference map is a different way of describing a utility function. An infinite number of isoquants make up an isoquant map. Each isoquant is associated with a different level of output, and the level of output increases as you move up and to the right in the figure.

Isoquants show the flexibility that firms have when making production decisions. In most cases, firms can obtain a particular output using various combinations of inputs. The manager of a firm must understand the nature of this flexibility. As we will see, this knowledge allows the manager to choose input combinations that minimize costs and maximize profit.

The Short Run Versus the Long Run

It is important to distinguish between the short and long run when talking about production and cost. The *short run* pertains to a period of time in which one or more factors of production cannot be changed. Factors that cannot be varied over this period are called *fixed inputs*. A firm's capital, for example, usually requires time to change—a new factory must be planned and built, and machinery and other equipment must be ordered and delivered, which can take a year or more. The *long run* is the amount of time sufficient to make all inputs variable. In the short run, firms vary the intensity with which they utilize a given plant and machinery; in the long run, they vary the size of the plant. All fixed inputs in the short run represent the outcomes of previous long-run decisions based on the firms' estimates of what they could profitably produce and sell. One must distinguish between the short and long run on a case-by-case basis. For example, the long run can be as brief as a day or two for a child's lemonade stand or as long as ten years for a petrochemical producer or an automobile manufacturer.

Figure 6.1 gives us a way to examine the difference between the short and long run. Suppose the firm is currently producing 55 units of food using 1 unit of labor and 3 units of capital (at point A), but it wants to expand its output to 90 units. Since labor costs $30 per hour, but capital costs only $10, the short-run total cost of producing 55 units is $60. In the long run, both capital and labor are variable inputs, so (for example) the additional output can be produced at E, at a cost of $110. This involves the use of one additional unit of labor and two additional units of capital. In the short run, however, capital cannot be changed. Therefore, the only way in which the 90 units of output can be produced is to increase labor input from 1 to 3, thereby moving from *A* to *C*. Unfortunately, the short-run cost of producing 90 units is $120, $10 higher than the long-run cost.

Firms continually make production decisions in the short run, while simultaneously planning how to alter their inputs in the long run. In the short run, it costs the firm $60 per hour to increase its output from 55 to 90 units. In the long run, however, this cost can be lowered to $50 per hour if two units of capital are added to the production process. Thus, our firm places its order for the additional capital, but it continues to produce 90 units with three units of labor. When the capital becomes available, the firm can reduce its labor input and increase its profit.

6.3 Production with One Variable Input (Labor)

Let's consider the case in which capital is fixed, but labor is variable, so that the firm can produce more output by increasing its labor input. Imagine, for example, that you are managing a clothing plant. You have a fixed amount of equipment, but you can hire more or less labor to sew and to run the machines. You have to decide how much labor to hire and how much clothing to produce. To make the decision, you will need to know how the amount of output Q increases (if at all), as the input of labor L increases.

Table 6.2 gives this information about the production function. It shows the amount of output that can be produced with different amounts of labor, and with capital fixed at ten units. (The first column shows the amount of labor, the second shows the fixed amount of capital, and the third shows output.) When labor input is zero, output is also zero. Then up to a labor input of eight units, output increases as labor is increased. Beyond that point, total output declines: while initially each unit of labor can take greater and greater advantage of the existing machinery and plant, after a certain point, additional labor is no longer useful and can indeed be counterproductive. (Five people can run an assembly line better than two, but ten people may get in each other's way.)

Average and Marginal Products

The contribution that labor makes to the production process can be described in terms of the average and marginal products of labor. The fourth column in Table 6.2 shows the *average product of labor* AP_L, which is the output per unit of input. The average product is calculated by dividing the total output Q by the total input of labor, L or Q/L. In our example the average product increases initially but falls when the labor input becomes greater than 4. The fifth column lists the *marginal product of labor* MP_L. This is the *additional* output produced as the labor input is increased one unit. For example, with capital fixed at 10 units, when the labor input increases from 2 to 3, total output increases from 30 to

TABLE 6.2 Production with One Variable Input

Amount of Labor (L)	Amount of Capital (K)	Total Output (Q)	Average Product (Q/L)	Marginal Product (ΔQ/ΔL)
0	10	0	—	—
1	10	10	10	10
2	10	30	15	20
3	10	60	20	30
4	10	80	20	20
5	10	95	19	15
6	10	108	18	13
7	10	112	16	4
8	10	112	14	0
9	10	108	12	−4
10	10	100	10	−8

60, creating an additional output of 30 (60 − 30) units. The marginal product of labor is written as $\Delta Q/\Delta L$ (i.e., the change in output ΔQ resulting from a one-unit increase in labor input ΔL). The marginal product of labor depends on the amount of capital used. If the capital input increased from 10 to 20, for example, the marginal product of labor would most likely increase. Like the average product, the marginal product first increases then falls, but it begins to decline just past the third unit of labor.

To summarize:

$$\text{Average Product of Labor } = \text{Output/Labor Input} = Q/L$$

$$\text{Marginal Product of Labor } = \text{Change in Output/Change in Labor Input} = \Delta Q/\Delta L$$

Figure 6.2 plots the information contained in Table 6.2. (We have connected all the points in the figure with solid lines.) Figure 6.2a shows that output increases until it reaches the maximum output of 112; thereafter it diminishes. That portion of the total output is dashed to denote that production past an output of eight is not technically efficient and therefore is not part of the production function. Technical efficiency rules out the possibility of negative marginal products. Figure 6.2b shows the average and marginal product curves. (The units of the vertical axis have changed from output to output per unit of labor.) Note that the marginal product is always positive when output is increasing, and it is negative when output is decreasing.

It is no coincidence that the marginal product curve crosses the horizontal axis of the graph at the point of maximum total product. This happens because adding a worker to a production line in a manner that slows up the line and actually decreases total output implies a negative marginal product for that worker.

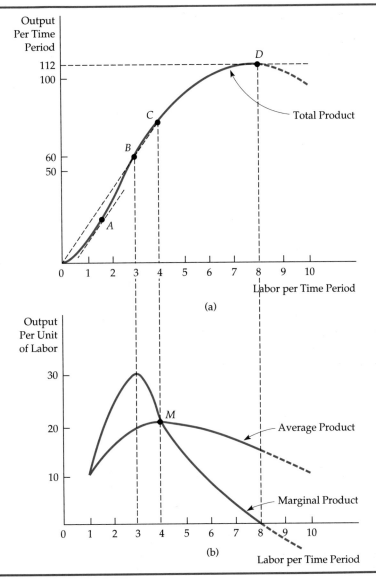

FIGURE 6.2 Production with One Variable Input.   When all inputs other than labor are fixed, the total product curve in part (a) shows the output produced for different amounts of labor input. The average and marginal products in part (b) are obtained directly from the total product curve. At point *B* in part (a) the average product of labor is given by the line from the origin to *B*.

The average product and marginal product curves are closely related, just as all average and marginal curves are. When the marginal product is greater than the average product, the average product is increasing, as shown between outputs 1 and 4 in Figure 6.2b. Suppose that the only employee of the firm can produce 10 units of product per day, so that initially 10 is the average product of labor. Then, a more productive employee is hired who can produce 20 units per day. The marginal product of labor, 20, is greater than the average, 10. And because both workers combine to produce 30 units in two days of labor, the new average product has increased to 15 units.

Similarly, when the marginal product is less than the average product, the average product must be decreasing, as shown between outputs 4 and 10 in Figure 6.2b. Finally, when the marginal product equals the average product, the average product curve reaches its maximum. This is shown at *M* in Figure 6.2b.[1]

To see the relationship between average and marginal product numerically, let's reexamine the data in Table 6.2. An increase in labor input *L* from 2 to 3 units yields a marginal product of 30. Because 30 is higher than the previously achieved average product of 15, the new average product increases, to 20. Similarly, when labor is increased from 3 to 4 units, the marginal product falls from 30 to 20. But this marginal product is equal to the previous average of 20, so the average does not change. This is the point at which the average product reaches its maximum. Finally, when labor is increased from 4 to 5 units, the marginal product falls from 20 to 15. Because this is less than the average of 20, the new average falls to 19.

There is an explicit geometric relationship between the total product and the average and marginal product curves, as Figure 6.2a shows. The average product of labor is the total product divided by the quantity of labor input. At *B* the average product is the output of 60 divided by the input of 3, or 20 units of output per unit of labor input. We can see that this average product is measured by the slope of the line running from the origin to *B* on the total product curve. In general, *the average product at a point on a total product curve is given by the slope of the line from the origin to that point.* A quick examination of the figure shows that the average product of labor reaches its maximum value at *B*, where the line from the origin has the greatest slope, and then decreases thereafter.

The marginal product of labor is the change in the total product in response to a small change in the input of labor. Geometrically, *the marginal product at a point on a total product curve is given by the slope of the total product curve at that point.* The slope of the total product curve, in turn, is given by the line drawn tangent to the curve. Thus, at *A*, the marginal product is 20, because the tangent to the total product curve has a slope of 20. By examining the slopes of the total product curve we can see that the marginal product of labor increases initially,

[1]This holds because the marginal product curve lies above the average product curve for all output levels less than this one and below the average product curve for all higher output levels.

reaches a peak at an output of 3, and then declines as we move up the total product curve to C and D. At D, when total output is maximized the slope of the tangent to the total product curve is 0, as is the marginal product. Beyond that point, the marginal product becomes negative.

The Law of Diminishing Returns

A diminishing marginal product of labor (and a diminishing marginal product of other inputs) is so prevalent that the phrase "the law of diminishing returns" is often used to describe it. The *law of diminishing returns* states that as the use of an input increases (with other inputs fixed), a point will eventually be reached at which the resulting additions to output decrease. When labor is used as an input to production (with capital fixed), small increments in labor input add substantially to output as workers are allowed to develop specialized tasks. Eventually, however, the law of diminishing returns applies. When there are too many workers, some jobs become superfluous, and the marginal product of labor falls.

The law of diminishing returns is relevant in the short run when at least one input is unchanged. The law describes a declining marginal product but not necessarily a negative one. Thus, in Figure 6.2 the law of diminishing returns applies to the production process for a level of employment of 3 or more, even though the marginal product of labor doesn't become negative until employment is greater than 8 units.

The law of diminishing returns applies to a given production technology. Over time, however, inventions and other improvements in technology may allow the entire output curve in Figure 6.2 to shift upward, so that more output can be achieved with the same inputs. Figure 6.3 illustrates this possibility. Initially the output curve is given by O_1, but an improvement in technology causes the curve to shift upward to the curve O_2, and further improvement allows the curve to become O_3.[2]

Suppose that over time as labor is increased in production, technological improvements are also being made. Then, output changes from A (with an input of 8 on curve O_1) to B (with an input of 9 on curve O_2) to C (with an input of 10 on O_3). The move from A to B to C relates an increase in labor input to an increase in output and makes it appear that there are not diminishing returns. But in fact, diminishing returns are present. For outputs greater than 8, each of the individual product curves exhibits diminishing returns to labor.

The shifting of the product curves hides the presence of diminishing returns and suggests that they need not have any negative long-run implications for economic growth. In fact, as we discuss in Example 6.1, confusion about the law of diminishing returns in the short run and improvements in technology

---

[2]Growth in capital can cause a similar shifting in total product curves.

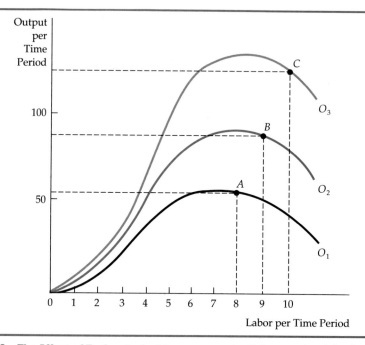

FIGURE 6.3 The Effect of Technological Improvement. Labor productivity (output per unit of labor) can increase if there are improvements in the technology, even though any given production process exhibits diminishing returns to labor. As we move from point A on curve O_1 to B on curve O_2 to C on curve O_3 over time, labor productivity increases.

in the long run led British economist Thomas Malthus to predict dire consequences from continued population growth.

EXAMPLE 6.1 MALTHUS AND THE FOOD CRISIS

The law of diminishing returns was central to the thinking of economist Thomas Malthus (1766–1834).[3] Malthus believed that the relatively fixed amount of land on our globe would not be able to supply enough food as population grew and as more laborers began to farm the land. Eventually as both the marginal and average productivity of labor fell and there would be more mouths to feed, mass hunger and starvation would result. Fortunately, Malthus was wrong (although he was right about the diminishing returns to labor).

Over the past century, technological improvements have altered the production of food in most countries (including developing countries such as India),

[3]Thomas Malthus, *Essay on the Principle of Population*, 1798.

TABLE 6.3 Index of World Food Consumption per Capita[4]	
Year	Index
1948–1952	100
1955	109
1960	115
1965	116
1970	123
1975	126
1978	128

so that the average product of labor has increased. As Table 6.3 shows, overall food production throughout the world has increased more or less steadily since the end of World War II.

Some of the increase in food production has been due to small increases in the amount of land devoted to farming. For example, from 1961 to 1975 the percentage of land devoted to agriculture increased from 32.9 percent to 33.3 percent in Africa, from 19.6 percent to 22.4 percent in Latin America, and from 21.9 percent to 22.6 percent in the Far East.[5] However, during the same period the percentage of land devoted to agriculture fell from 26.1 percent to 25.5 percent in North America, and from 46.3 percent to 43.7 percent in Western Europe. It seems clear that most of the improvement in food output is due to improved technology and not to increases in land used for agriculture.

Still, hunger remains a severe problem in some areas, such as Ethiopia and other African nations, in part because of the low productivity of labor there. Although other countries produce an agricultural surplus, mass hunger still occurs because of the difficulty of redistributing foods from more to less productive regions of the world, and because of the low incomes of those less productive regions.

Labor Productivity

We sometimes refer to the average product of labor as applied to an industry or to the economy as a whole as *labor productivity*. Because the average product measures output per unit of labor input, it is relatively easy to measure (because total labor input and total output are the only pieces of information you need)

[4]These data appear as Table 4–1 in Julian Simon, *The Ultimate Resource* (Princeton: Princeton University Press, 1981). The original source is the UN Food and Agriculture Organization, *Production Yearbook*, and *World Agricultural Situation*.

[5]See Julian Simon, *The Ultimate Resource*, p. 83.

TABLE 6.4 Labor Producitivity in Developed Countries[6]

	France	West Germany	Japan	Netherlands	United Kingdom	United States
	Output per Person (1984)					
	$12,643	$13,267	$12,235	$11,710	$11,068	$15,829
Years	Rate of Growth of Labor Productivity (%)					
1950–1973	4.65	4.88	7.67	3.62	2.54	2.12
1973–1984	2.16	2.29	2.94	0.96	1.43	0.55

and can provide useful comparisons across industries and for one industry over a long period. But productivity is especially important because it determines the real standard of living that a country can achieve for its citizens.

There is a simple link between productivity and the standard of living. In any particular year the aggregate value of goods and services produced by an economy is equal to the payments made to all factors of production, including wages, rental payments to capital, and profit to firms. But consumers ultimately receive these factor payments, whatever their form. As a result, consumers in the aggregate can increase their rate of consumption in the long run only by increasing the total amount they produce.

As Table 6.4 shows, the level of output per person in the United States is somewhat higher than in other leading developed nations. But two patterns over the post-World War II period have been disturbing. First, productivity growth in the United States has been less rapid than productivity growth in most other developed nations. Second, productivity growth in the past 15 to 20 years has been substantially lower in all developed countries than it has been in the past. Both these patterns can be seen clearly in the table.

Throughout the entire period 1950 to 1984, the rate of productivity growth in Japan has been the highest, followed by West Germany and France. United States productivity growth has been the lowest, even lower than that of the United Kingdom. How can this slowdown in growth be explained? And why has productivity growth in the United States been lower than in other developed countries? The most important source of growth in labor productivity is the growth in the stock of *capital*. An increase in capital means more and better machinery, so that each worker can produce more output for each hour of work on the job. Differences in the rate of growth of capital help to explain much of the data in Table 6.4. The greatest capital growth during the postwar period occurred in Japan and France, both of which were rebuilt substantially after World War II.

[6]For details, see Angus Maddison, "Growth and Slowdown in Advanced Capitalist Countries," *Journal of Economic Literature* 25 (1987): 649–698, Table A–4.

To some extent, therefore, the lower rate of growth of productivity in the United States as compared with Japan, France, and West Germany is the result of these countries need to catch up as a result of the war. Part of this catch-up process was inevitable—the United States had already shown an ability to utilize its natural resources effectively and a willingness to invest heavily in education and research and development. By following the lead of the highest productivity countries, other countries were able to improve their productivity growth substantially.

Productivity growth is also tied to the natural resource sector of the economy. As oil, natural gas, and other resource reserves began to be depleted, output per worker fell somewhat. Environmental regulations (e.g., the need to restore land to its original condition after strip mining for coal) magnified this effect as the public became more concerned with the importance of cleaner air and water.

These factors explain part, but not all, of productivity growth over time and across different countries. A full understanding of these differences remains an important research problem in economics.

EXAMPLE 6.2 THE STANDARD OF LIVING IN THE UNITED STATES: IS IT THREATENED?

Will the standard of living in the United States continue to improve, or will the economy barely keep future generations from being worse off than we are today? The answer depends on the labor productivity of U.S. workers, because the real incomes of U.S. consumers increase only as fast as productivity does.

From 1979 to 1985 productivity growth in the United States was 0.3 percent, the lowest of all major developed countries. What does this mean for the average U.S. worker? In a competitive international economy, this low growth will eventually lead to lower increases in workers' wages; otherwise, higher wages would have to be matched by higher prices. But these higher prices would not be competitive in today's world economy. The result is that workers will have to absorb most of the impact of low productivity growth.

We have seen how slow growth in capital investment leads to low productivity growth. But the decline in productivity growth in the United States has other causes particular to this country. This can best be understood if we look at three major production sectors of the economy.[7] First, during 1945–1965, many workers left farms and entered manufacturing. Agriculture has lower productivity than manufacturing, so the shift created productivity growth. (The ratio of agricultural to industrial productivity was about 0.40 in 1948, and has not changed much since.) By 1965 few people were left on the farms who could move to manufacturing, so this source of growth was exhausted.

---

[7]This discussion is based on Lester Thurow, "The Productivity Problem," *Technology Review* (1980): 40–51.

Second, the productivity of the U.S. construction sector has declined substantially. There is no consensus about the source of this decline—it may be due in part to problems with nuclear reactor construction, and in part to problems with the interstate highway system. Whatever the cause, construction productivity has fallen and does not seem likely to increase.[8]

Third, the movement of workers into the service sector of the economy has also dampened productivity growth in the United States, since productivity in the service sector is approximately 60 percent of the national average. By 1978, for example, about 35 percent of all hours of work were spent on service industry jobs, with a substantial portion of these hours devoted to nursing and health care and to lawyers and accountants.

Overall, this suggests that much of the slowdown in productivity growth was inevitable in the United States, and that not all of it was bad. Nursing care may be a low-productivity industry, but it is one that our society considers important. Other sources of low productivity growth include a relatively inexperienced labor force due to the postwar baby boom, and the inhibiting effects of certain government regulations involving health, safety, and the environment. Because the sources of low-productivity growth are varied and complex, the standard of living cannot be increased simply by reversing what has happened in the past. But the future need not be bleak. Capital can be increased by tax policies that stimulate investment. Greater and more creative efforts can be made to encourage productivity-enhancing research and development.

6.4 Production with Two Variable Inputs

Now that we have seen the relationship between production and productivity, let's reconsider the firm's production technology in the long-run setting, where two inputs (instead of one) are variable. We can examine the alternative ways of producing by looking at the shape of a series of isoquants.

The isoquants shown in Figure 6.4 are reproduced from Figure 6.1; they all slope downward because both labor and capital have positive marginal products. More of either input increases output; so if output is to be kept constant as more of one input is used, less of the other input must be used.

Diminishing Returns

There are diminishing returns to both labor and capital in this example as well. To see why there are diminishing returns to labor, for example, draw a horizontal line at a particular level of capital, say 3. Reading the levels of output

---

[8]An equally inauspicious story holds for the mining sector. Today, producers place particular emphasis on new wells, and it takes longer to obtain a barrel of oil from these wells. Coal mining has become more complex, especially in light of the importance of environmental and health concerns.

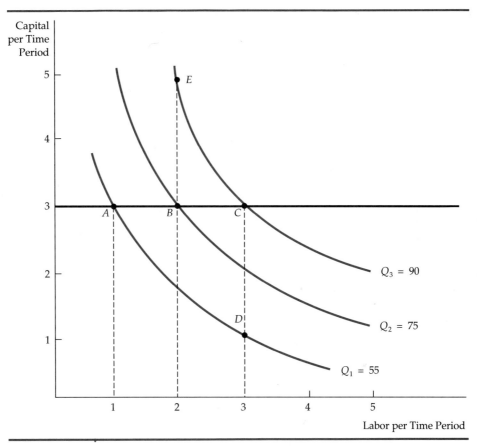

FIGURE 6.4   The Shape of Isoquants.   In the long run when both labor and capital are variable, both factors of production can exhibit diminishing returns. As we move from A to C, there are diminishing returns to labor, and as we move from D to C, there are diminishing returns to capital.

from each isoquant as labor is increased, we note that each additional unit of labor generates less and less additional output. For example, when labor is increased from 1 unit to 2 (from A to B), output increases by 20 (from 55 to 75). However, when labor is increased by an additional unit (from B to C), output increases by only 15 (from 75 to 90). Thus, there are diminishing returns to labor both in the long and the short run. Because adding one factor while holding the other factor constant eventually leads to lower and lower increments to output, the isoquant must become both steeper and steeper, as more capital is added in place of labor, and flatter and flatter when labor is added in place of capital.

There are also diminishing returns to capital. With labor fixed, the marginal product of capital decreases as capital is increased. For example, when capital is increased from 1 to 2 and labor is held constant at 3, the marginal product of capital is initially 20 $(75 - 55)$, but the marginal product falls to 15 $(90 - 75)$ when capital is increased from 2 to 3.

Substitution among Inputs

The slope of each isoquant indicates how the quantity of one input can be traded off against the quantity of the other, while keeping output constant. When the negative sign is removed, we call the slope the marginal rate of technical substitution (MRTS). The *marginal rate of technical substitution of labor for capital* is the amount by which the input of capital can be reduced when one extra unit of labor is used, so that output remains constant. This is analogous to the marginal rate of substitution (MRS) in consumer theory. Like the MRS, the MRTS is always measured as a positive quantity. In formal terms,

$$\text{MRTS} = -\text{Change in Capital Input/Change in Labor Input}$$

$$= -\Delta K / \Delta L$$

where ΔK and ΔL measure small changes in capital and labor along an isoquant (i.e., for Q constant).

Note that in Figure 6.5, the MRTS is equal to 2 when labor increases from 1 unit to 2, and output is fixed at 75. However, the MRTS falls to 1 when labor is increased from 2 units to 3, and then declines to $\frac{2}{3}$ and to $\frac{1}{3}$. Clearly, as more and more labor replaces capital, labor becomes less productive and capital becomes relatively more productive. So less capital needs to be given up to keep constant the output from production, and the isoquant becomes flatter.

Isoquants are convex—the MRTS diminishes as we move down along an isoquant. The diminishing MRTS tells us that the productivity that any one input can have is limited. As a lot of labor is added to the production process in place of capital, the productivity of labor falls. Similarly, when a lot of capital is added in place of labor, the productivity of capital falls. Production needs a balanced mix of both inputs.

As our discussion has just suggested, the MRTS is closely related to the marginal products of labor MP_L and capital MP_K. To see how, imagine adding some labor and reducing the amount of capital to keep output constant. The addition to output resulting from the increased labor input is equal to the additional output per unit of additional labor (the marginal product of labor) times the number of units of additional labor:

$$\text{Additional Output from Increased Use of Labor} = (MP_L)(\Delta L)$$

Similarly, the decrease in output resulting from the reduction in capital is the loss of output per unit reduction in capital (the marginal product of capital)

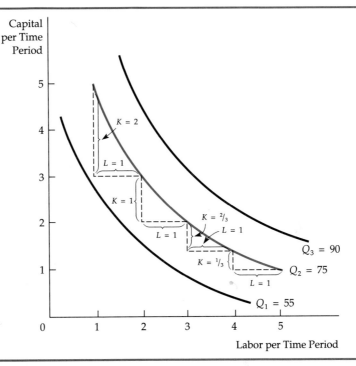

FIGURE 6.5 Marginal Rate of Technical Substitution. Isoquants are downward-sloping and convex like indifference curves. The slope of the isoquant at any point measures the marginal rate of technical substitution, the ability of the firm to replace capital with labor while maintaining the same level of output. On isoquant Q_2, the marginal rate of technical substitution falls from 2 to 1 to 2/3 to 1/3.

times the number of units of capital reduction:

Reduction in Output from Decreased Use of Capital $= (MP_K)(\Delta K)$

Because we are keeping output constant by moving along an isoquant, the total change in output must be zero. Thus,

$$(MP_L)(\Delta L) + (MP_K)(\Delta K) = 0$$

Now, by rearranging terms we see that

$$(MP_L)/(MP_K) = -(\Delta K/\Delta L) = MRTS \qquad (6.2)$$

Equation (6.2) tells us that as we move along an isoquant, continually replacing capital with labor in the production process, the marginal product of capital increases and the marginal product of labor decreases. The combined effect of both these changes is for the marginal rate of technical substitution to decrease and for the isoquant to become flatter.

Production Functions—Two Special Cases

Two extreme cases of production functions can be used to consider the possible range of input substitution in the production process. In the first case, shown in Figure 6.6, inputs to production are perfectly substitutable for one another. Here the MRTS is constant at all points on an isoquant. In this extreme case the same output can be produced with only labor, only capital, or a combination of both. For example, output Q_3 can be produced with capital (at A), labor (at C), or inputs of both (at B). This is usually not realistic, but in some cases provides a reasonable approximation of a firm's production process. For example, a toll booth on a road or bridge might be run automatically or manned by a toll collector. Another example is a musical instrument manufacturing process, which can rely almost entirely on machine tools for processing, or which can be accomplished with very few tools and highly skilled labor.

Figure 6.7 illustrates the opposite extreme, the *fixed-proportions production function*. In this case it is impossible to make any substitution among inputs. Each level of output requires a specific combination of labor and capital. Additional

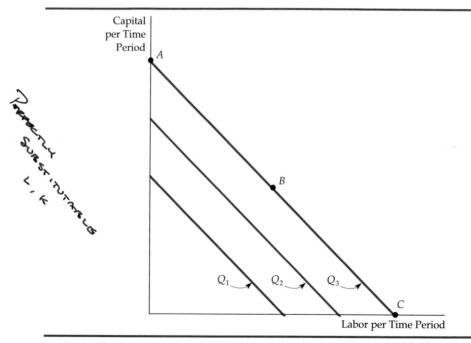

FIGURE 6.6 Production Function When Inputs Are Perfectly Substitutable. When the production isoquants are straight lines, the marginal rate of technical substitution is constant. This means that the rate at which capital and labor can be substituted for each other is the same whatever level of inputs is being used.

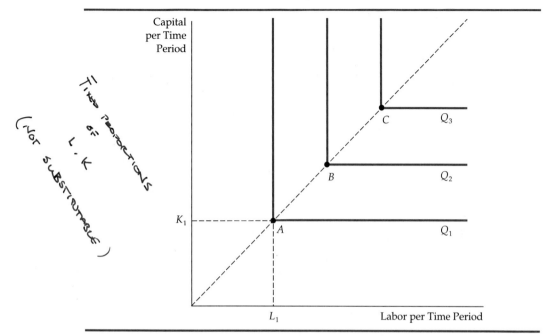

The handwritten margin notes read: "Fixed proportions of L, K (NOT SUBSTITUTABLE)"

FIGURE 6.7 **Fixed-Proportions Production Function.** When the production isoquants are L-shaped, only one combination of labor and capital can be used to produce a given output. At A, for example, labor L_1 and capital K_1 are the necessary inputs. The addition of more labor does not increase output, nor does the addition of more capital alone.

output cannot be obtained unless more capital and labor are added in specific proportions. As a result, the isoquants in Figure 6.7 are L-shaped. One example might be the reconstruction of concrete sidewalks using jackhammers. It takes one person to use a jackhammer—neither two people and one jackhammer nor one person and two jackhammers is likely to increase production. Another example might be taxicabs—under normal conditions, it takes one driver and one taxicab to provide the appropriate taxi service.

In Figure 6.7 points A, B, and C represent technically efficient combinations of inputs. For example, to produce output Q_1, a quantity of labor L_1 and capital K_1 can be used, as at A. If capital stays fixed at K_1, adding more labor does not change output. Nor does adding capital with labor fixed at L_2. Thus, on the vertical and the horizontal segments of the L-shaped isoquants, either the marginal product of capital or the marginal product of labor is zero. Higher output results only when both labor and capital are added, as in the move from input combination A to input combination B.

The fixed-proportions production function describes situations in which the methods of production available to firms are limited. For example, the production of a television show might involve a certain mix of capital (camera and sound equipment, etc.) and labor (producer, director, actors, etc.). To make more television shows, all inputs to production must be increased proportionally. In particular, it would be difficult to increase capital inputs at the expense of labor, since actors are necessary inputs to production (except perhaps for animated films). Likewise, it would be difficult to substitute labor for capital, since filmmaking today requires sophisticated film equipment.

EXAMPLE 6.3   A PRODUCTION FUNCTION FOR WHEAT

Crops can be produced using different methods. Food grown on large farms in the United States is usually produced with a *capital-intensive technology*, which involves substantial investments in capital, such as buildings and equipment, and relatively little input of labor. However, food can also be produced using very little capital (a hoe) and a lot of labor (several people with the patience and stamina to work the soil). One way to describe the agricultural production process is to show one isoquant (or more) that describes the combination of inputs that generate a given level of output (or several output levels). The description that follows comes from a production function for wheat that was estimated statistically.[9]

Figure 6.8 shows one isoquant associated with the production function, corresponding to an output of 1380 bushels of wheat per week. The manager of the farm can use this isoquant to decide whether it is profitable to hire more labor or use more machinery. Assume the farm is currently operating at A, with a labor input L of 50 hours and a capital input K of 10 machine-hours. The manager decides to experiment by using one fewer hour of machine time. To produce the same crop per week, he finds that he needs to replace this machine time by adding 26 hours of labor.

The results of this experiment tell the manager about the shape of the wheat production isoquant. When comparing points A (where $L = 50$ and $K = 10$) and B (where $L = 76$ and $K = 9$) in Figure 6.8, both of which are on the same isoquant, the manager finds that the marginal rate of technical substitution is equal to 0.04 ($-\Delta K/\Delta L = -(-1)/26 = .04$).

The MRTS tells the manager the nature of the trade-off between adding labor and reducing the use of farm machinery. Because the MRTS is substantially less than 1 in value, the manager knows that when the wage of a laborer is equal to the cost of running a machine, he ought to use more capital. (At his current

---

[9]The food production function on which this example is based is given by the equation $Q = 100(K^{.8}L^{.2})$, where Q is the rate of output in bushels of food per week, K is the quantity of machines in use per week, and L is the number of hours of labor per week. For a more detailed discussion of agricultural production functions, see E. O. Heady and J. L. Dillion, *Agricultural Production Functions* (Ames: Iowa State University Press, 1961).

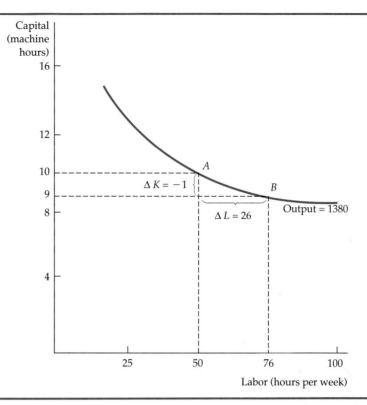

FIGURE 6.8   Isoquant Describing the Production of Wheat.   A wheat output of 1380 units can be produced with different combinations of labor and capital. The more capital-intensive production process is shown as point *A*, and the more labor-intensive process is given by *B*. The marginal rate of technical substitution between *A* and *B* is 1/26 = 0.04.

level of production, he needs 26 units of labor to substitute for 1 unit of capital.) In fact, he knows that unless labor is substantially less expensive than the use of a machine, his production process ought to become more capital-intensive.

The decision about how many laborers to hire and machines to use cannot be fully resolved until we discuss the costs of production in the next chapter. However, this example illustrates how knowledge about production isoquants and the marginal rate of technical substitution can help a manager. It also sug-gests why most farms in the United States and Canada, where labor is relatively expensive, operate in the range of production in which the MRTS is relatively low (with a high capital-to-labor ratio), while farms in developing countries in which labor is cheap operate with a higher MRTS (and a lower capital-to-labor ratio).[10] The exact labor/capital combination to use depends on the input prices, a subject we turn to in Chapter 7.

6.5 Returns to Scale

Understanding the nature of the firm's long-run operation is important in many settings, from managing private businesses to administering a public school, to regulating public and private utilities. For example, an analysis of the operation of high schools might lead one to conclude that the school program would be more effective (more courses, better administration and facilities) if the school system had one large high school with 3000 students rather than three small ones with 1000 students in each. A study of telephone companies might suggest that independent regional telephone companies could provide better local telephone service than a single national company.

The most useful place to begin a long-run analysis is with the scale of the firm's operation. The measure of increased output associated with increases in *all* inputs can tell us something about the long-run nature of the firm's production process. How does the output of the firm change as its inputs are proportionately increased? For example, if all inputs are doubled, does output double, or does it increase by more or by less? If output more than doubles (with doubled inputs), there are *increasing returns to scale*. This might arise because the larger scale of operation allows managers and workers to specialize in their tasks and makes use of more sophisticated, large-scale factories and equipment. The automobile assembly line is a famous example of increasing returns.

The presence of increasing returns to scale is an important issue from a public policy perspective. If there are increasing returns, then it is economically advantageous to have one large firm producing (at relatively low cost) than to have many small firms (at relatively high cost). Because this large firm can control the price that it sets, it may need to be regulated. For example, increasing returns in the provision of electricity is one reason why we have large, regulated power companies.

A second possibility with respect to the scale of production is that output may double when inputs are doubled. In this case, production is said to be subject to *constant returns to scale*. With constant returns to scale, the size of the firm's operation does not affect the productivity of its factors. The average and marginal productivity of the firm's inputs remains constant whether the plant

---

[10]With the production function given in footnote 9, it is not difficult (using the calculus) to show that the marginal rate of technical substitution is given by MRTS = $(MP_L/MP_K) = (1/4)(K/L)$. Thus, the MRTS decreases as the capital-to-labor ratio falls. For an interesting study of agricultural production in Israel, see Richard E. Just, David Zilberman, and Eithan Hochman, "Estimation of Multicrop Production Functions," *American Journal of Agricultural Economics* 65 (1983): 770–780.

is small or large. With constant returns to scale, one plant using a particular production process can easily be replicated, so that two plants produce twice as much output.

If there are no inputs that are unique and will not be available as the scale is increased, then constant returns to scale are guaranteed. For example, a large travel agency might have the same cost per client and use the same ratio of capital (office space) and labor (travel agents) as a small travel agency that services fewer clients.

Finally, output may less than double when all inputs double. This case of *decreasing returns to scale* is likely to apply to any firm with large-scale operations. Eventually, difficulties of management associated with the complexities of organizing and running a large-scale operation may lead to decreased productivity of both labor and capital. Communication between workers and managers can become difficult to monitor and the workplace more impersonal. Thus, decreasing returns are likely to be associated with the problems of coordinating tasks and maintaining a useful line of communication between management and workers. Or it may result because individuals cannot exhibit their entrepreneurial abilities in a large-scale operation.

The presence or absence of returns to scale is seen graphically in Figure 6.9. The production process is one in which labor and capital are used as inputs in the ratio of 5 hours of labor to 1 hour of machine time. The ray $0P$ from the origin describes the various combinations of labor and capital that can be used to produce output when the input proportions are kept constant.

At relatively low output levels, the firm's production function exhibits increasing returns to scale, as shown in the range $0A$ of the ray $0P$. When the input combination is 5 hours of labor and 1 hour of machine time, 10 units of output are produced (as shown in the lowest isoquant in the figure). When both inputs double, output triples from 10 to 30 units. Then when inputs increase by one-half again (from 10 to 15 hours of labor and 2 to 3 hours of machine time), output doubles from 30 to 60 units.

At relatively high output levels, the firm's production function exhibits decreasing returns to scale, as shown in the range AP of the ray $0P$. When the input combination increases by one-third, from 15 to 20 hours of labor and from 3 to 4 machine hours, output increases only by one-sixth, from 60 to 70 units. And when inputs increase by one-half, from 20 to 30 hours of labor and from 4 to 6 machine hours, output increases by only one-seventh, from 70 to 80 units.

Figure 6.9 shows that with increasing returns to scale, isoquants become closer and closer to one another as inputs increase proportionally. However, with decreasing returns to scale, isoquants become farther and farther from one another, because more and more inputs are needed. When there are constant returns to scale (not shown in Figure 6.9), isoquants are equally spaced.

Returns to scale vary substantially among firms in different industries in the United States and around the world. Other things being the same, the more substantial the returns to scale, the larger firms in an industry are likely to be.

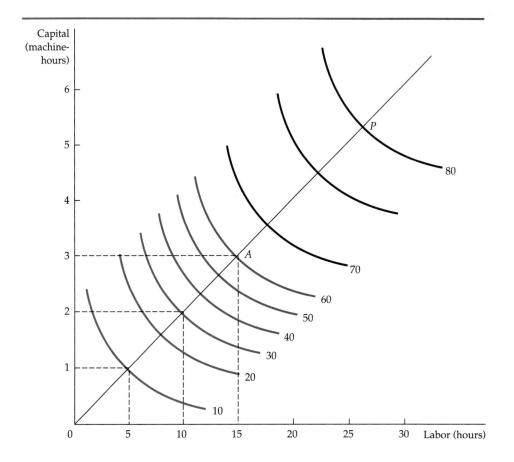

FIGURE 6.9 Returns to Scale. When a firm's production process exhibits increasing returns to scale as shown by a movement from 0 to *A* along ray 0*P*, the isoquants get closer and closer to one another. However, when there are decreasing returns to scale as shown by a move from *A* to *P*, the isoquants get farther and farther from one another.

Typically, manufacturing industries are more likely to have increasing returns to scale than service-oriented industries because manufacturing necessitates a substantial investment in capital equipment before firms can operate most efficiently. Services are quite labor-intensive and can usually be provided as efficiently in small quantities as they can on a large scale.

In many discussions of long-run production, the term *economies of scale* is used synonymously with the term *increasing returns to scale*. However, the appropriate use of the expression *economies of scale* applies when the scale of the operation increases but the firm is allowed sufficient time (say, one or two years) to produce most cheaply by substituting among inputs. Returns to sale refers to the expansion of a production when input proportions are held constant. Thus, a firm that can double its output using some multiple less than two of all its inputs enjoys increasing returns to scale. A firm that can double its output *at less than twice the cost* enjoys economies of scale. The term *economies of scale* thus includes increasing returns to scale as a special case, but it is more general because it allows for input combinations to be altered as the level of output changes.

EXAMPLE 6.4 RETURNS TO SCALE IN THE RAIL INDUSTRY

During most of this century, railroads have grown larger and larger, yet their financial problems have continued to mount.[11] Does this increase in size make good economic sense? If so, why do railroads continue to have difficulty competing with other forms of transportation? We can get some insight into these questions by looking at the economics of rail freight transportation.

To see whether there are economies of scale, we will measure input as *freight density*, the number of tons of railroad freight that are run per unit of time along a particular route. Output is given by the amount of a particular commodity shipped along this route within the specified time.[12] Then we can ask how the amount that can be shipped increases as we add to freight tonnage. We might expect increasing returns initially because as more freight is shipped, the railroad management can use its planning and organization to design the appropriate scheduling of the freight system efficiently. However, decreasing returns will arise at some point when there are so many freight shipments that scheduling gets difficult and rail speeds are reduced.

Most studies of the railroad industry indicate increasing returns to scale at low and moderate freight densities, but decreasing returns to scale begin to set in after a certain point (called the *efficient density*). Only when the density gets quite large is this phenomenon important, however. One study, for example,

---

[11]This example relies heavily on the analysis of railroad freight regulation by Theodore Keeler, *Railroads, Freight, and Public Policy* (Washington, D.C.: The Brookings Institution, 1983), chapter 3.

[12]Of course, a railroad is more complex than this, because it is likely to haul different products between different points and for differing durations. As a result, returns to scale can take different forms. For example, the firm can increase its scale by increasing the length of the freight haul. Or it can increase its scale by increasing the number of trips per year between two destinations, keeping the length of haul constant. The firm can also increase the quantity carried on each trip. Finally, the firm can increase the size of its entire operation. In Chapter 7 we will analyze the rail firm as a multiproduct firm in which the length of haul is variable.

TABLE 6.5 Freight Densities of Major Railroads (1980) (million tons per route-mile)	
Railroad	Density
Atchison, Topeka & Santa Fe	6.03
Baltimore & Ohio	4.46
Burlington Northern	6.11
Chicago and Northwestern	3.10
Colorado & Southern	10.66
Fort Worth & Denver	6.55
Kansas City Southern	5.96
Missouri Pacific	5.01
Southern Pacific	5.35
Union Pacific	7.87
Western Pacific	3.20

indicated increasing returns to scale up to the range of 8 to 10 million tons (per year) per route-mile, a very large freight density.[13]

To see the practical importance of these numbers, we have tabulated the freight densities of major U.S. railroads in Table 6.5. The table suggests that some railroads such as Colorado & Southern and Union Pacific have reached or surpassed the point of minimum efficient size (the point at which increasing returns to scale disappear). But many railroads in the United States operate at freight densities substantially below this.[14]

Since most rail companies have not surpassed their optimum size, it appears that the growth in the size of most rail firms has been economically advantageous. The financial problems of the railroad industry relate more to competition from other forms of transportation (especially in light of the regulation of alternatives such as trucking) than to the nature of the production process itself.

6.6 The Equal Marginal Rule: Using Inputs to Produce Several Products

Up to now we have assumed that the firm produced only one product. Most firms, however, produce several products, often through separate divisions.

[13]The study is by Ann F. Friedlaender and Richard H. Spady, *Freight Transport Regulation: Equity, Efficiency, and Competition in the Rail and Trucking Industries* (Cambridge: MIT Press, 1981). Another study concluded that the economies of scale could persist for up to 15 million ton-miles. See Theodore Keeler, "Railroad Costs, Returns to Scale, and Excess Capacity," *Review of Economics and Statistics* 56 (May 1974).

[14]Keeler (footnote 11) estimates, for example, that 75 percent of the nation's rail network was operating below 8 million ton-miles (per route-mile) in 1975.

For example, General Motors produces Chevrolets, Buicks, and Cadillacs, all in separate automotive divisions. Similarly, college athletic departments allocate their scarce resources among basketball, football, baseball, and other teams. We now extend our analysis of production to a firm that produces two products. For purposes of exposition we assume that the production is done in two separate divisions. The only link between the two divisions is that a single input is used in both. (In Chapter 7, we will treat the more general case in which there are economic advantages to joint production.)

Consider a toy-producing firm with two products—Division 1 produces a child's game (at output level Q_G), and Division 2 produces stuffed animals (at output level Q_A). To focus on production and not on sales, we presume that the firm can profitably sell all the games and stuffed animals that it produces at the same fixed price. However, in the short run the firm is limited by the available skilled labor that it can employ—only 40 full-time workers. How should this labor be allocated between the two divisions?

The simple answer to this question is that the 40 workers should be allocated to maximize the total output from the two divisions. (If the prices of the toys differed, we would be concerned about the value of the output.) To achieve this goal, the manager must use some inputs in both production processes, because there are diminishing returns to labor in the production of both outputs. Figure 6.10 illustrates the general rule for solving this allocation problem.

The figure shows the marginal product of labor in the production of games (MP_G), $\Delta Q_G/\Delta L$, and of stuffed animals (MP_A), $\Delta Q_A/\Delta L$. The horizontal axis shows the input of labor in full-time workers per week, and the vertical axis shows the marginal product of that labor input. In this example, although the marginal product for the games division is greater than the marginal product for the animals division for every amount of labor input, the firm still should not allocate all labor to producing games. This can be seen easily in the figure when we note that if all labor is allocated to the production of games, the marginal product of labor is -10. At the same time, the marginal product of labor in the production of animals is 24. Because the last input of labor in the production of games actually lowers output, some labor should be taken from the games division and allocated to the animals division. The net increase in output would be 34 (24 more animals and 10 more games).

But what allocation of labor maximizes output? Figure 6.10 shows the answer. When the labor input in the animal division is $L_A = 15$ and the labor input in the games division is $L_G = 25$, the entire labor input is utilized, *and* the marginal products of labor in the production of both games and animals are equalized (at 20). Formally,

$$MP_G = MP_A \tag{6.3}$$

We will see later how we arrived at this answer, but first let us see why the equalization of marginal products maximizes output. Consider what happens if the manager of the firm alters the labor inputs (from this point of equal

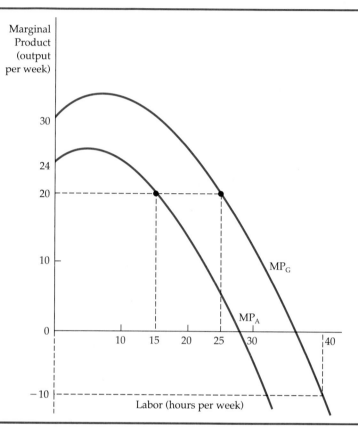

FIGURE 6.10 Allocation of Labor in a Two-Division Firm. When a firm allocates a single variable input, labor, toward the production of two products, the total output of the firm is maximized when the marginal product of labor is equal in each of the two divisions. In the figure, the total output of toys is maximized when the marginal product of labor in the production of games (MP_G) (20 units per week) is equal to the marginal product of labor in the production of animals (MP_A).

marginal products) by switching a unit of labor from the animals division to the games division. Since the marginal product of labor is falling, the additional output from the games division will be less than 20, and the output lost from the animals division will be greater than 20. On balance the firm will lose more from output than it will gain from such a move. More generally, as long as the marginal product of labor in one division of the firm is greater than the marginal product in another division, reallocating labor to the high marginal product division will increase output. The firm can maximize its output only when the marginal products of labor are equal in all divisions. This is another example of the *equal marginal rule* that we saw in our study of consumer theory. We will carry it forward to our analysis of the management and behavior of firms in forthcoming chapters.

EXAMPLE 6.5 **OPERATING AN OIL REFINERY**

In an oil refinery, crude oil is processed to produce refined oil products, such as gasoline, home heating oil, and kerosene. Because of the magnitude of the investment in plant and equipment and the high cost of stopping and starting the refining process, most refineries process the maximum possible amount of crude oil each day. The most important short-run production decision for an oil refinery is therefore to decide how much crude oil to allocate to produce each of the refinery's products, ranging from gasoline to jet and tanker fuel, kerosene, and asphalt. The production decision depends on the profit each of the oil products can generate in the firm. Profits, in turn, depend on the productivity of the oil refinery—its ability to obtain each oil product as effectively as possible from a barrel of crude oil.

Gasoline frequently generates a high profit for the firm in part because it is easy to refine initially. But as the portion of each barrel of crude oil allocated to gasoline production increases, the marginal product of crude oil in gasoline production (and the resulting profit) falls rapidly. As a result, rarely if ever will the refinery produce only gasoline with its crude oil input. Products such as kerosene have lower marginal products initially, but the rate of decline of their marginal product is lower than that of gasoline. Finally, crude oil used to produce tanker fuel has an even lower initial marginal product, which remains nearly constant irrespective of the percentage of a barrel of crude oil used.

The profit that crude oil can generate varies almost daily as market conditions and the prices of gasoline, heating oil, and other refined products change. (For example, heating oil prices tend to be higher in winter than in summer, while the opposite is true for gasoline.) As a result, a refinery manager regularly updates the appropriate mix of products for the refinery. But suppose the prices and the profits for the refined products are approximately equal, so that the manager is concerned with maximizing the amount of oil product that can be produced from the crude oil that flows through the refinery.

The following illustration suggests how the manager can make the *product-maximizing* decision. Suppose the marginal products of gasoline MP_g, kerosene MP_k, and tanker fuel MP_f are given by the following equations, which reflect diminishing marginal products of crude oil for each product:

$$MP_g = 1.0 - 1.0g$$

$$MP_k = 0.7 - 0.8k$$

$$MP_f = 0.6 - 0.4f$$

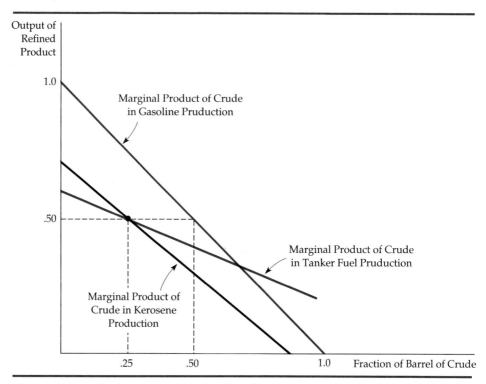

FIGURE 6.11 **Marginal Product of Crude Oil in a Refinery.** To maximize the total output of gasoline, kerosene, and tanker fuel in an oil refinery, the manager must allocate crude oil so as to equate the marginal product of crude oil in all three uses. Here, the maximum output is achieved when the marginal products are equal to 0.50.

where g, k, and f are the fractions of each barrel of crude oil to be allocated to produce gasoline, kerosene, and tanker fuel, respectively. The marginal products are measured in barrels of oil products, and are graphed in Figure 6.11. Because the refinery only processes three products, $g + k + f = 1$, and the managers must choose the fractions, g, k, and f that maximize total product. If we use the equal marginal rule, we must find values that equate the marginal product of crude oil in its three uses.

The optimal choice is to set $g = \frac{1}{2}$, $k = \frac{1}{4}$, and $f = \frac{1}{4}$, so that half the crude oil is allocated to gasoline and the other half is allocated equally to kerosene and tanker fuel. (The total outputs of refined products are gasoline = 0.375, kerosene = 0.150, and tanker fuel = 0.137.[15]) With this choice of inputs, we can check to see that the marginal product of crude oil is equal to 0.5 in all its

[15]The total outputs are calculated as the area under the marginal product curve between a crude oil input of 0 and the actual fraction utilized.

uses.[16] Any other allocation of a barrel of crude oil will result in a lower output for the firm. When all crude is allocated to gasoline, for example, its marginal product is zero, and the marginal products of kerosene and tanker fuel are 0.7 and 0.6, respectively. (Gasoline output is 0.5, but all other outputs are zero.) Clearly a reallocation of crude from gasoline to either kerosene or tanker fuel will increase total output (from 0.5 to 0.662). Similarly, when all crude is allocated to kerosene, the marginal product is −0.1, while the marginal product of gasoline is 1.0 and that of tanker fuel 0.6. A reallocation from kerosene to either gasoline or tanker fuel will increase total output (from 0.3 to 0.662).

One of the keys to the successful management of an oil refinery is a knowledge of the production technology, and in particular of the marginal product of crude oil in the production of various refinery products. With this understanding, and up-to-date information about the prices of oil products, oil refinery management can be very profitable.

*6.7. Measuring Production Functions

Information about the nature of firms' production functions can be obtained either from engineers who are expert in describing a particular firm's production capabilities or by statistical analyses of the production processes of a number of different firms (or one firm over time).

The engineering approach is most useful when a firm wishes to study its own production relationship. The data in such an approach are well understood because they apply to the particular firm. But the engineering approach often has limited applicability to other firms. Even within one firm, the data often describe only one technical aspect of the production process. As a result the technique may tell the firm little if anything about the presence of diseconomies of scale in the management of the entire production process.

The statistical approach is valuable if a manager or a policymaker wishes to examine production relationships that go beyond a particular plant or operation within a firm. There are two general methods for studying production relationships statistically. The first method uses *cross-section* data that describe the production of different firms in an industry at one point in time. The second approach uses *time-series* data that describe the production of one firm or an entire industry over time. Each approach has its own advantages and disadvantages, depending on the availability of data and the nature of the production process.

To see how the statistical approach might work with cross-section data, suppose we wish to characterize production in the automobile industry to see

---

[16]This solution can be obtained by trial and error or by setting the three marginal product equations equal to each other, and using the fact that f + g + k = 1. This yields three equations in three unknowns, so a solution is not difficult to find.

whether increasing returns to scale give larger companies a competitive advantage over smaller ones. We might obtain data for a particular year that record the aggregate amount of labor, the aggregate amount of capital, and the aggregate amount of materials that automobile companies such as GM, Ford, Chrysler, Toyota, Nissan, and Honda allocated toward production. These data could then be compared with the output of each firm in terms of number of finished cars per year to determine in summary fashion the nature of the production process. The particular technique used, *regression analysis*, is described in the Appendix to this book.

This statistical approach is complex, because firms' production techniques involve many types of labor, machines, and materials. There are also often varying degrees of subcontracting of tasks at different firms and alternative options to put on the cars before sale. Finally, production can involve waste and mismanagement, both of which must be considered in the statistical analysis. With proper care, useful information about production can be obtained if, for example, we aggregate labor into number of hours of a typical assembly-line job, and we measure capital by calculating an index that accounts for the fact that each firm will have different machines, different aged buildings, and so on. Materials inputs can also be aggregated, even though materials also vary from firm to firm.[17]

Suppose these empirical difficulties have been resolved satisfactorily, and we wish to measure the production function for automobiles. This production function will relate output Q to capital K and labor L. We begin by specifying the algebraic form of the production function. One widely used approach employs the *Cobb-Douglas production function*, which has the form

$$Q = AK^\alpha L^\beta \tag{6.4}$$

Here A is a constant that depends on the units in which inputs and output are measured, and α and β are constants that tell us about the relative importance of labor and capital in the production process. Ordinarily α and β are less than one, a result consistent with the fact that the marginal product of each input diminishes as that factor increases.[18]

The sum of the constants α and β has a special economic importance. If $\alpha + \beta = 1$, then the production function exhibits constant returns to scale; if $\alpha + \beta > 1$, then there are increasing returns to scale; and if $\alpha + \beta < 1$, there are decreasing returns to scale. To see this result, consider the experiment of dou-

---

[17]If a direct index of these inputs cannot be obtained, an indirect approach can be useful. One can obtain data on the total expenditure on an input such as labor, and then divide that total expenditure by an estimate of the average wage of labor in the automobile industry in the region in which the firm's plants are located. The result is an estimate of the total labor input of the firm.

[18]The Cobb-Douglas production function is sometimes written in its logarithmic form (by taking the logarithms of both sides of the equation for the production function): log (Q) = log (A) + α log (K) + β log (L). This form is more useful when a regression analysis is to be performed.

bling all inputs, so that K becomes $2K$, and L becomes $2L$. Then the new level of output Q' is given by

$$Q' = A(2K)^{\alpha}(2L)^{\beta} = A(2)^{\alpha}(K)^{\alpha}(2)^{\beta}(L)^{\beta}$$
$$= (2^{\alpha + \beta})AK^{\alpha}L^{\beta} = (2^{\alpha + \beta})Q \quad \text{(substituting the old value of } Q\text{)}$$

When $\alpha + \beta = 1$, $Q' = 2Q$, so output is doubled, and we have constant returns to scale. When $\alpha + \beta > 1$, output is more than doubled, there are increasing returns to scale, and so on.

As an example, consider the production function for railroads in the United States. This involves a more aggregated version of Example 6.5, because our concern lies with returns to scale in the industry rather than returns to scale in freight transportation. One estimate of the Cobb-Douglas production function for rail production that includes materials M as a third input yields the following form:[19]

$$Q = AK^{.12}L^{.89}M^{.28}$$

This production function exhibits increasing returns to scale, because the sum of the three relevant constants of the production function is greater than 1. (Recall that we also found increasing returns to scale in the previous example.) The rather high coefficient on the labor input tells us that if labor is increased by 1 percent in the production process, with capital and materials held constant, that output will increase by 0.89 percent.[20] On the other hand, a 1 percent increase in capital increases output by only 0.12 percent.

The Cobb-Douglas production function is valuable because it illustrates the way in which production functions can be measured. However, for two reasons, other more complex production functions are often used in place of the Cobb-Douglas function in industry studies. First, the Cobb-Douglas function does not allow for the realistic possibility that the firm's production process will exhibit increasing returns at low output level, constant returns at intermediate output levels, and decreasing returns at high output levels. Second, because a Cobb-Douglas production function implies that the MRTS varies as you move along each isoquant, it does not adequately describe production processes in which inputs are either extremely substitutable (straight-line isoquants) or barely substitutable at all (L-shaped isoquants).

Summary

1. A *production function* describes the maximum output a firm can produce for each specified combination of inputs.

[19]The source is A. A. Walters, "Production and Cost Functions," *Econometrica* (Jan. 1963).

[20]This percentage calculation is measured by the elasticity of output with respect to one input, say, labor. In general the elasticity is given by $(\Delta Q/\Delta L)(L/Q) = \alpha(Q/L)(L/Q) = \alpha$.

2. An *isoquant* is a curve that shows all combinations of inputs that yield a given level of output. Isoquants emphasize the flexibility that firms have in the production process. A firm's production function can be represented by a series of isoquants associated with different levels of output.

3. In the short run, one or more inputs to the production process are fixed, whereas in the long run all inputs are variable.

4. Production with a variable input, labor, can be usefully described in terms of the *average product of labor* (which measures the productivity of the average worker), and the *marginal product of labor* (which measures the productivity of the last worker added to the production process).

5. When one or more inputs are fixed, a variable input (usually labor) is likely to have a marginal product that diminishes as the level of input increases. The phrase "law of diminishing returns" emphasizes how common a diminishing marginal product is in production.

6. Isoquants always slope downward, because the marginal product of all inputs is positive. The shape of each isoquant can be described by the marginal rate of technical substitution at each point on the isoquant. The *marginal rate of technical substitution of labor for capital (MRTS)* is the amount by which the input of capital can be reduced when one extra unit of labor is used, so that output remains constant. The MRTS tells us about the firm's ability to substitute among inputs in the production process.

7. The standard of living that a country can attain for its citizens is closely related to its level of labor productivity. Recent decreases in the rate of productivity growth in developed countries are due in part to the lack of growth of capital investment.

8. The possibilities for substitution among inputs in the production process range from a production function in which inputs are perfectly substitutable to one in which the proportions of inputs to be used are fixed (a fixed-proportions production function).

9. In the long-run analysis, we tend to focus on the firm's choice of its scale or size of operation. Constant returns to scale mean that doubling all inputs leads to doubling output. Increasing returns to scale occur when output more than doubles when inputs are doubled, whereas decreasing returns to scale apply when output less than doubles.

10. The analysis of marginal products can also be applied to firms that produce two or more different products. The *equal marginal rule* tells us that the firm can maximize its output by allocating its variable input to equalize the marginal product of that input in all divisions of the firm.

11. Production functions can be measured from engineering studies, by using cross-section data for individual firms in an industry at one point in time, or by using time-series data for the entire industry over time. One useful production function is the Cobb-Douglas function, from which one can easily obtain direct measures of the presence or absence of returns to scale.

Questions for Review

1. What is a production function? How does a long-run production function differ from a short-run production function?

2. Why is the marginal product of labor likely to increase and then decline in the short run?

3. Diminishing returns to a single factor of production and constant returns to scale are not inconsistent. Discuss.

4. How does the curvature of an isoquant relate to the marginal rate of technical substitution along an isoquant?

5. If a firm has several divisions, what condition should the firm satisfy when allocating a fixed input toward the production of each of the divisions' products?

6. Can a firm have a production function that exhibits increasing returns to scale, constant returns to scale, and decreasing returns to scale as output increases? Discuss.

7. Give an example of a production process in which the short run involves a day or a week, and the long run any period longer than a week.

Exercises

1. Suppose a chair manufacturer is producing in the short run when equipment is fixed. The manufacturer knows that as the number of laborers used in the production process increases from 1 to 7, the number of chairs produced changes as follows: 10, 17, 22, 25, 26, 25, 23.
   a. Calculate the marginal and average product of labor for this production function.
   b. Does this production function exhibit diminishing returns to labor? Explain.
   c. Explain intuitively what might cause the marginal product of labor to become negative.

2. Suppose a political campaign manager has to decide whether to emphasize television advertisements or letters to potential voters in a reelection campaign. Describe the production function for campaign votes. How might information about this function (such as the shape of the isoquants) help the campaign manager to plan strategy?

3. Suppose you are a student with a fixed amount of time to prepare for two exams. Imagine that your function is to produce grades, and you are managing two divisions, one for each course in which you have an exam. How might information about the marginal product of labor in the preparation of each exam help you to allocate your study time?

4. Consider a firm that has a production process in which the inputs to production are perfectly substitutable in the long run. Can you tell whether the marginal rate of technical substitution is high or low, or is further information necessary? Discuss.

5. The marginal product of labor is known to be greater than the average product of labor at a given level of employment. Is the average product increasing or decreasing? Explain.

6. In Example 6.3 wheat is produced according to the production function $Q = 100(K^{.8}L^{.2})$.

   a. Beginnning with a capital input of 4 and a labor input of 49, show that the marginal product of labor and the marginal product of capital are both decreasing.

   b. Does this production function exhibit increasing, decreasing, or constant returns to scale?

7. The production function for the personal computers of DISK, Inc., is given by $Q = 10K^{.5}L^{.5}$, where Q is the number of computers produced per day, K is hours of machine time, and L is hours of labor input. DISK's competitor, FLOPPY, Inc., is using the production function $Q = 10K^{.6}L^{.4}$.

   a. If both companies use the same equal amounts of capital and labor, which will generate more output?

   b. Assume that capital is limited to 9 machine hours, but labor is unlimited in supply. In which company is the marginal product of labor the greater? Explain.

[Handwritten annotations in margins:]

4, 49
{ 660.2

{ 5, 50 / 1
{ 500

{ 1

(3, 48)

(522)

IN PROVING MP_L + MP_K -> START WITH

VALUES AT OPTIMAL, PRIOR, AND LATTER

(HERE, $K = 4$ $L = 48 = Q_0$
             -> 49 Q_1
               50   Q_2

DETERMINE DIFFERENCE BETWEEN

VALUES OF Q AT L = EACH VALUE -> DETERMINE

IF IT IS DECREASING.

CHAPTER 7

The Cost of Production

In the last chapter we examined the firm's production technology—the relationship that shows how factor inputs can be transformed into outputs. Now we will see how the production technology, together with the prices of factor inputs, determine the firm's costs of production.

Given their firm's production technology, managers must decide *how* to produce. As we saw, inputs can be combined in different ways to yield the same amount of output. For example, one can produce a certain quantity of output with a lot of labor and very little capital, with very little labor and a lot of capital, or with some other combination of the two. In this chapter we see how the optimal combination of factor inputs is chosen. We will also see how a firm's costs depend on its rate of output, and how they are likely to change over time.

We begin by explaining how cost is defined and measured, distinguishing between the concept of cost used by economists, who are concerned about the firm's performance, and by accountants, who may be more concerned with the firm's financial statements. We then examine how the characteristics of the firm's production technology affect costs, both in the short run when the firm can do little to change its capital stock, and in the long run when the firm can change all its factor inputs.

In Chapter 6 we showed how a firm can allocate its scarce resources between two divisions to maximize total output. In this chapter we examine the production of two outputs in greater detail and show how the concept of returns to scale applies more generally to the process of producing not just two but many different outputs. We also show how costs sometimes fall over time as managers and workers learn from experience, so that the production process becomes more efficient and less costly. Finally, we describe how to estimate cost functions and show how firms can use empirical information about costs.

7.1 Measuring Costs: Which Costs Matter?

Before we can analyze how costs are determined and why they change, we need to be clear about what we mean by costs and how we measure them. What items should be included as part of a firm's costs? Costs obviously include the wages a firm pays its workers and the rent it pays for office space. But what if the firm already owns an office building and doesn't have to pay rent? And how should we treat money that the firm spent two or three years ago (and can't recover) for equipment or for research and development? We'll answer these questions in the context of the economic decisions that managers make.

Economic Cost versus Accounting Cost

An economist thinks of cost differently from an accountant, who is concerned with the firm's financial statements. Accountants tend to take a retrospective look at a firm's finances, because they have to keep track of assets and liabilities and evaluate past performance. Accounting costs include actual expenses and depreciation expenses for capital equipment, which are determined on the basis of the allowable tax treatment by the Internal Revenue Service.

Economists—and we hope managers—on the other hand, take a forward-looking view of the firm. They are concerned with what costs are expected to be in the future, and with how the firm might be able to lower its costs and improve its profitability. They must therefore be concerned with *opportunity costs*, the costs associated with opportunities that are forgone by not putting the firm's resources to their highest valued use. Opportunity costs include the explicit outlays that a firm makes, but they include much more, as we will see.

Accountants and economists both include actual outlays, called *explicit costs*, in their calculations. Explicit costs include wages, salaries, and the costs of materials and property rentals. For accountants, explicit costs are important because they involve direct payments by a company to other firms and individuals that it does business with. These costs are relevant for the economist because the costs of wages and materials represent money that could have usefully been spent elsewhere. Explicit costs involve opportunity costs as well; for example, wages are the opportunity costs for labor inputs purchased in a competitive market.

Let's take a look at how economic costs can differ from accounting costs in their treatment of wages and economic depreciation. For example, consider an owner who manages her own retail store but chooses not to pay herself a salary. Although no monetary transaction has occurred (and thus would not appear as an accounting cost), the business nonetheless incurs an opportunity cost because the owner could have earned a competitive salary by working elsewhere.

Accountants and economists also treat depreciation differently. When estimating the future profitability of a business, an economist or manager is concerned with the capital cost of plant and machinery. This involves not only the explicit cost of buying and then running the machinery, but also the cost associated with wear and tear. When calculating past performance, accountants use tax rules to determine allowable depreciation in their cost and profit calculations. But these depreciation allowances need not reflect the actual wear and tear on the equipment. In fact, the rules for depreciation were changed substantially in the Tax Reform Act of 1986, while the actual rate of deterioration of physical plant and equipment remained unchanged.

Sunk Costs

Although opportunity costs are often hidden, they should always be taken into account when making economic decisions. Just the opposite is true of sunk costs—they are usually visible, but they should always be ignored when making economic decisions.

A *sunk cost* is an expenditure that has already been made and cannot be recovered.[1] Because it cannot be recovered, it should have no influence whatsoever on the firm's decisions. For example, consider the purchase of specialized equipment designed to order for a plant. We assume the equipment can be used to do only what it was originally designed for and can't be converted for alternative use or sold to another firm. The expenditure on this equipment is a sunk cost. Because it has no alternative use, its opportunity cost is zero. Thus it shouldn't be included as part of the firm's current or future costs.[2] Looking back, we see that the decision to buy this equipment may have been good or bad. It doesn't matter. It's water under the bridge, and shouldn't affect the firm's current decisions.

As another example, suppose a firm is considering moving its headquarters to a new city. Last year it paid $500,000 for an option to buy a building in the city; the option gives it the right to buy the building at a cost of $5,000,000, so that its total expenditure will be $5,500,000 if it indeed buys the building. Now it finds that a comparable building has become available in the same city at a price of $5,250,000. Which building should it buy? The answer is the original building. The $500,000 option is a sunk cost that should not affect the firm's current decision. The economic cost of the original property is $5,000,000 to the firm (because the sunk cost is not part of its economic cost), while the newer property has an economic cost of $5,250,000. Of course, if the new building cost $4,750,000, the firm should buy it, and forgo its option.

---

[1] It can also include an expenditure that must be made in the future because of a binding contractual agreement. Of course, if a firm goes bankrupt and no longer honors the agreement, the cost is no longer sunk.

[2] If, on the other hand, the equipment could be put to other use, or sold or rented to another firm, its current economic cost would be measured by the value from its next most profitable use.

EXAMPLE 7.1   CHOOSING THE LOCATION FOR A NEW LAW SCHOOL BUILDING

The Northwestern University Law School has long been located in Chicago, along the shores of Lake Michigan. However, the main campus of the university is located in the suburb of Evanston. In the mid-1970s the law school began planning the construction of a new building and needed to decide on an appropriate location. Should it be built on the current site in the city, where it would remain near the downtown law firms? Or should it be moved to Evanston, where it would become physically integrated with the rest of the university?

The downtown location had many prominent supporters. They argued in part that it was cost-effective to locate the new building in the city because the university already owned the land, whereas a large parcel of land would have to be purchased in Evanston if the building were to be built there. Does this argument make economic sense?

No. It makes the common mistake of failing to distinguish accounting costs from economic costs. From an economic point of view, it is very expensive to locate downtown because the opportunity cost of the valuable lakeshore location is high—that property could have been sold for enough money to buy the Evanston land with substantial funds left over.

In the end, Northwestern decided to keep the law school in Chicago. This was a costly decision. It may have been appropriate if the Chicago location was particularly valuable to the law school, but the decision was inappropriate if it was made on the presumption that the downtown land was without cost.

EXAMPLE 7.2   THE OPPORTUNITY COST OF WAITING IN A GASOLINE LINE

As a result of gasoline price controls in the spring of 1980, Chevron gasoline stations in California were required to lower their prices substantially below those of other major gasoline companies.[3] This allowed an experiment to be conducted in which consumers revealed information about the opportunity cost of their time.

In this experiment, 109 customers at one Chevron station and 61 customers at two competing stations nearby were surveyed.[4] The consumers could either

---

[3]This special treatment for Chevron stations occurred because these stations were owned and operated by Standard Oil of California. Stations owned by integrated oil companies such as SoCal were affected by the ceiling, but those operated by franchised dealers were not.

[4]The survey was by Robert T. Deacon and John Sonstelie, "Rationing by Waiting and the Value of Time: Results from a Natural Experiment," *Journal of Political Economy* 93 (1985): 627–647.

TABLE 7.1

Category	Opportunity Costs	
	Lower Bound	Upper Bound
Students	$ 7.15	$10.96
Part-time workers	3.52	5.39
Income $20,000–$30,000	6.51	9.44
Income $30,000–$40,000	8.93	13.70
Income over $40,000	11.26	17.26

buy high-priced gasoline with little or no wait, or wait almost 15 minutes longer to buy lower-priced Chevron gasoline.

Many respondents chose to wait in line for the lower-priced Chevron gasoline, presumably because they valued their time less than the savings they could obtain when they bought the lower-priced gasoline. Suppose, for example, that a motorist could save $0.25 per gallon by waiting for 20 minutes at the Chevron station, and that there would be no wait at the other stations. If she bought ten gallons of gasoline, the total savings would be $2.50. Because she chose to wait in line, the opportunity cost of her time must be less than $2.50 per 20 minutes, or $7.50 per hour. Suppose another person chose to buy gasoline at one of the stations where there was no waiting. Then the opportunity cost of his time must be at least $7.50 per hour. By using this general approach, and by noting that Chevron patrons bought 53 percent more gasoline than the patrons of the other two stations, we can estimate the opportunity cost of waiting time.

Table 7.1 provides some lower- and upper-bound estimates of the opportunity cost of time, in dollars per hour, obtained from the study. Part-time workers displayed the lowest value of time. They could earn additional money working, but that did not conflict with waiting in gas lines because their schedules were flexible. Students' opportunity costs are relatively high because class work is time consuming and because those students who work part time have relatively inflexible schedules and could be working more rather than waiting in gas lines. For all groups, the opportunity cost of time was found to increase with income. This is not surprising; we would expect that the higher the wage one can earn, the greater the opportunity cost of waiting in line to buy lower-priced gas.

This example shows that consumers' as well as firms' decisions are typically based on economic or opportunity cost and not on accounting cost. Everyone would have saved money at the Chevron gas station, and thus made an accounting profit, but many people chose not to because the opportunity cost was too high.

7.2 Costs in the Short Run

In the short run, some of the firm's inputs to production are fixed, yet others can be varied to change the rate of output. The *total cost* TC of producing a good then has two components: the *fixed cost* FC, which is borne by the firm whatever level of output it produces, and the *variable cost* VC, which varies with the level of output. Depending on circumstances, fixed costs may include expenditures for plant maintenance, insurance, and perhaps a minimal number of employees—these costs remain the same no matter how much the firm produces. Variable costs include expenditures for wages, salaries, and raw materials—these costs increase as output increases.

Fixed costs can be controlled in the long run but do not vary with the level of output in the short run. (They must be paid even if there is no output.) We will see in the next chapter that in the long run a firm may decide to go out of business and thereby forgo its outlays on fixed costs. Fixed costs are therefore an integral part of the decision-making process of the manager of a firm.

To decide how much to produce, managers of firms need to know how variable costs increase with the level of output. To address this issue, we need to develop some additional cost measures. We will use a specific example that typifies the cost situation of many firms. After we explain each of the cost concepts, we will describe how they relate to our analysis of the firm's production process in Chapter 6.

The data in Table 7.2 describe a firm with a fixed cost of $50. Variable cost increases with output, as does total cost. The total cost is the sum of the fixed cost in column (1) and the variable cost in column (2). From the cost figures given in columns (1) and (2), a number of additional cost variables can be defined.

Marginal Cost (MC) *Marginal cost—sometimes called incremental cost—is the increase in cost that results from producing one extra unit of output.* Because fixed cost does not change as the firm's level of output changes, marginal cost is just the increase in variable cost that results from an extra unit of output. We can therefore write marginal cost as

$$MC = \Delta VC/\Delta Q$$

Marginal cost tells us how much it will cost to expand the firm's output by one unit. In Table 7.2, marginal cost is calculated from either the variable cost column (2) or the total cost column (3). For example, the marginal cost of increasing output from 2 to 3 units is $20, because the variable cost of the firm increases from $78 to $98. (Total cost of production also increases by $20, from $128 to $148. Total cost differs from variable cost only by the fixed cost, which by definition does not change as output changes.)

Average Cost (AC) *Average cost is the cost per unit of output.* There are three types of average cost: average fixed cost, average variable cost, and average total cost. *Average fixed cost* AFC is the fixed cost (Column 1) divided by the level of output, FC/Q. For example, the average fixed cost of producing four units of output is $12.5 ($50/4). Because fixed cost is constant, average fixed cost declines as the rate of output increases.

Average variable cost (AVC) is variable cost divided by the level of output VC/Q. The average variable cost of producing five units of output is $26, $130 divided by 5. Finally, *average total cost* ATC is the total cost divided by the level of output TC/Q. Thus, the average total cost of producing at a rate of five units is $36, $180/5. Basically, average total cost tells us the per unit cost of production. By comparing the average total cost to the price of the product, we can determine whether production is profitable.

The Determinants of Short-Run Costs

Table 7.2 shows that variable and total costs increase with output. The rate at which these costs increase depends on the nature of the production process, and in particular on the extent to which production involves diminishing returns to variable factors. Recall from Chapter 6 that diminishing returns to labor occur when the marginal product of labor is decreasing. If labor is the only variable factor, what happens as we increase the firm's rate of output? To produce more output, the firm has to hire more labor. Then, if the marginal product of labor

TABLE 7.2 A Firm's Short-Run Costs

Rate of Output	Fixed Cost	Variable Cost	Total Cost	Marginal Cost (MC)	Average Fixed Cost (AFC)	Average Variable Cost (AVC)	Average Total Cost (ATC)
	(1)	(2)	(3)	(4)	(5)	(6)	(7)
0	50	0	50	—	—	—	—
1	50	50	100	50	50	50	100
2	50	78	128	28	25	39	64
3	50	98	148	20	16.7	32.7	49.3
4	50	112	162	14	12.5	28	40.5
5	50	130	180	18	10	26	36
6	50	150	200	20	8.3	25	33.3
7	50	175	225	25	7.1	25	32.1
8	50	204	254	29	6.3	25.5	31.8
9	50	242	292	38	5.6	26.9	32.4
10	50	300	350	58	5	30	35
11	50	385	435	85	4.5	35	39.5

decreases rapidly as the amount of labor hired is increased (owing to diminishing returns), greater and greater expenditures must be made to produce output at the faster rate. As a result, variable and total costs increase rapidly as the rate of output is increased. On the other hand, if the marginal product of labor decreases only slightly as the amount of labor is increased, costs will not rise so fast when the rate of output is increased.[5]

Let's look at this in more detail by concentrating on the costs of a firm that can hire as much labor as it wishes at a fixed wage w. Recall that marginal cost MC is the change in variable (or total) cost for a one-unit change in output (i.e., $\Delta VC/\Delta Q$). But the variable cost is the per-unit cost of the extra labor w times the amount of extra labor ΔL. It follows, then, that

$$MC = \Delta VC/\Delta Q = w\Delta L/\Delta Q$$

The marginal product of labor MP_L is the change in output resulting from a one-unit change in labor input, or $\Delta Q/\Delta L$. Therefore, the extra labor needed to obtain an extra unit of output is $\Delta L/\Delta Q = 1/MP_L$. As a result,

$$MC = w/MP_L \qquad (7.1)$$

Equation (7.1) states that in the short run, marginal cost is equal to the price of the input that is being varied divided by its marginal product. Suppose, for example, that the marginal product of labor is 3 and the wage rate is $30 per hour. Then, one hour of labor will increase output by 3 units, so that 1 unit of output will require ⅓ hour of labor, and will cost $10. The marginal cost of producing that unit of output is $10, which is equal to the wage, $30, divided by the marginal product of labor, 3. A low marginal product of labor means that a large amount of additional labor is needed to produce more output, which leads to a high marginal cost. A high marginal product means that the labor requirement is low, as is the marginal cost. More generally, whenever the marginal product of labor decreases, the marginal cost of production increases, and vice versa.[6]

The effect of the presence of diminishing returns in the production process can also be seen by looking at the data on marginal costs in Table 7.2. The marginal cost of additional output is high at first because the first few inputs to production are not likely to raise output much in a large plant with a lot of equipment. However, as the inputs become more productive, the marginal cost decreases substantially. Finally, marginal cost increases again for relatively high levels of output, owing to the effect of diminishing returns.

The law of diminishing returns also creates a direct link between the average

---

[5]We are implicitly assuming that labor (and other inputs) are hired in competitive markets, so that the payment per unit of factor used is the same no matter what the firm's output. Our analysis would be a bit more complicated if this were not the case.

[6]With two or more variable inputs, the relationship is more complex, but still the greater the productivity of factors, the less the variable costs that the firm must incur to produce its output.

variable cost of production and the average productivity of labor. Average variable cost AVC is equal to the variable cost per unit of output, or VC/Q. When L units of labor are used in the production process, the variable cost is wL. Thus,

$$AVC = wL/Q$$

Recall from Chapter 6 that the average product of labor AP_L is given by the output per unit of input Q/L. As a result, it follows that

$$AVC = w/AP_L \qquad (7.2)$$

Since the wage rate is fixed in our analysis, there is an inverse relationship between average variable cost and the average product of labor. Whenever the average product of labor is low, substantial inputs are needed to produce a given output, and the average variable cost of production is high. However, when the average product is high, the input requirements are low, as is the average variable cost of production.

With both marginal cost and average variable cost, there is a direct link between the productivity of factors of production and the costs of production. Marginal and average product tell us about the physical link between inputs and outputs. The comparable cost variables tell us about the budgetary implications of that production information.

The Shapes of the Cost Curves

Figure 7.1 shows a set of continuous curves that approximate the marginal and average cost data in Table 7.2.[7] Total fixed cost is $50; as a result the average fixed cost curve AFC falls continuously from $50 toward zero. The shape of the remaining short-run cost curves is determined by the relationship between the marginal and average cost curves. Whenever marginal cost lies below average cost, the average cost curve declines. Whenever marginal cost lies above average cost, the average cost curve increases. And when average cost is at a minimum, marginal cost equals average cost. Thus, marginal and average costs are another example of the average-marginal relationship described in Chapter 6 (with respect to marginal and average product). For example, at $20, marginal cost is below the average variable cost of $25, and the average is lowered. But when marginal cost is $30, which is greater than average cost ($25), the average increases. Finally, when marginal cost ($25) and average cost ($25) are the same, the average cost remains unchanged (at $25).

Marginal and average cost are important concepts. As we will see in the next chapter, they enter critically into the firm's choice of output level. Knowledge of short-run costs is particularly important for firms that operate in an environ-

---

[7]Because the marginal cost represents the change in cost associated with a change in output, we have plotted the marginal cost curve associated with the first unit of output by setting output equal to ½, for the second unit by setting output equal to 1½, and so on.

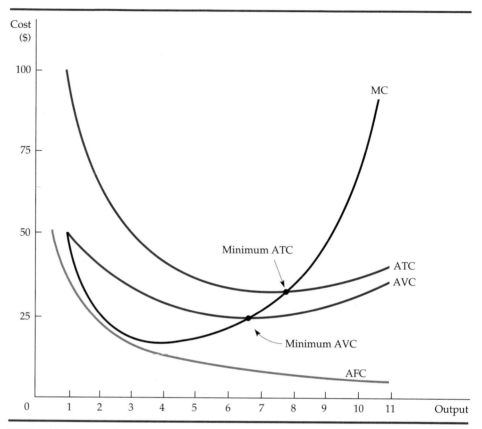

FIGURE 7.1   Short-Run Marginal and Average Costs.   Average variable cost AVC is the total variable cost divided by the number of units of output produced. Average total cost ATC is equal to average variable cost plus average fixed cost AFC. Marginal cost MC, the additional cost for every unit of output, crosses the average variable cost and average total cost curves at their minimum points.

ment in which demand conditions fluctuate considerably. If the firm is currently producing at a level of output at which marginal costs are sharply increasing, uncertainty about whether demand will increase in the future may lead the firm to alter its production process and perhaps incur additional costs now to avoid higher costs in the future.

7.3   Costs in the Long Run

In the long run the firm can change all its inputs. In this section we show how a manager chooses the combination of inputs that minimizes the cost of producing a given output. We will also seek to obtain information about the relationship between long-run cost and the level of output.

The Cost-Minimizing Input Choice

Let's begin by considering a fundamental problem that all firms face: *how to select inputs to produce a given output at minimum cost*. For simplicity, we will work with two variable inputs: labor (measured in hours of work) and capital (measured in hours of use of machinery). We assume that both labor and capital can be hired (or rented) in competitive markets. The price of labor is the wage rate w, and the price of capital is the rental rate for machinery r. We assume that capital is rented rather than purchased, so that we can put all business decisions on a comparable basis. For example, labor services might be hired at a wage of $12,000 per year, or capital might be "rented" for $75,000 per machine per year.

Because capital and labor inputs are competitively hired, we can take the price of inputs as fixed. We can then focus on the firm's optimal combination of factors, without worrying about whether large purchases will cause the price of an input to increase.[8]

The Isocost Line

We begin by looking at the costs of production, which can be represented by a firm's isocost lines. An *isocost line* includes all possible combinations of labor and capital that can be purchased for a given total cost. To see what an isocost line looks like, recall that the total cost TC of producing any particular output is given by the sum of the firm's labor cost wL and its capital cost rK:

$$TC = wL + rK \qquad (7.3)$$

For each different level of total cost, equation (7.3) describes a different isocost line. For example, in Figure 7.2, the isocost line C_0 describes all possible combinations of inputs that cost C_0 to purchase.

If we rewrite the total cost equation (7.3) as an equation for a straight line, we get

$$K = TC/r - (w/r)L$$

It follows that the isocost line has a slope of $\Delta K/\Delta L = -(w/r)$, which is the ratio of the wage rate to the rental cost of capital. This slope is similar to the slope of the budget line that the consumer faces (because it is determined solely by the prices of the goods in question, whether inputs or outputs). It tells us

---

[8]This might happen because of overtime or a relative shortage of capital equipment. We discuss the possibility of a relationship between the prices of factor inputs and the quantities demanded by a firm in Chapter 14.

that if the firm gave up a unit of labor (and recovered w dollars in cost) to buy w/r units of capital at a cost of r dollars per unit, its total cost of production would remain the same. For example, if the wage rate were $10 and the rental cost of capital $5, the firm could replace one unit of labor with two units of capital, with no change in total cost.

Choosing Inputs

Suppose we wish to produce output level Q_1. How can we do this at minimum cost? Look at the firm's production isoquant, labeled Q_1, in Figure 7.2. The problem is to choose the point on this isoquant that minimizes total costs.

Figure 7.2 illustrates the solution to this problem. Suppose the firm were to spend C_0 on inputs. Unfortunately, no combination of inputs can be purchased for expenditure C_0 that will allow the firm to achieve output Q_1. Output Q_1 can be achieved with the expenditure of C_2, however, either by using K_2 units of

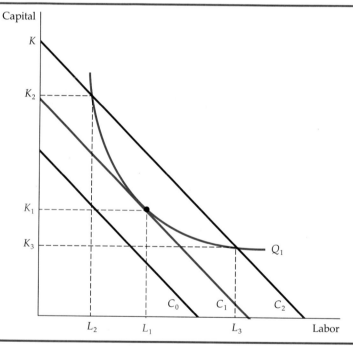

FIGURE 7.2   Producing a Given Output at Minimum Cost.   Isocost curves describe the combination of inputs to production that cost the same amount to the firm. Isocost curve C_1 is tangent to isoquant Q_1 and shows the firm that output Q_1 can be produced at minimum cost with labor input K_1 and capital input L_1. Other input combinations—L_2, K_2 and L_3, K_3—achieve the same output at higher cost.

capital and L_2 units of labor, or by using K_3 units of capital and L_3 units of labor. But C_2 is not the minimum cost. The same output Q_1 can be produced more cheaply than this, at a cost of C_1, by using K_1 units of capital and L_1 units of labor. In fact, isocost line C_1 is the lowest isocost line that allows output Q_1 to be produced. The point of tangency of the isoquant Q_1 and the isocost line C_1 tells us the cost-minimizing choice of inputs, L_1 and K_1, which can be read directly from the diagram. At this point, the slopes of the isoquant and the isocost line are just equal.

When the expenditure on all inputs increases, the slope of the isocost line does not change (because the prices of the inputs have not changed), but the intercept increases. Suppose, however, that the price of one of the inputs, such as labor, were to increase. Then, the slope of the isocost line $-(w/r)$ would increase in magnitude, and the isocost line would become steeper. Figure 7.3 shows this. Initially, the isocost line is C_1, and the firm minimizes its costs of producing output Q_1 at A by using L_1 units of labor and K_1 units of capital.

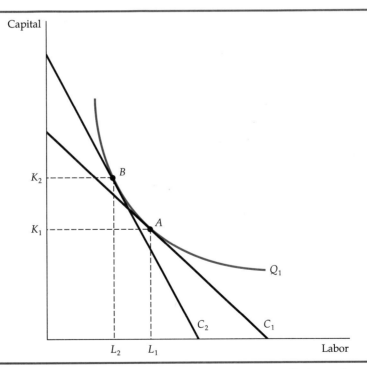

FIGURE 7.3 Input Substitution When an Input Price Changes. Facing an isocost curve C_1, the firm produces output Q_1 using L_1 units of labor and K_1 units of capital. When the price of labor increases, the isocost curves become steeper. Output Q_1 is now produced at B on isocost curve C_2, by using L_2 units of labor and K_2 units of capital.

When the price of labor increases, the isocost line becomes steeper. The isocost line C_2 reflects the higher price of labor. Facing this higher price of labor, the firm minimizes its cost of producing output Q_1 by producing at B, using L_2 units of labor and K_2 units of capital. The firm has responded to the higher price of labor by substituting capital for labor in the production process.

In our analysis of production technology, we showed that the marginal rate of technical substitution MRTS of labor for capital is the negative of the slope of the isoquant, and is equal to the ratio of the marginal products of labor and capital.

$$\text{MRTS} = -\Delta K / \Delta L = \text{MP}_L / \text{MP}_K \tag{7.4}$$

Above, we noted that the isocost line has a slope of $\Delta K / \Delta L = -w/r$. It follows that when a firm minimizes the cost of producing an output, the following condition holds:

$$\text{MP}_L / \text{MP}_K = w/r$$

Rewriting this condition slightly,

$$\text{MP}_L / w = \text{MP}_K / r \tag{7.5}$$

Equation (7.5) tells us that when costs are minimized, each dollar of input added to the production process will add an equivalent amount to output. Assume, for example, that the wage rate is $10 and the rental rate on capital is $2. If the firm chooses inputs so that the marginal product of labor and the marginal product of capital are equal to ten, it will want to hire less labor and rent more capital because capital is five times more expensive than labor. The firm can minimize its costs only when the production of an additional unit of output costs the same regardless of which additional input is used.

EXAMPLE 7.3 THE EFFECT OF EFFLUENT FEES ON FIRMS' INPUT CHOICES

Steel plants are often built on or near a river.[9] A river offers readily available, inexpensive transportation for both the iron ore that goes into the production process and the finished steel itself. A river also provides a cheap method of disposing of by-products of the production process (effluent). For example, a steel plant processes its iron ore for use in blast furnaces by grinding taconite deposits into a fine consistency. During this process, the ore is extracted by a magnetic field as a flow of water and fine ore pass through the plant. One by-product of this process—fine taconite particles—can be dumped in the river at relatively little cost to the firm, whereas alternative removal methods or private treatment plants are relatively expensive.

[9]This example was stimulated by a more general simulation analysis of water pollution. See Frank P. Stafford and Michael Aho, "River: Microeconomic Simulation of Pollution Control," Institute of Public Policy Studies Discussion Paper No. 132, University of Michigan, Dec. 1978.

Because the taconite particles are a nondegradable waste that can harm veg-
etation and fish, the Environmental Protection Agency (EPA) has considered
imposing an effluent fee—a per unit fee that the steel firm must pay for the
effluent that goes into the river. How should the manager of the firm respond
to the imposition of this effluent fee to minimize the costs of production?

Suppose that without regulation the steel firm is producing 2000 tons of steel
per day, while using 2000 machine-hours of capital and 10,000 gallons of water

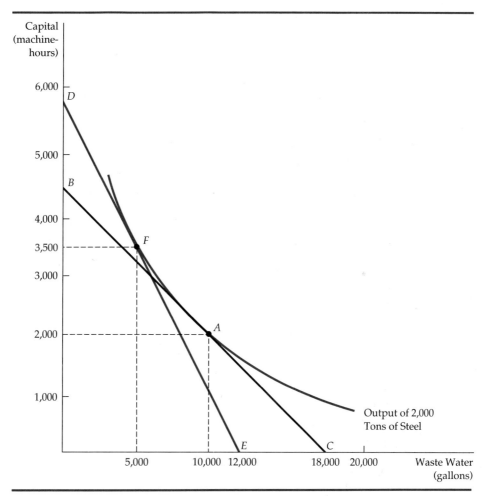

FIGURE 7.4   The Cost-Minimizing Response to an Effluent Fee.   When the firm is not
charged for dumping its waste water in a river, it chooses to produce a given output
using 10,000 gallons of waste water and 2,000 machine-hours of capital at *A*. However,
an effluent fee raises the cost of waste water, shifts the isocost curve from *BC* to *DE*,
and causes the firm to produce at *F*, with much less effluent.

(which contain taconite particles when returned to the river). The manager of the firm estimates that a machine-hour costs $40, and dumping each gallon of waste water in the river costs the firm $10. (The total cost of production is therefore $180,000—$80,000 for capital and $100,000 for waste water.) How should the manager respond to an EPA-imposed effluent fee of $10 per gallon of waste water dumped?

Figure 7.4 shows the cost-minimizing response. The vertical axis measures the firm's input of capital in machine-hours, and the horizontal axis measures the quantity of waste water in gallons. First, consider how the firm produces when there is no effluent fee. Point A represents the input of capital and the level of waste water that allows the firm to produce its quota of steel at minimum cost. Because the firm is minimizing cost, A lies on the isocost line BC, which is tangent to the isoquant. The slope of the isocost line is equal to $-\$10/\$40 = -0.25$ because a unit of capital costs four times more than a unit of waste water.

When the effluent fee is imposed, the cost of waste water increases from $10 per gallon to $20, because for every gallon of waste water (which costs $10), the firm has to pay the government an additional $10. The effluent fee increases the cost of waste water relative to capital. To produce the same output at the lowest possible cost, the manager must choose the isocost line with a slope of $-\$20/\$40 = -0.5$, which is tangent to the isoquant. In Figure 7.4, DE is the appropriate isocost line, and F gives the appropriate choice of capital and waste water. The move from A to F shows that with an effluent fee the use of an alternative production technology, which emphasizes the use of capital (3500 machine-hours) and uses less waste water (5000 gallons), is cheaper than the original process, which did not emphasize recycling. (The total cost of production has increased to $240,000—$140,000 for capital, $50,000 for waste water, and $50,000 for the effluent fee.)

We can learn two lessons from this decision. First, the more easily factors can be substituted in the production process, that is, the more easily the firm can deal with its taconite particles without using the river for waste treatment, the more effective the fee will be in reducing effluent. Second, the greater the degree of substitution, the more easily the firm can avoid the effluent fee. In our example, the fee would have been $100,000 had the firm not changed its inputs. However, the steel company pays only a $50,000 effluent fee by moving production from A to F.

Cost Minimization with Varying Output Levels

In the previous section we saw how a cost-minimizing firm selects a combination of inputs to produce a given level of output. Now we extend this analysis to see how the firm's costs depend on its output level. To do this we determine, for each output level, the firm's cost-minimizing input quantities and then calculate the resulting cost.

The cost-minimization exercise can be performed for every output that the firm is considering. Figure 7.5 shows a typical result of this analysis. Each of the points *A, B, C, D,* and *E* represents a tangency between an isocost curve and an isoquant for the firm. The curve, which moves upward and to the right from the origin, tracing out the points of tangency, is the firm's *expansion path*. The expansion path describes the combinations of labor and capital that the firm will choose to minimize costs for every output level. So long as the use of both inputs increases as output increases, the curve will look approximately as shown in Figure 7.5. The firm's expansion path gives information about the total costs of all variable inputs as the output of the firm changes. It tells us the lowest long-run total cost of producing each level of output.

7.4 Long-Run Versus Short-Run Cost Curves

We saw earlier (see Figure 7.1) that short-run average cost curves are U-shaped. We will see that long-run average cost curves are also U-shaped. But different economic factors explain the shapes of these curves. In this section, we discuss long-run average and marginal cost curves and highlight the differences between these curves and their short-run counterparts.

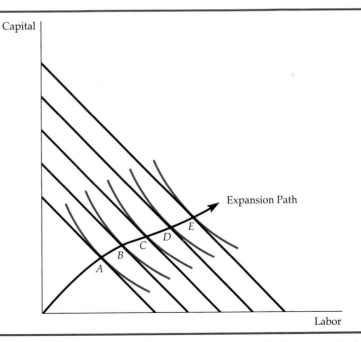

FIGURE 7.5   A Firm's Expansion Path.   The expansion path illustrates the least-cost combinations of labor and capital that can be used to produce each level of output in the long run when both inputs to production can be varied.

The Inflexibility of Short-Run Production

Recall that in the long run all inputs to the firm are variable, because its planning horizon is long enough to allow for a change in plant size. This added flexibility usually allows the firm to produce at a lower average cost than in the short run. To see why, we might compare the situation in which capital and labor are both flexible to the case in which capital is fixed in the short run.

Figure 7.6 shows the firm's production isoquants. Suppose capital is fixed at a level K_1 in the short run. To produce output Q_1, the firm would minimize costs by choosing labor equal to L_1, corresponding to the point of tangency with the isocost line AB. The inflexibility appears when the firm decides to increase

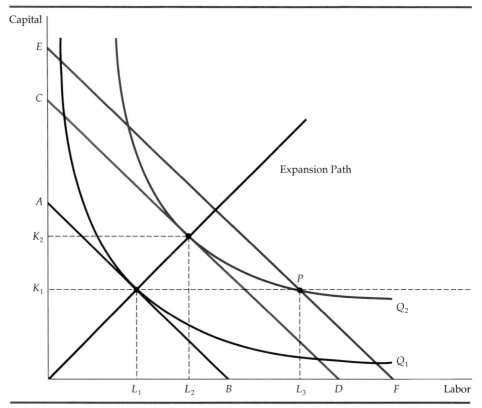

FIGURE 7.6 The Inflexibility of Short-Run Production. When a firm operates in the short run, its cost of production may not be minimized because of inflexibility in the use of capital inputs. Output is initially at level Q_1. In the short run output Q_2 can be produced only by increasing labor from L_1 to L_3, because capital is fixed at K_1. In the long run, the same output can be produced more cheaply by increasing labor from L_1 to L_2 and capital from K_1 to K_2.

its output to Q_2. If capital were not fixed, it would produce this output with capital K_2 and labor L_2. Its cost of production would be reflected by isocost line CD. However, the fixed capital forces the firm to increase its output by using capital K_1 and labor L_3 at P. Point P lies on the isocost line EF, which represents a higher cost than isocost line CD. The cost of production is higher when capital is fixed because the firm is unable to substitute relatively inexpensive capital for more costly labor when it expands its production.

This discussion shows why average costs of production are likely to be higher in the short run than in the long run. It also suggests why the factors that determine the shape of the long-run cost curves are different from the factors that shape the short-run curves.

The Shapes of Long-Run Cost Curves

In the long run, the ability to change the amount of capital allows the firm to reduce cost. To see how costs vary as the firm moves along its expansion path in the long run, we can look at the long-run average and marginal cost curves.[10] The most important determinant of the shape of the long-run average and marginal cost curves is whether there are increasing, constant, or decreasing returns to scale. Suppose, for example, that the firm's production process exhibits constant returns to scale at all levels of output. Then a doubling of inputs leads to a doubling of output. Because input prices remain unchanged as output increases, the average cost of production must be the same for all levels of output.

Suppose instead that the firm's production process is subject to increasing returns to scale. A doubling of inputs leads to more than a doubling of output. Then, the average cost of production falls with output, because a doubling of costs is associated with a more than twofold increase in output. By the same logic, when there are decreasing returns to scale, the average cost of production must be increasing with output.[11]

In the last chapter we saw that in the long run most firms' production technologies first exhibit increasing returns to scale, then constant returns to scale, and eventually decreasing returns to scale. Figure 7.7 shows a typical long-run average cost curve LAC consistent with this description of the production process. The long-run average cost curve is U-shaped, just like the short-run average cost curve, but the source of the U-shape is increasing and decreasing returns to scale, rather than diminishing returns to a production factor.

The long-run marginal cost curve LMC is determined from the long-run aver-

---

[10]We saw that in the short run, the shape of the average and marginal cost curves was determined primarily by diminishing returns. As we showed in Chapter 6, diminishing returns to each factor are consistent with constant (or even increasing) returns to scale.

[11]The relationship between returns to scale and long-run costs is somewhat more complicated, because firms have the option of changing input combinations as they expand their production.

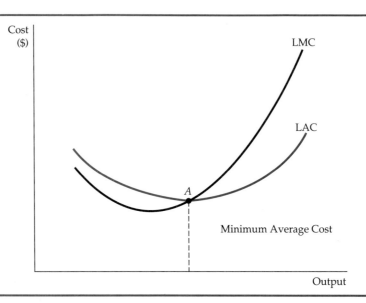

FIGURE 7.7   Long-Run Average and Marginal Cost.   When a firm is producing at an output at which the long-run average cost LAC is falling, the long-run marginal cost LMC is less than long-run average cost. When long-run average cost is increasing, long-run marginal cost is greater than long-run average cost.

age cost curve. It lies below the long-run average cost curve when LAC is falling, and above the long-run average cost curve when LAC is rising. The two curves intersect at A, where the long-run average cost curve achieves its minimum.

The Relationship Between Short-Run and Long-Run Costs

Figures 7.8 and 7.9 show the relationship between short-run and long-run cost. Assume a firm is uncertain about the future demand for its product and is considering three alternative plant sizes. The short-run average cost curves for the three plants are given by SAC_1, SAC_2, and SAC_3 in Figure 7.8. The decision is important because, once built, the size of a particular plant may not be able to be changed for some time.

Figure 7.8 shows the case in which there are constant returns to scale in the long run. If the firm were expecting to produce Q_1 units of output, then it should build the smallest plant. Its average cost of production would be $10; this is the minimum cost, because the short-run marginal cost SMC crosses short-run average cost SAC when both equal $10. If the firm is to produce Q_2 units of output, the middle-sized plant is best, and its average cost of production is again $10. If it is to produce Q_3, it moves to the third plant. With only these plant sizes,

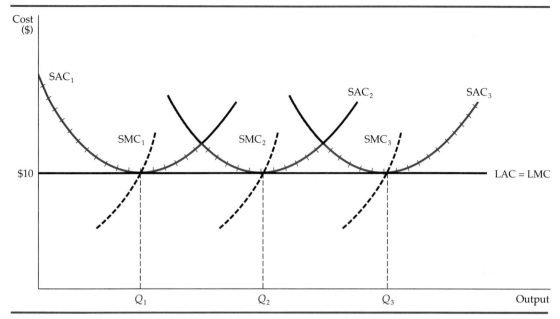

FIGURE 7.8 Long-Run Costs with Constant Returns to Scale. The long-run average cost curve LAC, which is identical to the long-run marginal cost curve LMC, is the envelope of the short-run average cost curves (SAC_1, SAC_2, and SAC_3 are shown). With constant returns to scale the long-run average cost curve consists of the minimum points of the short-run average cost curves.

any production choice between Q_1 and Q_2 will entail an increase in the average cost of production, as will any level of production between Q_2 and Q_3.

What is the firm's long-run cost curve? In the long run the firm can change the size of its plant, so if it was initially producing Q_1 and wanted to increase output to Q_2 or Q_3, it could do so with no increase in cost. The long-run average cost curve is therefore given by the cross-hatched portions of the short-run average cost curves because these show the minimum cost of production for any output level. The long-run average cost curve is the *envelope* of the short-run average cost curves—it envelops or surrounds the short-run curves.

Now suppose there are many choices of plant size, each of which has a short-run average cost curve that has its minimum at the $10 level. Again, the long-run average cost curve is the envelope of the short-run curves. In Figure 7.8 it is the straight line LAC.[12] Whatever the firm wants to produce, it can choose the plant size that allows it to produce that output at the minimum average cost of $10.

[12]Furthermore, because long-run average cost is constant, the long-run marginal cost LMC is also equal to the long-run average cost.

With increasing or decreasing returns to scale, the analysis is essentially the same, but the long-run average cost curve is no longer a horizontal line. Figure 7.9 illustrates the typical case in which the minimum average cost is lowest for a medium-sized plant. The long-run average cost curve, therefore, exhibits increasing returns to scale initially, but at higher output levels it exhibits decreasing returns. Once again, the cross-hatched lines show the envelope associated with the three plants.

To clarify the relationship between the short-run and the long-run cost curves, consider a firm that wants to produce output Q_1 in Figure 7.9. If it builds a small plant, the short-run average cost curve SAC_1 is relevant, so that the average cost of production (at B on SAC_1) is $8. A small plant is a better choice than a medium-sized plant with an average cost of production of $10 ($A$ on curve SAC_2). Point B would, therefore, become one point on the long-run cost function when only three plant sizes are possible. If plants of other sizes could be built, and at least one size allowed the firm to produce Q_1 at less than $8 per unit, then B would no longer be on the long-run cost curve.

In Figure 7.9, the envelope that would arise if plants of any size could be

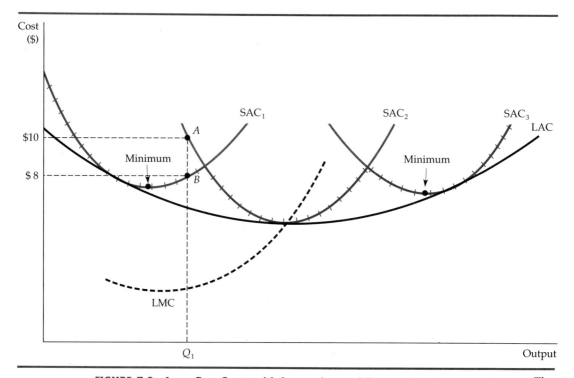

FIGURE 7.9 Long-Run Costs with Increasing and Decreasing Returns to Scale. The long-run average cost curve LAC is the envelope of the short-run average cost curves (SAC_1, SAC_2, and SAC_3). With increasing returns and decreasing returns, the minimum points of the short-run average cost curves do not lie on the long-run average cost curve.

built is given by the LAC curve, which is U-shaped. Note, once again, that the LAC curve never lies above any of the short-run average cost curves. Also note that the points of minimum average cost of the smallest and largest plants do *not* lie on the long-run average cost curve because there are increasing and decreasing returns to scale in the long run. For example, a small plant operating at minimum average cost is not efficient because a larger plant can take advantage of increasing returns to scale to produce at a lower average cost.

7.5 Production with Two Outputs—Economies of Scope

Many firms produce more than one product. Sometimes a firm's products are closely linked to one another—a chicken farm produces poultry and eggs, an automobile company produces automobiles, trucks, and tractors, and a university produces teaching and research. Other times, firms produce products that are physically unrelated. In both cases, however, a firm is likely to enjoy production or cost advantages when it produces two or more products rather than only one. These advantages could result from the joint use of inputs or production facilities, joint marketing programs, or possibly the cost savings of having common administration. In some cases, the production of one product gives an automatic and unavoidable by-product that is valuable to the firm. For example, sheet metal manufacturers produce scrap metal and shavings they can sell.

To study the economic advantages of joint production, let's consider an automobile company that produces two products, cars and tractors. Both products use capital (factories and machinery) and labor as inputs. Cars and tractors are not typically produced at the same plant, but they do share management resources, and both rely on similar machinery and similarly skilled labor. The managers of the company must choose how much of each product to produce. Figure 7.10 shows two *product transformation curves*. Each curve shows the various combinations of cars and tractors that can be produced with a given input of labor and machinery. Curve O_1 describes all combinations of the two outputs that can be produced with a relatively low level of inputs, and curve O_2 describes the output combinations associated with twice the inputs.

The product transformation curve has a negative slope because to get more of one output, the firm must give up some of the other output. For example, a firm that emphasizes car production will devote less of its resources to producing tractors. In this case, curve O_2 lies twice as far from the origin as curve O_1, signifying that this firm's production process exhibits constant returns to scale in the production of both commodities.[13]

[13]Our discussion would be more complex were we to incorporate the possibility of diseconomies or economies of scale. For a more general analysis of economies of scope, see Elizabeth E. Bailey and Ann F. Friedlaender, "Market Structure and Multiproduct Industries: A Review Article," *Journal of Economic Literature* 20 (Sept. 1982): 1024–1048, or John C. Panzar and Robert D. Willig, "Economies of Scope," *American Economic Review* 71 (May 1981): 268–272.

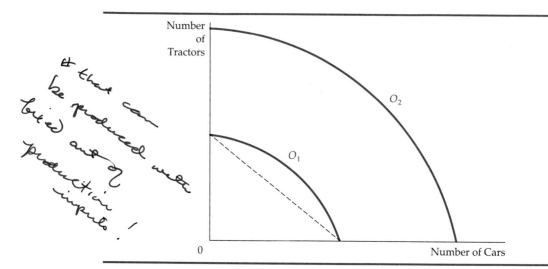

*et that can
be produced
tried and of
production
input.*

FIGURE 7.10 Product Transformation Curve. The product transformation curve describes the different combinations of two outputs that can be produced with a fixed amount of production inputs. The product transformation curves O_1 and O_2 are bowed out because there are economies of scope in production.

If curve O_1 were a straight line, joint production would entail no gains (or losses). One smaller company specializing in cars and another with an emphasis on tractors would generate the same output as the single company that produces both. However, the product transformation curve is bowed outward (or *concave*) because joint production usually has advantages that enable a single company to produce more cars and tractors with the same resources than would two companies producing each product separately. These production advantages involve the joint sharing of inputs. A single management is often able to schedule and organize production and to handle accounting and financial aspects more effectively than separate management could.

In general, *economies of scope* are present when the *joint output of a single firm is greater than the output that could be achieved by two different firms each producing a single product* (with equivalent production inputs allocated between the two firms). If a firm's joint output is *less* than could be achieved by separate firms, then its production process involves *diseconomies of scope*. This could occur if workers producing each product got in each other's way, or if the production of one product somehow conflicted with the production of the second product.

There is no direct relationship between increasing returns to scale and economies of scope. A two-output firm can enjoy economies of scope even if its production process involves decreasing returns to scale. Suppose, for example, that manufacturing flutes and piccolos jointly is cheaper than producing both separately. Yet, the production process involves highly skilled labor and is most effective if undertaken on a small scale. Likewise, a joint-product firm can have increasing returns to scale for each individual product, yet not enjoy economies of scope. Imagine, for example, a large conglomerate that owns several firms that produce efficiently on a large scale but that do not take advantage of economies of scope because they are administered separately.

The extent to which there are economies of scope can be determined by studying a firm's costs. For the company that produces both cars and tractors, curve C_1 in Figure 7.11 illustrates the total cost of producing 2000 vehicles, whether automobiles or tractors. Curve C_2, which denotes the total cost of producing 4000 vehicles, lies twice as far from the origin as C_1 because both production processes involve constant returns to scale.

Point A on curve C_1 measures the total cost of production when only tractors are produced, point B the total cost when only cars are produced. The total cost curve, which is bowed inward, or convex, is the mirror image of the concave product transformation curve and, like that curve, illustrates the presence of economies of scope. If a combination of inputs used by one firm generates more output than two independent firms would produce, then it costs less for a single firm to produce both products than it would cost the independent firms. The total cost of producing a combination of cars and tractors is less than the cost of producing both products separately.

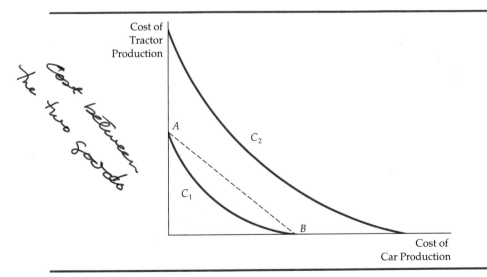

FIGURE 7.11 Economies of Scope in Production. The two-product cost isocost curves, C_1 and C_2, describe the various combinations of outputs that can be produced at equal cost. The isocost curves are bowed inward because there are economies of scope in production.

Note that if the cost curve in Figure 7.11 were a straight line, joint production would offer no cost savings and there would be no economies of scope. There would be diseconomies of scope, however, if the curve were bowed outward.

To measure the degree to which there are economies of scope, we should ask what percentage of the cost of production is saved when two (or more) products are produced jointly rather than individually. Equation (7.6) gives the *degree of economies of scope (SC)* that measures this savings in cost:

$$SC = \frac{C(Q_1) + C(Q_2) - C(Q_1 + Q_2)}{C(Q_1 + Q_2)} \tag{7.6}$$

$C(Q_1)$ represents the cost of producing output Q_1, $C(Q_2)$ the cost of producing output Q_2, and $C(Q_1 + Q_2)$ the joint cost of producing both outputs. With economies of scope, the joint cost is less than the sum of the individual costs, so that SC is greater than 0. With diseconomies of scope, SC is negative. In general, the larger the value of SC, the greater the economies of scope.

EXAMPLE 7.4 ECONOMIES OF SCOPE IN THE TRUCKING INDUSTRY

Suppose that you are managing a trucking firm that hauls loads of different sizes between cities.[14] In the trucking business, several related but distinct products can be offered depending on the size of the load and the length of the haul. First, any load, small or large, can be taken directly from one location to another without intermediate stops. Second, a load can be combined with other loads, which may go between different locations, and eventually be shipped indirectly from its origin to the appropriate destination. And each type of load, partial or full, may involve different lengths of haul.

This raises questions both about economies of scale and economies of scope. The scale question is whether large-scale, small, direct hauls are cheaper and more profitable than individual hauls by small truckers. The scope question is whether a large trucking firm enjoys cost advantages from operating both direct quick hauls and indirect, slower (but less expensive) hauls. Central planning and organization of routes could provide for economies of scope. The key to the presence of economies of scale is the fact that the organization of routes and the types of hauls we have described can be accomplished more efficiently

---

[14]This example is based directly on Judy S. Wang Chiang and Ann F. Friedlaender, "Truck Technology and Efficient Market Structure," *Review of Economics and Statistics* 67 (1985): 250–258.

when many hauls are involved. Then it will be more likely that hauls can be scheduled that allow most truckloads to be full, rather than half-full.

Studies of the trucking industry show that economies of scope are present. For example, an analysis of 105 trucking firms in 1976 looked at four distinct outputs: (1) short hauls with partial loads, (2) intermediate hauls with partial loads, (3) long hauls with partial loads, and (4) hauls with total loads. The results indicate that the degree of economies of scope SC was 1.576 for a reasonably large firm. However, the degree of economies of scope falls to 0.104 when the firm becomes very large. Large firms carry sufficiently large truckloads, so there is usually no advantage to stopping at an intermediate terminal to fill a partial load. A direct trip from the origin to the destination is sufficient. Apparently, however, other disadvantages are associated with the management of very large firms, so the economies of scope diminish in magnitude as the firm gets bigger. In any event, the ability to combine partial loads at an intermediate location lowers the firm's costs and increases its profitability.

The study suggests, therefore, that to compete in the trucking industry, a firm must be large enough to be able to combine loads at intermediate stopping points.

*7.6   Dynamic Changes in Costs—The Learning Curve

Our discussion has suggested one reason a large firm may have lower long-run average costs than a small firm—increasing returns to scale in production. It is tempting to conclude that firms that enjoy lower average costs over time are growing firms with increasing returns to scale. But this need not be true. In some firms, long-run average costs may decline over time because workers and managers absorb new technological information as they become more experienced at their jobs.

As management and labor gain experience with production, the firm's marginal and average cost of producing a given level of output falls for four reasons. First, workers often take longer to accomplish a given task the first few times they do it. As they become more adept, their speed increases. Second, managers learn to schedule the production process more effectively, from the flow of materials to the organization of the manufacturing itself. Third, engineers, who are initially very cautious in their product designs, may gain enough experience to be able to allow for tolerances in design that save costs without increasing defects. Better and more specialized tools and plant organization may also lower costs. Fourth, suppliers of materials may learn how to process materials required by the firm more effectively, and may pass on some of this advantage to the firm in the form of lower materials costs.

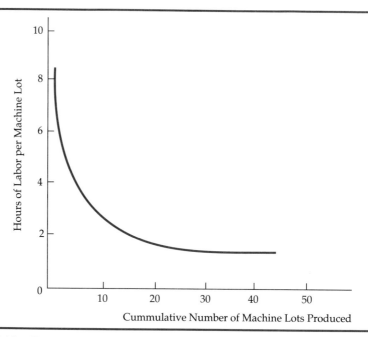

FIGURE 7.12 The Learning Curve. A firm's cost of production may fall over time as the managers and workers become more experienced and more effective at using the available plant and equipment. The learning curve shows the extent to which the hours of labor needed per unit of output (a machine in this case) falls as the cumulative output (number of machines) produced increases.

As a consequence, a firm "learns" over time as cumulative output increases. Managers use this learning process to help plan production and to forecast future costs. Figure 7.12 illustrates this process, in the form of a learning curve. A *learning curve* describes the relationship between a firm's cumulative output and the amount of inputs needed to produce a unit of output.

Figure 7.12 shows a learning curve for the production of machine tools by a manufacturer.[15] The horizontal axis measures the *cumulative* number of lots of machine tools that the firm has produced (a lot is a group of approximately 40 machines), and the vertical axis the number of hours of labor needed to produce each lot. Labor input per unit of output directly affects the firm's cost of production, because the fewer the hours of labor needed, the lower the marginal and average cost of production.

[15]This is based on Werner Z. Hirsch, "Manufacturing Progress Functions," *Review of Economics and Statistics*, 34 (May 1952): 143–155. The idea of a learning curve was first developed by T. P. Wright, who noted that the labor cost of producing the frame of an airplane declined with the number of frames produced. (T.P. Wright, "Factors Affecting the Cost of Airplanes," *Journal of Aeronautical Sciences* 3 (1936): 122–128.

The learning curve in the figure is based on the relationship

$$L = A + BN^{-\beta} \qquad (7.7)$$

where N is the cumulative units of output produced, L is the labor input per units of output, and A, B, and β are constants, with A and B positive, and β between 0 and 1. When N is equal to 1, L is equal to $A + B$, so that $A + B$ measures the labor input required to produce the first unit of output. When β equals 0, labor input per unit of output remains the same as the cumulative level of output increases, so there is no learning. When β is positive and N gets larger and larger, L becomes arbitrarily close to A, so that A represents the minimum labor input per unit of output after all learning has taken place.

The larger is β, the more important is the learning effect. With β equal to 0.5, for example, the labor input per unit of output falls proportionally to the square root of the cumulative output. This degree of learning can substantially reduce the firm's production costs as the form becomes more experienced.

In this machine tool example, the value of β is 0.32. For this particular learning curve, every doubling in cumulative output causes the difference between the input requirement and the minimum attainable input requirement to fall by about 20 percent.[16] As Figure 7.12 shows, the learning curve drops sharply as the cumulative number of lots produced increases to about 20. Beyond an output of 20 lots, the cost savings are relatively small.

Once the firm has produced 20 or more machine lots, the entire effect of the learning curve would be complete, and the usual analysis of costs could be employed. If, however, the production process were relatively new, then relatively high costs at low levels of output (and relatively low costs at higher levels) would indicate learning effects, and not increasing returns to scale. With learning, the costs of production for a mature firm are relatively low irrespective of the scale of the firm's operation. If a firm that produces machine tools in groups (or "lots") knows that it enjoys increasing returns to scale, it should produce its machines in very large lots to take advantage of the lower costs associated with size. If there is a learning curve, the firm can lower its costs by scheduling the production of many lots irrespective of the individual lot size.

Figure 7.13 shows this phenomenon. AC_1 represents the long-run average cost of production of a firm that enjoys increasing returns to scale in production. If there is a learning curve, the process of learning shifts the average cost curve downward, from AC_1 to AC_2 in the figure. The change in production from A to B along AC_1 leads to lower costs due to increasing returns to scale. The move from A on AC_1 to C on AC_2 leads to lower costs due to the learning curve.

The learning curve is crucial for a firm that wants to predict the cost of producing a new product. Suppose, for example, that a firm producing machine tools knows that its labor requirement per machine for the first ten machines is

---

[16]Specifically, because $(L - A) = BN^{-.31}$, it is easy to check that $0.8(L-A)$ is approximately equal to $B(2N)^{-.31}$.

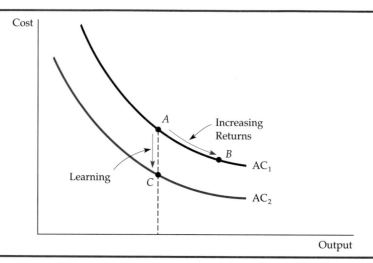

FIGURE 7.13 Increasing Returns to Scale versus Learning. A firm's average cost of production can decline over time because of growth of sales when increasing returns are present (a move from A to B on curve AC_1), or it can decline because there is a learning curve (a move from A on curve AC_1 to C on curve AC_2).

1.0, the minimum labor requirement A is equal to zero, and β is approximately equal to 0.32. Table 7.3 calculates the total labor requirement for producing 80 machines.

Because there is a learning curve, the per-unit labor requirement falls with increased production. As a result, the total labor requirement for producing more and more output increases in smaller and smaller increments. Therefore, a firm looking at the high initial labor requirement will obtain an overly pessimistic view of the business. Suppose the firm plans to be in business for a long time and the total labor requirement for each year's product is ten. In the first year of production, the labor requirement is ten, so the firm's costs will be high as it learns the business. But once the learning effect has taken place, production costs will be lower. After eight years, the labor requirement will be only 0.51, and per unit costs will be roughly half what they were in the first year of production. Thus, learning curve effects can be important for a firm deciding whether it is profitable to enter an industry.

EXAMPLE 7.5 THE LEARNING CURVE IN THE CHEMICAL PROCESSING INDUSTRY

Suppose you manage a firm that has just entered the chemical processing industry. You would face the following problem: Should you produce a relatively low level of output (and sell at a high price), or should you price your product

TABLE 7.3 Predicting the Labor Requirements of Producing a Given Output

Cumulative Output (N)	Per Unit Labor Requirement for each 10 units of output(L)[17]	Total Labor Requirement
10	1.00	10.0
20	.80	18.0 (10.0 + 8.0)
30	.70	25.0 (18.0 + 7.0)
40	.64	31.4 (25.0 + 6.4)
50	.60	37.4 (31.4 + 6.0)
60	.56	43.0 (37.4 + 5.6)
70	.53	48.3 (43.0 + 5.3)
80 and over	.51	53.4 (48.3 + 5.1)

lower and increase your rate of sales? The second alternative is particularly appealing if there is a learning curve in this industry. Then the increased volume will lower your average production costs in the long run and increase the firm's profitability.

To decide what to do, you can examine the available statistical evidence that distinguishes the components of the learning curve (learning new processes by labor, engineering improvements, etc.) from increasing returns to scale. A study of 37 chemical products from the late 1950s to 1972 reveals that cost reductions in the chemical processing industry were directly tied to the growth of cumulative industry output, to investment in improved capital equipment, and to a lesser extent to increasing returns to scale.[18] In fact, for the entire sample of chemical products, average costs of production fell at 5.5 percent per year.[19] The study reveals that for each doubling of plant scale, the average cost of production falls by 11 percent. For each doubling of cumulative output, however, the average cost of production falls by 27 percent. The evidence shows

---

[17]The numbers in this column were calculated from the equation $\log (L) = -0.322 \log (N/10)$, where L is the unit labor input and N is cumulative output.

[18]The study was by Marvin Lieberman, "The Learning Curve and Pricing in the Chemical Processing Industries," *Rand Journal of Economics* 15 (1984): 213–228.

[19]The author used the average cost AC of the chemical products, the cumulative industry output X, and the average scale of a production plant Z and estimated the relationship $\log (AC) = -0.387 \log (X) - 0.173 \log (Z)$. The -0.387 coefficient on cumulative output tells us that for every 1 percent increase in cumulative output, average cost decreases 0.387 percent. At the same time, the -0.173 coefficient on plant size tells us that for every 1 percent increase in plant size, cost decreases 0.173 percent.

clearly that learning effects are more important than increasing returns to scale in the chemical processing industry.[20]

Learning curve effects can be important in determining the shape of long-run cost curves and can thus help guide the firm's manager. The manager can use learning curve information to decide whether a production operation is profitable, and if it is profitable, to plan how large the plant operation and the volume of cumulative output need be before a positive cash flow will result.

*7.7 Estimating and Predicting Cost

A business that is expanding or contracting its operation needs to predict how costs will change as output changes. Estimates of future costs can be obtained from a *cost function*, which relates the cost of production to the level of output and other variables that the firm can control.

Suppose we wanted to characterize the short-run costs of production in the automobile industry. We could obtain data on the number of automobiles Q produced by each car company and relate this information to the variable costs of production VC. The use of variable cost, rather than total cost, avoids the problem of trying to allocate the fixed costs of a multiproduct firm's production process to the particular product being studied.[21]

Figure 7.14 shows a typical pattern of cost and output data. Each point on the graph relates the output of a particular auto company to that company's variable cost of production. To predict cost accurately, we need to determine as accurately as possible the underlying relationship between variable cost and output. Then, if a company expands its production, we can calculate what the associated cost is likely to be. The curve in the figure is drawn with this in mind—it provides a reasonably close fit to the cost data. (Typically, least-squares regression analysis would be used to fit the curve to the data.) But what shape

[20]By interpreting each of the two coefficients in footnote 19 in light of the levels of the output and plant size variables, one can allocate about 15 percent of the cost reduction to increases in the average scale of plants, and 85 percent to increases in the cumulative industry output. (Suppose plant scale doubled, while cumulative output increased by a factor of five during the period of study. Then costs would fall by 11 percent owing to the increased scale and by 62 percent owing to the increase in cumulative output.)

[21]If an additional piece of equipment is needed as output increases, then annual rental cost of the equipment should be counted as a variable cost. If, however, the same machine can be used at all output levels, then its cost is fixed and should not be included.

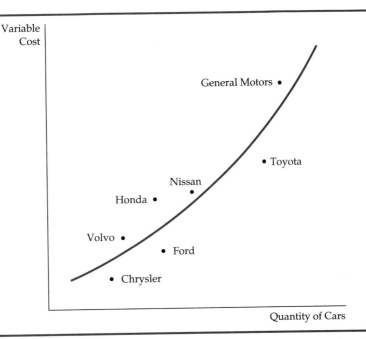

FIGURE 7.14 Total Cost Curve for the Automobile Industry. An empirical estimate of the total cost curve can be obtained by using data for individual firms in an industry. The total cost curve for automobile production is obtained by determining statistically the curve that best fits the points that relate the output of each firm to the total cost of production.

of curve is the most appropriate, and how do we represent that shape algebraically? The following discussion outlines some of the possibilities.

One cost function that might be chosen is

$$VC = \alpha + \beta Q \tag{7.8}$$

This *linear* relationship between cost and output is easy to use but is applicable only when the marginal cost is constant.[22] For every unit increase in output, variable cost increases by β, so the linear cost curve implies a constant marginal cost of production.

If we wish to allow for a U-shaped average cost curve and a marginal cost that is not constant, we must use a more complex cost function. One possibility,

---

[22]In statistical cost analyses, other variables might be added to the cost function to account for differences in input costs, production processes, product mix, etc. among firms.

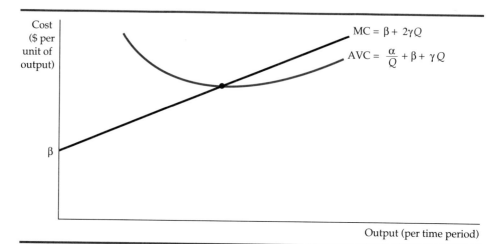

FIGURE 7.15 Quadratic Cost Function. A quadratic function is a useful specification for either short-run or long-run cost functions when the average cost curve is U-shaped and the marginal cost curve is linear.

shown in Figure 7.15, is the *quadratic* cost function, which relates total cost to output and output squared:

$$VC = \alpha + \beta Q + \gamma Q^2 \tag{7.9}$$

This implies a marginal cost curve of the form MC $= \beta + 2\gamma Q$.[23] Here, the relationship between marginal cost and output is linear—the marginal cost curve is a straight line. Marginal cost increases with output if γ is positive, and decreases with output if γ is negative. Average cost, given by AC $= \alpha/Q + \beta + \gamma Q$, is U-shaped when γ is positive.

If the marginal cost curve is not linear, we might use a *cubic* cost function:

$$VC = \alpha + \beta Q + \gamma Q^2 + \delta Q^3 \tag{7.10}$$

Figure 7.16 shows this cubic cost function. It implies U-shaped marginal as well as average cost curves.

As with production functions, cost functions can be difficult to measure. First, output data often represent an aggregate of different types of products. Total automobiles produced by General Motors, for example, involves different models of cars. Second, cost data are often obtained directly from accounting information that fails to reflect opportunity costs. Third, allocating maintenance

---

[23]Short-run marginal cost is given by $\Delta TVC/\Delta Q = \beta + \gamma\Delta(Q^2)/\Delta Q$. But $\Delta(Q^2)/\Delta Q = 2Q$. (Check this using the calculus or by numerical example.) Therefore, MC $= \beta + 2\gamma Q$.

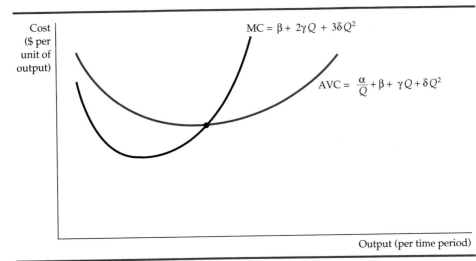

FIGURE 7.16 Cubic Cost Function. A cubic function is a useful specification for a short-run or long-run cost function when the average and the marginal cost curve are U-shaped.

and other plant costs to a particular product is difficult when the firm is a conglomerate that produces more than one product line. Problems like these can limit the accuracy of statistical cost studies.

Cost Functions and the Measurement of Scale Economies

Recall that economies of scale arise whenever the average cost of production less than doubles when output is doubled, whatever the combination of inputs. One way to measure scale economies is to use the *elasticity of cost* C *with respect to output* Q, E_C.

$$E_C = (\Delta C/C)/(\Delta Q/Q)$$

The cost-output elasticity is equal to one when costs increase proportionately with output, is greater than one when costs increase more rapidly than output, and is less than one when costs increase less rapidly than output. Therefore, we can define a *scale economies index* SCI as follows:

$$SCI = 1 - E_C \tag{7.11}$$

When $E_C = 1$, SCI = 0, and there are no economies of scale. When E_C is greater than one, SCI is negative, and there are diseconomies of scale. Finally, when E_C is less than one, SCI is positive, and there are economies of scale.

EXAMPLE 7.6   COST FUNCTIONS FOR ELECTRIC POWER

In 1955, consumers bought 369 kilowatt-hours (kwh) of electricity; by 1970 they were buying 1083 billion. Because there were fewer electric utilities in 1970, the output per firm had increased substantially. Was this increase in output the result of economies of scale or of other reasons? The question is important, because if it was the result of economies of scale, it would be economically inefficient for regulators to "break up" electric utility monopolies.

An interesting study of scale economies was based on the years 1955 and 1970 for investor-owned utilities with more than $1 million in revenues.[24] The cost of electric power was estimated by using a cost function that is somewhat more sophisticated than the quadratic and cubic functions discussed earlier, but the basic idea is the same.[25] Table 7.4 shows the resulting estimates of the Scale Economies Index (SCI). The results are based on a classification of all utilities into five size categories, with the median output (measured in kilowatt-hours) in each category listed.

The positive values of SCI tell us that all sizes of firms had some economies of scale in 1955. However, the magnitude of the economies of scale diminishes as firm size increases. The average cost curve associated with the 1955 study is drawn in Figure 7.17 and labeled 1955. The point of minimum average cost occurs at point *A* at an output of approximately 20 billion kilowatts. Because there were no firms of this size in 1955, no firm had exhausted the opportunity for returns to scale in production. Note, however, that the average cost curve is relatively flat from an output of 9 billion kilowatts and higher, a range in which 7 of 124 firms produced.

When the same cost functions were estimated with 1970 data, the cost curve, labeled 1970 in Figure 7.17, was the result. The graph shows clearly that the average costs of production fell from 1955 to 1970. (The data are in real 1970 dollars.) But the flat part of the curve now begins at about 15 billion kwh. By 1970, 24 of 80 firms were producing in this range. Thus, many more firms were operating in the flat portion of the average cost curve in which economies of

TABLE 7.4 Scale Economies in the Electric Power Industry					
Output (million kwh)	43	338	1109	2226	5819
Value of SCI, 1955	.41	.26	.16	.10	.04

[24]This example is based on Laurits Christensen and William H. Greene, "Economies of Scale in U.S. Electric Power Generation," *Journal of Political Economy* 84 (1976): 655–676.

[25]The translog cost function that was used provides a more general functional relationship than any of those we have discussed.

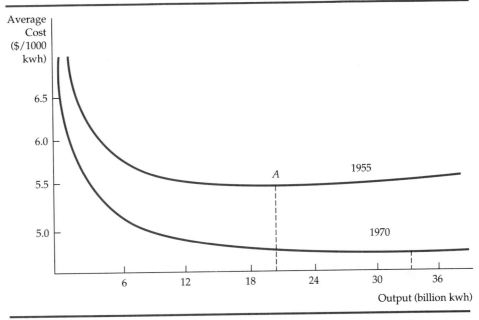

FIGURE 7.17 Average Costs of Production in the Electric Power Industry. The average cost of electric power in 1955 achieved a minimum at approximately 20 billion kilowatt-hours. By 1970 the average cost of production had fallen sharply and achieved a minimum at output of greater than 32 billion kilowatt-hours.

scale are not an important phenomenon. More important, most of the firms were producing in a portion of the 1970 cost curve that was flatter than their point of operation on the 1955 curve. (Five firms were at a point of diseconomies of scale: Consolidated Edison [SCI = −0.003], Detroit Edison [SCI = −0.004], Duke Power [SCI = −0.012], Commonwealth Edison [SCI = −0.014], and Southern [SCI = −0.028]). Thus, unexploited scale economies were much smaller in 1970 than in 1955.

This cost function analysis makes it clear that the decline in the cost of producing electric power cannot be explained by the ability of larger firms to take advantage of economies of scale. Rather, improvements in technology unrelated to the scale of the firms' operation and the decline in the real cost of energy inputs such as coal and oil are important reasons for the lower costs. The tendency toward lower average costs caused by a movement to the right along an average cost curve is minimal compared with the effect of technological improvement.

EXAMPLE 7.7 A COST FUNCTION FOR THE SAVINGS AND LOAN INDUSTRY

An understanding of returns to scale in the savings and loan industry is important for regulators who must decide whether mergers and takeovers are in the public interest, and for managers who must make internal decisions about the size of an association's operations. In both cases, the empirical estimation of a long-run cost function can be useful.[26]

Data were collected for 86 savings and loan associations for 1975 and 1976 in a region that includes Idaho, Montana, Oregon, Utah, Washington, and Wyoming. Output is difficult to measure in this case, because a savings and loan association provides a service to its customers, rather than a physical product. The output Q measure reported here (and used in other studies) is the total assets of each savings and loan association. In general, the larger the asset base of an association, the higher its profitability. Long-run average cost LAC is measured by average operating expense. Output and total operating costs are measured in hundreds of millions of dollars. Average operating costs are measured as a percentage of total assets.

A quadratic long-run average cost function was estimated for the year 1975, yielding the following relationship:

$$LAC = 2.38 - 0.6153Q + 0.0536Q^2$$

The estimated long-run average cost function is U-shaped and reaches its point of minimum average cost when the total assets of the savings and loan reach $574 million.[27] (At this point the average operating expenses of the savings and loan are 0.61 percent of its total assets.) Because almost all savings and loans in the region being studied had substantially less than $574 million in assets, the cost function analysis suggests that an expansion of savings and loans through either growth or mergers would be valuable.

How appropriate such a policy is cannot be fully evaluated here, however. To do so, we would need to take into account the possible social costs associated with the lessening of competition from growth or mergers, and we would need to assure ourselves that this particular cost function analysis accurately estimated the point of minimum average cost.[28]

---

[26]This example builds on J. Holton Wilson, "A Note on Scale Economies in the Savings and Loan Industry," *Business Economics* (Jan. 1981): 45–49.

[27]This can be seen by graphing the curve, or by differentiating the average cost function with respect to Q, setting it equal to 0, and solving for Q.

[28]The study by J. Holton Wilson suggests an alternative cost function approach that yields a much lower point of minimum average cost.

Summary

1. Managers, investors, and economists must take into account the opportunity costs associated with the use of the firm's resources—the costs associated with the opportunities forgone when the firm uses its resources in its next best alternative.

2. In the short run, one or more of the inputs of the firm are fixed. Total costs can be divided into fixed costs and variable costs. A firm's *marginal cost* is the additional variable cost associated with each additional unit of output. The *average variable cost* is the total variable cost divided by the number of units of output.

3. When there is a single variable input, as in the short run, the presence of diminishing returns determines the shape of the cost curves. In particular, there is an inverse relationship between the marginal product of the variable input and the marginal cost of production. The average variable cost and average total cost curves are U-shaped. The short-run marginal cost curve increases beyond a certain point, and cuts both average cost curves from below at their minimum points.

4. In the long run, all inputs to the production process are variable. As a result, the choice of inputs depends both on the relative costs of the factors of production and on the extent to which the firm can substitute among inputs in its production process. The cost-minimizing input choice is made by finding the point of tangency between the isoquant representing the level of desired output and an isocost line.

5. The firm's expansion path describes how its cost-minimizing input choices vary as the scale or output of its operation increases. As a result, the expansion path provides useful information relevant for long-run planning decisions.

6. The long-run average cost curve is the envelope of the firm's short-run average cost curves, and it reflects the presence or absence of returns to scale. When there are constant returns to scale and many plant sizes are possible, the long-run cost curve is horizontal, and the envelope consists of the points of minimum short-run average cost. However, when there are increasing returns to scale initially and then decreasing returns to scale, the long-run average cost curve is U-shaped, and the envelope does not include all points of minimum short-run average cost.

7. When a firm produces two (or more) outputs, it is important to note whether or not there are economies of scope in production. Economies of scope arise when the firm can produce any combination of the two outputs more cheaply than could two independent firms that each produced a single product. The degree of economies of scope is measured by the percentage in reduction in costs when one firm produces two products relative to the cost of producing them individually.

8. A firm's average cost of production can fall over time if the firm "learns" how to produce more effectively. The *learning curve* describes how much the input needed to produce a given output falls as the cumulative output of the firm increases.

9. Cost functions relate the cost of production to the level of output of the firm. Cost functions can be measured in both the short run and the long run by using either data for firms in an industry at a given time or data for an industry over time. A number of

functional relationships including linear, quadratic, and cubic can be used, depending on what the firm expects the shape of the cost curves to be.

Review Questions

1. A firm pays its accountant an annual retainer of $10,000. Is this an explicit or an implicit cost?

2. The owner of a small retail store does her own accounting work. How would you measure the opportunity cost of her work?

3. Suppose a chair manufacturer finds that the marginal rate of technical substitution of capital for labor in his production process is substantially greater than the ratio of the rental rate on machinery to the wage rate for assembly-line labor. How should he alter his use of capital and labor to minimize the cost of production?

4. Why are isocost lines straight lines? What might isocost lines look like if the market for labor and capital were not competitive?

5. If the marginal cost of production is increasing, does this tell you whether the average variable cost is increasing or decreasing? Explain.

6. If the marginal cost of production is greater than the average variable cost, does this tell you whether the average variable cost is increasing or decreasing? Explain.

7. If the firm's average cost curves are U-shaped, why does its average variable cost curve achieve its minimum at a lower level of output than the average total cost curve?

8. If a firm enjoys increasing returns to scale up to a certain output level, and then constant returns to scale, what can you say about the shape of the firm's long-run average cost curve?

9. How does a change in the price of one of the firm's inputs change the firm's long-run expansion path?

10. Distinguish between increasing returns to scale and economies of scope. Why can one be present without the other?

11. Distinguish between increasing returns to scale and the learning curve. Why can one be present without the other?

Exercises

1. A manufacturer of chairs hires its assembly-line labor for $22 an hour and calculates that the rental cost of its machinery is $110 per hour. Suppose that a chair can be produced using four hours of labor and machinery in any combination. If the firm is currently using three hours of labor for each hour of machine time, is it minimizing its costs of production? If so why? If not, how can it rectify the situation?

2. Assume a computer firm's marginal costs of production are constant at $1000 per computer. However, the fixed costs of production are equal to $10,000.

a. Calculate the firm's average variable cost and average total cost curves.

b. If the firm wanted to minimize the average total cost of production, would it choose to be very large or very small? Explain.

3. a. Suppose a firm must pay an annual franchise fee, which is a fixed sum, independent of whether it produces any output. How does this tax affect the firm's fixed, marginal, and average costs?

b. Now suppose the firm is charged a tax that is proportional to the number of items it produces. Again, how does this tax affect the firm's fixed, marginal, and average costs?

4. Suppose the economy takes a downturn and labor costs fall by 50 percent, and are expected to stay at that new level for a long time. Show graphically what this change in the relative price of labor and capital does to the firm's expansion path.

5. An oil refinery consists of different pieces of processing equipment, each of which differs in its ability to break down heavy sulfurized crude oil into final products. The refinery process is such that the marginal cost of producing gasoline is constant up to a point as crude oil is put through a basic distilling unit. However, as the unit fills up, the firm finds that in the short run there is a limit to the amount of crude oil that can be processed. The marginal cost of producing gasoline is also constant up to a capacity limit when crude oil is put through a more sophisticated hydrocracking unit. Graph the marginal cost of gasoline production when a basic distilling unit and a hydrocracker are used.

*6. Suppose the long-run total cost function for an industry is given by the cubic equation $TC = \alpha + \beta Q + \gamma Q^2 + \delta Q^3$. Show (using calculus) that this total cost function is consistent with a U-shaped average cost curve for at least some values of the parameters α, β, γ, and δ.

*7. A computer company produces hardware and software using the same plant and labor. The total cost of producing computer processing units H and software programs S is given by

$$TC = \alpha H + \beta S - \gamma HS$$

where α, β, and γ are positive. Is this total cost function consistent with the presence of increasing or decreasing returns to scale? economies or diseconomies of scope?

*8. A computer company's cost function, which relates its average cost of production AC to its cumulative output in thousands of computers CQ and its plant size in terms of thousands of computers produced per year Q, within the production range of 10,000 to 50,000 computers, is given by

$$AC = 10 - 0.1CQ + 0.3Q$$

a. Is there a learning curve effect?

b. Are there increasing or decreasing returns to scale?

c. The firm has produced 40,000 computers and is producing 10,000 computers this year. Next year it plans to increase its production to 12,000 computers. Will its average cost of production increase or decrease? Explain.

APPENDIX TO CHAPTER 7

Production and Cost Theory—
An Algebraic Treatment

This appendix presents an algebraic treatment of the basics of production and cost theory. As in the appendix to Chapter 4, we use the method of Lagrange multipliers to solve the firm's cost-minimizing problem.

Cost Minimization

The theory of the firm relies on the assumption that firms choose inputs to the production process that minimize the cost of producing output. If there are two inputs, capital K and labor L, the production function $F(K,L)$ describes the maximum output that can be produced for each possible combination of inputs. We assume that each of the factors in the production process has positive but decreasing marginal products. Writing the marginal product of capital as $\mathrm{MP}_K(K,L) = \partial F(K,L)/\partial K$, we assume that $\mathrm{MP}_K(K,L) > 0$ and $\partial \mathrm{MP}_K(K,L)/\partial K < 0$. Similarly, if the marginal product of labor is given by $\mathrm{MP}_L(K,L) = \partial F(K,L)/\partial L$, we assume that $\mathrm{MP}_L(K,L) > 0$ and $\partial \mathrm{MP}_L(K,L)/\partial L < 0$.

A competitive firm takes the prices of both labor w and capital r as given. Then the cost-minimization problem can be written as

$$\text{Minimize TC} = wL + rK \tag{A7.1}$$

subject to the constraint that a fixed output Q_0 be produced:

$$F(K,L) = Q_0 \tag{A7.2}$$

TC represents the cost of producing the fixed level of output Q_0, and w and r are the wage rate and price of capital, respectively.

To determine the firm's demand for the inputs capital and labor, we choose the values of K and L that minimize (A7.1) subject to (A7.2). We solve this constrained optimization problem using the method of Lagrange multipliers discussed in Appendix 4. In this case, the Lagrangian for this problem is

$$\Phi = wL + rK - \lambda[F(K,L) - Q_0] \tag{A7.3}$$

where λ is the Lagrange multiplier. Recall from Chapter 4 that by differentiating with respect to K, L, and then λ, and equating the derivatives to zero, we obtain the necessary conditions to achieve a maximum[1]:

$$\partial\Phi/\partial K = r - \lambda MP_K(K,L) = 0$$

$$\partial\Phi/\partial L = w - \lambda MP_L(K,L) = 0 \qquad (A7.4)$$

$$\partial\Phi/\partial\lambda = F(K,L) = Q_0$$

By combining the first two conditions we obtain

$$MP_K(K,L)/r = MP_L(K,L)/w \qquad (A7.5)$$

Equation (A7.5) tells us that if the firm is minimizing costs, it will choose its factor inputs to equate the ratio of the marginal product of each factor divided by its price. To see that this makes sense, suppose MP_K/r were greater than MP_L/w. Then the firm could reduce its cost while still producing the same output by using more capital and less labor.

Finally, we can combine the first two conditions of (A7.4) in a different way to evaluate the Lagrange multiplier:

$$\lambda = r/MP_K(K,L) = w/MP_L(K,L)$$

Suppose output increases by one unit. Because the marginal product of capital measures the extra output associated with an additional input of capital, $1/MP_K(K,L)$ measures the extra capital needed to produce one unit of output. Therefore, $r/MP_K(K,L)$ measures the additional input cost of producing an additional unit of output by increasing capital. Likewise, $w/MP_L(K,L)$ measures the additional cost of producing a unit of output using additional labor as an input. In both cases, the Lagrange multiplier is equal to the marginal cost of production, because it tells us how much the cost of production increases if the amount of production is increased by one unit.

Marginal Rate of Technical Substitution

Recall that an isoquant is a curve that represents the set of all input combinations that give the firm the same level of output, say, Q^*. Thus, the condition that $F(K,L) = Q^*$ represents a production isoquant. As input combinations are changed along an isoquant, the change in output must equal zero. This change in output is given by the total derivative of $F(K,L)$. Because output is constant along an isoquant (i.e., $dQ = 0$), we must have

$$MP_K(K,L)dK + MP_L(K,L)dL = dQ = 0 \qquad (A7.7)$$

[1]These conditions are necessary for an "interior" solution in which the firm uses positive amounts of both inputs. Of course, a firm could choose not to use one input at all.

It follows by rearrangement that

$$-dK/dL = \text{MRTS}_{LK} = MP_L(K,L)/MP_K(K,L) \qquad (A7.8)$$

where MRTS_{LK} is the firm's marginal rate of technical substitution between labor and capital.

Now, rewrite the condition given by (A7.5) to get

$$MP_L(K,L)/MP_K(K,L) = w/r \qquad (A7.9)$$

Because the left-hand side of (A7.8) represents the negative of the slope of the isoquant, it follows that at the point of tangency of the isoquant and the isocost line, the firm's marginal rate of technical substitution (which trades off inputs while keeping output constant) is equal to the ratio of the input prices (which represents the slope of the firm's isocost line). This is shown graphically in Figure 7.2.

We can look at this result another way by rewriting (A7.9) again:

$$MP_L/w = MP_K/r \qquad (A7.10)$$

Equation (A7.10) tells us that the marginal products of all production inputs must be equal when these marginal products are adjusted by the unit cost of each input. If the cost-adjusted marginal products were not equal, the firm could reallocate its inputs to produce the same output at a lower cost.

Duality in Production and Cost Theory

As in consumer theory, the firm's input decision has a dual nature. The optimum choice of K and L can be analyzed not only as the problem of choosing the lowest isocost line tangent to the production isoquant, but also as the problem of choosing the highest production isoquant tangent to a given isocost line. To see this, consider the following dual producer problem:

$$\text{Maximize } F(K,L)$$

subject to the cost constraint that

$$wL + rK = C_0 \qquad (A7.11)$$

The corresponding Lagrangian is given by

$$\Phi = F(K,L) - \mu(wL + rK - C_0) \qquad (A7.12)$$

where μ is the Lagrange multiplier. The necessary conditions for output maximization are:

$$MP_K(K,L) - \mu r = 0$$

$$MP_L(K,L) - \mu w = 0 \qquad (A7.13)$$

$$wL + rK - C_0 = 0$$

By solving the first two equations, we see that

$$MP_K(K,L)/r = MP_L(K,L)/w \qquad (A7.14)$$

which is identical to the condition that was necessary for cost minimization.

The Cobb-Douglas Production Function

Given a specific production function $F(K,L)$, conditions (A7.13) and (A7.14) can be used to derive the *cost function* $C(Q)$. To see this, let's work through the example of a Cobb-Douglas production function. This production function is

$$F(K,L) = AK^\alpha L^\beta$$

or, by taking the logs of both sides of the production function equation:

$$\log [F(K,L)] = \log (A) + \alpha \log (K) + \beta \log (K)$$

We assume that $\alpha < 1$ and $\beta < 1$, so that the firm has decreasing marginal products of labor and capital.[2] If $\alpha + \beta = 1$, the firm has *constant returns to scale*, because doubling K and L doubles F. If $\alpha + \beta > 1$, the firm has *increasing returns to scale*, and if $\alpha + \beta < 1$, it has *decreasing returns to scale*.

To find the amounts of capital and labor that the firm should utilize to minimize the cost of producing an output Q_0, we first write the Lagrangian:

$$\Phi = wL + rK - \lambda(AK^\alpha L^\beta - Q_0) \qquad (A7.15)$$

Differentiating with respect to L, K and λ, and setting those derivatives equal to 0, we obtain

$$\partial\Phi/\partial L = w - \lambda(\beta AK^\alpha L^{\beta-1}) = 0 \qquad (A7.16)$$

$$\partial\Phi/\partial K = r - \lambda(\alpha AK^{\alpha-1}L^\beta) = 0 \qquad (A7.17)$$

$$\partial\Phi/\partial \lambda = AK^\alpha L^\beta - Q_0 = 0 \qquad (A7.18)$$

From equation (A7.16) we have

$$\lambda = w/A\beta K^\alpha L^{\beta-1} \qquad (A7.19)$$

Substituting this into equation (A7.17) gives us

$$r\beta AK^\alpha L^{\beta-1} = w\alpha AK^{\alpha-1}L^\beta \qquad (A7.20)$$

or

$$L = \beta rK/\alpha w \qquad (A7.21)$$

---

[2] For example, the marginal product of labor is given by $MP_L = \partial[F(K,L)]/\partial L = \beta AK^\alpha L^{\beta-1}$, so that MP_L falls as L increases.

Now, use equation (A7.21) to eliminate L from equation (A7.18):

$$AK^\alpha\beta^\beta r^\beta K^\beta/\alpha^\beta w^\beta = Q_0 \tag{A7.22}$$

Rewrite this as

$$K^{\alpha+\beta} = (\alpha w/\beta r)^\beta Q_0/A \tag{A7.23}$$

or

$$K = [(\alpha w/\beta r)^{\beta/(\alpha+\beta)}](Q_0/A)^{1/(\alpha+\beta)} \tag{A7.24}$$

We have now determined the cost-minimizing quantity of capital. To determine the cost-minimizing quantity of labor, just substitute equation (A7.24) into equation (A7.21):

$$L = [(\beta r/\alpha w)^{\alpha/(\alpha+\beta)}](Q_0/A)^{1/(\alpha+\beta)} \tag{A7.25}$$

Note that if the wage rate w rises relative to the price of capital r, the firm will use more capital and less labor. If, say because of technological change, A increases (so the firm can produce more output with the same inputs), both K and L will fall.

We have shown how cost-minimization subject to an output constraint can be used to determine the firm's optimal mix of capital and labor. Now we will determine the firm's cost function. The total cost of producing *any output Q* can be obtained by substituting equations (A7.24) for K and (A7.25) for L into the equation $C = wL + rK$. After some algebraic manipulation we find that

$$C = [(w/\beta)^{\alpha/(\alpha+\beta)}(r/\alpha)^{\beta/(\alpha+\beta)}(1/(\alpha+\beta))][(Q/A)^{1/(\alpha+\beta)}] \tag{A7.26}$$

This *cost function* tells both how the total cost of production increases as the level of output Q increases, and also how cost changes as input prices change. When $\alpha + \beta$ equals 1, cost will increase proportionately with output, which means that the production process exhibits constant returns to scale. Likewise if $\alpha + \beta$ is greater than 1, there are decreasing returns to scale, and if $\alpha + \beta$ is less than 1, there are increasing returns to scale.

Now consider the dual problem of maximizing the output that can be produced with the expenditure of C_0 dollars. We leave it to you to work through this problem for the Cobb-Douglas production function, and show that equations (A7.24) and (A7.25) describe the cost-minimizing input choices. To get you started, note that the Lagrangian for this dual problem is $\Phi = AK^\alpha L^\beta - \mu(wL + rK - C_0)$.

Exercises

1. Of the following production functions, which exhibit increasing, constant, or decreasing returns to scale?

a. $F(K,L) = K^2L$
b. $F(K,L) = 10K + 5L$
c. $F(K,L) = (KL)^{.5}$

2. Suppose a production function is given by $F(K,L) = KL^2$, and that the price of capital is \$10 and the price of labor \$15. What combination of labor and capital minimizes the cost of producing any given output?

3. The production function for a product is given by $Q = 100KL$. If the price of capital is \$120 per day and the price of labor is \$30 per day, what is the minimum cost of producing 1000 units of output?

CHAPTER 8

Profit Maximization and Competitive Supply

The cost curves developed in the last chapter describe the minimum costs at which a firm can produce various amounts of output. With this knowledge, we can now turn to a fundamental problem that every firm faces: how much should be produced? In this chapter, we will see how a perfectly competitive firm chooses the level of output that maximizes its profit. We will also see how the output choice of individual firms leads to a supply curve for the entire industry.

Our discussion of production and cost in Chapters 6 and 7 applies to firms in all kinds of markets, but in this chapter we discuss only firms in perfectly competitive markets. In a perfectly competitive market all firms produce the identical product, and each firm is so small in relation to the industry that its production decisions have no effect on market price. New firms can easily enter the industry if they perceive a potential for profit, and existing firms can stay in business even if they start losing money.

We begin by showing how a competitive firm chooses its output in the short and long run. We then show how this output choice changes as the cost of production or the prices of the firm's inputs and output change. In this way, we show how to derive the *supply curve* for an individual competitive producer. We then aggregate the supply curves of individual firms to obtain the *industry* supply curve. In the short run, firms in an industry choose which level of output to produce to maximize profit. In the long run, firms not only make output choices, but also decide whether to be in a market at all. We will see that the prospect of high profits encourages firms to enter an industry, while losses encourage them to leave.

8.1 Do Firms Maximize Profit?

In the analysis that follows, we assume that the firm's sole objective is to maximize its profit over the long run. The assumption of profit maximization is frequently used in microeconomics because it predicts business behavior accurately and avoids unnecessary analytical complications. But whether firms do indeed maximize profit has been controversial and is worth discussing.

For smaller firms managed by their owners, profit is likely to dominate almost all the firm's decisions. In larger firms, however, managers who make day-to-day decisions usually have very little contact with the owners (i.e., the stockholders). As a result, the owners of the firm cannot monitor the managers' behavior on a regular basis. Managers then have some leeway in how they run the firm and can deviate from profit-maximizing behavior to some extent.

Managers may be more concerned with goals such as revenue maximization to achieve growth or the payment of dividends to satisfy shareholders than with profit maximization. Managers might also be overly concerned with the firm's short-run profit (perhaps to earn a promotion or a large bonus) at the expense of its longer-run profit, even though long-run profit maximization better serves the interests of the stockholders.[1] (We will discuss the implications of differences between the incentives of managers and owners of firms in greater detail in Chapter 18.)

Even so, the ability of any managers to pursue goals other than long-run profit maximization is limited. If they do, shareholders or the boards of directors can replace them, or the firm can be taken over by new management. In any case, firms that do not come close to maximizing profit are not likely to survive. Firms that do survive in competitive industries make long-run profit maximization one of their highest priorities.

Thus, our working assumption of profit maximization is sensible. Firms that have been in business for a long time are likely to care a lot about profit, whatever else their managers may appear to be doing. For example, a firm that subsidizes public television may seem public-spirited and altruistic. Yet, this beneficence is likely to be in the long-run financial interest of the firm because it generates goodwill for the firm and its products.

8.2 Demand, Average Revenue, and Marginal Revenue

Profit is the difference between revenue and cost. Thus, to determine the firm's profit-maximizing output level, we must analyze its revenues. (We analyzed its costs in Chapter 7.) Our discussion of revenues first treats the general case of a downward-sloping demand curve and then the special case of the demand curve faced by a competitive firm.

---

[1]To be more exact, maximizing the market value of the firm is a more appropriate goal than profit maximization, because value explicitly includes the stream of profits that the firm earns over time. It is the stream of profits that is of direct interest to the stockholders.

Marginal and Average Revenue

The total revenue R that a firm receives is equal to the price of the product P times the number of units sold Q:

$$R(Q) = PQ$$

Revenue is written $R(Q)$ rather than just R because revenue depends on output. *Marginal revenue* MR is the change in revenue $\Delta R(Q)$ resulting from a small increase in output ΔQ:

$$MR = \Delta R(Q)/\Delta Q$$

Finally, *average revenue* AR is the revenue per unit sold:

$$AR = R(Q)/Q$$

Table 8.1 shows the behavior of marginal and average revenue for a firm facing the following demand curve: $P = 6 - Q$. Note that average revenue is just price: $AR = R/Q = PQ/Q = P$.

For this demand curve, revenue is zero when the price is $6 because at that price nothing is sold. However, one unit is sold at a price of $5, and then revenue is $5. An increase in quantity from 1 to 2 increases revenue from $5 to $8, so that marginal revenue is $3. As quantity increases from 2 to 3, marginal revenue falls to $1, and when it increases from 3 to 4, marginal revenue becomes negative. Note that when marginal revenue is positive, revenue is increasing with quantity, but when marginal revenue is negative, revenue is decreasing.

When the demand curve is downward-sloping, the price (average revenue) is greater than marginal revenue because all units are sold at the same price. To increase sales by 1 unit, the price must fall, so that all units sold, not just the additional unit, earn less revenue. Note what happens in Table 8.1 when output is increased from 1 to 2 units and price is reduced to $4. Marginal revenue is $3: $4 (the revenue from the sale of the additional unit of output) less $1 (the loss of revenue from the sale of the first unit). Thus, marginal revenue ($3) is less than price ($4).

TABLE 8.1 Total, Marginal, and Average Revenue

Price	Quantity	Revenue	Marginal Revenue	Average Revenue
$6	0	$0	—	—
5	1	5	$5	$5
4	2	8	3	4
3	3	9	1	3
2	4	8	−1	2
1	5	5	−3	1

Figure 8.1 shows the relationship among total, average, and marginal revenue for the data in Table 8.1.[2] As we move down the demand curve, P falls and Q rises. Total revenue can increase or decrease, depending on the elasticity of demand. Demand is elastic in the upper portion of the curve (for Q less than 3), and here, marginal revenue is positive, because increasing output also increases revenue. However, demand is inelastic in the lower portion of the curve when marginal revenue is negative because increases in output (and decreases in price) reduce revenue.[3]

Algebraically, if the demand for the product is $P = 6 - Q$, then the revenue received by the firm is $PQ = 6Q - Q^2$. Average revenue is equal to $PQ/Q = 6 - Q$, which is the demand curve for the product. Marginal revenue is equal to $\Delta R(Q)/\Delta Q$, or $6 - 2Q$. You can check this with the data in Table 8.1.

The Demand Curve Facing A Competitive Firm

Because each firm in a competitive industry sells only a small fraction of the entire industry sales, *how much output the firm decides to sell will have no effect on the market price of the product.* The market price is determined by the *industry* demand and supply curves. Therefore, the competitive firm is a *price taker*: It knows that its production decision will have no effect on the price of the product. For example, when a farmer is deciding how many acres of wheat to plant in a given year, he can take the market price of wheat as given. That price will not be affected by his acreage decision.

Often, we will want to distinguish between market demand curves and the demand curves that individual firms face. When the two are used in the same analysis, market outputs Q and market demand curves D will be denoted by capital letters, and the outputs q and demand curves d of firms by lowercase letters.

Because the firm is a price taker, *the demand curve facing an individual competitive firm is given by a horizontal line.* In Figure 8.2a, the farmer's demand curve corresponds to a price of $4 per bushel of wheat. The horizontal axis measures the amount of wheat that the farmer can sell, and the vertical axis measures the

[2]If the demand curve is written so that price is a function of quantity, $P = a - bQ$, then the total revenue received PQ is given by $PQ = aQ - bQ^2$. The marginal revenue curve can be obtained using elementary calculus, because marginal revenue is the change in revenue associated with a change in quantity. Thus, marginal revenue $= d(PQ)/dQ = a - 2bQ$. In our case the marginal revenue curve is given by $MR = 6 - 2Q$. Whenever the demand curve is a straight line, the slope of the marginal revenue curve is twice the slope of the demand curve.

[3]It is easy to show the relationship between marginal revenue MR and price elasticity E_P using calculus. Because total revenue is PQ, marginal revenue is determined by calculating the change in PQ with respect to an increase in quantity: $MR = d(PQ)/dQ = P + Q(dP/dQ)$. Multiplying and dividing the last term on the right of the equal sign by P yields $MR = P + P(Q/P)(dP/dQ)$. Finally, substituting for the price elasticity yields $MR = P(1 - 1/E_P)$. When demand is price elastic, the expression on the right-hand side is positive. However, when demand is inelastic, the expression on the right-hand side is negative.

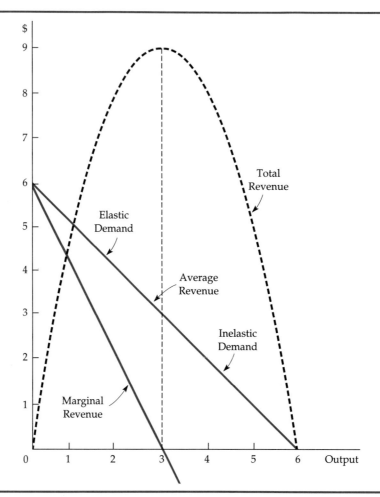

FIGURE 8.1   Marginal and Average Revenue.   A firm's demand curve describes the average revenue that the firm receives by selling its product. When the market demand for a product is downward-sloping, the marginal revenue curve also slopes downward and is below average revenue.

price. Compare the demand curve facing the firm (in this case, the farmer), designated *d* in Figure 8.2a, with the market demand curve *D* in Figure 8.2b.

The market demand curve shows how much wheat *all consumers* will buy at each possible price. The market demand curve is downward-sloping because consumers buy more wheat at a lower price. The demand curve facing the firm,

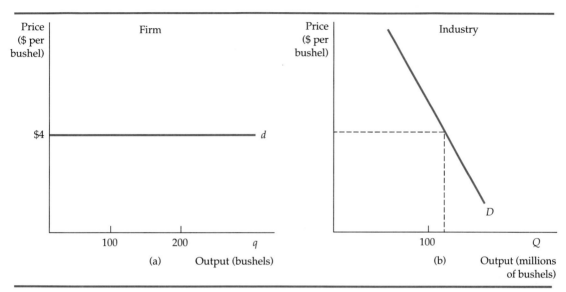

FIGURE 8.2   Demand Curve Faced by a Competitive Firm.   A competitive firm supplies only a small portion of the total output of all the firms in an industry. Therefore, the firm takes the market price of the product as given, choosing its output on the assumption that the price will be unaffected by the output choice. In part (a) the demand curve facing the firm is perfectly elastic, even though the market demand curve in part (b) is downward-sloping.

however, is horizontal because the firm's sales will have no effect on the price. Suppose the firm increased its sales from 100 to 200 bushels of wheat. This would have almost no effect on the market, because the industry output of wheat is 100 million bushels at $4 per bushel. Price is determined by the inter-action of all firms and consumers in the market, not by the output decision of a single firm.

Marginal and Average Revenue for a Competitive Firm

When an individual firm faces a horizontal demand curve, as in Figure 8.2a, then it can sell an additional unit of output without lowering price. As a result, the total revenue received increases by an amount equal to the price (one bushel of wheat sold for $4 yields additional revenue of $4 [i.e., MR $= \Delta R(q)/\Delta q = \Delta(4q)/\Delta q = 4$]). At the same time, the average revenue received by the firm is also $4, because each bushel of wheat produced will be sold at $4 (AR $= Pq/q = P = \$4$). Therefore, the demand curve d facing an individual firm in a com-petitive market is both its average revenue curve and its marginal revenue curve.

To summarize: When selling a large quantity requires a firm to lower its price, the demand curve (the average revenue curve) is downward-sloping, and the marginal revenue curve lies below the average revenue curve. When price is independent of the quantity sold (as for a perfectly competitive firm), the firm's demand, average revenue, and marginal revenue curves are all the same horizontal line.

8.3 Choosing Output in the Short Run

How should the manager of a profit-maximizing firm choose a level of output over the short run, when its plant size is fixed? Here we show how a firm can use information about revenue and cost to make a profit-maximizing output decision.

Profit Maximization

In the short run a firm operates with a fixed amount of capital and must choose the levels of its variable inputs (labor and materials) to maximize profit. Because of its importance, we will derive the profit-maximizing output level three different ways: numerically, graphically, and algebraically.

Table 8.2 shows a firm's revenue and cost information. The firm is selling its product in a competitive market at a market price of $40 per unit, regardless of the number of units it sells. Note that the firm's revenue increases proportionally with output, because average revenue (i.e., price) is constant. The fixed cost of production is $50, and total cost rises with output as Table 8.2 shows. The firm's profit π is the difference between revenue and total cost:

TABLE 8.2 A Firm's Short-run Revenues and Costs

Output (units)	Price ($/unit)	Revenue ($)	Total Cost ($)	Profit ($)	Marginal Cost ($)	Marginal Revenue ($)
0	40	0	50	−50	—	—
1	40	40	100	−60	50	40
2	40	80	128	−48	28	40
3	40	120	148	−28	20	40
4	40	160	162	−2	14	40
5	40	200	180	20	18	40
6	40	240	200	40	20	40
7	40	280	222	58	22	40
8	40	320	260	60	38	40
9	40	360	305	55	45	40
10	40	400	360	40	55	40
11	40	440	425	15	65	40

$$\pi(q) = R(q) - TC(q) \tag{8.1}$$

For low levels of output, the firm's profit is negative—revenue is insufficient to cover fixed and variable costs. As output increases, profit becomes positive and increases until output reaches 8 units. Beyond 8 units of production, profit falls, reflecting the rapid increase in the total cost of production. Observe that profit is maximized at $q^* = 8$, where MR is close to MC.

Figure 8.3 shows this graphically. Part (a) shows the revenue of the firm $R(q)$ as a straight line from the origin. Its slope is the change in revenue with respect to a change in output, which is marginal revenue. Similarly, the slope of the total cost (TC) curve is the change in cost with respect to a change in output, or marginal cost.

Part (b) shows the profit of the firm π, which is initially negative and increases to a maximum at output $q^* = 8$, and then declines. Note that when profit is maximized, the difference between R and TC (the line between A and B) is greatest (and positive). At that point the slope of the revenue curve—marginal revenue—is equal to the slope of the total cost curve—marginal cost. Thus, *profit is maximized when the marginal revenue of the firm is equal to the marginal cost of production. This condition holds for all firms, whether perfectly competitive or not.*

This condition should also be clear from Table 8.2. For all outputs up to 8, marginal revenue is greater than marginal cost. For any output up to 8, the firm should increase output further, because total profit will increase. At an output of 9, however, marginal cost becomes greater than marginal revenue, so that additional production would reduce profit rather than raise it. Table 8.2 does not show an output at which marginal revenue is exactly equal to marginal cost. It does show, however, that when $MR(q) > MC(q)$, output should be increased, and when $MR(q) < MC(q)$, it should be reduced. If the table could list output levels in small enough units, the rule that $MR(q) = MC(q)$ would hold exactly.

The same rule can be derived algebraically. Profit is

$$\pi(q) = R(q) - TC(q) \tag{8.2}$$

and is maximized at the point at which an additional increment to output just leaves profit unchanged (i.e., $\Delta\pi(q)/\Delta q = 0$):

$$\Delta\pi(q)/\Delta q = \Delta R(q)/\Delta q - \Delta TC(q)/\Delta q = 0 \tag{8.3}$$

$\Delta R(q)/\Delta q$ is the change in revenue associated with a change in output, or marginal revenue, and $\Delta TC(q)/\Delta q$ is marginal cost. Thus, we conclude that profit is maximized when[4]

$$\boxed{MR(q) = MC(q)}$$

[4]With calculus, our argument would be very similar. Whether or not the market is competitive, the firm maximizes $\pi = R(q) - TC(q)$ by choosing the level of q that satisfies the condition $d\pi/dq = dR/dq - dTC(q)/dq = 0$, or $MR(q) = MC(q)$.

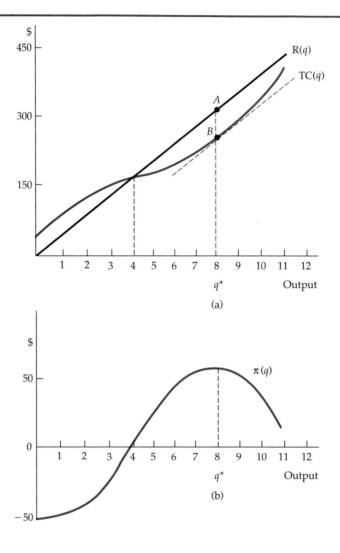

FIGURE 8.3 Profit Maximization in the Short Run.   A firm maximizes its profit at an output level at which the difference *AB* between revenues R and total costs TC is maximized. At that output level marginal revenue (the slope of the revenue curve) is equal to marginal cost (the slope of the cost curve). Part (a) shows that the profit-maximizing output is q^*, and part (b) shows that the profit curve π, which measures the difference between R and TC, reaches its peak at output q^*.

Profit Maximization by a Competitive Firm

Remember that the demand curve facing a firm in a competitive market is horizontal, so that marginal revenue and price are equal: $MR = P$. Therefore, the profit-maximization rule for the competitive firm is to choose output so that *price equals marginal cost*:

$$\text{Rule for competitive firm: } P = MC(q)$$

Note that this is a rule for setting output, not price, since competitive firms take price as fixed. However, we will see in Chapter 10 that the rule is a useful benchmark when we compare a noncompetitive firm's price with what the price would be if the market were competitive. The rule can also help regulators decide what prices to set when they are regulating noncompetitive firms.

The marginal revenue and marginal cost curves in Figure 8.4 also show this rule for profit maximization. The average and marginal revenue curves are drawn as horizontal lines at a price equal to $40. In this figure, we have drawn the average cost curve AC, the average variable cost curve AVC, and the marginal cost curve MC so that we can see the firm's profit more easily.

Profit is maximized at point A, associated with an output $q^* = 8$ and a price of $40, because marginal revenue is equal to marginal cost at this point. At a lower output, say, $q_1 = 7$, marginal revenue is greater than marginal cost, so profit could be increased by increasing output. The shaded area between $q_1 = 7$ and q^* shows the lost profit associated with producing at q_1. At a higher output, say, q_2, marginal cost is greater than marginal revenue; thus, reducing output saves a cost that exceeds the reduction in revenue. The shaded area between q^* and $q_2 = 9$ shows the lost profit associated with producing at q_2.

The MR and MC curves cross at an output of q_0 as well as q^*. At q_0, however, profit is clearly not maximized. An increase in output beyond q_0 increases profit because marginal cost is well below marginal revenue. So the condition for profit maximization is that *marginal revenue equals marginal cost at a point at which the marginal cost curve is rising rather than falling*.

The Short-Run Profitability of a Competitive Firm

Figure 8.4 also shows the competitive firm's short-run profit. The distance AB is the difference between price and average cost at the output level q^*, which is the average profit per unit of output. Segment BC measures the total number of units produced. Therefore, rectangle $ABCD$ is the firm's total profit.

A firm need not always earn a profit in the short run, as Figure 8.5 shows. One major change from Figure 8.4 is the increased fixed cost of production. This raises average total cost but does not change the average variable cost and marginal cost curves. At the profit-maximizing output q^*, the price P is less than

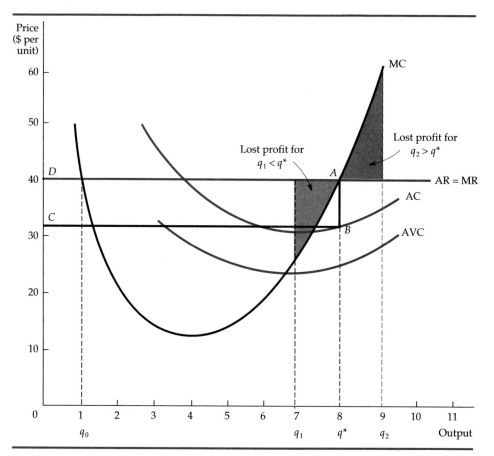

FIGURE 8.4 A Competitive Firm Making Positive Profit. In the short run the competitive firm maximizes its profit by choosing an output q^* at which its marginal cost MC is equal to the price P (or marginal revenue MR) of its product. The profit of the firm is measured by the rectangle $ABCD$. Any lower output q_1, or higher output q_2, will lead to lower profit.

average cost, so that line segment AB measures the average *loss* from production. Likewise, the shaded rectangle $ABCD$ now measures the firm's loss.

Why doesn't a firm that earns a loss leave the industry entirely? A firm might operate at a loss *in the short run* because it expects to earn a profit in the future as the price of its product increases or the costs of production fall. In fact, a firm has two choices in the short run; it can produce some output, or it can shut down its production temporarily. It will choose the more profitable (or the less unprofitable) of the two alternatives. In particular, a firm will find it profitable to shut down (produce no output) when the price of its product is less than the minimum average variable cost. In this situation, revenues from production will not cover variable costs, and losses will increase.

Figure 8.5 illustrates the case in which some production is appropriate. The output q^* is at the point where short-run losses are minimized. It is cheaper in this case to operate at q^* rather than to produce no output, because price exceeds average variable cost at q^*. Each unit produced yields more revenue than cost, thereby generating higher profit than if the firm were to produce nothing. (Total profit is still negative, however, because *fixed costs* are high.) Line segment *AE* measures the difference between price and average variable cost, and rectangle *AEFD* measures the additional profit that can be earned by producing at q^* rather than at 0.

To see this another way, recall that the difference between average cost AC and average variable cost AVC is average fixed cost AFC. Therefore, in Figure 8.5, line segment *BE* represents the average fixed cost, and rectangle *CBEF* represents the total fixed cost of production. When the firm produces no output, its loss is equal to its total fixed cost *CBEF*. But when it produces at q^*, its loss

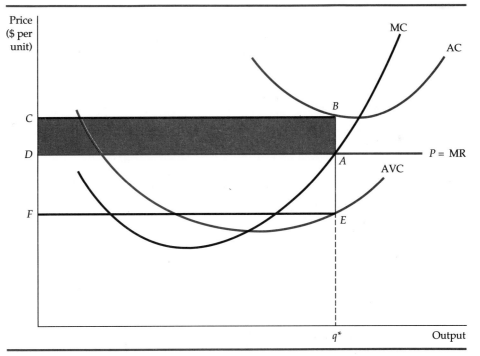

FIGURE 8.5 A Competitive Firm Incurring Losses. In the short run a competitive firm may produce at a loss, if it can still generate revenues that more than cover its variable costs. The firm minimizes its losses by producing at q^*, with losses *ABCD*. If the firm were to shut down, it would incur even greater losses equal to the fixed costs of production *CBEF*.

is reduced to the rectangle *ABCD*. Fixed costs, which are irrelevant to the firm's production decision in the short run, are crucial when determining whether the firm ought to leave the industry in the long run.

To summarize: The competitive firm produces no output if price is less than minimum average variable cost. When it does produce, it maximizes profit by choosing the output level at which price is equal to marginal cost. At this output level, profit is positive if price is greater than average total cost. The firm may operate at a loss in the short run. However, if it expects to continue to lose money over the long run, it will go out of business.

EXAMPLE 8.1 SOME COST CONSIDERATIONS FOR MANAGERS

The application of the rule that marginal revenue should equal marginal cost depends on the manager's ability to estimate marginal cost.[5] To obtain useful measures of cost, managers should keep three guidelines in mind.

First, *avoid the use of average variable cost as a proxy or substitute for marginal cost.* When marginal and average costs are nearly constant, there is little difference between them. However, when marginal and average costs are increasing sharply, the use of average variable cost can be very misleading when deciding how much to produce. Suppose, for example, that a company has the following cost information:

Current output: 100 units per day, of which 25 units are produced during overtime
Materials cost: $500 per day
Labor cost: $2000 per day (regular) plus $1000 per day (overtime)

Average variable cost is easily calculated—it is the labor and materials cost ($3500) divided by the 100 units per day, or $35 per unit. But the appropriate cost is marginal cost, which could be calculated as follows: Materials cost per unit is likely to be constant whatever the output level, so that marginal materials cost is $500/100 = $5 per unit. Since the marginal cost of labor is likely to involve overtime work only, it is obtained by noting that 25 of the 100 units were produced during the overtime period. The average overtime pay per unit of production, $1000/25 = $40 per unit, provides a good estimate of the marginal cost of labor. Therefore, the marginal cost of producing an additional unit of output is $45 per unit (the marginal materials cost plus the marginal labor cost), substantially greater than the average variable cost of $35. If the manager relied on average variable cost, too much output would be produced.

Second, *a single item on a firm's accounting ledger may have two components, only one of which involves marginal costs.* Suppose, for example, that a manager is trying to cut back production. She reduces the number of hours that some employees

---

[5]This example draws on the discussion of costs and managerial decision making in Thomas Nagle, *The Strategy and Tactics of Pricing* (Englewood Cliffs, N.J.: Prentice-Hall, 1987), chapter 2.

work and lays off others. But the salary of an employee who is laid off may not be an accurate measure of the marginal cost of production when cuts are made, because union contracts often require the firm to pay laid-off employees part of their salary. In this case, the marginal cost of increasing production is not the same as the savings in marginal cost when production is decreased. The savings in cost when production is decreased is the labor cost after the required layoff salary has been subtracted.

Third, *all opportunity costs must be included in determining marginal cost*. Suppose a department store wants to sell children's furniture. Instead of building a new selling area, the manager decides to use part of the third floor, which had been used for applicances, for the furniture. The marginal cost of this space is the profit that would have been earned had the store continued to sell appliances there, per unit of furniture sold. This opportunity cost measure may be substantially greater than what the store actually paid for that part of the building.

These three guidelines can help a manager to measure marginal cost correctly. Failure to do so can cause production to be too high or too low, and thereby reduce profit.

8.4   The Competitive Firm's Short-Run Supply Curve

A *supply curve* for a firm tells us how much output it will produce at every possible price. We have seen that firms will increase output to the point at which price is equal to marginal cost, but they will shut down if price is below average variable cost. Therefore, for positive output the firm's supply curve is the portion of the marginal cost curve that lies above the average variable cost curve. Since the marginal cost curve cuts the average variable cost curve at its minimum point (recall our discussion in Chapter 7 of marginal and average cost), *the firm's supply curve is its marginal cost curve above the point of minimum average variable cost*. For any P greater than minimum AVC, the profit-maximizing output can be read directly from the graph. At a price P_1 in Figure 8.6, for example, the quantity supplied will be q_1, and at P_2 it will be q_2. For P less than (or equal to) minimum AVC, the profit-maximizing output is equal to zero. In Figure 8.6 the entire supply curve is the cross-hatched portion of the vertical axis and the marginal cost curve.

Short-run supply curves for competitive firms slope upwards for the same reason that marginal costs increase—the presence of diminishing returns to one or more factors of production. As a result, an increase in the market price will induce those firms already in the market to increase the quantitites they produce. The higher price makes the additional production profitable and also increases the firm's *total* profit, because it applies to all units that the firm produces.

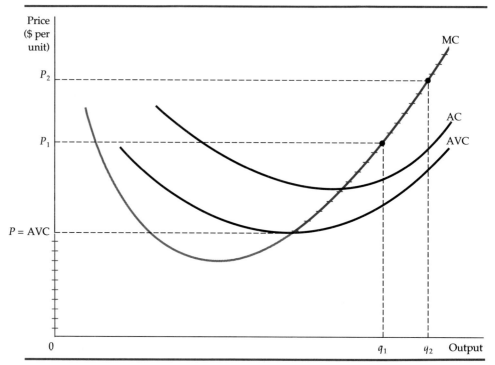

FIGURE 8.6 The Short-Run Supply Curve of a Competitive Firm. In the short run the firm chooses its output so that marginal cost MC is equal to price, so long as it covers its variable costs of production. The short-run supply curve is given by the cross-hatched portion of the marginal cost curve.

The Firm's Response to an Input Price Change

When the price of a product changes, the firm changes its output level, so that the marginal cost of production remains equal to the price. Often, however, output price changes at the same time that the prices of *inputs* change. In this section we show how the firm's output decision changes in response to a change in the prices of one of the firm's inputs.

Figure 8.7 shows a firm's marginal cost curve that is initially given by MC_1 when the firm faces a price of $5 for its product. The firm maximizes its profit by producing an output of q_1. Now suppose the price of one of the firm's inputs increases. This causes the marginal cost curve to shift upward from MC_1 to MC_2, because it now costs more to produce each unit of output. The new profit-maximizing output is q_2, at which $P = MC_2$. Thus, the higher input price causes the firm to reduce its output.

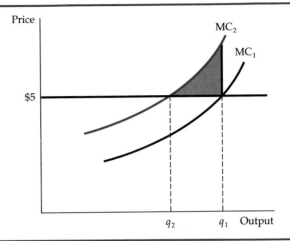

FIGURE 8.7 The Response of a Firm to a Change in Input Price. When the marginal cost of production for a firm increases (from MC_1 to MC_2), the level of output that maximizes profit falls (from q_1 to q_2).

If the firm had continued to produce at q_1, it would have incurred a loss on the last unit of production. In fact, all production beyond q_2 reduces profit. The shaded area in the figure gives the total savings to the firm (or equivalently, the reduction in lost profit) associated with the reduction in output from q_1 to q_2.

EXAMPLE 8.2 THE SHORT-RUN PRODUCTION OF PETROLEUM PRODUCTS

Suppose you are managing an oil refinery and (to simplify) you have decided to produce a particular combination of refinery products, including gasoline, jet fuel, and residual fuel oil for home heating. A substantial amount of crude oil is available, but the amount of product that you refine depends on the capacity of the refinery and the cost of production. How much of the product mix should you refine each day?[6]

Information about the marginal cost of production of the refinery is essential to making a sound decision. Figure 8.8 shows the marginal cost curve for short-run production (SMC). The marginal cost of production increases with output, but in a series of uneven segments rather than as a smooth curve. The increase

---

[6]This example is based on James M. Griffin, "The Process Analysis Alternative to Statistical Cost Functions: An Application to Petroleum Refining," *American Economic Review* 62 (1972): 46–56. The numbers have been updated and applied to a particular refinery.

is in segments because the refinery uses different processing units to turn crude oil into finished products. When a particular processing unit reaches capacity, output can be increased only by substituting a more expensive process. For example, gasoline can be produced from light crude oils rather inexpensively in a processing unit called a "thermal cracker." When this unit becomes full, additional gasoline can still be produced (from heavy as well as light crude oil) but at a higher cost. In Figure 8.8 the first capacity constraint comes into effect when production reaches about 9700 barrels a day. A second capacity constraint becomes important when production increases beyond 10,700 barrels a day.

Deciding how much output to produce now becomes relatively easy. Suppose the mix of refined products can be sold for $23 per barrel. Since the marginal cost of production is close to $24 for the first unit of output, at a price of $23 no crude oil should be run through the refinery. If, however, the price of the

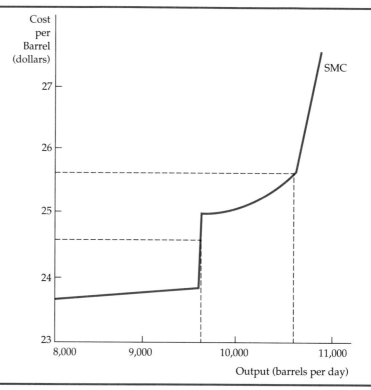

FIGURE 8.8 The Short-Run Production of Petroleum Products. The marginal cost of producing a mix of petroleum products from crude oil increases sharply at several levels of output as the refinery shifts from one processing unit to another. As a result, the output level can be insensitive to some changes in price and very sensitive to others.

product mix is between $24 and $25, you should produce 9700 barrels a day (filling the thermal cracker). Finally, if the price is above $25, you should use the more expensive refining unit and expand production toward 10,700 barrels a day.

Because the cost function rises in steps, you know that your production decisions need not change much in response to small changes in the price of the product. You will typically utilize sufficient crude oil to fill the appropriate processing unit until price increases (or decreases) substantially. Then you need simply calculate whether the increased price warrants using an additional, more expensive processing unit.

8.5   The Short-Run Market Supply Curve

The *short-run market supply curve* shows the amount of output that the industry will produce in the short run for every possible price. The industry's output is the sum of the quantities supplied by all the individual firms. Therefore, the market supply curve can be obtained by adding their supply curves. Figure 8.9 shows how this is done when there are only three firms, all of which have different short-run production costs. Each firm's marginal cost curve is drawn only for the portion that lies above its average variable cost curve. (We have shown only three firms to keep the graph simple, but the same analysis applies when there are many firms.)

At any price below P_1, the industry will produce no output, because P_1 is the minimum average variable cost of the lowest-cost firm. Between P_1 and P_2, only firm 3 will produce, so the industry supply curve will be identical to that portion of firm 3's marginal cost curve MC_3. At price P_2, the industry supply will be the sum of the quantity supplied by all three firms. Firm 1 supplies 2 units, firm 2 supplies 5 units, and firm 3 supplies 8 units; thus, industry supply is 15 units. At price P_3, firm 1 supplies 4 units, firm 2 supplies 7 units, and firm 3 supplies 10 units; in total the industry supplies 21 units. Note that the industry supply curve is upward-sloping but has a kink at price P_2. With many firms in the market, however, the kink becomes unimportant, so we usually draw industry supply curves as smooth, upward-sloping curves.

Finding the industry supply curve is not always as simple as adding up a set of firm supply curves. As price rises, all firms in the industry expand their output. This additional output increases the demand for inputs to production and may lead to higher input prices. As we saw in Figure 8.7, increasing input prices shifts the firms' marginal cost curves upward. For example, an increased demand for beef could also increase demand for corn and soybeans (which are used to feed cattle), and thereby cause the prices of these crops to rise. In turn, the higher input prices would cause beef firms' marginal cost curves to shift

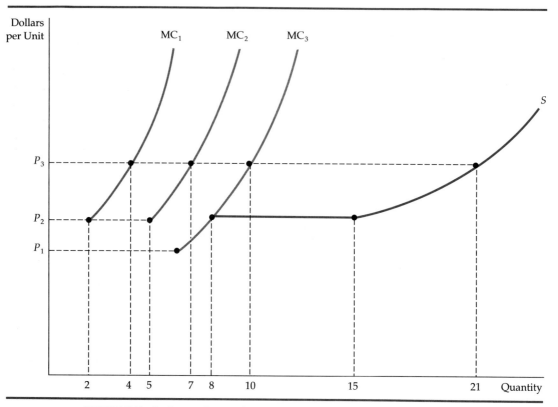

FIGURE 8.9   Industry Supply in the Short Run.   The short-run industry supply curve is the horizontal summation of the supply curves of the individual firms. Because the third firm has a lower average variable cost curve than the first two firms, the market supply curve S begins at price P_1 and follows the marginal cost curve of the third firm MC_3 until price equals P_2, where there is a kink. For all prices above P_2, the industry supply curve is the sum of the quantity supplied by each of the three firms.

upward. This lowers each firm's output choice (for any given market price) and causes the industry supply curve to be less responsive to changes in output price than it would otherwise be.

Elasticity of Market Supply

The price elasticity of market supply measures the sensitivity of industry output to market price. Recall from Chapter 2 that the elasticity of supply E_S is the percentage change in quantity supplied Q in response to a 1 percent change in price P:

$$E_S = (\Delta Q/Q)/(\Delta P/P)$$

Because marginal cost curves are upward-sloping, the short-run elasticity of supply is always positive. When marginal costs increase rapidly in response to increases in output, the elasticity of supply is low. Firms are then capacity-constrained and find it costly to increase output. However, when marginal costs increase slowly in response to increases in output, supply is relatively elastic, and a small price increase induces firms to produce substantially more output.

At one extreme is the case of *perfectly inelastic supply*, which arises when the industry's plant and equipment are so fully utilized that new plants must be built (as they will be in the long run) to achieve greater output. At the other extreme is the case of *perfectly elastic supply*, which arises when marginal costs are constant. This might apply, for example, to taxi service in an unregulated market. People can always buy another cab and hire a driver at the same cost, no matter how many cabs are in the market.

EXAMPLE 8.3 THE SHORT-RUN WORLD SUPPLY OF COPPER

In the short run the shape of the markets supply curve for a mineral such as copper depends on how the cost of mining varies within and among the world's major producers. Costs of mining, smelting, and refining copper differ because of differences in labor and transportation costs and differences in the copper content of the ore. Table 8.3 summarizes some of the relevant cost and production data for the largest copper-producing nations.[7]

These data can be used to plot the world supply curve for copper. The supply curve is a short-run curve because it takes the existing mines as fixed. Figure 8.10 shows how this curve is constructed for the six countries listed in the table. The complete world supply curve would, of course, incorporate data for all copper-producing countries. Also, note that the curve in Figure 8.10 is an ap-

TABLE 8.3 The World Copper Industry (1985)

Country	Annual Production (thousand metric tons)	Marginal Cost (dollars per pound)
Canada	724.4	.88
Chile	1356.4	.58
Peru	397.2	.79
United States	1007.3	.68
Zaire	560.0	.49
Zambia	363.0	.54

[7]The USSR is excluded because of data limitations. The source is the U.S. Department of the Interior, Bureau of Mines, *Minerals Yearbook*, 1985, Tables 4 and 31. For further information on the world copper industry, see Ferdinand E. Banks, *The World Copper Market: An Economic Analysis* (Cambridge, Mass.: Ballinger, 1974).

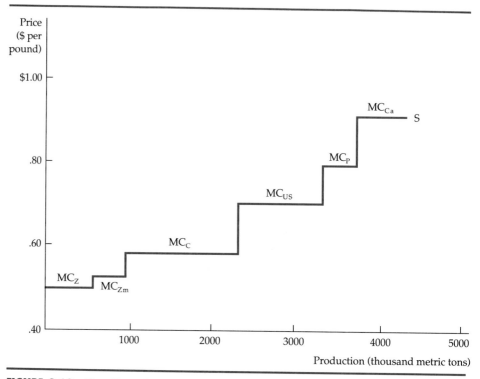

FIGURE 8.10   The Short-Run World Supply of Copper. The supply curve for world copper is obtained by summing the marginal cost curves for each of the major copper-producing countries. The supply curve slopes upward because the marginal cost of production ranges from a low of 49 cents per pound in Zaire to a high of 88 cents per pound in Canada.

proximation. The marginal cost number for each country is an average for all copper producers in that country. In the United States, for example, some producers had a marginal cost greater than $0.68, and some less than $0.68.

The lowest-cost copper is mined in Zaire, where the marginal cost of refined copper was about 49 cents per pound.[8] Curve MC_Z describes this marginal cost curve. The curve is horizontal until Zaire's capacity to mine copper is reached. Curve MC_{Zm} describes Zambia's supply curve (marginal cost is 54 cents per pound). Likewise, curves MC_C, MC_{US}, MC_P, and MC_{Ca} represent the marginal cost curves for Chile, the United States, Peru, and Canada, respectively.

The world supply curve, denoted S, is obtained by summing each nation's supply curve horizontally. The slope and the elasticity of the supply curve depend on the price of copper. At relatively low prices, such as 60 to 75 cents

[8]We are presuming that marginal and average costs of production are approximately the same.

per pound, the supply curve is quite elastic, because small price increases lead to substantial increases in refined copper. But for higher prices, say, above $1.00 per pound, the supply curve becomes quite inelastic because at such prices all producers would be operating at capacity.

Producer Surplus in the Short Run

In Chapter 4 we measured consumer surplus as the difference between the maximum that a person would pay for an item and its market price. The price of the good represents the person's opportunity cost of consuming that good. An analogous concept applies to firms. If marginal cost is rising, the price of the product is greater than marginal cost for every unit produced except the last one. As a result, the firm earns a surplus on all but the last unit of output. The *producer surplus* of a firm is the sum over all units of production of the

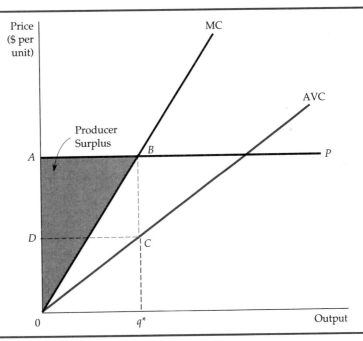

FIGURE 8.11   Producer Surplus for a Firm.   The producer surplus for a firm is measured by the shaded area below the market price and above the marginal cost curve, between outputs 0 and q^*, the profit-maximizing output. Alternatively, it is equal to rectangle *ABCD*, because the sum of all marginal costs up to q^* is equal to the variable costs of producing q^*.

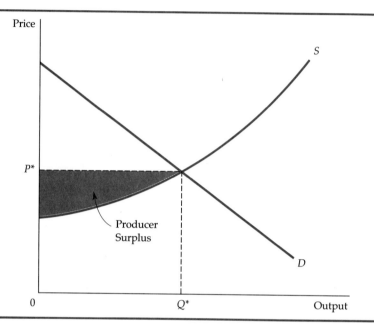

FIGURE 8.12 Producer Surplus in an Industry. The producer surplus for an industry is the area below the market price line and above the market supply curve, between 0 and output Q^*.

difference between the market price of the good and the marginal cost of production.

Figure 8.11 illustrates producer surplus for a firm that has increasing marginal and average variable costs. The profit-maximizing output q^* occurs when $P = MC$. Producer surplus is given by the shaded area under the firm's horizontal demand curve and above its marginal cost curve, from zero output to the profit-maximizing output q^*.

The sum of the marginal costs of producing all levels of output up to q^* is equal to the sum of the variable costs of producing q^*. Marginal costs reflect increments to costs associated with increases in output; since fixed costs do not vary with output, the sum of all marginal costs must equal the sum of the firm's variable costs. Thus, producer surplus can alternatively be defined as the difference between the firm's revenue and its total variable costs. In Figure 8.11, producer surplus is also given by the rectangle $ABCD$.

The extent to which firms enjoy producer surplus depends on their costs of production. Higher-cost firms have lower amounts of producer surplus, and vice versa. We can sum up all these individual effects by applying the concept of producer surplus to market supply. In Figure 8.12 the market supply curve begins at the vertical axis at a point that represents the average variable cost of the lowest-cost firm in the industry. Producer surplus is the area that lies below the market price of the product and above the supply curve between the output levels 0 and Q^*.

Producer surplus is measured by the difference between revenues and *variable* costs. Producer surplus will be greater than economic profit to the extent that the firm has incurred any fixed costs, or more generally to the extent that the firm has any opportunity costs associated with production that do not involve explicit outlays. We will describe the difference between producer surplus and profit in more detail after we analyze the firm's output decision in the long run.

8.6 Choosing Output in the Long Run

In the long run a firm can alter all its inputs, including the size of the plant. It can decide to shut down (i.e., to *exit* the industry) or to begin to produce a product for the first time (i.e., to *enter* an industry). Because we are concerned here with competitive markets, we allow for *free entry* and *free exit*. In other

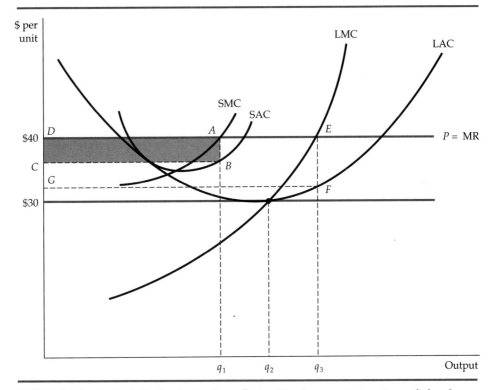

FIGURE 8.13 Output Choice in the Long Run. The firm maximizes its profit by choosing the output at which price is equal to long-run marginal cost LMC. In the diagram, the firm increases its profit from *ABCD* to *EFGD* by increasing its output in the long run.

words, we are assuming that firms may enter or exit without any legal restriction or any entry cost apart from the direct costs of production and investment in new capital.

Figure 8.13 shows how a competitive firm makes its long-run, profit-maximizing output decision. As in the short run, it faces a horizontal demand curve. (In Figure 8.13 the firm takes the market price of $40 as given.) Its short-run average (total) cost curve SAC and short-run marginal cost curve SMC are low enough for the firm to make a positive profit, given by rectangle $ABCD$, by producing an output of q_1, where SMC = MR. The long-run average cost curve LAC reflects the presence of increasing returns to scale up to output level q_2 and decreasing returns to scale at higher output levels. The long-run marginal cost curve LMC cuts the long-run average cost from below at q_2, the point of minimum long-run average cost.

If the firm believes the market price will remain at $40, it will want to increase the size of its plant to produce an output q_3 at which its *long-run* marginal cost is equal to the $40 price. When this expansion is complete, the firm's profit margin will increase from AB to EF, and its total profit will increase from $ABCD$ to $EFGD$. Output q_3 is profit-maximizing for the firm because at any lower output, say, q_2, the marginal revenue from additional production is greater than the marginal cost, so expansion is desirable. But at any output greater than q_3, marginal cost is greater than marginal revenue, so additional production would reduce profit. In summary, *the long-run output of a profit maximizing competitive firm is where long-run marginal cost is equal to price.*

Note that the higher the market price, the higher the profit that the firm can earn. Correspondingly, as the price of the product falls from $40 to $30, so does the profit of the firm. At a price of $30, the firm's profit-maximizing output is q_2, the point of long-run minimum average cost. In this case the firm earns zero economic profit. As we show below, this means that investors in the firm earn a competitive return on their investment.

Zero Profit

As we saw in Chapter 7, it is important to distinguish between accounting profit and economic profit. Accounting profit is measured by the difference between the firm's revenues and costs, including actual outlays and depreciation expenses. Economic profit takes account of opportunity costs. One such opportunity cost is the return that the owners of the firm could make if their capital were invested elsewhere.

A firm earning a negative economic profit should consider going out of business if it does not expect to improve its financial picture. However, a firm that earns zero economic profit need not go out of business, because zero profit means the firm is earning a reasonable return on its investment. Of course, investors would like to earn a positive economic profit—that is what encourages entrepreneurs to develop and commercialize new ideas. But in competitive markets, as we will see, economic profit tends toward zero. This tendency signifies not that the firms in the industry are performing poorly, but that the industry is competitive.

Long-Run Competitive Equilibrium

Figure 8.13 shows how a $40 price induces a firm to increase its output and gives the firm a positive profit. Because profit is calculated net of the opportunity cost of investment, a positive profit means an unusually high return on investment. This high return causes investors to direct resources away from other industries and into this one—there will be *entry* into the market. Eventually the increased production associated with new entry causes the market supply curve to shift to the right, so that market output increases and the market price of the product falls. Figure 8.14 illustrates this. In part (b) of the figure, the supply curve has shifted from S_1 to S_2, causing the price to fall from P_1 ($40) to P_2 ($30).

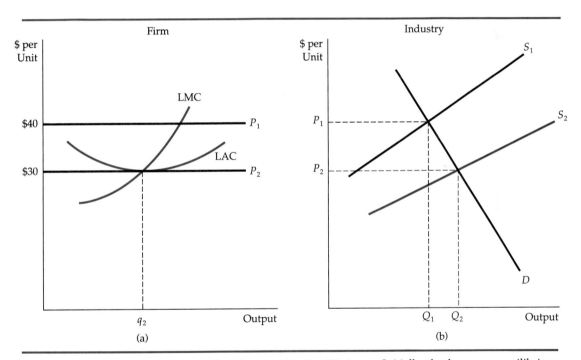

FIGURE 8.14 Long-Run Competitive Equilibrium. Initially the long-run equilibrium price of a product is $40 per unit, as shown in part (b) as the intersection of demand curve D and supply curve S_1. Part (a) shows that firms earn a positive profit, because their long-run average cost reaches a minimum of $30 (at q_1). This positive profit encourages entry of new firms and causes a shift to the right in the supply curve to S_2. The long-run equilibrium occurs at a price of $30, because the firm earns zero profit, and there is no incentive to enter or exit the industry.

In part (a), which applies to a single firm, the long-run average cost curve is tangent to the horizontal price line at output q_2.

When a firm earns zero profit, it has no incentive to exit the industry, and other firms have no special incentive to enter. A *long-run competitive equilibrium* occurs when three conditions hold. First, all firms in the industry are maximizing profit. Second, no firm has an incentive either to enter or exit the industry, because all firms in the industry are earning zero economic profit. Third, the price of the product is such that the quantity supplied by the industry is equal to the quantity demanded by consumers.

A puzzle is associated with the dynamic process that leads to long-run equilibrium. Firms enter the market because of the opportunity to earn positive profit, and they exit because of losses. Yet, in long-run equilibrium, firms earn zero profit. Why do firms exit or enter if they know that eventually they will be no better or worse off than if they do nothing? The answer is it can take a long time to reach a long-run equilibrium, and a substantial profit (or loss) can be made in the short run. The first firm to enter a profitable industry can earn much more short-run profit for its investors than can firms that enter later. Similarly, the first firm to exit an unprofitable industry can save its investors lots of money. Thus, the concept of long-run equilibrium tells us the *direction* that firms' behavior is likely to take. The idea of an eventual zero-profit, long-run equilibrium should not discourage a manager whose reward depends on the short-run profit that the firm earns.

To see why all the conditions for long-run equilibrium must hold, assume that all firms have identical costs, and consider what happens if too many firms enter the industry in response to an opportunity for profit. Then the supply curve in Figure 8.14b will shift further to the right, and price will fall below $30, say, to $25. At that price, however, firms will lose money. As a result, some firms will exit the industry. Firms will continue to exit until the market supply curve shifts back to S_2. Only when there is no incentive to exit or enter the industry can a market be in long-run equilibrium.

Now suppose that all firms in the industry do not have identical cost curves. One firm has a patent or new idea that lets it produce at a lower average cost than all other firms. Then, it is consistent with long-run equilibrium for that firm to be earning a positive *accounting* profit (and to enjoy a higher producer surplus than other firms). As long as other investors and firms cannot acquire the patent or idea that lowers costs, they have no incentive to enter the industry. And as long as the process is particular to this product and this industry, the fortunate firm has no incentive to exit the industry. The distinction between accounting profit and economic profit is important here. If the new idea or invention is profitable, other firms in the industry will pay to use that idea. (Or they might attempt to buy the entire firm to acquire the idea.) The increased value of the patent thus represents an opportunity cost to the firm—it could sell the rights to the patent rather than use it. If all firms are equally efficient otherwise, once this opportunity cost is accounted for, the *economic* profit of the firm falls to zero.[9]

There are other instances in which firms earning positive accounting profit may be earning zero economic profit. Suppose, for example, that a clothing store happens to be located near a large shopping center. The additional flow of customers may substantially increase the store's accounting profit because the cost of the land is based on its historical cost. However, as far as economic profit is concerned, the cost of the land should reflect its opportunity cost, which in this case is its current market value. When the opportunity cost of land is included, the profitability of the clothing store is no higher than that of its competitors.

Thus, the condition that economic profit be zero is essential for the market to be in a long-run equilibrium. Positive economic profit, by definition, represents an opportunity for investors and an incentive to enter the industry. Positive accounting profit, however, may signal that firms already in the industry possess valuable assets, skills, or ideas, and this will not necessarily encourage entry by other firms.

Economic Rent

Some firms earn higher accounting profit than other firms because they have access to factors of production that are in limited supply; these might include land and natural resources, entrepreneurial skill, or other creative talent. What makes economic profit zero in these situations is the willingness of other firms to buy or rent the factors of production that are in limited supply. Economic *rent* is the difference between what firms are willing to pay for an input to production in a competitive market less the minimum amount necessary to buy that input. Since rent represents the excess of accounting profit over opportunity cost, rent is generally *not* equal to zero.

For an example, suppose that two firms in an industry own their land outright; the minimum cost of obtaining the land is zero. One firm is located on a river and can ship its products for $10,000 a year less than the other firm, which is inland. Then, the $10,000 higher profit of the first firm is due to the $10,000 per year economic rent associated with its river location. The rent is created because the land along the river is valuable, and other firms would be willing to pay for it. Eventually, the competition for this specialized factor of production will increase its value to $10,000. Land rent—the difference between $10,000 and the zero cost of obtaining the land—is also $10,000. Note that while the economic rent has increased, the economic profit of the firm on the river has become zero.

[9]If the firm with the patent is more efficient than other firms, then it will be earning a positive profit. But if the patent holder is less efficient, it should sell off the patent and go out of business.

The zero economic profit tells the firm located on the river that it should remain in the industry only if it is at least as efficient in production as other firms. It also tells possible entrants to the industry that entry will be profitable only if they can produce more efficiently than firms already producing.

Producer Surplus in the Long Run

When a firm is earning a positive accounting profit but there is no incentive for other firms to enter or exit the industry, this profit must reflect economic rent. Recall that producer surplus measures the difference between the market price a producer receives and the marginal cost of production. Thus, in the long run (in a competitive market) *the producer surplus that a firm earns consists of the economic rent that it enjoys.*

Suppose, for example, that a baseball team has a franchise, which makes it the only team in a particular city. The team will earn a substantial accounting

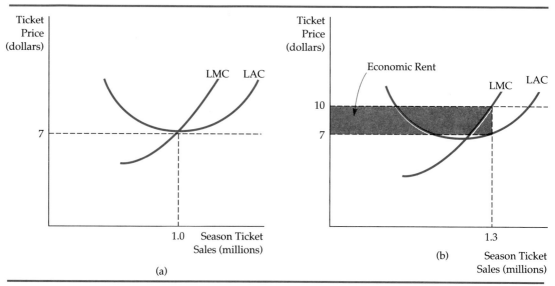

FIGURE 8.15   Firms Earn Zero Profit in Long-Run Equilibrium.   In long-run equilibrium all firms earn zero economic profit. In part (a) a baseball team in a city with other competitive sports teams sells enough tickets, so that price ($7) is equal to marginal and average cost. In part (b) there are no other competitors, so a $10 price can be charged. The team increases its sales to the point at which the average cost of production plus the average economic rent is equal to the ticket price. When the opportunity cost associated with owning the franchise is taken into account, the team earns zero economic profit.

profit. This profit will include some economic rent because the team is more valuable with the franchise than it would be if entry into the local baseball market were unrestricted. The producer surplus earned by the baseball team would include its economic profit and the rent that reflects the difference between the current value of the team and what its value would be if an unlimited number of franchises were available.

Figure 8.15 shows that firms that earn economic rent earn the same economic profit as firms that do not earn rent. Part (a) shows the economic profit of a baseball team located in a city with several competing teams. The average price of a ticket is $7, and costs are such that the team earns zero economic profit. Part (b) shows the profit of a team with the same costs, but in a city with no competing teams. Because it is the only team in town, it can sell tickets for $10 apiece, and thereby earn an accounting profit of close to $3 on each ticket. However, the rent associated with the desirable location represents a cost to the firm—an opportunity cost—because it could sell its franchise to another team. As a result, the economic profit in the city without competition is also zero.

8.7 The Industry's Long-Run Supply Curve

In our analysis of short-run supply, we first derived the firm's supply curve and then showed how the horizontal summation of individual firms' supply curves generated a market supply curve. We cannot analyze long-run supply in the same way, however, because in the long run firms enter and exit the market as the market price changes. This makes it impossible to sum up supply curves—we don't know which firms' supplies to add.

To determine long-run supply, we assume all firms have access to the available production technology. Output is increased by using more inputs, not by invention. We also assume, for simplicity, that the conditions underlying the market for inputs to production do not change when the industry expands or contracts. For example, an increased demand for labor does not increase a union's ability to negotiate a better wage contract for its workers.

The shape of the long-run supply curve depends on the extent to which increases and decreases in industry output affect the prices that the firms must pay for inputs into the production process. It is thus useful to distinguish among three types of industries: constant-cost, increasing-cost, and decreasing-cost.

Constant-Cost Industry

Figure 8.16a and 8.16b show the derivation of the long-run supply curve for a constant-cost industry. Assume that the industry is initially in long-run equilibrium at the intersection of market demand curve D_1 and market supply curve

S_1, in part (b) of the figure. Point A at the intersection of demand and supply is on the long-run supply curve S_L, because it tells us that the industry will produce Q_1 units of output when the long-run equilibrium price is P_1.

To obtain other points on the long-run supply curve, suppose the market demand for the product unexpectedly increases, say, because of a tax cut. A typical firm is initially producing at an output of q_1, where P_1 is equal to long-run marginal cost and long-run average cost. But the firm is also in short-run equilibrium, so that price also equals short-run marginal cost. Suppose that the tax cut shifts the market demand curve from D_1 to D_2. Demand curve D_2 intersects supply curve S_1 at C. As a result, the price increases from P_1 to P_2.

Part (a) shows how this price increase affects a typical firm in the industry. When the price increases to P_2, the firm follows its short-run marginal cost curve and increases its output to q_2. This output choice maximizes profit because it satisfies the condition that price equal short-run marginal cost. If every firm responds this way, each firm will be earning a positive profit in short-run equilibrium. This profit will be attractive to investors and will cause existing firms to expand their operations and new firms to enter the market.

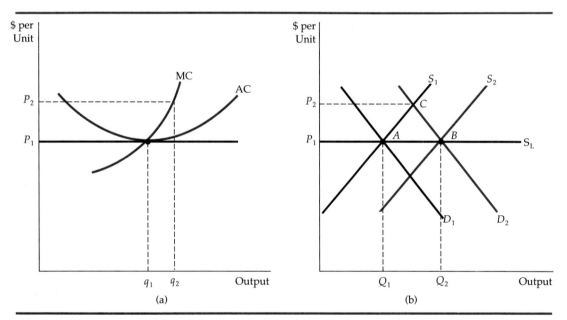

FIGURE 8.16   Long-Run Supply in a Constant-Cost Industry.   In (b) the long-run supply curve in a constant-cost industry is a horizontal line S_L. When demand increases, initially causing a price rise, the firm initially increases its output from q_1 to q_2 in (a). But, the entry of new firms causes a shift to the right in supply. Because input prices are unaffected by the increased output of the industry, entry occurs until the original price is obtained.

Thus, the total output of the industry will increase. Thus, in Figure 8.16b the short-run supply curve shifts to the right, from S_1 to S_2. This shift causes the market to move to a new long-run equilibrium at the intersection of D_2 and S_2. For this intersection to be a long-run equilibrium, output must expand just enough so that firms are earning zero profit, and the incentive to enter or exit the industry disappears.

In a constant-cost industry the additional inputs necessary to produce the higher output can be purchased without an increase in the per unit price. This might happen, for example, if unskilled labor is a major input in production, and the market wage of unskilled labor is unaffected by the increase in the demand for labor. Since the prices of inputs have not changed, the firms' cost curves are also unchanged; the new equilibrium must be at a point such as B in Figure 8.16b, at which price is equal to P_1, the original price before the unexpected increase in demand occurred.

The long-run supply curve for a constant-cost industry is, therefore, a horizontal line at a price that is equal to the long-run minimum average cost of production. At any higher price, there would be positive profit, increased entry, increased short-run supply, and thus downward pressure on price. Remember that in a constant-cost industry, input prices do not change when conditions change in the output market. Constant-cost industries can have horizontal long-run average cost curves.

Increasing-Cost Industry

In an increasing-cost industry, the prices of some or all inputs to production increase as the industry expands and the demand for the inputs grows. This might arise, for example, if the industry uses skilled labor, which becomes in short supply as the demand for it increases. Or the firm might require mineral resources that are available only on certain types of land, so that the cost of land as an input increases with output. Figure 8.17 shows the derivation of long-run supply, which is similar to the previous constant-cost derivation. The industry is initially in long-run equilibrium at A in part (b). When the demand curve unexpectedly shifts from D_1 to D_2, the short-run price of the product increases to P_2, and industry output increases from Q_1 to Q_2. A typical firm shown in part (a) increases its output from q_1 to q_2 in response to the higher price by moving along its short-run marginal cost curve. The higher profit that this and other firms earn induces new firms to enter the industry.

As new firms enter and output expands, the increased demand for inputs causes some or all input prices to increase. The short-run market supply curve shifts to the right as before, but not as much, and the new equilibrium at B results in a price P_3 that is higher than the initial price P_1. The higher market price is needed to ensure that firms earn zero profit in long-run equilibrium because the higher input prices raise the firms' short-run and long-run cost

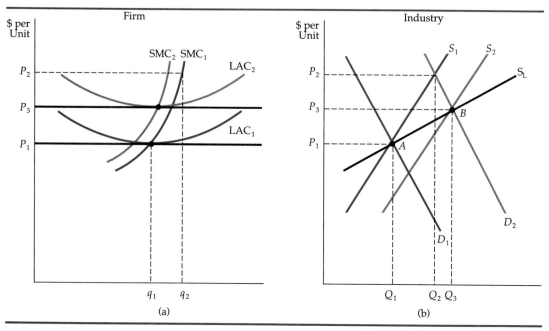

FIGURE 8.17 Long-Run Supply in an Increasing-Cost Industry. In (b), the long-run supply curve in an increasing-cost industry is an upward-sloping curve S_L. When demand increases, initially causing a price rise, the firms increase their output from q_1 to q_2 in (a). Then, the entry of new firms causes a shift to the right in supply. Because input prices increase as a result, the new long-run equilibrium occurs at a higher price than the initial equilibrium.

curves. Figure 8.17a illustrates this. The long-run average cost curve shifts up from LAC_1 to LAC_2, while the short-run marginal cost curve shifts (to the left) from SMC_1 to SMC_2. The new long-run equilibrium price P_3 is equal to the new long-run minimum average cost. As in the constant-cost case, the higher short-run profit caused by the initial increase in demand disappears in the long run as firms increase their output and input costs rise.

The new long-run equilibrium at B in Figure 8.17b is, therefore, on the long-run supply curve for the industry. *In an increasing-cost industry, the long-run industry supply curve is upward-sloping.* The industry produces more output, but only at the higher price needed to compensate for the increase in input costs. The term "increasing cost" refers to the upward shift in the firms' long-run average cost curves, not to the positive slope of the cost curve itself.

Decreasing-Cost Industry

The industry supply curve can also be downward-sloping. In this case, the unexpected increase in demand causes industry output to expand as before. But as the industry grows larger, it can take advantage of its size to obtain some of its inputs more cheaply. For example, a larger industry may allow for an improved transportation system or for a better, less expensive financial network. In this case firms' average cost curves shift downward (even though firms do not enjoy economies of scale), and the market price of the product falls. The lower market price and the lower average cost of production induce a new long-run equilibrium with more firms, more output, and a lower price. Therefore, *in a decreasing-cost industry, the long-run supply curve for the industry is downward-sloping.*

It is tempting to use the decreasing-cost argument to explain why certain products, such as computers have fallen in price over time. But other explanations are usually more persuasive. For example, lower computer prices can be explained by improvements in technology which lower production costs, or by a learning curve. The long-run downward-sloping supply curve arises only when expansion itself lowers input prices, or when firms can use scale or scope economies to produce at lower cost.

The Short-Run and Long-Run Effects of a Tax

In Chapter 6 we saw that a tax on a firm's input (in the form of an effluent fee) creates an incentive for the firm to change the way it uses inputs in its production process. Now we consider how a firm responds to a tax on its output. To simplify the analysis, assume that the firm uses a fixed-proportions production technology. If the firm is a polluter, the output tax can be a useful way to reduce the firm's effluent, but the tax might be imposed just to raise revenue.

First, suppose the output tax is imposed only on this firm and thus does not affect the market price of the product. We will see that the tax on output encourages the firm to reduce its output.[10] Figure 8.18 shows the relevant short-run cost curves for a firm enjoying positive economic profit by producing an output of q_1 and selling its product at the market price P_1. Because the tax is assessed for every unit of output, it raises the firm's marginal cost curve from MC_1 to $MC_2 = MC_1 + t$, where t is the tax per unit of the firm's output. The tax also raises the average variable cost curve by the amount t.

A close look at Figure 8.18 shows us that the output tax can have two possible effects. First, if the tax is less than the firm's profit margin, the firm will maximize its profit by choosing an output at which its marginal cost plus the tax is equal to the price of the product. The firm's output falls from q_1 to q_2, and the implicit effect of the tax is to shift the firm's short-run supply curve upward (by the amount of the tax). Second, if the tax is greater than the firm's profit margin,

---

[10]One study that documents the beneficial aspects of effluent fees is James A. Seagraves, "Industrial Waste Discharges," *Journal of Environmental Engineering Division* 99 (Dec. 1973): 873–881.

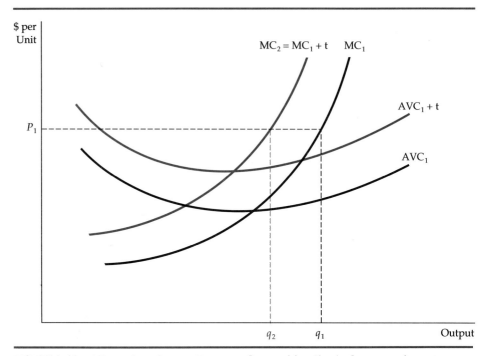

FIGURE 8.18 Effect of an Output Tax on a Competitive Firm's Output. An output tax raises the firm's marginal cost curve by the amount of the tax. The firm will reduce its output to the point at which the marginal cost plus the tax is equal to the price of the product.

then the average variable cost curve will rise, and the minimum average variable cost will be greater than the market price of the product. The firm will then choose not to produce.

Now suppose all firms in the industry are taxed and face similar cost conditions. Since each firm reduces its output at the current market price, the total output supplied by the industry will also fall, causing the price of the product to increase. Figure 8.19 illustrates this where an upward shift in the supply curve, from S_1 to $S_2 = S_1 + t$, causes the market price of the product to increase from P_1 to P_2. This increase in the price of the product diminishes some of the effects that we described previously. Firms will reduce their output less than they would without a price increase.

Output taxes may also encourage some firms (those whose costs are somewhat higher than others) to exit the industry. Figure 8.20 shows the long-run effects of the tax. Part (a) of the figure shows that the fee raises the long-run average cost curve for each firm. This makes production unprofitable for some firms, which choose to exit the industry in search of greater profit elsewhere.

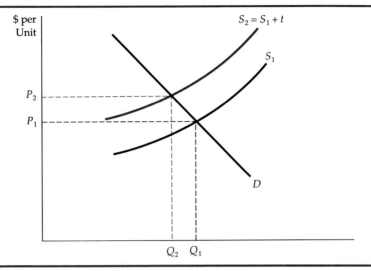

FIGURE 8.19 Effect of an Output Tax on Industry Output. An output tax placed on all firms in a competitive market shifts the short-run supply curve for the industry upward by the amount of the tax. This raises the market price of the product and lowers the total output of the industry.

This results in a shift to the left in the market supply curve, shown in part (b), which assumes increasing costs. The market price of the product increases from P_1 to P_2, and the quantity sold in the market falls from Q_1 to Q_2.

When the dust settles, the long-run equilibrium will have fewer firms and less output (and less effluent produced), because the output tax has reduced the relative profitability of production in the industry and has encouraged some investors to look elsewhere.[11]

Long-Run Elasticity of Supply

The elasticity of long-run industry supply is defined in the same way as short-run elasticity. It is equal to the percentage change in output ($\Delta Q/Q$) that results from a percentage change in price ($\Delta P/P$). In a constant-cost industry, the long-run supply curve is horizontal and the long-run supply elasticity is infinitely large. (A small increase in price will induce an extremely large increase in output.) In an increasing-cost industry, however, the long-run supply elasticity will

[11]Theoretically, although total market output will decline, each of the firms that remains in the market could produce more output and generate more effluent if the increase in the price associated with this increasing cost case is greater than the upward shift in the long-run average cost curve. But if policy is directed toward total industrial pollution, the response of the industry, not of individual firms, is important.

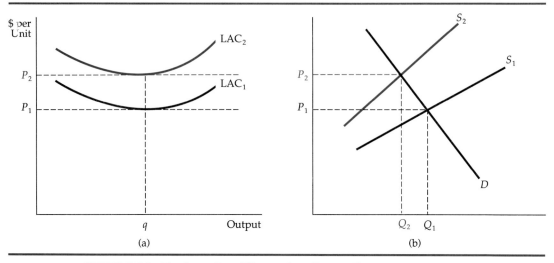

FIGURE 8.20 The Long-Run Effects of an Output Tax. In the long run the output tax will raise the average cost curve in (a) from LAC_1 to LAC_2. As firms exit the industry because of lower profit, the aggregate supply curve in (b) shifts upward and to the left. In the long-run equilibrium, quantity demanded and quantity supplied are equated at a higher price and a lower output.

be positive. Because industries can adjust and expand in the long run, we would generally expect long-run elasticities of supply to be larger than short-run elasticities.[12] The magnitude of the elasticity will depend on the extent to which input costs increase as the market expands. For example, an industry that depends on inputs that are widely available is likely to have a high long-run supply elasticity. Another industry that depends on inputs in short supply may have a much lower long-run elasticity.

EXAMPLE 8.4 THE LONG-RUN SUPPLY OF HOUSING

The production of both owner-occupied and rental housing provides an interesting example of the broad range of possible supply elasticities. People buy or rent housing to obtain the services that a house provides—a place to eat and sleep, comfort, and so on. If the price of housing services were to rise in one area of the country, the quantity of services provided could increase substantially.

First, consider the supply of owner-occupied housing in suburban or rural

---

[12]In some cases the opposite is true. Consider the elasticity of supply of scrap metal from a durable good like copper. Recall from Chapter 2 that because there is an existing stock of scrap, the long-run elasticity of supply will be *smaller* than the short-run elasticity.

areas where land is not scarce. Here, the price of land does not increase substantially as the quantity of housing supplied increases. Likewise, the costs associated with construction are not likely to increase, because there is a national market for lumber and other materials. Therefore, the long-run elasticity of the supply of housing is likely to be very large, approximating a constant-cost industry. In fact, one recent study found the long-run supply curve to be nearly horizontal.[13]

When the elasticity of supply is measured within urban areas only, where land costs do rise as the demand for housing services increases, the long-run elasticity of supply is still likely to be large because land costs make up only about one quarter of total housing costs. In one study of urban housing supply, the price elasticity was found to be 5.3.[14]

The market for rental housing is different, however. The construction of rental housing is often restricted by local zoning laws. Many communities outlaw it entirely, while others limit it to certain areas. Because urban land on which most rental housing is located is restricted and valuable, the long-run elasticity of supply of rental housing is substantially lower than the long-run supply of owner-occupied housing. As the price of rental housing services rises, new high-rise rental units are built and older units are renovated, which increases the quantity of rental services. With urban land becoming more valuable as housing density increases, and with the cost of construction soaring with the height of buildings, the increased demand causes the inputs to the production of rental housing to rise in cost. In this increasing-cost case, the elasticity of supply can be substantially less than one. In one study of rental housing, the authors found the supply elasticity to be between 0.3 and 0.7.[15]

8.8 When Is a Market Perfectly Competitive?

Apart from agriculture, few real-world markets are perfectly competitive in the sense that each firm faces a perfectly horizontal demand curve for a homogeneous product, and that firms can freely enter or exit the industry. Nevertheless, the analysis that we have just completed is useful because many markets are *almost* perfectly competitive: Firms in these markets face highly elastic demand curves, and entry and exit are relatively easy. Firms in such markets want to

[13]See James R. Follain, Jr., "The Price Elasticity of the Long-Run Supply of New Housing Construction," *Land Economics* (May 1979): 190–199.

[14]See Barton A. Smith, "The Supply of Urban Housing," *Journal of Political Economy* 40, No. 3 (Aug. 1976): 389–405.

[15]See Frank deLeeuw and Nkanta Ekanem, "The Supply of Rental Housing," *American Economic Review* 61 (Dec. 1971): 806–817, table 5.2.

set output so that the marginal cost of production is approximately equal to price.

A simple rule of thumb to describe whether a market is close to being perfectly competitive would be helpful. Unfortunately, we have no such rule, and it is important to understand why. Consider the most obvious candidate for such a rule: an industry with many firms (say at least 10 to 20). Unfortunately, the presence of many firms is neither necessary nor sufficient for an industry to approximate perfect competition, because firms can collude to fix prices, especially if they are selling a homogenous product.

The presence of only a few firms in a market also does not rule out competitive behavior. Suppose, for example, five firms are in the market but market demand for the product is very elastic. Then, the demand curve facing each firm is likely to be nearly horizontal, and the firms will behave *as if* they were operating in a perfectly competitive market.

Now suppose that the demand curve is relatively inelastic, and the five firms each sell 100 units of output. The demand curve facing one firm may still be very elastic if the supply curves of the other four firms are also very elastic. For example, consider what happens if one firm decides to drop its price from $20 to $19. The other firms in the market also lower their price. If the supply curve of the other firms is elastic, they will reduce their output substantially, say, from 400 to 300 units in total. Since the market demand is inelastic, total sales will remain at 500. Therefore, the first firm will be able to increase its sales, from 100 to 200, and will act as if it were facing a nearly horizontal demand curve.

Contestable Markets

A recent idea in microeconomics is that even when only one firm is in a market, that firm can act as if it were competitive. In this view, competition among firms *within* a market is less important than the competition *for* a market. Even though the market is so small that only one firm can operate profitably in it, there may be substantial competition to determine which firm will enter the market, and what price that firm will charge. In a *contestable market* new firms may enter the market under essentially the same cost conditions as a firm that is already in the market. A firm can also exit the market without losing any investment in capital that is specific to that market and valueless elsewhere.[16]

Suppose, for example, that we are considering the market for airplane flights between two small cities. It may be economical for there to be only one flight

---

[16]The theory is developed in William J. Baumol, John C. Panzar, and Robert D. Willig, *Contestable Markets and the Theory of Industry Structure* (1982), and criticized in William G. Shepherd, "Contestability vs. Competition," *American Economic Review* 74 (Sept. 1984): 572–587.

each day, a condition that requires a single firm to provide service. Two competing airlines would fly with many empty seats and lose money. Yet this market might be contestable. A major expense of establishing an air route is the cost of the airplanes needed to fly it. But the cost of airplanes is not specific to any particular route. If a firm loses control over the route to a competitor, it can move its airplanes to other routes with relatively little expense. Put somewhat differently, little or none of the costs of production are *sunk costs*. In general, the easier exit is, and the lower the sunk costs are, the more likely it is that the market will be contestable.

Most markets in which there is a monopoly are not contestable, however, because the incumbent firm does have sunk costs. Then, the incumbent has a competitive advantage over any prospective newcomer to the business and, as a result, can charge a price higher than marginal cost.

For instance, suppose that a firm has a local monopoly over cable television. It is economical for one firm to provide cable service because laying cable and providing individual hookups to cable subscribers involve substantial economies of scale. But the market is not fully contestable because some of the costs incurred by the cable company are sunk costs, which cannot be transferred if the company were to move its business elsewhere. The cable itself can be reutilized, but much of the labor involved in moving it would be wasted, and some of the cable and other materials associated with the hookups in each house would be valueless if the company had to exit the business. Because some of the investment is sunk, a new firm competing for the business would have to bid high enough to cover all its costs, whereas the incumbent firm could set a slightly lower price and make a substantial profit above and beyond its variable costs.

This discussion should make it clear that firms may behave competitively in many situations. Unfortunately, no simple indicator signifies when a market approximates perfect competition. Often it is necessary to analyze the number and size of firms and their strategic interactions, as we will do in Chapters 12 and 13.

Summary

1. The managers of firms can operate in accordance with a complex set of objectives and under various constraints. However, we can assume that firms act is if they are maximizing their long-run profit.

2. Because a firm in a competitive market has a small share of total industry output, it makes its output choice under the assumption that the demand for its own output is horizontal, in which case the demand curve and the marginal revenue curve are identical.

3. In general, the market demand curve for a product (which is the average revenue curve) is downward-sloping. In this case, the marginal revenue curve is steeper than the average revenue curve.

4. In the short run a competitive firm maximizes its profit by choosing an output at which price is equal to (short-run) marginal cost, so long as price is greater than or equal to the firm's minimum average variable cost of production.

5. The short-run market supply curve is the horizontal summation of the supply curves of the firms in an industry. It can be characterized by the elasticity of supply—the percentage change in quantity supplied in response to a percentage change in price.

6. The producer surplus for a firm is the difference between the revenue of a firm and the minimum cost that would be necessary to produce the profit-maximizing output. In both the short run and the long run, producer surplus is the area under the horizontal price line and above the marginal cost of production for the firm.

7. Economic rent is the payment for a factor of production less the minimum amount necessary to hire that factor. In the long run in a competitive market, producer surplus is equal to the economic rent.

8. In the long run, profit-maximizing, competitive firms choose the output at which price is equal to long-run marginal cost.

9. A long-run competitive equilibrium occurs when (i) firms maximize profit; (ii) all firms earn zero economic profit, so that there is no incentive to enter or exit the industry; and (iii) the quantity of the product demanded is equal to the quantity supplied.

10. The long-run supply curve for a firm is horizontal when the industry is a constant-cost industry in which the increased demand for inputs to production (associated with an increased demand for the product) has no effect on the market price of the inputs. But the long-run supply curve for a firm is upward-sloping in an increasing-cost industry, where the increased demand for inputs causes the market price of some or all inputs to production to rise.

11. Many markets may approximate perfectly competitive markets in the sense that one or more firms act as if they face a nearly horizontal demand curve for their product. However, the number of firms in an industry is not a good indicator of the extent to which that industry is competitive.

Questions for Review

1. Explain why a firm that incurs losses would choose to produce rather than shut down.

2. The supply curve for a firm in the short run is the short-run marginal cost curve (above the point of minimum average variable cost). Explain why the supply curve in the long run is *not* the long-run marginal cost curve (above the point of minimum average total cost).

3. In long-run equilibrium all firms in the industry earn zero economic profit. Why is this true?

4. What is the difference between economic profit and producer surplus?

5. Why do firms enter an industry when they know that in the long run economic profit will be zero?

6. An increase in the demand for video films increases the salaries of actors and actresses substantially. Is the long-run supply curve for films likely to be horizontal or upward-sloping? Explain.

7. True or false: A firm should always produce at an output at which long-run average cost is minimized. Explain.

8. Can there be constant returns to scale in an industry with an upward-sloping supply curve? Explain.

9. What assumptions are necessary for a market to be perfectly competitive? In light of what you have learned in this chapter, describe why each of these assumptions is important.

10. The government passes a law that allows a substantial subsidy for every acre of land used to grow tobacco. How does this program affect the long-run supply curve for tobacco?

Exercises

1. From the data in Table 8.2, show what happens to the firm's output choice and profit if the price of the product falls from $40 to $35.

2. Again, from the data in Table 8.2, show what happens to the firm's output choice and profit if the fixed cost of production increases from $50 to $100, and then to $150. What general conclusion can you reach about the effects of fixed costs on the firm's output choice?

3. Suppose you are the manager of a watchmaking firm operating in a competitive market. Your cost of production is given by $C = 100 + Q^2$, where Q is the level of output and C is total cost. (The marginal cost of production is $2Q$. The fixed cost of production is $100.)
   a. If the price of watches is $60, how many watches should you produce to maximize profit?
   b. What will the profit level be?
   c. At what minimum price will the firm produce a positive output?

4. Use the same information as in Exercise 3 to answer the following.
   a. Derive the firm's short-run supply curve. (Hint: You may want to plot the appropriate cost curves.)
   b. If 100 identical firms are in the market, what is the industry supply curve?

5. A sales tax of $1 per unit of output is placed on one firm whose product sells for $5 in a competitive industry.
   a. How will this tax affect the cost curves for the firm?
   b. What will happen to the firm's price, output, and profit in the short run?
   c. What will happen in the long run?

6. A sales tax of 10 percent is placed on half the firms (the polluters) in a competitive industry. The revenue is paid to the remaining firms (the nonpolluters) as a 10 percent subsidy on the value of output sold.

a. Assuming that all firms have identical cost curves before the sales tax–subsidy policy, what do you expect to happen to the price of the product, the output of each of the firms, and industry output? Explain.

b. Can such a policy *always* be achieved with a balanced budget in which tax revenues are equal to subsidy payments? Why? Explain.

CHAPTER 9

The Analysis of Competitive Markets

In Chapter 2 we saw how supply and demand curves can help us describe and understand the behavior of competitive or quasi-competitive markets. In Chapters 3 to 8 we saw how these curves are derived and what determines their shapes. With this foundation, we return to supply-demand analysis and show how it can be applied to a wide variety of economic problems—problems that might concern a consumer faced with a purchasing decision, a firm faced with a long-range planning problem, or a government agency that has to design a policy and evaluate its likely impact.

We begin by showing how consumer and producer surplus can be used to study the *welfare effects* of a government policy—in other words, who gains and who loses from the policy, and by how much. We also use consumer and producer surplus to demonstrate the *efficiency* of a competitive market—why the equilibrium price and quantity in a competitive market maximizes the aggregate economic welfare of producers and consumers.

Then we apply supply-demand analysis to a variety of problems. Very few markets in the United States have been untouched by government interventions of one kind or another, so most of the problems that we will study deal with the effects of such interventions. Our objective is not simply to solve these problems, but to show you how to use the tools of economic analysis to deal with others like them on your own. We hope you will begin to understand how to calculate the response of markets to changing economic conditions or government policies and to evaluate the resulting gains and losses to consumers and producers. The examples that we provide along the way should help in this regard, but we also urge you to work through some of the exercises at the end of the chapter.

9.1 Evaluating the Gains and Losses from Government Policies— Consumer and Producer Surplus

We saw at the end of Chapter 2 that a price ceiling causes the quantity of a good demanded to rise (consumers want to buy more, given the lower price) and the quantity supplied to fall (producers are not willing to supply as much given the lower price), so that a shortage results. But we also know that those consumers who can still buy the good will be better off because they will now pay less. (Presumably, this was the objective of the policy in the first place.) But if we also take into account those who cannot obtain the good, how much better off are consumers *as a whole*? Might they be worse off? And if we lump consumers and producers together, will their total welfare be greater or lower, and by how much? To answer questions like these, we need a way to measure the gains and losses from government interventions and the changes in market price and quantity such interventions cause.

Our method is to calculate the changes in *consumer and producer surplus* that result from an intervention. In Chapter 4 we saw that consumer surplus measures the aggregate net benefit that consumers obtain from a competitive market. In Chapter 8 we saw how *producer surplus* measures the aggregate net benefit to producers, namely, their aggregate profits plus rents. Here we will see how useful a tool consumer and producer surplus is.

Review of Consumer and Producer Surplus

In an unregulated, competitive market, consumers and producers buy and sell at the prevailing market price. But remember, for some consumers the value of the good *exceeds* this market price; they would pay more for the good if they had to. As a result, they receive a benefit, or value, beyond what they pay. *Consumer surplus* is the total benefit or value that consumers receive beyond what they pay for the good.

For example, suppose the market price is $5 per unit, as in Figure 9.1. Some consumers probably value this good very highly and would pay much more than $5 for it. Consumer A, for example, would pay up to $10 for the good. However, because the market price is only $5, he enjoys a net benefit of $5— the $10 value he places on the good, less the $5 he must pay to obtain it. Consumer B values the good somewhat less highly. She would be willing to pay $7, and thus enjoys a $2 net benefit. Finally, Consumer C values the good at exactly the market price, $5. He is indifferent between buying or not buying the good, and if the market price were one cent higher, he would forgo the purchase. Consumer C therefore obtains no net benefit.[1]

---

[1] Of course, some consumers attach a value to the good that is *less* than $5. These consumers make up the part of the demand curve to the right of the equilibrium market quantity Q_0 and will not purchase the good.

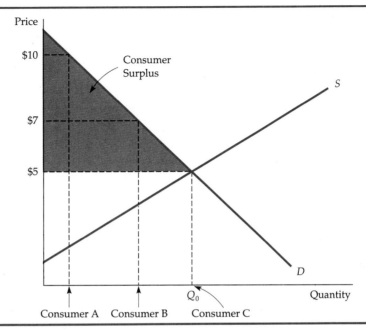

FIGURE 9.1   Illustration of Consumer Surplus.   Consumer A would pay $10 for a good whose market price is $5, and therefore enjoys a benefit of $5. Consumer B enjoys a benefit of $2, and Consumer C, who values the good at exactly the market price, enjoys no benefit. Consumer surplus, which measures the total benefit to all consumers, is the shaded area between the demand curve and the market price.

Consumer surplus is the total net benefit that all consumers purchasing the good enjoy. For consumers in the aggregate, it is the *area between the demand curve and the market price* (i.e., the shaded area in Figure 9.1). And because consumer surplus measures the total net benefit to consumers, we can measure the gain or loss to consumers from a government intervention by measuring the resulting change in consumer surplus.

Producer surplus is the analogous measure for producers. Some producers are producing units at a cost just equal to the market price. Other units, however, could be produced for less than the market price, and indeed would still be produced and sold even if the market price were lower. Producers therefore enjoy a benefit—a surplus—from selling those units. For each unit, this surplus is the difference between the market price the producer receives and the marginal cost of producing this unit. It represents the profit on the unit, plus any rents accruing to factors of production.

For the market as a whole, producer surplus is *the area above the supply curve up to the market price;* this is the total profit plus factor rents that lower-cost producers enjoy by selling at the market price. In Figure 9.2 it is the lower

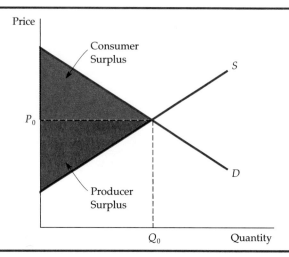

FIGURE 9.2   Consumer and Producer Surplus.   Producer surplus measures the aggregate profits of producers, plus rents to factor inputs. It is the area between the supply curve and the market price. Together, consumer and producer surplus measure the welfare benefit of a competitive market.

shaded triangle. And because producer surplus measures the total net benefit to producers, we can measure the gain or loss to producers from a government intervention by measuring the resulting change in producer surplus.

Application of Consumer and Producer Surplus

To see how consumer and producer surplus can be used to evaluate government policies, let us return to the example of *price controls* that we first encountered toward the end of Chapter 2. Recall that by depressing production and increasing demand, price controls create excess demand.

Figure 9.3 replicates Figure 2.20, except that it also shows the changes in consumer and producer surplus that result from the government price control policy. Some consumers have been rationed out of the market because of price controls, and production and sales fall from Q_0 to Q_1. Those consumers who can still purchase the good can now do so at a lower price, so they enjoy an *increase* in consumer surplus, which is given by shaded rectangle A. However, some consumers can no longer buy the good. Their *loss* of consumer surplus is given by shaded triangle B. The net change in consumer surplus is therefore A − B. In Figure 9.3, rectangle A is larger than triangle B, so the net change in consumer surplus is positive.

What about the change in producer surplus? Those producers who are still in the market and producing quantity Q_1 are now receiving a lower price. They

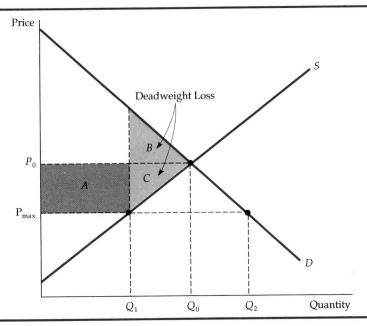

FIGURE 9.3 Change in Consumer and Producer Surplus from Price Controls. The price of a good has been regulated to be no higher than P_{max}, which is below the market-clearing price P_0. The gain to consumers is the difference between rectangle A and triangle B. The loss to producers is the sum of rectangle A and triangle C. Triangles B and C together measure the deadweight loss from price controls.

have lost producer surplus of an amount given by rectangle A. However, total production has also dropped. This represents an additional loss of producer surplus and is given by triangle C. Therefore, the total change in producer surplus is $-A - C$. Producers clearly lose as a result of price controls.

Is this loss to producers from price controls offset by the gain to consumers? No—as Figure 9.3 shows, price controls result in a net loss of total surplus, which we call a *deadweight loss*. Recall that the change in consumer surplus is $A - B$ and that the change in producer surplus is $-A - C$, so the *total* change in surplus is $(A - B) + (-A - C) = -B - C$. We thus have a deadweight loss, which is given by the two triangles B and C in Figure 9.3. This deadweight loss is an inefficiency caused by price controls; the loss of producer surplus exceeds the gain in consumer surplus.

If politicians value consumer surplus more highly than producer surplus, this deadweight loss may not carry much political weight. However, if the demand curve is very inelastic, price controls can result in a *net loss of consumer surplus*, as is illustrated in Figure 9.4. In that figure triangle B, which measures the loss to consumers who have been rationed out of the market, is larger than rectangle

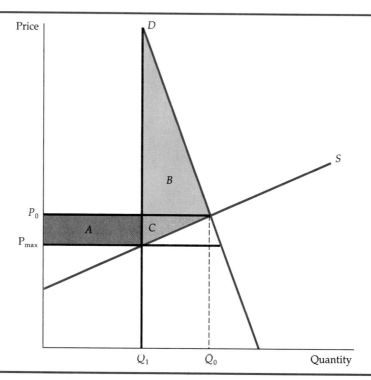

FIGURE 9.4 **Effect of Price Controls When Demand is Inelastic.** If demand is sufficiently inelastic, triangle B can be larger than rectangle A. In this case, consumers suffer a net loss from price controls.

A, which measures the gain to consumers able to buy the good. Here, consumers value the good highly, and those who are rationed out suffer a large loss.

The demand for gasoline is fairly inelastic in the short run (but much more elastic in the long run). During the summer of 1979, gasoline shortages occurred as a result of oil price controls that prevented domestic gasoline prices from increasing to rising world levels. Consumers sometimes spent hours waiting in line to buy gasoline. This may have been a good example of price controls making consumers—the group the policy was presumably intended to protect—worse off.

EXAMPLE 9.1   PRICE CONTROLS AND THE NATURAL GAS SHORTAGE

In Example 2.7 of Chapter 2, we saw that during the 1970s price controls created a large excess demand for natural gas. But how much did consumers gain from those controls, how much did producers lose, and what was the deadweight loss to the country? We can answer these questions by calculating the resulting changes in consumer and producer surplus.

Once again we base our analysis on the numbers for 1975 and calculate the gains and losses that apply to that year. Refer to Example 2.7, where we showed that the supply and demand curves can be approximated as follows:

$$Supply: \quad Q^S = 14 + 2P_G + 0.25P_O$$

$$Demand: \quad Q^D = -5P_G + 3.75P_O$$

where Q^S and Q^D are the quantities supplied and demanded, each measured in trillions of cubic feet (Tcf), P_G is the price of natural gas in dollars per thousand cubic feet ($/mcf), and P_O is the price of oil in dollars per barrel ($/b). As the reader can verify by setting Q^S equal to Q^D, given that the price of oil was $8 per barrel, the equilibrium free market price and quantity are $2.00 per mcf and

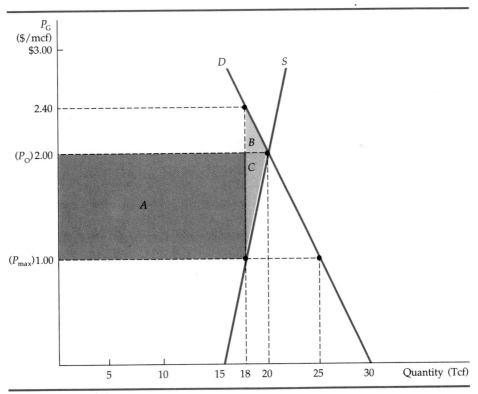

FIGURE 9.5   Effects of Natural Gas Price Controls.   The market-clearing price of natural gas is $2.00 per mcf, and the maximum allowable price is $1.00. A shortage of $25 - 18 = 7$ trillion cubic feet results. The gain to consumers is rectangle A minus triangle B, and the loss to producers is rectangle A plus triangle C.

20 Tcf, respectively. Under the regulations, however, the maximum allowable price was $1.00 per mcf.

Figure 9.5 shows these supply and demand curves and free market and regulated prices. Rectangle A and triangles B and C measure the changes in consumer and producer surplus resulting from price controls. By calculating the areas of the rectangle and triangles, we can determine the gains and losses from controls.

To do the calculations, first note that 1 Tcf is equal to 1 billion mcf. (We must put the quantities and prices in common units.) Also, by substituting the quantity 18 Tcf into the equation for the demand curve, we can determine that the vertical line at 18 Tcf intersects the demand curve at a price of $2.40 per mcf. Then we can calculate the areas as follows:

$$A = (18 \text{ billion mcf}) \times (\$1/\text{mcf}) = \$18 \text{ billion}$$

$$B = (\tfrac{1}{2}) \times (2 \text{ billion mcf}) \times (\$0.40/\text{mcf}) = \$0.4 \text{ billion}$$

$$C = (\tfrac{1}{2}) \times (2 \text{ billion mcf}) \times (\$1/\text{mcf}) = \$1 \text{ billion}$$

(The area of a triangle is one half the product of its altitude and its base.)

The 1975 change in consumer surplus resulting from price controls was therefore $A - B = 18 - 0.4 = \$17.6$ billion. The change in producer surplus was $-A - C = -18 - 1 = -\$19$ billion. And finally the deadweight loss for the year was $-B - C = -0.4 - 1 = -\$1.4$ billion.

The amount $1.4 billion per year is a significant loss to society, but in fact this number understates the true loss resulting from natural gas price controls. Our analysis was a *partial equilibrium* one, which means that it ignored the spillover effects that natural gas shortages had on other markets. For example, during the 1970s much of the excess demand for natural gas ($25 - 18 = 7$ Tcf) wound up as an increased demand for oil and oil products. This increased both American dependence on imported oil and the losses resulting from domestic price controls on oil. Calculating these additional losses is beyond the scope of this example, but you should be aware that they exist.

9.2 The Efficiency of a Competitive Market

We just saw how price controls create a deadweight loss: When the government requires that producers charge a price below that which clears the market, the *aggregate* welfare of consumers and producers taken together is reduced. Of course, this does not mean that such a policy is bad; it may achieve objectives that policymakers and the public think are important. However, there is a cost to such a policy—taken together, producer and consumer surplus is reduced by the amount of the deadweight loss.

You might think that a competitive market is better left alone, if the only objective is to maximize the total welfare of consumers and producers. This is sometimes, but not always, the case. In two situations government intervention can increase the total welfare of consumers and producers in a competitive market. The first is when the actions of either consumers or producers result in costs or benefits that do not show up as part of the market price. Such costs or benefits are called *externalities* because they are "external" to the market. An example of an externality is the cost to society of environmental pollution by a producer of industrial chemicals. Without government intervention, such a producer will have no incentive to consider the social cost of this pollution. We will examine externalities and the proper government response to them in Part 4 of this book.

Market failure is the second situation in which government intervention can improve on the outcome of a freely functioning competitive market. Loosely speaking, market failure means that prices fail to provide the proper signals to consumers and producers, so that the market does not operate as we have described it. For example, market failure can occur when consumers lack information about the quality or nature of a product, and therefore cannot make utility-maximizing purchasing decisions. Government intervention (e.g., the requirement of "truth in labeling") may then be desirable. Market failure will also be discussed in Part 4.

Without externalities or market failure, an unregulated competitive market does indeed lead to the welfare-maximizing price and output level. To see this, let us consider what happens if price is constrained to be something other than the equilibrium market-clearing price.

We have already examined the effects of a price ceiling (i.e., a price held below the market-clearing one). Production falls (from Q_0 to Q_1 in Figure 9.6), and there is a corresponding loss of total surplus (the deadweight loss triangles B and C in the figure). Too little is produced, and consumers and producers in the aggregate are worse off.

Now suppose instead that the government required the price to be *above* the market-clearing one, say, P_2 instead of P_0. As Figure 9.7 shows, producers would like to produce more at this higher price (Q_2 instead of Q_0), but consumers will now buy less (Q_3 instead of Q_0). If we assume that producers produce only what can be sold, the market output level will be Q_3, and again, there is a net loss of total surplus. In Figure 9.7, rectangle A now represents a transfer from consumers to producers (who now receive a higher price), but triangles B and C are again a deadweight loss. Because of the higher price, some consumers are no longer buying the good (a loss of consumer surplus given by triangle B), and some producers are no longer producing it (a loss of producer surplus given by triangle C).

In fact, the deadweight loss triangles B and C in Figure 9.7 give an optimistic assessment of the efficiency cost of policies that force price above market-clearing levels. Some producers, enticed by the high price P_2, might increase their

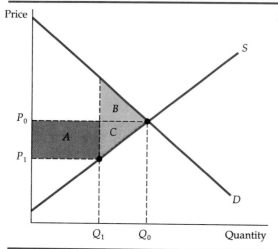

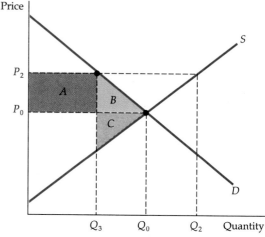

FIGURE 9.6   Welfare Loss When Price Is Held Below Market-Clearing Level.   When price is regulated to be no higher than P_1, the deadweight loss given by triangles B and C results.

FIGURE 9.7   Welfare Loss When Price Is Held Above Market-Clearing Level.   When price is regulated to be no lower than P_2, only Q_3 will be demanded. If Q_3 is produced, the deadweight loss is given by triangles B and C. At price P_2, producers would like to produce more than Q_3. If they do, the deadweight loss will be even larger.

capacity and output levels, which would result in unsold output. (This actually happened in the airline industry when fares were regulated to be above market-clearing levels by the Civil Aeronautics Board.) Or to satisfy producers, the government might buy up unsold output so production can be maintained at Q_2 or close to it. (This is what happens with U.S. agriculture.) In both cases the total welfare loss will significantly exceed triangles B and C.

We will examine minimum prices, price supports, and related policies in some detail in the next few sections. Besides showing how supply-demand analysis can be used to understand and assess these policies, we will discuss examples of how deviations from the competitive market equilibrium lead to efficiency costs, and how large those costs can be.

EXAMPLE 9.2   THE MARKET FOR HUMAN KIDNEYS

Should people have the right to sell parts of their bodies? The U.S. Congress believes the answer is no. In 1984 it passed the National Organ Transplantation Act, which prohibits the sale of organs for transplantation. Organs may only be donated.

Although the law prohibits their sale, it does not make organs valueless.

Instead, it prevents those who supply organs (living persons or the families of the deceased) from reaping their economic value. It also creates a shortage of organs. Each year about 8,000 kidneys, 20,000 corneas, and 1,200 hearts are transplanted in the United States, but there is considerable excess demand for these organs, and many potential recipients must do without them. Some of these potential recipients die as a result.

To understand the effects of this law, let's consider the supply and demand for kidneys. First the supply curve. Even at a price of zero (the effective price under the 1984 act), donors supply about 8,000 kidneys per year. But many other people who need kidney transplants cannot obtain them because of a lack of donors. It has been estimated that 4,000 more kidneys would be supplied if the price were $20,000. This implies the following linear supply curve[2]:

$$Supply:\quad Q^S = 8,000 + 0.2P$$

It is expected that at a price of $20,000 the demand for kidneys would be 12,000 per year. Like supply, demand is relatively price inelastic; a reasonable estimate for the elasticity of demand at the $20,000 price is -0.33. This implies the following linear demand curve:

$$Demand:\quad Q^D = 20,000 - .4P$$

These supply and demand curves are plotted in Figure 9.8, which shows the market-clearing price and quantity of $20,000 and 12,000, respectively.

Because the 1984 act prohibits the sale of kidneys, supply is limited to 8,000 (the number of kidneys that people donate). This constrained supply is shown as the vertical line S'. How does this affect the welfare of kidney suppliers and recipients?

First consider suppliers. Those who provide kidneys fail to receive the $20,000 each kidney is worth, a loss of surplus represented by rectangle A, and equal to $(8,000)(\$20,000) = \$160$ million. Also, some people who would supply kidneys if they were paid for them do not, and they lose an amount of surplus represented by triangle C, and equal to $(\frac{1}{2})(4,000)(\$20,000) = \$40$ million. So the total loss to suppliers is $200 million.

What about recipients? Presumably the 1984 act intended to treat the kidney as a gift to the recipient. If this were indeed the case, those recipients who could obtain kidneys would *gain* rectangle A ($160 million) because they would not have to pay the $20,000. Those who cannot obtain kidneys lose surplus of an amount given by triangle B and equal to $40 million. This would imply a net increase in the surplus of recipients of $160 - \$40 = \$120$ million. It also implies a deadweight loss equal to the areas of triangles B and C (i.e., $80 million).

This deadweight loss represents a large efficiency cost, but it is not the end

---

[2] The supply curve is of the form $Q = a + bP$. When $P = 0$, $Q = 8,000$, so $a = 8,000$. If $P = \$20,000$, $Q = 12,000$, so $b = (12,000 - 8,000)/20,000 = 0.2$. At a price of $20,000 the elasticity of supply is 0.33.

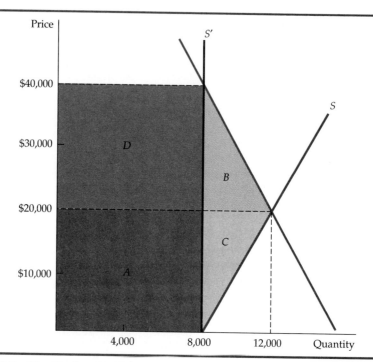

FIGURE 9.8 The Market for Kidneys, and Effect of the 1984 National Transplantation Act. The market-clearing price is $20,000; at this price, about 12,000 kidneys per year would be supplied. The 1984 act effectively makes the price zero. About 8,000 kidneys per year are still donated; this constrained supply is shown as S'. The loss to suppliers is given by rectangle A and triangle C. If consumers received kidneys at no cost, their gain would be given by rectangle A less triangle B. In practice, kidneys are often rationed on the basis of willingness to pay, and many recipients pay most or all of the $40,000 price that clears the market when supply is constrained. Rectangles A and D measure the total value of kidneys when supply is constrained.

of the story. With excess demand, there is no way to insure that recipients will indeed receive their kidneys as gifts, as the 1984 act intends. In practice, kidneys are often rationed on the basis of willingness to pay, and many recipients end up paying all or most of the $40,000 price that is needed to clear the market when supply is constrained to 8,000. A good part of the value of the kidneys—rectangles A and D in the figure—is then captured by hospitals and middlemen. As a result, the law reduces the surplus of recipients, as well as of suppliers.[3]

[3]These issues are discussed in Emanuel Thorne and Gilah Langner, "The Body's Value Has Gone Up," *New York Times*, Sept. 8, 1986. They point out, for example, that in 1984–1985 many hospitals were performing nearly 30 percent of kidney transplants on foreigners who were allowed to jump the queue of Americans, and who were charged surgeons' and hospital fees nearly twice as high as for Americans.

There are, of course, arguments in favor of prohibiting the sale of organs.[4] One argument stems from the problem of imperfect information; if people receive payment for organs, they may hide adverse information about their health histories. This argument is probably most applicable to the donation versus sale of blood, where there is a possibility of transmitting hepatitis, AIDS, or other viruses. But even here screening (at a cost that would be included in the market price) may be more efficient than prohibiting sales. This issue, in fact, has been central to the debate in the United States over blood policy.

A second argument is that it is simply unfair to allocate a basic necessity of life on the basis of ability to pay. This argument transcends economics. However, two points should be kept in mind. First, when the price of a good that has a significant opportunity cost is forced to zero, there is bound to be a reduced supply and excess demand. Second, it is not clear why live organs should be treated differently from close substitutes; artificial limbs, for example, are for sale, but real kidneys are not.

Many complex ethical and economic issues are involved in the sale of organs. These issues are important, and this example is not intended to sweep them away. Economics, the dismal science, simply shows us that human organs have economic value that cannot be ignored, and that prohibiting their sale imposes a cost on society that must be weighed against the benefits.

9.3 Minimum Prices

As we have seen, government policy sometimes seeks to *raise* prices above market-clearing levels, rather than lower them. Examples include the former regulation of the airlines by the Civil Aeronautics Board, the minimum wage law, and a variety of agricultural policies. (Most import quotas and tariffs also have this intent, as we will see in Section 9.5.) One way to raise price above the market-clearing level is by direct regulation—simply make it illegal to charge a price lower than a specific minimum level.

Look back to Figure 9.7. If producers correctly anticipate that they can sell only the lower quantity Q_3, the net welfare loss will be given by triangles B and C. But as we explained, producers might not limit their output to Q_3. What happens if producers think they can sell all they want at the higher price, and produce accordingly?

This situation is illustrated in Figure 9.9, where P_{min} denotes a minimum price set by the government. The quantity supplied is now Q_2, and the quantity demanded is Q_3, the difference representing an excess, unsold supply. Now let us follow the resulting changes in consumer and producer surplus.

[4]For a detailed and very illuminating analysis of the strengths and weaknesses of these arguments, see Susan Rose-Ackerman, "Inalienability and the Theory of Property Rights," *Columbia Law Review* 85 (June 1985): 931–969.

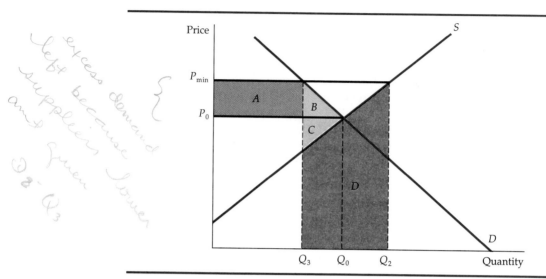

(handwritten margin notes) excess supply because at P_{min}; left because demand lower. Q_2 - Q_3

FIGURE 9.9   Price Minimum.   Price is regulated to be no lower than P_{min}. Producers would like to supply Q_2, but consumers will buy only Q_3. If producers indeed produce Q_2, the amount $Q_2 - Q_3$ will go unsold and will be $A - C - D$. In this case, producers as a group may be worse off.

Those consumers who still purchase the good must now pay a higher price and so suffer a loss of surplus, which is given by rectangle A in Figure 9.9. Some consumers have also dropped out of the market because of the higher price, with a corresponding loss of surplus given by triangle B. The total change in consumer surplus is therefore

$$\Delta C.S. = -A - B$$

Consumers clearly are worse off as a result of this policy.

What about producers? Producers now receive a higher price for the units they sell, and that results in an increase of surplus, given by rectangle A. (Rectangle A represents a transfer of money from consumers to producers.) But the drop in sales from Q_0 to Q_3 results in a loss of surplus, which is given by triangle C. Finally, consider the cost to producers of expanding production from Q_0 to Q_2. Because they sell only Q_3, there is no revenue to cover the cost of producing $Q_2 - Q_3$. This cost is the area under the supply curve from Q_3 to Q_2, and is represented by the shaded trapezoid D.[5] So unless producers respond to unsold output by cutting production, the total change in producer surplus will be given by

$$\Delta P.S. = A - C - D$$

[5]Remember that the supply curve is the aggregate marginal cost curve for the industry. The supply curve therefore gives us the additional cost of producing each incremental unit, so the area under the supply curve from Q_3 to Q_2 is the cost of producing the quantity $Q_2 - Q_3$.

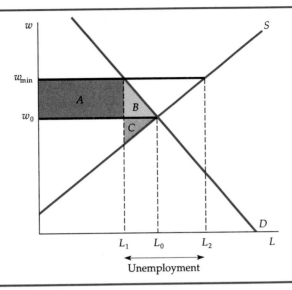

FIGURE 9.10 The Minimum Wage. The market-clearing wage is w_0, but firms are not allowed to pay less than w_{min}. This results in unemployment of an amount $L_2 - L_1$, and a deadweight loss given by triangles B and C.

Given that trapezoid D can be quite large, a price minimum can even result in a net loss of surplus to producers alone! And although producers may cut output, they will probably not cut back to Q_3. Each producer sees the high price, and hopes he can sell all its output at that price, leaving competitors with the unsold inventories. As a result, this form of government intervention can cause producers' profits to fall because of the cost of excess production.

Another example of a government-imposed price minimum is the minimum wage law. This is illustrated in Figure 9.10, where the supply curve corresponds to the supply of labor, and the demand curve is the demand for labor. The wage is set at w_{min}, a level higher than the wage w_0 that would prevail in an unregulated labor market. As a result, those workers who can find jobs obtain a higher wage. However, some people who want to work will be unable to. The policy results in unemployment, which in the figure is $L_2 - L_1$.

EXAMPLE 9.3 AIRLINE REGULATION

During 1976–1981 the airline industry in the United States changed dramatically. Until that time fares and routes had been tightly regulated by the Civil Aeronautics Board (CAB). The CAB set most fares considerably above what would have prevailed in a free market. It also restricted entry, so that many routes were served by only one or two airlines. But in 1976 the CAB started to liberalize fare regulation. In 1977 it approved the first "Super Saver" fares. In 1978 it allowed airlines to set fares as much as 10 percent above or 50 percent below a CAB standard fare, and in 1980 this "zone of reasonableness" was expanded to give airlines unlimited downward flexibility and more upward flexibility over fares. Also, shortly after passage of the Airline Deregulation Act in October 1978, the CAB essentially gave airlines the ability to serve any routes they wished, and since then many new airlines began scheduled interstate service. By 1981 the industry had been completely deregulated, and the CAB itself was dissolved in 1982.

Many airline executives feared that deregulation would lead to chaos in the industry, with competitive pressure causing sharply reduced profits and bankruptcies. After all, the original rationale for CAB regulation was to provide "stability" for an industry that was considered vital to the U.S. economy. And one might think that by holding price above its market-clearing level, profits would be higher than they would be in a free market.

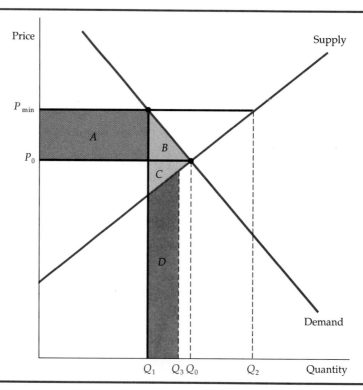

FIGURE 9.11   Effect of Airline Regulation by the Civil Aeronautics Board. At price P_{min}, airlines would like to supply quantity Q_2, well above the quantity Q_1 that consumers will buy. Here they supply Q_3. Trapezoid D measures the cost of unsold output. Airline profits may have been lower as a result of CAB regulation because triangle C and trapezoid D can together exceed rectangle A. In addition, consumers lose $A + B$.

Deregulation did lead to major changes in the industry. Some airlines merged or went out of business, but many more new airlines entered the industry. And although prices fell considerbly (bringing a huge benefit to consumers), profits overall did not fall much because the CAB's minimum prices had caused major inefficiencies and artificially high costs. The effect of minimum prices is illustrated in Figure 9.11, where P_0 and Q_0 are the market-clearing price and quantity, P_{min} is the minimum price set by the CAB, and Q_1 is the amount demanded at this higher price. The problem was that at price P_{min}, airlines wanted to supply a quantity Q_2, much larger than Q_1. And although they did not expand output to Q_2, they did expand it well beyond Q_1—to Q_3 in the figure—hoping to sell this quantity at the expense of competitors. As a result, load factors (the average percentage of seats filled) were low, and so were profits. (Trapezoid D measures the cost of unsold output.)

Table 9.1 gives some key numbers that illustrate the evolution of the industry. Although the number of carriers increased dramatically after deregulation, so did passenger load factors, while the passenger-mile rate (the revenue per passenger-mile flown) fell only slightly in real (inflation-adjusted) terms after 1975. And what about costs? The real cost index indicates that even after adjusting for inflation, costs increased by about 25 percent from 1975 to 1982. But this was due to the sharp increase in fuel costs (caused by the increase in oil prices) that occurred during this period, and it had nothing to do with deregulation. The last line in Table 9.1 is the real cost index after adjusting for fuel cost increases. This is what costs would have been had oil prices increased only at the rate of inflation. This index *fell* during the period.

What, then, did airline deregulation do for consumers and producers? As new airlines entered the industry and fares went down, consumers clearly benefited. (The increase in consumer surplus is given by rectangle A and triangle B in Figure 9.11.[7]) As for the airlines, they had to learn to live in a more competitive—and therefore more turbulent—environment, and some firms did not sur-

TABLE 9.1 Airline Industry Data[6]

	1970	1975	1980	1982	1984
Number of carriers	39	33	63	98	95
Passenger load factor (%)	50	54	59	59	59
Passenger-mile rate (constant 1975 dollars)	.095	.077	.074	.071	.072
Real cost index (1975 = 100)	98	100	120	125	123
Real cost index corrected for fuel cost increases	113	100	94	96	95

[6]Source: Department of Commerce, *U.S. Statistical Abstract*, 1986.

[7]The benefit to consumers was somewhat smaller than this because *quality* declined as planes became more crowded and delays and cancellations more frequent.

vive. But overall, airlines became so much more cost-efficient that producer surplus may have increased. The total welfare gain from deregulation was positive, and quite large.[8]

9.4 Price Supports and Production Quotas

Besides imposing a minimum price, the government can increase the price of a good in other ways. Much of American agricultural policy is based on a system of *price supports*, often combined with incentives to reduce or restrict production. In this section we examine how these policies work and their impact on consumers, producers, and the federal budget.

Price Supports

In the United States, price supports aim to increase the prices of dairy products, tobacco, corn, peanuts, etc., so that the producers of those goods can receive higher incomes. One way to do this is for the governmemt to set a support price P_s and then buy up whatever output is needed to keep the market price at this level. Figure 9.12 illustrates this. Let us examine the resulting gains and losses to producers, consumers, and the government.

At price P_s, consumer demand falls to Q_1, but supply increases to Q_2. To maintain this price and avoid having inventories pile up in producer warehouses, the government must buy the quantity $Q_g = Q_2 - Q_1$. In effect the government adds its demand Q_g to the demand of consumers, and producers can sell all they want at price P_s.

Those consumers who purchase the good must pay the higher price P_s instead of P_0, and so they suffer a loss of consumer surplus given by rectangle A. Other consumers no longer buy the good or buy less of it, and their loss of surplus is given by triangle B. So as with the minimum price that we examined above, consumers lose, in this case by an amount

$$\Delta \text{C.S.} = -A - B$$

On the other hand producers gain (which is why such a policy is implemented). Producers are now selling a larger quantity Q_2 instead of Q_0, and at

---

[8]Detailed studies of the effects of deregulation include John M. Trapani and C. Vincent Olson, "An Analysis of the Impact of Open Entry on Price and the Quality of Service in the Airline Industry," *Review of Economics and Statistics* 64 (Feb. 1982): 118–138; David R. Graham, Daniel P. Kaplan, and David S. Sibley, "Efficiency and Competition in the Airline Industry," *Bell Journal of Economics* (spring 1983): 118–138; S. Morrison and Clifford Whinston, *The Economic Effects of Airline Deregulation* (Washington, D.C.: Brookings Institution, 1986); and Nancy L. Rose, "Financial Influences on Airline Safety," MIT Sloan School Working Paper, #1890–87, May 1987.

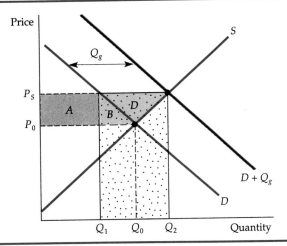

FIGURE 9.12 Price Supports. To maintain a price P_s above the market-clearing price P_0, the government buys a quantity Q_g. The gain to producers is $A + B + D$. The loss to consumers is $A + B$. The cost to the government is the speckled rectangle $P_s(Q_2 - Q_1)$.

a higher price P_s. Observe from Figure 9.12 that producer surplus increases by the amount

$$\Delta\text{P.S.} = A + B + D$$

But there is also a cost to the government (which must be paid for by taxes, and so is ultimately a cost to consumers). The cost to the government is $(Q_2 - Q_1)P_s$, which is what the government must pay for the output it purchases. In Figure 9.12 this is the large speckled rectangle. (This cost may be reduced if the government can "dump" some of its purchases [i.e., sell them abroad at a low price]. But this hurts the ability of domestic producers to sell in foreign markets, and it is domestic producers that the government is trying to please in the first place.)

What is the total welfare cost of this policy? To find out, we must add the change in consumer surplus to the change in producer surplus and then subtract the cost to the government. You can verify that the total change in welfare is

$$\Delta\text{C.S.} + \Delta\text{P.S.} - \text{Cost to Govt.} = D - (Q_2 - Q_1)P_s$$

In terms of Figure 9.12, society as a whole is worse off by an amount given by the large speckled rectangle, less triangle D.

As we will see in Example 9.4, this welfare loss can be extremely large. But the most unfortunate part of this policy is that there is a much more efficient way (i.e., less costly to society) to make farmers better off. If the objective is to give farmers an additional income equal to $A + B + D$, it is far less costly to society to give them this money directly, rather than via price supports. Since consumers are losing $A + B$ anyway with price supports, by giving the money to farmers directly, society saves the large speckled rectangle, less triangle D. Then why doesn't the government make farmers better off by simply giving them money? Perhaps because price supports are a less obvious giveaway, and therefore politically more attractive.[9]

Production Quotas

Besides entering the market and buying up output, thereby increasing total demand, the government can also cause the price of a good to rise by *reducing supply*. It can do this by decree—the government simply sets quotas on how much each firm can produce. By setting the appropriate quotas, the price can then be forced up to any arbitrary level.

This is exactly how many city governments maintain high taxi fares. They limit total supply by requiring each taxicab to have a medallion, and then limit the total number of medallions. Who gains from this? Taxicab companies that own the valuable medallions. Who loses? The consumer, of course.[10]

Another example of such a policy is the control of liquor licenses by state governments. By requiring any bar or restaurant that serves alcohol to have a liquor license and then by limiting the number of licenses, entry by new res tauranteurs is limited, which allows those who have the licenses to earn higher prices and profit margins.

In U.S. agricultural policy, output is reduced by incentives, rather then outright quotas. *Acreage limitation programs* give farmers financial incentives (in the form of direct income transfers) to leave some of their acreage idle. Figure 9.13 shows how prices can be increased by reducing supply in this way. Note that by limiting the acreage planted, the supply curve becomes completely inelastic at the quantity Q_1, and the market price is increased from P_0 to P_s.

Figure 9.13 also shows the changes in consumer and producer surplus re-

---

[9]In practice, price supports for many agricultural commodities are effected through the use of nonrecourse loans. The loan rate (say, per bushel of wheat) is in effect a price floor. The loan is usually for about nine months. If during this period market prices are not sufficiently high, farmers can forfeit their grain to the government (specifically to the Commodity Credit Corporation) as *full payment for the loan*. And, of course, farmers have the incentive to do this unless the market price rises above the support price.

[10]For example, as of 1986 New York City had not issued any new taxi medallions for half a century. Only 11,800 taxis were permitted to cruise the city's streets, the same number as in 1935! As a result, a medallion could be rented for $350 per week, or sold outright for over $100,000. It shouldn't be a surprise, then, that the city's taxicab companies have fought vigorously against phasing out medallions in favor of an open system. Washington, D.C. has such an open system: an average taxi ride there costs about half of what it does in New York, and taxis are far more available.

sulting from this policy. Note that once again the change in consumer surplus is

$$\Delta C.S. = -A - B$$

Farmers now receive a higher price for the production Q_1, which corresponds to a gain in surplus of rectangle A. But because production is reduced from Q_0 to Q_1, there is a loss of producer surplus corresponding to triangle C. Finally, farmers receive money from the government as an incentive to reduce production. Thus, the total change in producer surplus is now

$$\Delta P.S. = A - C + \text{payments for not producing}$$

The cost to the government is a payment sufficient to give farmers an incentive to reduce output to Q_1. That incentive must be at least as large as $B + C + D$ because that is the additional profit that could be made by planting, *given the higher price* P_s. (Remember that the higher price P_s gives farmers an incentive to produce *more*, but the government is trying to get them to produce *less*.) So the cost to the government is at least $B + C + D$ and the total change in producer surplus is therefore

$$\Delta P.S. = A - C + B + C + D = A + B + D$$

This is the same change in producer surplus as with price supports maintained by government purchases of output. (Refer to Figure 9.12.) Farmers,

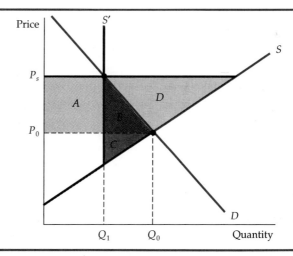

FIGURE 9.13 Acreage Limitations. To maintain a price P_s above the market-clearing price P_0, the government gives producers a financial incentive to reduce output to Q_1. For the incentive to work, it must be at least as large as $B + C + D$, the additional profit earned by planting, given the higher price P_s. The cost to the government is therefore at least $B + C + D$.

then, should be indifferent between the two policies because they end up gaining the same amount of money from each. Consumers should also be indifferent, aside from their concern about taxes, because they lose the same amount of money.

But which policy costs the government more? The answer depends on whether the sum of triangles $B + C + D$ in Figure 9.13 is larger or smaller than $(Q_2 - Q_1)P_s$ (the large speckled rectangle) less triangle D in Figure 9.12. Usually it will be smaller, so that an acreage limitation program costs the government (and society) less than price supports maintained by government purchases.

Still, even an acreage limitation program is more costly to society than simply handing the farmers money. The total change in welfare (ΔC.S. + ΔP.S. − Cost to Govt.) under the acreage limitation program is

$$\Delta\text{Welfare} = -A - B + A + B + D - B - C - D = -B - C$$

Society would clearly be better off if the government simply gave the farmers $A + B + D$, leaving price and output alone. Farmers would then gain $A + B + D$, the government would lose $A + B + D$, for a total welfare change of zero, instead of a loss of $B + C$. Unfortunately, economic efficiency is not always the objective of government policy.[11]

EXAMPLE 9.4 SUPPORTING THE PRICE OF WHEAT

In Example 2.2 of Chapter 2, we began to examine the market for wheat in the United States. Using simple linear demand and supply curves, we found that the market-clearing price of wheat was about $3.46 in 1981, but it fell to about $1.80 by 1985 because of a large drop in export demand. In fact, government price support programs kept the actual price of wheat much higher—about $3.70 in 1981, and about $3.20 in 1985. How did these programs work, how much did they end up costing consumers, and how much did they add to the federal budget deficit?

First, let us examine the market in 1981. In that year there were no effective limitations on the production of wheat, and price was increased by government purchases. How much would the government have had to buy to get the price from $3.46 to $3.70? To answer this, first write the equations for supply, and

---

[11]In 1983 the Reagan administration introduced the *Payment-in-Kind Program* (PIK). Under this program, producers who had already reduced acreage under the Reduced Acreage Program could keep fallow an additional 30 percent of their base acreage. A corn producer, for example, would then be given corn directly from government reserves at an amount equal to 80 percent of the normal yield on the number of fallow acres. The farmer could then sell that corn in the market for cash. The objective of PIK was to remove more land from production (thereby maintaining higher prices by reducing output), and reduce government stocks of grain, which had been growing rapidly. Unfortunately, the program did not deal with the fundamental problem: Price supports, whether maintained by government purchases or by incentives to reduce output, are inefficient.

for total (domestic plus export) demand:

1981 Supply:	$Q_S = 1800 + 240P$
1981 Demand:	$Q_D = 3550 - 266P$

By equating supply and demand, you can check that the market-clearing price is $3.46, and that the quantity produced is 2630 million bushels. Figure 9.14 illustrates this.

To increase the price to $3.70, the government must buy a quantity of wheat Q_g. *Total* demand (private plus government) will then be

1981 Total Demand:	$Q_{DT} = 3550 - 266P + Q_g$

Now equate supply with this total demand:

$$1800 + 240P = 3550 - 266P + Q_g$$

or

$$Q_g = 506P - 1750$$

This equation can be used to determine the required quantity of government wheat purchases Q_g as a function of the desired support price P. So to achieve a price of $3.70, the government must buy

$$Q_g = (506)(3.70) - 1750 = 122 \text{ million bushels}$$

Note in Figure 9.14 that these 122 million bushels are the difference between supply at the $3.70 price (2688 million bushels) and private demand (2566 million bushels). The figure also shows the gains and losses to consumers and producers. Recall that consumers lose rectangle A and triangle B. The reader can verify that rectangle A is $(3.70 - 3.46)(2566) = \$616$ million, and triangle B is $(\frac{1}{2})(3.70 - 3.46)(2630 - 2566) = \$8$ million, so that the total cost to consumers is $624 million.

The cost to the government is the $3.70 it pays for the wheat times the 122 million bushels it buys, or $452 million. The total cost of the program is then $624 + $452 = $1076 million. This can be compared with the gain to producers, which is rectangle A plus triangles B and C. You can verify that this gain is $638 million.

Price supports for wheat were clearly expensive in 1981. To increase the surplus of farmers by $638 million, consumers and taxpayers together had to pay $1076 million. But in fact taxpayers paid even more. Wheat producers were also given subsidies of about 30 cents per bushel, which adds up to another $806 million.

In 1985 the situation became even worse because of the drop in export demand. In that year the supply and demand curves were as follows:

1985 Supply:	$Q_S = 1800 + 240P$
1985 Demand:	$Q_D = 2580 - 194P$

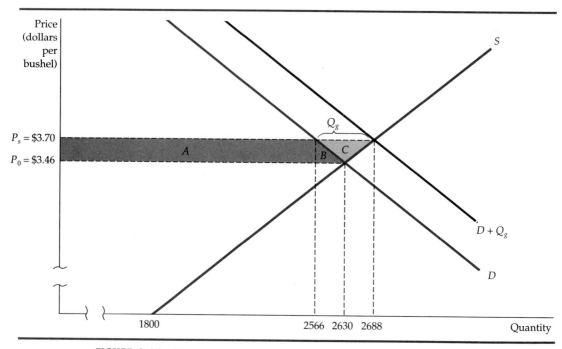

FIGURE 9.14 The Wheat Market in 1981. By buying 122 million bushels of wheat, the government increased the market-clearing price from $3.46 per bushel to $3.70.

You can verify that the market-clearing price and quantity were $1.80 and 2232 million bushels, respectively.

To increase the price to $3.20, the government bought wheat and imposed a production quota of about 2425 million bushels. (Farmers who wanted to take part in the subsidy program—and most did—had to agree to limit their acreage.) Figure 9.15 illustrates this situation. At the quantity 2425 million bushels, the supply curve becomes vertical. Now to determine how much wheat Q_g the government had to buy, set this quantity of 2425 equal to total demand:

$$2425 = 2580 - 194P + Q_g$$

or

$$Q_g = -155 + 194P$$

Substituting $3.20 for P, we see that Q_g must be 466 million bushels. This cost the government $(3.20)(466) = \$1491$ million.

Again, this is not the whole story. The government also provided a subsidy of 80 cents per bushel, so that producers again received about $4.00 for their wheat.[12] Since 2425 million bushels were produced, that subsidy cost an addi-

[12]The administration later decided to reduce the support price but increase the direct income subsidy, so farmers came out about the same. Is this a sensible change?

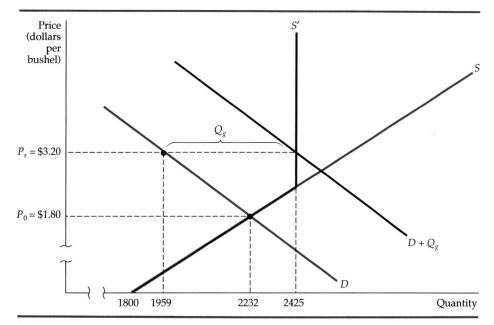

FIGURE 9.15   The Wheat Market in 1985.   In 1985 the demand for wheat was much lower than in 1981, so the market-clearing price was only $1.80. To increase the price to $3.20, the government bought 466 million bushels and also imposed a production quota of 2425 million bushels.

tional $1940 million. In all, U.S. wheat programs cost taxpayers nearly $3.5 billion in 1985.

Of course, there was also a loss of consumer surplus and a gain of producer surplus. You can calculate what they were.

9.5   Import Quotas and Tariffs

Many countries use import quotas and tariffs to keep the domestic price of a product above world levels and thereby enable the domestic industry to enjoy higher profits than it would under free trade. Unfortunately, the cost to society from this protection can be high, with the loss to consumers exceeding the gain to domestic producers. Let us use supply and demand curves to see what an import quota or tariff does.

Without a quota or tariff, a country will import a good when its world price is below the market price that would prevail if there were no imports. Figure 9.16 illustrates this. S and D are the domestic supply and demand curves. If there were no imports, the domestic price and quantity would be P_0 and Q_0,

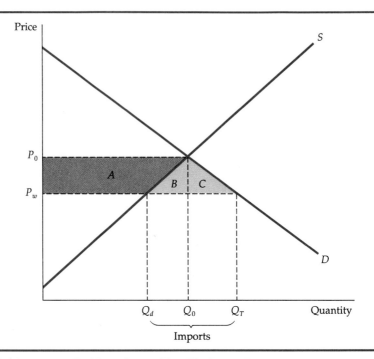

FIGURE 9.16   Import Tariff or Quota That Eliminates Imports.   In a free market, the domestic price equals the world price P_w. A total Q_T is consumed, of which Q_d is produced domestically, and the rest imported. By eliminating imports, the price is increased to P_0. The gain to producers is trapezoid A. The loss to consumers is $A + B + C$, so the deadweight loss is $B + C$.

which equate supply and demand. But the world price P_w is below P_0, so domestic consumers have an incentive to purchase from abroad, which they will do if imports are not restricted. How much will be imported? The domestic price will fall to the world price P_w, and at this lower price domestic production will fall to Q_d, and domestic consumption will rise to Q_T. Imports are then the difference between domestic consumption and domestic production, $Q_T - Q_d$.

Now suppose the government, bowing to pressure from the domestic industry, eliminates imports from this market by imposing a quota of zero (i.e., forbidding any importation of the good). What are the gains and losses from such a policy?

With no imports allowed, the domestic price will rise to P_0. Consumers who still purchase the good (in quantity Q_0) will pay more and will lose an amount of surplus given by trapezoid A and triangle B. Also, given this higher price, some consumers will no longer buy the good, so there is an additional loss of consumer surplus, given by traingle C. The total change in consumer surplus is therefore

$$\Delta C.S. = -A - B - C$$

What about producers? Output is now higher (Q_0 instead of Q_d) and is sold at a higher price (P_0 instead of P_w). Producer surplus therefore increases by the amount of trapezoid A:

$$\Delta \text{P.S.} = A$$

The change in total surplus, $\Delta \text{C.S.} + \Delta \text{P.S.}$, is therefore $-B - C$. Once again there is a deadweight loss—consumers lose more than producers gain.

Imports could also be reduced to zero by imposing a large enough tariff. The tariff would have to be equal to or greater than the difference between P_0 and P_w. With a tariff of this size, there will be no imports and therefore no government revenue from tariff collections, so the effect on consumers and producers would be the same as with a quota.

More often, government policy is designed to reduce, but not eliminate, imports. Again, this can be done with either a tariff or a quota, as Figure 9.17 shows. Without a tariff or quota, the domestic price will equal the world price P_w, and imports will be $Q_T - Q_d$. Now suppose a tariff of T dollars per unit is imposed on imports. Then the domestic price will rise to P^* (the world price plus the tariff); domestic production will rise; and domestic consumption will fall.

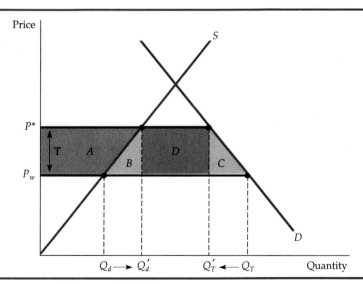

FIGURE 9.17   Import Tariff or Quota (general case).   By reducing imports, the domestic price is increased from P_w to P^*. This can be achieved by a quota, or by a tariff T = P^* − P_w. Trapezoid A again measures the gain to domestic producers. The loss to consumers is $A + B + C + D$. If a tariff is used, the government gains D, the revenue from the tariff, so the net domestic loss is $B + C$. If a quota is used instead, rectangle D becomes part of the profits of foreign producers, and the net domestic loss is $B + C + D$.

In Figure 9.17 this tariff leads to a change of consumer surplus given by

$$\Delta C.S. = -A - B - C - D$$

The change in producer surplus is again

$$\Delta P.S. = A$$

Finally, the government will collect revenue in the amount of the tariff times the quantity of imports, which is rectangle D. The total change in welfare, $\Delta C.S.$ plus $\Delta P.S.$ plus the revenue to the government, is therefore $-A - B - C - D + A + D = -B - C$. Triangles B and C again represent the deadweight loss from restricting imports.

Suppose the government used a quota instead of a tariff to restrict imports: Foreign producers are permitted to ship only a specific quantity ($Q_T' - Q_d'$ in Figure 9.17) to the United States. Foreign producers can then charge the higher price P^* for their U.S. sales. The changes in U.S. consumer and producer surplus will then be the same as with the tariff, but instead of the U.S. government collecting the revenue given by rectangle D, this money will go to the foreign producers as higher profits. Compared with the tariff, the United States as a whole will be even worse off, losing D as well as the deadweight loss B and C.[13]

This is exactly what happened with automobile imports from Japan in the 1980s. The Reagan administration, under pressure from domestic automobile producers, negotiated "voluntary" import restraints, under which the Japanese agreed to restrict their shipments of cars to the United States. The Japanese could therefore sell those cars that were shipped at a price higher than the world level and capture a higher profit margin on each one. The United States would have been better off by simply imposing a tariff on these imports.

EXAMPLE 9.5 THE SUGAR QUOTA

In recent years the world price of sugar has been as low as 4 cents per pound, while the United States price has been above 25 cents per pound. Why? The U.S. government protects the $3 billion domestic sugar industry, which would virtually be put out of business if it had to compete with low-cost foreign producers, by restricting imports. This has been good news for U.S. sugar producers. It has even been good news for some foreign sugar producers—those whose successful lobbying efforts have given them big shares of the quota. But

---

[13]Alternatively, an import quota can be maintained by rationing imports to U.S. importing firms or trading companies. These middlemen would have the rights to import a fixed amount of the good each year. Of course, these rights are valuable because the middleman can buy the product on the world market at price P_w and then sell it at price P^*. The aggregate value of these rights is therefore just given by rectangle D. If the government *sells* the rights for this amount of money, it can capture the same revenue it would receive with a tariff. But if these rights are given away, as sometimes happens, the money will go instead as a windfall to middlemen.

like most policies of this sort, it has been bad news for consumers.

To see just how bad, let's look at the sugar market in 1983. Here are the relevant data for that year:

U.S. production: 11.4 billion pounds
U.S. consumption: 17.8 billion pounds
U.S. price: 22 cents per pound
World price: 8.5 cents per pound

At these prices and quantities, the price elasticity of U.S. supply is 1.67, and the price elasticity of U.S. demand is -0.2.[14]

We will fit linear supply and demand curves to these data, and then use them to calculate the effects of the quotas. You can verify that the following U.S. supply curve is consistent with a production level of 11.4 billion pounds, a price of 22 cents/lb, and a supply elasticity of 1.67[15]:

$$U.S.\ Supply: \qquad Q_S = -6.2 + 0.8P$$

where quantity is measured in billions of pounds and price in cents per pound. Similarly, the -0.2 demand elasticity together with the data for U.S. consumption and U.S. price give the following linear demand curve:

$$U.S.\ Demand: \qquad Q_D = 22.2 - 0.2P$$

These supply and demand curves are plotted in Figure 9.18. At the 8.5 cent world price, U.S. production would have been negligible, and U.S. consumption would have been 20.5 billion pounds, almost all of this imports. But fortunately for U.S. producers, imports were limited to only 6.4 billion pounds, which pushed the price up to 22 cents.

What did this cost U.S. consumers? The lost consumer surplus is given by the sum of trapezoid A, triangles B and C, and rectangle D. You should go through the calculations to verify that trapezoid A is equal to $810 million, traingle B to $729 million, triangle C to $182 million, and rectangle D to $864 million, so that the total cost to consumers in 1983 was about $2.5 billion.

How much did producers gain from this policy? Their increase in surplus is given by trapezoid A (i.e., $810 million). The $864 million of rectangle D was a gain for those foreign producers who succeeded in obtaining large allotments of the quota because they received a higher price for their sugar. Triangles B and C represent a deadweight loss of $911 million.

---

[14]These elasticity estimates are based on Morris E. Morkre and David G. Tarr, *Effects of Restrictions on United States Imports: Five Case Studies and Theory*, U.S. Federal Trade Commission Staff Report, June 1981, as well as the studies that they cite. For a general discussion of sugar quotas and other aspects of U.S. agricultural policy, see D. Gale Johnson, *Agricultural Policy and Trade* (New York: New York University Press, 1985).

[15]Turn to Section 2.5 of Chapter 2 to review how to fit linear supply and demand functions to data of this kind.

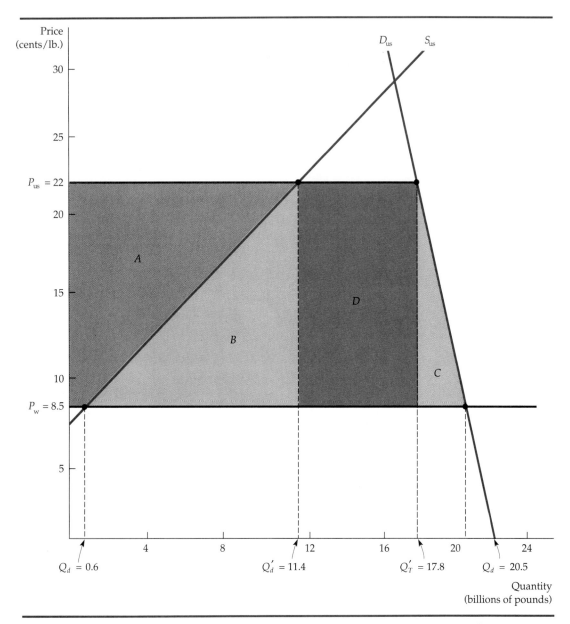

FIGURE 9.18 Impact of Sugar Quota in 1983. At the world price of 8.5 cents per pound, 20.5 billion pounds of sugar would have been consumed in the United States, of which all but 0.6 billion pounds would have been imported. By restricting imports to 6.4 billion pounds, the U.S. price was increased to 22 cents. The cost to consumers, $A + B + C + D$, was about $2.5 billion. The gain to domestic producers is trapezoid A, $810 million. Rectangle D, $864 million, was a gain to foreign producers who obtained quota allotments. Triangles B and C represent the deadweight loss of $911 million.

9.6 The Impact of a Tax or Subsidy

What would happen to the price of widgets if the government imposed a $1 tax on every widget sold? Many people would answer that the price would increase by a dollar, with consumers now paying a dollar more per widget than they would have paid without the tax. But this answer is wrong.

Or consider the following question. The government wants to impose a 50 cent per gallon tax on gasoline and is considering two methods of collecting the tax. Under Method 1, the owner of each gas station would deposit the tax money (50 cents times the number of gallons sold) in a locked box, for a government agent to collect. Under Method 2 the consumer would lock up the tax (50 cents times the number of gallons purchased) until it was collected by the government. Which method costs the consumer more? Many people would answer that Method 2 does, but this answer is also wrong.

The burden of a tax (or the benefit of a subsidy) falls partly on the consumer and partly on the producer. Furthermore, it really does not matter who puts the money in the collection box (or sends the check to the government)—Methods 1 and 2 above both cost the consumer the same amount of money. As we will see, the share of a tax borne by consumers depends on the shapes of the supply and demand curves, and in particular on the relative elasticities of supply and demand. As for our first question, a $1 tax on widgets would indeed cause the price of widgets to rise, but usually by *less* than a dollar, and sometimes by *much* less. To understand why, let us use supply and demand curves to see how consumers and producers are affected when a tax is imposed on a product, and what happens to price and quantity.

For simplicity we will consider a *specific tax* (i.e., a tax of a certain amount of money *per unit sold*). This is in constrast to an *ad valorem* (i.e., proportional) tax, such as a state sales tax. (The analysis of an ad valorem tax is roughly the same and yields the same qualitative results.) Examples of specific taxes include federal and state taxes on gasoline and cigarettes.

Suppose the government imposes a tax of t cents per unit on widgets. Assuming everyone obeys the law, the government must then receive t cents for every widget sold. *This means that the price the consumer pays must exceed the net price the seller receives by t cents.* Figure 9.19 illustrates this simple accounting relationship—and its implications. Here, P_0 and Q_0 represent the market price and quantity *before* the tax is imposed. P_b is the price that consumers pay, and P_s is the net price that sellers receive *after* the tax is imposed. Note that $P_b - P_s = t$, so the government is happy.

How do we determine what the market quantity will be after the tax is imposed, and how much of the tax is borne by consumers and how much by producers? First, remember that what consumers care about is the price that they must pay: P_b. The amount that consumers will buy is given by the demand curve; it is the quantity that we read off of the demand curve given a price P_b.

Similarly, what producers care about is the net price they receive, P_s. Given P_s, the quantity they will produce is read off the supply curve. Finally, we know that the quantity that producers sell must equal the quantity that consumers buy—a single quantity is bought and sold. The solution, then, is to find the quantity that corresponds to a price of P_b on the demand curve, and a price of P_s on the supply curve, such that the difference $P_b - P_s$ is equal to the tax t. In Figure 9.19 this quantity is shown as Q_1.

Who bears the burden of the tax? In Figure 9.19, this burden is shared roughly equally by consumers and producers. The market price (the price consumers must pay) rises by half of the tax. And the price that producers receive falls by roughly half of the tax.

As Figure 9.19 shows, *four conditions* must be satisfied after the tax is in place. First, the quantity sold and the buyer's price P_b must lie on the demand curve (because consumers are interested only in the price they must pay). Second, the quantity sold and the seller's price P_s must lie on the supply curve (because producers are concerned only with the amount of money they receive net of the tax). Third, the quantity demanded must equal the quantity supplied (Q_1 in the figure). And fourth, the difference between the price the buyer pays and

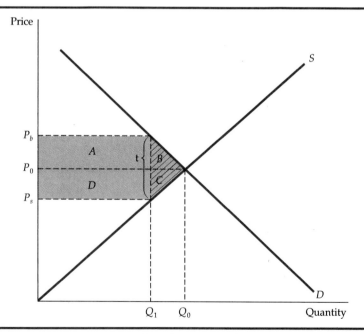

FIGURE 9.19   Incidence of a Tax. P_b is the price (including the tax) paid by buyers. P_s is the price that sellers receive, net of the tax. Here the burden of the tax is split about evenly between buyers and sellers. Buyers lose $A + B$, sellers lose $D + C$, and the government earns $A + D$ in revenue. The deadweight loss is $B + C$.

the price the seller receives must equal the tax t. These conditions can be summarized by the following four equations:

$$Q^D = Q^D(P_b) \tag{9.1a}$$

$$Q^S = Q^S(P_s) \tag{9.1b}$$

$$Q^D = Q^S \tag{9.1c}$$

$$P_b - P_s = t \tag{9.1d}$$

If we know the demand curve $Q^D(P_b)$, the supply curve $Q^S(P_s)$, and the size of the tax t, we can solve these equations for the buyers' price P_b, the sellers' price P_s, and the total quantity demanded and supplied. Although this task might appear to be difficult, in fact it is easy, as we demonstrate in Example 9.6.

Figure 9.19 also shows us that a tax results in a *deadweight loss*. Observe that because buyers pay a higher price, there is a change in consumer surplus given by

$$\Delta C.S. = -A - B$$

And because sellers now receive a lower price, there is a change in producer surplus given by

$$\Delta P.S. = -C - D$$

Government tax revenue is $(t)(Q_1)$, the sum of rectangles A and D. The total change in welfare, ΔC.S. plus ΔP.S. plus the revenue to the goverment, is therefore $-A - B - C - D + A + D = -B - C$. Triangles B and C represent the deadweight loss from the tax.

In Figure 9.19 the burden of the tax is shared about evenly between consumers and producers, but this is not always the case. If demand is relatively inelastic and supply is relatively elastic, the burden of the tax will fall mostly on consumers. Figure 9.20a shows why: It takes a relatively large increase in price to get consumers to reduce demand by even a small amount, whereas only a small price decrease is needed to reduce the quantity producers supply. Figure 9.20b shows the opposite: If demand is relatively elastic and supply is relatively inelastic, the burden of the tax will fall mostly on producers.

So even if we have only estimates of the elasticities of demand and supply at a point or for a small range of prices and quantities, as opposed to the entire demand and supply curves, we can still roughly determine who will bear the greatest burden of a tax (whether the tax is actually in effect or is only under discussion as a policy option). In general, *a tax falls mostly on the buyer if E_d/E_s is small, and mostly on the seller if E_d/E_s is large.*

It is not difficult to calculate the exact percentage of the tax borne by producers and by consumers. To do this, we use the following "pass-through"

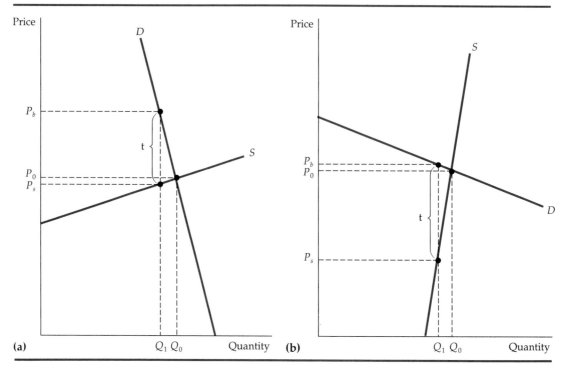

FIGURE 9.20   Impact of a Tax Depends on Elasticities of Supply and Demand.   (a) If demand is very inelastic relative to supply, the burden of the tax falls mostly on buyers. (b) If demand is very elastic relative to supply, the tax falls mostly on sellers.

formula:

$$\text{Pass-through fraction} = E_S/(E_S - E_D)$$

This formula tells us what fraction of the tax is passed through to consumers in the form of higher prices.[16] For example, when demand is totally inelastic, so that E_D is zero, the pass-through fraction is 1, and all the tax is borne by consumers. And when demand is totally elastic, the pass-through fraction is zero, and producers bear all the tax.

A *subsidy* can be analyzed in much the same way as a tax—in fact, you can think of a subsidy as a *negative tax*. With a subsidy, the sellers' price *exceeds* the buyers' price, and the difference between the two is the amount of the subsidy. As you would expect, the effect of a subsidy on the quantity produced and consumed is just the opposite of the effect of a tax—the quantity will increase. Figure 9.21 illustrates this. At the presubsidy market price P_0, the elasticities

---

[16]Correspondingly, the fraction of the tax borne by producers is given by: $-E_D/(E_S - E_D)$.

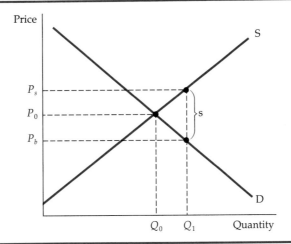

FIGURE 9.21 Subsidy. A subsidy can be thought of as a negative tax. Like a tax, the benefit of a subsidy is split between buyers and sellers, depending on the relative elasticities of supply and demand.

of supply and demand are roughly equal; as a result, the benefit of the subsidy is shared roughly equally between consumers and producers. As with a tax, this is not always the case. In general, *the benefit of a subsidy accrues mostly to consumers if E_d/E_s is small, and mostly to producers if E_d/E_s is large.*

As with a tax, given the supply curve, the demand curve, and the size of the subsidy s, one can solve for the resulting prices and quantity. The same four conditions apply for a subsidy as with a tax, but now the difference between the sellers' price and the buyers' price is equal to the subsidy. Again, we can write these conditions algebraically:

$$Q^D = Q^D(P_b) \tag{9.2a}$$

$$Q^S = Q^S(P_s) \tag{9.2b}$$

$$Q^D = Q^S \tag{9.2c}$$

$$P_s - P_b = s \tag{9.2d}$$

To make sure you understand how to analyze the impact of a tax or subsidy, you might find it helpful to work through one or two examples, such as Exercises 9.5 and 9.6 at the end of this chapter.

EXAMPLE 9.6 A TAX ON GASOLINE

During the 1980 presidential campaign, John Anderson, an independent candidate, proposed a 50 cent per gallon tax on gasoline. The idea of a gasoline tax, both to raise government revenue and to reduce oil consumption and U.S. dependence on oil imports from the Persian Gulf, has been widely discussed since then. Let's determine how a 50 cent tax would affect the price and consumption of gasoline.

We will do this analysis in the setting of market conditions during the middle of 1986—when gasoline was selling for about $1 per gallon, and total consumption was about 100 billion gallons per year (bg/yr).[17] We will also use intermediate-run elasticities (i.e., elasticities that would apply to a period of about three to six years after a price change).

A reasonable number for the intermediate-run elasticity of gasoline demand is -0.5 (see Example 2.3 in Chapter 2). We can use this elasticity figure, together with the $1 and 100 bg/yr price and quantity numbers to calculate a linear demand curve for gasoline. (Refer to Chapter 2, Section 2.5, for a review of how to do this.) You can verify that the following demand curve fits these data:

$$\text{Gasoline Demand:} \qquad Q^D = 150 - 50P$$

Gasoline is refined from crude oil, some of which is produced domestically and some imported.[18] The supply curve for gasoline will therefore depend on the world price of oil, on domestic oil supply, and on the cost of refining. The details are beyond the scope of this example, but a reasonable number for the elasticity of supply is 0.4. You should verify that this elasticity, together with the $1 and 100 bg/yr price and quantity, gives the following linear supply curve:

$$\text{Gasoline Supply:} \qquad Q^S = 60 + 40P$$

You should also verify that these demand and supply curves imply a market price of $1.00 and quantity of 100 bg/yr.

We can use these linear demand and supply curves to calculate the effect of a $0.50 per gallon tax. First, we write the four conditions that must hold, as given by equations (9.1a-d):

$$Q^D = 150 - 50P_b \qquad \text{(Demand)}$$

$$Q^S = 60 + 40P_s \qquad \text{(Supply)}$$

$$Q^D = Q^S \qquad \text{(Supply must equal demand)}$$

$$P_b - P_s = 0.50 \qquad \text{(Government must receive \$0.50/gallon)}$$

Now combine the first three equations to equate supply and demand:

$$150 - 50P_b = 60 + 40P_s$$

We can rewrite the last of the four equations as $P_b = P_s + 0.50$, and substitute

---

[17]Of course, this price varied across regions, and across grades of gasoline, but we can ignore this here. Quantities of oil and oil products are often measured in barrels; there are 42 gallons in a barrel, so the 1986 quantity figure could also be written as 2.4 billion barrels per year.

[18]Some gasoline is also imported directly from foreign refineries.

this for P_b in the above equation:

$$150 - 50(P_s + 0.50) = 60 + 40P_s$$

Now we can rearrange this and solve for P_s:

$$50P_s + 40P_s = 150 - 25 - 60$$

$$90P_s = 65, \text{ or } P_s = .72$$

Remember that $P_b = P_s + 0.50$, so $P_b = 1.22$. Finally, we can determine the total quantity from either the demand or supply curve. Using the demand curve (and the price $P_b = 1.22$), we find that $Q = 150 - (50)(1.22) = 150 - 61$, or $Q = 89$ bg/yr. This represents an approximately 11 percent decline in gasoline consumption. Figure 9.22 illustrates these calculations and the effect of the tax.

The burden of this tax would be split roughly evenly between consumers and producers; consumers would pay about 22 cents per gallon more for the gasoline they bought, and producers would receive about 28 cents per gallon

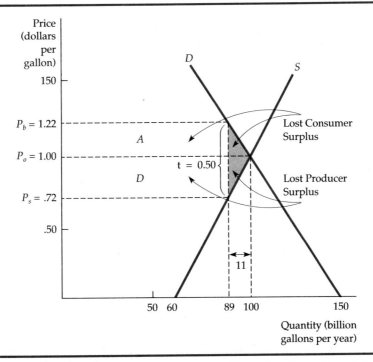

FIGURE 9.22   Impact of 50 Cent Gasoline Tax.   The price of gasoline at the pump increases from $1.00 per gallon to $1.22, and the quantity sold falls from 100 to 89 billion gallons per year. The annual revenue from the tax is $(0.50)(89) = \$44.5$ billion. The two shaded triangles show the deadweight loss of $2.75 billion per year.

less. It should not be surprising, then, that both consumers and producers opposed such a tax, and politicians representing both groups fought the proposal every time it came up. But note that the tax would raise significant revenue for the government. The annual revenue from the tax would be $(t)(Q) = (0.50)(89) = \$44.5$ billion per year.

The cost to consumers and producers, however, will be more than the $44.5 billion in tax revenue. Figure 9.22 shows the deadweight loss from this tax as the two shaded triangles. The two rectangles A and D represent the total tax collected by the government, but the total loss of consumer and producer surplus is larger.

Before deciding whether or not a gasoline tax is desirable, it is important to know how large the resulting deadweight loss is likely to be. We can easily calculate this from Figure 9.22. Combining the two small triangles into one large one, we see that the area is

$$(\tfrac{1}{2}) \times (\$0.50/\text{gallon}) \times (11 \text{ billion gallons/year})$$

$$= \$2.75 \text{ billion per year}$$

This deadweight loss is about 6 percent of the government revenue resulting from the tax, and must be balanced against any additional benefits that the tax might bring.

Summary

1. Simple models of supply and demand can be used to analyze a wide variety of government policies. Specific policies that we have examined include price controls, minimum prices, price support programs, production quotas or incentive programs to limit output, import tariffs and quotas, and taxes and subsidies.

2. In each case, consumer and producer surplus is used to evaluate the gains and losses to consumers and producers. Applying the methodology to natural gas price controls, airline regulation, price supports for wheat, and the sugar quota, we found that these gains and losses can be quite large.

3. When government imposes a tax or subsidy, price usually does not rise or fall by the full amount of the tax or subsidy. Also, the incidence of a tax or subsidy is usually split between producers and consumers. The fraction that each group ends up paying or receiving depends on the relative elasticities of supply and demand.

4. Government intervention generally leads to a deadweight loss; even if consumer welfare and producer welfare are weighted equally, there will be a net loss from government policies that shift welfare from one group to the other. In some cases this deadweight loss will be small, but there are other cases—price supports and import quotas are examples—for which it is large. This deadweight loss is a form of economic inefficiency that must be taken into account when policies are designed and implemented.

5. Government intervention in a competitive market is not always a bad thing. Government—and the society it represents—might have other objectives besides economic efficiency. In addition, there are situations in which government intervention can *improve* economic efficiency. This includes externalities and cases of market failure. These situations, and the way government can respond to them, are discussed in Part 4 of the book.

Review Questions

1. What is meant by deadweight loss? Why does a price ceiling usually result in a deadweight loss?

2. Suppose the supply curve for a good was completely inelastic. If the government imposed a price ceiling below the market-clearing level, would a deadweight loss result? Explain why or why not.

3. Does a price ceiling necessarily make consumers better off? Under what conditions might it make them worse off?

4. Suppose the government regulates the price of a good to be no lower than some minimum level. Can such a minimum price make producers as a whole worse off? Explain.

5. How are production limits used in practice to raise the prices of the following goods or services: (i) taxi rides, (ii) drinks in a restaurant or bar, (iii) wheat or corn?

6. Suppose the government wants to increase the incomes of farmers. Why do price supports or acreage limitation programs cost society more than simply giving the farmers money?

7. Suppose the government wants to limit imports of a certain good. Is it preferable to use an import quota or a tariff? Why?

8. The burden of a tax is shared by producers and consumers. Under what conditions will consumers pay most of the tax? Under what conditions will producers pay most of it? What determines the share of a subsidy that benefits consumers?

9. Why does a tax create a deadweight loss? What determines the size of the deadweight loss?

Exercises

1. Some people have suggested raising the minimum wage, perhaps with a government subsidy to employers to help finance the higher wage. This exercise examines the economics of a minimum wage and wage subsidies. Suppose the supply of labor is given by

$$L^S = 10w$$

where L^S is the quantity of labor (in millions of persons employed each year), and w is the wage rate (in dollars per hour). The demand for labor is given by

$$L^D = 60 - 10w$$

a. What will the free market wage rate and employment level be? Suppose the government sets a minimum wage of $4 per hour. How many people would then be employed?

b. Suppose that instead of a minimum wage, the government offered a subsidy of $1 per hour for each employee. (The subsidy would be paid directly to the company.) What will the total level of employment be now? What will the equilibrium wage rate be?

2. About 100 million pounds of jelly beans are consumed in the United States each year, and the price has been about 50 cents per pound. However, jelly bean producers feel that their incomes are too low, and they have convinced the government that price supports are in order. The government will therefore buy up as many jelly beans as necessary to keep the price at $1.00 per pound. However, government economists are worried about the impact of this program, because they have no estimates of the elasticities of jelly bean demand or supply.

a. Could this program cost the government *more* than $50 million per year? Under what conditions? Could it cost *less* than $50 million per year? Under what conditions? Illustrate with a diagram.

b. Could this program cost consumers (in terms of lost consumer surplus) *more* than $50 million per year? Under what conditions? Could it cost consumers *less* than $50 million per year? Under what conditions? Again, use a diagram to illustrate.

3. In 1983 the Reagan administration introduced a new agricultural program called the Payment-in-Kind Program. To examine how the program worked, let's consider the wheat market.

a. Suppose the demand function is $Q^D = 28 - 2P$ and the supply function is $Q^S = 4 + 4P$, where P is the price of wheat in dollars per bushel, and Q is the quantity in billions of bushels. Find the free market equilibrium price and quantity.

b. Now suppose the government wants to lower the supply of wheat by 25 percent from the free market equilibrium by paying farmers to withdraw land from production. However, the payment is made in wheat rather than in dollars—hence the name of the program. The wheat comes from the government's vast reserves that resulted from previous price support programs. The amount of wheat paid is equal to the amount that could have been harvested on the land withdrawn from production. Farmers are free to sell this wheat on the market. How much is now produced by farmers? How much is indirectly supplied to the market by the government? What is the new market price? How much do farmers gain? Do consumers gain or lose?

c. Had the government not given the wheat back to the farmers, it would have stored or destroyed it. Do taxpayers gain from the program? What potential problems does the program create?

4. The domestic supply and demand curves for hula beans are as follows:

Supply:	$P = 50 + Q$
Demand:	$P = 200 - 2Q$

where P is the price in cents per pound, and Q is the quantity in millions of pounds. We are a small country in the world hula bean market, where the current price (which will not be affected by anything we do) is 60 cents per pound. Congress is considering a tariff of 40 cents per pound. Compute the domestic price of hula beans that will result if the tariff is imposed. Also compute the dollar gain or loss to domestic consumers, domestic producers, and government revenue from the tariff.

5. You know that if a tax is imposed on a particular product, the burden of the tax is shared by producers and consumers. You also know that the demand for automobiles is characterized by a stock adjustment process. Suppose a special 20 percent sales tax is suddenly imposed on automobiles. Will the share of the tax paid by consumers rise, fall, or stay the same over time? Explain briefly. Repeat for a 50 cent per gallon gasoline tax.

6. Suppose the market for widgets can be described by the following equations:

Demand:	$P = 10 - Q$
Supply:	$P = Q - 4$

where P is the price in dollars per unit, and Q is the quantity in thousands of units. Then

    a. What is the equilibrium price and quantity?
    b. Suppose the government imposes a tax of \$1 per unit to reduce widget consumption and raise government revenues. What will the new equilibrium quantity be? What price will the buyer pay? What amount per unit will the seller receive?
    c. Suppose the government has a change of heart about the importance of widgets to the happiness of the American public. The tax is removed, and a subsidy of \$1 per unit is granted to widget producers. What will the equilibrium quantity be? What price will the buyer pay? What amount per unit (including the subsidy) will the seller receive? What will be the total cost to the government?

7. In Example 9.1 we calculated the gains and losses from price controls on natural gas, and found that there was a deadweight loss of \$1.4 billion. This calculation was based on a price of oil of \$8 per barrel. If the price of oil had been \$12 per barrel, what would the free market price of gas be? How large a deadweight loss would have resulted if the maximum allowable price had been \$1.00 per mcf?

8. Example 9.5 describes the effects of the sugar quota in 1983. At that time, imports were limited to 6.4 billion pounds, which pushed the price in the United States up to 22 cents per pound. Suppose imports had been limited to only 4 billion pounds and that the demand and supply functions were unchanged. What would the U.S. price have been as a result? By how much would domestic producers have gained and consumers have lost?

PART III

Market Structure and Competitive Strategy

Part III examines a broad range of markets and explains how the pricing, investment, and output decisions of firms depend on market structure and the behavior of competitors.

Chapters 10 and 11 examine market power—the ability to affect price, either by a seller or a buyer. We will see how market power arises, how it differs across firms, how it affects the welfare of consumers and producers, and how it can be limited by government. We will also see how firms can design pricing strategies to take advantage of their market power.

Chapters 12 and 13 deal with markets in which the number of firms is limited. We will examine a variety of such markets, ranging from monopolistic competition, in which many firms sell differentiated products, to cartels, in which a group of firms coordinate their decisions and act as a monopolist. We are particularly concerned with markets in which there are only a few firms. Then, each firm must design its pricing, output, and investment strategies, keeping in mind how its competitors are likely to react. We will develop and apply principles from game theory to analyze such strategies.

Chapter 14 shows how markets for factor inputs such as labor and raw materials operate. We will examine the firm's input decisions, and how those decisions depend on the structure of the input market. Chapter 15 then focuses on the firm's capital investment decisions. We will see how the firm can value the profits it expects an investment to yield in the future, and then compare this value with the cost of the investment to determine whether the investment is worthwhile.

CHAPTER 10

Market Power: Monopoly and Monopsony

In a perfectly competitive market, there are enough sellers and buyers of a good so that no single seller or buyer can affect its price. Price is determined by the market forces of supply and demand. Individual firms take the market price as a given in deciding how much to produce and sell, and consumers take it as a given in deciding how much to buy.

The subjects of this chapter, *monopoly* and *monopsony*, are the polar opposites of perfect competition. A *monopoly* is a market that has only one seller, but many buyers. A *monopsony* is just the opposite—a market with many sellers, but only one buyer. Monopoly and monopsony are closely related, which is why we cover them in the same chapter.

We first discuss the behavior of a monopolist. Because a monopolist is the sole producer of a product, the market demand curve relates the price that the monopolist receives to the quantity it offers for sale. We will see how a monopolist can take advantage of its control over price and how the profit-maximizing price and quantity differ from what would prevail in a competitive market. In general, the monopolist's quantity will be lower and its price higher than the competitive quantity and price (and greater than marginal cost). This imposes a cost on society, because fewer consumers buy the product, and those who do pay more for it. This is why the antitrust laws forbid firms from monopolizing most markets. When increasing returns to scale make monopoly desirable—for example, with local electric power companies—we will see how the government can then maximize social welfare by regulating the monopolist's price.

Pure monopoly is rare, but in many markets only a few firms compete with each other. The interactions of firms in such markets can be complicated and often involve aspects of strategic gaming, a topic covered in Chapters 12 and 13. However, the firms may be able to affect price and may find it profitable to charge a price higher than marginal cost. These firms have *monopoly power*. We will discuss the determinants of monopoly power, its measurement, and its implications for pricing.

Next we will turn to *monopsony*. Unlike a competitive buyer, the price that a monopsonist pays is a function of the quantity that it purchases. The monopsonist's problem is to choose the quantity that maximizes its net benefit from the purchase—the value derived from the good less the money paid for it. By showing how the choice is made, we will demonstrate the close parallel between monopsony and monopoly.

Pure monopsony is also unusual. But many markets have only a few buyers, who can purchase the good for less than would be paid in a competitive market. These buyers have *monopsony power*. Typically this occurs in markets for inputs to production. For example, the three large U.S. car manufacturers have monopsony power in the markets for tires, car batteries, and other parts. We will discuss the determinants of monopsony power, its measurement, and its implications for pricing.

Monopoly and monopsony power are two forms of *market power*. Market power refers to the ability—by a seller or a buyer—to affect the price of a good.[1] Since sellers or buyers have at least some market power (in most real-world markets), we need to understand how market power works and its implications for firms and consumers.

10.1 Monopoly

As the sole producer of a product, a monopolist is in a unique position. If the monopolist decides to raise the price of the product, it need not worry about competitors who, by charging a lower price, would capture a larger share of the market at the monopolist's expense. The monopolist *is* the market and has complete control over the amount of output offered for sale.

But this does not mean that the monopolist can charge as high a price as it wants—at least not if its objective is to maximize profit. This textbook is a case in point. The Macmillan Publishing Company owns the copyright and is therefore a monopoly producer of this book. Then why doesn't it sell the book for $350 a copy? Because most of you would refuse to buy it, and Macmillan would earn a much lower profit.

To maximize profit, the monopolist must first determine the characteristics of market demand, as well as its costs. Knowledge of demand and cost is crucial for a firm's economic decision making. Given this knowledge, the monopolist

---

[1] The courts often use the term "monopoly power" to mean a substantial amount of market power, and in particular enough to warrant scrutiny under the antitrust laws. Economists, however, find this distinction difficult to make. In this book we use "monopoly power" to mean market power on the part of sellers, whether substantial or not.

must then decide how much to produce and sell. The price per unit the monopolist receives then follows directly from the market demand curve. (Equivalently, the monopolist can determine price, and the quantity it will sell at that price follows from the market demand curve.)

The Monopolist's Output Decision

What quantity should the monopolist produce? In Chapter 8 we saw that to maximize profit, a firm must set output so that marginal revenue is equal to marginal cost. This is the solution to the monopolist's problem. In Figure 10.1, the market demand curve D is the monopolist's average revenue curve. It specifies the price per unit that the monopolist receives as a function of its output level. Also shown are the corresponding marginal revenue curve MR and the average and marginal cost curves, AC and MC.[2] Marginal revenue and marginal cost are equal at quantity Q^*. Then from the demand curve we find the price P^* that corresponds to this quantity Q^*.

How can we be sure that Q^* is the profit-maximizing quantity? Suppose the monopolist produces a smaller quantity Q_1 and receives the corresponding higher price P_1. As Figure 10.1 shows, marginal revenue would then exceed marginal cost, so if the monopolist produced a little more than Q_1, it would receive extra profit (MR − MC) and thereby increase its total profit. In fact, the monopolist could keep increasing output, adding more to its total profit until output Q^*, at which point the incremental profit earned from producing one more unit is zero. So the smaller quantity Q_1 is not profit maximizing, even though it allows the monopolist to charge a higher price. By producing Q_1 instead of Q^*, the monopolist's total profit would be smaller by an amount equal to the shaded area below the MR curve and above the MC curve, between Q_1 and Q^*.

In Figure 10.1, the larger quantity Q_2 is likewise not profit maximizing. At this quantity marginal cost exceeds marginal revenue, so if the monopolist produced a little less than Q_2, it would increase its total profit (by MC − MR). The monopolist could increase its profit even more by reducing output all the way to Q^*. The increased profit achieved by producing Q^* instead of Q_2 is given by the area below the MC curve and above the MR curve, between Q^* and Q_2.

We can also see algebraically that Q^* maximizes profit. Profit π is the difference between revenue and cost, both of which are functions of Q:

$$\pi(Q) = R(Q) - C(Q)$$

As Q is increased from zero, profit will increase until it reaches a maximum, and then begin to decrease. Thus, the profit-maximizing Q is such that the

---

[2]This analysis applies to both the short and long run, so we haven't bothered to distinguish the two.

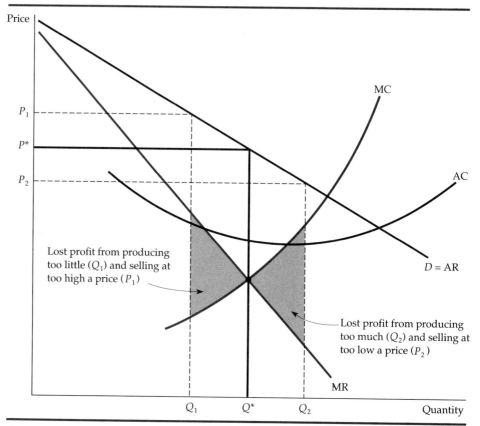

FIGURE 10.1 Profit Is Maximized When Marginal Revenue Equals Marginal Cost. Q^* is the output level at which MR = MC. If the firm produces a smaller output, say, Q_1, it sacrifices some profit because the extra revenue that could be earned from producing and selling the units between Q_1 and Q^* exceeds the cost of producing them. Similarly, expanding output from Q^* to Q_2 would reduce profits, because the additional cost would exceed the additional revenue.

incremental profit resulting from a small increase in Q is just zero (i.e., $\Delta\pi/\Delta Q = 0$). Then

$$\Delta\pi/\Delta Q = \Delta R/\Delta Q - \Delta C/\Delta Q = 0$$

But $\Delta R/\Delta Q$ is marginal revenue, and $\Delta C/\Delta Q$ is marginal cost, so the profit-maximizing condition is that MR − MC = 0, or MR = MC.

A Numerical Example

To grasp this result more clearly, let's work through a numerical example. Suppose the cost function is

$$C(Q) = 50 + Q^2$$

(i.e., there is a fixed cost of $50, and variable cost is Q^2). Then average cost is $C(Q)/Q = 50/Q + Q$, and marginal cost is $\Delta C/\Delta Q = 2Q$. And suppose demand is given by

$$P(Q) = 40 - Q$$

so that revenue is $R(Q) = P(Q)Q = 40Q - Q^2$, and marginal revenue is MR $= \Delta R/\Delta Q = 40 - 2Q$. By setting marginal revenue equal to marginal cost, you can verify that profit is maximized when $Q = 10$, which corresponds to a price of $30.

These cost and revenue functions are plotted in Figure 10.2a, as is the profit function $\pi(Q) = R(Q) - C(Q)$. Note that when the firm produces little or no output, profit is negative because of the fixed cost. Profit increases as Q increases, until it reaches a maximum of $150 at $Q^* = 10$, and then decreases as Q is increased further. And at the point of maximum profit, the slopes of the revenue and cost functions are the same. (Note that the tangent lines rr′ and cc′ are parallel.) The slope of the revenue function is $\Delta R/\Delta Q$, or marginal revenue, and the slope of the cost function is $\Delta C/\Delta Q$, or marginal cost. Profit is maximized when marginal revenue equals marginal cost, so the slopes are equal.

Figure 10.2b shows the corresponding average and marginal revenue curves, and average and marginal cost curves. Marginal revenue and marginal cost intersect at $Q^* = 10$. At this quantity, average cost is $15 per unit and price is $30 per unit, so average profit is $30 - $15 = $15 per unit. Since 10 units are sold, profit is $(10)($15) = 150, the area of the shaded rectangle.

A Rule of Thumb for Pricing

We know that price and output should be such that marginal revenue equals marginal cost, but how can the manager of a firm find the correct price and output level in practice? Most managers have only limited knowledge of the average and marginal revenue curves that their firms face. Similarly, they might know only the firm's marginal cost over a limited output range. We therefore want to translate the condition that marginal revenue should equal marginal cost into a rule of thumb that can be more easily applied in practice.

To do this, we first rewrite the expression for marginal revenue:

$$\text{MR} = \frac{\Delta R}{\Delta Q} = \frac{\Delta(PQ)}{\Delta Q}$$

Note that the extra revenue from an incremental unit of quantity, $\Delta(PQ)/\Delta Q$, has two components. Producing one extra unit and selling it at price P brings in revenue $(1)(P) = P$. But the firm faces a downward-sloping demand curve, so producing and selling this extra unit also results in a small drop in price $\Delta P/\Delta Q$, which reduces the revenue from *all* units sold (i.e., a change in revenue

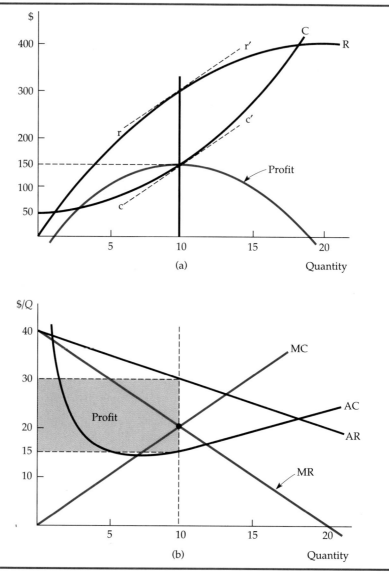

FIGURE 10.2 Example of Profit Maximization. Part (a) shows total revenue R, total cost C, and profit, the difference between the two. Part (b) shows average and marginal revenue and average and marginal cost. Marginal revenue is the slope of the total revenue curve, and marginal cost is the slope of the total cost curve. The profit-maximizing output is $Q^* = 10$, the point where marginal revenue equals marginal cost. At this output level, the slope of the profit function is zero, and the slopes of the total revenue and total cost curves are equal. The profit per unit is $15, the difference between average revenue and average cost. Because 10 units are produced, total profit is $150.

$Q[\Delta P/\Delta Q]$). Thus,

$$MR = P + Q\frac{\Delta P}{\Delta Q} = P + P\left(\frac{Q}{P}\right)\left(\frac{\Delta P}{\Delta Q}\right)$$

We obtained the expression on the right by taking the term $Q(\Delta P/\Delta Q)$ and multiplying and dividing it by P. Recall that the elasticity of demand is defined as $E_d = (P/Q)(\Delta Q/\Delta P)$. Thus, $(Q/P)(\Delta P/\Delta Q)$ is the reciprocal of the elasticity of demand, $1/E_d$, measured at the profit-maximizing output, and

$$MR = P + P(1/E_d)$$

Now, since the firm's objective is to maximize profit, we can set marginal revenue equal to marginal cost:

$$P + P(1/E_d) = MC$$

which can be rearranged to give us

$$\boxed{\frac{P - MC}{P} = -\frac{1}{E_d}} \qquad (10.1)$$

This relationship provides a rule of thumb for pricing. The left-hand side, $(P - MC)/P$, is the markup over marginal cost as a percentage of price. The relationship says that this markup should equal minus the inverse of the elasticity of demand.[3] (This will be a positive number because the elasticity of demand is negative.) Equivalently, we can rearrange this equation to express price directly as a markup over marginal cost:

$$P = \frac{MC}{1 + (1/E_d)} \qquad (10.2)$$

For example, if the elasticity of demand is -4 and marginal cost is \$9 per unit, price should be \$9/(1 − ¼) = \$9/.75 = \$12 per unit.

How does the price set by a monopolist compare with the price under competition? In Chapter 8 we saw that in a perfectly competitive market, price equals marginal cost. A monopolist charges a price that exceeds marginal cost, but by an amount that depends inversely on the elasticity of demand. As the markup equation (10.1) shows, if demand is extremely elastic, E_d is a large negative number, and price will be very close to marginal cost, so that a monopolized market will look much like a competitive one. In fact, when demand is very elastic, there is little benefit to being a monopolist.

---

[3]Remember that this markup equation applies at the point of a profit maximum. If both the elasticity of demand and marginal cost vary considerably over the range of outputs under consideration, you may have to know the entire demand and marginal cost curves to determine the optimum output level. On the other hand, this equation can be used to check whether a particular output level and price are optimal.

Shifts in Demand

In a competitive market there is a clear relationship between price and the quantity supplied. That relationship is the supply curve, which, as we saw in Chapter 8, represents the marginal cost of production for the industry as a whole. The supply curve tells us how much will be produced at every price.

A monopolized market has no supply curve. In other words, there is no one-to-one relationship between price and the quantity produced. The reason is that the monopolist's output decision depends not only on marginal cost, but also on the shape of the demand curve. As a result, shifts in demand do not trace out a series of prices and quantities as happens with a competitive supply curve. Instead, shifts in demand can lead to changes in price with no change in output, changes in output with no change in price, or changes in both.

This is illustrated in Figure 10.3a and 10.3b. In both parts of the figure, the demand curve is initially D_1, the corresponding marginal revenue curve is MR_1, and the monopolist's initial price and quantity are P_1 and Q_1. In Figure 10.3a the demand curve is shifted down and rotated; the new demand and marginal revenue curves are shown as D_2 and MR_2. Note that MR_2 intersects the marginal cost curve at the same point that MR_1 does. As a result, the quantity produced stays the same. Price, however, falls to P_2.

In Figure 10.3b the demand curve is shifted up and rotated. The new marginal revenue curve MR_2 intersects the marginal cost curve at a larger quantity, Q_2 instead of Q_1. But the shift in the demand curve is such that the price charged is exactly the same.

Shifts in demand usually cause changes in both price and quantity. But the special cases shown in Figure 10.3 illustrate an important distinction between monopoly and competitive supply. A competitive industry supplies a specific quantity at every price. No such relationship exists for a monopolist, which, depending on how demand shifts, might supply several different quantities at the same price, or the same quantity at different prices.

The Effect of a Tax

A tax on output can also affect a monopolist very differently than it affects a competitive industry. In Chapter 9 we saw that when a specific (i.e., per unit) tax is imposed on a competitive industry, the market price rises by an amount that is less than the tax, and that the burden of the tax is shared by producers and consumers. Under monopoly, however, price can rise by *more* than the amount of the tax.

Analyzing the effect of a tax on a monopolist is straightforward. Suppose a specific tax of t dollars per unit is levied, so that the monopolist must remit t dollars to the government for every unit it sells. Therefore, the firm's marginal (and average) cost is increased by the amount of the tax t. If MC was the firm's original marginal cost, its optimal production decision is now given by

$$MR = MC + t$$

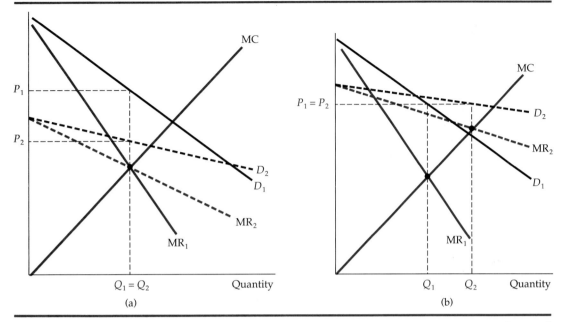

(a)

(b)

FIGURE 10.3a Shift in Demand Leads to Change in Price but Same Output. Demand curve D_1 shifts to new demand curve D_2. But the new marginal revenue curve MR_2 intersects marginal cost at the same point that the old marginal revenue curve MR_1 did. The profit-maximizing output therefore remains the same, although price falls from P_1 to P_2.

FIGURE 10.3b Shift in Demand Leads to Change in Output but Same Price. The new marginal revenue curve MR_2 intersects marginal cost at a higher output level Q_2. But because demand is now more elastic, price remains the same.

Graphically, we shift the marginal cost curve upwards by an amount t, and find the new intersection with marginal revenue. Figure 10.4 shows this. Here Q_0 and P_0 are the quantity and price before the tax is imposed, and Q_1 and P_1 are the quantity and price after the tax.

Shifting the marginal cost curve upwards results in a smaller quantity and higher price. Sometimes price increases by less than the tax, but not always—in Figure 10.4, price increases by *more* than the tax. This would be impossible in a competitive market, but it can happen with a monopolist because the relationship between price and marginal cost depends on the elasticity of demand. Suppose, for example, that a monopolist faces a constant elasticity demand curve, with elasticity -2. Equation (10.2) then tells us that price will equal twice marginal cost. With a tax t, marginal cost increases to MC + t, so price increases to 2(MC + t) = 2MC + 2t, i.e., it rises by twice the amount of the tax.

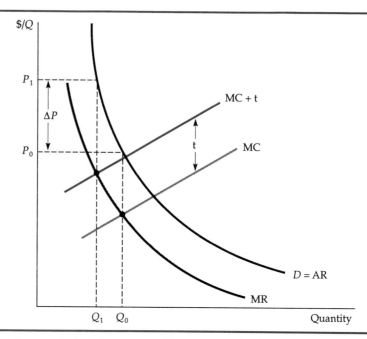

FIGURE 10.4   Effect of Excise Tax on Monopolist.   With a tax t per unit, the firm's effective marginal cost is increased to MC + t. A tax can therefore be analyzed by shifting the marginal cost curve up by amount t. In this example, the increase in price ΔP is larger than the tax t.

10.2   Monopoly Power

Pure monopoly is rare. Markets in which several firms compete with one another are much more common. We will say more about the forms this competition can take in Chapters 12 and 13. But we should explain here why in a market with only several firms, each firm is likely to face a downward-sloping demand curve, and therefore will produce so that price exceeds marginal cost.

Suppose, for example, that four firms produce toothbrushes, which have the market demand curve shown in Figure 10.5a. Let's assume that these four firms are producing an aggregate of 20,000 toothbrushes per day (5,000 per day each), and selling them at $1.50 each. Note that market demand is relatively inelastic; you can verify that at this $1.50 price, the elasticity of demand is −1.5.

Now suppose that Firm A is deciding whether to lower its price to increase sales. To make this decision, it needs to know how its sales would respond to a change in its price. In other words, it needs some idea of the demand curve *it* faces, as opposed to the *market* demand curve. A reasonable possibility is shown in Figure 10.5b, where the firm's demand curve D_A is much more elastic

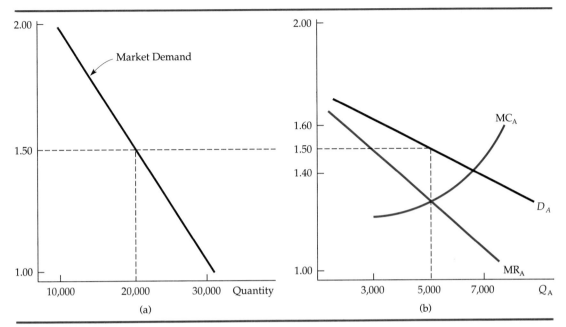

FIGURE 10.5a   Market Demand for Toothbrushes.   FIGURE 10.5b   Demand for Tooth-brushes as Seen by Firm A.   At a market price of $1.50, elasticity of market demand is −1.5. Firm A, however, sees a much more elastic demand curve D_A because of competition from other firms. At a price of $1.50, Firm A's demand elasticity is −6. Still, Firm A has some monopoly power. It's profit-maximizing price is $1.50, which exceeds marginal cost.

than the market demand curve. (At the $1.50 price the elasticity is −6.0.) The firm might anticipate that by raising price from $1.50 to $1.60, its sales will drop, say, from 5000 units to 3000, as consumers buy more toothbrushes from the other firms. (If *all* firms raised their prices to $1.60, sales for Firm A would fall only to 4500.) But for several reasons sales won't drop to zero, as they would in a perfectly competitive market. First, Firm A's toothbrushes might be a little different from its competitors, so some consumers will pay a bit more for them. Second, the other firms might also raise their prices. Similarly, Firm A might anticipate that by lowering its price from $1.50 to $1.40, it can sell more, perhaps 7000 toothbrushes instead of 5000. But it will not capture the entire market. Some consumers might still prefer the competitors' toothbrushes, and the competitors might also lower their prices.

So Firm A's demand curve depends on how much its product differs from its competitors' products and on how the four firms compete with one another. We will discuss product differentiation and interfirm competition in Chapters 12 and 13. But one important point should be clear: *Firm A is likely to face a demand curve that is more elastic than the market demand curve, but not infinitely elastic like the demand curve facing a perfectly competitive firm.*

Given knowledge of its demand curve, how much should Firm A produce? The same principle applies: The profit-maximizing quantity equates marginal revenue and marginal cost. In Figure 10.5b that quantity is 5000 units, and the corresponding price is $1.50, which exceeds marginal cost. So although Firm A is not a pure monopolist, *it does have monopoly power*—it can profitably charge a price greater than marginal cost. Of course, its monopoly power is less than it would be if it had driven away the competition and monopolized the market, but it might still be substantial.

This raises two questions. First, how can we *measure* monopoly power, so that we can compare one firm with another? (So far we have been talking about monopoly power only in *qualitative* terms.) Second, what are the *sources* of monopoly power, and why do some firms have more monopoly power than others? We address both these questions below, although a more complete answer to the second question will be provided in Chapters 12 and 13.

Measuring Monopoly Power

Remember the important distinction between a perfectly competitive firm and a firm with monopoly power: For the competitive firm, price equals marginal cost, but price exceeds marginal cost for the firm with monopoly power. Therefore, a natural way to measure monopoly power is to examine the extent to which the profit-maximizing price exceeds marginal cost. In particular, we can use the markup ratio of price minus marginal cost to price that we introduced earlier as part of a rule of thumb for pricing. This measure of monopoly power was introduced by economist Abba Lerner in 1934 and is called *Lerner's Degree of Monopoly Power*[4]:

$$L = (P - MC)/P$$

This Lerner index always has a value between zero and one. For a perfectly competitive firm, $P = MC$ and $L = 0$. The larger L is, the greater the degree of monopoly power.

This index of monopoly power can also be expressed in terms of the elasticity of demand facing the firm. Using equation (10.1), we know that

$$L = (P - MC)/P = -1/E_d \qquad (10.3)$$

Remember, however, that E_d is now the elasticity of the *firm's* demand curve, and not the market demand curve. In the toothbrush example discussed above,

[4]Abba P. Lerner, "The Concept of Monopoly and the Measurement of Monopoly Power," *Review of Economic Studies* 1 (June 1934): 157–175.

the elasticity of demand for Firm A is -6.0, and the degree of monopoly power is $\frac{1}{6} = 0.167$.[5]

Note that considerable monopoly power does not necessarily imply high profits. Profit depends on *average* cost relative to price. Firm A might have more monopoly power than firm B, but might earn lower profits because it has much higher average costs.

The Rule of Thumb for Pricing

In the previous section we saw how the relationship among price, marginal cost, and the elasticity of demand can be used as a rule of thumb for pricing by a monopolist. In particular, equation (10.2) allowed us to compute price as a simple markup over marginal cost:

$$P = \frac{MC}{1 + (1/E_d)}$$

This relationship provides a rule of thumb for any firm with monopoly power, if we remember that E_d is the elasticity of demand for the *firm*, and not the elasticity of *market* demand.

It is harder to determine the elasticity of demand for the firm than for the market because the firm must consider how its competitors will react to price changes. Essentially, the manager must estimate the percentage change in the firm's unit sales that is likely to result from a 1 percent change in the price the firm charges. This estimate might be based on a formal model, or it might be based on the manager's intuition and experience.

Given an estimate of the firm's elasticity of demand, the manager can calculate the proper markup. If the firm's elasticity of demand is large, this markup will be small (and we can say that the firm has very little monopoly power). If the firm's elasticity of demand is small, this markup will be large (and the firm will have considerable monoply power). Figure 10.6a and 10.6b illustrates these two extremes.

---

[5]The Lerner index is useful to measure the extent of monopoly power, but three problems can arise when it is applied to the analysis of public policy toward firms. First, because marginal cost is difficult to measure, average variable cost is often used instead in Lerner index calculations. (Marginal revenue, however, can be used instead of marginal cost.) Second, the Lerner index measures the extent to which monopoly power has actually been exercised; if the firm prices below its optimal price (possibly to avoid legal scrutiny), its potential monopoly power will not be noted by the index. Third, the index ignores dynamic aspects of pricing like effects of the learning curve, shifts in demand, etc. This is discussed in R. S. Pindyck, "The Measurement of Monopoly Power in Dynamic Markets," *Journal of Law and Economics* 28 (April 1985): 193–222.

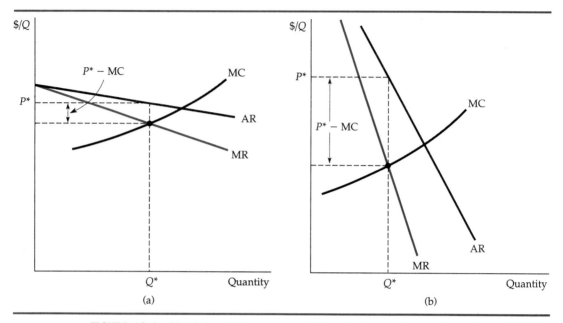

FIGURE 10.6 Elasticity of Demand and Price Markup. The markup $(P - MC)/P$ is equal to minus the inverse of the elasticity of demand. If demand is elastic as in part (a), the markup is small, and the firm has little monopoly power. The opposite is true if demand is inelastic, as in part (b).

EXAMPLE 10.1 MARKUP PRICING: SUPERMARKETS TO DESIGNER JEANS

Three examples should help clarify the use of markup pricing. Consider a retail supermarket chain. Although the elasticity of market demand for food is small (about −1), several supermarkets usually serve most areas, so no single supermarket can raise its prices very much without losing many customers to other stores. As a result, the elasticity of demand for any one supermarket is often as large as −10. Substituting this number for E_d in equation (10.2), we find $P = MC/(1 - 0.1) = MC/(0.9) = (1.11)MC$. In other words, the manager of a typical supermarket should set prices about 11 percent above marginal cost. For a reasonably wide range of output levels (over which the size of the store and the number of its employees will remain fixed), marginal cost includes the cost of purchasing the food at wholesale, together with the costs of storing the food, arranging it on the shelves, etc. For most supermarkets the markup is indeed about 10 or 11 percent.

Small convenience stores, which often open on Sundays or even 24 hours a day, typically charge higher prices than supermarkets. Why? Because a convenience store faces a less elastic demand curve. Its customers are generally less price sensitive. They might need a quart of milk or a loaf of bread late at night, or find it inconvenient to drive to the supermarket. The elasticity of demand for a convenience store is about -5, so the markup equation implies that its prices should be about 25 percent above marginal cost, as indeed they typically are.

The Lerner index, $(P - MC)/P$, tells us that the convenience store has more monopoly power, but does it make larger profits? No. Because its volume is far smaller and its average fixed costs are larger, it usually earns a much smaller profit than a large supermarket, despite its higher markup.

Finally, consider the producer of designer jeans. Although many companies produce blue jeans, some consumers will pay much more for jeans with a designer label. Just how much more they will pay—or more exactly, how much sales will drop in response to higher prices—is a question that the producer must carefully consider because it is critical in determining the price at which the clothing will be sold (at wholesale to retail stores, which then mark up the price further for sale to their customers). With designer jeans, demand elasticities in the range of -3 to -4 are typical for the major labels. This means that price should be 33 to 50 percent higher than marginal cost. Marginal cost is typically \$8 to \$12 per pair, and the wholesale price is in the \$12 to \$18 range.

EXAMPLE 10.2 HOW TO PRICE PRERECORDED VIDEO CASSETTES

During the mid-1980s, the number of households owning video cassette recorders (VCRs) grew rapidly, as did the markets for rentals and sales of prerecorded cassettes. Although many more video cassettes are rented through small retail outlets than are sold outright, the market for sales is large and growing. Producers, however, found it difficult to decide what price to charge for their cassettes. As a result, popular movies were selling for vastly different prices. Table 10.1 shows the retail price in February 1985 for what were then some of the best-selling video cassettes.[6]

Note that *The Empire Strikes Back* was selling for nearly \$80, while *Star Trek*, a film that appealed to the same audience and was about as popular, sold for only about \$25. These price differences reflected uncertainty and a wide divergence of views on pricing by producers. The issue was whether lower prices would induce consumers to buy the video cassettes, rather than rent them. Because producers do not share in the retailers' revenues from rentals, they should charge a low price for cassettes only if that will induce enough consumers to buy them. Because the market was young, producers had no good

---

[6]"Video Producers Debate the Value of Price Cuts," *New York Times*, Feb. 19, 1985.

TABLE 10.1

Title	Retail Price ($)
Purple Rain	29.98
Raiders of the Lost Ark	24.95
Jane Fonda Workout	59.95
The Empire Strikes Back	79.98
An Officer and A Gentleman	24.95
Star Trek: The Motion Picture	24.95
Star Wars	39.98

estimates of the elasticity of demand, so they based prices on hunches or trial and error.

As the market matured, however, sales data and market research studies put pricing decisions on firmer ground. The data and studies strongly indicated that demand was elastic, and that the profit-maximizing price was in the range of $20 to $30. By 1988, many producers had begun moving to lower prices across the board, and sales and profits increased as a result.

10.3 Sources of Monopoly Power

Why do some firms have considerable monopoly power, and other firms have little or none? Remember that monopoly power is the ability to set price above marginal cost, and the amount by which price exceeds marginal cost depends inversely on the firm's elasticity of demand. As equation (10.3) shows, the less elastic its demand curve, the more monopoly power a firm has. The ultimate determinant of monopoly power is therefore the firm's elasticity of demand. The question is, why do some firms (e.g., a supermarket chain) face a demand curve that is more elastic, while others (e.g., a producer of designer clothing) face one that is less elastic?

Three factors determine a firm's elasticity of demand. First is the *elasticity of market demand*. The firm's own demand will be at least as elastic as market demand, so the elasticity of market demand limits the potential for monopoly power. Second is the *number of firms* in the market. If there are many firms, it is unlikely that any one firm will be able to affect price significantly. Third is the *interaction among firms*. Even if only two or three firms are in the market, each firm will be unable to profitably raise price very much if the rivalry among them is aggressive, with each firm trying to capture as much of the market as it can. Let's examine each of these three determinants of monopoly power.

The Elasticity of Market Demand

If there is only a single firm—a pure monopolist—its demand curve is the market demand curve. Then the firm's degree of monopoly power depends completely on the elasticity of market demand. More often, however, several firms compete with one another; then the elasticity of market demand sets a lower limit on the elasticity of demand for each firm. Recall our example of the toothbrush producers that was illustrated in Figure 10.5. The market demand for toothbrushes might not be very elastic, but each firm's demand will be more elastic. How much more depends on how the firms compete with one another. (In Figure 10.5, the elasticity of market demand is -1.5, and the elasticity of demand for each firm is -6.) But no matter how the firms compete, the elasticity of demand for each firm could never become smaller than -1.5.

The demand for oil is fairly inelastic (at least in the short run), which is why OPEC could raise oil prices far above marginal production cost during the 1970s and early 1980s. The demands for such commodities as coffee, cocoa, tin, and copper are much more elastic, which is why attempts by producers to cartelize those markets and raise prices have largely failed. In each case, the elasticity of market demand limits the potential monopoly power of individual producers.

The Number of Firms

The second determinant of a firm's demand curve, and hence its monopoly power, is the number of firms in the market. Other things being equal, the monopoly power of each firm will fall as the number of firms increases. As more and more firms compete, each firm will find it harder to raise prices and avoid losing sales to other firms.

What matters, of course, is not just the total number of firms, but the number of "major players" (i.e., firms that have a significant share of the market). For example, if only two large firms account for 90 percent of sales in a market, with another 20 firms accounting for the remaining 10 percent, the two large firms might have considerable monopoly power. When only a few firms account for most of the sales in a market, the market is highly *concentrated*.[7]

It is sometimes said (not always jokingly) that the greatest fear of American business is competition. That may or may not be true. But we would certainly expect that when only a few firms are in a market, their managers would prefer that no new firms enter the market. An increase in the number of firms can only reduce the monopoly power of each incumbent firm. An important aspect of competitive strategy (discussed in detail in Chapter 13) is finding ways to create *barriers to entry*—conditions that deter entry by new competitors.

---

[7]A statistic called the *concentration ratio*, which measures the fraction of sales accounted for by, say, the four largest firms, is often used to describe the concentration of a market. Concentration is one, but not the only, determinant of market power.

Sometimes there are natural barriers to entry. For example, one firm may have a *patent* on the technology needed to produce a particular product. This makes it impossible for other firms to enter the market, at least until the patent expires.[8] Other legally created rights work in the same way—a *copyright* can limit the sale of a book, music, or a computer software program to a single company, and the need for a government *license* can prevent new firms from entering the market for telephone service, television broadcasting, or interstate trucking. Finally, *economies of scale* may make it too costly for more than a few firms to supply the entire market. In some cases the economies of scale may be so large that it is most efficient for a single firm—a *natural monopoly*—to supply the entire market. We will discuss scale economies and natural monopoly in more detail shortly.

The Interaction Among Firms

How competing firms interact is also an important—and sometimes the most important—determinant of monopoly power. Suppose there are four firms in a market, and consider how they might compete with one another. They might, for example, compete very aggressively, undercutting one another's prices to capture a greater market share. This would probably drive prices down to nearly competitive levels. Each firm will be afraid to raise its price for fear of being undercut and losing its market share, and thus it will have little or no monopoly power.

However, the firms might not compete very much. They might even collude (in violation of the antitrust laws). At the extreme, they might form a *cartel* and explicitly agree to limit output and raise prices. Raising prices in concert rather than individually is more likely to be profitable, so collusion can generate substantial monopoly power.

Firms can thus interact in several ways. At this stage we simply want to point out that other things being equal, monopoly power is smaller when firms compete aggressively, and is larger when they cooperate.

Remember that a firm's monopoly power often changes over time, as its operating conditions (market demand and cost), its behavior, and the behavior of its competitors change. Monopoly power must therefore be thought of in a dynamic context. For example, the market demand curve might be very inelastic in the short run but much more elastic in the long run. (This is the case with oil, which is why OPEC had considerable short-run but less long-run monopoly power.) Furthermore, real or potential monopoly power in the short run can make an industry more competitive in the long run. Large short-run profits can induce new firms to enter an industry, thereby reducing monopoly power over the longer term.

---

[8]In the United States, patents last for 17 years.

10.4 The Social Costs of Monopoly Power

In a competitive market, price equals marginal cost, while monopoly power implies that price exceeds marginal cost. Because monopoly power results in higher prices and lower quantities produced, we would expect it to make consumers worse off and the firm better off. But suppose we value the welfare of consumers the same as that of producers. Does monopoly power make consumers and producers in the aggregate better or worse off?

We can answer this question by comparing the consumer and producer surplus that results when a competitive industry produces a good with the surplus that results when a monopolist supplies the entire market.[9] (We assume that the competitive market and the monopolist have the same cost curves.) Figure 10.7 shows the average and marginal revenue curves and marginal cost curve

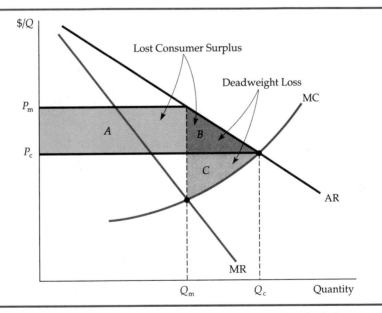

FIGURE 10.7 Deadweight Loss from Monopoly Power. The shaded rectangle and triangles show changes in consumer and producer surplus when moving from competitive price and quantity, P_c and Q_c, to a monopolist's price and quantity, P_m and Q_m. Because of the higher price, consumers lose $A + B$, and producer gains $A - C$. The total change in surplus is $-B - C$. This is the deadweight loss from monopoly power.

[9]If there were two or more firms, each with some monopoly power, the analysis would be more complex. However, the basic results would be the same.

for the monopolist. To maximize profit, the firm produces at the point where marginal revenue equals marginal cost, so that the price and quantity are P_m and Q_m. In a competitive market, price must equal marginal cost, so the competitive price and quantity, P_c and Q_c, are found at the intersection of the average revenue (demand) curve and the marginal cost curve. Now let's examine how surplus changes if we move from the competitive price and quantity, P_c and Q_c, to the monopoly price and quantity, P_m and Q_m.

Under monopoly the price is higher and consumers buy less. Because of the higher price, those consumers who buy the good lose surplus of an amount given by rectangle A. Those consumers who do not buy the good at price P_m but will buy at price P_c also lose surplus, of an amount given by triangle B. The total loss of consumer surplus is therefore A + B. The producer, however, gains rectangle A by selling at the higher price but loses triangle C, the additional profit it would have earned by selling $Q_c - Q_m$ at price P_c. The total gain in producer surplus is therefore A - C. Subtracting the loss of consumer surplus from the gain in producer surplus, we see a net loss of surplus given by B + C. This is the *deadweight loss from monopoly power*. Even if the monopolist's profits were taxed away and redistributed to the consumers of its products, there would be an inefficiency because output would be lower than under competition. The deadweight loss is the social cost of this inefficiency.

There may be an additional social cost of monopoly power that goes beyond the deadweight loss in triangles B and C. The firm may spend large amounts of money in a socially unproductive way to acquire, maintain, or exercise its monopoly power. This might involve advertising, lobbying, and legal efforts to avoid government regulation or antitrust scrutiny. Or it might mean installing but not utilizing extra productive capacity to convince potential competitors that they will be unable to sell enough to make entry worthwhile. Roughly speaking, the economic incentive to incur these costs should bear a direct relation to the gains to the firm from having monopoly power (i.e., rectangle A minus triangle C). Therefore, the larger the transfer from consumers to the firm (rectangle A), the larger the social cost of monopoly.

Price Regulation

Because of its social cost, antitrust laws prevent firms from accumulating excessive amounts of monopoly power. We will say more about the antitrust laws at the end of the chapter. Here, we examine another means by which society can limit monopoly power—price regulation.

We saw in Chapter 9 that in a competitive market, price regulation always results in a deadweight loss. This need not be the case, however, when a firm has monopoly power. On the contrary, price regulation can eliminate the deadweight loss that results from monopoly power.

Figure 10.8 illustrates the effects of price regulation. P_m and Q_m are the price and quantity that would result without regulation. Now suppose the price is

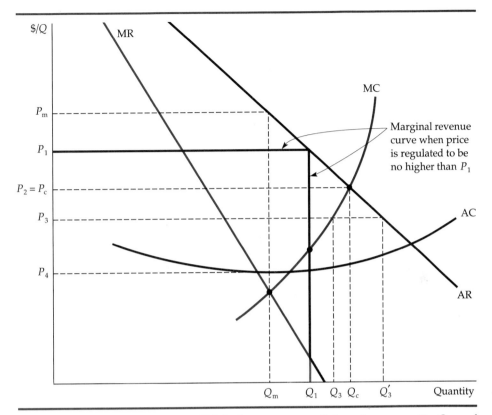

FIGURE 10.8 Price Regulation. If left alone, a monopolist produces quantity Q_m and charges price P_m. When the government imposes a price ceiling of P_1, the firm's average and marginal revenue are constant and equal to P_1 for output levels up to Q_1. For larger output levels, the old average and marginal revenue curves apply. The new marginal revenue curve is therefore given by the dark line, which intersects the marginal cost curve at Q_1. When price is lowered to P_c, at the point where marginal cost intersects average revenue, output increases to its maximum Q_c. This is the same output level that would be produced by a competitive industry. Lowering the price further, to P_3, reduces output to Q_3 and causes a shortage, $Q'_3 - Q_3$.

regulated to be no higher than P_1. Since the firm can charge no more than P_1 for output levels up to Q_1, its new average revenue curve is a horizontal line at P_1. For output levels greater than Q_1, the new average revenue curve is identical to the old average revenue curve because at these output levels the firm will charge less than P_1, and so it would be unaffected by the regulation.

The firm's new marginal revenue curve corresponds to its new average revenue curve, and is shown by the dark line in the figure. For output levels up to Q_1, marginal revenue is equal to average revenue. For output levels greater than Q_1, the new marginal revenue curve is identical to the old curve. The firm will produce quantity Q_1, because that is where its marginal revenue curve intersects its marginal cost curve. You can verify that at price P_1 and quantity Q_1, the deadweight loss from monopoly power is reduced.

As the price is lowered further, the quantity produced continues to increase and the deadweight loss to decline. At price P_c, where average revenue and marginal cost intersect, the quantity produced has increased to the competitive level, and the deadweight loss from monopoly power has been eliminated. Reducing the price even more, say, to P_3, results in a *reduction* in quantity. This is equivalent to imposing a price ceiling on a competitive industry. A shortage develops, $(Q'_3 - Q_3)$, as well as a deadweight loss from regulation. As the price is lowered further, the quantity produced continues to fall and the shortage grows. Finally, if the price is lowered below P_4, the minimum average cost, the firm loses money and goes out of business.

Price regulation is most often practiced for *natural monopolies* such as local

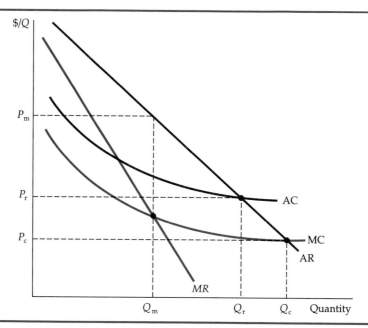

FIGURE 10.9   Regulating the Price of a Natural Monopoly.   A firm is a natural monopoly because it has economies of scale (declining average and marginal costs) over its entire output range. If price were regulated to be P_c, the firm would lose money and go out of business. Setting the price at P_r yields the largest possible output consistent with the firm's remaining in business; excess profit is zero.

utility companies. Figure 10.9 illustrates natural monopoly. Note that average cost is declining everywhere, so marginal cost is always below average cost. Unregulated, the firm would produce Q_m at P_m. Ideally, the regulatory agency would like to push the firm's price down to the competitive level P_c, but then the firm could not meet its average cost and would go out of business. The best alternative is therefore to set the price at P_r, where average cost and average revenue intersect. Then the firm earns no monopoly profit and output is as large as it can be without driving the firm out of business.

Regulation in Practice

Recall that the competitive price (P_c in Figure 10.8) is found where the firm's marginal cost and average revenue (demand) curves intersect. Likewise, for a natural monopoly the minimum feasible price (P_r in Figure 10.9) is found where average cost and demand intersect. Unfortunately it is often difficult to determine these prices accurately in practice because the firm's demand and cost curves may shift as market conditions evolve.

As a result, the regulation of a monopoly is usually based on the rate of return that it earns on its capital. The regulatory agency determines an allowed price, so that this rate of return is in some sense "competitive" or "fair." This is called *rate-of-return regulation:* The maximum price allowed is based on the (expected) rate of return that the firm will earn.[10]

Unfortunately, difficult problems—problems that gladden the hearts of lawyers and accountants—arise when implementing rate-of-return regulation. First, although it is a key element in determining the firm's rate of return, the firm's undepreciated capital stock is difficult to value. Second, a "fair" rate of return must be based on the firm's actual cost of capital, but that cost in turn depends on the behavior of the regulatory agency (and on investors' perceptions of what future allowed rates of return will be).

The difficulty of agreeing on a set of numbers to be used in rate-of-return calculations often leads to delays in the regulatory response to changes in cost and other market conditions, as well as long and expensive regulatory hearings. The major beneficiaries are usually lawyers, accountants, and, occasionally, economic consultants. The net result is *regulatory lag*—the delays of a year or more that are usually required to change the regulated price.

In the 1950s and 1960s, regulatory lag worked to the advantage of regulated firms. During those decades costs were typically falling (usually as a result of

---

[10]Regulatory agencies typically use a formula that looks something like the following to determine price:

$$P = \text{AVC} + (D + T + sK)/Q,$$

where AVC is average variable cost, Q is output, s is the allowed rate of return, D is depreciation, T is taxes, and K is the firm's current capital stock. The idea is to set s at some "fair" or "competitive" level, and then determine a corresponding price.

scale economies achieved as firms grew), so regulatory lag meant that these firms could, at least for a while, enjoy actual rates of return greater than those ultimately deemed "fair" at the end of regulatory proceedings. Beginning in the early 1970s, however, the situation changed, and regulatory lag worked to the detriment of regulated firms. For example, when oil prices were rising rapidly, electric utilities needed to raise their prices. Regulatory lag caused many of these firms to earn rates of return well below the "fair" rates they had been earning earlier.

10.5 Monopsony

So far our discussion of market power has focused entirely on the seller side of the market. Now we turn to the *buyer* side. We will see that if there are not too many buyers, they can also have market power and use it profitably to affect the price they pay for a product.

First, a few terms. *Monopsony* refers to a market in which there is a single buyer. An *oligopsony* is a market with only a few buyers. With one or only a few buyers, some buyers may have *monopsony power*, which is a buyer's ability to affect the price of a good. It enables the buyer to purchase the good for less than the price that would prevail in a competitive market.

Suppose you are trying to decide how much of a good to purchase. You could apply the basic marginal principle—keep purchasing units of the good until the last unit purchased gives you additional value, or utility, just equal to the cost of that last unit. In other words, on the margin, additional benefit should just be offset by additional cost.

Recall from Chapter 4 that a person's demand curve measures marginal value, or marginal utility, as a function of the quantity purchased. Therefore, your *marginal value* schedule is your *demand* curve for the good. But your marginal cost of buying additional units of the good depends on whether you are a competitive buyer or a buyer with monopsony power.

Suppose you are a competitive buyer, which means that you have no influence over the price of the good. Then the cost of each unit you buy is the same, no matter how many units you purchase—it is the market price of the good. Figure 10.10a illustrates this. In that figure the price you pay per unit is your *average expenditure* per unit, and it is the same for all units. But what is your *marginal expenditure* per unit? As a competitive buyer, your marginal expenditure is equal to your average expenditure, which in turn is equal to the market price of the good.

Figure 10.10a also shows your marginal value schedule (i.e., your demand curve). Now how much of the good should you buy? You should buy until the marginal value of the last unit is just equal to the marginal expenditure on that unit. So you should purchase quantity Q^* at the intersection of the marginal expenditure and demand curves.

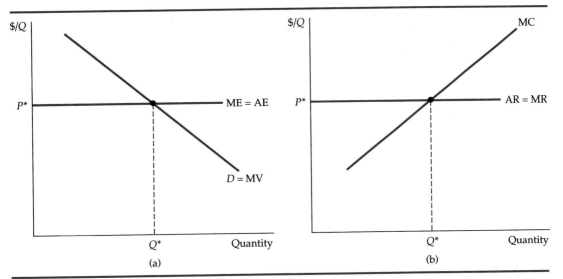

FIGURE 10.10 Competitive Buyer Compared to Competitive Seller. The competitive buyer in part (a) takes market price P^* as given. Therefore, marginal expenditure and average expenditure are constant and equal, and the quantity purchased is found by equating price to marginal value (demand). The competitive seller in part (b) also takes price as given. Marginal revenue and average revenue are constant and equal, and quantity sold is found by equating price to marginal cost.

This is another way of saying that under competitive conditions, a person's demand curve describes how much that person will buy as a function of the market price. We have introduced the concepts of marginal and average expenditure because they will make it easier to understand what happens when buyers have monopsony power. But before considering that situation, let's look at the analogy between competitive buyer conditions and competitive seller conditions. Figure 10.10b shows how a perfectly competitive seller decides how much to produce and sell. Since the seller takes the market price as given, both average and marginal revenue are equal to the price. The profit-maximizing quantity is found at the intersection of the marginal revenue and marginal cost curves.

Now suppose that you are the *only* buyer of the good. You again face a market supply curve, which tells you how much producers are willing to sell as a function of the price you pay. Should the quantity you purchase be at the point where your marginal value curve intersects the market supply curve? No. If you want to maximize your net benefit from purchasing the good, you should purchase a smaller quantity, which you will obtain at a lower price.

To determine how much to buy, set the marginal value from the last unit

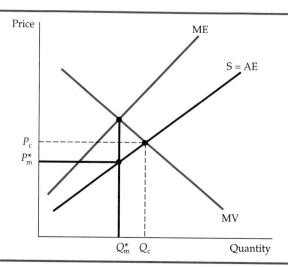

FIGURE 10.11 Monopsonist Buyer. The market supply curve is the monopsonist's average expenditure curve AE. Average expenditure is rising, so marginal expenditure lies above it. The monopsonist purchases quantity Q_m^* where marginal expenditure and marginal value (demand) intersect. The price paid per unit P_m^* is then found from the average expenditure (supply) curve. In a competitive market, price and quantity, P_c and Q_c, are both higher. They are found at the point where average expenditure (supply) and marginal value (demand) intersect.

purchased equal to the marginal expenditure on that unit.[11] But note that the market supply curve is not the marginal expenditure curve. The market supply curve tells you how much you must pay *per unit*, as a function of the total number of units you buy. In other words, the supply curve is the *average expenditure* curve. And since this average expenditure curve is upward-sloping, the marginal expenditure curve must lie above it because the decision to buy an extra unit raises the price that must be paid for *all* units, including the extra one.[12]

Figure 10.11 illustrates this. The optimal quantity for the monopsonist to buy

---

[11]Mathematically, we can write the net benefit NB from the purchase as NB = $V - C$, where V is the value to the buyer of the purchase and C is the cost. Net benefit is maximized when $\Delta NB/\Delta Q$ = 0. Then

$$\Delta NB/\Delta Q = \Delta V/\Delta Q - \Delta C/\Delta Q = MV - ME = 0$$

so that MV = ME.

[12]Given a supply curve, we can obtain the marginal expenditure schedule algebraically as follows. Write the supply curve with price on the left-hand side: $P = P(Q)$. Then total expenditure E is price times quantity, or $E = P(Q)Q$. Marginal expenditure is the change in total expenditure resulting from a small change in Q:

$$ME = \Delta E/\Delta Q = P(Q) + Q(\Delta P/\Delta Q)$$

The supply curve is upward-sloping, so $\Delta P/\Delta Q$ is positive, and marginal expenditure is greater than average expenditure.

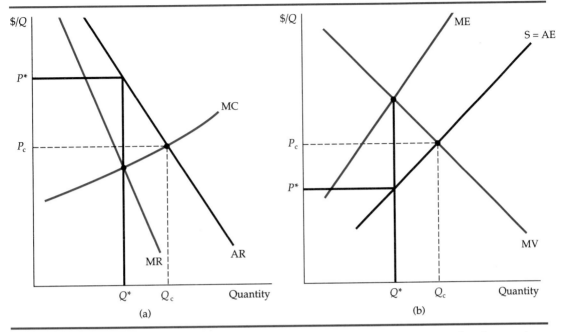

FIGURE 10.12 Monopoly and Monopsony. These diagrams show the close analogy between monopoly and monopsony. (a) The monopolist produces where marginal revenue intersects marginal cost. Average revenue exceeds marginal revenue, so that price exceeds marginal cost. (b) The monopsonist produces where marginal expenditure intersects marginal value. Marginal expenditure exceeds average expenditure, so that marginal value exceeds price.

Q_m^* is found at the intersection of the demand and marginal expenditure curves. And the price that the monopsonist pays is found from the supply curve; it is the price P_m^* that brings forth the supply Q_m^*. Finally, note that this quantity Q_m^* is less, and the price P_m^* is higher, than the quantity and price that would prevail in a competitive market, Q_c and P_c.

Monopsony and Monopoly Compared

Monopsony is easier to understand if you compare it with monopoly. Figure 10.12a and 10.12b illustrates this comparison. Note that a monopolist can charge a price above marginal cost because it faces a downward-sloping demand, or average revenue curve, so that marginal revenue is less than average revenue. Equating marginal cost with marginal revenue leads to a quantity Q^* that is less than what would be produced in a competitive market, and a price P^* that is higher than the competitive price P_c.

The monopsony situation is exactly analogous. As Figure 10.12b illustrates, the monopsonist can purchase a good *at a price below its marginal value* because the supply, or average expenditure curve, it faces is upward-sloping, so that marginal expenditure is greater than average expenditure. Equating marginal value with marginal expenditure leads to a quantity Q^* that is less than what would be bought in a competitive market, and a price P^* that is lower than the competitive price P_c.

10.6 Monopsony Power

Much more common than pure monopsony are markets with only a few firms competing among themselves as buyers, so that each firm has some monopsony power. For example, the three major U.S. automobile manufacturers compete with one another as buyers of tires. Because each of them accounts for a large share of the tire market, each has some monopsony power in that market. General Motors, the largest of the three firms, might be able to exert considerable monopsony power when contracting for supplies of tires (and other automotive parts).

Measuring Monopsony Power

To find a measure of monopsony power, let's draw an analogy with monopoly power. We saw that a firm with monopoly power sets price above marginal cost, so that a natural measure of monopoly power is the extent to which price exceeds marginal cost. Now, remember the distinction between a competitive buyer and a buyer with monopsony power: For a competitive buyer, price is equal to marginal value, but price is below marginal value for a buyer with monopsony power. So a natural measure of monopsony power is the extent to which marginal value exceeds price.

With a little algebra, one can derive the following equation, which is analogous to equation (10.1)[13]:

$$\frac{MV - P}{P} = \frac{1}{E_s} \tag{10.4}$$

In a competitive market, price and marginal value are equal, but a buyer with monopsony power can purchase the good at a price below marginal value. The left-hand side of equation (10.4) measures the difference between marginal value

---

[13]Recall that MV = ME. We can write marginal expenditure as

$$ME = \Delta \text{Expenditure}/\Delta Q = \Delta(PQ)/\Delta Q = P + Q(\Delta P/\Delta Q)$$

Here $P(Q)$ represents the *supply* curve facing the firm (so $\Delta P/\Delta Q$ is positive). Now multiply and divide the last term by P, and use the fact that $(Q/P)(\Delta P/\Delta Q)$ is the reciprocal of the elasticity of supply:

$$ME = P + P(Q/P)(\Delta P/\Delta Q) = P + P(1/E_s) = MV$$

Rearranging gives equation (10.4).

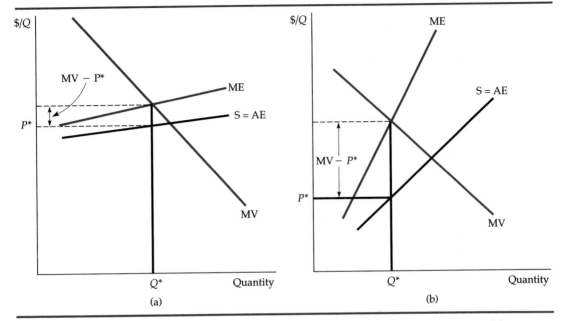

FIGURE 10.13   Elastic versus Inelastic Supply, and Monopsony Power.   Monopsony power depends on elasticity of supply. When supply is elastic, as in part (a), marginal expenditure and average expenditure do not differ by much, so price is close to what it would be in a competitive market. The opposite is true when supply is inelastic, as in part (b).

and price in percentage terms and provides a measure of monopsony power analogous to Lerner's degree of monopoly power. It can be thought of as a percentage "markdown" due to monopsony power. The size of this markdown is inversely proportional to the elasticity of supply facing the buyer. If supply is very elastic (E_s is large), the markdown will be small, and the buyer has little monopsony power. If supply is very inelastic, the markdown will be large, and the buyer has considerable monopsony power. Figure 10.13a and 10.13b illustrates these two cases.

Sources of Monopsony Power

What determines the degree of monopsony power in a market? Again, we can draw analogies with monopoly and monopoly power. We saw that monopoly power depends on three things: the elasticity of market demand, the number of sellers in the market, and how those sellers interact. Monopsony power depends on similar things: the elasticity of market supply, the number of buyers in the market, and how those buyers interact.

First consider the *elasticity of market supply*. A monopsonist benefits because it faces an upward-sloping supply curve, so that marginal expenditure exceeds average expenditure. The less elastic the supply curve, the greater is the difference between marginal expenditure and average expenditure, and the more monopsony power the buyer has. If only one buyer is in the market—a pure monopsonist—its monopsony power is completely determined by the elasticity of market supply. If supply is highly elastic, monopsony power is small, and there is little gain in being the only buyer.

Most markets have more than one buyer, and the *number of buyers* is an important determinant of monopsony power. When the number of buyers is very large, no single buyer can have much influence over price. Thus, each buyer faces an extremely elastic supply curve, and the market is almost completely competitive. The potential for monopsony power arises when the number of buyers is limited.

Finally, monopsony power is determined by the *interaction among buyers*. Suppose three or four buyers are in the market. If those buyers compete aggressively, they will bid up the price close to their marginal value of the product, and thus they will have little monopsony power. On the other hand, if those buyers compete less aggressively, or even collude, prices will not be bid up very much, and the buyers' degree of monopsony power might be nearly as high as if there were only one buyer.

So as with monopoly power, there is no simple way to predict how much monopsony power buyers will have in a market. We can count the number of buyers, and we can often estimate the elasticity of supply, but that is not enough. Monopsony power also depends on the interaction among buyers, which can be more difficult to ascertain.

The Social Costs of Monopsony Power

Because monopsony power results in lower prices and lower quantities purchased, we would expect it to make the buyer better off and sellers worse off. But suppose we value the welfare of buyers and sellers equally. How is aggregate welfare affected by monopsony power?

We can answer this question by comparing the consumer and producer surplus that results from a competitive market to the surplus that results when a monopsonist is the sole buyer. Figure 10.14 shows the average and marginal expenditure curves and marginal value curve for the monopsonist. The monopsonist's net benefit is maximized by purchasing a quantity Q_m at a price P_m such that marginal value equals marginal expenditure. In a competitive market, price equals marginal value, so the competitive price and quantity, P_c and Q_c, are found where the average expenditure and marginal value curves intersect. Now let's see how surplus changes if we move from the competitive price and quantity, P_c and Q_c, to the monopsony price and quantity, P_m and Q_m.

With monopsony, the price is lower and less is sold. Because of the lower price, sellers lose an amount of surplus given by rectangle A. In addition, sellers lose surplus of an amount given by triangle C because of the reduced sales. The

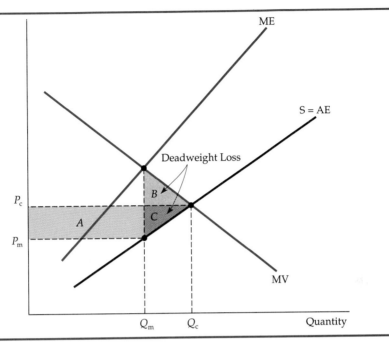

FIGURE 10.14 Deadweight Loss from Monopsony Power. The shaded rectangle and triangles show changes in consumer and producer surplus when moving from competitive price and quantity, P_c and Q_c, to monopsonist's price and quantity, P_m and Q_m. Because both price and quantity are lower, there is an increase in buyer (consumer) surplus given by $A - B$. Producer surplus falls by $A + C$, so there is a deadweight loss given by triangles B and C.

total loss of producer (seller) surplus is therefore $A + C$. The buyer gains surplus of an amount given by rectangle A by buying at a lower price. However, the buyer buys less, Q_m instead of Q_c, and so loses surplus of an amount given by triangle B. The total gain in surplus to the buyer is therefore $A - B$. All together, then, we see a net loss of surplus given by $B + C$. This is the *deadweight loss from monopsony power*. Even if the monopsonist's gains were taxed away and redistributed to the producers, there would be an inefficiency because output would be lower than under competition. The deadweight loss is the social cost of this inefficiency.

Bilateral Monopoly

What happens when a monopolist meets a monopsonist? It's hard to say. We call a market with only one seller and only one buyer a *bilateral monopoly*. If you think about such a market, you'll see why it is difficult to predict what the price and quantity will be. Both the buyer and the seller are in a *bargaining* situation. Unfortunately, no simple rule determines who, if anyone, will get the better part of the bargain. One party might have more time and patience, or might be able to convince the other party that it will walk away if the price is too low or too high.

Bilateral monopoly is rare. Markets in which a few producers have some monopoly power and sell to a few buyers who have some monopsony power are more common. Although bargaining may still be involved, we can apply a rough principle here: Monopsony power and monopoly power will tend to counteract each other. In other words, the monopsony power of buyers will reduce the effective monopoly power of sellers, and vice versa. This does not mean that the market will end up looking perfectly competitive; monopoly power might be large, for example, and monopsony power small, so that the residual monopoly power would still be significant. But in general, monopsony power will push price closer to marginal cost, and monopoly power will push price closer to marginal value.

EXAMPLE 10.3 MONOPSONY POWER IN U.S. MANUFACTURING

Monopoly power, as measured by the price-cost margin $(P - MC)/P$, varies considerably across manufacturing industries in the United States. Some industries have price-cost margins close to zero, while in other industries the price-cost margins are as high as 0.4 or 0.5. These variations are due in part to differences in the determinants of monopoly power—in some industries market demand is more elastic than in others; some industries have more sellers than others; and in some industries sellers compete more aggressively than in others. But something else can help explain these variations in monopoly power— differences in monopsony power among the firms' customers.

The role of monopsony power was investigated in a statistical study of 327 U.S. manufacturing industries.[14] The study sought to determine the extent to which variations in price-cost margins could be attributed to variations in monopsony power by buyers in each industry. Although the degree of buyers' monopsony power could not be measured directly, data were available for variables that help determine monopsony power, such as buyer concentration (the fraction of total sales going to the three or four largest firms) and the average annual size of orders by buyers.

The study found that buyers' monopsony power had an important effect on the price-cost margins of sellers and could significantly reduce any monopoly power that sellers might otherwise have. Take, for example, the concentration of buyers, an important determinant of monopsony power. In industries where only four or five buyers account for all or nearly all sales, the price-cost margins

---

[14]The study was by Steven H. Lustgarten, "The Impact of Buyer Concentration in Manufacturing Industries," *Review of Economics and Statistics* 57 (May 1975): 125–132.

of sellers would on average be as much as 10 percentage points lower than in comparable industries where hundreds of buyers account for the sales.

A good example of monopsony power in manufacturing is the market for automobile parts and components, such as brakes and radiators. There are only three major car producers in the United States. Each typically buys an individual part from at least three, and often as many as a dozen, suppliers. In addition, for a standardized product such as brakes, each automobile company usually produces part of its needs itself, so that it is not totally reliant on outside firms. This puts GM, Ford, and Chrysler in an excellent bargaining position with respect to their suppliers. Each supplier must compete for sales against five or ten other suppliers, but each can sell to at most three buyers. (For a specialized part, a single auto company may be the *only* buyer.) As a result, the automobile companies have considerable monopsony power.

This monopsony power becomes evident from the conditions under which suppliers must operate. To obtain a sales contract, a supplier must have a track record of reliability, in terms of both the quality of its products and its ability to meet tight delivery schedules. Suppliers are also often required to respond to changes in volume, as auto sales and hence production levels fluctuate. Finally, pricing negotiations are notoriously difficult; a potential supplier will sometimes lose a contract because its bid is a penny per item higher than those of its competitors. Not surprisingly, producers of parts and components usually have little or no monopoly power.[15]

10.7 Limiting Market Power: The Antitrust Laws

We have seen that market power—whether of sellers or buyers—leads to a deadweight loss. Excessive market power also raises problems of equity and fairness; if a firm has significant monopoly power, it will profit at the expense of consumers. In theory, the firm's excess profits could be taxed away and redistributed to the buyers of its products, but such a redistribution is often impossible in practice. It is difficult to determine what portion of a firm's profit is attributable to monopoly power, and it is even more difficult to locate all the buyers and reimburse them in proportion to their purchases. So in addition to the deadweight loss, excessive market power can lead to a socially objectionable transfer of money.

How, then, can society prevent market power from becoming excessive? For a natural monopoly such as an electric utility company, we saw that direct price

---

[15]For a more detailed discussion of the market for automobile parts and components, see Michael E. Porter, "Note on Supplying the Automobile Industry," Harvard Business School Case No. 9–378–219, July 1981.

regulation is the answer. But more generally, the answer is to prevent firms from acquiring excessive market power in the first place. In the United States, this is done via the antitrust laws.

The primary objective of the antitrust laws is to promote a competitive economy by prohibiting actions that restrain, or are likely to restrain, competition, and by restricting the forms of market structure that are allowable.

Monopoly power can arise in a number of ways, each of which is regulated under the antitrust laws. Section 1 of the Sherman Act (which was passed in 1890) prohibits contracts, combinations, or conspiracies in restraint of trade. One obvious example of an illegal combination is an explicit agreement among producers to restrict their outputs and "fix" price above the competitive level. But *implicit* collusion can also be construed as violating the law. Firm A and Firm B need not meet or talk on the telephone to violate the Sherman Act; the publication of pricing information that leads to an implicit understanding can suffice.[16]

Section 2 of the Sherman Act makes it illegal to monopolize or to attempt to monopolize a market and prohibits conspiracies that result in monopolization. The Clayton Act (1914) did much to pinpoint the kinds of practices that are likely to be anticompetitive. For example, the Clayton Act makes it unlawful to require the buyer or lessor of a good not to buy from a competitor. And it makes *predatory pricing*—pricing designed to drive current competitors out of business and to discourage new entrants—illegal.

Monopoly power can also be achieved by a merger of firms into a larger and more dominant firm, or by one firm acquiring or taking control of another firm by purchasing its stock. The Clayton Act prohibits mergers and acquisitions if they "substantially lessen competition," or "tend to create a monopoly."

The antitrust laws also limit the activities of firms that have legally obtained monopoly power. For example, the Clayton Act, as amended by the Robinson-Patman Act (1936), makes it illegal to discriminate by charging buyers of essentially the same product different prices. (As we will see in the next chapter, price discrimination is in fact a common practice. It becomes the target of antitrust action when monopoly power is substantial.)

Another important component of the antitrust laws is the *Federal Trade Commission Act* (1914, amended in 1938, 1973, 1975), which created the Federal Trade Commission (FTC). This act supplements the Sherman and Clayton acts by fostering competition through a whole set of prohibitions against unfair and anticompetitive practices, such as deceptive advertising and labeling, agreements with retailers to exclude competing brands, etc. Because these prohibi-

---

[16]The Sherman Act applies not only to American firms, but to foreign firms as well (to the extent that a conspiracy to restrain trade could affect U.S. markets). However, foreign governments (or firms operating under their government's control) are not subject to the act, so OPEC need not fear the wrath of the Justice Department.

tions are interpreted and enforced in administrative proceedings before the FTC, the act provides powers that are very broad and reach further than other antitrust laws.

The antitrust laws are actually phrased vaguely in terms of what is and what is not allowed. The laws are intended to provide a general statutory framework to give the Justice Department, the FTC, and the courts wide discretion in interpreting and applying them. This is important because it is difficult to know in advance what might be an impediment to competition, and this ambiguity creates a need for common law (i.e., courts interpreting statutes) and supplemental provisions and rulings (e.g., by the FTC and the Justice Department).

Enforcement of the Antitrust Laws

The antitrust laws are enforced in three ways. The first is through the Antitrust Division of the Department of Justice. As an arm of the executive branch, its enforcement policies closely reflect the view of whatever administration is in power. As the result of an external complaint or an internal study, the department can decide to institute a criminal proceeding, bring a civil suit, or both. The result of a criminal action can be fines for the corporation and fines or jail sentences for individuals. For example, individuals who conspire to monopolize can be deemed guilty of a *felony*. (This means a jail sentence—something to remember if you are planning to parlay your knowledge of microeconomics into a successful business career!) The result of a civil action is to force a corporation to cease its anticompetitive practices.

The second means of enforcement is through the administrative procedures of the Federal Trade Commission. Again, action can occur as the result of an external complaint or from the FTC's own initiative. Should the FTC decide that action is required, it can either request a voluntary understanding to comply with the law, or it can decide to seek a formal commission order, requiring compliance.

The last and the most common means of enforcement is via *private proceedings*. Individuals or companies can sue for *treble (threefold) damages* inflicted on their business or property. The possibility of having to pay treble damages can be a strong deterrent to would-be violators of the laws. Individuals or companies can also ask the courts for an injunction to force a wrongdoer to cease anticompetitive actions.

The U.S. antitrust laws are more stringent and far-reaching than those of most other countries. Some people have argued that the laws have prevented American industry from competing effectively in international markets. The laws certainly constrain American business, and they may at times have put American firms at a disadvantage in world markets. But this must be weighed against their benefits. The laws have been crucial for maintaining competition, and competition is essential for economic efficiency and growth.

EXAMPLE 10.4 A PHONE CALL ABOUT PRICES

In 1981 and early 1982, American Airlines and Braniff Airways were competing fiercely with each other for passengers. A fare war broke out as the firms undercut each other's prices to capture market share. On February 21, 1982, Robert Crandall, president and chief executive officer of American Airlines, made a phone call to Howard Putnam, president and chief executive of Braniff Airways. To Mr. Crandall's later surprise, the call had been taped. It went something like this[17]:

Mr. Crandall: I think it's dumb as hell for Christ's sake, all right, to sit here and pound the @!#$%&! out of each other and neither one of us making a !@#$%! dime.

Mr. Putnam: Well . . .

Mr. Crandall: I mean, you know, goddamn, what the hell is the point of it?

Mr. Putnam: But if you're going to overlay every route of American's on top of every route that Braniff has—I just can't sit here and allow you to bury us without giving our best effort.

Mr. Crandall: Oh sure, but Eastern and Delta do the same thing in Atlanta and have for years.

Mr. Putnam: Do you have a suggestion for me?

Mr. Crandall: Yes, I have a suggestion for you. Raise your goddamn fares 20 percent. I'll raise mine the next morning.

Mr. Putnam: Robert, we . . .

Mr. Crandall: You'll make more money and I will, too.

Mr. Putnam: We can't talk about pricing!

Mr. Crandall: Oh @!#$%&!*, Howard. We can talk about any goddamn thing we want to talk about.

Mr. Crandall was wrong. Corporate executives cannot talk about anything they want. Talking about prices and agreeing to fix them is a clear violation of Section 1 of the Sherman Act. Mr. Putnam must have known this because he promptly rejected Mr. Crandall's suggestion. After learning about the call, the Justice Department filed a suit accusing Mr. Crandall of violating the antitrust laws by proposing to fix prices.

Proposing to fix prices is not enough to violate Section 1 of the Sherman Act. The two parties must *agree* to collude for the law to be violated. Therefore, because Mr. Putnam had rejected Mr. Crandall's proposal, Section 1 had not been violated. The court later ruled, however, that a proposal to fix prices could be an attempt to monopolize part of the airline industry, and if so would violate

---

[17]According to the *New York Times*, Feb. 24, 1983.

Section 2 of the Sherman Act. American Airlines promised the Justice Department never again to engage in such an activity.

Summary

1. Market power is the ability of sellers or buyers to affect the price of a good.

2. Market power comes in two forms. When sellers charge a price that is above marginal cost, we say that they have monopoly power, and we measure the amount of monopoly power by the extent to which price exceeds marginal cost. When buyers can obtain a price that is below their marginal value of the good, we say they have monopsony power, and we measure the amount of monopsony power by the extent to which marginal value exceeds price.

3. Monopoly power is determined in part by the number of firms competing in the market. If there is only one firm—a pure monopoly—monopoly power depends entirely on the elasticity of market demand. The less elastic demand is, the more monopoly power the firm will have. When there are several firms, monopoly power also depends on how the firms interact. The more aggressively they compete, the less monopoly power each firm will have.

4. Monopsony power is determined in part by the number of buyers in the market. If there is only one buyer—a pure monopsony—monopsony power depends on the elasticity of market supply. The less elastic supply is, the more monopsony power the buyer will have. When there are several buyers, monopsony power also depends on how aggressively the buyers compete for supplies.

5. Market power can impose costs on society. Monopoly and monopsony power both cause production to be below the competitive level, so that there is a deadweight loss of consumer and producer surplus.

6. Sometimes, scale economies make pure monopoly desirable. But the government will still want to regulate price to maximize social welfare.

7. More generally, we rely on the antitrust laws to prevent firms from obtaining excessive market power.

Review Questions

1. Suppose a monopolist was producing at a point where its marginal cost exceeded its marginal revenue. Explain how it should adjust its output level to increase its profit.

2. We write the percentage markup of price over marginal cost as $(P - MC)/P$. For a profit-maximizing monopolist, how does this markup depend on the elasticity of demand? Why can this markup be viewed as a measure of monopoly power?

3. Why is there no market supply curve under monopoly?

4. Why might a firm have monopoly power even if it is not the only producer in the market?

5. What are some of the sources of monopoly power? Give an example of each.

6. What factors determine how much monopoly power an individual firm is likely to have? Explain each one briefly.

7. Why is there a social cost to monopoly power? If the gains to producers from monopoly power could be redistributed to consumers, would the social cost of monopoly power be eliminated? Explain briefly.

8. Why will a monopolist's output increase if the government forces it to lower its price? If the government wants to set a price ceiling that maximizes the monopolist's output, what price should it set?

9. How should a monopsonist decide how much of a product to buy? Will it buy more or less than a competitive buyer? Explain briefly.

10. What is meant by the term "monopsony power"? Why might a firm have monopsony power even if it is not the only buyer in the market?

11. What are some sources of monopsony power? What factors determine how much monopsony power an individual firm is likely to have?

12. Why is there a social cost to monopsony power? If the gains to buyers from monopsony power could be redistributed to sellers, would the social cost of monopsony power be eliminated? Explain briefly.

13. How do the antitrust laws limit market power in the United States? Give examples of the major provisions of the laws.

14. Explain briefly how the U.S. antitrust laws are actually enforced.

Exercises

1. Caterpillar Tractor is one of the largest producers of farm tractors in the world. They hire you to advise them on their pricing policy. One of the things the company would like to know is how much a 5 percent increase in price is likely to reduce sales. What are the main facts you would want to know to help the company with their problem? Explain why these facts are important.

2. Will an increase in the demand for a monopolist's product always result in a higher price? Explain. Will an increase in the supply facing a monopsonist buyer always result in a lower price? Explain.

3. A firm faces the following average revenue (demand) curve:

$$P = 100 - 0.01Q$$

where Q is weekly production and P is price, measured in cents per unit. The firm's cost function is given by $C = 50Q + 30,000$. Assuming the firm maximizes profits

a. What is the level of production, price, and total profit per week?

b. The government decides to levy a tax of 10 cents per unit on this product. What will the new level of production, price, and profit be as a result?

4. A monopolist faces the demand curve $P = 11 - Q$, where P is measured in dollars per unit and Q in thousands of units. The monopolist has a constant average cost of $6 per unit.

   a. Draw the average and marginal revenue curves, and the average and marginal cost curves. What are the monopolist's profit-maximizing price and quantity, and what is the resulting profit? Calculate the firm's degree of monopoly power using the Lerner index.

   b. A government regulatory agency sets a price ceiling of $7 per unit. What quantity will be produced, and what will the firm's profit be? What happens to the degree of monopoly power?

   c. What price ceiling yields the largest level of output? What is that level of output? What is the firm's degree of monopoly power at this price?

5. One of the more important antitrust cases of this century involved the Aluminum Company of America (Alcoa) in 1945. At that time, Alcoa controlled about 90 percent of primary aluminum production in the United States, and the company had been accused of monopolizing the aluminum market. In its defense, Alcoa argued that although it indeed controlled a large fraction of the primary market, secondary aluminum (i.e., aluminum produced from the recycling of scrap) accounted for roughly 30 percent of the total supply of aluminum, and many competitive firms were engaged in recycling. Therefore, Alcoa argued, it did not have much monopoly power.

   a. Provide a clear argument *in favor* of Alcoa's position.

   b. Provide a clear argument *against* Alcoa's position.

   c. The 1945 decision by Judge Learned Hand has been called "one of the most celebrated judicial opinions of our time." Do you know what Judge Hand's ruling was?

*6. A monopolist faces the following demand curve:

$$Q = 144/P^2$$

where Q is the quantity demanded and P is price. Its *average variable cost* is

$$AVC = Q^{1/2}$$

and its *fixed cost* is 5.

   a. What is its profit-maximizing price and quantity? What is the resulting profit?

   b. Suppose the government regulates the price to be no greater than $4 per unit. How much will the monopolist produce, and what will its profit be?

   c. Suppose the government wants to set a ceiling price that induces the monopolist to produce the largest possible output. What price will do this?

CHAPTER 11

Pricing with Market Power

As we explained in Chapter 10, market power is quite common. Many industries have only a few producers, so that each producer has some monopoly power. And many firms, as buyers of raw materials, labor, or specialized capital goods, have some monopsony power in the markets for these factor inputs. The problem the managers of these firms face is how to use their market power most effectively. They must decide how to set prices, choose quantities of factor inputs, and determine output in both the short and long run to maximize the firm's profit.

Managers of a firm with market power have a harder job than those who manage perfectly competitive firms. A firm that is perfectly competitive in output markets has, by definition, no influence over market price. As a result, its managers need only worry about the cost side of the firm's operations, choosing output so that price is equal to marginal cost. But the managers of a firm with monopoly power must also worry about the characteristics of demand. Even if they set a single price for the firm's output, they must obtain at least a rough estimate of the elasticity of demand to determine what that price (and corresponding output level) should be. Furthermore, we will see that one can often do much better by using a more complicated pricing strategy, for example, charging different prices to different customers. To design such a pricing strategy, managers need ingenuity and even more information about market demand.

In this chapter we will see how firms with market power set prices. We begin by explaining the basic objective of every pricing strategy—capturing consumer surplus and converting it into additional profit for the firm. Then we discuss the most common way to do this—by using *price discrimination*. Here different prices are charged to different customers, sometimes for the same product, and sometimes for small variations in the product. Because price discrimination is widely practiced in one form or another, it is important to understand how it works.

Next, we discuss the *two-part tariff*. Here customers must pay in advance for the right to purchase units of the good at a later time (and at additional cost). The classic example of this is an amusement park, where customers pay a fee to enter, and then an additional fee for each ride they go on. Although amusement parks may seem like a rather specialized market, there are many other examples of two-part tariffs: the price of a Gillette (or Schick) razor, which gives the owner the opportunity to purchase Gillette (or Schick) razor blades; the price of a Polaroid camera, which gives the owner the opportunity to purchase Polaroid film; or the monthly subscription cost of a mobile telephone, which gives users the opportunity to make phone calls from their automobiles, paying by the message unit as they do so.

Finally, we discuss *bundling*. This pricing strategy simply involves tying products together and selling them as a package. For example: a personal computer that comes bundled with several software packages; a one-week vacation in Hawaii in which the airfare, rental car, and hotel are bundled and sold at a single package price; or a luxury car, in which the air conditioning, power windows, and stereo are "standard" features.

11.1 Capturing Consumer Surplus

All the pricing strategies that we will examine have one thing in common—they are ways of capturing consumer surplus and transferring it to the producer. You can see this more clearly in Figure 11.1. Suppose the firm sold all its output at a single price. To maximize profit, it would pick a price P^* and corresponding output Q^* at the intersection of its marginal cost and marginal revenue curves. The firm would then be profitable, but its managers might wonder if they could make it even more profitable.

They know that some customers (in region A of the demand curve) would pay more than P^*. Raising price, however, would mean losing some customers, selling a lesser quantity, and earning smaller profits. Similarly, other potential customers are not buying the firm's product because they will not pay a price as high as P^*. Many of them, however, would pay prices higher than the firm's marginal cost. (These customers are in region B of the demand curve.) By lowering its price, the firm could sell to some of these customers, but it would then earn less revenue from its existing customers, and again profits would shrink.

How can the firm capture the consumer surplus (or at least part of it) from its customers in region A, and perhaps also sell profitably to some of its potential customers in region B? Charging a single price clearly will not do the trick. However, the firm might charge different prices to different customers, according to where the customers are along the demand curve. For example, some customers in the upper end of region A would be charged the higher price P_1, some in region B would be charged the lower price P_2, and some in between would be charged P^*. This is the basis of *price discrimination*—charging different

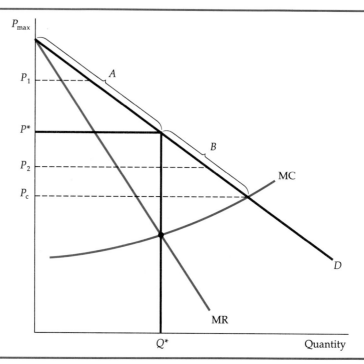

FIGURE 11.1   Capturing Consumer Surplus.   If a firm can charge only one price for all its customers, that price will be P^* and the quantity produced will be Q^*. Ideally, the firm would like to charge more to consumers willing to pay more than P^*, thereby capturing some of the consumer surplus under region A of the demand curve. The firm would also like to sell to consumers willing to pay prices lower than P^*, but only if that does not entail lowering the price to other consumers. In that way the firm could also capture some of the surplus under region B of the demand curve. Pricing strategies are ways of capturing consumer surplus.

prices to different customers. The problem, of course, is to identify the different customers, and to get them to pay different prices. We will see how this can be done in the next section.

The other pricing techniques that we will discuss in this chapter—two-part tariffs and bundling—also expand the range of the firm's market to include more customers and to capture more consumer surplus. In each case we will examine the amount by which the firm's profit can be increased, as well as the effect on consumer welfare. (As we will see, when there is a high degree of monopoly power these pricing techniques can sometimes make both consumers and the producer better off.) We turn first to price discrimination.

11.2 Price Discrimination

Price discrimination can take three broad forms, which we call first-, second-, and third-degree price discrimination. Let's examine each of them.

First-Degree Price Discrimination

Ideally, a firm would like to charge a different price to each of its customers. If it could, it would charge each customer the maximum price that customer is willing to pay for each unit bought. We call this maximum price the customer's *reservation price*. The practice of charging each customer his or her reservation price is called perfect *first-degree price discrimination*.[1] Let's see how it affects the firm's profit.

First, we need to know the profit the firm earns when it charges only the single price P^* in Figure 11.2. To find out, we can add the profit on each incremental unit produced and sold, up to the total quantity Q^*. This incremental profit is the marginal revenue less the marginal cost for each unit. In Figure 11.2, this marginal revenue is highest and marginal cost lowest for the first unit. For each additional unit, marginal revenue falls and marginal cost rises, so the firm produces the total output Q^*, where marginal revenue and marginal cost are equal. Producing any more than Q^* would raise marginal cost above marginal revenue, and would thus reduce profits. Total variable profit is simply the sum of the profits on each incremental unit produced, and therefore, it is given by the diagonally shaded area in Figure 11.2, between the marginal revenue and marginal cost curves.[2] Consumer surplus, which is the area between the average revenue curve and the price P^* that customers pay, is shown as a dark triangle.

Now, what happens if the firm can perfectly price discriminate? Since each consumer is charged exactly what he or she is willing to pay, the marginal revenue curve is no longer relevant to the firm's output decision. Instead, the incremental revenue earned from each additional unit sold is simply the price paid for that unit, and is therefore given by the demand curve.

Price discrimination, however, does not affect the firm's cost structure, and the cost of each additional unit is again given by the firm's marginal cost curve. Therefore, *the profit from producing and selling each incremental unit is now the*

---

[1] We are assuming that each customer buys one unit of the good. If a customer bought more than one unit, the firm would have to charge different prices for each of the units.

[2] Recall that total profit π is the difference between total revenue R and total cost C, so incremental profit is just $\Delta\pi = \Delta R - \Delta C = MR - MC$. Total variable profit is found by summing all the $\Delta\pi$s, and thus it is the area between the MR and MC curves. This ignores fixed costs, but fixed costs are independent of the firm's output and pricing decisions.

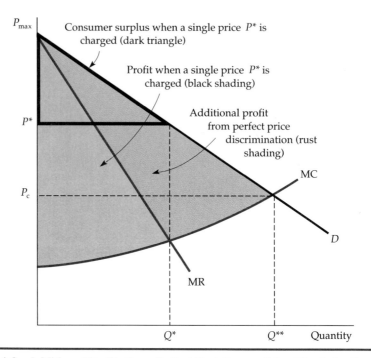

FIGURE 11.2 Additional Profits from Perfect First-Degree Price Discrimination. Here the firm charges every consumer his or her reservation price, so it is profitable to expand output to Q^{**}. When only a single price, P^*, is charged, the firm's variable profit is the area between the marginal revenue and marginal cost curves. With perfect price discrimination, this profit expands to the area between the demand curve and the marginal cost curve.

difference between demand and marginal cost. As long as demand exceeds marginal cost, the firm can increase its profits by expanding production, and it will do so until it produces a total output Q^{**}. At Q^{**} demand is equal to marginal cost, and producing more reduces profit.

Total profit is now given by the area between the demand and marginal cost curves.[3] Note from Figure 11.2 that total profit is now much larger. (The additional profit resulting from price discrimination is shown by the horizontally shaded area.) Note also that since every customer is being charged the maximum amount that he or she is willing to pay, all consumer surplus has been captured by the firm.

[3]Incremental profit is again $\Delta\pi = \Delta R - \Delta C$, but because the price each customer pays is independent of the prices all other customers pay, ΔR is given by the price to each customer (i.e., the average revenue curve), so $\Delta\pi = AR - MC$. Total profit is the sum of these $\Delta\pi$s and so is given by the area between the AR and MC curves.

However, a firm will probably not be able to charge each and every customer a different price (unless there are only a few customers).[4] First, the firm usually does not know the reservation price of each customer. Second, even if the firm could ask how much each customer would be willing to pay, it probably would not receive honest answers. After all, it is in the customers' interest to claim that they would pay very little (because then they would be charged a low price). In practice, then, perfect first-degree price discrimination is almost never possible.

Sometimes, however, firms can discriminate imperfectly by charging a few different prices based on estimates of their customers' reservation prices. This happens frequently when professionals, such as doctors, lawyers, accountants, or architects, who know their clients reasonably well, are the "firms." Then the client's willingness to pay can be assessed, and fees set accordingly. For example, a doctor may offer a reduced fee to a low-income patient whose willingness (or ability) to pay or whose insurance coverage is low, but charge higher fees to upper-income or better-insured patients. And an accountant, having just completed a client's tax returns, is in an excellent position to estimate how much the client is willing to pay for the service.

Another example is a car salesperson, who typically works with a 15 percent profit margin. The salesperson can give part of this away to the customer by making a "deal," or can insist that the customer pay the sticker price for the car. A good salesperson knows how to size up customers and determine whether they will look elsewhere for a car if they don't receive a sizable discount. The customer who is likely to leave and shop around receives a big discount (from the salesperson's point of view, a small profit is better than no sale and no profit), but the customer in a hurry is offered little or no discount. In other words, a successful car salesperson knows how to price discriminate!

Figure 11.3 illustrates this kind of imperfect first-degree price discrimination. Here, if only a single price were charged, it would be P_4. Instead, six different prices are charged, the lowest of which, P_6, is just above the point where marginal cost intersects the demand curve. Note that those customers who would not have been willing to pay a price of P_4 or greater are actually better off in this situation—they are now in the market and may be enjoying at least some consumer surplus. In fact, if price discrimination brings enough new customers into the market, consumer welfare can increase, so that both the producer and consumers are better off.

Second-Degree Price Discrimination

In some markets, each consumer purchases many units of the good over any given period, and the consumer's demand declines with the number of units

---

[4]And even if it could, this might violate the antitrust laws. The Clayton Act prohibits price discrimination unless it is "affirmatively justified" (e.g., leads to lower costs).

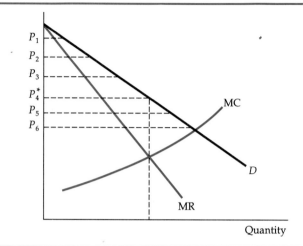

FIGURE 11.3   First-Degree Price Discrimination in Practice.   A firm usually cannot accurately identify the reservation price of each and every consumer. But sometimes reservation prices can be roughly identified. Here, six different prices are charged. The firm earns higher profits, but some consumers may also enjoy welfare gains. With a single price P_4^*, there are fewer consumers. The consumers who now pay P_5 or P_6 may have a surplus.

purchased. Examples include water, heating fuel, and electricity. Consumers may each purchase a few hundred kilowatt-hours of electricity a month, but their willingness to pay declines with increasing consumption. (The first hundred kilowatt-hours may be worth a lot to the consumer—operating a refrigerator and providing for minimal lighting. Conservation becomes easier with the additional units, and may be worthwhile if the price is high.) In this situation, a firm can discriminate according to the quantity consumed. This is called *second-degree price discrimination,* and it works by charging different prices for different quantities or "blocks" of the same good or service.

An example of second-degree price discrimination is block pricing by electric power companies. If there are significant scale economies so that average and marginal costs are declining, the state agency that controls the company's rates may encourage block pricing. By expanding output and achieving greater scale economies, consumer welfare can be increased, even allowing for greater profit to the company. The reason is that prices are reduced overall, while the savings from the lower unit costs still permit the power company to make a reasonable profit.

Figure 11.4 illustrates second-degree price discrimination for a firm with declining average and marginal costs. If a single price were charged, it would be P_0, and the quantity produced would be Q_0. Instead, three different prices are

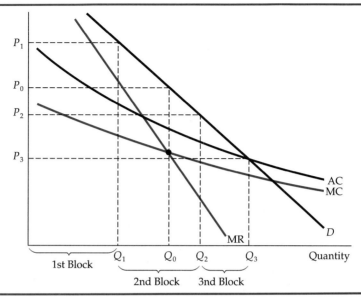

FIGURE 11.4 Second-Degree Price Discrimination. Different prices are charged for different quantities, or "blocks," of the same good. Here, there are three blocks, with corresponding prices P_1, P_2, and P_3. There are also economies of scale, and average and marginal costs are declining. Second-degree price discrimination can then make consumers better off by expanding output and lowering cost.

charged, based on the quantities purchased. The first block of sales is priced at P_1, the second at P_2, and the third at P_3.

Third-Degree Price Discrimination

A well-known liquor company has what seems to be a strange pricing practice. The company produces a vodka that it advertises as one of the smoothest and best-testing available. This vodka is called "Three Star Golden Crown," and it is sold for about $12 a bottle.[5] However, the company also takes some of this same vodka and bottles it under the name "Old Sloshbucket," which is sold for about $4 a bottle. Why does it do this? Has the president of the company been spending too much time near the vats?

Perhaps, but this liquor company is also practicing *third-degree price discrimination*, and it does it because the practice is profitable. This form of price discrimination divides consumers into two or more groups with separate demand curves for each group. This is the most prevalent form of price discrimination

[5]We have changed the names to protect the innocent.

and examples abound: regular versus "special" airline fares; the premium versus nonpremium brand of liquor, canned food or frozen vegetables; discounts to students and senior citizens; and so on.

In each case, some characteristic is used to divide consumers into distinct groups. For example, for many goods, students and senior citizens are usually willing to pay less on average than the rest of the population (because their incomes are lower), and identity can be readily established (via college ID or Social Security cards). Likewise, to separate vacationers from business travelers (whose companies are usually willing to pay much higher fares), airlines can put restrictions on special low-fare tickets, such as requiring advance purchase. With the liquor company, or the premium versus nonpremium (e.g., supermarket label) brand of food, the label itself divides consumers; many consumers are willing to pay more for a name brand, even though the nonpremium brand is identical or nearly identical (and in fact is sometimes manufactured by the same company that produced the premium brand).

If third-degree price discrimination is feasible, how should the firm decide what price to charge each group of consumers? Let's think about this intuitively in two steps. First, we know that however much is produced, total output should be divided between the groups of customers so that the marginal revenues for each group are equal. Otherwise, the firm would not be maximizing profit. For example, if there are two groups of customers and the marginal revenue for the first group, MR_1, exceeds the marginal revenue for the second group, MR_2, the firm could clearly do better by shifting output from the second group to the first. It would do this by lowering the price to the first group and raising the price to the second group. So whatever the two prices are, they must be such that the marginal revenues for the different groups are equal.

Second, we know that *total* output must be such that the marginal revenue for each group of consumers is equal to the marginal cost of production. Again, if this were not the case, the firm could increase its profit by raising or lowering total output (and lowering or raising its prices to both groups). For example, suppose the marginal revenues were the same for each group of consumers, but marginal revenue exceeded the marginal cost of production. The firm could then make a greater profit by increasing its total output. It would lower its prices to both groups of consumers, so that the marginal revenues for each group fell (but were still equal to each other), and approached marginal cost (which would increase as total output increased).

Let's look at this algebraically. Let P_1 be the price charged to the first group of consumers, P_2 the price charged to the second group, and $C(Q_T)$ the total cost of producing output $Q_T = Q_1 + Q_2$. Then total profit is given by

$$\pi = P_1 Q_1 + P_2 Q_2 - C(Q_T)$$

The firm should increase its sales to each group of consumers, Q_1 and Q_2, until the incremental profit from the last unit sold is zero. First, we set incremental profit for sales to the first group of consumers equal to zero:

$$\frac{\Delta\pi}{\Delta Q_1} = \frac{\Delta(P_1Q_1)}{\Delta Q_1} - \frac{\Delta C}{\Delta Q_1} = 0$$

here $\Delta(P_1Q_1)/\Delta Q_1$ is the incremental revenue from an extra unit of sales to the first group of consumers (i.e., MR_1). The next term, $\Delta C/\Delta Q_1$, is the incremental cost of producing this extra unit, i.e., marginal cost, MC. We thus have

$$MR_1 = MC$$

Similarly, for the second group of consumers, we must have

$$MR_2 = MC$$

Putting these relations together, we see that prices and output must be set so that

$$\boxed{MR_1 = MR_2 = MC} \qquad (11.1)$$

Again, marginal revenue must be equal across groups of consumers and must equal marginal cost.

Managers may find it easier to think in terms of the relative prices that should be charged to each group of consumers, and to relate these prices to the elasticities of demand. Recall that we can write marginal revenue in terms of the elasticity of demand as

$$MR = P(1 + 1/E_d)$$

Then $MR_1 = P_1(1 + 1/E_1)$ and $MR_2 = P_2(1 + 1/E_2)$, where E_1 and E_2 are the elasticities of demand for the firm's sales in the first and second markets, respectively. Now equating MR_1 and MR_2 gives us the following relationship that must hold for the prices:

$$\boxed{\frac{P_1}{P_2} = \frac{(1 + 1/E_2)}{(1 + 1/E_1)}} \qquad (11.2)$$

As you would expect, the higher price will be charged to consumers with the lower demand elasticity. For example, if the elasticity of demand for consumers in group 1 is -2, and the elasticity for consumers in group 2 is -4, we will have $P_1/P_2 = (1 - \frac{1}{4})/(1 - \frac{1}{2}) = (\frac{3}{4})/(\frac{1}{2}) = 1.5$. In other words, the price charged to the first group of consumers should be 1.5 times as high as the price charged to the second group.

Figure 11.5 illustrates third-degree price discrimination. Note that the demand curve D_1 for the first group of consumers is less elastic than the curve for the second group, and the price charged to the first group is likewise higher. The total quantity produced, $Q_T = Q_1 + Q_2$, is found by summing the marginal revenue curves MR_1 and MR_2 horizontally, which yields the dashed curve MR_T,

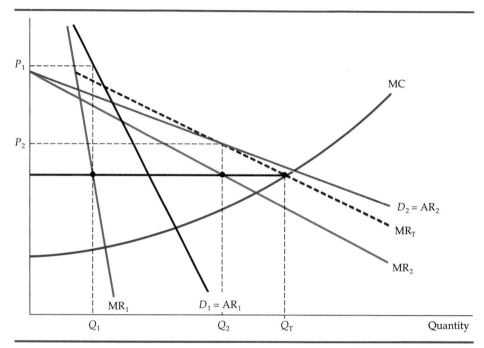

FIGURE 11.5 Third-Degree Price Discrimination. Consumers are divided into two groups, with separate demand curves for each group. The optimal prices and quantities are such that the marginal revenue from each group is the same and equal to marginal cost. Here group 1, with demand curve D_1, is charged P_1, and group 2, with the more elastic demand curve D_2, is charged the lower price P_2. Marginal cost depends on the total quantity produced Q_T. Note that Q_1 and Q_2 are such that $MR_1 = MR_2 = MC$.

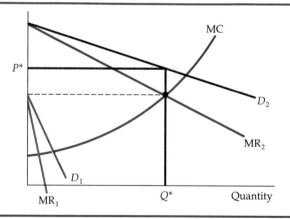

FIGURE 11.6 No Sales to Smaller Market. Even if second-degree price discrimination is feasible, it doesn't always pay to sell to both groups of consumers if marginal cost is rising. Here, the first group of consumers, with demand D_1, are not willing to pay much for the good. It is unprofitable to sell to them because the price would have to be too low to compensate for the resulting increase in marginal cost.

and finding its intersection with the marginal cost curve. Since MC must equal MR_1 and MR_2, we can draw a horizontal line leftwards from this intersection to find the quantities Q_1 and Q_2.

It may not always be worthwhile for the firm to try to sell to more than one group of consumers. In particular, if demand is small for the other group of consumers and marginal cost is rising steeply, the increased cost of producing and selling to this other group may outweigh the increase in revenue. Thus, in Figure 11.6, the firm is better off charging a single price P^* and selling only to the larger group of consumers because the additional cost of serving the smaller market would outweigh the additional revenue.

EXAMPLE 11.1   THE ECONOMICS OF COUPONS AND REBATES

The producers of processed foods and related consumer goods often issue coupons that let one buy the product at a discount. These coupons are usually distributed as part of an advertisement for the product, and they may appear in a newspaper or magazine, or as part of a promotional mailing. For example, a coupon for a particular breakfast cereal might be worth 25 cents toward the purchase of a box of the cereal. Why do firms issue these coupons? Why not just lower the price of the product, and thereby save the costs of printing and collecting the coupons?

Coupons provide a means of price discrimination. Studies show that only about 20 to 30 percent of all consumers regularly bother to clip, save, and use coupons when they go shopping. These consumers tend to be more sensitive to price than those who ignore coupons. They generally have more price-elastic demands and lower reservation prices. So by issuing coupons, a cereal company can separate its customers into two groups, and in effect charge the more price-sensitive customers a lower price than the other customers.

Rebate programs work the same way. For example, Kodak ran a program in which a consumer could mail in a form together with the proof of purchase of three rolls of film, and receive a rebate of $1.50. Why not just lower the price of film by 50 cents a roll? Because only those consumers with relatively price-sensitive demands bother to send in the material and request a rebate. Again, the program is a means of price discrimination.

Can consumers really be divided into distinct groups in this way? Table 11.1 shows the results of a statistical study in which, for a variety of products, price elasticities of demand were estimated for users and nonusers of coupons.[6] This study confirms that users of coupons tend to have more price-sensitive demands. It also shows the extent to which the elasticities differ for the two groups of consumers, and how the difference varies from one product to another.

[6]The study is by Chakravarthi Narasimhan, "A Price Discrimination Theory of Coupons," *Marketing Science* (Spring 1984).

TABLE 11.1 Price Elasticities of Demand for Users Versus Nonusers of Coupons

Product	Price Elasticity	
	Nonusers	Users
Toilet tissue	−0.60	−0.66
Stuffing/dressing	−0.71	−0.96
Shampoo	−0.84	−1.04
Cooking/salad oil	−1.22	−1.32
Dry mix dinners	−0.88	−1.09
Cake mix	−0.21	−0.43
Cat food	−0.49	−1.13
Frozen entrees	−0.60	−0.95
Gelatin	−0.97	−1.25
Spaghetti sauces	−1.65	−1.81
Creme rinse/conditioner	−0.82	−1.12
Soups	−1.05	−1.22
Hot dogs	−0.59	−0.77

These elasticity estimates by themselves do not tell a firm what price to set and how large a discount to offer through its coupons because they pertain to *market demand,* not the demand for the firm's particular brand. For example, Table 11.1 indicates that the elasticity of demand for cake mix is −0.21 for nonusers of coupons and −0.43 for users. But the elasticity of demand for any of the eight or ten major brands of cake mix on the market will be far larger than either of these numbers—about eight or ten times as large, as a rule of thumb.[7] So for any one brand of cake mix, say, Pillsbury, the elasticity of demand for users of coupons might be about −4, versus about −2 for nonusers. From equation (11.2) we can therefore determine that the price to nonusers of coupons should be about 1.5 times the price to users. In other words, if a box of cake mix sells for $1.50, the company should offer coupons that give a 50 cent discount.

EXAMPLE 11.2 HOW TO SET AIRLINE FARES

Travelers are often amazed at the variety of fares available for a round-trip flight from New York to Paris. For example, the first-class fare was recently almost $2,000; the regular (unrestricted) economy fare was about $1,200; and special discount fares (often requiring the purchase of a ticket several weeks in advance and/or a stay of at least one week) could be bought for as little as $500. Although

---

[7]This rule of thumb follows if interfirm competition can be described by the Cournot model, which we will discuss in Chapter 12.

TABLE 11.2 Elasticities of Demand for Air Travel by Fare Category: U.S./Europe

| | Fare Category | | |
Elasticity	First-Class	Regular Economy	Excursion
Price	−0.45	−1.30	−1.83
Income	1.50	1.38	2.37

first-class service is not the same as economy service with a minimum stay requirement, the difference would not seem to warrant a price that is four times as high. Why, then, do airlines set fares this way?

The reason is that these fares provide an important and very profitable form of price discrimination for airlines. The gains from discriminating are large, and to maximize profits these fares should indeed differ considerably because different types of customers, with very different elasticities of demand, purchase these different types of tickets. Table 11.2 shows estimates of the price (and income) elasticities of demand for three categories of service between the United States and Europe: first-class, regular economy, and excursion.[8] (An excursion fare requires minimum and maximum stays, but no prepurchase.)

Note that the demand for excursion fares is about four times as price elastic as first class service. Of course, these elasticities pertain to market demand, and with several airlines competing for transatlantic customers, the elasticities of demand for each airline will be larger. But the *relative* sizes of elasticities across the three categories of service should be about the same. When elasticities of demand differ so widely, it should not be surprising that airlines set such different fares for different categories of service.

Price discrimination has become especially sophisticated for flights within the United States. A wide variety of fares is available, depending on how far in advance the ticket is bought, the percentage of the fare that is refundable if the trip is changed or cancelled, and whether the trip includes a weekend stay.[9] The objective of the airlines has been to discriminate more finely among travelers with different reservation prices. As American Airlines' vice-president of pricing and product planning explained it, "You don't want to sell a seat to a guy for $69 when he is willing to pay $400."[10] At the same time, an airline would rather sell a seat for $69 than leave it empty.

[8] These estimates are from a study by J. M. Cigliano, "Price and Income Elasticities for Airline Travel: The North Atlantic Market," *Business Economics* 15 (Sept. 1980): 17–21.

[9] Airlines also allocate the number of seats on each flight that will be available for each fare category. This is based on the total demand and mix of passengers expected for each flight. Methods for doing this are discussed in Peter P. Belobaba, "Airline Yield Management: An Overview of Seat Inventory Control," *Transportation Science* 21 (May 1987): 63–73.

[10] "The Art of Devising Air Fares," *New York Times*, March 4, 1987.

11.3   Intertemporal Price Discrimination and Peak-Load Pricing

Intertemporal price discrimination is an important and widely practiced pricing strategy closely related to third-degree price discrimination. Here consumers are separated into different groups with different demand functions by being charged different prices at different points in time.

To see how intertemporal price discrimination works, think about how an electronics company might price a new, technologically advanced piece of equipment, such as video cassette recorders during the 1970s, compact disc players in the early 1980s, and most recently, digital tape players. In Figure 11.7, D_1 is the (inelastic) demand curve for a small group of consumers who value the product highly and do not want to wait to buy it (e.g., stereo buffs who value the high-quality sound from a compact disc player). D_2 is the demand curve for the broader group of consumers who are more willing to forgo the product if the price is too high. The strategy, then, is to initially offer the product at the high price P_1, selling mostly to consumers on demand curve D_1. Later, after this first group of consumers has bought the product, the price is lowered

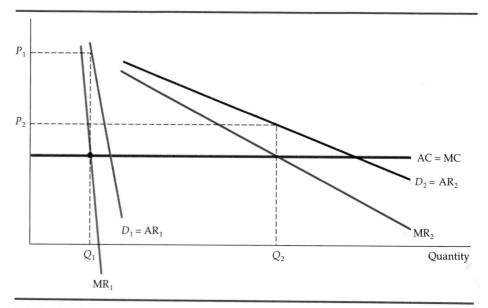

FIGURE 11.7   Intertemporal Price Discrimination.   Here, consumers are divided into groups by changing the price over time. Initially, the price is high, and the firm captures surplus from consumers who have a high demand for the good and are unwilling to wait to buy it. Later, the price is reduced to appeal to the mass market.

to P_2, and sales are made to the larger group of consumers on demand curve D_2.[11]

There are other examples of intertemporal price discrimination. One involves charging a high price for a first-run movie, then lowering the price after the movie has been out a year and is playing in the suburbs. Another, practiced almost universally by publishers, is to charge a high price for the hardcover edition of a book, and then to release the paperback version at a much lower price about a year later. Many people think that the lower price of the paperback is due to a much lower cost of production, but this is not true. Once a book has been edited and typeset, the marginal cost of printing an additional copy, whether hardcover or paperback, is quite low, perhaps a dollar or so. The paperback version is sold for much less money not because it is much cheaper to print, but because high-demand consumers have already purchased the hardbound edition, and the remaining consumers generally have more elastic demands.

Peak-load pricing is a form of intertemporal price discrimination based on efficiency. For some goods and services, demand peaks at particular times—for roads and tunnels during commuter rush hours, for electricity during late summer afternoons, and for ski resorts and amusement parks on weekends. Marginal cost is also high during these peak periods because of capacity constraints. Prices should thus be higher during peak periods.

This is illustrated in Figure 11.8, where D_1 is the demand curve for the peak period, and D_2 is the demand curve for the nonpeak period. The firm sets marginal revenue equal to marginal cost for each period, obtaining the high price P_1 for the peak period, and the lower price P_2 for the nonpeak period, with corresponding quantities Q_1 and Q_2. This increases the firm's profits above what they would be if it charged one price for all periods. It is also more efficient—the sum of producer and consumer surplus is greater because prices are closer to marginal cost.[12]

Note that peak-load pricing is different from third-degree price discrimination. With third-degree price discrimination, marginal revenue has to be equal for each group of consumers and equal to marginal cost. The reason is that the costs of serving the different groups are not independent. For example, with unrestricted versus discounted air fares, increasing the number of seats sold at discounted fares affects the cost of selling unrestricted tickets—marginal cost

---

[11]The prices of new electronic products also come down over time because costs fall as producers start to achieve greater scale economies and move down the learning curve. But even if costs did not fall, producers can make more money by first setting a high price and then reducing it over time, thereby discriminating and capturing consumer surplus.

[12]The efficiency gain from peak-load pricing is important. If the firm were a regulated monopolist (e.g., an electric utility), the regulatory agency should set the prices P_1 and P_2 at the points where the *demand* curves, D_1 and D_2, intersect the marginal cost curve, rather than where the marginal revenue curves intersect marginal cost. Consumers then realize the entire efficiency gain.

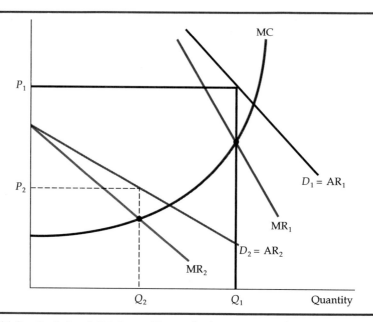

FIGURE 11.8   Peak-Load Pricing.   Demands for some goods and services increase sharply during particular times of the day or year. Charging a higher price P_1 during the peak periods is more profitable for the firm than charging a single price at all times. It is also more efficient because marginal cost is higher during peak periods.

rises rapidly as the airplane fills up. But this is not so with peak-load pricing (and for that matter, with most instances of intertemporal price discrimination). Selling more tickets for the ski lifts or amusement park on a weekday does not significantly raise the cost of selling tickets on the weekend. Similarly, selling more electricity during the off-peak period will not significantly increase the cost of selling electricity during the peak period. As a result, price and sales in each period can be determined independently by setting marginal cost equal to marginal revenue for each period.

Movie theaters, which charge more for the evening show than for the matinee, are another example of this. For most movie theaters the marginal cost of serving customers during the matinee is independent of the marginal cost during the evening. The owner of a movie theater can determine the optimal prices for the evening and matinee shows independently, using estimates of demand in each period and of marginal cost.

EXAMPLE 11.3   HOW TO PRICE A BEST-SELLING NOVEL

Publishing both hardbound and paperback editions of a book allows publishers to price discriminate. As they do with most goods, consumers differ considerably in their willingness to pay for books. For example, some consumers want to buy a new best seller as soon as it is released, even if the price is $20. Other consumers, however, will wait a year until the book is available in paperback for $4 or $5. But how should a publishing company decide that $20 is the right price for the new hardbound edition and $5 is the right price for the paperback edition? And how long should it wait before bringing out the paperback edition?

The key is to divide consumers into two groups, so that those who are willing to pay a high price do so, and only those unwilling to pay a high price wait and buy the paperback. This means that significant time must be allowed to pass before the paperback is released. If consumers know that the paperback will be available within a few months, they will have little incentive to buy the hardbound edition.[13] On the other hand, the publisher cannot wait too long to bring out the paperback edition, or else interest in the book will wane and the market will dry up. As a result, publishers typically wait a year to a year and a half before releasing the paperback edition.

What about price? Setting the price of the hardbound edition is difficult because, except for a few authors whose books always seem to sell, a publisher has little data from which to estimate demand for a book that is about to be published, other than the sales of similar successful books in the past. But usually only aggregate data are available for each category of book. So most new novels, for example, are released at fairly similar prices. It is clear, however, that those consumers willing to wait for the paperback edition have demands that are far more elastic than those of bibliophiles. It is not surprising, then, that paperback editions sell for so much less than hardbound ones.[14]

11.4 The Two-Part Tariff

The two-part tariff is related to price discrimination and provides another means of extracting consumer surplus. It requires consumers to pay a fee up front for the right to buy a product. Consumers then pay an additional fee for each unit of the product they wish to consume. The classic example of this is an amuse-

---

[13]This is not strictly true. Some consumers will buy the hardbound edition even if the paperback is already available because it is more durable and more attractive on a bookshelf. This must be taken into account when setting prices, but it is of secondary importance compared with intertemporal price discrimination.

[14]In many cases, the hardbound and paperback editions are published by different companies. The author's agent auctions the rights to the two editions, but the contract for the paperback specifies a delay to protect the sales of the hardbound edition. The principle still applies, however. The length of the delay and the prices of the two editions are chosen to intertemporally price discriminate.

ment park.[15] You pay an admission fee to enter, and you also pay a certain amount for each ride you go on. The owner of the park has to decide whether to charge a high entrance fee and a low price for the rides, or alternatively, to admit people for free but charge high prices for the rides.

The two-part tariff has been applied in many settings: tennis and golf clubs (you pay an annual membership fee, plus a fee for each use of a court or round of golf); the rental of large mainframe computers (you pay a flat monthly fee plus a fee for each unit of processing time consumed); basic telephone service (you pay a monthly hook-up fee plus a fee for message units); a Polaroid camera (you pay for the camera, which lets you productively consume the film, which you pay for by the package); and safety razors (you pay for the razor, which lets you productively consume the blades that fit only that brand of razor).

The problem for the firm is how to set the entry fee (which we denote by T) versus the usage fee (which we denote by P). Assuming that the firm has some market power, should it set a high entry fee and low usage fee, or vice versa? To see how a firm can solve this problem we need to understand the basic principles involved.

Let us begin with an artificial but very simple case. Suppose only one consumer is in the market (or many consumers with identical demand curves). Suppose also that the firm knows this consumer's demand curve. Now, remember that the firm wants to capture as much consumer surplus as possible. In this case, the solution is straightforward: set the usage fee P equal to marginal cost, and the entry fee T equal to the total consumer surplus for each consumer. Thus, in Figure 11.9, the consumer pays T^* (or a bit less) to use the product, and $P^* = $ MC per unit consumed. With the fees set this way, the firm captures *all* the consumer surplus as its profit.

Now, suppose there are two different consumers (or two groups of identical consumers). The firm, however, can set only *one* entry fee and one usage fee. The firm would thus no longer want to set the usage fee equal to marginal cost. If it did, it could make the entry fee no larger than the consumer surplus of the consumer with the smaller demand (or else it would lose that consumer), and this would not give a maximum profit. Instead, the firm should set the usage fee *above* marginal cost, and then set the entry fee equal to the remaining consumer surplus of the consumer with the smaller demand.

Figure 11.10 illustrates this. With the optimal usage fee at P^* greater than MC, the firm's profit is $2T^* + (P^* - MC)(Q_1 + Q_2)$. (There are two consumers and each pays T^*.) You can verify that this profit is more than twice the area of triangle ABC, the consumer surplus of the consumer with the smaller demand when $P = $ MC. To determine the exact values of P^* and T^*, the firm would need to know (in addition to its marginal cost) the demand curves D_1 and D_2.

---

[15]And indeed, this form of pricing was first analyzed in detail by Walter Oi in his article, "A Disneyland Dilemma: Two-Part Tariffs for a Mickey Mouse Monopoly," *Quarterly Journal of Economics* (Feb. 1971): 77–96.

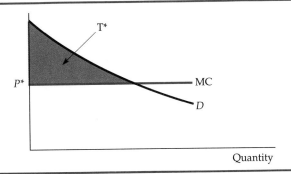

FIGURE 11.9 Two-Part Tariff with a Single Consumer. The consumer has demand curve D. The firm maximizes profit by setting usage fee P equal to marginal cost and entry fee T equal to the entire surplus of the consumer.

It would then write down its profit as a function of P and T, and choose the two prices that maximize this function. (See Exercise 5 for an example of how to do this.)

Most firms, however, face a variety of consumers with heterogeneous demands. Unfortunately, there is no simple formula to calculate the optimal two-

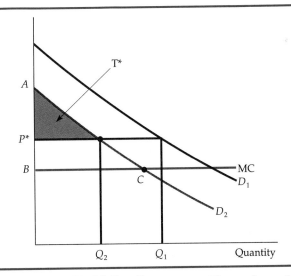

FIGURE 11.10 Two-Part Tariff with Two Consumers. The profit-maximizing usage fee P^* will exceed marginal cost. The entry fee T^* is equal to the surplus of consumer with the smaller demand. The resulting profit is $2T^* + (P^* - MC)(Q_1 + Q_2)$. Note that this profit is larger than twice the area of triangle ABC.

part tariff in this case; the design of the two-part tariff usually involves trial and error. But there is always a trade-off: A lower entry fee means more entrants and thus more profit from sales of the item. However, as the entry fee becomes smaller and the number of entrants larger, the profit derived from the entry fee will fall. The problem, then, is to pick an entry fee that results in the optimum number of entrants, i.e., the fee that allows for maximum profit. In principle, one can do this by starting with a price for sales of the item P, finding the optimum entry fee T, and then estimating the resulting profit. The price P is then changed, and the corresponding entry fee calculated, along with the new profit level. By iterating in this way, one can sometimes approach the optimal two-part tariff.

Figure 11.11 illustrates this. Here, the firm's profit π is divided into two components, each of which is plotted as a function of the entry fee T, assuming a fixed sales price P. The first component π_a is the profit from receipt of the entry fee, and is equal to the revenue $n(T)T$, where $n(T)$ is the number of entrants. (Note that very high T implies a very small n.) Initially, as T is in-

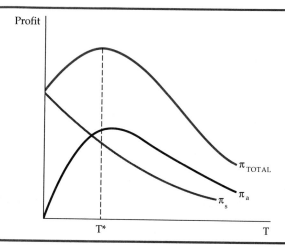

FIGURE 11.11 Two-Part Tariff with Many Different Consumers. Total profit π is the sum of the profit from the entry fee π_a and the profit from sales π_s. Both π_a and π_s depend on T, the entry fee:

$$\pi = \pi_a + \pi_s = n(T)T + (P - MC)Q(n)$$

where n is the number of entrants and depends on the entry fee T, and Q is the rate of sales, which is greater the larger is n. Here, T^* is the profit-maximizing entry fee, given P. There is no simple formula to calculate optimum values for P and T. One approach is to start with a number for P, find the optimum T, and then estimate the resulting profit. P is then changed and the corresponding T is recalculated, along with the new profit level.

creased from zero, the revenue $n(T)T$ rises. Eventually, however, further increases in T will make n so small that $n(T)T$ falls.[16] The second component, π_s, is the profit from sales of the item itself at price P, and is equal to $(P - MC)Q$, where Q is the rate at which entrants purchase the item. Q will be larger the larger the number of entrants n. Therefore, π_s falls when T is increased because a higher T reduces n.

Given P, we determine the optimal (profit-maximizing) T^*. We then change P, find a new T^*, and determine whether profit is now higher or lower. This is repeated until profit has been maximized.

Obviously, more data are needed to design an optimal two-part tariff than to choose a single price. Knowing marginal cost and the aggregate demand curve is not enough. It is impossible (in most cases) to determine the demand curve of every consumer, but one would at least like to know by how much individual demands differ from one another. If consumers' demands for your product are fairly homogeneous, you would want to charge a price P that is close to marginal cost, and make the entry fee T large. This is the ideal situation from the firm's point of view because most of the consumer surplus could then be captured. On the other hand, if consumers have heterogeneous demands for your product, you would probably want to set P substantially above marginal cost, and charge a lower entry fee T. But then, the two-part tariff is a much less effective means of capturing consumer surplus; setting a single price may do almost as well.

Firms are perpetually searching for innovative pricing strategies, and a few have devised and introduced a two-part tariff with a "twist"—the entry fee T entitles the customer to a certain number of free units. For example, if you buy a Gillette razor, several blades are usually included in the package. And the monthly lease fee for a large mainframe computer usually includes some free usage before usage is charged. This twist lets the firm set a higher entry fee T without losing as many small consumers. These small consumers might pay little or nothing for usage under this scheme, so the higher entry fee will capture their surplus without driving them out of the market, while also capturing more of the surplus of the large consumers.

EXAMPLE 11.4 POLAROID CAMERAS

In 1971 Polaroid introduced its new SX-70 camera. This camera was sold, not leased, to individual consumers. Nevertheless, because it sold its film separately, Polaroid could apply a two-part tariff to the pricing of the SX-70. Let us examine how this pricing device gave Polaroid greater profits than would have

---

[16]Note that $\pi_a = n(T)T$ is much like the revenue function $R(Q) = P(Q)Q$. $R(Q)$ increases in Q when Q is small, but eventually when Q is large enough and P is small enough, further decreases in P and increases in Q will reduce R.

been possible if its camera had used ordinary roll film, and how Polaroid might have determined the optimal prices for each part of its two-part tariff. Some time later, Kodak entered the market with a competing self-developing film and camera.[17] We will also consider the effect of Kodak's entry into the market on Polaroid's prices and profits.

First, let's make it clear why the pricing of the SX-70 (and Polaroid's other cameras and film as well) involved a two-part tariff. Polaroid had a monopoly on both its camera and the film. (Only Polaroid film could be used in the camera.) Consumers bought the camera and film to take instant pictures: The camera was the "entry fee" that provided access to the consumption of instant pictures, which was what consumers ultimately demanded.[18] In this sense, the price of the camera was very much like the entry fee at an amusement park. However, while the marginal cost of allowing someone entry into the park is close to zero, the marginal cost of producing a camera was significantly above zero, and thus had to be taken into account when designing the two-part tariff.

It was important that Polaroid have a monopoly on the film as well as the camera. If the camera had used ordinary roll film, competitive forces would have pushed the price of film close to its marginal cost. If all consumers had had identical demands, Polaroid could still have captured all the consumer surplus by setting a high price for the camera (equal to the surplus of each consumer). But in practice, consumers were heterogeneous, and the optimal two-part tariff required a price for the film well above marginal cost. (In fact Polaroid got—and still gets—most of its profits from film rather than cameras.) Polaroid needed its monopoly on the film to maintain this high price.

How should Polaroid have selected its prices for the camera and film? It could have begun with some analytical spadework. Its profit is given by

$$\pi = PQ + NT - C_1(Q) - C_2(N)$$

where P is the price of the film, T is the price of the camera, Q is the quantity of film sold, N is the number of cameras sold, and $C_1(Q)$ and $C_2(N)$ are the costs for producing film and cameras, respectively.

Polaroid wanted to maximize its profit π, taking into account that Q and N depend on P and T. Given a heterogeneous base of potential consumers, this dependence on P and T might only have been guessed at initially, drawing on knowledge of related products. Later, a better understanding of demand and of how Q and N depend on P and T might have been possible as the firm accumulated data from its sales experience. Knowledge of C_1 and C_2 may have

---

[17]In 1984 the courts ruled that Kodak's camera and film involved a patent infringement, and Kodak was forced to withdraw from the instant picture market in 1985. However, it played an important role in this market for nearly a decade.

[18]We are simplifying here. In fact some consumers obtain utility just from owning the camera, even if they take few or no pictures. Adults, like children, enjoy new toys, and can obtain pleasure from the mere possession of a technologically innovative good.

been easier to come by, perhaps from engineering and statistical studies (as discussed in Chapter 7).

Given some initial guesses or estimates for $Q(P)$, $N(T)$, $C_1(Q)$ and $C_2(N)$, Polaroid could have calculated the profit-maximizing prices P and T. It could also have determined how sensitive these profit-maximizing prices were to uncertainty over demand and cost. This could have provided a guideline for trial-and-error pricing experiments. Over time these experiments would also have told Polaroid more about demand and cost, so that it could refine its design of the two-part tariff.[19]

Did the entry of Kodak with a competing instant camera and film mean that Polaroid lost its ability to use a two-part tariff to extract consumer surplus? No—only Polaroid film could be used in Polaroid cameras, and Polaroid still had some monopoly power to exploit. However, its monopoly power was reduced, the amount of consumer surplus that could potentially be extracted was smaller, and prices had to be changed. With demand now more elastic, Polaroid would have wanted to reduce the price of its cameras significantly (which is indeed what it did). Assuming that consumers remained more or less as heterogeneous as before, Polaroid might also have wanted to reduce the price of its film.

11.5 Bundling

You have probably seen the 1939 film, *Gone with the Wind*. It is a classic that is nearly as popular now as it was then. Yet we would guess that you have not seen *Getting Gertie's Garter*, a flop that the same film company (Loews) also produced in 1939. And we would also guess that you didn't know that these two films were priced in what was then an unusual and innovative way.[20]

Movie theaters that leased *Gone with the Wind* also had to lease *Getting Gertie's Garter*. (Movie theaters pay the film companies or their distributors a daily or weekly fee for the films they lease.) In other words, these two films were *bundled*, i.e., sold as a package.[21] Why would the film company do this?

You might think that the answer is obvious: *Gone with the Wind* was a great film and *Gertie* was a lousy film, so bundling the two forced movie theaters to lease *Gertie*. But this answer doesn't make economic sense. Suppose a theater's reservation price (the maximum price it will pay) for *Gone with the Wind* is $12,000

---

[19]Setting prices for a product such as a Polaroid camera is clearly not a simple matter. We have ignored the *dynamic* behavior of cost and demand: how production costs fall as the firm moves down its learning curve, and how demand changes over time as the market begins to saturate.

[20]For those readers who claim to know all this, our final trivia question is: Who played the role of Gertie in *Getting Gertie's Garter?*

[21]Another term for bundling is *block booking*.

per week, and its reservation price for *Gertie* is $3,000 per week. Then the most it would pay for *both* films is $15,000, whether it takes the films individually or as a package.

Bundling makes sense when *customers have heterogeneous demands,* and when the firm cannot price discriminate. With films, different movie theaters serve different groups of patrons and therefore may well have different demands for films. For example, the theater might appeal to different age groups, who have different relative film preferences.

To see how a film company can use this heterogeneity to its advantage, suppose there are *two* movie theaters, and their reservation prices for our two films are as follows:

	Gone with the Wind	Getting Gertie's Garter
Theater A	$12,000	$3,000
Theater B	$10,000	$4,000

If the films are rented separately, the maximum price that could be charged for *Wind* is $10,000 because charging more than this would exclude Theater B. Similarly, the maximum price that could be charged for *Gertie* is $3,000. Charging these two prices would yield $13,000 from each theater, for a total of $26,000 in revenue. But suppose the films are *bundled.* Theater A values the *pair* of films at $15,000 ($12,000 + $3,000), and Theater B values the pair at $14,000 ($10,000 + $4,000). So we can charge each theater $14,000 for the pair of films, and earn a total revenue of $28,000. Clearly, we can earn more revenue ($2,000 more) by bundling the films.

Why is bundling more profitable than selling the films separately? Because (in this example) the *relative* valuations of the two films are reversed. In other words, although both theaters would pay much more for *Wind* than for *Gertie,* Theater A would pay more than Theater B for *Wind* ($12,000 vs. $10,000), while Theater B would pay more than Theater A for *Gertie* ($4,000 vs. $3,000). In technical terms, we say that the demands are *negatively correlated*—the customer willing to pay the most for *Wind* is willing to pay the least for *Gertie.* To see why this is critical, suppose Theater A would pay more for *both* films:

	Gone with the Wind	Getting Gertie's Garter
Theater A	$12,000	$4,000
Theater B	$10,000	$3,000

The most that Theater A would pay for the pair of films is now $16,000, but the most that Theater B would pay for the pair is only $13,000. So if the films were bundled, the maximum price that could be charged for the package is $13,000, yielding a total revenue of $26,000, the same as by selling the films separately.

Now, suppose a firm is selling two different goods to many consumers. To analyze the possible advantages of bundling, we will use a simple diagram to describe the preferences of the consumers in terms of their reservations prices and their consumption decisions given the prices charged. In Figure 11.12 the horizontal axis is r_1, which is the reservation price of a consumer for good 1, and the vertical axis is r_2, which is the reservation price for good 2. The figure shows the reservation prices for three consumers. Consumer a is willing to pay up to $3.25 for good 1 and up to $6 for good 2; consumer b is willing to pay $8.25 for good 1 and up to $3.25 for good 2; and consumer c is willing to pay up to $10 for each of the goods. In general, the reservation prices for any number of consumers can be plotted this way.

Suppose there are many consumers, and the products are sold separately, at prices P_1 and P_2, respectively. Figure 11.13 shows how consumers can be divided into groups in terms of their consumption decisions. Consumers in region A of the graph have reservation prices that are above the prices being charged for each of the goods, and so will buy both goods. Consumers in region B have a reservation price for good 2 that is above P_2, but a reservation price for good 1 that is below P_1; they will buy only good 2. Similarly, consumers in region D will buy only good 1. Finally, consumers in region C have reservation prices below the prices charged for each of the goods, and so will buy neither good.

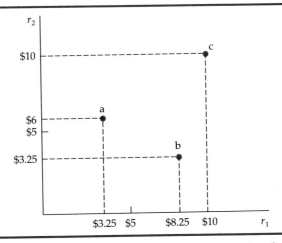

FIGURE 11.12 Reservation Prices. Reservation prices r_1 and r_2 for two goods are shown for three consumers, labeled a, b, and c. Consumer a is willing to pay up to $3.25 for good 1 and up to $6 for good 2.

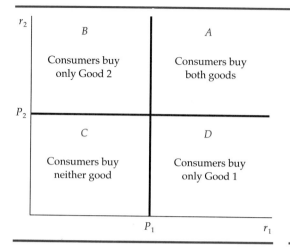

FIGURE 11.13   Consumption Decisions When Products Are Sold Separately.   The reservation prices of consumers in region A exceed the prices P_1 and P_2 charged for the two goods, and so these consumers buy both goods. Consumers in regions B and D buy only one of the goods, and consumers in Region C buy neither good.

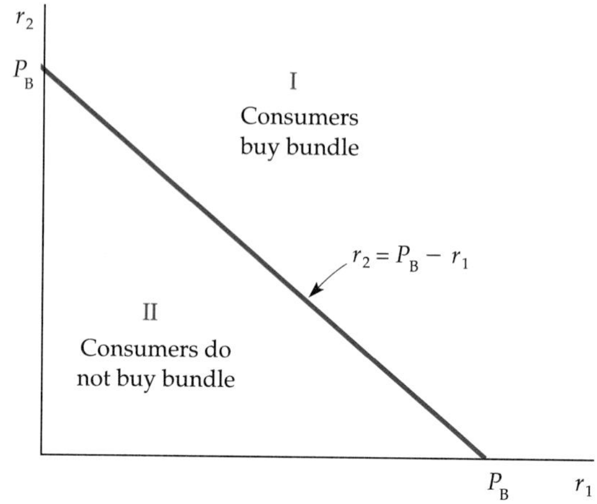

FIGURE 11.14   Consumption Decisions When Products Are Bundled.   Consumers compare the *sum* of their reservation prices, $r_1 + r_2$, with the price of the bundle P_B. They buy the bundle only if $r_1 + r_2$ is at least as large as P_B.

Now suppose the goods are sold as a bundle, for a total price of P_B. We can then divide the graph into two regions, as in Figure 11.14. Any given consumer will buy the bundle only if its price is less than or equal to the sum of that consumer's reservation prices for the two goods. The dividing line is therefore the equation $P_B = r_1 + r_2$, or equivalently, $r_2 = P_B - r_1$. Consumers in region I have reservation prices that add up to more than P_B, so they will buy the bundle. Consumers in region II have reservation prices that add up to less than P_B, so they will not buy the bundle.

Depending on the prices charged, some of the consumers in region II of Figure 11.14 might have bought one of the goods if they had been sold separately. These consumers are lost to the firm, however, when it sells the goods as a bundle. The firm, then, has to determine whether it can do better by bundling.

In general, the effectiveness of bundling depends on how negatively correlated demands are. In other words, it works best when consumers who have a high reservation price for good 1 have a low reservation price for good 2, and vice versa. Figures 11.15a and b show two extremes. In Figure 11.15a each point represents the two reservation prices of a consumer. Note that the demands for the two goods are perfectly positively correlated—consumers with a high reservation price for good 1 also have a high reservation price for good 2. If the

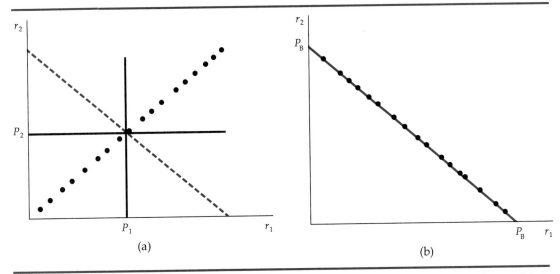

FIGURE 11.15 Reservation Prices. In (a), demands are perfectly positively correlated, so the firm does not gain by bundling. It would earn the same profit as by selling the goods separately. In (b), demands are perfectly negatively correlated. Bundling is the ideal strategy—all the consumer surplus can be extracted.

firm bundles and charges a price $P_B = P_1 + P_2$, it will make the same profit it would if it sold the goods separately at prices P_1 and P_2. In Figure 11.15b, on the other hand, demands are perfectly negatively correlated—a higher reservation price for good 2 implies a proportionately lower one for good 1. In this case, bundling is the ideal strategy. By charging the price P_B shown in the figure, the firm can capture *all* the consumer surplus.

Figure 11.16, which shows the movie example that we introduced at the beginning of this section, illustrates how the demands of the two movie theaters are negatively correlated. (Theater A will pay relatively more for *Gone with the Wind*, but Theater B will pay relatively more for *Getting Gertie's Garter.*) This makes it more profitable to rent the films as a bundle, priced at $14,000.

Mixed Bundling

So far, we have assumed that the firm has two options to sell the goods either separately or as a bundle. But there is a third option, called *mixed bundling*. As the name suggests, the firm offers its products both separately and as a bundle, with a package price below the sum of the individual prices. Mixed bundling is often the ideal strategy when demands are only somewhat negatively correlated, and/or when marginal production costs are significant. (Thus far, we have assumed that marginal production costs are zero.)

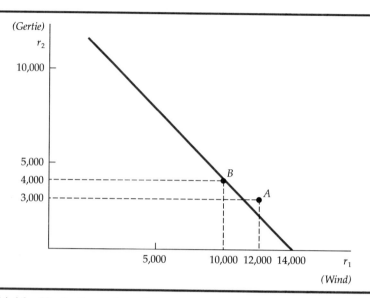

FIGURE 11.16   Movie Example.   Consumers *A* and *B* are two movie theaters. The diagram shows their reservation prices for the films *Gone with the Wind* and *Getting Gertie's Garter*. Demands are negatively correlated, so bundling pays.

In Figure 11.17, mixed bundling is the most profitable strategy. Here, demands are perfectly negatively correlated, but there are significant marginal costs. (The marginal cost of producing good 1 is $20, and the marginal cost of producing good 2 is $30.) Four consumers are shown, labeled *A* through *D*. Now, let's compare three strategies—selling the goods separately at prices P_1 = $60 and P_2 = $90; selling the goods only as a bundle (a strategy that we will refer to as "pure bundling") at a price of $100; or mixed bundling, where the goods are sold separately at prices P_1 = P_2 = $89.95, or as a bundle at a price of $100.

Table 11.3 shows these three strategies and their resulting profits. (You can try other prices for P_1, P_2, and P_B to verify that those given in the table maximize profits for each strategy.) When the goods are sold separately, only consumers *C* and *D* buy good 1, and only consumer *A* buys good 2, so that the total profit is 2(60 − 20) + 1(90 − 30) = $140. With pure bundling, all four consumers buy the bundle for $100, so that total profit is 4(100 − 20 − 30) = $200. As we should expect, pure bundling is better than selling the goods separately, because consumers' demands are negatively correlated. But what about mixed bundling? Now consumer *D* buys only good 1 for $89.95, consumer *A* buys only good 2 for $89.95, and consumers *B* and *C* buy the bundle for $100. Total profit is now (89.95 − 20) + (89.95 − 30) + 2(100 − 20 − 30) = $229.90.

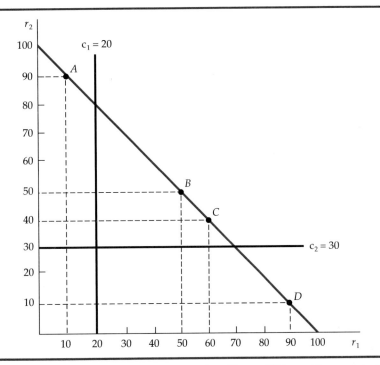

FIGURE 11.17 Example of Mixed versus Pure Bundling. With positive marginal costs, mixed bundling may be more profitable than pure bundling. That is the case in this example. Consumer A has a reservation price for good 1 that is below marginal cost c_1, and consumer D has a reservation price for good 2 that is below marginal cost c_2. With mixed bundling, consumer A is induced to buy only good 2, and consumer D is induced to buy only good 1, reducing the firm's costs.

Here, mixed bundling is the most profitable strategy, even though demands are perfectly negatively correlated (i.e., all four consumers have reservation prices on the line $r_2 = 100 - r_1$). The reason is that for each good, marginal production cost exceeds the reservation price of one consumer. For example, consumer A has a reservation price of $90 for good 2, but a reservation price of

TABLE 11.3				
	P_1	P_2	P_B	Profit
Sell separately	$60	$90	—	$140
Pure bundling	—	—	$100	$200
Mixed bundling	$89.95	$89.95	$100	$229.90

only $10 for good 1. Since the cost of producing a unit of good 1 is $20, the firm would prefer that consumer *A* buy only good 2, and not the bundle. It can achieve this by offering good 2 separately for a price just below consumer *A's* reservation price, while also offering the bundle at a price acceptable to consumers *B* and *C*.

Mixed bundling would *not* be the preferred strategy in this example if marginal costs were zero because then there would be no benefit in excluding consumer *A* from buying good 1 and consumer *D* from buying good 2. We leave it to you to demonstrate this (see Exercise 8).[22]

EXAMPLE 11.5 THE COMPLETE DINNER VS. À LA CARTE: A RESTAURANT'S PRICING PROBLEM

Many restaurants offer complete dinners as well as an à la carte menu. Why? Most customers go to a restaurant knowing roughly how much they are willing to spend for dinner (and choose the restaurant accordingly). However, the customers that enter a restaurant have different preferences. For example, some value an appetizer very highly, but could happily skip the dessert. Other customers have just the opposite preferences—they attach little value to the appetizer, but dessert is essential. And finally, some customers attach moderate values to both the appetizer and dessert. What pricing strategy lets the restaurant capture as much consumer surplus as possible from these heterogeneous customers? The answer, of course, is mixed bundling.

For a restaurant, mixed bundling means offering both complete dinners (the appetizer, main course, and dessert come as a package) and an à la carte menu (the customer buys the appetizer, main course, and dessert separately). This allows the à la carte menu to be priced to capture consumer surplus from customers who value some dishes much more highly than other dishes. (Such customers would correspond to consumers *A* and *D* in Figure 11.18.) At the same time, the complete dinner retains those customers who have lower variations in their reservation prices for different dishes (e.g., customers who attach a moderate value to both the appetizer and dessert).

For example, if the restaurant expects to attract customers willing to spend about $20 for dinner, it might charge about $5 for the appetizers, about $14 for

[22]For a more detailed discussion of bundling, see William J. Adams and Janet L. Yellin, "Commodity Bundling and the Burden of Monopoly," *Quarterly Journal of Economics* 90 (Aug. 1976): 475–498. In some instances a firm with monopoly power will find it profitable to bundle its product with the product of another firm. This is discussed in Richard L. Schmalensee, "Commodity Bundling by Single-Product Monopolies," *Journal of Law and Economics* 25 (April 1982): 67–71. Bundling can also be profitable when the products have interdependent demands (i.e., are substitutes or complements). See Arthur Lewbel, "Bundling of Substitutes or Complements," *International Journal of Industrial Organization* 3 (1985): 101–107.

a typical main dish, and about $4 for dessert. It could also offer a complete dinner, which includes an appetizer, main course, and dessert, for $20. Then, the customer who loves dessert but couldn't care less about an appetizer will order only the main dish and dessert, and spend $18 (and the restaurant will save the cost of preparing an appetizer). At the same time, another customer who attaches a moderate value (say, $3 or $3.50) to both the appetizer and dessert will buy the complete dinner.

Unfortunately for consumers, perhaps, creative pricing can be more important than creative cooking for the financial success of a restaurant. Successful restaurateurs know their customers' demand characteristics and use that knowledge to design a pricing strategy that extracts as much consumer surplus as possible.

Tying

Another pricing technique, called tying, is related to bundling but should not be confused with it. *Tying* works as follows. Suppose a firm sells a product (such as a copying machine), the use of which requires the consumption of a secondary product (such as paper). The consumer that buys the first product is also required to buy the secondary product from the same company. This requirement is usually imposed through a contract. Note that tying is different from bundling. With bundling, the consumer might have been happy to buy just one of the products. With tying, however, the first product is useless without access to the secondary product.

Why do firms use this pricing practice? One of the main benefits of tying is that it often allows a firm to *meter demand*, and thus to practice price discrimination more effectively. For example, during the 1950s, when Xerox had a monopoly on copying machines but not on paper, customers who leased a Xerox copier also had to buy Xerox paper. This allowed Xerox to meter consumption (customers who used a machine intensively bought more paper), and thereby apply a two-part tariff to the pricing of its machines. Also during the 1950s, IBM required customers that leased its mainframe computers to use paper computer cards made only by IBM. By pricing these cards well above marginal cost, IBM was effectively charging higher prices for computer usage to customers with larger demands.[23]

Tying can also have other uses. An important one is to protect customer goodwill connected with a brand name. This is why franchises are often required to purchase inputs from the franchiser. For example, Mobil Oil requires

---

[23]However, antitrust actions forced IBM to discontinue this pricing practice.

its service stations to sell only Mobil motor oil, Mobil batteries, etc. Similarly, until recently, a McDonald's franchisee had to purchase all materials and supplies—from the hamburgers to the paper cups—from McDonald's, thus ensuring product uniformity and protecting the brand name.[24]

Summary

1.   Firms with market power are in an enviable position because they have the potential to earn large profits, but realizing that potential may depend critically on the firm's pricing strategy. Even if the firm sets a single price, it needs an estimate of the elasticity of demand for its output. More complicated strategies, which can involve setting several different prices, require even more information about demand.

2.   A pricing strategy aims to enlarge the customer base that the firm can sell to, and capture as much consumer surplus as possible. There are a number of ways to do this, and they usually involve setting more than a single price.

3.   Ideally, the firm would like to perfectly price discriminate, i.e., charge each customer his or her reservation price. In practice this is almost always impossible. On the other hand, various forms of imperfect price discrimination are often used to increase profits.

4.   The two-part tariff is another means of capturing consumer surplus. Customers must pay an "entry" fee, which allows them to buy the good at a per unit price. The two-part tariff is most effective when customer demands are relatively homogeneous.

5.   When demands are heterogeneous and negatively correlated, bundling can be an effective pricing technique. With pure bundling, two or more different goods are sold only as a package. With mixed bundling, the customer can buy the goods individually or as a package.

6.   Tying is related to pure bundling, but it should not be confused with it. With tying, a primary product is useless without access to a secondary product.

7.   History has shown entrepreneurs to be quite adept at designing new and innovative pricing strategies. We leave it to you to come up with twists and enhancements to the pricing techniques that have been described in this chapter.

Review Questions

1. Suppose a firm can practice perfect, first-degree price discrimination. What is the lowest price it will charge, and what will its total output be?

---

[24]In some cases, the courts ruled that tying is not necessary to protect customer goodwill and is anticompetitive, so now a McDonald's franchisee can buy supplies from any McDonald's approved source. For a discussion of some of the antitrust issues involved in franchise tying, see Benjamin Klein and Lester F. Saft, "The Law and Economics of Franchise Tying Contracts," *Journal of Law and Economics* 28 (May 1985): 345–361.

2. How does a car salesperson practice price discrimination? How does the ability to discriminate correctly affect his or her earnings?

3. Electric utilities often practice second-degree price discrimination. Why might this improve consumer welfare?

4. Give some examples of third-degree price discrimination. Can third-degree price discrimination be effective if the different groups of consumers have different levels of demand but the same price elasticities?

5. Show why optimal, third-degree price discrimination requires that marginal revenue for each group of consumers equal marginal cost. Use this condition to explain how a firm should change its prices and total output if the demand curve for one group of consumers shifted outward, so that marginal revenue for that group increased.

6. How is peak-load pricing a form of price discrimination? Can it make consumers better off? Give an example.

7. How can a firm determine an optimal two-part tariff if it has two customers with different demand curves? (Assume that it knows the demand curves.)

8. Why is the pricing of a Gillette safety razor a form of a two-part tariff? Must Gillette be a monopoly producer of its blades as well as its razors? Suppose you were advising Gillette on how to determine the two parts of the tariff. What procedure would you suggest?

9. Why did Loews bundle *Gone with the Wind* and *Getting Gertie's Garter?* What characteristic of demands is needed for bundling to increase profits?

10. How does mixed bundling differ from pure bundling? Under what conditions is mixed bundling preferred to pure bundling? Why do many restaurants practice mixed bundling (by offering a complete dinner as well as an à la carte menu) instead of pure bundling?

11. How does tying differ from bundling? Why might a firm want to practice tying?

Exercises

1. Price discrimination requires the ability to sort customers and the ability to prevent arbitrage. Explain how the following can function as price discrimination schemes; discuss both sorting and arbitrage.

    a. A requirement that airline travelers spend at least one Saturday night away from home to qualify for a low fare.

    b. Insisting on delivering cement to buyers, and basing prices on buyers' locations.

    c. Selling food processors along with coupons that can be sent to the manufacturer to obtain a $10 rebate.

    d. Offering temporary price cuts on bathroom tissue.

    e. Charging high-income patients more than low-income patients for plastic surgery.

2. Suppose a monopolist can produce any level of output it wishes at a constant average and marginal cost of $5 per unit. Assume that the monopolist sells its goods in two different markets that are far apart. The demand curve in the first market is given by

$$Q_1 = 55 - P_1$$

and the demand curve in the second market is given by

$$Q_2 = 70 - 2P_2$$

a. If the monopolist can keep the two markets separate, what level of output should it produce and what price should it charge in each market? What is its profit?

*b. How would the answer change if consumers could transport the good between the two markets for $5 per unit? What would be the monopolist's profit in this situation? Finally, how would your answer change if transportation costs were zero?

3. Sal's satellite company broadcasts TV to subscribers in Los Angeles and New York. The demand functions for each of these are

$$Q_{NY} = 50 - (\tfrac{1}{3})P_{NY}$$

$$Q_{LA} = 80 - (\tfrac{2}{3})P_{LA}$$

where Q is in thousands of subscriptions per year, and P is the subscription price per year. The cost of providing Q units of service is given by

$$C = 1000 + 30Q$$

where $Q = Q_{NY} + Q_{LA}$.

a. What are the profit-maximizing prices and quantities for the New York and Los Angeles markets?

b. As a consequence of a new satellite that the Pentagon recently deployed, people in Los Angeles receive Sal's New York broadcasts, and people in New York receive Sal's Los Angeles broadcasts. As a result, anyone in New York or Los Angeles can receive Sal's broadcasts by subscribing in either city. What will be the new equalization levels of prices and quantities for the New York and Los Angeles markets?

c. In which of the above situations, a. or b., is Sal better off? In terms of consumer surplus, which situation is preferred by people in New York and which is preferred by people in Los Angeles? Why?

4. Many retail video stores offer two alternative plans for renting films:

a. A two-part tariff: Pay an annual membership fee (e.g., $40), and then pay a small fee for the daily rental of each film (e.g., $2 per film per day).

b. A straight rental fee: Pay no membership fee, but pay a higher daily rental fee (e.g., $4 per film per day).

What is the logic behind the two-part tariff in this case? Why offer the customer a choice of two plans, rather than simply a two-part tariff?

5. As the owner of the only tennis club in an isolated wealthy community, you must decide on membership dues and fees for court time. There are two types of tennis players. "Serious" players have demand

$$Q_1 = 6 - P$$

where Q_1 is court hours per week and P is the fee per hour for each individual player.

There are also "occasional" players with demand

$$Q_2 = 3 - (\tfrac{1}{2})P$$

Assume that there are 1000 players of each type. You have plenty of courts, so that the marginal cost of court time is zero. You have fixed costs of $5000 per week. Serious and occasional players look alike, so you must charge them the same prices.

a. Suppose that to maintain a "professional" atmosphere, you want to limit membership to serious players. How should you set the *annual* membership dues and court fees (assume 52 weeks/year) to maximize profits, keeping in mind the constraint that only serious players choose to join? What are profits (per week)?

b. A friend tells you that you could make much greater profits by not encouraging both types of players to join. Is the friend right? What annual dues and court fees would maximize profits? What would these profits be per week?

c. Suppose that over the years, young, upwardly mobile professionals move to your community, all of whom are serious players. You believe there are now 3000 serious players and 1000 occasional players. Is it still profitable to cater to the occasional player? What are the profit-maximizing annual dues and court fees? What are profits per week?

6. When pricing automobiles for wholesale delivery to dealers, American car companies typically charge a much higher percentage markup over cost for "luxury option" items (such as a vinyl roof, carpeting, decorative trim, etc.) than for the car itself and more "basic" options such as power steering and automatic transmission. Explain why.

7. Figure 11.12 shows the reservation prices of three consumers for two goods. Assuming that marginal production cost is zero for both goods, can the producer make the most money by selling the goods separately, by bundling, or by "mixed" bundling (i.e., offering the goods separately or as a bundle)? What prices should be charged?

8. Go back to the example in Figure 11.17. Suppose the marginal costs c_1 and c_2 were zero. Show that in this case pure bundling is the most profitable pricing strategy, and not mixed bundling. What price should be charged for the bundle, and what will the firm's profit be?

9. On October 22, 1982, an article appeared in the *New York Times* about IBM's pricing policy. The previous day IBM had announced major price cuts on most of its small and medium-sized computers. The article said:

> IBM probably has no choice but to cut prices periodically to get its customers to purchase more and lease less. If they succeed, this could make life more difficult for IBM's major competitors. Outright purchases of computers are needed for ever larger IBM revenues and profits, says Morgan Stanley's Ulric Weil in his new book, *Information Systems in the '80's*. Mr. Weil declares that IBM cannot revert to an emphasis on leasing.

a. Provide a brief but clear argument *in support* of the claim that IBM should try "to get its customers to purchase more and lease less."

b. Provide a brief but clear argument *against this claim.*

c. What factors determine whether leasing or selling is preferable for a company like IBM? Explain briefly.

10. You are selling two goods, 1 and 2, to a market consisting of three consumers with reservation prices as follows:

	Reservation Price ($)	
Consumer	for 1	for 2
A	10	70
B	40	40
C	70	10

The unit cost of each product is 20.

a. Compute the optimal prices and profits for (i) selling the goods separately, (ii) pure bundling, and (iii) mixed bundling.

b. Which strategy yields the highest profits? Why?

11. Your firm produces two products, the demands for which are independent. Both products are produced at zero marginal cost. You face four consumers (or groups of consumers) with the following reservation prices:

Consumer	Good 1 ($)	Good 2 ($)
A	30	90
B	40	60
C	60	40
D	90	30

a. Consider three alternative pricing strategies: (i) selling the goods separately; (ii) pure bundling; (iii) mixed bundling. For *each strategy*, determine the optimal prices to be charged and the resulting profits. Which strategy is best?

b. Now suppose the production of each good entails a marginal cost of $35. How does this change your answers to (a)? Why is the optimal strategy now different?

APPENDIX TO CHAPTER 11

Transfer Pricing
in the Integrated Firm

So far we have studied the firm's pricing decision assuming that it sells its output in an *external market*, i.e., to consumers or to other firms. Many firms, however, are *vertically integrated*—they contain several divisions, with some divisions producing parts and components that other divisions use to produce the finished product.[1] For example, each of the major U.S. automobile companies has "upstream" divisions that produce engines, brakes, radiators, and other components that the "downstream" divisions use to produce the finished products. *Transfer pricing* refers to the valuation of these parts and components within the firm. *Transfer prices* are internal prices at which the parts and components from upstream divisions are "sold" to downstream divisions. Transfer prices must be chosen correctly because they are the signals that divisional managers use to determine output levels.

This Appendix shows how a profit-maximizing firm chooses its transfer prices and divisional output levels. We will also examine other issues raised by vertical integration. For example, suppose a computer firm's upstream division produces memory chips that are used by a downstream division to produce the final product. If other firms also produce these chips, should our firm obtain all its chips from the upstream division, or should it also buy some on the outside market? Should the upstream division produce more chips than is needed by the downstream division, selling the excess in the market? If it does, should the transfer price for chips supplied to the downstream division differ from the price on the open market? And finally, how should the firm coordinate the operations of the upstream and downstream divisions? In particular, can we design incentives for the divisions, so that the firm's profit is maximized?

We begin with the simplest situation—there is no outside market for the output of the upstream division, i.e., the upstream division produces a good that is neither produced nor used by any other firm. Next we consider the complications that arise when there is an outside market for the output of the upstream division.

---

[1] A firm is *horizontally integrated* when it has several divisions that produce the same product or closely related products. Many firms are both vertically and horizontally integrated.

Transfer Pricing When There is No Outside Market

Consider a firm that has three divisions. Two of these are upstream divisions that produce inputs to a downstream processing division. The two upstream divisions produce quantities Q_1 and Q_2, and have total costs $C_1(Q_1)$ and $C_2(Q_2)$. The downstream division produces a quantity Q using the production function

$$Q = f(K, L, Q_1, Q_2)$$

where K and L are capital and labor inputs, and Q_1 and Q_2 are the intermediate inputs from the upstream divisions. Excluding the costs of the inputs Q_1 and Q_2, the downstream division has a total production cost $C_d(Q)$. The total revenue from sales of the final product is $R(Q)$.

We assume there are *no outside markets* for the intermediate inputs Q_1 and Q_2. (They can be used only by the downstream division.) Then the firm has two problems. First, what quantities Q_1, Q_2, and Q maximize its profit? Second, we want to design an incentive scheme that will decentralize the firm's management. In particular, we want to determine a set of optimal transfer prices P_1 and P_2, so that *if each division maximizes its own divisional profit, the profit of the overall firm will also be maximized.*

To solve these problems, note that the firm's total profit is

$$\pi(Q) = R(Q) - C_d(Q) - C_1(Q_1) - C_2(Q_2) \tag{A11.1}$$

Now, what is the level of Q_1 that maximizes this profit? It is the level at which *the cost of the last unit of Q_1 is just equal to the additional revenue it brings to the firm.* The cost of producing one extra unit of Q_1 is the marginal cost $\Delta C_1/\Delta Q_1 = MC_1$. How much extra revenue results from the unit? An extra unit of Q_1 allows the firm to produce more final output Q of an amount $\Delta Q/\Delta Q_1 = MP_1$, the marginal product of Q_1. An extra unit of final output results in additional revenue $\Delta R/\Delta Q = MR$, but it also results in additional cost by the downstream division, of an amount $\Delta C_d/\Delta Q = MC_d$. Thus, the *net marginal revenue* NMR_1 that the firm earns from an extra unit of Q_1 is $(MR - MC_d)MP_1$. Setting this equal to the marginal cost of the unit, we obtain the following rule for profit maximization[2]:

$$\boxed{NMR_1 = (MR - MC_d)MP_1 = MC_1} \tag{A11.2}$$

Going through the same steps for the second intermediate input gives

$$\boxed{NMR_2 = (MR - MC_d)MP_2 = MC_2} \tag{A11.3}$$

[2]Using calculus, we can obtain this by differentiating equation (A11.1) with respect to Q_1:

$$d\pi/dQ_1 = (dR/dQ)(\partial Q/\partial Q_1) - (dC_d/dQ)(\partial Q/\partial Q_1) - dC_1/dQ_1$$

$$= (MR - MC_d)MP_1 - MC_1$$

Setting $d\pi/dQ = 0$ to maximize profit gives equation (A11.2).

Note from equations (A11.2) and (A11.3) that it is *incorrect* to determine the firm's final output level Q by setting marginal revenue equal to marginal cost for the downstream division, i.e., by setting $MR = MC_d$. Doing so would ignore the cost of producing the intermediate input. (MR exceeds MC_d because this cost is positive.) Also, note that equations (A11.2) and (A11.3) are standard conditions of marginal analysis—the output of each upstream division should be such that its marginal cost is equal to its marginal contribution to the profit of the overall firm.

Now, what transfer prices P_1 and P_2 should be "charged" to the downstream division for its use of the intermediate inputs? Remember that if each of the three divisions uses these transfer prices to maximize its own divisional profit, the profit of the overall firm should be maximized. The two upstream divisions will maximize their divisional profits, π_1 and π_2, which are given by

$$\pi_1 = P_1 Q_1 - C_1(Q_1)$$

and

$$\pi_2 = P_2 Q_2 - C_2(Q_2)$$

Since the upstream divisions take P_1 and P_2 as given, they will choose Q_1 and Q_2 so that $P_1 = MC_1$ and $P_2 = MC_2$. Similarly, the downstream division will maximize

$$\pi(Q) = R(Q) - C_d(Q) - P_1 Q_1 - P_2 Q_2$$

Since the downstream division also takes P_1 and P_2 as given, it will choose Q_1 and Q_2 so that

$$(MR - MC_d)MP_1 = NMR_1 = P_1 \qquad (A11.4)$$

and

$$(MR - MC_d)MP_2 = NMR_2 = P_2 \qquad (A11.5)$$

Note that by setting the transfer prices equal to the respective marginal costs ($P_1 = MC_1$ and $P_2 = MC_2$), the profit-maximizing conditions given by equations (A11.2) and (A11.3) will be satisfied. We therefore have a simple solution to the transfer pricing problem: *Set each transfer price equal to the marginal cost of the respective upstream division.* Then when each division is told to maximize its own profit, the quantities Q_1 and Q_2 that the upstream divisions will want to produce will be the same quantities that the downstream division will want to "buy," ınd they will maximize the total profit of the firm.

We can illustrate this graphically with the following example. Race Car Motors, Inc., has two divisions. The upstream Engine Division produces engines, and the downstream Assembly Division puts together automobiles, using one engine (and a few other parts) in each car. In Figure A11.1, the average revenue curve AR is Race Car Motors' demand curve for cars. (Note that the firm has monopoly power in the automobile market.) MC_A is the marginal cost of assem-

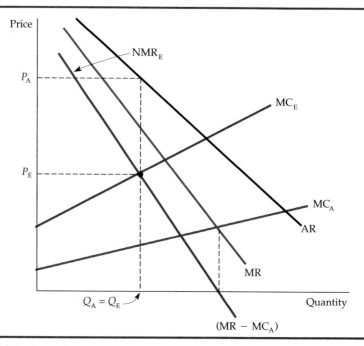

FIGURE A11.1 Race Car Motors, Inc.   The firm's upstream division should produce a quantity of engines Q_E that equates its marginal cost of engine production MC_E with the downstream division's net marginal revenue of engines NMR_E. Since the firm uses one engine in every car, NMR_E is the difference between the marginal revenue from selling cars and the marginal cost of assembling them, i.e., $MR - MC_A$. The optimal transfer price for engines P_E equals the marginal cost of producing them. Finished cars are sold at price P_A.

bling automobiles, *given the engines* (i.e., it does not include the cost of the engines). Since the car requires one engine, the marginal product of the engines is one, so that the curve labeled $MR - MC_A$ is also the net marginal revenue curve for engines: $NMR_E = (MR - MC_A)MP_E = MR - MC_A$.

The profit-maximizing number of engines (and number of cars) is given by the intersection of the net marginal revenue curve NMR_E with the marginal cost curve for engines MC_E. Having determined the number of cars it will produce, and knowing its divisional cost functions, the management of Race Car Motors can now set the transfer price P_E that correctly values the engines used to produce its cars. It is this transfer price that should be used to calculate divisional profit (and year-end bonuses for the divisional managers).

Transfer Pricing with a Competitive Outside Market

Now suppose there is a *competitive* outside market for the intermediate good produced by an upstream division. Since the outside market is competitive, there is a single market price at which one can buy or sell the good. Therefore, *the marginal cost of the intermediate good is simply the market price.* Since the optimal transfer price must equal marginal cost, it must also equal the competitive market price.

To make this clear, let's return to Race Car Motors. Suppose there is a competitive market for the engines that Race Car Motors produces and uses in its cars. If the market price is low, Race Car Motors may want to buy some or all of its engines in the market; if it is high, it may want to sell engines in the market. Figure A11.2 illustrates the first case. For quantities below $Q_{E,1}$, the

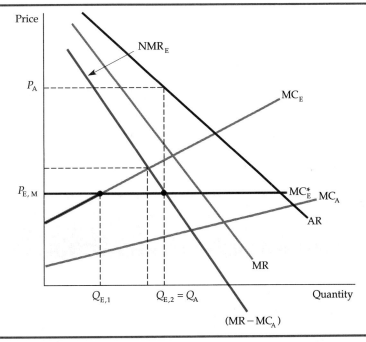

FIGURE A11.2 Race Car Motors Buys Engines in a Competitive External Market. The firm's marginal cost of engines MC_E^* is the upstream division's marginal cost for quantities up to $Q_{E,1}$ and the market price $P_{E,M}$ for quantities above $Q_{E,1}$. The downstream division should use a total of $Q_{E,2}$ engines to produce an equal number of cars; at this quantity, the marginal cost of engines equals net marginal revenue. $Q_{E,2} - Q_{E,1}$ of these engines are bought in the external market. The upstream division "pays" the downstream division the transfer price $P_{E,M}$ for the remaining $Q_{E,1}$ engines.

upstream division's marginal cost of producing engines MC_E is below the market price $P_{E,M}$, and for quantities above $Q_{E,1}$ it is above the market price. The firm should obtain engines at least cost, so the marginal cost of engines MC_E^* is the upstream division's marginal cost for quantities up to $Q_{E,1}$ and the market price for quantities above $Q_{E,1}$. Note that Race Car Motors uses more engines and produces more cars than it would have had there not been an external engine market. The downstream division now buys $Q_{E,2}$ engines and produces an equal number of automobiles. However, it "buys" only $Q_{E,1}$ of these engines from the upstream division, and buys the rest on the open market.

It might appear strange that Race Car Motors should have to go into the open market to buy engines, when it can make those engines itself. If it made all its own engines, however, its marginal cost of producing engines would exceed the competitive market price, and although the profit of the upstream division would be higher, *the total profit of the firm would be lower*.

Figure A11.3 shows the case where Race Car Motors *sells* engines in the

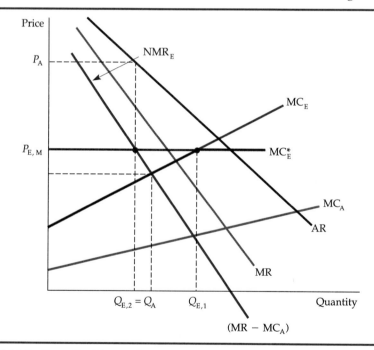

FIGURE A11.3   Race Car Motors Sells Engines in a Competitive External Market. The optimal transfer price is again the market price $P_{E,M}$. This price is above the point at which MC_E intersects NMR_E, so the upstream division sells some of its engines in the external market. The upstream division produces $Q_{E,1}$ engines, the quantity at which MC_E equals $P_{E,M}$. The downstream division uses only $Q_{E,2}$ of these, the quantity at which NMR_E equals $P_{E,M}$. Compared with Figure A11.1, in which there is no external market, more engines but fewer cars are produced.

external market. Now the competitive market price $P_{E,M}$ is above the transfer price that the firm would have set had there not been an external market. In this case the upstream Engine Division produces $Q_{E,1}$ engines, but only $Q_{E,2}$ engines are used by the downstream division to produce automobiles. The rest are sold in the external market at the price $P_{E,M}$.

Note that compared with a situation in which there is no external engine market, Race Car Motors is producing more engines but fewer cars. Why not produce this larger number of engines, but use all of them to produce more cars? Because the engines are too valuable. On the margin, the net revenue that can be earned from selling them in the external market is higher than the net revenue from using them to build additional cars.

Transfer Pricing with a Noncompetitive External Market

Now suppose there is an external market for the output of the upstream division, but that market is not competitive—the firm has monopoly power. We can apply the same principles to determine the optimal production levels and transfer prices, but we must be careful when measuring net marginal revenue. We'll use our example of Race Car Motors to illustrate this.

Suppose the engine produced by the upstream Engine Division is a special one that only Race Car Motors can make. There is an external market for this engine, however, so Race Car Motors can be a monopoly supplier to that market and can also produce engines for its own use. What is the optimal transfer price for use of the engines by the downstream division, and at what price (if any) should engines be sold in the external market?

The trick is to determine the firm's net marginal revenue from the sale of engines. In Figure A11.4, $D_{E,M}$ is the external market demand curve for engines, and $MR_{E,M}$ is the corresponding marginal revenue curve. Race Car Motors therefore has two sources of marginal revenue from the production and sale of an additional engine—the marginal revenue $MR_{E,M}$ from sales in the external market and the net marginal revenue ($MR - MC_A$) from the use of the engines by the downstream division. By summing these two curves horizontally, we obtain the *total net marginal revenue curve for engines*; it is the dark line labeled NMR_E.

The intersection of the marginal cost and total net marginal revenue curves gives the quantity of engines $Q_{E,1}$ that the upstream division should produce and the optimal transfer price P_E^*. (Again, the optimal transfer price is equal to marginal cost.) But note that only $Q_{E,2}$ of these engines are used by the downstream division to make cars. (This is the quantity at which the downstream division's net marginal revenue, $MR - MC_A$, is equal to the tranfer price P_E^*.) The remaining engines $Q_{E,3}$ are sold in the external market. However, they are not sold at the transfer price P_E^*. Instead the firm exercises its monopoly power and sells them at the higher price $P_{E,M}$.

Why pay the upstream division only P_E^* per engine when the firm is selling

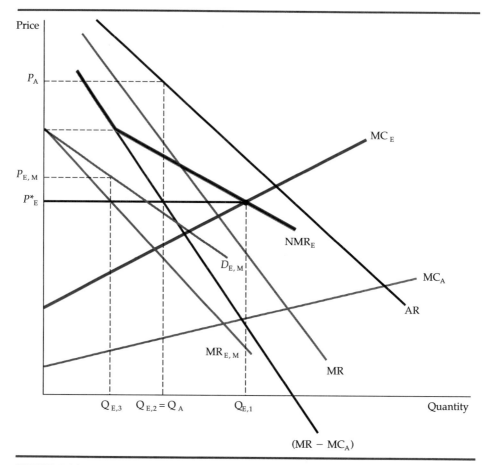

FIGURE A11.4 Race Car Motors Is a Monopoly Supplier of Engines to an External Market. $D_{E,M}$ is the external market demand curve for engines, and $MR_{E,M}$ is the corresponding marginal revenue curve. Race Car Motors has two sources of marginal revenue from producing engines—the marginal revenue $MR_{E,M}$ from sales in the external market and the net marginal revenue ($MR - MC_A$) from the use of the engines by the downstream division. The *total net marginal revenue curve for engines* NMR_E is the horizontal sum of these two marginal revenues. The optimal transfer price P_E^* and the quantity of engines that the upstream division produces $Q_{E,1}$ are found at the intersection of MC_E and NMR_E. Only $Q_{E,2}$ of these engines are used by the downstream division to make cars, the quantity at which the downstream division's net marginal revenue, $MR - MC_A$, is equal to the transfer price P_E^*. The remaining engines $Q_{E,3}$ are sold in the external market at the price $P_{E,M}$.

these same engines in the external market at the higher price $P_{E,M}$? Because if the upstream division is paid more than P_E^* (and thereby encouraged to produce more engines), the marginal cost of engines will rise and exceed the net marginal revenue from their use by the downstream division. And if the price charged in the outside market were lowered, the marginal revenue from sales in that market would fall below marginal cost. At the prices P_E^* and $P_{E,M}$, marginal revenues and marginal cost are equal: $MR_{E,M} = (MR - MC_A) = MC_E$.

A Numerical Example

Let's go through a numerical example to clarify the solution to the transfer pricing problem. Suppose Race Car Motors has the following demand for its automobiles:

$$P = 20,000 - Q$$

so that its marginal revenue is

$$MR = 20,000 - 2Q$$

The downstream division's cost of assembling cars is

$$C_A(Q) = 8,000Q$$

so that the division's marginal cost is $MC_A = 8,000$. The upstream division's cost of producing engines is

$$C_E(Q_E) = 2Q_E^2$$

so that the division's marginal cost is $MC_E(Q_E) = 4Q_E$.

(a) First, suppose there is *no external market* for the engines. How many engines and cars should the firm produce, and what should the transfer price for engines be? To solve this problem, we set the net marginal revenue for engines equal to the marginal cost of producing engines. Since each car has one engine, $Q_E = Q$, and the net marginal revenue of engines is

$$NMR_E = MR - MC_A = 12,000 - 2Q_E$$

Now set NMR_E equal to MC_E:

$$12,000 - 2Q_E = 4Q_E$$

so that $6Q_E = 12,000$, and $Q_E = 2,000$. The firm should therefore produce 2,000 engines and 2,000 cars. The optimal transfer price is the marginal cost of these 2,000 engines: $P_E = 4Q_E = \$8,000$.

(b) Now suppose that there is an *external competitive market* in which engines can be bought or sold for $6,000. Because this is below the $8,000 transfer price that is optimal when there is no external market, the firm should buy some of its engines outside. Its marginal cost of engines, and the optimal transfer price, is now \$6,000. Set this \$6,000 marginal cost equal to the net marginal revenue of engines:

$$6,000 = NMR_E = 12,000 - 2Q_E$$

Thus the total quantity of engines and cars is now 3,000. Note that the company now produces more cars (and sells them at a lower price) because its cost of engines is lower. Also, note that since the transfer price for the engines is now \$6,000, the upstream Engine Division supplies only 1,500 engines (because $MC_E(1,500) = \$6,000$). The remaining 1,500 engines are bought in the external market.

(c) Now suppose that Race Car Motors is the only producer of these engines, but can sell them in an external market. Demand in the external market is given by:

$$P_{E,M} = 10,000 - Q_E$$

so that the marginal revenue from sales in the market is:

$$MR_{E,M} = 10,000 - 2Q_E$$

To determine the optimal transfer price, we find the *total* net marginal revenue by horizontally summing $MR_{E,M}$ with the net marginal revenue from "sales" to the downstream division, $12,000 - 2Q_E$, as in Figure 11A.4. For outputs Q_E greater than 1,000, this is:

$$NMR_{E,Total} = 11,000 - Q_E$$

Now set this equal to the marginal cost of producing engines:

$$11,000 - Q_E = 4Q_E$$

Therefore the total quantity of engines produced should be $Q_E = 2,200$.

How many of these engines should go to the downstream division, and how many to the external market? First, note that the marginal cost of producing these 2,200 engines, and therefore the optimal transfer price, is $4Q_E = \$8,800$. Now set this equal to the marginal revenue from sales in the external market:

$$8,800 = 10,000 - 2Q_E$$

or $Q_E = 600$. Therefore 600 engines should be sold in the external market. Finally, set this \$8,800 transfer price equal to the net marginal revenue from "sales" to the downstream division:

$$8,800 = 12,000 - 2Q_E$$

or $Q_E = 1,600$. So 1,600 engines should be supplied to the downstream division for use in the production of 1,600 cars.

Exercises

1. Review the numerical example about Race Car Motors. Calculate the profit earned by the upstream division, the downstream division, and the firm as a whole in each of the three cases examined: (a) no external market for engines; (b) a competitive market for engines in which the market price is $6,000; and (c) the firm is a monopoly supplier of engines to an external market. In which case does Race Car Motors earn the most profit? In which case does the upstream division earn the most? the downstream division?

2. Ajax Computer makes a specialized computer for climate control in office buildings. The company makes the computer using a microprocessor produced by its upstream division, together with other parts bought in outside competitive markets. The microprocessor is produced at a constant marginal cost of $500, and the marginal cost of assembling the computer (including the cost of the other parts) by the downstream division is a constant $700. The firm has been selling the computer for $2000, and until now there has been no outside market for the microprocessor.

    a. Suppose an outside market for the microprocessor develops and Ajax has monopoly power in that market, selling microprocessors for $1000 each. Assuming that demand for the microprocessor is unrelated to the demand for the Ajax computer, what transfer price should Ajax apply to the microprocessor for its use by the downstream division? Should its production of computers be increased, decreased, or left unchanged? Explain briefly.

    b. How would your answer to (a) change if the demands for the computer and the microprocessors were competitive, i.e., some of the people who buy the microprocessors use them to make climate control systems of their own?

CHAPTER 12

Monopolistic Competition and Oligopoly

In the last two chapters, we saw how firms with monopoly power can choose prices and output levels to maximize profit. We also saw that monopoly power does not require a firm to be a pure monopolist. In many industries several firms compete, but each firm has at least some monopoly power—it has control over price and will charge a price that exceeds marginal cost.

In this chapter we examine market structures other than pure monopoly that can give rise to monopoly power. We begin with *monopolistic competition*. A monopolistically competitive market is similar to a perfectly competitive market in that there are many firms, and entry by new firms is not restricted. But it differs from perfect competition in that the product is *differentiated*—each firm sells a brand or version of the product that differs in quality, appearance, or reputation, and each firm is the sole producer of its own brand. The amount of monopoly power the firm has depends on its success in differentiating its product from those of other firms. Examples of monopolistically competitive industries abound: toothpaste, laundry detergent, and soft drinks are a few.

The second form of market structure we will examine is *oligopoly*. In oligopolistic markets, only a few firms compete with one another, and entry by new firms is impeded. The product that the firms produce might be differentiated, as with automobiles, or it might not be, as with steel. Monopoly power and profitability in oligopolistic industries depends in part on how the firms interact. For example, if the interaction tends to be more cooperative than competitive, the firms could charge prices well above marginal cost and earn large profits.

In some oligopolistic industries, firms do cooperate, but in others firms compete aggressively, even though this means lower profits. To see why, we need to consider how oligopolistic firms decide on output and prices. These decisions are complicated because each firm must operate *strategically*—when making a decision, it must weigh the probable reactions of its competitors. To understand oligopolistic markets, we must therefore introduce some basic concepts of gaming and strategy. Later, in Chapter 13, we develop these concepts more fully.

The third form of market structure we examine is a *cartel*. In a cartelized market, some or all of the firms explicitly collude—they coordinate their prices and output levels to maximize their *joint* profits. Cartels can arise in markets that would otherwise be competitive, as with OPEC, or oligopolistic, as with the international bauxite cartel.

At first glance a cartel may seem like a pure monopoly. After all, the firms in a cartel appear to operate as though they were parts of one big company. But a cartel differs from a monopoly in two important respects. First, since cartels rarely control the entire market, they must consider how their pricing decisions will affect noncartel production levels. Second, the members of a cartel are *not* part of one big company, and they may be tempted to "cheat" their partners by undercutting price and grabbing a bigger share of the market. As a result, many cartels tend to be unstable and represent a market structure that is often temporary.

12.1 Monopolistic Competition

In many industries, the products that firms make are differentiated. For one reason or another, consumers view each firm's brand as different from those of other firms. Crest toothpaste, for example, is different from Colgate, Aim, and a dozen other toothpastes. The difference is partly flavor, partly consistency, and partly reputation—the consumer's image (correct or incorrect) of the relative decay-preventing efficacy of Crest. As a result, some consumers (but not all) will pay more for Crest.

Because Procter and Gamble is the sole producer of Crest, it has monopoly power. But Procter and Gamble's monopoly power is limited because consumers can easily substitute other brands for Crest if its price rises. Although consumers who prefer Crest will pay more for it, most of them will not pay very much more. The typical Crest user might pay 25 or even 50 cents a tube more, but probably not a dollar more. For most consumers, toothpaste is toothpaste, and the differences among brands are small. Therefore, the demand curve for Crest toothpaste, though downward-sloping, is fairly elastic. (A reasonable estimate of the elasticity of demand for Crest is -10.) Because of its limited monopoly power, Procter and Gamble will charge a price higher, but not much higher, than marginal cost. The situation is similar for Tide detergent, Scott paper towels, and Canada Dry ginger ale.

The Makings of Monopolistic Competition

A monopolistically competitive market has two key characteristics: First, firms compete by selling differentiated products, which are highly substitutable with one another but not perfect substitutes. (In other words, the cross-price elasticities of demand are large but not infinite.) Second, there is *free entry and exit*—it is relatively easy for new firms to enter the market with their own brands of the product and for existing firms to leave if their products become unprofitable.

To see why free entry is an important requirement, let's compare the markets for toothpaste and automobiles. The toothpaste market is monopolistically competitive, but the automobile market is better characterized as an oligopoly. It is relatively easy for other firms to introduce new brands of toothpaste that might compete with Crest, Colgate, and so on. This limits the profitability of producing Crest or Colgate. If the profits were large, other firms would spend the necessary money (for development, production, advertising, and promotion) to introduce new brands of their own, which would reduce the market shares and profitability of Crest and Colgate.

The automobile market is also characterized by product differentiation. However, the large scale economies involved in production make entry by new firms difficult. Hence, until the mid-1970s when Japanese producers became important competitors, the three major U.S. auto makers had the market largely to themselves.

There are numerous other examples of monopolistic competition besides toothpaste. Soap, shampoo, deodorants, shaving cream, vitamins, cold remedies, and many other items found in a drugstore are sold in monopolistically competitive markets. The markets for skis, tennis rackets, bicycles, and other sporting goods are likewise monopolistically competitive. So is most retail trade, since goods are sold in many different retail stores that compete with one another by differentiating their services according to location, availability and expertise of salespeople, credit terms, etc. Because entry is relatively easy, new stores will enter if profits are high in a neighborhood because it has only a few stores.

Equilibrium in the Short Run and the Long Run

As with monopoly, in monopolistic competition firms face downward-sloping demand curves and therefore have monopoly power. But this does not mean that monopolistically competitive firms will earn large profits. Monopolistic competition is also similar to perfect competition. There is free entry, so the potential to earn profits will attract new firms with competing brands, driving profits down to zero.

To make this clear, let's examine the equilibrium price and output level for a monopolistically competitive firm in the short and long run. Figure 12.1a shows the short-run equilibrium. Because the firm's product differs from its competitors', its demand curve D_{SR} is downward-sloping. (This is the *firm's* demand curve, not the market demand curve, which is more steeply sloped.) The profit-maximizing quantity Q_{SR} is found at the intersection of the marginal revenue and marginal cost curves. Since the corresponding price P_{SR} exceeds

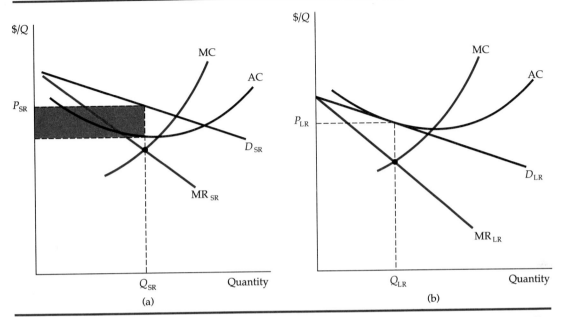

FIGURE 12.1   A Monopolistically Competitive Firm in the Short and Long Run.   Because the firm is the only producer of its brand, it faces a downward-sloping demand curve; price exceeds marginal cost, and the firm has monopoly power. In the short run, price also exceeds average cost, and the firm earns profits as shown by the shaded rectangle. In the long run, these profits attract new firms with competing brands into the industry. The firm's market share falls, and its demand curve shifts downward. In long-run equilibrium, price equals average cost, so the firm earns zero profit, even though it has monopoly power.

average cost, the firm earns a profit, as shown by the shaded rectangle in the figure.

In the long run, this profit will induce entry by other firms. As they introduce competing brands, this firm will lose market share and sales; its demand curve will shift down, as in Figure 12.1b. (In the long run, the average and marginal cost curves may also shift. We have assumed for simplicity that costs do not change.) The long-run demand curve D_{LR} will be just tangent to the firm's average cost curve. Now profit maximization implies the quantity Q_{LR}, the price P_{LR}, and *zero profit* because price is equal to average cost. The firm still has monopoly power; its long-run demand curve is downward-sloping because the firm's particular brand is still unique. But the entry and competition of other firms have driven its profit to zero.

More generally, firms may have different costs, and some brands will be more distinctive than others. In this case firms may charge slightly different prices, and some will earn small profits.

Monopolistic Competition and Economic Efficiency

Perfectly competitive markets are desirable because they are economically efficient—as long as nothing impedes the workings of the market, the total surplus of consumers and producers is as large as possible. Monopolistic competition is similar to competition in some respects, but is it an efficient market structure? To answer this question, let's compare the long-run equilibrium of a monopolistically competitive industry to the long-run equilibrium of a perfectly competitive industry.

Figure 12.2a and 12.2b shows that there are two sources of inefficiency in a monopolistically competitive industry. First, unlike perfect competition, the equilibrium price exceeds marginal cost. This means that the value to consumers of additional units of output exceeds the cost of producing those units. If output were expanded to the point where the demand curve intersects the marginal cost curve, total surplus could be increased by an amount equal to the shaded area in Figure 12.2b. This should not be surprising. We saw in Chapter 10 that

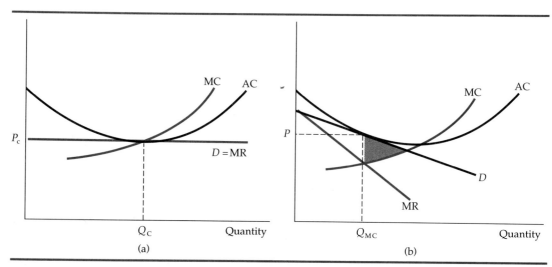

FIGURE 12.2 Comparison of Monopolistically Competitive Equilibrium and Perfectly Competitive Equilibrium. Under perfect competition, price equals marginal cost, but under monopolistic competition, price exceeds marginal cost, so there is a deadweight loss (of surplus) as shown by the shaded area in 12.2b. In both types of markets, entry occurs until profits are driven to zero. Under perfect competition the demand curve facing the firm is horizontal, so the zero-profit point occurs at the point of minimum average cost. Under monopolistic competition, however, the demand curve is downward-sloping, so the zero-profit point is to the left of the point of minimum average cost. In evaluating monopolistic competition, these inefficiencies must be balanced against the gains to consumers from product diversity.

monopoly power creates a deadweight loss, and monopoly power exists in monopolistically competitive markets.

Second, note in Figure 12.2 that the monopolistically competitive firm operates with *excess capacity;* its output level is smaller than that which minimizes average cost. Entry of new firms drives profits to zero in both perfectly competitive and monopolistically competitive markets. In a perfectly competitive market, each firm faces a horizontal demand curve, so the zero-profit point occurs at minimum average cost, as Figure 12.2a shows. In a monopolistically competitive market, however, the demand curve is downward-sloping, so the zero-profit point occurs to the left of minimum average cost. This excess capacity is inefficient because average costs could be reduced if there were fewer firms.

These inefficiencies make consumers worse off. Is monopolistic competition then a socially undesirable market structure that should be regulated? The answer for two reasons is probably not.

First, in most monopolistically competitive markets, monopoly power is small. Usually, enough firms compete, with brands that are sufficiently substitutable for one another, so that no single firm will have substantial monopoly power. Any deadweight loss from monopoly power should therefore also be small. And because firms' demand curves will be fairly elastic, the excess capacity will be small, too.

Second, whatever inefficiency there is must be balanced against an important benefit that monopolistic competition provides—product diversity. Most consumers value the ability to choose among a wide variety of competing products and brands that differ in various ways. The gains from product diversity can be large and may easily outweigh the inefficiency costs resulting from downward-sloping demand curves.

EXAMPLE 12.1 MONOPOLISTIC COMPETITION IN THE MARKETS FOR COLAS AND COFFEE

The markets for soft drinks and coffee illustrate the characteristics of monopolistic competition. Each market has a variety of brands that differ slightly but are close substitutes for one another. Each brand of cola, for example, tastes a little different from the next. (Can you tell the difference between Coke and Pepsi? Between Coke and Royal Crown Cola?) And each brand of ground coffee has a slightly different flavor, fragrance, and caffeine content. Most consumers develop their own preferences; you might prefer Maxwell House coffee to the other brands and buy it regularly. However, these brand loyalties are usually limited. If the price of Maxwell House were to rise substantially above those of other brands, you and most other consumers who had been buying Maxwell House would probably switch brands.

Just how much monopoly power does General Foods, the producer of Maxwell House, have with this brand? In other words, how elastic is the demand

TABLE 12.1 Elasticities of Demand for Brands of Colas and Coffee

	Brand	Elasticity of Demand
Colas:	Royal Crown	−2.4
	Coke	−5.2 to −5.7
Ground Coffee:	Hills Brothers	−7.1
	Maxwell House	−8.9
	Chase & Sanborn	−5.6

for Maxwell House? For General Foods, this is an important question. As we saw in Chapters 10 and 11, General Foods must estimate the elasticity of demand for Maxwell House to set its optimal price, and so, too, must other coffee producers determine the elasticities of demand for their brands.

Most large companies carefully study the demands for their product as part of their market research. (In Chapter 4 we reviewed some of the methods for estimating product demands.) Company estimates are usually proprietary, but a study of the demands for various brands of colas and ground coffee used a simulated shopping experiment to determine how market shares for each brand would change in response to specific changes in price.[1] Table 12.1 summarizes the results by showing the elasticities of demand for several brands.

First, note that among the colas, Royal Crown is much less price elastic than Coke. Although it has a small share of the cola market, its taste is more distinctive than that of Coke, Pepsi, and other brands, so consumers who buy it have stronger brand loyalty. But because Royal Crown has more monopoly power than Coke does not mean that it is more profitable. Profits depend on fixed costs and volume, as well as price. Even if its average profit is smaller, Coke will generate more profit because it has a much larger share of the market.

Second, note that coffees as a group are more price elastic than colas. There is less brand loyalty among coffees than among colas because the differences among coffees are less perceptible than the differences among colas. Compared with different brands of colas, fewer consumers notice or care about the differences between Hills Brothers and Maxwell House coffees.

With the exception of Royal Crown, all the colas and coffees are very price elastic. With elasticities on the order of −5 to −9, each brand has only limited monopoly power. This is typical of monopolistic competition.

---

[1] The study was by John R. Nevin, "Laboratory Experiments for Estimating Consumer Demand: A Validation Study," *Journal of Marketing Research* 11 (Aug. 1974): 261–268. The experiment consisted of simulated shopping trips. Consumers had to choose the brands they preferred from a variety of prepriced brands. The trips were repeated several times, each time with different prices.

12.2 Oligopoly

In an oligopolistic market, the product may or may not be differentiated. What matters is that only a few firms account for most or all of total production. In some oligopolistic markets, some or all of the firms earn substantial profits over the long run because *barriers to entry* make it difficult or impossible for new firms to enter the market. Oligopoly is a prevalent form of market structure. Examples of oligopolistic industries in the United States include automobiles, steel, aluminum, petrochemicals, electrical equipment, and computers.

Why might barriers to entry arise? We discussed some of the reasons in Chapter 10. Scale economies may make it unprofitable for more than a few firms to coexist in the market; patents or access to a technology may exclude potential competitors; and the need to spend money for name recognition and market reputation may obstruct entry by new firms. These are "natural" entry barriers—they are basic to the structure of the particular market. In addition, incumbent firms may take *strategic actions* to deter entry by newcomers. For example, they might threaten to flood the market and drive prices down if entry occurs, and to make that threat credible, they can construct excess production capacity. We will discuss strategic actions of this sort in the next chapter. Here, simply note that entry barriers—whether natural or created by incumbent firms—can arise.

Managing an oligopolistic firm is complicated because pricing, output, advertising, and investment decisions involve important strategic considerations. Because only a few firms are competing, each firm must carefully consider how its actions will affect its rivals, and how its rivals are likely to react.

Suppose, for example, because of sluggish car sales, Ford is considering a 10 percent price cut to stimulate demand. It must think carefully about how GM and Chrysler will react. They might not react at all, or they might cut their prices only slightly, in which case Ford could enjoy a substantial increase in sales, largely at the expense of its competitors. Or they might match Ford's price cut, in which case all three automakers will sell more cars but might make much lower profits because of the lower prices. Another possibility is that GM and Chrysler will cut their prices by even more than Ford did. They might cut price by 15 percent to punish Ford for rocking the boat, and this in turn might lead to a price war and to a drastic fall in profits for all three firms. Ford must carefully weigh all these possibilities. In fact, for almost any major economic decision a firm makes—setting price, determining production levels, undertaking a major promotion campaign, or investing in new production capacity—it must try to determine the most likely response of its competitors.

These strategic considerations can be complex. When making decisions, each firm must weigh its competitors' reactions, knowing that these competitors will also weigh *its* reactions to *their* decisions. Furthermore, decisions, reactions, reactions to reactions, and so forth are dynamic, evolving over time. When the managers of a firm evaluate the potential consequences of their decisions, they must assume that their competitors are as rational and intelligent as they are. Then, they must put themselves in their competitors' place and consider how they would react.

The Cournot Model

We will start to explore this kind of thinking with a simple model of *duopoly*—two firms competing with each other—first introduced by the French economist Augustin Cournot in 1838.[2] Suppose the firms produce a homogeneous good and know the market demand curve. *Each firm must decide how much to produce, and the two firms make their decisions at the same time.* When making its production decisions, each firm must remember that its competitor is *also* deciding how much to produce, and that the price it receives will depend on the total production of both firms.

The essence of the Cournot model is that *each firm treats the output level of its competitor as fixed, and then decides how much to produce.* To see how this works, let's consider the output decision of Firm 1. Suppose Firm 1 thinks that Firm 2 will produce nothing. Then Firm 1's demand curve is the market demand curve. In Figure 12.3, this is shown as $D_1(0)$, which means the demand curve for Firm 1, assuming Firm 2 produces zero. Figure 12.3 also shows the corresponding marginal revenue curve $MR_1(0)$. We have assumed that Firm 1's marginal cost MC_1 is constant. As shown in the figure, Firm 1's profit-maximizing output is 50 units, the point where $MR_1(0)$ intersects MC_1. So if Firm 2 produces zero, Firm 1 should produce 50.

Suppose, instead, that Firm 1 thinks Firm 2 will produce 50 units. Then Firm 1's demand curve is the market demand curve shifted to the left by 50. In Figure 12.3 this is labeled $D_1(50)$, and the corresponding marginal revenue curve is labeled $MR_1(50)$. Firm 1's profit-maximizing output is now 25 units, the point where $MR_1(50) = MC_1$. Now, suppose Firm 1 thinks Firm 2 will produce 75 units. Then Firm 1's demand curve is the market demand curve shifted to the left by 75. It is labeled $D_1(75)$ in Figure 12.3, and the corresponding marginal revenue curve is labeled $MR_1(75)$. Firm 1's profit-maximizing output is now 12.5 units, the point where $MR_1(75) = MC_1$. Finally, suppose Firm 1 thinks Firm 2 will produce 100 units. Then Firm 1's demand and marginal revenue curves (not shown in the figure) would intersect its marginal cost curve on the vertical axis; if Firm 1 thinks that Firm 2 will produce 100 units or more, it should produce nothing.

To summarize: If Firm 1 thinks Firm 2 will produce nothing, it will produce 50; if it thinks Firm 2 will produce 50, it will produce 25; if it thinks Firm 2 will produce 75, it will produce 12.5; and if it thinks Firm 2 will produce 100, then

[2]A. Cournot, *Recherches sur les Principes Mathématiques de la Théorie des Richesse* (Paris, 1838). English translation by N. Bacon (New York: Macmillan, 1897).

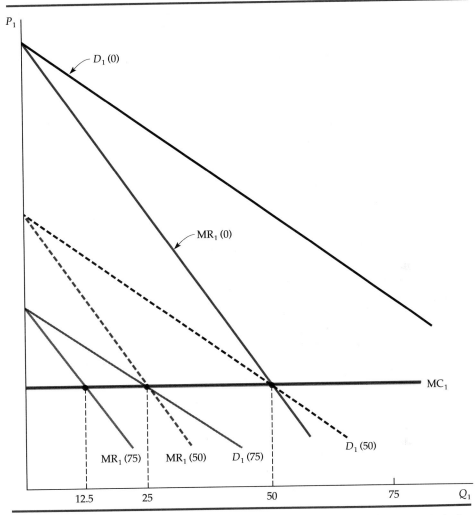

FIGURE 12.3 Firm 1's Output Decision. Firm 1's profit-maximizing output choice depends on how much it thinks Firm 2 will produce. If it thinks Firm 2 will produce nothing, its demand curve, labeled $D_1(0)$, is the market demand curve. The corresponding marginal revenue curve is labeled $MR_1(0)$, and it intersects Firm 1's marginal cost curve MC_1 at an output of 50 units. If Firm 1 thinks Firm 2 will produce 50 units, its demand curve is shifted to the left by this amount. This demand curve is labeled $D_1(50)$, and the corresponding marginal revenue curve is labeled $MR_1(50)$. Profit maximization now implies an output of 25 units. $D_1(75)$ and $MR_1(75)$ are Firm 1's demand and marginal revenue curves when it thinks Firm 2 will produce 75 units. Then Firm 1 will produce only 12.5 units.

it will produce nothing. *Firm 1's profit-maximizing output is thus a decreasing schedule of how much it thinks Firm 2 will produce.* We call this schedule Firm 1's *reaction curve,* and we denote it by $Q_1^*(Q_2)$. This curve is plotted in Figure 12.4, where each of the four output combinations we found above is shown as an *x*.

We can go through the same kind of analysis for Firm 2 (i.e., determine Firm 2's profit-maximizing quantity given various assumptions about how much Firm 1 will produce). The result will be a reaction curve for Firm 2, i.e., a schedule $Q_2^*(Q_1)$ that relates its output to the output it thinks Firm 1 will produce. If Firm 2's marginal cost curve is different from that of Firm 1, its reaction curve will also differ in form from that of Firm 1. For example, Firm 2's reaction curve might look like the one drawn in Figure 12.4.

How much will each firm produce? Each firm's reaction curve tells it how

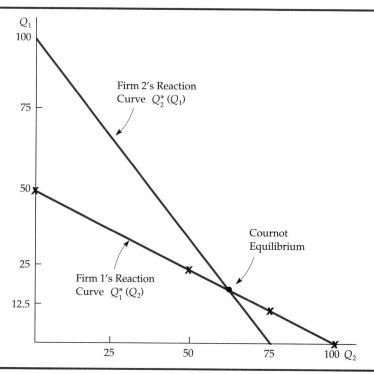

FIGURE 12.4 Reaction Curves and Cournot Equilibrium. Firm 1's reaction curve shows how much it will produce as a function of how much it thinks Firm 2 will produce. (The *x*s, at $Q_2 = 0$, 50, and 75, correspond to the examples shown in Figure 12.3.) Firm 2's reaction curve shows its output as a function of how much it thinks Firm 1 will produce. In Cournot equilibrium, each firm correctly assumes how much its competitor will produce, and thereby maximizes its own profits. Therefore, neither firm will move from this equilibrium.

much to produce, given the output of its competitor. In equilibrium, each firm sets output according to its own reaction curve, so the equilibrium output levels are found at the *intersection* of the two reaction curves. We call the resulting set of output levels a *Cournot equilibrium.* In this equilibrium, each firm correctly assumes how much its competitor will produce, and it maximizes profits accordingly.

A Cournot equilibrium is an example of what game theorists call a *Nash equilibrium.* In the Nash equilibrium of a game, each player is doing the best it can, *given what its opponents are doing.* As a result, no player has any incentive to change its behavior. In the Cournot equilibrium, each duopolist is producing an amount that maximizes its profit *given what its competitors are producing,* so neither duopolist has any incentive to change its output. (We will discuss the Nash equilibrium concept in detail in Chapter 13.)

Suppose the firms are initially producing output levels that differ from the Cournot equilibrium. Should we expect them to adjust their outputs until the Cournot equilibrium is reached? Unfortunately, the Cournot model says nothing about the dynamics of the adjustment process. In fact, during any adjustment process, the model's central assumption that each firm can assume its competitor's output is fixed would not hold. Neither firm's output would be fixed, because both firms would be adjusting their outputs. We need different models to understand dynamic adjustment, and we will examine some in Chapter 13.

When is it rational for each firm to assume that its competitor's output is fixed? It is rational if the two firms are choosing their outputs only once because then their outputs cannot change. It is also rational once they are in the Cournot equilibrium because then neither firm would have any incentive to change its output. We will therefore confine ourselves to the behavior of firms in equilibrium.

Example: A Linear Demand Curve

Let's work through a specific example—when two identical firms face a linear market demand curve. This will help clarify the meaning of a Cournot equilibrium and let us compare it with both the competitive equilibrium and the equilibrium that would result if the firms colluded and chose their output levels cooperatively rather than competitively.

Suppose our duopolists face the following market demand curve:

$$P = 30 - Q$$

where Q is the *total* production of both firms (i.e., $Q = Q_1 + Q_2$). Also, suppose both firms have zero marginal cost:

$$MC_1 = MC_2 = 0$$

Then we can determine the reaction curve for Firm 1 as follows. To maximize profit, the firm sets marginal revenue equal to marginal cost. Firm 1's total revenue R_1 is given by

$$R_1 = PQ_1 = (30 - Q)Q_1$$
$$= 30Q_1 - (Q_1 + Q_2)Q_1$$
$$= 30Q_1 - Q_1^2 - Q_2Q_1$$

The firm's marginal revenue MR_1 is just the incremental revenue ΔR_1 resulting from an incremental change in output ΔQ_1:

$$MR_1 = \Delta R_1/\Delta Q_1 = 30 - 2Q_1 - Q_2$$

Now, setting MR_1 equal to zero (the firm's marginal cost), and solving for Q_1, we find:

$$\textit{Firm 1's Reaction Curve:} \quad Q_1 = 15 - \frac{1}{2}Q_2 \qquad (12.1)$$

You can go through the same calculation for Firm 2:

$$\textit{Firm 2's Reaction Curve:} \quad Q_2 = 15 - \frac{1}{2}Q_1 \qquad (12.2)$$

The equilibrium output levels are the values for Q_1 and Q_2 that are at the intersection of the two reaction curves, i.e., that are the solution to equations (12.1) and (12.2). By replacing Q_2 in equation (12.1) with the expression on the right-hand side of (12.2), you can verify that the equilibrium output levels are

$$\textit{Cournot Equilibrium:} \quad Q_1 = Q_2 = 10$$

The total quantity produced is therefore $Q = Q_1 + Q_2 = 20$, so the equilibrium market price is $P = 30 - Q = 10$.

Figure 12.5 shows the Cournot reaction curves and this Cournot equilibrium. Note that Firm 1's reaction curve shows its output Q_1 in terms of Firm 2's output Q_2. Similarly, Firm 2's reaction curve shows Q_2 in terms of Q_1. (Since the firms are identical, the two reaction curves have the same form. They look different because one gives Q_1 in terms of Q_2, and the other gives Q_2 in terms of Q_1.) The Cournot equilibrium is at the intersection of the two curves. At this point each firm is maximizing its own profit, given its competitor's output.

We have assumed that the two firms compete with each other. Suppose, instead, that the antitrust laws were relaxed and the two firms could collude. They would set their outputs to maximize *total profit*, and presumably they would split that profit evenly. Total profit is maximized by choosing total output Q so that marginal revenue equals marginal cost, which in this example is zero. Total revenue for the two firms is

$$R = PQ = (30 - Q)Q = 30Q - Q^2$$

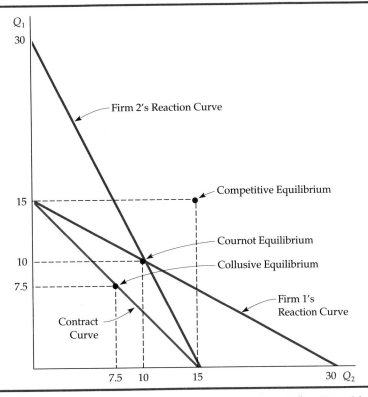

FIGURE 12.5 Duopoly Example. The demand curve is $P = 30 - Q$, and both firms have zero marginal cost. In Cournot equilibrium, each firm produces 10. The contract curve shows combinations of Q_1 and Q_2 that maximize *total* profits. If the firms collude and share profits equally, they will each produce 7.5. Also shown is the competitive equilibrium, in which price equals marginal cost, and profit is zero.

so marginal revenue is

$$MR = \Delta R/\Delta Q = 30 - 2Q$$

Setting MR equal to zero, we see that total profit is maximized when $Q = 15$.

Any combination of outputs Q_1 and Q_2 that add up to 15 maximizes total profit. The curve $Q_1 + Q_2 = 15$, called the *contract curve*, is therefore the set of outputs Q_1 and Q_2 that maximize total profit. This curve is also shown in Figure 12.5. If the firms agree to share the profits equally, they will each produce half of the total output:

$$Q_1 = Q_2 = 7.5$$

As you would expect, both firms now produce less—and earn higher profits—than in the Cournot equilibrium. Figure 12.5 shows this collusive equilibrium and the *competitive* output levels found by setting price equal to marginal cost. (You can verify that they are $Q_1 = Q_2 = 15$, which implies that each firm makes zero profit.) Note that the Cournot outcome is much better (for the firms) than perfect competition, but not as good as the outcome from collusion.

12.3 First Mover Advantage—The Stackelberg Model

We have assumed that our two duopolists make their output decisions at the same time. Now let's see what happens if one of the firms can set its output first. There are two questions of interest. First, would the firm *want* to set its output first? In other words, it is advantageous to go first? Second, what is the resulting equilibrium (i.e., how much will each firm produce)?

Again, we assume both firms have zero marginal cost, and that the market demand curve is given by $P = 30 - Q$, where Q is the total output. *Suppose Firm 1 sets its output first, and then Firm 2, after observing Firm 1's output, makes its output decision.* In setting output, *Firm 1 must therefore consider how Firm 2 will react.* This is different from the Cournot model, in which neither firm has any opportunity to react.

Let's begin with Firm 2. Because it makes its output decision *after* Firm 1, it takes Firm 1's output as fixed. Therefore, Firm 2's profit-maximizing output is given by its Cournot reaction curve, which we found to be

$$\text{Firm 2's Reaction Curve:} \quad Q_2 = 15 - \frac{1}{2}Q_1 \tag{12.2}$$

What about Firm 1? To maximize profit, it chooses Q_1 so that its marginal revenue equals its marginal cost of zero. Recall that Firm 1's revenue is

$$R_1 = PQ_1 = 30Q_1 - Q_1^2 - Q_2Q_1 \tag{12.3}$$

Because R_1 depends on Q_2, Firm 1 must anticipate how much Firm 2 will produce. Firm 1 knows, however, that Firm 2 will choose Q_2 according to the reaction curve (12.2). Substituting equation (12.2) for Q_2 into equation (12.3), we find that Firm 1's revenue is

$$R_1 = 30Q_1 - Q_1^2 - Q_1\left(15 - \frac{1}{2}Q_1\right)$$

$$= 15Q_1 - \frac{1}{2}Q_1^2$$

so its marginal revenue is

$$MR_1 = \Delta R_1/\Delta Q_1 = 15 - Q_1 \tag{12.4}$$

Setting $MR_1 = 0$ gives $Q_1 = 15$. And from Firm 2's reaction curve (12.2), we find that $Q_2 = 7.5$. Firm 1 produces twice as much as Firm 2 and makes twice as much profit. *Going first gives Firm 1 an advantage.* This may appear counter-intuitive: It seems disadvantageous to announce your output first. Why then is going first a strategic advantage?

The reason is that announcing first creates a fait accompli—no matter what your competitor does, your output will be large. To maximize profit, your competitor must take your large output level as given and set a low level of output for itself. (If your competitor produced a large level of output, this would drive price down, and you would both lose money. So unless your competitor views "getting even" as more important than making money, it would be irrational for it to produce a large amount.) This kind of "first mover advantage" occurs in many strategic situations, as we will see in Chapter 13.

The Cournot and Stackelberg models are alternative representations of oligopolistic behavior. Which model is the more appropriate depends on the industry. For an industry composed of roughly similar firms, none of which has a strong operating advantage or leadership position, the Cournot model is probably the more appropriate. On the other hand, some industries are dominated by a large firm that usually takes the lead in introducing new products or setting price; the mainframe computer market is an example, with IBM the leader. Then the Stackelberg model may be more realistic.

12.4 Price Competition

We have assumed that our oligopolistic firms compete by setting quantities. This is reasonable if the firms are producing a homogeneous good.[3] In most oligopolistic industries, however, there is some degree of product differentiation, and competition occurs along price dimensions.[4] For example, for GM, Ford, and Chrysler, price is a key strategic variable, and each firm chooses its price with its competitors in mind.

[3]The *Bertrand model* of oligopoly assumes that firms produce a homogeneous good but compete by setting prices, with each firm taking the prices of its competitors as fixed, and the firm with the lowest price capturing all the sales. In this case, each firm has an incentive to undercut the price of its competitor, until price is driven down to marginal cost. However, there is no natural way to determine market shares in equilibrium. For example, if all firms charge the same price, so that consumers are indifferent among the firms, what share of total sales will go to each one? Quantity competition is therefore more realistic when a homogeneous good is produced. Also, it has been shown that if firms compete by first setting output *capacities*, and then setting price, the Cournot equilibrium in quantities again results. See David Kreps and Jose Scheinkman, "Quantity Precommitment and Bertrand Competition Yield Cournot Outcomes," *Bell Journal of Economics* 14 (1983): 326–338.

[4]Product differentiation can exist even for a seemingly homogeneous product. Consider gasoline, for example. Although gasoline itself is a homogeneous good, service stations differ in terms of location, use of credit cards, and services (such as checking the oil, etc.). Thus, gasoline prices may differ from one service station to another.

The Cournot model that we developed for quantity competition can also be applied to price competition. We can illustrate this with the following simple example. Suppose each of two duopolists has fixed costs of $20 but zero variable costs, and that they face the same demand curves:

$$\text{Firm 1's Demand:} \quad Q_1 = 12 - 2P_1 + P_2 \qquad (12.5a)$$

$$\text{Firm 2's Demand:} \quad Q_2 = 12 - 2P_2 + P_1 \qquad (12.5b)$$

where P_1 and P_2 are the prices that Firms 1 and 2 charge, respectively, and Q_1 and Q_2 are the resulting quantities that they sell. Note that the quantity each firm can sell decreases when the firm raises its own price, but increases when its competitor charges a higher price.

If both firms set their prices at the same time, we can use the Cournot model to determine the resulting equilibrium. Each firm will choose its own price, taking its competitor's price as fixed. Now consider Firm 1. Its profit π_1 is its revenue P_1Q_1 less its fixed cost of $20. Substituting for Q_1 from the demand curve of equation (12.5a), we have

$$\pi_1 = P_1Q_1 - 20 = 12P_1 - 2P_1^2 + P_1P_2 - 20$$

At what price P_1 is this profit maximized? The answer depends on P_2, which Firm 1 assumes is fixed. However, whatever price Firm 2 is charging, Firm 1's profit is maximized when the incremental profit from a very small increase in its own price is just zero. Taking P_2 as fixed, Firm 1's profit-maximizing price is therefore given by

$$\Delta\pi_1/\Delta P_1 = 12 - 4P_1 + P_2 = 0$$

This can be rewritten to give the following pricing rule, or *reaction curve*, for Firm 1:

$$\text{Firm 1's Reaction Curve:} \quad P_1 = 3 + (\tfrac{1}{4})P_2$$

This tells Firm 1 what price to set, given the price P_2 that Firm 2 is setting. We can similarly find the following pricing rule for Firm 2:

$$\text{Firm 2's Reaction Curve:} \quad P_2 = 3 + (\tfrac{1}{4})P_1$$

These reaction curves are drawn in Figure 12.6. The Cournot equilibrium is at the point where the two reaction curves cross; you can verify that each firm is then charging a price of $4, and earning a profit of $12. *At this point, since each firm is doing the best it can given the price its competitor has set, neither firm has an incentive to change its price.*

Now, suppose the two firms colluded. Instead of choosing their prices in-

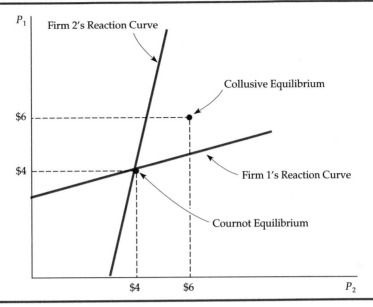

FIGURE 12.6 Cournot Equilibrium in Prices. Here two firms sell a differentiated product, and each firm's demand depends on its own price and its competitor's price. The two firms choose their prices at the same time, and each takes its competitor's price as given. Firm 1's reaction curve gives its profit-maximizing price as a function of the price that Firm 2 sets, and similarly for Firm 2's reaction curve. The Cournot equilibrium is at the intersection of the two reaction curves; when each firm is charging a price of $4, it is doing the best it can given its competitor's price, and it has no incentive to change price. Also shown is the collusive equilibrium. If the firms cooperatively set price, they would choose $6.

dependently, they both decide to charge the same price, which will be the price that maximizes both of their profits. You can verify that the firms would then charge a price of $6, and that the firms would be better off colluding because each would now earn a profit of $16.[5] Figure 12.6 shows this collusive equilibrium.

[5]The firms have the same costs, so they will charge the same price P. Total profits are given by

$$\pi_T = \pi_1 + \pi_2 = 24P - 4P^2 + 2P^2 - 40 = 24P - 2P^2 - 40.$$

This is maximized when $\Delta\pi_T/\Delta P = 0$. $\Delta\pi_T/\Delta P = 24 - 4P$, so the joint profit-maximizing price is $P = 6$. Each firm's profit is then

$$\pi_1 = \pi_2 = 12P - P^2 - 20 = 72 - 36 - 20 = \$16$$

EXAMPLE 12.2 A PRICING PROBLEM FOR PROCTER & GAMBLE

When Procter & Gamble, Inc. (P&G) planned to enter the Japanese market for Gypsy Moth Tape, it knew its production costs and understood the market demand curve, but found it hard to determine the right price to charge because two other firms—Kao Soap, Ltd., and Unilever, Ltd.—were also planning to enter the market. All three firms would be choosing their prices at about the same time, and P&G had to take this into account when setting its own price.[6]

Because all three firms were using the same technology for producing Gypsy Moth Tape, they had the same production costs. Each firm faced a fixed cost of $480,000 per month and a variable cost of $1 per unit. From market research, P&G ascertained that its demand curve for monthly sales was given by

$$Q = 3375P^{-3.5}(P_U)^{.25}(P_K)^{.25}$$

where Q is monthly sales in thousands of units, and P, P_U, and P_K are P&G's, Unilever's, and Kao's prices, respectively. Now, put yourself in P&G's position. Assuming that Unilever and Kao face the same demand conditions, *with what price should you enter the market, and how much profit should you expect to earn?*

You might begin by calculating the profit you would earn as a function of the price you charge, under alternative assumptions about the prices that Unilever and Kao will charge. Using the demand curve and cost numbers given above, we have done these calculations for you and tabulated the results in Table 12.2. Each entry shows your profit, in thousands of dollars per month, for a particular combination of prices (but in each case assumes that Unilever and Kao set the same price). For example, if you charge $1.30 and Unilever and Kao both charge $1.50, you will earn a profit of $15,000 per month.

Remember that in all likelihood, the managers of Unilever and Kao are going through the same calculations and considerations that you are and probably have their own versions of Table 12.2. Now suppose your competitors charge $1.50 or more. As the table shows, you would want to charge only $1.40 because that gives you the highest profit. (For example, if they charged $1.50, you would make $29,000 per month by charging $1.40, but only $20,000 by charging $1.50, and $15,000 by charging $1.30.) So you would not want to charge $1.50 (or more). Assuming that your competitors have gone through the same reasoning, you should not expect them to charge $1.50 (or more) either.

What if your competitors charge $1.30? Then you will lose money, but you will lose the least money ($6,000 per month) by charging $1.40. Your competitors would therefore not expect you to charge $1.30, and by the same reasoning, you should not expect them to charge a price this low. What price lets you do the best you can, given your competitors' prices? It is $1.40. This is also the

---

[6]This example is based on classroom material developed by Professor John Hauser of MIT. To protect P&G's proprietary interests, some of the facts about the product and the market have been altered. The fundamental description of P&G's problem, however, is accurate.

TABLE 12.2 P&G's Profit (in thousands of $ per month)

P&G's Price ($)	Their (Equal) Prices ($)							
	1.10	1.20	1.30	1.40	1.50	1.60	1.70	1.80
1.10	−226	−215	−204	−194	−183	−174	−165	−155
1.20	−106	−89	−73	−58	−43	−28	−15	−2
1.30	−56	−37	−19	2	15	31	47	62
1.40	−44	−25	−6	12	29	46	62	78
1.50	−52	−32	−15	3	20	36	52	68
1.60	−70	−51	−34	−18	−1	14	30	44
1.70	−93	−76	−59	−44	−28	−13	1	15
1.80	−118	−102	−87	−72	−57	−44	−30	−17

price at which your competitors are doing the best *they* can, so it is the Cournot equilibrium.[7] As the table shows, in this equilibrium you and your competitors each make a profit of $12,000 per month.

If you could *collude* with your competitors, you could make larger profits. You would all then agree to set a price $1.50, and each of you would earn $20,000. (This collusive agreement might be hard to enforce—you could increase your profit further at your competitors' expense by dropping your price below theirs, and your competitors might think about doing the same to you.)

12.5 Competition versus Collusion: The Prisoners' Dilemma

A Cournot equilibrium is a *noncooperative* equilibrium—each firm makes the decisions that give it the highest possible profit, given the actions of its competitors. As we have seen, the resulting profits earned by each firm are higher than they would be under perfect competition, but lower than if the firms colluded.

Collusion is, however, illegal, and most managers prefer to stay out of jail and not pay stiff fines. But if cooperation can lead to higher profits, why don't firms cooperate *without* explicitly colluding? In particular, if you and your competitor can both figure out the profit-maximizing price you would agree to charge *if you were to collude, why not just set that price and hope your competitor will do the same?* If your competitor *does* do the same, you will both make more money.

The problem is that your competitor might *not* choose to set price at the

[7]This Cournot equilibrium can also be derived algebraically from the demand curve and cost data above. We leave this as an exercise.

collusive level. In fact, it probably *won't* set price at the collusive level. Why not? *Because your competitor would do better by choosing the Cournot price, even if it knew that you are going to set price at the collusive level.*

To understand this, let's go back to our example of price competition from the last section. The firms in that example each have a fixed cost of $20, have zero variable cost, and face the following demand curves:

$$\text{Firm 1's Demand:} \quad Q_1 = 12 - 2P_1 + P_2 \tag{12.6a}$$

$$\text{Firm 2's Demand:} \quad Q_2 = 12 - 2P_2 + P_1 \tag{12.6b}$$

We found that in the Cournot equilibrium, each firm will charge a price of $4 and earn a profit of $12, whereas if the firms collude they will charge a price of $6 and earn a profit of $16. Now suppose the firms do not collude, but that Firm 1 charges the $6 collusive price, hoping that Firm 2 will do the same. If Firm 2 *does* do the same, it will earn a profit of $16. But what if it charges the $4 price instead? Then, Firm 2 would earn a profit of

$$\pi_2 = P_2Q_2 - 20 = (4)[12 - (2)(4) + 6] - 20 = \$20$$

Firm 1, on the other hand, will earn a profit of

$$\pi_1 = P_1Q_1 - 20 = (6)[12 - (2)(6) + 4] - 20 = \$4$$

So if Firm 1 charges $6 but Firm 2 charges only $4, Firm 2's profit will increase to $20. And it will do so at the expense of Firm 1's profit, which will fall to $4. Clearly, Firm 2 does best by charging only $4. And similarly, Firm 1 does best by charging only $4. If Firm 2 charges $6 and Firm 1 charges $4, Firm 1 will earn a $20 profit, and Firm 2 will earn only $4.

Table 12.3 summarizes the results of these different pricing possibilities. In deciding what price to set, the two firms are playing a *noncooperative game*—each firm independently does the best it can, taking its competitor into account. Table 12.3 is called the *payoff matrix* for this game because it shows the profit (or payoff) to each firm given its decision and the decision of its competitor. For example, the upper left-hand corner of the payoff matrix tells us that if both firms charge $4, each firm will make a $12 profit. The upper right-hand corner tells us that if Firm 1 charges $4 and Firm 2 charges $6, Firm 1 will make $20, and Firm 2 will make $4.

TABLE 12.3 Payoff Matrix for Pricing Game

		Firm 2	
		Charge $4	Charge $6
Firm 1	Charge $4	$12, $12	$20, $4
	Charge $6	$4, $20	$16, $16

This payoff matrix can clarify the answer to our original question: Why don't firms behave cooperatively, and thereby earn higher profits, even if they can't collude? In this case, cooperating means *both* firms charging $6 instead of $4, and thereby earning $16 instead of $12. The problem is that each firm always makes more money by charging $4, *no matter what its competitor does.* As the payoff matrix shows, if Firm 2 charges $4, Firm 1 does best by charging $4. And if Firm 2 charges $6, Firm 1 still does best by charging $4. Similarly, Firm 2 always does best by charging $4, no matter what Firm 1 does. As a result, unless the two firms can sign an enforceable agreement to charge $6, neither firm can expect its competitor to charge $6, and both will charge $4.

A classic example in game theory, called the *Prisoners' Dilemma,* illustrates the problem oligopolistic firms face. It goes as follows: Two prisoners have been accused of collaborating in a crime. They are in separate jail cells and cannot communicate with each other. Each has been asked to confess to the crime. If both prisoners confess, each will receive a prison term of five years. If neither confesses, the prosecution's case will be difficult to make, so the prisoners can expect to plea bargain and receive a term of two years. On the other hand, if one prisoner confesses and the other does not, the one who confesses will receive a term of only one year, while the other will go to prison for ten years. If you were one of these prisoners, what would you do—confess or not confess?

The payoff matrix in Table 12.4 summarizes the possible outcomes. (Note that the "payoffs" are negative; the entry in the lower right-hand corner of the payoff matrix means a two-year sentence for each prisoner.) As the table shows, these prisoners face a dilemma. If they could only both agree not to confess (in a way that would be binding), then each would go to jail for only two years. But they can't talk to each other, and even if they could, can they trust each other? If Prisoner A does not confess, he risks being taken advantage of by his former accomplice. After all, *no matter what Prisoner A does, Prisoner B comes out ahead by confessing.* Similarly, Prisoner A always comes out ahead by confessing, so Prisoner B must worry that by not confessing, she will be taken advantage of. Therefore, both prisoners will probably confess, and go to jail for five years.

Oligopolistic firms often find themselves in a Prisoners' Dilemma. They must decide whether to compete aggressively, attempting to capture a larger share of the market at their competitor's expense, or to "cooperate" and compete

TABLE 12.4 Payoff Matrix for Prisoners' Dilemma

		Prisoner B	
		Confess	Don't Confess
Prisoner A	Confess	−5, −5	−1, −10
	Don't Confess	−10, −1	−2, −2

more passively, coexisting with their competitors and settling for the market share they currently hold, and perhaps even implicitly colluding. If the firms compete passively, setting high prices and limiting output, they will make higher profits than if they compete aggressively.

Like our prisoners, however, each firm has an incentive to "fink" and undercut its competitors, and each knows that its competitors have the same incentive. As desirable as cooperation is, each firm worries—with good reason—that if it competes passively, its competitor might compete aggressively, taking the lion's share of the market. In the pricing problem illustrated in Table 12.3, both firms do better by "cooperating" and charging a high price. But the firms are in a Prisoners' Dilemma, where neither firm can trust or expect its competitor to set a high price.

EXAMPLE 12.3 PROCTER & GAMBLE IN A PRISONERS' DILEMMA[8]

In Example 12.2, we examined the problem that arose when P&G, Unilever, and Kao Soap were all planning to enter the Japanese market for Gypsy Moth Tape at the same time. They all faced the same cost and demand conditions, and each firm had to decide on a price that took its competitors into account. In Table 12.2, we tabulated the profits to P&G corresponding to alternative prices that it and its competitors might charge. We argued that P&G should expect its competitors to charge a price of $1.40, and should do the same.

P&G would be better off if it *and its competitors* all charged a price of $1.50. This is clear from the payoff matrix in Table 12.5. (This payoff matrix is the portion of Table 12.2 corresponding to prices of $1.40 and $1.50, with the payoffs to P&G's competitors also tabulated.) If all the firms charge $1.50, they will each make a profit of $20,000 per month, instead of the $12,000 per month they make by charging $1.40. Then why don't they charge $1.50?

TABLE 12.5 Payoff Matrix for Pricing Problem

		Unilever and Kao[9]	
		Charge $1.40	Charge $1.50
P&G	Charge $1.40	$12, $12	$29, $11
	Charge $1.50	$3, $21	$20, $20

[8]As in Example 12.2, some of the facts about the product and the market have been altered to protect P&G's proprietary interests.

[9]Assumes that Unilever and Kao both charge the same price. Entries represent profits in thousands of dollars per month.

Because these firms are in a Prisoners' Dilemma. No matter what Unilever and Kao do, P&G makes more money by charging $1.40. For example, if Unilever and Kao charge $1.50, P&G can make $29,000 per month by charging $1.40, versus $20,000 by charging $1.50. This is also true for Unilever and for Kao. For example, if P&G charges $1.50 and Unilever and Kao both charge $1.40, they will each make $21,000, instead of $20,000.[10] As a result, P&G knows that if it sets a price of $1.50, its competitors will have a strong incentive to undercut and charge $1.40. P&G will then have only a small share of the market and will make only $3,000 per month profit. Should P&G make a leap of faith and charge $1.50? If you were faced with this dilemma, what would you do?

12.6 Implications of the Prisoners' Dilemma for Oligopolistic Pricing

Does the Prisoners' Dilemma doom oligopolistic firms to aggressive competition and low profits? Not necessarily. Although our imaginary prisoners have only one opportunity to confess, most firms set output and price over and over again, continually observing their competitors' behavior and adjusting their own accordingly. This allows firms to develop reputations from which trust can arise. As a result, oligopolistic coordination and cooperation can sometimes prevail.

Take, for example, an industry made up of only three or four firms that have coexisted for a long time. Over the years, the managers of those firms might grow tired of losing money because of price wars, and an implicit understanding might arise in which all the firms maintain high prices, and no firm makes a serious attempt to take market share from its competitors. Although each firm might be tempted to undercut its competitors, the managers know that the gains from this will be short-lived. They know their competitors will retaliate, and the result will be renewed warfare, and lower profits over the long run.

This resolution of the Prisoners' Dilemma occurs in some industries, but not in others. Sometimes managers are not content with the moderately high profits resulting from implicit collusion and prefer to compete aggressively to try and capture most of the market. Sometimes implicit understandings are just too difficult to reach. For example, firms might have different costs and different assessments of market demand, so that they disagree about what the "correct" collusive price is. Firm A might think the "correct" price is $10, while Firm B thinks it is $9. When it sets a $9 price, Firm A might view this as an attempt to undercut, and might retaliate by lowering its price to $8, so a price war begins.

As a result, in many industries implicit collusion is short-lived. There is often a fundamental layer of mistrust, so warfare erupts as soon as one firm is perceived by its competitors to be "rocking the boat" by changing its price or doing too much advertising.

---

[10]If P&G and Kao both charged $1.50 and *only* Unilever undercut and charged $1.40, Unilever would make $29,000 per month. It is especially profitable to be the only firm charging the low price.

Price Rigidity

Because implicit collusion tends to be fragile, oligopolistic firms usually have a strong desire for stability, particularly with respect to price. This is why *price rigidity* is often a characteristic of oligopolistic industries. Even if costs or demand change, firms are reluctant to change price. If costs fall or market demand declines, firms are reluctant to lower price because that might send the wrong message to their competitors, and thereby set off a round price warfare. And if costs or demand rise, firms are reluctant to raise price because they are afraid that their competitors might not also raise their prices.

This price rigidity is the basis of the well-known "kinked demand curve" model of oligopoly. According to this model, each firm faces a demand curve kinked at the currently prevailing price P^*. (See Figure 12.7.) At prices above P^* the demand curve is very elastic. The reason is that the firm believes that if it raises its price above P^*, other firms will not follow suit, and it will therefore lose sales and much of its market share. On the other hand, the firm believes

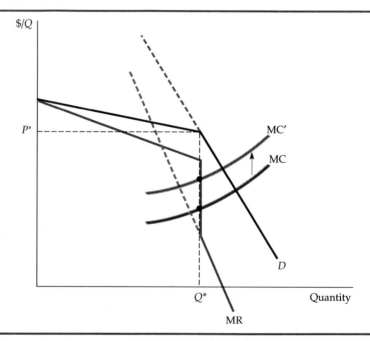

FIGURE 12.7 The Kinked Demand Curve. Each firm believes that if it raises its price above the current price P^*, none of its competitors will follow suit, so it will lose most of its sales. Each firm also believes that if it lowers price, everyone will follow suit, and its sales will increase only to the extent that market demand increases. As a result, the firm's demand curve D is kinked at price P^*, and its marginal revenue curve MR is discontinuous at that point. If marginal cost increases from MC to MC', the firm will still produce the same output level Q^* and charge the same price P^*.

that if it lowers its price below P^*, other firms will follow suit because they will not want to lose *their* shares of the market, so that sales will expand only to the extent that a lower market price increases total market demand.

Because the firm's demand curve is kinked, its marginal revenue curve is discontinuous. (The bottom part of the marginal revenue curve corresponds to the less elastic part of the demand curve, as shown by the dashed portions of each curve.) As a result, the firm's costs can change without resulting in a change in price. As shown in the figure, marginal cost could increase, but it would still equal marginal revenue at the same output level, so that price stays the same.

The kinked demand curve model is attractively simple, but it does not really explain oligopolistic pricing. It says nothing about how firms arrived at price P^* in the first place, and why they didn't arrive at some different price. It is useful mainly as a description of price rigidity, rather than an explanation of it.[11] The explanation for price rigidity comes from the Prisoners' Dilemma and from firms' desires to avoid mutually destructive price competition.

Price Leadership

One of the main impediments to implicitly collusive pricing is that it is difficult for firms to agree (without talking with one another) on what the price should be. Agreement becomes particularly problematic when cost and demand conditions are changing and the "correct" price is thus also changing. *Price leadership* is a form of implicit collusion that gets around this problem. Under price leadership, one firm sets the price, and the other firms, the "price followers," go along with it. This arrangement solves the problem of agreeing on price—just charge what the "leader" is charging.

What price will the leader set? It depends on whether the other firms, in addition to matching price, restrain production so that market shares remain about the same, or instead produce more at the higher price. If the other firms restrain production, the leader can set the joint profit-maximizing price (for example, $6 in Table 12.3). Or the leader might be a *dominant firm*, which sets a price that maximizes its own profit, with the other firms producing all they want at that price.

Figure 12.8 shows how a dominant firm sets its price. Here, D is the market demand curve, and S_F is the supply curve (i.e., the aggregate marginal cost curve) of followers. The leader must determine *its* demand curve D_L. As the figure shows, this is just the difference between market demand and the supply of followers. For example, at price P_1 the supply of followers is just equal to market demand, so the leader can sell nothing at this price. At a price of P_2 or

---

[11]Also, the model has not stood up well to empirical tests; there is evidence that rival firms do match price increases as well as decreases. The earliest tests were by George Stigler, "The Kinky Oligopoly Demand Curve and Rigid Prices," *Journal of Political Economy* 55 (Oct. 1947): 432–449.

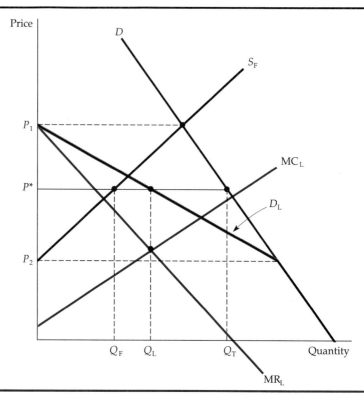

FIGURE 12.8 Price Leadership by a Dominant Firm. One firm, the leader, sets price, and the other firms sell as much as they want at that price. The leader's demand curve D_L is the difference between market demand D and the supply of followers S_F. The leader produces a quantity Q_L at the point where its marginal revenue MR_L is equal to its marginal cost MC_L. The corresponding price is P^*. At this price, followers sell Q_F, so that total sales is Q_T.

less, followers will not supply any of the good, so the leader faces the market demand curve. At prices between P_1 and P_2, the leader faces the curve D_L.

Corresponding to D_L is the leader's marginal revenue curve MR_L. MC_L is the leader's marginal cost curve. To maximize its profit, the leader produces quantity Q_L at the intersection of MR_L and MC_L. From the demand curve D_L, we find price P^*. At this price, followers sell a quantity Q_F, so that the total quantity sold is $Q_T = Q_L + Q_F$.

Price leadership requires one firm to be the leader. Since firms cannot communicate about this directly, it is often natural for the largest firm to become the leader. That has been the case in the automobile industry, where General Motors has traditionally been the price leader. However, in some industries, different firms will be the leader from time to time, as Example 12.4 illustrates.

EXAMPLE 12.4 PRICE LEADERSHIP AND PRICE RIGIDITY IN COMMERCIAL BANKING

Commercial banks borrow money from individuals and companies that deposit funds in checking accounts, savings accounts, and certificates of deposit. They then use this money to make loans to household and corporate borrowers. By lending at an interest rate higher than the rate they pay on their deposits, they earn a profit.

The largest commercial banks in the United States—Bank of America, Bankers Trust Co., Chase Manhattan Bank, Chemical Bank, Citibank, Manufacturers Hanover Trust Co., Morgan Guaranty Trust Co., and Wells Fargo, among others—compete with each other to make loans to large corporate clients. The main form of competition is over price, in this case the interest rate they charge corporate clients for loans. If competition becomes aggressive, the interest rates they charge fall, and so do their profits. To avoid aggressive competition, a form of price leadership has evolved.

The interest rate that banks charge large corporate clients is called the *prime*

TABLE 12.6 The Prime Rate[12]

Date	Bank	Rate Change
December 18, 1984	Manufacturers Hanover	11 ¼ → 10 ¾
December 19, 1984	Bankers Trust	11 ¼ → 10 ¾
December 20, 1984	All others	11 ¼ → 10 ¾
January 15, 1985	Manufacturers Hanover	10 ¾ → 10 ½
January 16, 1985	All others	10 ¾ → 10 ½
May 16, 1985	Bankers Trust	10 ½ → 10
May 17, 1985	Citibank, Chase	10 ½ → 10
May 18, 1985	All others	10 ½ → 10
June 19, 1985, A.M.	Morgan Guaranty	10 → 9 ½
June 19, 1985, P.M.	All others	10 → 9 ½
March 7, 1986, A.M.	Chase Manhattan	9 ½ → 9
March 7, 1986, P.M.	All others	9 ½ → 9
April 22, 1986, A.M.	Chase Manhattan	9 → 8 ½
April 22, 1986, P.M.	All others	9 → 8 ½
July 14, 1986, A.M.	Chemical Bank	8 ½ → 8
July 14, 1986, P.M.	All others	8 ½ → 8
August 26, 1986	Wells Fargo	8 → 7 ½
August 27, 1986	All others	8 → 7 ½

[12]Source: *Wall Street Journal*, various issues.

rate.[13] This rate is widely cited in newspapers and business publications, and is therefore a convenient focal point for price leadership. Most of the largest banks charge the same or nearly the same prime rate, and they avoid making frequent changes in the rate that might be destabilizing and lead to competitive warfare. The prime rate changes only when money market conditions have changed enough so that other interest rates have risen or fallen substantially. When that happens, one of the major banks (the leader) announces a change in its rate, and the other banks quickly follow suit. Different banks take on the role of

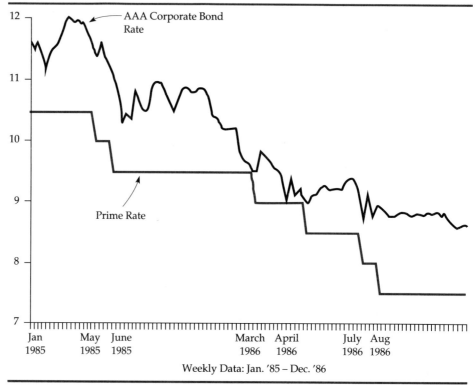

Weekly Data: Jan. '85 – Dec. '86

FIGURE 12.9   Prime Rate vs. Corporate Bond Rate.   The prime rate is the rate that major banks charge their largest corporate customers for short-term loans. It changes only infrequently, because banks are reluctant to undercut one another. When a change does occur, it begins with one bank, and other banks follow suit within a day or two. The corporate bond rate is the return on long-term corporate bonds. Because these bonds are widely traded, this rate fluctuates with market conditions.

[13]The prime rate is a variable interest rate that applies when a corporate client is given a line of credit. For example, Bank of America might tell the General Dynamics Corporation that it can borrow up to $10 million at the bank's prime rate. It is a variable rate in that if the bank's prime rate goes up, General Dynamics will have to pay more interest on however much of this $10 million it has in fact borrowed.

leader from time to time, but when one bank announces a change, the other banks follow within two or three days.

Table 12.6 shows the evolution of the prime rate from late 1984 through the middle of 1986, which was a period of falling interest rates. Note that on December 18, 1984, for example, Manufacturers Hanover lowered its prime rate from 11 ¼ percent to 10 ¾ percent, and all the other major banks followed suit within two days. On May 16, 1985, Bankers Trust was the first to lower its rate, this time from 10 ½ to 10 percent, and again all the other banks followed suit within two days. On several occasions, all banks changed their rates within the same day.

Table 12.6 also shows that changes in the prime rate were relatively infrequenty. Other market interest rates were fluctuating considerably during this period, but the prime rate changed only after the other rates had changed substantially. Figure 12.9 shows this by comparing the prime rate with the rate on high-grade, long-term corporate bonds during 1985 and 1986.[14] Note the long periods during which the prime rate did not change.

12.7 Cartels

Producers in a cartel explicitly agree to cooperate in setting prices and output levels. Not all the producers in an industry need to join the cartel, and most cartels involve only a subset of producers. But if enough producers adhere to the cartel's agreements, and if market demand is sufficiently inelastic, the cartel may drive prices well above competitive levels.

Cartels are often international. The U.S. antitrust laws prohibit American companies from colluding, but the antitrust laws of other countries are much weaker, and are sometimes poorly enforced. Furthermore, nothing prevents countries, or companies owned or controlled by foreign governments, from forming a cartel. For example, the OPEC cartel is an international agreement among oil-producing countries, which for over a decade succeeded in raising world oil prices far above what they would have been otherwise.

Other international cartels have also succeeded in raising prices. For example, during the mid-1970s, the International Bauxite Association (IBA) quadrupled bauxite prices, and a secretive international uranium cartel pushed up uranium prices. Some cartels had longer successes: From 1928 through the early 1970s a cartel called Mercurio Europeo kept the price of mercury close to monopoly levels, and an international cartel monopolized the iodine market from 1878 through 1939. However, most cartels have failed to raise prices. An international copper cartel operates to this day, but it has never had a significant impact on

[14]Figure 12.8 shows the AAA corporate bond rate, which is the average rate on long-term bonds issued by the most creditworthy corporations. We discuss interest rates in more detail in Chapter 15.

copper prices. And cartel attempts to drive up the prices of tin, coffee, tea, and cocoa have also failed.[15]

Why do some cartels succeed while others fail? There are two requisites for cartel success. First, a stable cartel organization must be formed whose members agree on price and production levels and then adhere to that agreement. Unlike our prisoners in the Prisoners' Dilemma, cartel members can talk to each other to formalize an agreement. This does not mean, however, that agreeing is easy. Different members may have different costs, different assessments of market demand, and even different objectives, and they may therefore want to set price at different levels. Furthermore, each member of the cartel will be tempted to "cheat" by lowering its price slightly to capture a larger market share than what it was allotted. Most often, only the threat of a long-term return to competitive prices deters cheating of this sort. But if the profits from cartelization are large enough, that threat may be sufficient.

The second requisite for success is the potential for monopoly power. Even if a cartel can solve its organizational problems, there will be little room to raise price if it faces a highly elastic demand curve. Potential monopoly power may be the most important condition for success; if the potential gains from cooperation are large, cartel members will have more incentive to solve their organizational problems.

The Analysis of Cartel Pricing

Only rarely do *all* the producers of a good combine to form a cartel. A cartel usually accounts for only a portion of total production and must take the supply response of competitive (noncartel) producers into account when setting price. Cartel pricing is thus best analyzed by using the dominant firm model discussed earlier. We will apply this model to two cartels, the OPEC oil cartel and the CIPEC copper cartel.[16] This will help us understand why OPEC was so successful in raising price, while CIPEC was not.

Figure 12.10 illustrates the case of OPEC. Total Demand TD is the total world demand curve for crude oil, and S_c is the competitive (non-OPEC) supply curve. The demand for OPEC oil D_{OPEC} is the difference between total demand and competitive supply, and MR_{OPEC} is the corresponding marginal revenue curve. MC_{OPEC} is OPEC's marginal cost curve; OPEC has much lower production costs than do non-OPEC producers. OPEC's marginal revenue and marginal cost are equal at quantity Q_{OPEC}, which is the quantity that OPEC will produce. We see from OPEC's demand curve that the price will be P^*, at which competitive supply is Q_c.

---

[15]See Robert S. Pindyck, "The Cartelization of World Commodity Markets," *American Economic Review* 69 (May 1979): 154–158; and Jeffrey K. MacKie-Mason and R. S. Pindyck, "Cartel Theory and Cartel Experience in International Minerals Markets," in *Energy: Markets and Regulation* (Cambridge, Mass.: MIT Press, 1986).

[16]CIPEC is the French acronym for International Council of Copper Exporting Countries.

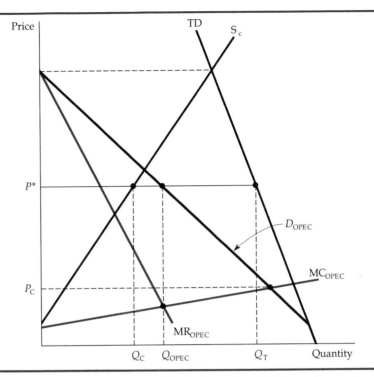

FIGURE 12.10 The OPEC Oil Cartel. TD is the total world demand curve for oil, and S_c is the competitive (non-OPEC) supply curve. OPEC's demand D_{OPEC} is the difference between the two. Because both total demand and competitive supply are inelastic, OPEC's demand is inelastic. OPEC's profit-maximizing quantity Q_{OPEC} is found at the intersection of its marginal revenue and marginal cost curves; at this quantity, OPEC charges price P^*. If OPEC producers had not cartelized, price would be P_c, where OPEC's demand and marginal cost curves intersect.

Suppose petroleum-exporting countries had not formed a cartel and instead had produced competitively. Price would then have equaled marginal cost. We can therefore determine the competitive price from the point where OPEC's demand curve intersects its marginal cost curve. That price, labeled P_c, is much lower than the cartel price P^*. Because both total demand and non-OPEC supply are inelastic, the demand for OPEC oil is also fairly inelastic; thus the cartel has substantial monopoly power. It used that power to drive prices well above competitive levels.

In Chapter 2 we stressed the importance of distinguishing between short-run and long-run supply and demand, and that distinction is important here. The total demand and non-OPEC supply curves in Figure 12.10 apply for a short- or intermediate-run analysis. In the long run, both demand and supply will be much more elastic, which means that OPEC's demand curve will also be much more elastic. As a result, we would expect that in the long run OPEC would be unable to maintain a price that is so much above the competitive level.

Indeed, during 1982–1987, oil prices fell in real terms, largely because of the long-run adjustment of demand and non-OPEC supply.

Figure 12.11 provides a similar analysis of CIPEC. CIPEC consists of four copper-producing countries: Chile, Peru, Zambia, and Zaire, which collectively account for about a third of world copper production. In these countries production costs are lower than those of non-CIPEC producers, but except for Chile, not much lower. In Figure 12.11 CIPEC's marginal cost curve is therefore drawn only a little below the non-CIPEC supply curve. CIPEC's demand curve D_{CIPEC} is the difference between total demand TD and non-CIPEC supply S_c. CIPEC's marginal cost and marginal revenue curves intersect at quantity Q_{CIPEC}, with the corresponding price P^*. Again, the competitive price P_c is found at the point where CIPEC's demand curve intersects its marginal cost curve. Note that this price is very close to the cartel price P^*.

Why can't CIPEC increase copper prices much? As Figure 12.11 shows, the total demand for copper is more elastic than for oil. (Other materials, such as aluminum, can easily be substituted for copper.) Also, competitive supply is much more elastic. Even in the short run, non-CIPEC producers can easily

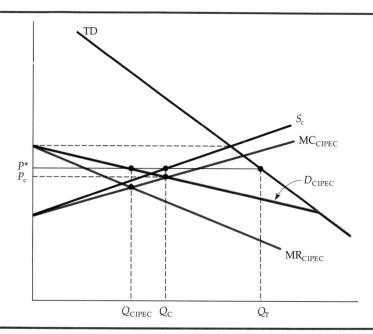

FIGURE 12.11 The CIPEC Copper Cartel. TD is the total demand for copper, and S_c is the competitive (non-CIPEC) supply curve. CIPEC's demand curve D_{CIPEC} is the difference between the two. Both total demand and competitive supply are relatively elastic, so CIPEC's demand curve is elastic, and CIPEC has very little monopoly power. Note that CIPEC's optimal price P^* is not very different from the competitive price P_c.

expand supply if prices should rise (in part because of the availability of supply from scrap metal). Thus CIPEC's potential monopoly power is small.[17]

As the examples of OPEC and CIPEC illustrate, successful cartelization requires two things. First, the total demand for the good must not be very price elastic. Second, either the cartel must control nearly all the world's supply, or if it doesn't, the supply of noncartel producers must not be price elastic. Most international commodity cartels have failed because few world markets meet both these conditions.

EXAMPLE 12.5 THE CARTELIZATION OF INTERCOLLEGIATE ATHLETICS

Many people think of intercollegiate athletics as an extracurricular activity for college students, and a diversion for fans. They assume that universities support athletics avidly because it gives amateur athletes a chance to develop their skills and play football or basketball before a large audience, and also provides entertainment and promotes school spirit and alumni support. Although it does these things, intercollegiate athletics is also a big—and an extremely profitable—industry.

Like any industry, intercollegiate athletics has firms and consumers. The "firms" are the universities that support and finance teams. The inputs to production are the coaches, student athletes, and capital in the form of stadiums and playing fields. The consumers are the fans who buy tickets to games, and the TV and radio networks that pay to broadcast the games. There are many firms and consumers, which suggests that the industry is competitive. But the persistently high level of profits in this industry is inconsistent with competition—a large state university can regularly earn more than $6 million a year in profits from football games alone.[18] This profitability is the result of monopoly power, obtained via cartelization.

The cartel organization is the National Collegiate Athletic Association (NCAA). The NCAA restricts competition in a number of important activities. To reduce bargaining power by student athletes, the NCAA creates and enforces rules regarding eligibility and terms of compensation. To reduce output competition by firms, it limits the number of games that can be played each season and the number of teams that can participate in each division. And to limit price competition, the NCAA has, until 1984, been the sole negotiator for all football television contracts, thereby monopolizing one of the main sources of industry revenues.[19]

---

[17]For more detailed analysis of both OPEC and CIPEC, see Robert S. Pindyck, "Gains to Producers from the Cartelization of Exhaustible Resources," *Review of Economics and Statistics* (May 1978): 238–251.

[18]See "In Big-Time College Athletics, the Real Score Is in Dollars," *New York Times*, March 1, 1987.

[19]See James V. Koch, "The Intercollegiate Athletics Industry," in Walter Adams, *The Structure of American Industry*, 7th ed. (New York: Macmillan, 1986). Koch provides a detailed and informative discussion of the nature of this industry and the behavior of the NCAA cartel.

Has the NCAA been a successful cartel? Like most cartels, its members have occasionally broken its rules and regulations. But until 1984, it has increased the monopoly power of this industry well above what it would have been otherwise. In 1984, however, the Supreme Court ruled that the NCAA's monopolization of football television contracts was illegal, and that individual universities could negotiate their own contracts. As a result, more college football is shown on television, and the revenues to the schools has dropped somewhat. But although the Supreme Court's ruling reduced the NCAA's monopoly power, it did not eliminate it. Intercollegiate athletics remains very profitable, thanks to the cartel.

Summary

1. In a monopolistically competitive market, firms compete by selling differentiated products, which are highly substitutable. New firms can enter or exit easily. Firms have only a small amount of monopoly power. In the long run, entry will occur until profits are driven to zero. Firms then produce with excess capacity (i.e., at output levels below those that minimize average cost.)

2. In an oligopolistic market, only a few firms account for most or all of production. Barriers to entry allow some firms to earn substantial profits, even over the long run. Economic decisions involve strategic considerations—each firm must consider how its actions will affect its rivals, and how they are likely to react.

3. In the Cournot model of oligopoly, firms make their output decisions at the same time, each taking the other's output as fixed. In equilibrium, each firm is maximizing its profit, given the output of its competitor, so no firm has an incentive to change its output. Each firm's profit is higher than under perfect competition, but less than what it would earn by colluding.

4. In the Stackelberg model, one firm sets its output first. That firm has a strategic advantage and earns a higher profit. It knows it can choose a large output, and its competitors will have to choose small outputs if they want to maximize profits.

5. The Cournot model can also be applied to markets in which firms produce substitute goods and compete by setting price. In equilibrium, each firm maximizes its profit, given the prices of its competitors, and so has no incentive to change price.

6. Firms would earn higher profits by collusively agreeing to raise prices, but the antitrust laws prohibit this. They might all set a high price without colluding, each hoping its competitors will do the same, but they are in a Prisoners' Dilemma, which makes this unlikely. Each firm has an incentive to cheat by lowering its price and capturing sales from its competitors.

7. The Prisoners' Dilemma creates price rigidity in oligopolistic markets. Firms are reluctant to change prices for fear of setting off a round of price warfare.

8. Price leadership is a form of implicit collusion that sometimes gets around the Prisoner's Dilemma. One firm sets price, and the other firms follow with the same price.

9. In a cartel, producers explicitly collude in setting prices and output levels. Successful cartelization requires that the total demand for the good not be very price elastic, and that either the cartel control most supply or else the supply of noncartel producers be inelastic.

Review Questions

1. What are the characteristics of a monopolistically competitive market? What happens to the equilibrium price and quantity in such a market if one firm introduces a new, improved product?

2. Why is the firm's demand curve flatter than the total market demand curve in monopolistic competition? Suppose a monopolistically competitive firm is making a profit in the short run. What will happen to its demand curve in the long run?

3. Some experts have argued that too many brands of breakfast cereal are on the market. Give an argument in support of this view. Give an argument against this view.

4. Why is the Cournot equilibrium stable (i.e., why don't firms have any incentive to change their output levels once in equilibrium)? Even if they can't collude, why don't firms set their outputs at the joint profit-maximizing levels (i.e., the levels they would have chosen had they colluded)?

5. In the Stackelberg model, the firm that sets output first has an advantage. Explain why.

6. Explain the meaning of a Cournot equilibrium when firms are competing with respect to price. Why is the equilibrium stable? Why don't the firms raise their prices to the level that maximizes joint profits?

7. The kinked demand curve describes price rigidity. Explain how the model works. What limitations does it have? Why does price rigidity arise in oligopolistic markets?

8. Why does price leadership sometimes evolve in oligopolistic markets? Explain how the price leader determines a profit-maximizing price.

9. Why has the OPEC oil cartel succeeded in raising prices substantially, while the CIPEC copper cartel has not? What conditions are necessary for successful cartelization? What organizational problems must a cartel overcome?

Exercises

1. Suppose all the firms in a monopolistically competitive industry were merged into one large firm. Would that new firm produce as many different brands? Would it produce only a single brand? Explain.

2. A monopolist can produce at a constant average (and marginal) cost of $AC = MC = 5$. The firm faces a market demand curve given by $Q = 53 - P$.
    a. Calculate the profit-maximizing price and quantity for this monopolist. Also calculate the monopolist's profits.

b. Suppose a second firm enters the market. Let Q_1 be the output of the first firm and Q_2 be the output of the second. Market demand is now given by

$$Q_1 + Q_2 = 53 - P$$

Assuming that this second firm has the same costs as the first, write the profits of each firm as functions of Q_1 and Q_2.

c. Suppose (as in the Cournot model) each firm chooses its profit-maximizing level of output under the assumption that its competitor's output is fixed. Find each firm's "reaction curve" (i.e., the rule that gives its desired output in terms of its competitor's output).

d. Calculate the Cournot equilibrium (i.e., the values of Q_1 and Q_2 for which both firms are doing as well as they can given their competitor's output). What are the resulting market price and profits of each firm?

*e. Suppose there are N firms in the industry, all with the same constant marginal cost, $MC = 5$. Find the Cournot equilibrium. How much will each firm produce, what will be the market price, and how much profit will each firm earn? Also, show that as N becomes large, the market price approaches the price that would prevail under perfect competition.

3. This exercise is a continuation of Exercise 2. We return to two firms with the same constant average and marginal cost, $AC = MC = 5$, facing the market demand curve $Q_1 + Q_2 = 53 - P$. Now we will use the Stackelberg model to analyze what will happen if one of the firms makes its output decision ahead of the other one.

a. Suppose Firm 1 is the Stackelberg leader (i.e., makes its output decisions ahead of Firm 2). Find the reaction curves that tell each firm how much to produce in terms of the output of its competitor.

b. How much will each firm produce, and what will its profit be?

4. Consider the following duopoly. Demand is given by $P = 10 - Q$, where $Q = Q_1 + Q_2$. The firms' cost functions are $C_1(Q_1) = 4 + 2Q_1$ and $C_2(Q_2) = 3 + 3Q_2$.

a. Suppose both firms have entered the industry. What is the joint profit-maximizing level of output? How much will be produced by each firm? How would your answer change if the firms have not yet entered the industry?

b. What is each firm's equilibrium output and profit if they behave noncoooopera-tively? Use the Cournot model. Draw the firms' reaction curves and show the equilibrium.

c. How much should Firm 1 be willing to pay to purchase Firm 2 if collusion is illegal but the takeover is not?

*5. Two firms compete by choosing price. Their demand functions are

$$Q_1 = 20 - P_1 + P_2$$

and

$$Q_2 = 20 + P_1 - P_2$$

where P_1 and P_2 are the prices charged by each firm, and Q_1 and Q_2 are the resulting demands. (Note that the demand for each good depends only on the difference in prices; if the two firms colluded and set the same price, they could make that price as high as they want, and earn infinite profits.) Marginal costs are zero.

a. Suppose the two firms set their prices at the *same time*. Find the resulting Cournot equilibrium. What price will each firm charge, how much will it sell, and what will its profit be? (Hint: Maximize the profit of each firm with respect to its price.)

b. Suppose Firm 1 sets its price *first*, and then Firm 2 sets its price. What price will each firm charge, how much will it sell, and what will its profit be?

c. Suppose you are one of these firms, and there are three ways you could play the game: (i) Both firms set price at the same time. (ii) You set price first. (iii) Your competitor sets price first. If you could choose among these, which would you prefer. Explain why.

6. The dominant firm model can help us understand the behavior of some cartels. Let us apply this model to the OPEC oil cartel. We will use isoelastic curves to describe world oil demand W and noncartel (competitive) supply S. Reasonable numbers for the price elasticities of world demand and noncartel supply are $-\frac{1}{2}$ and $\frac{1}{2}$, respectively. Then, expressing W and S in millions of barrels per day (mb/d), we could write

$$W = 160P^{-1/2}$$

and

$$S = 3\frac{1}{3}P^{1/2}$$

Note that OPEC's net demand is given by $D = W - S$.

a. Sketch the world demand curve W, the non-OPEC supply curve S, OPEC's net demand curve D, and OPEC's marginal revenue curve. For purposes of approximation, assume OPEC's production cost is zero. Indicate OPEC's optimal price, OPEC's optimal production, and non-OPEC production on the diagram. Now, show on the diagram how the various curves will shift, and how OPEC's optimal price will change if non-OPEC supply becomes more expensive because reserves of oil start running out.

b. Calculate OPEC's optimal (profit-maximizing) price. (Hint: Because OPEC's cost is zero, just write the expression for OPEC revenue and find the price that maximizes it.)

c. Suppose the oil-consuming countries were to unite and form a "buyers' cartel" to gain monopsony power. What can we say, and what can't we say, about the impact this would have on price?

*7. Monopolistically competitive firms often advertise to help differentiate their products from those of competitors and thereby increase demand. Firms must choose their level of advertising expenditures together with the choice of price and output. To see this, consider a firm with monopoly power that faces the demand curve

$$P = 100 - 3Q + 4A^{1/2}$$

and has the total cost function

$$C = 4Q^2 + 10Q + A$$

where A is the level of advertising expenditures, and P and Q are price and output.

a. Find the values of A, Q, and P that maximize this firm's profit.

b. Calculate the Lerner index of monopoly power, $L = (P - MC)/P$, for this firm at its profit-maximizing levels of A, Q, and P.

CHAPTER 13

Game Theory and Competitive Strategy

Unlike a pure monopoly or a perfectly competitive firm, most firms must consider the likely responses of competitors when they make strategic decisions about price, advertising expenditure, investment in new capital, and other variables. Although we began to explore some of these strategic decisions in the last chapter, there are many questions about market structure and firm behavior that we have not yet addressed. For example, why do firms tend to collude in some markets and compete aggressively in others? How do some firms manage to deter entry by potential competitors? And how should firms make pricing decisions when demand or cost conditions are changing, or new competitors are entering the market?

To answer these questions, we need to extend our analysis of strategic decision making by firms. The development and application of game theory is one of the most exciting areas in microeconomics. This chapter explains some of this theory and shows how it can be used to understand how markets evolve and operate, and how managers should think about the strategic economic decisions they continually face. We will see, for example, what happens when oligopolistic firms must set and adjust prices strategically over time, so that the Prisoners' Dilemma, which we discussed in Chapter 12, is repeated over and over. We will discuss how firms can make strategic moves that give them an advantage over their competitors or the edge in a bargaining situation. And we'll see how firms can use threats, promises, or more concrete actions to deter entry by potential competitors.

13.1 Gaming and Strategic Decisions

First, we should clarify what gaming and strategic decision making are all about. In essence, we are concerned with the following question: *If I believe that my competitors are rational and act to maximize their own profits, how should I take their behavior into account when making my own profit-maximizing decisions?*

As we will see, this question can be difficult to answer, even under conditions of complete symmetry and perfect information (i.e., my competitors and I have the same cost structure and are fully informed about each others' costs, about demand, etc.). Moreover, we will be concerned with more complex situations in which firms have different costs, different types of information, and various degrees and forms of competitive "advantage" and "disadvantage."

Noncooperative vs. Cooperative Games

The economic games that firms play can be either *cooperative* or *noncooperative.* A game is *cooperative* if the players can negotiate binding contracts that allow them to plan joint strategies. A game is *noncooperative* if negotiation and enforcement of a binding contract are not possible.

An example of a cooperative game is the bargaining between a buyer and a seller over the price of a rug. If the rug costs $100 to produce and the buyer values the rug at $200, a cooperative solution to the game is possible, because an agreement to sell the rug at any price between $101 and $199 will maximize the sum of the buyer's consumer surplus and the seller's profit, while making both parties better off. Another cooperative game would involve two firms in an industry, which negotiate a joint investment to develop a new technology (where neither firm would have enough know-how to succeed on its own). If the firms can sign a binding contract to divide the profits from their joint investment, a cooperative outcome that makes both parties better off is possible.[1] An example of a noncooperative game is a situation in which two competing firms take each other's likely behavior into account and independently determine a pricing or advertising strategy to win market share.[2]

Note that the fundamental difference between cooperative and noncooperative games lies in the contracting possibilities. In cooperative games binding contracts are possible; in noncooperative games they are not.

We will be concerned mostly with noncooperative games. In any game, however, the most important aspect of strategy design is *understanding your opponent's point of view, and (assuming your opponent is rational) deducing how he or she is likely to respond to your actions.* This may seem obvious—of course, one must understand an opponent's point of view. Yet even in simple gaming situations, people often ignore or misjudge their opponents' positions and the rational responses those positions imply. Example 13.1 illustrates this.

In the material that follows, we will examine simple games that involve pricing, advertising, and investment decisions. The games are simple in that, *given*

---

[1] Bargaining over a rug is called a *constant sum* game because no matter what the selling price, the sum of consumer surplus and profit will be the same. Negotiating over a joint venture is a *nonconstant sum* game: The total profits that result from the venture will depend on the outcome of the negotiations, e.g., the resources that each firm devotes to the venture.

[2] If the total size of the market were fixed, the game would be constant sum. If the total size of the market depended on the pricing strategies, the game would be nonconstant sum.

some behavioral assumption, we can determine the best strategy for each firm. However, even for these simple games, we will find that the "correct" behavioral assumptions are not easy to make, and will depend on how the game is played (e.g., how long firms stay in business, the extent to which they develop reputations, etc.). Therefore, when reading this chapter, you should try to understand the basic issues involved in the design and analysis of strategic decisions.

EXAMPLE 13.1 ACQUIRING A COMPANY

You represent Company A (the acquirer), which is considering acquiring Company T (the target).[3] You plan to offer cash for all of Company T's shares, but you are unsure what price to offer. The complication is this: The value of Company T, indeed, its viability, depends on the outcome of a major oil exploration project that it is currently undertaking. If the project fails, Company T under current management will be worth nothing. But if it succeeds, Company T's value under current management could be as high as $100/share. All share values between $0 and $100 are considered equally likely.

It is well known, however, that Company T will be worth considerably more under the progressive management of Company A than under current management. In fact, whatever the ultimate value under current management, *Company T will be worth 50 percent more under the management of Company A.* If the project fails, Company T is worth $0/share under either management. If the exploration project generates a $50/share value under current management, the value under Company A will be $75/share. Similarly, a $100/share value under Company T implies a $150/share value under Company A, and so on.

You must determine what price Company A should offer for Company T's shares. This offer must be made *now, before* the outcome of the exploration project is known. From all indications, Company T would be happy to be acquired by Company A, *for the right price.* You expect Company T to delay a decision on your bid until the exploration results are in and then accept or reject your offer before news of the drilling results reaches the press.

Thus, *you (Company A) will not know the results of the exploration project when submitting your price offer, but Company T will know the results when deciding whether to accept your offer. Also, Company T will accept any offer by Company A that is greater than the (per share) value of the company under current management.* As the representative of Company A, you are considering price offers in the range $0/share (i.e., making no offer at all) to $150/share. *What price per share should you offer for Company T's stock?*

Note: The typical response—to offer between $50 and $75 per share—is

---

[3]This is a revised version of an example designed by Max Bazerman for a course at MIT. We appreciate his making it available.

wrong. The correct answer to this problem appears at the end of this chapter, but we urge you to try to answer it on your own.

13.2 Dominant Strategies

How can we decide on the best strategy for playing a game? How can we determine a game's likely outcome? We need something to help us determine how the rational behavior of each player will lead to an equilibrium solution. Some strategies may be successful if competitors make certain choices, but will fail if they make other choices. Other strategies, however, may be successful whatever competitors choose to do. We begin our discussion of game theory with the concept of a *dominant strategy—one that is optimal for a player no matter what an opponent does.*

The following example illustrates this in a duopoly setting. Suppose Firms A and B sell competing products and are deciding whether to undertake advertising campaigns. Each firm, however, will be affected by its competitor's decision. The possible outcomes of the game are illustrated by the payoff matrix in Table 13.1. (Recall that the payoff matrix summarizes the possible outcomes of the game; the first number in each cell is the payoff to A and the second is the payoff to B.) Observe from this payoff matrix that if both firms decide to advertise, Firm A will make profits of 10, and Firm B will make profits of 5. If Firm A advertises and Firm B doesn't, Firm A will earn 15, and Firm B will earn zero. And similarly for the other two possibilities.

What strategy should each firm choose? First, consider Firm A. It should clearly advertise because no matter what Firm B does, Firm A does best by advertising. (If Firm B advertises, A earns a profit of 10 if it advertises, but only 6 if it doesn't. And if B does not advertise, A earns 15 if it advertises, but only 10 if it doesn't.) Thus, advertising is a dominant strategy for Firm A. The same is true for Firm B; no matter what Firm A does, Firm B does best by advertising. Therefore, assuming that both firms are rational, we know that the outcome for this game is that *both firms will advertise.* This outcome is easy to determine because both firms have dominant strategies.

TABLE 13.1 Payoff Matrix for Advertising Game

		Firm B	
		Advertise	Don't Advertise
Firm A	Advertise	10,5	15,0
	Don't Advertise	6,8	10,2

TABLE 13.2 Modified Advertising Game

		Firm B	
		Advertise	Don't Advertise
Firm A	Advertise	10,5	15,0
	Don't Advertise	6,8	20,2

However, not every game has a dominant strategy for each player. To see this, let's change our advertising example slightly. The payoff matrix in Table 13.2 is the same as in Table 13.1, except for the bottom right-hand corner—if neither firm advertises, Firm B will again earn profits of 2, but Firm A will earn profits of 20 (perhaps because Firm A's ads are largely defensive, designed to refute Firm B's claims, and expensive; so by not advertising, Firm A can reduce its expenses considerably).

Now Firm A has no dominant strategy. *Its optimal decision depends on what Firm B does.* If Firm B advertises, then Firm A does best by advertising; but if Firm B does not advertise, Firm A also does best by not advertising. Now suppose both firms must make their decisions at the same time. What should Firm A do?

To answer this, Firm A must put itself in Firm B's shoes. What decision is best from Firm B's point of view, and what is Firm B likely to do? The answer is clear: Firm B has a dominant strategy—advertise, no matter what Firm A does. (If Firm A advertises, B earns 5 by advertising and 0 by not advertising. If A doesn't advertise, B earns 8 if it advertises and 2 if it doesn't.) Therefore, Firm A can conclude that Firm B will advertise. This means that Firm A should itself advertise (and thereby earn 10 instead of 6). The equilibrium is again that both firms will advertise. It is the logical outcome of the game because Firm A is doing the best it can, given Firm B's decision; and Firm B is doing the best it can, given Firm A's decision.

13.3 The Nash Equilibrium Concept

To determine the likely outcome of a game, we have been seeking "self-enforcing," or "stable," strategies. Dominant strategies are stable, but in many games one or more players do not have a dominant strategy. We therefore need a more general solution concept—the *Nash equilibrium*.[4]

[4]This equilibrium concept is named after John Nash, who introduced it in 1951. Our discussion of the Nash equilibrium, and of game theory in general, is at an introductory level. For a more detailed but nontechnical discussion of game theory and its application, see Morton D. Davis, *Game Theory: A Nontechnical Introduction* (New York: Basic Books, 1983). For a more technical, in-depth coverage, see James W. Friedman, *Game Theory with Applications to Economics* (New York: Oxford University Press, 1986), and Guillermo Owen, *Game Theory* (New York: Academic Press, 1982).

A Nash equilibrium is a set of strategies (or actions) such that *each player believes (correctly) that it is doing the best it can given the actions of its opponents.* Since each player has no incentive to deviate from its Nash strategy, the strategies are stable. In the example shown in Table 13.2, the Nash equilibrium is that both firms advertise. It is a Nash equilibrium because, given the decision of its competitor, each firm is satisfied that it has made the best decision possible, and has no incentive to change its decision.

In Chapter 12 we used a *Cournot equilibrium* to analyze the output and pricing decisions of oligopolistic firms. In a Cournot equilibrium, each firm sets output or price while taking the output or price of its competitor as fixed. Once the firms have reached a Cournot equilibrium, no firm has an incentive to change its output or price unilaterally because each firm is doing the best it can given the decisions of its competitors. Therefore, a Cournot equilibrium is also a Nash equilibrium.[5]

It is helpful to compare the concept of a Nash equilibrium with that of an equilibrium in dominant strategies:

Dominant Strategies: I'm doing the best I can *no matter what you do.*
                              You're doing the best you can *no matter what I do.*

Nash Equilibrium: I'm doing the best I can *given what you are doing.*
                              You're doing the best you can *given what I am doing.*

Note that a dominant strategy equilibrium is a special case of a Nash equilibrium.

In the advertising game of Table 13.2, there is a single Nash equilibrium—both firms advertise. In general, a game does not have to have a single Nash equilibrium. Sometimes there is no Nash equilibrium, and sometimes there are several (i.e., several sets of strategies are stable and self-enforcing). A few more examples will help clarify how a Nash equilibrium works.[6]

Consider the following "product choice" problem. Two breakfast cereal companies face a market in which two new variations of cereal can be successfully introduced—provided each variation is introduced by only one firm. There is a market for a new "crispy" cereal and for a new "sweet" cereal, but each firm has the resources to introduce only one new product. Then the payoff matrix for the two firms might look like the one in Table 13.3.

In this game each firm is indifferent about which product it produces, so long as it does not introduce the same product as its competitor. If coordination were possible, the firms would probably agree to divide the market. But what will happen if the firms must behave *noncooperatively?* Suppose that somehow—perhaps through a news release or other form of communication—Firm 1 indicates it is about to introduce the sweet cereal, and Firm 2 (after hearing this)

---

[5] A Stackelberg equilibrium is also a Nash equilibrium. In the Stackelberg model, the rules of the game are different: One firm makes its output decision before its competitor does. Under these rules, each firm is doing the best it can given the decision of its competitor.

[6] Several of these examples were developed by Professor Garth Saloner at MIT.

TABLE 13.3 Product Choice Problem

| | | Firm 2 | |
		Crispy	Sweet
Firm 1	Crispy	$-5,-5$	10,10
	Sweet	10,10	$-5,-5$

indicates it will introduce the crispy one. Now, given the action it believes its opponent is taking, neither firm has an incentive to deviate from its proposed action. If it takes the proposed action, its payoff is 10, but if it deviates—given that its opponent's action remains unchanged—its payoff will be -5. Therefore, the strategy set given by the bottom left-hand corner of the payoff matrix is stable and constitutes a Nash equilibrium: Given the strategy of its opponent, each firm is doing the best it can and has no incentive to deviate.

Note that the upper right-hand corner of the payoff matrix is also a Nash equilibrium, which might occur if Firm 1 indicated it was about to produce the crispy cereal. Each Nash equilibrium is stable because *once the strategies are chosen*, no player will unilaterally deviate from them. However, without more information, we have no way of knowing which equilibrium (crispy/sweet vs. sweet/crispy) is likely to result—or if *either* will result. Of course, both firms have a strong incentive to reach *one* of the two Nash equilibria—if they both introduce the same type of cereal, they will both lose money. The fact that the two firms are not allowed to collude does not mean that they will not reach a Nash equilibrium. As an industry develops, understandings usually evolve as firms "signal" each other about the paths the industry is to take. We will describe examples of such "understandings" later in this chapter.

The concept of a Nash equilibrium relies heavily on individual rationality. Each player's choice of strategy depends not only on its own rationality, but also on that of its opponent. This can be a limitation, as the example in Table 13.4 shows.

TABLE 13.4

| | | Player 2 | |
		Left	Right
Player 1	Top	1,0	1,1
	Bottom	$-1000,0$	2,1

TABLE 13.5 Prisoners' Dilemma

| | | Prisoner B | |
		Confess	Don't Confess
Prisoner A	Confess	−5, −5	−1, −10
	Don't Confess	−10, −1	−2, −2

In this game, playing "right" is a dominant strategy for Player 2 because by using this strategy Player 2 will do better (earning 1 rather than 0), no matter what Player 1 does. Thus, Player 1 should expect Player 2 to play the "right" strategy. In this case Player 1 would do better by playing "bottom" (and earning 2) than by playing "top" (and earning 1). Clearly the outcome (bottom, right) is a Nash equilibrium for this game, and you can verify that it is the only Nash equilibrium. But note that Player 1 had better be sure that Player 2 understands the game and is rational. If Player 2 should happen to make a mistake and play "left," it would be extremely costly to Player 1.

If you were Player 1, what would you do? If you tend to be cautious, and you are concerned that Player 2 might not be fully informed or rational, you might choose to play "top," in which case you will be assured of earning 1, and you will have no chance of losing 1000. Such a strategy is called a *maximin strategy*, because it *maximizes the minimum gain that can be earned*. If both players used maximin strategies, the outcome would be (top, right). A maximin strategy is conservative, but not profit-maximizing (since Player 1 earns a profit of 1 rather than 2). Note that if Player 1 *knew for certain* that Player 2 was using a maximin strategy, it would prefer to play "bottom" (and earn 2), instead of following the maximin strategy of playing "top."

What is the Nash equilibrium for the Prisoners' Dilemma discussed in Chapter 12? Table 13.5 shows the payoff matrix for the Prisoners' Dilemma. (The payoffs are negative because they represent years in jail.) For the two prisoners, the ideal outcome is one in which neither confessed, so that they both get two years in prison. However, confessing is a *dominant strategy* for each prisoner—it yields a higher payoff regardless of the strategy of the other prisoner. Dominant strategies are also maximin strategies. Therefore, the outcome in which both prisoners confess is both a Nash equilibrium and a maximin solution. Thus, in a very strong sense it is rational for each prisoner to confess.

Before concluding this section, we should note that we have been analyzing noncooperative, egotistical games. Each player maximizes its own payoff whether it hurts or helps the other player. (With cooperation, some or all of the players might benefit.) It is in this sense that we say each player is playing "rationally."

13.4 Repeated Games

We saw in Chapter 12 that in oligopolistic markets, firms often find themselves in a Prisoners' Dilemma when making output or pricing decisions. Can firms find a way out of this dilemma, so that oligopolistic coordination and cooperation (whether explicit or implicit) could prevail?

To answer this question, we must recognize that the Prisoners' Dilemma, as we have described it so far, is static and thus limited. Although some prisoners may have only one opportunity in life to confess or not, most firms set output and price over and over again. In real life, firms play a *repeated game.* With each repetition of the Prisoners' Dilemma, firms can develop reputations about their behavior, and study the behavior of their competitors.

How does repetition change the likely outcome of the game? Suppose you are Firm 1 in the Prisoners' Dilemma illustrated by the payoff matrix in Table 13.6. If you and your competitor both charge a high price, you will both make higher profits than if you both charged a low price. However, you are afraid to charge a high price because if your competitor undercuts you and charges a low price, you will lose a lot of money and, to add insult to injury, your competitor will get rich. But suppose this game is repeated over and over again—for example, you and your competitor simultaneously announce your prices on the first day of every month. Should you then play the game differently? Should you change your price over time, perhaps in response to your competitor's behavior?

In an interesting study, Robert Axelrod asked game theorists around the world to come up with the best strategy they could think of to play this game in a repeated manner.[7] (A possible strategy might be: "I'll start off with a high price, then lower my price, but then if my competitor lowers its price, I'll raise mine for a while before lowering it again, etc."). Then, in a computer simulation, Axelrod played these strategies off against one another to see which worked best.

As you would expect, any given strategy would work better against some strategies than it would against others. The objective, however, was to find the strategy that was most robust, i.e., would work best on average against *all,* or almost all, other strategies. The result was surprising. The strategy that worked best was extremely simple—it was a *"tit-for-tat"* strategy: I start out with a high price, which I maintain so long as you continue to "cooperate" and also charge a high price. As soon as you lower your price, however, I follow suit and lower mine. If you later decide to cooperate and raise your price again, I'll immediately raise my price as well.

Why does this tit-for-tat strategy work best? In particular, can I expect that using the tit-for-tat strategy will induce my competitor to behave cooperatively (and charge a high price)?

[7]See Robert Axelrod, *The Evolution of Cooperation* (New York: Basic Books, 1984).

TABLE 13.6 Pricing Problem

		Firm 2	
		Low Price	High Price
Firm 1	Low Price	10,10	100, −50
	High Price	−50,100	50,50

Suppose the game is *infinitely repeated*. In other words, my competitor and I repeatedly set price month after month, *forever*. Cooperative behavior (i.e., charging a high price) is then the rational response to a tit-for-tat strategy. (This assumes that my competitor knows, or can figure out, that I am using a tit-for-tat strategy.) To see why, suppose that in one month my competitor sets a low price and undercuts me. During that month it will, of course, make a large profit. But the competitor knows that the following month I will set a low price, so that its profit will fall, and will remain low as long as we both continue to charge a low price. Since the game is infinitely repeated, the cumulative loss of profits that results must inevitably outweigh any short-term gain that accrued during the first month of undercutting. Thus, it is not rational to undercut.

In fact, with an infinitely repeated game, my competitor does not even have to be sure that I am playing tit-for-tat to make cooperation the rational strategy for it to follow. Even if the competitor believes there is only some chance that I am playing tit-for-tat, it will still be rational for it to start by charging a high price, and maintain the high price as long as I do. The reason is that with infinite repetition of the game, the *expected* gains from cooperation will outweigh those from undercutting. This will be true even if the probability that I am playing tit-for-tat (and so will continue cooperating) is small.

Now suppose the game is repeated a *finite* number of times—say N months. (N can be large as long as it is finite.) If my competitor (Firm 2) is rational, *and believes that I am rational*, it would reason as follows: "Because Firm 1 is playing tit-for-tat, I (Firm 2) cannot undercut—that is, *until the last month*. I *should* undercut in the last month because then I can make a large profit that month, and afterwards the game is over, so that Firm 1 cannot retaliate." "Therefore," figures Firm 2, "I will charge a high price until the last month, and then I will charge a low price."

However, since I (Firm 1) have also figured this out, I also plan to charge a low price in the last month. Of course, Firm 2 can figure this out as well, and therefore *knows* I will charge a low price in the last month. But then what about the next-to-last month? Firm 2 figures that it should undercut and charge a low price in the next-to-last month, because there will be no cooperation anyway in the last month. But, of course, I have figured this out too, so I *also* plan to charge a low price in the next-to-last month. And because the same reasoning applies to each preceding month, the only rational outcome is for both of us to charge a low price every month.

Since most of us do not expect to live forever, the tit-for-tat strategy seems of little value; once again we are stuck in the Prisoners' Dilemma without a way out. However, there *is* a way out if my competitor *has even a slight doubt about my "rationality."*

Suppose my competitor thinks (it need not be certain) that I am playing tit-for-tat. It also thinks that *perhaps* I am playing tit-for-tat "blindly," or with limited rationality, in the sense that I have failed to work out the logical implications of a finite time horizon as discussed above. My competitor thinks, for example, that perhaps I have not figured out that it will undercut me in the last month, so that I should also charge a low price in the last month, so that it should charge a low price in the next-to-last month, and so on. *"Perhaps,"* thinks my competitor, "Firm 1 will play tit-for-tat blindly, charging a high price as long as I charge a high price." Then (if the time horizon is long enough), it *is* rational for my competitor to maintain a high price until the last month (when it will undercut me).

Note that we have stressed the word "perhaps." My competitor need not be sure that I am playing tit-for-tat "blindly," or even that I am playing tit-for-tat at all. Just the *possibility* of this can make cooperative behavior a good strategy (until near the end) if the time horizon is long enough. Although my competitor's conjecture about how I am playing the game might be wrong, cooperative behavior is profitable *in expected value terms*. With a long time horizon, the sum of current and future profits, weighted by the probability that the conjecture is correct, can exceed the sum of profits from warfare, even if the competitor is the first to undercut.[8]

Thus, in a repeated game the Prisoners' Dilemma can have a cooperative outcome. In most markets the game is, in fact, repeated over a long time, and managers have doubts about how "perfectly rationally" they and their competitors operate. As a result, in some industries, particularly those in which only a few firms compete over a long period under stable demand and cost conditions, cooperation prevails, even though no contractual arrangements are made. In many other industries, however, there is little or no cooperative behavior.

Sometimes cooperation breaks down or never begins because there are too many firms. More often, the failure to cooperate is the result of rapidly shifting demand or cost conditions. Uncertainties about demand or costs make it difficult for the firms in the industry to reach an implicit understanding of what cooperation should entail. (Remember that an *explicit* understanding, arrived at

---

[8]After all, if I am wrong and my competitor charges a low price, I can shift my strategy at the cost of only one period's profit, a minor cost in light of the substantial profit that I can make if we both choose to set a high price. These results on the repeated Prisoners' Dilemma were first developed by David Kreps, Paul Milgrom, John Roberts, and Robert Wilson, "Rational Cooperation in the Finitely Repeated Prisoners' Dilemma," *Journal of Economic Theory* 27 (1982): 245–252.

through meetings and discussions, could lead to an antitrust conviction.) Suppose, for example, that cost differences or different beliefs about demand lead one firm to conclude that cooperation means charging $50, but lead a second firm to think it means charging $40. If the second firm charges $40, the first firm might view that as a grab for market share and respond in tit-for-tat fashion with a $35 price. A price war could then develop.

EXAMPLE 13.2 OLIGOPOLISTIC COOPERATION IN THE WATER METER INDUSTRY

For the past 30 years, almost all the water meters sold in the United States have been produced by four American companies: Rockwell International, Badger Meter, Neptune Water Meter Company, and Hersey Products. Rockwell has had about a 35 percent share of the market, and the other three firms have together had about a 50 to 55 percent share.[9]

Most buyers of water meters are municipal water utilities, who install the meters in residential and commercial establishments so that they can measure water consumption and bill consumers accordingly. Since the cost of the water meters is a small part of the total cost of providing water, the utilities are concerned mainly that the meters be accurate and reliable. The price of the meters is thus not a primary issue, and demand is very price inelastic. Utilities also tend to have long-standing relationships with suppliers and are reluctant to shift from one supplier to another. This creates a barrier to entry because any new entrant will find it difficult to lure customers from existing firms. Substantial economies of scale create a second barrier to entry: To capture a significant share of the market, a new entrant would have to invest in a large factory. This virtually precludes entry by new firms.

With inelastic demand and little threat of entry by new firms, the existing four firms could earn substantial monopoly profits if they set prices cooperatively. If, on the other hand, they compete aggressively, with each firm cutting price to try and increase its own share of the market, profits would fall to nearly competitive levels. The firms are thus in a Prisoners' Dilemma. Can cooperation prevail?

It can and *has* prevailed since the 1960s. Remember that the same four firms have been playing a *repeated game* for decades. Demand has been stable and predictable (the use of water meters has grown steadily along with population growth), and over the years the firms have been able to assess their own and each other's costs. In this situation, tit-for-tat strategies work well; it pays each firm to cooperate, as long as its competitors are cooperating.

So, the firms operate as though they were members of a country club. There is almost never any attempt to undercut price, and each firm appears satisfied

[9]This example is based in part on Nancy Taubenslag, "Rockwell International," Harvard Business School Case No. 9–383–019, July 1983.

with its share of the market. And while the business may appear dull, it is certainly profitable. All four firms have been earning returns on their investments that far exceed those in more competitive industries.

EXAMPLE 13.3   COMPETITION AND COLLUSION IN THE AIRLINE INDUSTRY

In March 1983, American Airlines, whose president, Robert Crandall, had become notable for his use of the telephone (see Example 10.4), proposed that all airlines adopt a uniform fare schedule based on mileage. The rate per mile would depend on the length of the trip, with the lowest rate of 15 cents per mile for trips over 2,500 miles, higher rates for shorter trips, and the highest rate, 53 cents per mile, for trips under 250 miles. For example, a one-way coach ticket from Boston to Chicago, a distance of 932 miles, would cost $233 (based on a rate of 25 cents per mile for trips between 751 and 1,000 miles).

This proposal would do away with the many different fares (some heavily discounted) then available. The cost of a ticket from one city to another would depend only on the number of miles between those cities. As a senior vice-president of American Airlines said, "The new streamlined fare structure will help reduce fare confusion." Most other major airlines reacted favorably to the plan and began to adopt it. A vice-president of TWA said, "It's a good move. It's very businesslike." United Airlines quickly announced that it would adopt the plan on routes where it competes with American, which includes most of its system, and TWA and Continental said that they would adopt it for all of their routes.[10]

Why did American Airlines propose this fare structure, and what made it so attractive to the other airlines? Was it really to "help reduce fare confusion"? No, the aim was to reduce price competition and achieve a collusive pricing arrangement. Prices had been driven down by competitive undercutting, as airlines competed for market share. And as Robert Crandall had learned less than a year earlier, fixing prices over the telephone is illegal. Instead, the companies would implicitly fix prices by agreeing to use the same formula for fares.

The plan failed, a victim of the Prisoners' Dilemma. Only two weeks after the plan was announced and adopted by most airlines, Pan Am, which was dissatisfied with its small share of the U.S. market, dropped its fares. American, United, and TWA, afraid of losing their own shares of the market, quickly dropped their fares to match Pan Am. The price-cutting continued, and fortunately for consumers, the plan was soon dead.[11]

---

[10]"American to Base Fares on Mileage," *New York Times*, March 15, 1983; "Most Big Airlines Back American's Fare Plan," *New York Times*, March 17, 1983.

[11]"Pan Am Drops Its U.S. Fares," *New York Times*, March 31, 1983.

This episode exemplifies the problem of oligopolistic pricing. One economist summarized it accurately: "You can't blame American Airlines for trying. After all, it is the American Way to try to cartelize prices with a simple formula. But it is also in the great tradition of open competition in this country to frustrate any such establishment of cartel prices by competitive chiseling."[12]

13.5 Threats, Commitments, and Credibility

We turn now to a broader set of strategic economic decisions: *What actions can a firm take to gain advantage in the marketplace?* For example, how might a firm deter entry by potential competitors, or induce existing competitors to raise prices, reduce output, or leave the market altogether? Or, how might a firm reach an implicit agreement with its competitors that is heavily weighted in its own favor?

Behavior that gives a firm this kind of advantage is called a *strategic move.* Perhaps the best definition of a strategic move was that given by Thomas Schelling, who was the first to explain the concept and its implications in 1960: "A strategic move is one that influences the other person's choice in a manner favorable to one's self, by affecting the other person's expectations on how one's self will behave. One constrains the partner's choice by constraining one's own behavior."[13]

The idea of constraining your own behavior to gain a strategic advantage may seem paradoxical, but we'll soon see that it is not. To see how various kinds of strategic moves can give one an economic advantage in the marketplace, we will discuss a few examples in detail.

The Advantage of Moving First

To begin, let's reexamine the product choice problem that we first discussed in Section 13.3. This involves two breakfast cereal companies who face a market in which two new variations of cereal can be successfully introduced, as long as each firm introduces only one variation. This time, let's change the payoff matrix slightly. As Table 13.7 shows, the new sweet cereal will inevitably be a better seller than the new crispy cereal, earning a profit of 20 rather than 10 (perhaps because consumers prefer sweet things to crispy things). Both the new

[12]Paul W. MacAvoy, "A Plan That Won't Endure Competition," *New York Times*, April 3, 1983.

[13]Thomas C. Schelling, *The Strategy of Conflict* (New York: Oxford University Press, 1960), p. 160. (1980 edition published by Harvard University Press.) For a general discussion of strategic moves as an element of business planning and strategy, see Michael E. Porter, *Competitive Strategy* (New York: Free Press, 1980).

TABLE 13.7 Modified Product Choice Problem

| | | Firm 2 | |
		Crispy	Sweet
Firm 1	Crispy	$-5, -5$	10, 20
	Sweet	20, 10	$-5, -5$

cereals will still be profitable, however, as long as each is introduced by only one firm. (Compare Table 13.7 with Table 13.3.)

Suppose that both firms, in ignorance of each other's intentions, must announce their decisions independently and simultaneously. Both will then probably introduce the sweet cereal—and both will lose money.

Now suppose, instead, that *one* of the two firms can introduce a new cereal first. That firm clearly has an advantage. It will introduce the sweet cereal, knowing that the only rational response for the other firm is to introduce the crispy cereal. Thus, whichever firm can gear up its production first will do better. (This is another example of "first-mover advantage." Recall that in the Stackelberg model from Chapter 12, the firm that makes its output decision before its competitors makes a higher profit.)

But even if both firms require the same amount of time to gear up production, each has an incentive to *commit itself first to the sweet cereal.* The key word is "commit." If Firm 1 simply announces it will produce the sweet cereal, Firm 2 will have little reason to believe it. After all, Firm 2, knowing the incentives, can make the same announcement louder and more vociferously. Firm 1 must constrain its own behavior—Firm 2 must be convinced that Firm 1 has *no choice* but to produce the sweet cereal. Such an action by Firm 1 might include an expensive advertising campaign describing the new sweet cereal well before its introduction, thereby putting Firm 1's reputation on the line. Firm 1 might also sign a contract for the forward delivery of a large quantity of sugar (and make the contract public, or at least send a copy to Firm 2). The idea is for Firm 1 to *commit itself* to produce the sweet cereal. Commitment is a strategic move that will induce Firm 2 to make the decision Firm 1 wants it to make—to produce the crispy cereal.

Why can't Firm 1 simply *threaten* Firm 2, vowing to produce the sweet cereal even if Firm 2 does the same? Because Firm 2 has little reason to believe the threat and can make the same threat itself. A threat is useful only if it is credible. The following example should help make this clear.

Empty Threats

Suppose Firm 1 produces personal computers that can be used both as word processors and to do other tasks. Firm 2 produces only dedicated word processors. As the payoff matrix in Table 13.8 shows, as long as Firm 1 charges a high

TABLE 13.8 Pricing of Computers and Word Processors

		Firm 2	
		High Price	Low Price
Firm 1	High Price	100,80	80,100
	Low Price	20,0	10,20

price for its computers, both firms can make a good deal of money. Even if Firm 2 charges a low price for its word processors, many people will still buy Firm 1's computers (because they can do so many other things), although some will be induced by the price differential to buy the dedicated word processor instead. However, if Firm 1 charges a low price for its computers, Firm 2 will also have to charge a low price (or else make zero profit), and the profit of both firms will be significantly reduced.

Firm 1 would prefer the outcome in the upper left-hand corner of the matrix. For Firm 2, however, charging a low price is clearly a dominant strategy. Thus, the outcome in the upper right-hand corner will prevail (no matter which firm sets its price first).

Firm 1 would probably be viewed as the "dominant" firm in this industry, because its pricing actions will have the greatest impact on overall industry profits. Then, can't Firm 1 induce Firm 2 to charge a high price by *threatening* to charge a low price itself if Firm 2 charges a low price? No, as the payoff matrix in Table 13.8 makes clear. *Whatever* Firm 2 does, Firm 1 will be much worse off if it charges a low price. As a result, its threat is not credible.

Commitment and Credibility

Sometimes firms can make a threat credible. To see how, consider the following example. Race Car Motors, Inc., produces cars, and Far Out Engines, Ltd., produces specialty car engines. Far Out Engines sells most of its engines to Race Car Motors, and a few to a limited outside market. Nonetheless, it depends heavily on Race Car Motors, and makes its production decisions in response to the production plans of Race Car Motors.

We thus have a game in which Race Car Motors is the "leader." It will decide what kind of cars to build, and Far Out Engines will then decide what kind of engines to produce. (A game in which one of the players moves first, and the other players moves second, is called a *sequential game*.) The payoff matrix in Table 13.9a shows the possible outcomes of this game. (Profits are in millions of dollars.) The payoff matrix makes it clear that Race Car Motors will do best by deciding to produce small cars. It knows that in response to this, Far Out Engines will produce small engines, most of which Race Car Motors will then

TABLE 13.9a Production Choice Problem

		Race Car Motors	
		Small Cars	Big Cars
Far Out Engines	Small Engines	3,6	3,0
	Big Engines	1,1	8,3

buy for its new cars. As a result, Far Out Engines will make $3 million, and Race Car Motors will earn $6 million.

Far Out Engines, however, would much prefer the outcome in the lower right-hand corner of the payoff matrix. If it could produce big engines, *and* Race Car Motors produced big cars and therefore bought the big engines, it would make $8 million. (Race Car Motors, however, would make only $3 million.) Can Far Out Engines induce Race Car Motors to produce big cars instead of small ones?

Suppose Far Out Engines *threatens* to produce big engines no matter what Race Car Motors does, and no other engine producer can easily satisfy the needs of Race Car Motors. If Race Car Motors believed the threat, it would want to produce big cars, since it would have trouble finding engines for its small cars, and would therefore earn only $1 million instead of $3 million. But the threat is not credible. Once Race Car Motors announced its intentions to produce small cars, Far Out Engines would have no incentive to carry out its threat.

Far Out Engines must make a strategic move to make its threat credible. This means visibly and irreversibly reducing some of *its own* payoffs in the matrix, so that its choices become constrained. In particular, Far Out Engines must reduce its profits from small engines (the payoffs in the top row of the matrix). It might do this by *shutting down or destroying some of its small engine production capacity*. This would result in the payoff matrix shown in Table 13.9b. Now Race Car Motors *knows* that whatever kind of car it produces, Far Out Engines will produce big engines. (If Race Car Motors produces the small cars, Far Out Engines will sell the big engines as best it can to other car producers, and will make only $1 million. But this is better than making no profits by producing small engines. Race Car Motors will also have to look elsewhere for its engines,

TABLE 13.9b Modified Production Choice Problem

		Race Car Motors	
		Small Cars	Big Cars
Far Out Engines	Small Engines	0,6	0,0
	Big Engines	1,1	8,3

so its profit will also be lower, at $1 million.) Now it is clearly in Race Car Motor's interest to produce the large cars. By making a strategic move that *seemingly puts itself at a disadvantage,* Far Out Engines has improved the outcome of the game.

Strategic commitments of this kind can be effective, but they are risky and depend heavily on the committing firm's having accurate knowledge of the payoff matrix and the industry. Suppose, for example, that Far Out Engines commits itself to producing big engines, but is surprised to find that another firm can produce small engines at a low cost. The commitment may then lead Far Out Engines to bankruptcy rather than to continued high profits.

Developing a *reputation* can also give one a strategic advantage, and developing the right kind of reputation can be viewed as a strategic move. Again, consider Far Out Engines' desire to produce big engines for Race Car Motors' big cars. Suppose the managers of Far Out Engines develop a reputation for being irrational—perhaps downright crazy. They threaten to produce big engines no matter what Race Car Motors does. (Refer to Table 13.9a.) Now the threat might be credible without any further action; after all, you can't be sure that an irrational manager will always make a profit-maximizing decision. In gaming situations, the party that is known (or thought) to be a little crazy can have a significant advantage. The game of "chicken" (two cars careen toward each other, and the first driver to swerve to the side is the loser) is a dramatic example of this.

Developing a reputation can be an especially important strategy in a repeated game. A firm might find it advantageous to behave irrationally for several plays of the game. This might give it a reputation that will allow it to increase its long-run profits substantially.

EXAMPLE 13.4 WAL-MART STORES' PREEMPTIVE INVESTMENT STRATEGY

Wal-Mart Stores, Inc., is an enormously successful chain of discount retail stores started by Sam Walton in 1969.[14] Its success was unusual in the industry. During the 1960s and 1970s, rapid expansion by existing firms and the entry and expansion of new firms made discount retailing increasingly competitive. During the 1970s and 1980s, industrywide profits fell, and large discount chains—including such giants as King's, Korvette's, Mammoth Mart, W.T. Grant, and Woolco—went bankrupt. Wal-Mart Stores, however, kept on growing (from 153 stores in 1976 to 1009 in 1986) and became even more profitable. By the end of 1985, Sam Walton was one of the richest people in the United States.[15]

---

[14]This example is based on information in Pankaj Ghemawat, "Wal-Mart Stores' Discount Operations," Harvard Business School, 1986.

[15]In October 1985 he and his children owned stock in Wal-Mart worth about $2.8 billion. Walton's net worth increased to over $4 billion by April 1986, and *Forbes* magazine called him the nation's richest person.

TABLE 13.10 The Discount Store Preemption Game

		Company X	
		Enter	Don't Enter
Wal-Mart	Enter	−10, −10	20, 0
	Don't Enter	0, 20	0, 0

How did Wal-Mart Stores succeed where others failed? The key is in Wal-Mart's expansion strategy. To charge less than ordinary department stores and small retail stores, discount stores rely on size, no frills, and high inventory turnover. Through the 1960s, the conventional wisdom held that a discount store could succeed only in a city with a population of 100,000 or more. Sam Walton disagreed and decided to open his stores in small Southwestern towns; by 1970 there were 30 Wal-Mart stores in small towns in Arkansas, Missouri, and Oklahoma. The stores succeeded because Wal-Mart had created 30 "local monopolies." Discount stores that had opened in larger towns and cities were competing with other discount stores, which drove prices and profit margins down. These small towns, however, had room for only one discount operation. Wal-Mart could undercut the nondiscount retailers but never had to worry that another discount store would open and compete with it.

By the mid-1970s other discount chains realized that Wal-Mart had a profitable strategy: Open a store in a small town that could support only one discount store and enjoy a local monopoly. There are a lot of small towns in the United States, so the issue became who would get to each town first. Wal-Mart now found itself in a *preemption game* of the sort illustrated by the payoff matrix in Table 13.10. As the matrix shows, if Wal-Mart enters a town, but Company X doesn't, Wal-Mart would make 20 and Company X would make 0. Similarly, if Wal-Mart doesn't enter but Company X does, Wal-Mart makes 0 and Company X makes 20. But if Wal-Mart and Company X *both* enter, *they will both lose 10.*

This game has two Nash equilibria—the lower left-hand corner and the upper right-hand corner. Which equilibrium results depends on *who moves first.* If Wal-Mart moves first, it can enter, knowing that the rational response of Company X will be not to enter, so that Wal-Mart will be assured of earning 20. *The trick is therefore to preempt*—to set up stores in other small towns quickly, before Company X (or Companies Y or Z) can do so. That is exactly what Wal-Mart did. By 1986 it had 1009 stores in operation and was earning an annual profit of $450 million, while other discount chains were going under.[16]

---

[16]"Wal-Mart Net Climbs 38.5%," *New York Times*, March 5, 1987; "Many Bullish On Wal-Mart," *New York Times*, June 10, 1987.

13.6 Entry Deterrence

We have seen that barriers to entry, which are an important source of monopoly power and profits, sometimes arise naturally. For example, economies of scale, patents and licenses, or access to critical inputs can create entry barriers. However, firms themselves can sometimes deter entry by potential competitors.

To deter entry, *the incumbent firm must convince any potential competitor that entry will be unprofitable.* To see how this might be done, put yourself in the position of an incumbent monopolist facing a prospective entrant, Firm X. Suppose that to enter the industry, Firm X will have to pay a (sunk) cost of $40 million to build a plant. You, of course, would like to induce Firm X to stay out of the industry. If X stays out, you can continue to charge a high price and enjoy monopoly profits. As shown in the upper right-hand corner of the payoff matrix in Table 13.11a, you would then earn $100 million in profits.

If Firm X does enter the market, you must make a decision. You can be "accommodating," maintaining a high price in the hope that X will do the same. You will then earn only $50 million in profit because you will have to share the market. The new entrant X will earn a *net* profit of $10 million: $50 million less the $40 million cost of constructing a plant. (This outcome is shown in the upper left-hand corner of the payoff matrix.) Alternatively, you can increase your production capacity, produce more, and force price down. Increasing production capacity is costly, however, and lower prices will mean lower revenues. Warfare will therefore mean lower profits for both you and Firm X. As Table 13.11a shows, your profit will fall to $30 million, and Firm X will have a net loss of $10 million: the $30 million that it earns from sales less the $40 million for the cost of its plant.

If Firm X thinks you will be accommodating and maintain a high price after entry, it will find it profitable to enter and will do so. Suppose you threaten to expand output and fight a price war to keep X out. If X believed the threat, it would not enter the market because it would expect to lose $10 million. However, the threat is not credible. As Table 13.11a shows (and as the potential competitor knows), *once entry has occurred, it will be in your best interest to accommodate and maintain a high price.* Firm X knows this, and its rational move is to

TABLE 13.11a Entry Possibilities

		Potential Entrant	
		Enter	Stay Out
Incumbent	High Price (Accommodation)	50,10	100,0
	Low Price (Warfare)	30, −10	40,0

TABLE 13.11b Entry Deterrence

| | | Potential Entrant | |
		Enter	Stay Out
Incumbent	High Price (Accommodation)	20,10	70,0
	Low Price (Warfare)	30, −10	40,0

enter the market; the outcome will be the upper left-hand corner of the payoff matrix.

But what if you can make an irrevocable commitment that would alter your incentives once entry occurred—a commitment that would give you little choice but to charge a low price if entry occurred? In particular, suppose you invest *now*, rather than later, in the extra capacity needed to increase output and engage in competitive warfare should entry occur. We'll assume that this extra capacity will cost $30 million to build, maintain, and operate. Of course, if you later maintain a high price (whether or not X enters), this added cost will reduce your payoffs.

We now have a new payoff matrix, as shown in Table 13.11b. Now your threat to engage in competitive warfare if entry occurs is *completely credible*, as a result of your decision to invest in additional capacity. Because you have the additional capacity, you will do better in competitive warfare, if entry occurs, than you would by maintaining a high price. The potential competitor now knows that entry will result in warfare, so it is rational for it to stay out of the market. You can therefore maintain a high price, and earn a profit of $70 million, having deterred entry.[17]

Might an incumbent monopolist deter entry without making the costly move of installing additional production capacity? Earlier we saw that a reputation for irrationality can bestow a strategic advantage. Suppose the incumbent firm has such a reputation. Suppose also that with vicious price-cutting, this firm has eventually driven out every entrant in the past, even though it incurred (rationally unwarranted) losses in doing so. Its threat might then indeed be credible. A rational firm considering entry must take its opponent's irrationality into account when making decisions. In this case the incumbent's irrationality suggests to the potential competitor that it might be better off by staying away.

Of course, if the game described above were to be *indefinitely repeated*, then the incumbent might have a *rational* incentive to carry out the threat of warfare whenever entry actually occurs. The reason is that short-term losses from war-

---

[17]This use of investment in excess capacity to deter entry is discussed in more detail in Avinash Dixit, "Recent Developments in Oligopoly Theory," *American Economic Review* 72 (May 1982): 12–16. For a general discussion of capacity expansion, see Marvin B. Lieberman, "Strategies for Capacity Expansion," *Sloan Management Review* (Summer 1987): 19–27.

fare might be outweighed by longer-term gains from preventing entry. Furthermore, the potential competitor, making the same calculations, might find the incumbent's threat of warfare credible and decide to stay out of the market. Now the incumbent relies on its reputation for being rational—and in particular for being far-sighted—to provide the credibility needed to deter entry. But whether this works depends on the time horizon and the relative gains and losses associated with accommodation and warfare.

We have seen that the attractiveness of entry depends largely on how incumbents can be expected to react.[18] In general, incumbents cannot be expected to maintain output at the preentry level once entry has occurred. Eventually, incumbents may back off and reduce output, raising price to a new joint profit-maximizing level. Because potential entrants know this, incumbent firms must create a credible threat of warfare to deter entry. A reputation for irrationality can help do this. Indeed, this seems to be the basis for much of the entry-preventing behavior that goes on in actual markets. The potential entrant must consider that *rational* industry discipline can break down after entry occurs.

There is a useful analogy here to *nuclear deterrence*.[19] Consider the problem of using a nuclear threat to deter the Soviets from invading Western Europe. If they invaded, would the United States actually respond with nuclear weapons, knowing that the Soviets would then respond in kind? It is not rational for the United States to respond this way, so the threat of nuclear response might not appear credible. But this assumes that everyone is rational. The Soviets might have good reason to fear an *irrational* response by the United States. Even if an irrational response is viewed as having a very small probability, it can deter a Soviet attack on Europe, given the costliness of an error. The United States can thus gain by promoting the idea that it will act irrationally, or that events might get out of control once an invasion occurs. This is the "rationality of irrationality."

EXAMPLE 13.5 DU PONT DETERS ENTRY IN THE TITANIUM DIOXIDE INDUSTRY

Titanium dioxide is a whitener used in paints, paper, and other products. In the early 1970s, Du Pont and National Lead each accounted for about a third of U.S. titanium dioxide sales; another seven firms produced the remainder. In

---

[18]In older theories, established firms were assumed to maintain their output levels when entry occurs. This gave a key role to scale economies. To see how, suppose a new entrant enters at *minimum efficient scale* (MES). Then, the larger the MES is relative to total industry output, the more price will be depressed by the new entrant. The potential entrant, figuring this out, will see less of an incentive to enter. Thus, *the greater the MES, the higher price can be above the competitive level without attracting new entry*. In this way, high MES (scale economies) becomes an effective entry barrier.

[19]This analogy was made in F. M. Scherer, *Industrial Market Structure and Economic Performance*, 2nd ed. (Boston: Houghton Mifflin, 1980), p. 246.

1972, Du Pont was weighing whether to expand its capacity. The industry was changing, and with the right strategy, those changes might enable Du Pont to capture more of the market and dominate the industry.[20]

Three factors had to be considered. First, although the future demand for titanium dioxide was uncertain, it was expected to grow substantially. Second, the government had announced that new environmental regulations would be imposed. And third, the prices of raw materials used to make titanium dioxide were rising. The new regulations and the higher input prices would have a major effect on production cost, and give Du Pont a cost advantage both because its production technology was less sensitive to the change in input prices and because its plants were in areas that made disposal of corrosive wastes much less difficult than it would be for other producers. Because of these cost changes, Du Pont anticipated that National Lead and some of the other producers would have to shut down part of their capacity. Du Pont's competitors would in effect have to "reenter" the market by building new plants. Could Du Pont deter them from doing this?

In 1972, Du Pont's Executive Committee considered the following strategy: invest nearly $400 million in increased production capacity to try to capture 64 percent of the market by 1985. The production capacity that would be put on line would be much more than what was actually needed. The idea was to *deter Du Pont's competitors from investing.* Scale economies and movement down the learning curve would give Du Pont a cost advantage.[21] This would make it hard for other firms to compete, and would make credible the implicit threat that Du Pont would fight in the future, rather than accommodate.

The strategy was sensible, and it seemed to work for a few years. By 1975, however, things began to go awry. First, demand grew much less than expected, so that there was excess capacity industrywide. Second, the environmental regulations were only weakly enforced, so that Du Pont's competitors did not have to shut down capacity as expected. And finally, Du Pont's strategy led to antitrust action by the Federal Trade Commission in 1978. (The FTC claimed that Du Pont was attempting to monopolize the market. Du Pont won the case, but the decline in demand made its victory moot.)

---

[20]This example is based on Pankaj Ghemawat, "Capacity Expansion in the Titanium Dioxide Industry," *Journal of Industrial Economics* 33 (Dec. 1984): 145–163; and P. Ghemawat "Du Pont in Titanium Dioxide," Harvard Business School, Case No. 9–385–140, June 1986.

[21]The learning curve refers to cost reductions that take place as a result of experience with a production technology. It is discussed in Chapter 7.

EXAMPLE 13.6 DIAPER WARS

For more than a decade, the disposable diaper industry in the United States has been dominated by just two firms: Procter & Gamble, with an approximately 65 percent market share, and Kimberly-Clark, with another 20 to 25 percent.[22] How do these firms compete? And why haven't other firms been able to enter and take a significant share of this $3 billion per year market?

Even though there are only two major firms, competition is intense. The competition occurs mostly in the form of *cost-reducing innovation*. The key to success is to perfect the manufacturing process, so that a plant can manufacture diapers in high volume and at low cost. This is not as simple as it might seem. Packing cellulose fluff for absorbency, adding an elastic gatherer, and binding, folding, and packaging the diapers—at a rate of about 3,000 diapers per minute and at a cost of about 6 to 8 cents per diaper—requires an innovative, carefully designed, and finely tuned process. Furthermore, small technological improvements in the manufacturing process can result in a significant competitive advantage. If a firm can shave its production cost even slightly, it can reduce price and capture market share. As a result, both firms are forced to spend heavily on R&D in a race to reduce cost.[23]

The payoff matrix in Table 13.12 illustrates this. If both firms spend aggressively on R&D, they can expect to maintain their current market shares. P&G will then earn a profit of 40, and Kimberly (with a smaller market share) will earn 20. If neither firm spends money on R&D, their costs and prices would remain constant, and the money saved from R&D would become part of profits. P&G's profit would increase to 60, and Kimberly's to 40. However, if one firm continues to do R&D and the other firm doesn't, the innovating firm will eventually capture most of its competitor's market share. (For example, if Kimberly does R&D and P&G doesn't, P&G can expect to lose 20, while Kimberly's profit increases to 60.) The two firms are therefore in a Prisoners' Dilemma; spending money on R&D is a dominant strategy for each firm.

The ongoing R&D expenditures by P&G and Kimberly-Clark also serve to deter entry. In addition to brand name recognition, these two firms have accumulated so much technological know-how and manufacturing proficiency that they would have a substantial cost advantage over any firm just entering the market. Besides building new factories, an entrant would have to spend a considerable amount on R&D to capture even a small share of the market. After it began producing, a new firm would have to continue to spend heavily on

---

[22]Procter & Gamble makes Pampers, Ultra Pampers, and Luvs. Kimberly-Clark has only one major brand, Huggies.

[23]See Michael E. Porter, "The Disposable Diaper Industry," Harvard Business School Case 9–380–175, July 1981, and "Innovation Key to Diaper War," *New York Times*, Nov. 25, 1986. Recently P&G developed a superabsorbent chemical to replace the cellulose fluff, allowing for a thinner and lighter diaper.

TABLE 13.12 Competing Through R&D

		Kimberly-Clark R&D	No R&D
P&G	R&D	40,20	80, −20
	No R&D	−20,60	60,40

R&D to reduce its costs over time. Entry would be profitable only if P&G and Kimberly-Clark stop doing R&D, so that the entrant could catch up and eventually gain a cost advantage. But as we have seen, no rational firm would expect this to happen.[24]

13.7 Bargaining Strategy

In looking at the Prisoners' Dilemma and related problems, we have assumed that collusion was limited by an inability to make an enforceable agreement. Clearly, alternative outcomes are possible (and likely) if firms or individuals can make promises that can be enforced. The Prisoners' Dilemma illustrated by the pricing problem shown in Table 13.6 is a good example of this. If there were no antitrust laws and both firms could make an enforceable agreement about pricing, they would both charge a high price and make profits of 50. Here, the bargaining problem is simple.

Other bargaining situations that often arise in economics are more complicated, however, and the outcome can depend on the ability of either side to make a strategic move that alters its relative bargaining position. For example, consider two firms that are each planning to introduce one of two products, which happen to be complementary goods. As the payoff matrix of Table 13.13

TABLE 13.13 Production Decision

		Firm 2 Produce A	Produce B
Firm 1	Produce A	40,5	50,50
	Produce B	60,40	5,45

[24]Example 15.3 in Chapter 15 examines in more detail the profitability of capital investment by a new entrant in the diaper market.

TABLE 13.14 Decision to Join Consortium

		Firm 2	
		Work Alone	Enter Consortium
Firm 1	Work Alone	10,10	10,20
	Enter Consortium	20,10	40,40

shows, Firm 1 has an advantage in producing A, so that if both firms produce A, Firm 1 will be able to maintain a lower price and will make much higher profits. Similarly, Firm 2 has an advantage in producing product B. As should be clear from the payoff matrix, if the two firms could agree about who will produce what, the only rational outcome would be that in the upper right-hand corner. Firm 1 produces A, Firm 2 produces B, and both firms make profits of 50. Indeed, even *without cooperation* this outcome will result, whether Firm 1 or Firm 2 moves first or both firms move simultaneously. The reason is that producing B is a dominant strategy for Firm 2, so (A, B) is the only Nash equilibrium.

Firm 1 would, of course, prefer the outcome in the lower left-hand corner of the payoff matrix. But in the context of this limited set of decisions, it cannot achieve that outcome. Suppose, however, that Firms 1 and 2 are also bargaining over a second issue—whether to join a research consortium that a third firm is trying to form. Table 13.14 shows the payoff matrix for this decision problem. Clearly, the dominant strategy is for both firms to enter the consortium, thereby obtaining increased profits of 40.

Now consider the following strategic move for Firm 1. Firm 1 *links the two bargaining problems* by announcing that it will join the consortium *only* if Firm 2 agrees to produce product A. (How can Firm 1 make this threat credible?) In this case it is indeed in Firm 2's interest to agree to produce A (with Firm 1 producing B), in return for Firm 1's participation in the consortium. This example illustrates how a strategic move can be used in bargaining, and why combining issues in a bargaining agenda can sometimes benefit one side at the other's expense.

Two people bargaining over the price of a house is another good illustration of how a strategic move can improve one's bargaining position.[25] Suppose I, as a potential buyer, do not want to pay more than $100,000 for a house that is actually worth $150,000 to me. The seller is ultimately willing to part with the house at any price above $90,000 but would like to receive the highest price she can. If I am the only bidder for the house, how can I make the seller think I will walk away rather than pay more than $100,000?

---

[25]This example is due to Thomas Schelling, *The Strategy of Conflict.*

I might declare—in effect promise—that I will never, ever pay more than $100,000 for that house. But is such a promise credible? It is if the seller knows that I have a *strong reputation* for toughness and steadfastness, if she knows that I have never, ever broken my word on a promise of this sort. In fact, *the development of a tough reputation* can be viewed as a strategic move to improve one's position in all bargaining situations of this sort.

But suppose I have no such reputation. Then the seller knows that I have every incentive to make the promise (making it costs nothing), but little incentive to keep it (since this will probably be our only business transaction together). As a result, this promise by itself is not likely to improve my bargaining position.

The promise can work, however, if it is combined with a strategic move that gives it credibility. Such a strategic move must reduce my flexibility—limit my options—so that I have no choice but to keep the promise. A possible move would be to make an enforceable bet with a third party—for example, "If I pay more than $100,000 for that house, I'll pay you $60,000." Alternatively, if I am buying the house on behalf of my company, the company might insist on authorization by the Board of Directors for a price above $100,000, and announce that the board will not meet again for several months. In both cases, my promise becomes credible because I have destroyed my ability to break it. The result is less flexibility—and more bargaining power.

Summary

1. Games can be cooperative or noncooperative. A game is cooperative if the players can communicate with one another and arrange binding contracts; otherwise it is noncooperative. In playing either kind of game, however, the most important aspect of strategy design is understanding your opponent's position, and (if your opponent is rational) correctly deducing the likely response to your actions. Misjudging an opponent's position is a common mistake, as Example 13.1, "Acquiring a Company," illustrates.[26]

2. A Nash equilibrium is a set of strategies such that each player is doing the best it can, given the strategies of the other players. An equilibrium in dominant strategies is a special case of a Nash equilibrium; a dominant strategy is optimal no matter what the other players do. A Nash equilibrium relies on the rationality of each player. A maximin strategy is more conservative because it maximizes the minimum possible outcome.

[26]Here is the solution to Company A's problem: *It should offer nothing for Company T's stock.* To see why, remember that Company T will accept an offer only if it is greater than the per share value under current management. Suppose you offer $50. Then Company T will accept this offer only if the results of the exploration project result in a per share value of $50 or less. Any values between $0 and $150 are equally likely. Therefore the *expected value* of Company T's stock, *given that it accepts the offer*, i.e., given that the outcome of the exploration project leads to a value less than $50, is $25, so that under the management of Company A the value would be $(1.5)(\$25) = \$37.5$, which is less than $50. In fact, for any price P, if the offer is accepted, Company A can expect a value of only $(\frac{3}{4})P$.

3. Strategies that are not optimal for a one-shot game may be optimal for a repeated game. Depending on the number of repetitions, a "tit-for-tat" strategy, in which one plays cooperatively as long as one's competitor does the same, may be optimal for the repeated Prisoners' Dilemma.

4. In some strategic situations, the player that moves first has an advantage. Players may then have an incentive to try to precommit themselves to particular actions before their competitors can do the same.

5. An empty threat is a threat that one would have no incentive to carry out. If one's competitors are rational, empty threats are of no value. To make a threat credible, it is sometimes necessary to constrain one's later behavior, so that there would indeed be an incentive to carry out the threat. Such an action is called a "strategic move." Developing a reputation is sometimes a strategic move.

6. To deter entry, an incumbent firm must convince any potential competitor that entry will be unprofitable. This may be done by giving credibility to the threat that entry will be met by price warfare.

7. Bargaining situations are examples of cooperative games. As with noncooperative games, in bargaining one can sometimes gain a strategic advantage by limiting one's flexibility.

Review Questions

1. What is the difference between a cooperative and a noncooperative game? Give an example of each.

2. What is a dominant strategy? Why is an equilibrium in dominant strategies stable?

3. Explain the meaning of a Nash equilibrium. How does it differ from an equilibrium in dominant strategies?

4. How does a Nash equilibrium differ from a game's maximin solution? In what situations is a maximin solution a more likely outcome than a Nash equilibrium?

5. What is a "tit-for-tat" strategy? Why is it a rational strategy for the infinitely repeated Prisoners' Dilemma?

6. Consider a game in which the Prisoners' Dilemma is repeated 10 times, and both players are rational and fully informed. Is a tit-for-tat strategy optimal in this case? Under what conditions would such a strategy be optimal?

7. Suppose you and your competitor are playing the pricing game shown in Table 13.6. Both of you must announce your prices at the same time. Might you improve your outcome by promising your competitor that you will announce a high price?

8. What is meant by "first-mover advantage"? Give an example of a gaming situation with a first-mover advantage.

9. What is a "strategic move"? How can the development of a certain kind of reputation be a strategic move?

10. Can the threat of a price war deter entry by potential competitors? What kinds of strategic moves might a firm take to make this threat credible?

11. A strategic move limits one's flexibility and yet gives one an advantage. Why? How might a strategic move give one an advantage in bargaining?

Exercises

1. In many oligopolistic industries, the same firms compete over a long period of time, setting prices and observing each other's behavior repeatedly. Given that the number of repetitions is large, why don't collusive outcomes typically result?

2. Two computer firms, A and B, are planning to market network systems for office information management. Each firm can develop either a fast, high-quality system (H), or a slower, low-quality system (L). Market research indicates that the resulting profits to each firm for the alternative strategies are given by the following payoff matrix:

		Firm B	
		H	L
Firm A	H	30,30	50,35
	L	40,60	20,20

a. If both firms make their decisions at the same time and follow *maximin* (low-risk) strategies, what will the outcome be?

b. Suppose both firms try to maximize profits, but Firm A has a head start in planning, and therefore can commit first. Now what will the outcome be? What will the outcome be if Firm B has the head start in planning and can commit first?

c. Getting a head start costs money (you have to gear up a large engineering team). Now consider the *two-stage* game in which *first*, each firm decides how much money to spend to speed up its planning, and *second*, it announces which product (H or L) it will produce. Which firm will spend more to speed up its planning? How much will it spend? Should the other firm spend *anything* to speed up its planning? Explain briefly.

3. Many industries are often plagued by overcapacity—firms simultaneously make major investments in capacity expansion, so that total capacity far exceeds demand. This happens in industries in which demand is highly volatile and unpredictable, but also in industries in which demand is fairly stable. What factors lead to overcapacity? Explain each briefly.

4. You are a duopolist producer of a homogeneous good. Both you and your competitor have *zero* marginal costs. The market demand curve is given by

$$P = 30 - Q$$

where $Q = Q_1 + Q_2$. Q_1 is your output, and Q_2 is your competitor's output. Your competitor has also read this book.

a. Suppose you are to play this game only once. If you and your competitor must announce your outputs at the same time, how much will you choose to produce? What do you expect your profit to be? Explain.

b. Suppose you are told that you must announce your output before your competitor does. How much will you produce in this case, and how much do you think your competitor will produce? What do you expect your profit to be? Is announcing first an advantage or disadvantage? Explain briefly. *How much would you pay* to be given the option of announcing either first or second?

c. Suppose instead that you are to play the first round of a *series of ten rounds* (with the same competitor). In each round you and your competitor announce your outputs at the same time. You want to maximize the sum of your profits over the ten rounds. How much will you produce *in the first round?* How much would you expect to produce in the tenth round? The ninth round? Explain briefly.

d. Once again you will play a series of ten rounds. This time, however, in each round your competitor will announce its output before you announce yours. How will your answers to (c) change in this case?

CHAPTER 14

Markets for Factor Inputs

So far as we have concentrated on *output markets*, i.e., markets for goods and services that firms sell and consumers purchase. In this chapter we discuss *factor markets*—markets for labor, raw materials, and other inputs to production. Much of our material will be familiar, because the same forces that shape supply and demand in output markets also affect factor markets.

We have seen that output markets can differ greatly in their structure. Some markets are perfectly or almost perfectly competitive, while in others producers have market power. The same is true for factor markets. We will examine three different factor market structures: (1) perfectly competitive factor markets, (2) markets in which buyers of factors have monopsony power, and (3) markets in which sellers of factors have monopoly power. We will also point out instances in which equilibrium in the factor market depends on how much market power there is in *output* markets.

14.1 Competitive Factor Markets

A competitive factor market is one in which there are a large number of sellers and buyers of the factor of production. Because no single seller or buyer can affect the price of the factor, each of them is a price taker. For example, if individual firms that buy lumber to construct homes purchase a small share of the total volume of lumber available, their purchasing decision will have no effect on its price. Similarly, if suppliers of lumber each control a small share of the market, their supply decisions will not affect the price of the lumber they sell.

We begin by analyzing the demands for a factor by individual firms. These demands are added to get market demand. We then shift to the supply side of the market and show how market price and input levels are determined.

Demand for a Factor Input When Only One Input Is Variable

Demand curves for factors of production are downward-sloping, just like demand curves for the final goods that result from the production process, but for a different reason. Unlike consumers' demands for goods and services, factor demands (such as the demand for labor) are *derived demands*—they depend on, and are derived from, the firm's level of output and the costs of inputs (such as the wage rate). For example, the demand of Apple Computer for computer programmers is a derived demand that depends not only on the current salaries of programmers, but also on how many computers and how much software Apple expects to sell.

To analyze factor demands, we will use the material from Chapter 7 that shows how a firm chooses its production inputs. We will assume that the firm produces its output using two inputs, capital K and labor L, that can be purchased at the prices r (the rental cost of capital) and w (the wage rate), respectively.[1] We will also suppose that the firm has its plant and equipment in place (as in a short-run analysis), but must decide how much labor to hire.

The firm has already hired a certain number of workers and wants to know whether it is profitable to hire one additional worker. Hiring this additional worker is worthwhile if the additional revenue is greater than the cost. The additional revenue from an incremental unit of labor is called the *marginal revenue product of labor*, and is denoted MRP_L. We know that the firm should hire more labor if the MRP_L is at least as large as the wage cost w.

How do we measure the MRP_L? It's the additional output obtained from the additional unit of labor, multiplied by the additional revenue from an extra unit of output. The additional output is given by the marginal product of labor MP_L and the additional revenue by the marginal revenue MR. Thus[2]

$$MRP_L = (MP_L)(MR) \tag{14.1}$$

This important result holds for any competitive factor market, whether the output market is competitive or not. However, to examine the characteristics of the MRP_L, let's begin with the case of a perfectly competitive output (and input) market. In a competitive output market, a firm will sell all its output at the market price P. The marginal revenue from the sale of an additional unit of output is then equal to P. In this case the marginal revenue product of labor is equal to the marginal product of labor times the price of the product:

$$MRP_L = (MP_L)(P) \tag{14.2}$$

---

[1] We implicitly assume that all inputs to production are identical in quality. Differences in workers' skills and abilities are discussed in Chapter 17.

[2] The marginal revenue product is $\Delta R/\Delta L$, where L is the number of units of labor input and R is revenue. Note that $MP_L = \Delta Q/\Delta L$, and $MR = \Delta R/\Delta Q$, where Q is output. Therefore, $MRP_L = \Delta R/\Delta L = (\Delta R/\Delta Q)(\Delta Q/\Delta L) = (MR)(MP_L)$.

The higher of the two curves in Figure 14.1 represents the MRP_L curve for a firm in a competitive output market in which firms have no monopoly power. Note that the marginal product of labor falls as the number of hours of labor increases because there are diminishing returns to labor. The marginal revenue product curve thus slopes downward, even though the price of the product is constant.

The lower curve in Figure 14.1 is the MRP_L curve when the firm has monopoly power in the output market. When firms have monopoly power, they must lower the price of all units of the product to sell more of it. As a result, marginal revenue is always less than price ($MR < P$), and marginal revenue falls as output increases. Thus, the marginal revenue product curve slopes downward in this case because the marginal revenue curve *and* the marginal product curve both slope downward.

Let's compare the MRP_L curve without monopoly power with the same curve in which the firm has monopoly power. The MRP_L curve with monopoly power is steeper than the MRP_L curve without monopoly power and lies below it.

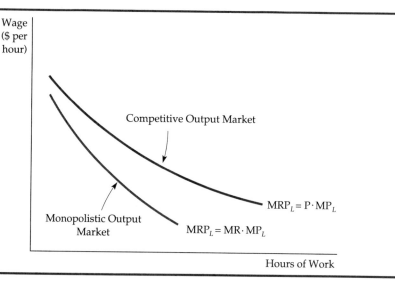

FIGURE 14.1   Marginal Revenue Product.   In a competitive factor market in which the producer of the product is a price taker, the buyer's demand for that input is given by the marginal revenue product curve. The marginal revenue product curve falls because the marginal product of labor falls as labor increases. When the producer of the product has monopoly power, the demand for the input is also given by the marginal revenue product curve, but the marginal revenue product curve falls because both the marginal product of labor and marginal revenue fall. As a result, the marginal revenue product curve is more inelastic when the producer has monopoly power than the marginal revenue product curve in the competitive case.

Formally,

$$\text{MRP}_L \text{ (Monopoly Power)} = (\text{MP}_L)(\text{MR}) < (\text{MP}_L)(P)$$

$$= \text{MRP}_L \text{ (No Monopoly Power)}$$

One implication of this result is that, for any given wage, firms with monopoly power in their output market will hire fewer workers than similar firms that have no monopoly power.

The concept of marginal revenue product can be applied to the hiring of workers by firms. However competitive the output market, the marginal revenue product tells us how much the firm will pay to hire an additional unit of labor. As long as the MRP_L is greater than the wage rate, the firm should hire an additional unit of labor. If the marginal revenue product is less than the wage rate, the firm should lay off workers. Only when the marginal revenue product is equal to the wage will the firm have hired the profit-maximizing amount of labor. So the profit-maximizing condition is

$$\text{MRP}_L = w \qquad (14.3)$$

Figure 14.2 illustrates this condition. The demand for labor curve D_L is the MRP_L. Note that the quantity of labor demanded increases as the wage rate falls. Since the labor market is perfectly competitive, the firm can hire as many workers as it wants at the market wage w^*, so that the supply of labor curve

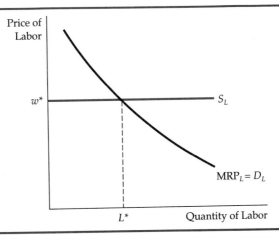

FIGURE 14.2 Hiring by a Firm in the Labor Market (with capital fixed). In the competitive labor market, a firm faces a perfectly elastic supply of labor S_L, and can hire as many workers as it wants at a wage rate w^*. The firm's demand for labor D_L is given by the marginal revenue product of labor MRP_L. The profit-maximizing firm will hire L^* units of labor at the point at which the marginal revenue product of labor is equal to the wage.

facing the firm S_L is a horizontal line. The profit-maximizing amount of labor that the firm hires, L^*, is at the intersection of the supply and demand curves.

Figure 14.3 shows how the quantity of labor demanded changes in response to a drop in the market wage rate from w_1 to w_2. The wage rate might decrease if more people entering the labor force are looking for jobs for the first time (as happened, for example, when all the baby boomers came of age). The quantity of labor demanded by the firm is initially L_1, at the intersection of MRP_L and S_1. However, when the supply of labor curve shifts from S_1 to S_2 and the wage falls from w_1 to w_2, the quantity of labor demanded increases from L_1 to L_2.

Factor markets are similar to output markets in many ways. For example, the factor market profit-maximizing condition that the marginal revenue product of labor be equal to the wage rate is analogous to the output market condition that marginal revenue be equal to marginal cost. To see why this is true, recall that $MRP_L = (MP_L)(MR)$ and divide both sides of equation (14.3) by the marginal product of labor. We then get

$$MR = w/MP_L \qquad (14.4)$$

Since MP_L measures the additional output per unit of input, the right-hand side of equation (14.4) measures the cost of an additional unit of output (the wage rate multiplied by the labor needed to produce one unit of output), i.e., the marginal cost of production. Equation (14.4) shows that both the hiring and

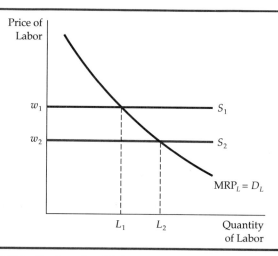

FIGURE 14.3   A Shift in the Supply of Labor.   When the supply of labor facing the firm is S_1, the firm hires L_1 units of labor at wage w_1. But when the market wage rate decreases and the supply of labor shifts to S_2, the firm maximizes its profit by moving along the demand for labor curve until the new wage rate w_2 is equal to the marginal revenue product of labor, and L_2 units of labor are hired.

output choices of the firm follow the same rule—inputs or outputs are chosen so that the marginal revenue (from the sale of output) is equal to marginal cost (from the purchase of inputs). This result holds in both competitive and non-competitive markets.

The Demand for a Factor Input When Several Inputs Are Variable

When the firm simultaneously chooses quantities of two or more variable inputs (as in a long-run analysis), the hiring problem becomes more difficult because a change in the price of one input will change the demand for others. Suppose, for example, that both labor and assembly-line machinery are variable inputs to producing farm equipment, and we wish to determine the firm's demand for labor curve. As the wage rate falls, more labor will be demanded even if the firm's investment in machinery is unchanged. But as labor becomes less expensive, the marginal cost of producing the farm equipment falls, which makes it profitable for the firm to increase its output. As a result, the firm is likely to invest in additional machinery to expand its production capacity. Expanding the use of machinery causes the marginal revenue product of labor curve to shift to the right, which in turn causes the quantity of labor demanded to increase.

Figure 14.4 illustrates this. Suppose that when the wage rate is $20 per hour, the firm hires 100 worker-hours, as shown by point A on the MRP_{L1} curve. Now consider what happens when the wage rate falls to $15 per hour. Because the marginal revenue product of labor is now greater than the wage rate, the firm will demand more labor. But the MRP_{L1} curve describes the demand for labor when the use of machinery is fixed. The lower wage will encourage the firm to hire more machinery as well as labor. Because there is more machinery, the marginal product of labor will increase (with more machinery, workers can be more productive), and the marginal revenue product curve will shift to the right (to MRP_{L2}). Thus, when the wage rate falls, the firm will use 140 hours of labor as shown by point C, rather than 120 hours as given by B.[3] A and C are two points on the firm's demand for labor curve (with machinery variable) D_L. Note that as constructed, the demand for labor curve is more elastic than either of the two marginal product of labor curves (which presume no change in the amount of machinery). Thus, the greater elasticity of demand for labor when capital inputs are variable in the long run (compared with the short run when capital is fixed) is due to the fact that firms can substitute capital for labor in the production process.

[3]In this case labor and capital are complements, in the sense that an increase in the use of labor increases the marginal product of capital. However, if labor and capital are substitutes, the marginal product of capital will fall. To the extent that the firm chooses to use less capital, the marginal product of labor will increase (because the two are substitutes), so that the marginal revenue product curve shifts to the right as before.

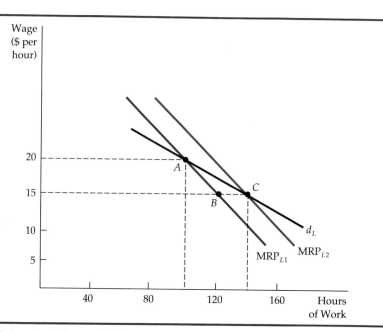

FIGURE 14.4 Firm's Demand Curve for Labor (with variable capital). When two or more inputs are variable, a firm's demand for one input depends on the marginal revenue product of both inputs. As a result, the demand curve is obtained by choosing points from the appropriate marginal revenue product curves as the price of the input changes. When the wage rate is $20, A represents one point on the firm's demand for labor curve. When the wage rate falls to $15, the marginal revenue product curve shifts from MRP_{L1} to MRP_{L2}, generating a new point C on the firm's demand for labor curve. Thus, A and C are on the demand for labor curve, but B is not.

The Market Demand Curve

When we aggregated the individual demand curves of consumers to obtain the market demand curve for a product like food or clothing, we were concerned with a single industry. However, a factor input like skilled labor is demanded by firms in many different industries. To obtain the total market demand for labor curve, we must therefore first determine each industry's demand for labor, then add the industry demand curves horizontally. The second step is straightforward. Adding industry demand curves for labor to obtain a market demand curve for labor is just like adding individual product demand curves to obtain the market demand curve for that product. So let's concentrate our attention on the more difficult first step.

The first step—determining industry demand—takes into account that the level of output produced by the firm and its product price both change as the prices of the inputs to production change. It is easiest to determine market demand when there is a single producer of the product. Then, the marginal revenue product curve is the industry demand curve for the input. With many firms, however, the analysis is more complex because of the possible interaction among the firms. To illustrate this problem, consider the demand for labor when output markets are perfectly competitive. In this case, the marginal revenue product of labor is the product of the price of the good and of the marginal product of labor (see equation 14.2), as is shown by the curve MRP_{L1} in Figure 14.5.

Suppose initially that the wage rate for labor is $15 per hour, and the firm demands 100 worker-hours of labor. Now suppose the wage rate for this firm falls to $10 per hour. If no other firms could hire workers at the lower wage, then our firm would hire 150 worker-hours of labor (simply by finding the point on the MRP_{L1} curve that corresponds to the $10 per hour wage rate). But if the wage rate falls for all firms in an industry, the industry as a whole will hire more labor. In turn, this will lead to more output from the industry and a shift to the right of the industry supply curve. This shift in supply will lead to a lower market price for the product.

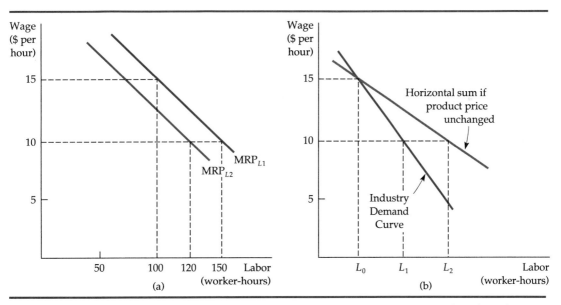

FIGURE 14.5 The Industry Demand for Labor. The demand curve for labor of a competitive firm MRP_{L1} in part (a) assumes that the product price is given. But as the wage rate falls from $15 to $10 per hour, the product price also falls and the firm's demand curve shifts downward to MRP_{L2}. As a result, the industry demand curve, shown in part (b), is more inelastic than the demand curve that would be obtained if the product price were assumed to be unchanged.

In Figure 14.5a, when product price falls, the original marginal revenue product curve shifts to the left, from MRP_{L1} to MRP_{L2}. This leads to a smaller firm demand for labor than we originally expected—120 worker-hours rather than 150. Consequently, industry demand for labor will be smaller than if only one firm were able to hire workers at the lower wage. Figure 14.5b illustrates this. The lighter line shows the horizontal sum of the individual firms' demands for labor that would be obtained if the price of the product does not change as the wage falls. The darker line shows the industry demand curve for labor, which takes into account that the price of the product will fall as all firms expand their output in response to the lower wage rate. The industry demand for labor is L_0 worker-hours when the wage rate is $15 per hour. When the wage falls to $10 per hour, the industry demand increases to L_1, a smaller increase than L_2, which would occur if the product price were fixed. The aggregation of industry demand curves into the market demand curve for labor is the final step—to complete it we simply add the labor demanded in all industries.

Finally, the derivation of the market demand curve for labor (or any other input) is essentially the same when the output market is monopolistically competitive or oligopolistic. The only difference is that it is more difficult to predict the change in product price in response to a change in the wage rate, because each firm in the market is likely to be pricing strategically (as we have shown in Chapters 12 and 13), rather than taking product price as given.

EXAMPLE 14.1   THE DEMAND FOR JET FUEL

Throughout the 1970s fuel costs for U.S. airlines increased rapidly, in tandem with rising world oil prices. Whereas fuel costs made up 12.4 percent of total operating costs in 1971, fuel's share of operating costs rose to 24.6 percent in 1979. As we would expect, the amount of jet fuel used by airlines during this period fell as its price rose. Thus, the output of the airline industry, as measured by the number of ton-miles (one ton-mile is short for one ton of passengers, baggage, or freight transported one mile), rose by 29.6 percent, while the amount of jet fuel consumed increased by only 8.8 percent.

Understanding the demand for jet fuel is important to managers of oil refineries who must decide how much jet fuel to produce, and to managers of airlines, who must project how their fuel purchases and costs will change when fuel prices rise. A recent study provides some information about this factor demand.[4]

The effect of the increase in fuel costs on the airline industry depends on the ability of airlines either to cut fuel usage by reducing weight (by carrying less

---

[4]This example is drawn from Joseph M. Cigliano, "The Demand for Jet Fuel by the U.S. Domestic Trunk Airlines," *Business Economics* (Sept. 1982): 32–36.

TABLE 14.1 Short-Run Price Elasticity of Demand for Jet Fuel

Airline	Elasticity	Airline	Elasticity
American	−.06	Braniff	−.10
Continental	−.09	Delta	−.15
Eastern	−.07	National	−.03
Northwest	−.07	Pan American	.00
TWA	−.10	United	−.10

excess fuel) and flying slower (reducing drag and increasing engine efficiency) or to pass on their higher costs in prices to customers. Thus, the price elasticity of demand for jet fuel depends both on the ability to conserve fuel and on the elasticities of demand and supply of travel.

To measure the short-run elasticity of demand for jet fuel, we use as the quantity of fuel demanded the number of gallons of fuel used by an airline in all markets within its domestic route network. The price of jet fuel is measured in dollars per gallon. A statistical analysis of demand must control for factors other than price that can explain why some firms demand more fuel than others. One factor takes into account that some airlines are using more fuel-efficient jet aircraft, while others are not. A second factor is the length of the flights. The shorter the flight, the more fuel consumed per mile of travel. Both these factors were included in a statistical analysis that relates the quantity of fuel demanded to its price, using (quarterly) data for 1971 through 1979.[5] Table 14.1 shows some price elasticities.[6] All elasticities are short run, because they apply to a limited period and do not account for the introduction of new types of aircraft.

The jet fuel price elasticities for the airlines range in value from 0 (for Pan Am) to −.15 (for Delta). Overall, the results show that the demand for jet fuel as an input to the production of airline flight-miles is very inelastic. This is not surprising—in the short run, there is no good substitute for jet fuel. The long-run elasticity of demand is higher, however, because airlines can eventually introduce more energy-efficient airplanes.

Figure 14.6 shows the short- and long-run demands for jet fuel. The short-run demand curve, MRP_{SR} is quite inelastic because it is difficult to substitute

[5]The study controls for the number of trips taken, so that the elasticities measured do not reflect the possibility that higher fuel prices may lead to fewer trips.

[6]Because each regression was estimated in a log-linear form, the regression coefficient is the price elasticity of demand.

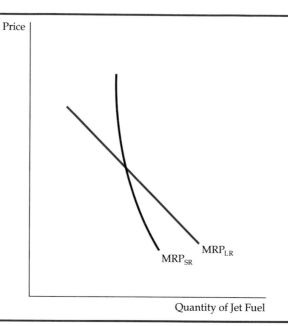

FIGURE 14.6 The Short- and Long-run Demand for Jet Fuel. The short-run demand for jet fuel MRP$_{SR}$ is more inelastic than the long-run demand MRP$_{LR}$. In the short run, airlines cannot reduce fuel consumption much when fuel prices increase. In the long run, however, the airlines can take longer, more fuel-efficient routes and put more fuel-efficient planes into service. This allows them to reduce fuel consumption in response to increased fuel prices.

other inputs for fuel in the short run. The long-run demand curve MRP$_{LR}$ is more elastic, because there are more possibilities for substitution in the long run.

The Supply of Inputs to a Firm

When the market for a factor input is perfectly competitive, a firm can purchase as much of that input as it wants at a fixed price. The input supply curve facing a firm is then perfectly elastic, as in Figures 14.2 and 14.7b. In Figure 14.7b a firm is buying fabric at $10 per yard to weave into clothing. Because the firm is only a small part of the fabric market, it can buy all it wants without affecting the price.

The supply curve facing a firm in any market tells us what price per unit the firm will have to pay to purchase a quantity of input. Thus, the supply curve

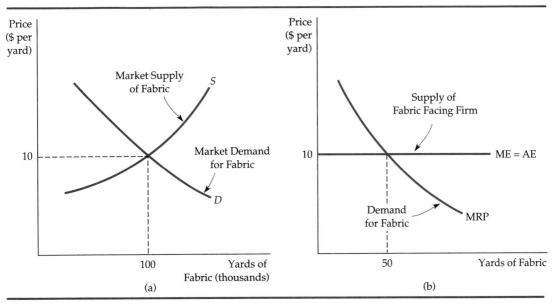

FIGURE 14.7 A Firm's Input Supply in a Competitive Factor Market. In a competitive factor market, a firm can buy any amount of the input it wants without affecting the price. Therefore, the firm faces a perfectly elastic supply curve for that input. As a result, the quantity of the input purchased by the producer of the product is determined by the intersection of the input demand and supply curves. In part (a) the industry quantity demanded and quantity supplied of fabric are equated at a price of $10 per yard. In part (b) the firm faces a horizontal marginal expenditure curve at a price of $10 per yard of fabric, and chooses to buy 50 yards.

AE is an *average expenditure curve* (just as the demand curve facing a firm is an average revenue curve), because it represents the expenditure that the firm must make per unit of input that it purchases. The *marginal expenditure curve* ME, on the other hand, represents the expenditure of the firm for each *additional* unit of input it buys. (The marginal expenditure curve in a factor market is analogous to the marginal revenue curve in the output market.) When the factor market is competitive, the average expenditure and marginal expenditure curves are identical horizontal curves, just as the marginal and average revenue curves are identical (and horizontal) for a competitive firm in the output market.

How much of the input should a firm facing a competitive factor market purchase? As long as the marginal revenue product curve lies above the marginal expenditure curve, profit can be increased by purchasing more of the input because the benefit of an additional unit (MRP) exceeds the cost (ME). However, when the marginal revenue product curve lies below the marginal expenditure curve, some units yield benefits that are less than cost. Therefore, profit maximization requires that *marginal revenue product be equal to marginal expenditure:*

$$ME = MRP \qquad (14.5)$$

When we considered the special case of a competitive output market, we saw that the firm bought inputs such as labor up to the point at which the marginal revenue product is equal to the price of the input w, as in equation (14.3). Thus, in the competitive case, the condition for profit maximization is that the price of the input be equal to marginal expenditure:

$$ME = w \qquad (14.6)$$

In our example, the price of the fabric ($10 per yard) is determined in the competitive fabric market shown in Figure 14.7a, at the intersection of the demand and supply curves. Figure 14.7b shows the amount of fabric purchased by a firm at the intersection of the marginal expenditure and marginal revenue product curves. When 50 yards of fabric are purchased, the marginal expenditure of $10 is equal to the marginal revenue obtained from the sale of the clothing made possible by the increased use of fabric in the production process. If less than 50 yards of fabric were purchased, the firm would be forgoing an opportunity to make an additional profit from clothing sales. If more than 50 yards were purchased, the cost of the fabric would be greater than the additional revenue that the firm would receive when it sold the extra clothing.

The Market Supply of Inputs

The market supply curve for a factor is usually upward-sloping. We saw in Chapter 8 that the market supply of a good sold in a competitive market is upward-sloping when the marginal cost of production is increasing. The same argument applies here, because inputs such as fabric are usually produced with increasing marginal cost as well.

When the factor input is labor, however, people rather than firms are making supply decisions. Then, utility maximization rather than profit maximization becomes the operative goal. In the discussion that follows we show that the market supply curve for labor can be upward-sloping, but that it may also, as in Figure 14.8, be *backward-bending,* i.e., a higher wage rate can lead to *less* labor being supplied.

To see why a labor supply curve may be backward-bending, let's consider how a worker decides how many hours a day (or weeks a year) to work. The day is divided into hours of work and hours of leisure. Leisure is a generic term that describes nonwork activities, including sleeping and eating. We can assume that leisure is enjoyable but that work benefits the worker only through the

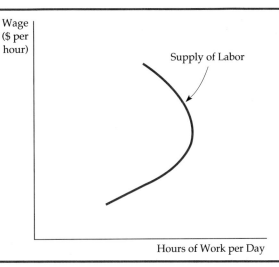

FIGURE 14.8 Backward-Bending Supply of Labor.   When the wage rate increases, the hours of work supplied increase initially but eventually decrease as individuals choose to enjoy more leisure and to work less. The backward-bending portion of the labor supply curve arises when the income effect associated with the higher wage (which encourages more leisure) is greater than the substitution effect (which encourages more work).

income that is earned. We also assume that a worker can choose how many hours per day to work.

The wage rate therefore measures the price that the worker places on leisure time, because the wage is the amount of money that the worker gives up to enjoy leisure. As the wage rate increases, the price of leisure also increases. Recall from our analysis of consumer demand in Chapter 4 that a price change brings about both a substitution effect (a change in relative price with utility held constant) and an income effect (a change in utility with relative prices unchanged). Here, these two effects occur when the wage rate is increased. There is a substitution effect because the higher price of leisure encourages workers to substitute work for leisure. An income effect occurs because the higher wage rate increases the worker's real income. With this higher income, the worker can buy more of many goods, one of which is leisure. If more leisure is purchased, then the income effect encourages the laborer to work fewer hours. In addition, if the income effect is large enough, the worker will work less as the wage rate increases. Income effects can be very large because wages are the primary determinant of most people's income. When a higher wage leads a worker to work fewer hours because of the large income effect, the result is the backward-bending supply curve.

Figure 14.9 shows the work-leisure decision that leads to the backward-bending supply curve for labor. The horizontal axis shows hours of leisure per day,

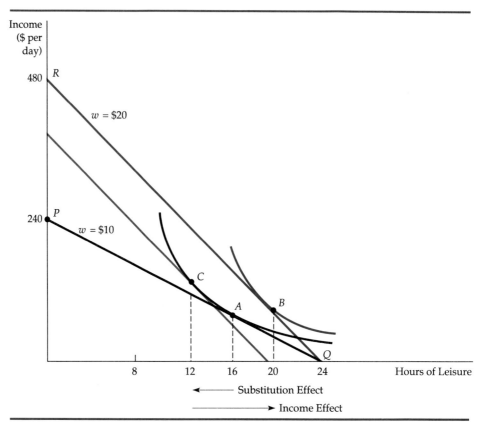

FIGURE 14.9 Substitution and Income Effects of a Wage Increase. When the wage rate increases from $10 to $20 per hour, the worker's budget line shifts from *PQ* to *RQ*. In response, the worker moves from *A* to *B*, while decreasing work hours from 8 to 4. The reduction in hours worked arises because the income effect outweighs the substitution effect. In this case, the supply of labor curve is backward-bending.

the vertical axis income generated by work. (We assume there are no other sources of income.) Initially the wage rate is $10 per hour, and the budget line is given by *PQ*. Point *P*, for example, shows that the individual who works a 24-hour day earns an income of $240.

The worker maximizes utility by choosing point *A*, and by enjoying 16 hours of leisure per day (with 8 hours of work) and earning $80. When the wage rate increases to $20 per hour, the budget line rotates about the horizontal intercept to line *RQ*. (Only 24 hours of leisure are possible.) Now the worker maximizes utility at *B* by choosing 20 hours of leisure per day (with 4 hours of work), while earning $80 in the process. Were only the substitution effect to arise, the higher wage rate would encourage the worker to work 12 hours (at *C*) instead of 8.

However, the income effect works in the opposite direction. It overcomes the substitution effect and lowers the work day from 8 to 4 hours.[7]

In real life, a backward-bending labor supply curve might apply to a college student working during the summer to earn living expenses for the school year. As soon as a target level of earnings is reached, the student stops working and allocates more time to leisure activities. An increase in the wage rate will then lead to fewer hours worked because it enables the student to reach the target level of earnings faster.

EXAMPLE 14.2 LABOR SUPPLY FOR ONE- AND TWO-EARNER HOUSEHOLDS

One of the most dramatic changes in the labor market in the twentieth century has been the increase in women's participation in the labor force. Women made up 29 percent of the labor force in 1950 and 42 percent in 1980. Married women account for a substantial portion of this increase. The increased role of women in the labor market has also had a major impact on housing markets: Where to live and work has increasingly become a joint husband and wife decision. The complex nature of the work choice was analyzed in a study that compared the work decisions of unmarried females (94 in all) with the work decisions of heads of households and spouses in 397 families.[8]

One way to describe the work decisions of the various family groups is to calculate labor supply elasticities. Each elasticity relates the numbers of hours worked to the wage that the head of household was paid, and also to the wage of the other member of the household if it included two earners. (Other sources of income and housing choices are also taken into account.) Table 14.2 summarizes the results.

When a higher wage rate leads to fewer hours worked, the labor supply curve is backward-bending because the income effect, which encourages more leisure, outweighs the substitution effect, which encourages more work. The elasticity of labor supply is then negative. Table 14.2 shows that heads of one-earner families with children and two-earner families (with or without children) all have backward-bending labor supply curves, with elasticities ranging from −.002 to −.078. Most single-earner heads of households are on the upward-sloping portion of their labor supply curve, with the largest elasticity of .106 associated with single women with children. Married women (listed as spouses of heads of households) are also on the backward-bending portion of the labor supply curve, with elasticities of −.028 and −.086. This suggests that higher wages for women in two-earner families will discourage, rather than encourage,

[7]An empirical analysis of the labor-leisure choice appears in L. F. Dunn, "An Empirical Indifference Function for Income and Leisure," *Review of Economics and Statistics* 58 (Nov. 1978): 533–540.

[8]The study was by Janet E. Kohlhase, "Labor Supply and Housing Demand for One- and Two-Earner Households," *Review of Economics and Statistics* 68 (1986): 48–56.

TABLE 14.2 Elasticities of Labor Supply (hours worked)

Group	Head's Hours with Respect to Head's Wage	Spouse's Hours with Respect to Spouse's Wage	Head's Hours with Respect to Spouse's Wage
Unmarried males (no children)	.026		
Unmarried females (with children)	.106		
Unmarried females (no children)	.011		
One-earner family (with children)	− .078		
One-earner family (no children)	.007		
Two-earner family (with children)	− .002	− .086	− .004
Two-earner family (no children)	− .107	− .028	− .059

more work. The work decision of the head of the household is also responsive to the wage of the spouse: The household head works fewer hours when his or her spouse earns a higher wage.

14.2 Equilibrium in a Competitive Factor Market

A competitive factor market is in equilibrium when the price of the input equates the quantity demanded to the quantity supplied. Figure 14.10a shows such an equilibrium for a labor market. At point A, the equilibrium wage rate is w_C, and the equilibrium quantity supplied is L_C. Because there is complete information in our model of competition, all workers receive the identical wage and generate the identical marginal revenue product of labor wherever they are employed. If any worker had a wage greater than his or her marginal product, a firm would find it profitable to offer that worker a higher wage. As we will see in Chapter 17, however, when information is limited, employers can discriminate against workers.

If the output market is also perfectly competitive, the demand curve for the input measures the benefit that consumers of the product place on the additional use of the input in the production process. The wage rate also reflects the cost to the firm and to society of using an additional unit of the input. Thus, at A in Figure 14.10a, the marginal benefit of an hour of labor (its marginal revenue product MRP_L) is equal to its marginal cost (the wage rate w). Therefore, when

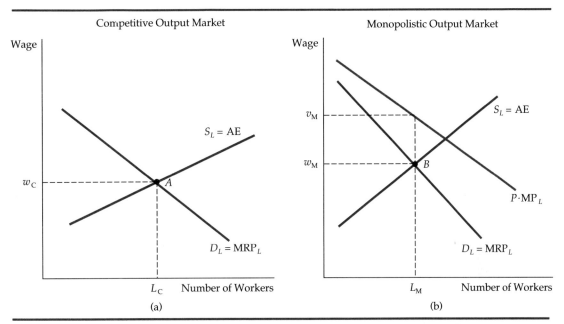

FIGURE 14.10 Labor Market Equilibrium. In a competitive labor market in which the output market is competitive, the equilibrium wage w_C is given by the intersection of the demand for labor (marginal revenue product) curve and the supply of labor (average expenditure) curve. The equilibrium is shown by point A in part (a) of the figure. Part (b) shows that when the producer of the product has monopoly power, the marginal value of a worker v_M is greater than the wage w_M, so that not enough workers are employed. (Point B determines the quantity of labor that the firm hires and the wage rate paid.)

the output and input markets are both perfectly competitive, resources are used efficiently because the difference between total benefits and total costs is maximized. This condition for efficient use of resources often appears in another form. From equation (14.2) we know that in a competitive labor market, the marginal revenue product is equal to the price of the product times the marginal product of labor, $MRP_L = (P)(MP_L)$. Since a competitive labor market is efficient, this condition is required for efficiency. It states that the additional revenue received by the firm from employing an additional unit of labor equals the social benefit of the additional output that labor unit produces.

When the output market is not perfectly competitive, the condition $MRP_L = (P)(MP_L)$ no longer holds. Note in Figure 14.10b that the curve representing the price of the product multiplied by the marginal product of labor $[(P)(MP_L)]$ lies above the marginal revenue product curve $[(MR)(MP_L)]$. Point B represents the equilibrium wage w_M and the equilibrium labor supply L_M. But $(P)(MP_L)$ is the value that consumers place on additional inputs of labor. Therefore, when L_M

laborers are employed, the marginal cost to the firm w_M is less than the marginal benefit to society v_M. Thus, the firm is maximizing its profit, but because its output is less than the efficient level of output, its input use is also less than the efficient level. Net benefits (total benefits minus total costs) would increase if the firm or firms with market power hired more factor inputs and thereby increased output.

Economic Rent

The concept of economic rent helps explain how factor markets work. When discussing output markets in Chapter 8, we defined economic rent as the payments received by a firm over and above the minimum cost of producing its output. For a factor market *economic rent* is *the difference between the payments made to a factor of production and the minimum amount that must be spent to obtain the use of that factor*. Figure 14.11 illustrates the concept of economic rent as applied to a competitive labor market, but the concept also applies to other factor markets. The equilibrium price of labor is w^*, and the quantity of labor supplied is L^*.

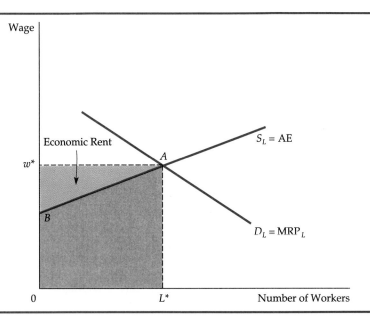

FIGURE 14.11   Economic Rent.   The economic rent associated with the employment of labor is given by the excess of wages paid above the minimum amount needed to be paid to hire workers. The equilibrium wage is given by A, at the intersection of the labor supply and labor demand curves. Because the supply curve (AE) is upward-sloping, some workers would have accepted jobs for a wage less than w^*. The shaded area ABw^* represents the economic rent received by all workers.

The supply of labor curve is the upward-sloping average expenditure curve, and the demand for labor is the downward-sloping marginal revenue product curve. Because the supply curve tells us how much labor will be supplied at each wage rate, the minimum expenditure needed to employ L^* units of labor is given by the shaded region AL^*OB, the area below the supply curve to the left of the equilibrium labor supply L^*.

In perfectly competitive markets all workers are paid the wage w^*. This wage is required to get the last or "marginal" worker to supply his or her labor, but all other "inframarginal" workers earn rents, because their wage is greater than the wage that would be needed to get them to work. Since total wage payments are equal to the rectangle $0w^*AL^*$, the economic rent earned by labor is given by the area Bw^*A. From the worker's point of view, economic rent is quite similar to consumer surplus, because consumer surplus represents the additional value in consumption above and beyond the cost of purchasing a good.

Note that if the supply curve were infinitely elastic, economic rent would be zero. Rents arise only when supply is somewhat inelastic. In fact, when supply

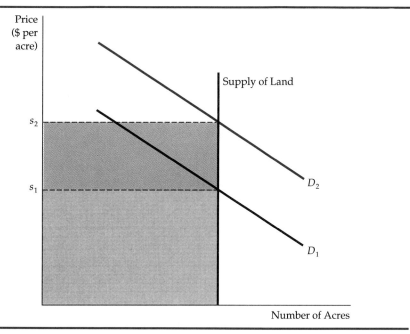

FIGURE 14.12   Land Rents.   When the supply of land is perfectly inelastic, the market price of land is determined at the point of intersection of the demand curve, and the entire value of the land is an economic rent. When demand is given by D_1, the economic rent per acre is given by s_1, and when demand is increased to D_2, the economic rent increases to s_2.

is perfectly inelastic, all payments to a factor of production are economic rents because the factor will be supplied no matter what price is paid. One frequent example of an inelastically supplied factor is land, as Figure 14.12 shows.

The supply curve in Figure 14.12 is perfectly inelastic because land used to produce housing (or for agriculture) is fixed, at least in the short run. With land inelastically supplied, the price of land is determined entirely by the demand for it. In the figure, the demand for land is given by D_1, and its price per unit is s_1. Total land rent is given by the dark shaded rectangle. But when the demand for land increases to D_2, the rental value per unit of land increases to s_2, and the total land rent includes the lighter shaded area as well. Thus, an increase in the demand for land (a shift to the right in the demand curve) leads to a higher rental price for it, and a higher economic rent.

EXAMPLE 14.3   PAY IN THE MILITARY

The U.S. Army has been having a major personnel problem. During the Civil War, roughly 90 percent of the armed forces were unskilled workers involved in ground combat. But since then the nature of warfare has evolved, so that ground combat forces now make up only 16 percent of the armed forces. Meanwhile, changes in technology have led to a severe shortage in skilled technicians, trained pilots, computer analysts, mechanics, and others needed to operate sophisticated military equipment. Why has such a shortage developed, and why has the military been unable to keep its skilled personnel? A recent study provides some answers.[9]

The rank structure of the army has remained essentially unchanged over the years. It includes nine enlisted ranks, but only six officer ranks. Among the officer ranks, pay increases are determined primarily by the number of years of service. As a result, officers with differing skill levels and abilities are usually paid similar salaries. Because of this uniform wage structure, some skilled workers are underpaid relative to what they could receive in the private sector. As a result, skilled workers who join the army because of salaries that are initially high find that their marginal revenue products are eventually higher than their wages. Some remain in the army, but many leave.

Figure 14.13 shows the inefficiency that results from the army's pay policy. The equilibrium wage rate w^* is the wage that equates the demand for labor to the supply. Because of inflexibility in its pay structure, however, the army pays the wage w_0, which is below the equilibrium wage. At w_0, demand is greater than supply, and there is a shortage of skilled labor. By contrast, competitive labor markets pay more productive workers higher wages than their less productive counterparts. But how can the army attract and keep its skilled labor force?

[9]See Walter Y. Oi, "Paying Soldiers: On a Wage Structure for a Large Internal Labor Market," unpublished, undated paper.

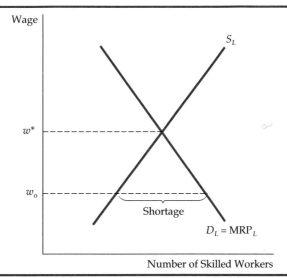

FIGURE 14.13 The Shortage of Skilled Military Personnel. When the wage w^* is paid to military personnel, the labor market is in equilibrium. When the wage is kept below w^*, at w_0, however, there is a shortage of personnel, because the quantity of labor demanded is greater than the quantity supplied.

The army's choice of wage structure affects the nation's ability to maintain an effective fighting force. In response to its personnel problems, the army has begun to change its salary structure by expanding the number and size of its reenlistment bonuses. Selective reenlistment bonuses targeted at skilled jobs for which there are shortages can be an effective recruiting device. The immediate bonuses create more of an incentive than the somewhat uncertain promise of higher wages in the future. As the demand for skilled military jobs increases, we can expect the army to make greater use of these reenlistment bonuses and other market-based incentives.

14.3 Factor Markets with Monopsony Power

In some factor markets individual buyers of factors have monopsony power—i.e., they can influence price. For example, we saw in Chapter 10 that U.S. automobile companies have considerable monopsony power as buyers of parts and components. GM, Ford, and Chrysler buy large quantities of brakes, radiators, tires, and other parts and can negotiate lower prices than smaller purchasers might pay. Similarly, IBM has monopsony power in the market for disk drives, because it purchases so many drives for its computers.

Throughout this section we will assume that the output market is perfectly competitive. Also, because a single buyer is easier to visualize than several buyers who all have some monopsony power, we will restrict our attention to pure monopsony.

Marginal and Average Expenditure

When a firm buys a factor input in a competitive market, the marginal and average expenditure curves are identical. But when the firm is a monopolist, the marginal and average expenditure curves are not the same, as Figure 14.14 shows.

The factor supply curve facing the monopsonist is the market supply curve. (It shows how much of the factor suppliers are willing to sell as the price of the

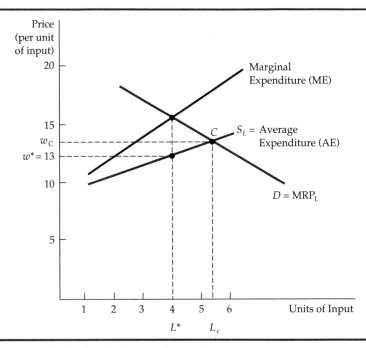

FIGURE 14.14 Marginal and Average Expenditure. When the buyer of an input has monopsony power, the marginal expenditure curve lies above the average expenditure curve, because the firm raises the input price as more of the input is bought. The number of units of input purchased is given by L^*, at the intersection of the marginal revenue product and marginal expenditure curves. The wage rate at which the marginal revenue product is equal to the average expenditure w^* is lower than the competitive wage w_c.

factor increases.) Because the monopsonist pays the same price for each unit, the supply curve is its *average expenditure* curve. The average expenditure curve is upward-sloping because the monopsonist must pay a higher price if it wants to buy more of the factor. For a profit-maximizing firm, however, it is the *marginal expenditure curve* that is relevant for the decision about how much of the factor to buy. Recall from Chapter 10 that the marginal expenditure curve lies above the average expenditure curve because when the firm increases the price of the factor to hire more units, the firm must pay *all* units that higher price, not just the last unit hired.

The Input Purchasing Decision of the Firm

How much of the input should the firm buy? It should buy up to the point where marginal expenditure equals marginal revenue product. Here the benefit from the last unit bought (MRP) is just equal to the cost (ME). Figure 14.14 illustrates this for a labor market. Note that the monopsonist hires L^* units of labor; at that point ME $=$ MRP_L. The wage rate w^* that workers are paid is given by finding the point on the average expenditure or supply curve associated with L^* units of labor.

As we showed in Chapter 10, a buyer with monopsony power maximizes net benefit (utility less expenditure) from a purchase by buying up to the point where marginal value (MV) is equal to marginal expenditure:

$$MV = ME$$

For a firm buying a factor input, MV is just the marginal revenue product of the factor MRP. So we have

$$MRP = ME \tag{14.7}$$

This condition is analogous to the profit-maximizing output decision that marginal revenue equal marginal cost. But when buying an input, marginal revenue is calculated on the basis of the additional output that results from using an additional unit of input.

Note from Figure 14.14 that the monopsonist hires less labor than a firm or group of firms with no monopsony power. In a competitive labor market, L_c workers would be hired, because at that level the quantity of labor demanded (given by the marginal revenue product curve) is equal to the quantity of labor supplied (given by the average expenditure curve). Note also that the monopsonistic firm will be paying its workers a wage w^* that is less than the wage w_c that would be paid in a competitive market.

Monopsony power can arise in different ways. One source can be the specialized nature of a firm's business. If the firm buys a component that no other firm buys, it is likely to be a monopsonist in the market for that component. One source of monopsony power in labor markets can be the business's location—it may be the only major employer within an area. Another source of monopsony power is an agreement among the buyers of a factor to form a cartel to limit purchases of the factor, so they can buy it at a price lower than the competitive price. As we will see in Example 14.4, the market for major league baseball players is an example of this.

Few firms in our economy are pure monopsonists. But firms (or individuals) often have some monopsony power either because they buy products in large volume or have some advantage over other potential purchasers of the product. The government is a monopsonist when it hires volunteer soldiers or buys missiles, aircraft, and other specialized equipment for the army. A mining firm or other company that is the only major employer in a community also has monopsony power in the local labor market. Even in these cases, however, monopsony power may be limited, because the government competes to some extent with other firms that offer similar jobs, and the mining firm competes to some extent with companies in nearby communities.

EXAMPLE 14.4   MONOPSONY POWER IN THE MARKET FOR BASEBALL PLAYERS

In the United States, major league baseball is exempt from the antitrust laws, the result of a Supreme Court decision that goes hand in hand with the more general decision by Congress not to apply the antitrust laws to labor problems.[10] This antitrust exemption allowed baseball team owners (before 1975) to operate a monopsonistic cartel. Like all cartels, this one depended on an agreement among owners. This agreement involved an annual draft of players and a *reserve clause* that effectively tied each player to one team for life, thereby eliminating most interteam competition for players. Under the reserve clause, once a player was drafted by a team, he could not play for another team unless rights were sold to that team. As a result, baseball owners had monopsony power in negotiating new contracts with their players—the only alternative to signing an agreement was to give up the game or play it outside the United States.

During the 1960s and early 1970s, baseball players' salaries were substantially below the market value of their marginal products (determined in part by the incremental attention that better hitting or pitching might achieve). For example, players receiving a salary of approximately $42,000 in 1969 would have received a salary of $300,000 were the players' market perfectly competitive.

Fortunately for the players, and unfortunately for the owners, there was a strike in 1972 followed by a lawsuit by one player (Curt Flood of the St. Louis Cardinals) and an arbitrated labor-management agreement. This process eventually led in 1975 to an agreement by which baseball players could become free agents after playing for a team for five years. The reserve clause was no longer

---

[10]This example builds on a recent analysis of the structure of baseball players' salaries by Roger Noll, who has kindly supplied us with the relevant data. See also G. W. Scully, "Pay and Performance in Major League Baseball," *American Economic Review* (Dec. 1974): 915–930.

in effect and a highly monopsonistic labor market became much more competitive.

The result was an interesting experiment in labor market economics. Between 1975 and 1980 the market for baseball players adjusted to a new post-reserve clause equilibrium. Whereas before 1975 expenditures on players' contracts made up approximately 25 percent of all team expenditures, the pool of funds allocated to salaries increased to 40 percent by the year 1980. Moreover, the average player's salary doubled in real terms. By 1987, the average baseball player was earning $410,732, an incredible increase from the monopsonistic wages of the late 1960s. (In 1969, for example, the average baseball salary was approximately $42,000. When adjusted for inflation this comes to approximately $130,000 in 1987.)

14.4 Monopoly Power in Factor Markets

Just as buyers of inputs can have monopsony power, sellers of inputs can have monopoly power. In the extreme, the seller of an input may be a monopolist, as when a firm has a patent to produce a computer chip that no other firm can duplicate. There are relatively few pure monopolies in factor markets, but in many industries firms have some monopoly power in the sale of products that other firms will use as factors of production. Because the most important example of monopoly power in factor markets involves labor unions, we will concentrate most of our attention there.[11] In the subsections that follow, we briefly describe how a labor union, which is a monopolist in the sale of labor services, might increase the well-being of its members and at the same time substantially affect nonunionized workers.

Monopoly Power over the Wage Rate

Figure 14.15 shows a demand for labor curve in a market with no monopsony power—it aggregates the marginal revenue products of firms that compete to buy labor. The labor supply curve describes how union members would supply labor *if* the union exerted no monopoly power. Then the labor market would be competitive, and L^* workers would be hired for a wage of w^* (point A).

[11]For a general discussion of the power of unions, see Richard B. Freeman and James L. Medoff, *What Do Unions Do?* (New York: Basic Books, 1984), chapter 3. Union monopoly has evidently been declining. The membership of unions in the United States has diminished substantially over the past several decades. Today only about 20 percent of all workers belong to unions, and evidence suggests that union wages are at best 10 to 15 percent higher than comparable nonunion wages.

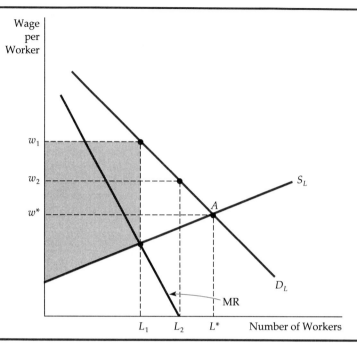

FIGURE 14.15 Monopoly Power of Sellers of Labor. When the seller of a labor input (a labor union) is a monopolist, it chooses among the points on the buyer's demand for labor curve D_L. The seller can maximize the number of workers hired, at L^*, by agreeing that workers will work at wage w^*. The quantity of labor L_1 that maximizes the rent that employees earn is determined by the intersection of the marginal revenue and supply of labor curves. Union members will receive a wage rate of w_1, corresponding to the quantity of labor L_1 on the firm's demand curve for labor. Finally, if the union wishes to maximize total wages paid to workers, it should allow L_2 union members to be employed at a wage rate of w_2, because the marginal revenue to the union will then be zero.

Because of its monopoly power, however, the union can choose any wage rate and the corresponding quantity of labor supplied (just as a monopolist seller of output chooses price and the corresponding quantity of output). If the union wanted to maximize the number of workers hired, it would choose the competitive outcome at A. Suppose, however, that the union wished to obtain a higher than competitive wage. Then, it could restrict its membership to L_1 workers. As a result, the firm would pay a wage rate of w_1. Those union members who work are better off, while those people who do not work are worse off.

Is a policy of restrictive union membership worthwhile? Yes, if the union wishes to maximize the economic rent that its workers receive. By restricting membership, the union would be acting analogously to a firm that restricts output to maximize profit. Profit to a firm represents the revenue it receives less its opportunity costs. Rent to a union represents the wages its members earn in excess of their opportunity cost. To maximize rent, the union must choose the number of workers hired so that the marginal revenue to the union (the additional wages earned) is equal to the extra cost of inducing the worker to work. In Figure 14.15 this involves choosing the quantity of labor at which the marginal revenue curve MR crosses the supply curve (because the supply curve represents the opportunity cost of workers being employed). We have chosen the wage-employment combination of w_1 and L_1 with this in mind. The shaded area below the demand for labor curve, above the supply of labor curve, and to the left of L_1 represents the economic rent that workers receive.

A rent-maximizing policy can benefit nonunion workers if they can find non-union jobs. However, if these jobs are not available, rent maximization may create too sharp a distinction between winners and losers. An alternative objective is to maximize the aggregate wages that all workers receive. To achieve this goal, in the example in Figure 14.15, the number of workers hired is increased from L_1 until the marginal revenue to the union is equal to zero. Because any further employment decreases total wage payments, aggregate wages are maximized when the wage is equal to w_2 and the number of workers is equal to L_2.

A Two-Sector Model of Labor Employment

When the union uses its monopoly power to increase its members' wages, the number of unionized workers who are hired falls. Because these workers either move to the nonunion sector or choose not to join the union initially, it is important to understand what happens in the nonunionized part of the economy.

Suppose that in the market for a certain type of skilled labor, the total supply of unionized and nonunionized workers is fixed. In Figure 14.16 the market supply of labor in both sectors is given by S_L. The demand for labor by firms in the unionized sector is given by D_U, and the demand in the nonunionized sector by D_{NU}. The total market demand is the horizontal sum of the demands in the two sectors, and is given by D_L.

Suppose the union chooses to increase the wage of its workers above the competitive wage w^*, to w_U. At that wage rate, the number of workers hired in the unionized sector falls by an amount ΔL_U, as shown on the horizontal axis. As these workers find employment in the nonunionized sector, the wage rate in the nonunionized sector adjusts until the labor market is in equilibrium. The new wage rate in the nonunionized sector, w_{NU}, was chosen so that the additional number of workers hired in the nonunionized sector, ΔL_{NU}, is equal to the number of workers who left the unionized sector.

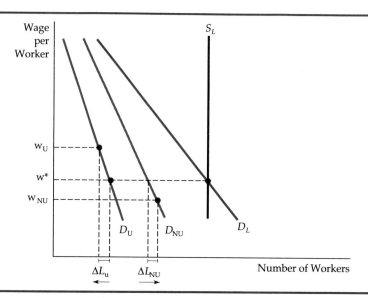

FIGURE 14.16   Wage Determination in Unionized and Nonunionized Sectors.   When
a monopolistic union raises the wage in the unionized sector of the economy from w^*
to w_U, employment in that sector falls, as shown by the movement along the demand
curve D_U. For the total supply of labor, given by S_L, to remain unchanged, the wage in
the nonunionized sector must fall from w^* to w_{NU}, as shown by the movement along
the demand curve D_{NU}.

Figure 14.16 shows an adverse consequence of a union strategy directed
toward raising union wages—nonunionized wages fall. Unionization can improve working conditions and provide useful information to workers and management. But when the demand for labor is not perfectly inelastic, union workers are helped at the expense of nonunion workers.

Bilateral Monopoly in the Labor Market

The adverse effects of union wage policies by a monopolistic union depend to
some extent on our assumption that the input market was otherwise competitive. To see this, we now consider the consequences of union wage policies
when the buyers of labor also have monopsony power.

As we discussed in Chapter 10, *bilateral monopoly*, is a market in which a
monopolist sells to a monopsonist. In a labor market, bilateral monopoly might
arise when representatives from a union and companies that hire a certain type
of worker meet to negotiate wages. Figure 14.17 shows a typical bilateral bargaining situation. The S_L curve represents the supply curve for skilled labor,
and the firm's demand curve for labor is given by the marginal revenue product
curve D_L.

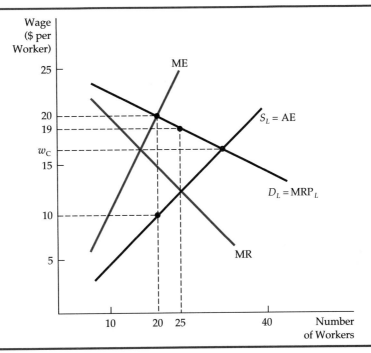

FIGURE 14.17 Bilateral Monopoly. When the seller of labor is a monopolist and the buyer of labor a monopsonist, the wage rate that is negotiated will be between a high of $19 (determined by the intersection of the marginal revenue and average expenditure curves) and a low of $10 (determined by the intersection of the marginal revenue product curve and marginal expenditure curves).

If the union had no monopoly power, the monopsonist would make its hiring decision on the basis of its marginal expenditure curve ME, choosing to hire 20 workers and paying them $10 per hour. When 20 workers are hired, the marginal revenue product of labor is equal to the marginal expenditure of the firm.

The seller of labor faces a demand curve D_L that describes the firm's hiring plans as the wage rate varies. The union chooses a point on the demand curve that maximizes its members' wages. Because the wage paid to all workers falls as the number hired increases, the marginal revenue curve MR describes the additional wages that the union gets for its members as the number of employees hired increases.

The supply curve S_L tells the union the minimum payment necessary to encourage workers to offer their labor to firms in the industry. Suppose the union wishes to maximize the economic rent of its members. To do so, the union views the supply curve as the marginal cost of labor. To maximize the rent that is earned, the union chooses a wage of $19, because $19 is the wage that equates the marginal revenue (the marginal increase in wages) to the marginal cost (the increase in the minimum wages needed to hire the labor). At $19, the firms would hire 25 workers.

In summary, firms are willing to pay a wage of $10 and hire 20 workers, but the union is demanding a wage of $19 and wants the firm to hire 25 workers. What happens in this case? The result depends on the bargaining strategies of the two parties. If the union can make a credible threat to strike, it might secure a wage closer to $19 than to $10. If the firms can make a credible threat to hire nonunion labor, they might secure a wage closer to $10. If both parties can make credible threats, the resulting agreement might be close to the competitive outcome (wage w_c) of about $15 in Figure 14.17.[12]

EXAMPLE 14.5   THE DECLINE OF PRIVATE SECTOR UNIONISM

For several decades, labor unions have experienced increasingly difficult times, with both their membership and bargaining power declining.[13] A decline in union monopoly power can lead to different responses by union negotiators, and can have a number of different effects on the wage rate and level of employment by unions. During the 1970s most of the effect was felt on union wages: Levels of employment did not change much, but the differential between union and nonunion wages decreased substantially. We would have expected the same pattern to occur in the 1980s, because of the heavily publicized wage freezes and the rapid growth of two-tier wage provisions, in which newer union members are paid less than their more experienced counterparts.

Surprisingly, however, the union-management bargaining process changed during this period. From 1979 to 1984 the level of unionized employment fell from 27.8 percent to 19.0 percent. Yet, the union-nonunion wage differential remained relatively stable and in fact grew wider in some industries. For example, the union wage rate in mining, forestry, and fisheries declined only from 25 percent higher than the nonunion wage in 1979 to 24 percent higher in 1984. On the other hand, the union wage rate in manufacturing increased slightly from approximately 14 percent higher than the nonunion wage in 1979 to 16 percent in 1984.

One explanation for this pattern of wage-employment responses is a change in union strategy—a move to maximize the individual wage rate rather than

---

[12]There is no guarantee that monopoly power and monopsony power will cancel each other, nor that the total number of workers hired will be near the competitive level, because both the monopolist and the monopsonist want to limit the number of workers hired. In "Unions and Monopoly Profits," *Review of Economics and Statistics* 67 (1985): 34–42, Thomas Karier shows that unions tend to reduce profits in highly concentrated industries, but they have little or no effect on profits in more competitive industries.

[13]This example is based on Richard Edwards and Paul Swaim, "Union-Nonunion Earnings Differentials and the Decline of Private-Sector Unionism," *American Economic Review* 76 (May 1986): 97–102.

the total wages paid to all union members. However, the demand for unionized employees has probably become increasingly elastic over time as firms find it easier to substitute capital for skilled labor in the production process. Faced with an elastic demand for its services, the union would have little choice but to maintain the wage rate of its members and to allow employment levels to fall substantially. Of course, the substitution of nonunion for union workers may cause further losses in the bargaining power of labor unions. How this will affect the differential between union and nonunion wages remains to be seen.

Summary

1. In a competitive input market, the demand for an input is given by the marginal revenue product, the product of the firm's marginal revenue and the marginal product of the input.

2. A firm in a competitive labor market will hire workers to the point at which the marginal revenue product of labor is equal to the wage rate. This is analogous to the profit-maximizing output condition that production be increased to the point at which marginal revenue is equal to marginal cost.

3. The market demand for an input is the horizontal sum of the demands for that input by all industries. Industry demand, however, is not the horizontal sum of the demands of all the firms in the industry. An appropriate determination of industry demand must take into account that the market price of the product will change in response to the change in the price of an input.

4. When factor markets are competitive, the buyer of an input assumes that its purchases will have no effect on the price of the input. As a result, the marginal expenditure and average expenditure curves that the firm faces are both perfectly elastic.

5. The market supply of a factor such as labor need not be upward-sloping. A backward-bending labor supply curve can result if the income effect associated with a higher wage rate (more leisure is demanded because leisure is a normal good) is greater than the substitution effect (less leisure is demanded because the price of leisure has gone up).

6. Economic rent is the difference between the payments to factors of production and the minimum payment that would be needed to employ those factors. In a labor market, rent is measured by the area below the wage level and above the marginal expenditure curve.

7. When a buyer of an input has monopsony power, the marginal expenditure curve lies above the average expenditure curve, which reflects that the monopsonist must pay a higher price to attract more of the input into employment.

8. Labor unions are an important example of the case in which the sellers of an input have monopoly power. When the input seller is a monopolist, the seller chooses the point on the marginal revenue product curve that best suits its objective. For labor unions, max-

imization of employment, total economic rent, and total wages are three plausible objectives.

9. When a monopolistic union bargains with a monopsonistic employer, the wage rate depends on the nature of the bargaining process. There is no reason to believe, however, that the two forces will cancel each other so that the competitive outcome would be achieved.

Questions for Review

1. Why is a firm's demand for labor curve more inelastic when the firm has monopoly power in the output market than when the firm is producing competitively?

2. Why may a labor supply curve be backward-bending?

3. How is a computer company's demand for computer programmers a derived demand?

4. Compare the hiring choices of a monopsonistic and a competitive employer of workers. Which will hire more workers, and which will pay the higher wage? Explain.

5. Rock musicians sometimes earn over $1 million per year. Can you explain this large income in terms of economic rent?

6. Explain what happens to the demand for one input when the use of a complementary input increases.

7. For a monopsonist, what is the relationship between the supply of an input and the marginal expenditure on that input?

8. Currently the National Football League has a system for drafting college players by which each player is picked by only one team and must sign with that team or not play in the league. What would happen to the wages of newly drafted and more experienced football players if the draft system were repealed, so that all teams could compete for college players?

9. Why are wages and employment levels indeterminate when the union has monopoly power and the firm has monopsony power?

Exercises

1. Suppose a firm's production function is given by $Q = 12L - L^2$, for $L = 0$ to 6, where L is labor input per day and Q is output per day. Derive and draw the firm's demand for labor curve if the output sells for $10 in a competitive market. How many workers will the firm hire when the wage rate is $30 per day? $60 per day? (Hint: The marginal product of labor is $12 - 2L$.)

2. Suppose there are two groups of workers, unionized and nonunionized. Congress passes a law that requires all workers to join the union. What do you expect to happen to the wage rates of formerly nonunionized workers and those workers who were origi-nally unionized? What have you assumed about the union's behavior?

3. Workers with incomes between $0 and $10,000 currently do not pay federal income taxes. Suppose a new government program guarantees each worker $5,000, whether or not he or she earns any income. For all earned income up to $10,000, the worker must pay a 50 percent tax to the government. Draw the budget line facing the worker under this new program. How is the program likely to affect the labor supply curve of workers?

4. The demand for labor by an industry is given by the curve $L = 1200 - 10w$, where L is the labor demanded per day and w is the wage rate. The supply curve is given by $L = 20w$. What is the equilibrium wage rate and quantity of labor hired? What is the economic rent earned by workers?

5. The demand for labor by an industry is given by the curve $L = 1200 - 10w$, where L is the labor demanded per day and w is the wage rate. The supply curve is given by $L = 20w$. Suppose the only labor available is controlled by a monopolistic labor union that wishes to maximize the rents that union members earn. What will be the quantity of labor employed and the wage rate? How does your answer compare with your answer in question 4? Discuss. (Hint: The union's marginal revenue curve is given by $L = 600 - 5w$.)

C H A P T E R   1 5

Investment, Time, and Capital Markets

In Chapter 14 we saw how firms decide on the quantities of factor inputs to employ, and how the prices of those inputs are determined. In competitive markets, firms compare the marginal revenue product of each factor to its cost to decide how much to purchase each month. The decisions of all firms determine the market demand for each factor, and the market price is the one that equates the quantity demanded with the quantity supplied. For factor inputs such as labor and raw materials, this picture is reasonably complete, but not so for capital. The reason is that capital is *durable*—it can last and contribute to production for years after it is purchased.

Firms sometimes rent capital much the way they hire workers. For example, a firm might rent office space for a monthly fee, just as it hires a worker for a monthly wage. But more often, capital expenditures involve the purchases of factories and equipment that are expected to last for years. For example, a firm might pay $10 million today to build a factory that it expects to use over the next 20 years.

This introduces the element of *time*. When a firm decides whether to build a factory or purchase machines, it must compare the outlays it would have to make *now* with the additional profit the new capital will generate *in the future*. To make this comparison, the firm must address the following question: *How much are future profits worth today?* This problem does not arise when hiring labor or purchasing raw materials. To make those choices, the firm need only compare its *current* expenditure on the factor, e.g., the wage or the price of steel, with the factor's *current* marginal revenue product.

In this chapter we will learn how to calculate the current value of future flows of money. This is the basis for our study of the firm's investment decisions. Most of these decisions involve comparing an outlay today with profits that will be received in the future; we will see how firms can make this comparison and determine whether the outlay is warranted. Often, the future profits resulting from a capital investment are uncertain; they may be higher or lower than anticipated. We will see how firms can take this kind of uncertainty into account.

We will also examine other intertemporal decisions that firms sometimes face. For example, producing a depletable resource such as coal or oil today means that less will be available to produce in the future. How should a producer take this into account? And how long should a timber company let the trees on its land grow before harvesting them for lumber?

The answers to these investment and production decisions depend in part on the *interest rate* that one pays or receives when borrowing or lending money. We will discuss what determines interest rates, and why interest rates, such as those on government bonds, corporate bonds, or savings accounts, differ.

15.1 Stocks versus Flows

Before proceeding, we must be clear about how to measure capital and other factor inputs that firms purchase. Capital is measured as a *stock*, i.e., a quantity of plant and equipment that the firm owns. For example, if a firm owns an electric motor factory worth $10 million, we say that it has a *capital stock* worth $10 million. Inputs of labor and raw materials, on the other hand, are measured as *flows*, as is the output of the firm. For example, this same firm might use 20,000 man-hours of labor and 50,000 pounds of copper *per month* to produce 8,000 electric motors *per month*. (The choice of monthly units is arbitrary; we could just as well have expressed these quantities in weekly or annual terms, for example, 240,000 man-hours of labor per year, 600,000 pounds of copper per year, and 96,000 motors per year.)

Let's look at this producer of electric motors in more detail. Both total variable cost and the rate of output are flows. Suppose the wage rate is $15 per hour and the price of copper is $0.80 per pound. Then total variable cost is (20,000)($15) + (50,000)($0.80) = $340,000 *per month*. Average variable cost, on the other hand, is a cost *per unit*: ($340,000 per month)/(8,000 units per month) = $42.50 per unit.

Suppose the firm sells its electric motors for $52.50 each. Then its average profit is $52.50 − $42.50 = $10.00 per unit, and its total profit is $80,000 *per month*. (Note that this is also a flow.) To make and sell these motors, however, the firm needs capital—the factory that it built for $10 million. *Thus, the firm's $10 million capital stock allows it to earn a flow of profit of $80,000 per month.*

Was the $10 million investment in this factory a sound decision? To answer this question, we need to translate the $80,000 per month profit flow into a number that we can compare with the factory's $10 million cost. Suppose the factory is expected to last for 20 years. Then, simply put, the problem is, What is the value today of $80,000 per month for the next 20 years? If that value is greater than $10 million, the investment was profitable.

A profit of $80,000 per month for 20 years comes to ($80,000)(20)(12) = $19.2 million. That would make the factory seem like an excellent investment. But is $80,000 five years—or 20 years—from now worth $80,000 today? No, because money today can be invested—in a bank account, a bond, or other interest-bearing assets—to yield more money in the future. As a result, $19.2 million received over the next 20 years is worth *less* than $19.2 million today.

15.2 Present Discounted Value

We will return to the $10 million electric motor factory in Section 15.4, but first we must address a basic problem: *How much is $1 paid in the future worth today?* The answer depends on the *interest rate*, the rate at which one can borrow or lend money.

Suppose the interest rate is R. (Don't worry about which interest rate this actually is; later, we'll discuss how to choose among the various types of interest rates.) Then $1 today can be invested to yield $(1 + R)$ dollars a year from now. Therefore, $1 + R$ dollars is the *future value* of $1 today. Now, what is the value today, i.e., the *present discounted value* (PDV), of $1 paid one year from now? The answer is easy, once we see that $1 + R$ dollars one year from now is worth $(1 + R)/(1 + R) = \$1$ today. Therefore, *$1 a year from now is worth $\$1/(1 + R)$ today.* This is the amount of money that will yield $1 after one year if invested at the rate R.

What is the value today of $1 paid *two* years from now? If $1 were invested today at the interest rate R, it would be worth $1 + R$ dollars after one year, and $(1 + R)(1 + R) = (1 + R)^2$ dollars at the end of two years. Since $(1 + R)^2$ dollars two years from now is worth $1 today, $1 two years from now is worth $\$1/(1 + R)^2$ today. Similarly, $1 paid three years from now is worth $\$1/(1 + R)^3$ today, and $1 paid n years from now is worth $\$1/(1 + R)^n$ today.[1] We can summarize this as follows:

$$\text{PDV of \$1 paid after 1 year} = \frac{\$1}{(1 + R)}$$

$$\text{PDV of \$1 paid after 2 years} = \frac{\$1}{(1 + R)^2}$$

$$\text{PDV of \$1 paid after 3 years} = \frac{\$1}{(1 + R)^3}$$

$$\vdots$$

$$\text{PDV of \$1 paid after } n \text{ years} = \frac{\$1}{(1 + R)^n}$$

[1] We are assuming that the annual rate of interest R is constant from year to year. Suppose the annual interest rate were expected to change, so that R_1 is the rate in year 1, R_2 is the rate in year 2, and so forth. After two years, $1 invested today would be worth $(1 + R_1)(1 + R_2)$, so that the PDV of $1 received two years from now is $\$1/(1 + R_1)(1 + R_2)$. Similarly, the PDV of $1 received n years from now is $\$1/(1 + R_1)(1 + R_2)(1 + R_3) \ldots (1 + R_n)$.

TABLE 15.1 PDV of $1 Paid in the Future

Interest Rate	1 Year	2 Years	5 Years	10 Years	20 Years	30 Years
0.01	$0.990	$0.980	$0.951	$0.905	$0.820	$0.742
0.02	0.980	0.961	0.906	0.820	0.673	0.552
0.03	0.971	0.943	0.863	0.744	0.554	0.412
0.04	0.962	0.925	0.822	0.676	0.456	0.308
0.05	0.952	0.907	0.784	0.614	0.377	0.231
0.06	0.943	0.890	0.747	0.558	0.312	0.174
0.07	0.935	0.873	0.713	0.508	0.258	0.131
0.08	0.926	0.857	0.681	0.463	0.215	0.099
0.09	0.917	0.842	0.650	0.422	0.178	0.075
0.10	0.909	0.826	0.621	0.386	0.149	0.057
0.15	0.870	0.756	0.497	0.247	0.061	0.015
0.20	0.833	0.694	0.402	0.162	0.026	0.004

Table 15.1 shows, for different interest rates, the present value of $1 paid after 1, 2, 5, 10, 20, and 30 years. Note that for interest rates above 6 or 7 percent, $1 paid 20 or 30 years from now is worth very little today; but this is not the case for low interest rates. For example, if R is 3 percent, the PDV of $1 paid 20 years from now is about 55 cents. Put another way, if 55 cents were invested now at the rate of 3 percent, it would yield about $1 after 20 years.

Valuing Payment Streams

We can now determine the present value of a stream of payments over time. For example, consider the two payment streams in Table 15.2. Stream A comes to $200: $100 paid now and $100 a year from now. Stream B comes to $220: $20 paid now, $100 a year from now, and $100 two years from now. Which of these two payment streams would you prefer to receive? The answer depends on the interest rate.

To calculate the present discounted value of these two streams, we compute and add the present values of each year's payment:

TABLE 15.2 Two Payment Streams

	Today	1 Year	2 Years
Payment Stream A:	$100	$100	0
Payment Stream B:	$20	$100	$100

$$\text{PDV of Stream A} = \$100 + \frac{\$100}{(1 + R)}$$

$$\text{PDV of Stream B} = \$20 + \frac{\$100}{(1 + R)} + \frac{\$100}{(1 + R)^2}$$

Table 15.3 shows the present values of the two streams for interest rates of 5, 10, 15, and 20 percent. As the table shows, which stream is preferred depends on the interest rate. For interest rates of 10 percent or less, Stream B is worth more; for interest rates of 15 percent or more, Stream A is worth more. The reason is that the total amount paid out in Stream A is smaller, but it is paid out sooner.

TABLE 15.3 PDV of Payment Streams

	$R = .05$	$R = .10$	$R = .15$	$R = .20$
PDV of Stream A:	$195.24	$190.90	$186.96	$183.33
PDV of Stream B:	205.94	193.54	182.57	172.77

EXAMPLE 15.1 THE VALUE OF LOST EARNINGS

In legal cases involving accidents, victims or their heirs (if the victim is killed) sue the injuring party (or an insurance company) to recover damages. In addition to recompensing pain, suffering, and emotional distress, those damages include the future income that the injured or deceased person would have earned had the accident not occurred. To see how the present value of these lost earnings can be calculated, let's examine an actual 1986 accident case. (The names and some of the data have been changed to preserve anonymity.)

Harold Jennings died in an automobile accident on January 1, 1986, at the age of 53. His family sued the driver of the other car for negligence. A major part of the damages they asked to be awarded was the present value of the earnings that Mr. Jennings would have received from his job as an airline pilot had he not been killed. The calculation of present value was typical of cases like this.

Had he worked in 1986, Mr. Jennings' salary would have been $85,000, and the normal age of retirement for an airline pilot is age 60. To calculate the present value of Mr. Jennings' lost earnings, we need to take several things into account. First, Mr. Jennings' salary would probably have increased over the years. Second, we cannot be sure that he would have lived to retirement had the accident not occurred; he might have died from some other cause. The PDV of his lost earnings until retirement at the end of 1993 is therefore

TABLE 15.4 Calculating Lost Wages

Year	$W_0(1 + g)^t$	$(1 - m_t)$	$1/(1 + R)^t$	$W_0(1 + g)^t(1 - m_t)/(1 + R)^t$
1986	$ 85,000	.991	1.000	$84,235
1987	91,800	.990	.917	83,339
1988	99,144	.989	.842	82,561
1989	107,076	.988	.772	81,671
1990	115,642	.987	.708	80,810
1991	124,893	.986	.650	80,043
1992	134,884	.985	.596	79,185
1993	145,675	.984	.547	78,408

$$PDV = W_0 + \frac{W_0(1 + g)(1 - m_1)}{(1 + R)} + \frac{W_0(1 + g)^2(1 - m_2)}{(1 + R)^2}$$
$$+ \cdots + \frac{W_0(1 + g)^7(1 - m_7)}{(1 + R)^7}$$

where W_0 is his salary in 1986, g is the annual percentage rate at which his salary is likely to have grown (so that $W_0(1 + g)$ would be his salary in 1987, $W_0(1 + g)^2$ would be his salary in 1988, etc.), and $m_1, m_2, \ldots, m_7$ are *mortality rates*, i.e., the probabilities that he would have died from some other cause by 1987, 1988, . . . , 1993.

To calculate this PDV, we need to know the mortality rates $m_1, \ldots, m_7$, the expected rate of growth of Mr. Jennings' salary g, and the interest rate R. Mortality data are available from insurance tables that provide death rates for men of similar age and race.[2] As a value for g, we can use 8 percent, the average rate of growth of wages for airline pilots over the past decade. Finally, for the interest rate we can use the rate on government bonds, which in 1986 was about 9 percent. (We will say more about how one chooses the correct interest rate to discount future cash flows in Sections 15.4 and 15.5.) Table 15.4 shows the details of the present value calculation.

By summing the last column we obtain a PDV of $650,252. If Mr. Jennings's family were successful in proving that the defendant was at fault, and there were no other damage issues involved in the case, they could recover this amount as compensation.[3]

---

[2]See, for example, the *Statistical Abstract of the United States*, 1980, Table No. 108.

[3]Actually, this sum should be reduced by the amount of Mr. Jennings' wages that would have been spent on his own consumption, and therefore would not benefit his wife or children.

15.3 The Value of a Bond

A bond is a contract in which a borrower agrees to pay the bondholder (the lender) a stream of money. For example, a corporate bond (a bond issued by a corporation) might make "coupon" payments of $100 per year for the next ten years, and then a principal payment of $1000 at the end of 10 years.[4] How much would you pay for such a bond? To find out how much the bond is worth, we simply compute the present value of the payment stream:

$$PDV = \frac{\$100}{(1 + R)} + \frac{\$100}{(1 + R)^2} + \frac{\$100}{(1 + R)^3} + \cdots + \frac{\$100}{(1 + R)^{10}} + \frac{\$1000}{(1 + R)^{10}}$$

(15.1)

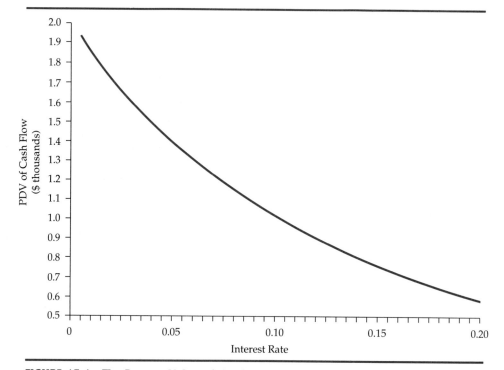

FIGURE 15.1 The Present Value of the Cash Flow from a Bond. Because most of the bond's payments occur in the future, the present discounted value of a bond declines as the interest rate increases. For example, when the interest rate is 5 percent, the PDV of a ten-year bond paying $100 per year on a principal of $1000 is $1386.

[4]In the United States the coupon payments on most corporate bonds are made in semiannual installments. We will assume that the payments are made annually to keep the arithmetic simple.

Once again, the present value depends on the interest rate. Figure 15.1 shows the value of the bond—the present value of its payment stream—for interest rates up to 20 percent. Note that the higher the interest rate, the lower the value of the bond. At an interest rate of 5 percent, the bond is worth about $1386, but at an interest rate of 15 percent, its value is only $749.

Perpetuities

A *perpetuity* is a bond that pays out a fixed amount of money each year, *forever*. How much is a perpetuity that pays $100 per year worth? The present value of the payment stream is given by

$$PDV = \frac{\$100}{(1 + R)} + \frac{\$100}{(1 + R)^2} + \frac{\$100}{(1 + R)^3} + \frac{\$100}{(1 + R)^4} + \cdots$$

where the summation has an infinite number of terms.

Fortunately, it isn't necessary to calculate and add up all these terms to find the value of this perpetuity; the summation can be expressed in terms of a simple formula[5]:

$$PDV = \$100/R \qquad (15.2)$$

So if the interest rate is 5 percent, the perpetuity is worth $100/(.05) = $2000, but if the interest rate is 20 percent, the perpetuity is worth only $500.

The Effective Yield on a Bond

Many corporate and most government bonds are traded in the *bond market*. The value of a traded bond can be determined directly by looking at its market price, since this is what buyers and sellers agree that the bond is worth.[6] Thus, most often we know the value of a bond, but to compare the bond with other investment opportunities, we would like to determine the interest rate consistent with that value.

Equations (15.1) and (15.2) show how the values of two different bonds depend on the interest rate used to discount future payments. These equations can be "turned around" to relate the interest rate to the bond's value. This is particularly easy to do for the perpetuity. Suppose the market price—and hence the value—of the perpetuity is P. Then from equation (15.2), $P = \$100/R$, and $R = \$100/P$. So if the price of the perpetuity is $1000, we know that the interest rate is $R = \$100/\$1000 = 0.10$, or 10 percent. This interest rate is called the

---

[5]Let x be the PDV of $1 per year in perpetuity, so $x = 1/(1 + R) + 1/(1 + R)^2 + \ldots$. Then $x(1 + R) = 1 + 1/(1 + R) + 1/(1 + R)^2 + \ldots$, so $x(1 + R) = 1 + x$, $xR = 1$, and $x = 1/R$.

[6]The prices of actively traded corporate and U.S. government bonds are shown daily in newspapers such as the *Wall Street Journal* and the *New York Times*.

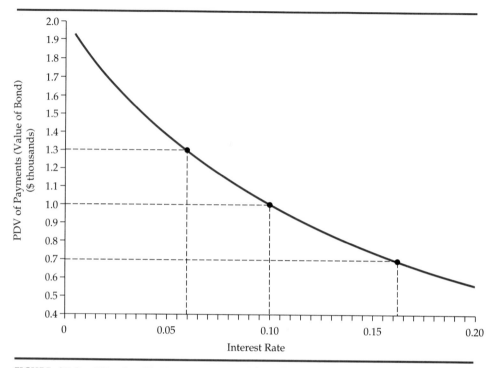

FIGURE 15.2   Effective Yield on a Bond.   The effective yield is the interest rate that equates the present value of the bond's payment stream with the bond's market price. The figure shows the present value of the payment stream as a function of the interest rate, so the effective yield can be found by drawing a horizontal line at the level of the bond's price. For example, if the price of this bond were $1000, its effective yield would be about 10 percent. If the price were $1300, the effective yield would be about 7 percent, and if the price were $700, the effective yield would be 17.4 percent.

effective yield, or *rate of return*. It is the percentage return that one receives by investing in the perpetuity.

For the ten-year coupon bond in equation (15.1), calculating the effective yield is a bit more complicated. If the price of the bond is P, we write equation (15.1) as

$$P = \frac{\$100}{(1 + R)} + \frac{\$100}{(1 + R)^2} + \frac{\$100}{(1 + R)^3} + \cdots + \frac{\$100}{(1 + R)^{10}} + \frac{\$1000}{(1 + R)^{10}}$$

Given the price P, this equation must be solved for R. Although no simple formula expresses R in terms of P in this case, there are methods (sometimes available on hand-held calculators) for calculating R numerically. Figure 15.2, which plots the same curve that is in Figure 15.1, shows how R depends on P for this bond. Note that if the price of the bond is $1000, the effective yield is

10 percent. If the price rises to $1300, the figure shows that the effective yield drops to about 6 percent. If the price falls to $700, the effective yield rises to over 16 percent.

Yields can differ considerably among different bonds. Corporate bonds generally yield more than government bonds, and as Example 15.2 shows, the bonds of some corporations yield much more than the bonds of others. One of the most important reasons for this is that different bonds carry different degrees of risk. The U.S. government is less likely to *default* (fail to make interest or principal payments) on its bonds than is a private corporation. And some corporations are financially stronger and therefore less likely to default on their bonds than others. As we saw in Chapter 5, the more risky an investment is, the greater the return that an investor demands. As a result, riskier bonds have higher yields.

EXAMPLE 15.2   THE YIELDS ON CORPORATE BONDS

To see how corporate bond yields are calculated, and how they can differ from one corporation to another, let's examine the yields for two coupon bonds— one issued by IBM and the other by Bethlehem Steel. Each has a *face value* of $1000, which means that when the bond matures, the holder receives a principal payment of that amount. Each bond makes a "coupon" (i.e., interest) payment every six months.

We calculate the bond yields using the closing prices on August 4, 1987. The following information on the bonds appeared on the bond page of the newspapers on August 5:

For IBM:

IBM   10¼ 95 9.6   20   107   107 107 +½

And for Bethlehem Steel:

BethSt   9s00   12.9   136   71⅜   70   70   . . .

What do these numbers mean? For IBM, 10¼ refers to the coupon payments *over one year*. This bond pays $5.125 every six months, for a total of $10.25 per year. The number 95 means the bond matures in 1995 (at which time the holder receives $100 in principal). The next number, 9.6, is the annual coupon divided by the bond's closing price (i.e., 10.25/107). The number 20 refers to the number of these IBM bonds traded that day. The next three numbers, 107, 107, and 107, are the high, low, and closing prices for the bond. Finally, the +½ means that the closing price was ½ point higher than the preceding day's close.[7]

---

[7]These bonds actually have a face value of $1000, not $100. The prices and coupon payments are listed as though the face value were $100 to save space. To get the actual prices and payments, just multiply the numbers that appear in the newspaper by ten.

What is the yield on this bond? For simplicity, we'll assume the coupon payments are made annually, instead of every six months. (The error that this introduces is very small.) Because the bond matures in 1995, payments will be made for 1995–1987 = eight years. The yield is then given by the following equation:

$$107 = \frac{10.25}{(1 + R)} + \frac{10.25}{(1 + R)^2} + \frac{10.25}{(1 + R)^3} + \cdots + \frac{10.25}{(1 + R)^8} + \frac{100}{(1 + R)^8}$$

This equation must be solved for R. You can check (by substituting and seeing whether the equation is satisfied) that the solution is $R^* = 9.0$ percent.

The yield on the Bethlehem Steel bond is found in the same way. This bond makes coupon payments of $9 per year, matures in the year 2000, and had a price of $70. Since the bond has 13 years to mature, the equation for its yield is

$$70 = \frac{9}{(1 + R)} + \frac{9}{(1 + R)^2} + \frac{9}{(1 + R)^3} + \cdots + \frac{9}{(1 + R)^{13}} + \frac{100}{(1 + R)^{13}}$$

The solution to this equation is $R^* = 14.2$ percent.

Why is the yield on the Bethlehem Steel bond so much higher than that on the IBM bond? Because it is much riskier. In 1987 and for several years before, steel prices were depressed, and Bethlehem Steel was not profitable. Given its uncertain financial situation, investors required a higher return before they would hold Bethlehem Steel's bonds.

15.4   The Net Present Value Criterion for Capital Investment Decisions

One of the most common and important decisions that firms make is to invest in new capital. Millions of dollars may be invested in a factory or machines that will last—and affect the firm's profits—for many years. The future cash flows that the investment will generate are often uncertain. And once the factory has been built, the firm usually cannot disassemble and resell it to recoup its investment—it becomes a sunk cost.

How should a firm decide whether a particular capital investment is worthwhile? It should calculate the present value of the future cash flows that it expects to receive from the investment, and compare it with the cost of the investment. This is the *Net Present Value (NPV) criterion*:

NPV Criterion: Invest if the present value of the expected future cash flows from an investment is larger than the cost of the investment.

Suppose a capital investment costs C and is expected to generate profits over the next ten years of amounts $\pi_1, \pi_2, \ldots, \pi_{10}$. Then we write the net present value as

$$\text{NPV} = -C + \frac{\pi_1}{(1 + R)} + \frac{\pi_2}{(1 + R)^2} + \frac{\pi_3}{(1 + R)^3} + \cdots + \frac{\pi_{10}}{(1 + R)^{10}} \quad (15.3)$$

where R is the *discount rate* that we use to discount the future stream of profits. (R might be a market interest rate, or it might be some other rate; we will discuss how to choose it shortly.) Equation (15.3) describes the net benefit to the firm from the investment. The firm should make the investment only if that net benefit is positive, i.e., *only if NPV > 0.*

What discount rate should the firm use? The answer depends on the alternative ways that the firm could use its money. For example, instead of this investment, the firm might invest in another piece of capital that generates a different stream of profits. Or it might invest in a bond that yields a different return. As a result, we can think of R as the *firm's opportunity cost of capital.* Had the firm not invested in this project, it could have earned a return by investing in something else. *The correct value for R is therefore the return that the firm could earn on a "similar" investment.*

By "similar" investment, we mean one with the same *risk.* As we saw in Chapter 5, the more risky an investment, the greater the return one expects to receive from it. Therefore, the opportunity cost of investing in this project is the return that one could earn from another project or asset of similar riskiness.

We'll see how to evaluate the riskiness of an investment in the next section. For now, let's assume that this project has *no risk* (i.e., the firm is sure that the future profit flows will be π_1, π_2, etc.). Then the opportunity cost of the investment is the *risk-free return,* e.g., the return one could earn on a government bond. If the project is expected to last for ten years, the firm could use the annual interest rate on a ten-year government bond to compute the NPV of the project, as in equation (15.3).[8] If the NPV is zero, the benefit from the investment would just equal the opportunity cost, so the firm should be indifferent between investing and not investing. If the NPV is greater than zero, the benefit exceeds the opportunity cost, so the investment should be made.

The Electric Motor Factory

In Section 15.1, we discussed a decision to invest $10 million in a factory to produce electric motors. This factory would enable the firm to use labor and copper to produce 8,000 motors per month for 20 years, at a cost of $42.50 each. The motors could be sold for $52.50 each, for a profit of $10 per unit, or $80,000 per month. We will assume that after 20 years the factory will be obsolete, but it can be sold for scrap for $1 million. Is this a good investment? To find out, we must calculate its net present value.

---

[8]This is an approximation. To be precise, the firm should use the rate on a one-year bond to discount π_1, the rate on a two-year bond to discount π_2, etc.

We will assume for now that the $42.50 production cost and the $52.50 price at which the motors can be sold are certain, so that the firm is sure it will receive $80,000 per month, or $960,000 per year, in profit. We also assume that the $1 million scrap value of the factory is certain. The firm should therefore use a risk-free interest rate to discount future profits. Writing the cash flows in millions of dollars, the NPV is

$$
\text{NPV} = -10 + \frac{.96}{(1 + R)} + \frac{.96}{(1 + R)^2} + \frac{.96}{(1 + R)^3}
$$
$$
+ \cdots + \frac{.96}{(1 + R)^{20}} + \frac{1}{(1 + R)^{20}} \tag{15.4}
$$

Figure 15.3 shows the NPV as a function of the discount rate R. Note that at the rate R^*, which is about 7.5 percent, the NPV is equal to zero.[9] For discount rates below 7.5 percent, the NPV is positive, so the firm should invest in the factory. For discount rates above 7.5 percent, the NPV is negative, and the firm should not invest.

Real versus Nominal Discount Rates

In the example above, we assumed that future cash flows are certain, so that the discount rate R should be a risk-free interest rate, such as the rate on U.S. government bonds. Suppose that rate happened to be 9 percent. Does that mean the NPV is negative and the firm should not invest?

To answer this question, we must distinguish between real and nominal discount rates, and between real and nominal cash flows. Let's begin with the cash flows. In Chapter 1 we discussed real versus nominal prices, and we explained that the real price is *net of inflation*, whereas the nominal price includes inflation. In our example, we assumed that the electric motors coming out of the factory could be sold for $52.50 each over the next 20 years. We said nothing, however, about the effect of inflation. Is the $52.50 a real price, net of inflation, or does it include inflation? As we will see, the answer to this question can be critical.

Let's assume that the $52.50 price—and the $42.50 production cost—are in *real* terms. (This means that if we expect a 5 percent annual rate of inflation, the nominal price of the motors will increase from $52.50 in the first year to $(1.05)(52.50) = 55.13 in the second year, to $(1.05)(55.13) = 57.88 in the third year, and so on.) Therefore, our profit of $960,000 per year is also in real terms.

Now let's turn to the discount rate. *If the cash flows are in real terms, the discount rate must also be in real terms.* The reason is that the discount rate is the opportunity cost of the investment. If inflation is not included in the cash flows from the investment, it should not be included in the opportunity cost either.

---

[9]The rate R^* is sometimes referred to as the *internal rate of return* on the investment.

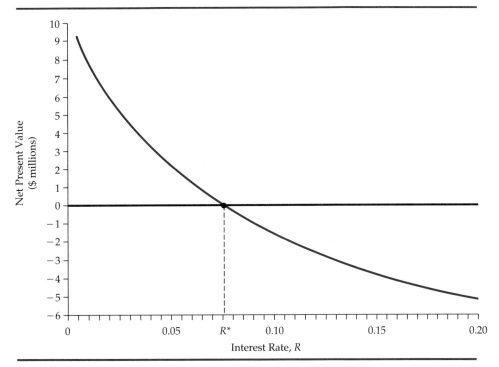

FIGURE 15.3   Net Present Value of a Factory.   The NPV of a factory is the present discounted value of all the cash flows involved in building and operating it. Here it is the PDV of the flow of future profits less the current cost of construction. Note that the NPV declines as the interest rate increases. At the interest rate R^*, the NPV is zero.

In our example, the discount rate should therefore be the *real* interest rate on government bonds. The nominal interest rate (9 percent) is the rate that we see in the newspapers; it includes inflation. *The real interest rate is the nominal rate minus the expected rate of inflation.*[10] If we expect inflation to be 5 percent per year on average, the real interest rate would be $9 - 5 = 4$ percent. This is the discount rate that should be used to calculate the NPV of the investment in the electric motor factory. Note from Figure 15.3 that at this rate the NPV is clearly positive, so the investment should be undertaken.

When using the NPV rule to evaluate investments, the numbers in the calculations may be in real or in nominal terms, as long as they are consistent. If cash flows are in real terms, the discount rate should also be in real terms. If a nominal discount rate is used, the effect of future inflation must also be included in the cash flows.

[10]People can have different views about future inflation, and may therefore have different estimates of the real interest rate.

Negative Future Cash Flows

Factories and other production facilities can take several years to build and equip. Then, the cost of the investment will also be spread out over several years, instead of occurring only at the outset. In addition, some investments are expected to result in *losses*, rather than profits, for the first few years. (For example, demand may be low until consumers learn about the product, or costs may start high and fall only when managers and workers have moved down the learning curve.) Negative future cash flows create no problem for the NPV rule; they are simply discounted just like positive cash flows.

For example, now let's suppose that our electric motor factory will take a year to build: $5 million is spent right away and another $5 million is spent next year. Also, suppose the factory is expected to *lose* $1 million in its first year of operation and $0.5 million in its second year. Afterwards, it will earn $0.96 million a year until year 20, when it will be scrapped for $1 million, as before. (All these cash flows are in real terms.) Now the net present value is

$$\text{NPV} = -5 - \frac{5}{(1 + R)} - \frac{1}{(1 + R)^2} - \frac{.5}{(1 + R)^3} + \frac{.96}{(1 + R)^4} + \frac{.96}{(1 + R)^5}$$

$$+ \cdots + \frac{.96}{(1 + R)^{20}} + \frac{1}{(1 + R)^{20}} \tag{15.5}$$

Suppose the real interest rate is 4 percent. Should the firm build this factory? You can confirm that the NPV is positive, so this project is a good investment.

15.5 Adjustments for Risk

We have seen that a risk-free interest rate is an appropriate discount rate for future cash flows that are certain. For most projects, however, future cash flows are far from certain. For example, for our electric motor factory, we would expect uncertainty over future copper prices, over the future demand and hence the price of motors, and even over future wage rates. Thus, the firm cannot know what its profits from the factory will be over the next 20 years. Its best estimate of profits might be $960,000 per year, but actual profits may turn out to be higher or lower than this. How should the firm take this uncertainty into account when calculating the net present value of the project?

A common practice is to increase the discount rate by adding a *risk premium* to the risk-free rate. The idea is that the owners of the firm are risk averse, which makes future cash flows that are risky worth less than those that are certain. Increasing the discount rate takes this into account by reducing the present value of those future cash flows. But how large should the risk premium be? We discuss this below.

Diversifiable versus Nondiversifiable Risk

Adding a risk premium to the discount rate must be done with care. If the firm's managers are operating in the stockholders' interests, they must distinguish between two kinds of risk—*diversifiable* and *nondiversifiable risk*.[11] Diversifiable risk can be eliminated by investing in many projects or by holding the stocks of many companies. Nondiversifiable risk cannot be eliminated in this way. *Only nondiversifiable risk affects the opportunity cost of capital, and should enter into the risk premium.*

To understand this, recall from Chapter 5 that diversifying can eliminate many risks. For example, I cannot know whether the result of a coin flip will be heads or tails. But I can be reasonably sure that of a thousand coin flips, roughly half will be heads. Similarly, an insurance company that sells me life insurance cannot know how long I will live. But by selling life insurance to thousands of people, it can be reasonably sure about the fraction of those people that will die each year.

Much the same is true about capital investment decisions. Although the profit flow from a single investment may be very risky, if the firm invests in dozens of projects (as most large firms do), its overall risk will be much less. Furthermore, even if the company invests in only one project, the stockholders can easily diversify by holding the stocks of a dozen or more different companies, or by holding a mutual fund that invests in many stocks. So the stockholders, i.e., the owners of the firm, can eliminate diversifiable risk.

Because investors can eliminate diversifiable risk, they cannot expect to earn a return higher than the risk-free rate by bearing it. (No one will pay you for bearing a risk that there is no need to bear.) And indeed, assets that have only diversifiable risk tend on average to earn a return close to the risk-free rate. Now, remember that the discount rate for a project is the opportunity cost of investing in that project, rather than in some other project or asset with *similar risk characteristics*. Therefore, if the project's only risk is diversifiable, the opportunity cost is the risk-free rate, *and no risk premium should be added to the discount rate.*

What about nondiversifiable risk? First, let's be clear about how it can arise. For a life insurance company, the possibility of a major war poses nondiversifiable risk. A war may increase mortality rates sharply, and the company could not expect that an "average" number of its customers would die each year, no matter how many customers it had. As a result, most insurance policies, whether for life, health, or property, do not cover losses resulting from acts of war.

---

[11]Diversifiable risk is also called *nonsystematic risk,* and nondiversifiable risk is called *systematic* risk. Adding a simple risk premium to the discount rate may cause problems, which sometimes make it an incorrect way of dealing with risk. We do not deal with those problems here; the interested reader should refer to a standard text in corporate finance. A good one is Richard Brealey and Stewart Myers, *Principles of Corporate Finance* (New York: McGraw-Hill, 1986).

For capital investments, nondiversifiable risk arises because firms' profits, and profits from individual projects, tend to depend on the overall economy. When economic growth is strong, corporate profits tend to be higher. (For our electric motor factory, the demand for motors is likely to be strong, so profits increase.) On the other hand, profits tend to fall in a recession. Because the profits of most companies tend to reflect the economy, and because future economic growth is uncertain, diversification cannot eliminate all risk. Investors should (and indeed can) earn a higher return by bearing this risk.

To the extent that a project has nondiversifiable risk, the opportunity cost of investing in that project is higher than the risk-free rate, and a risk premium must be included in the discount rate. Let's see how the size of that risk premium can be determined.

The Capital Asset Pricing Model

The *Capital Asset Pricing Model* (CAPM) measures the risk premium for a capital investment by comparing the expected return on that investment with the expected return on the entire stock market. To understand the model, suppose, first, that you invest in the entire stock market (say, through a mutual fund). Then your investment would be completely diversified, and you would bear no diversifiable risk. You would, however, bear nondiversifiable risk because the stock market tends to move with the overall economy. (The stock market reflects expected future profits, which depend in part on the economy.) As a result, the expected return on the stock market is higher than the risk-free rate. Denoting the expected return on the stock market by r_m and the risk-free rate by r_f, the risk premium on the market is $r_m - r_f$. This is the additional expected return one can expect to earn by bearing the nondiversifiable risk associated with the stock market.

Now consider the nondiversifiable risk associated with one asset, such as a company's stock. We can measure that risk in terms of the extent to which the return on the asset tends to be *correlated* with (move in the same direction as) the return on the stock market as a whole. For example, one company's stock might have almost no correlation with the market as a whole. On average, the price of that stock would move independently of changes in the market, so it would have little or no nondiversifiable risk. The return on that stock should therefore be about the same as the risk-free rate. Another stock, however, might be highly correlated with the market. Its price changes might even amplify changes in the market as a whole. That stock would have substantial nondiversifiable risk, perhaps more than the stock market as a whole, in which case its return on average will exceed the market return r_m.

The CAPM summarizes this relationship between expected returns by the following equation:

$$r_i - r_f = \beta(r_m - r_f)$$ (15.6)

where r_i is the expected return on an asset. The equation says that the risk premium on the asset (its expected return less the risk-free rate) is proportional to the risk premium on the market. The constant of proportionality, β, is called the *asset beta*. It measures how sensitive the asset's return is to market movements and therefore the asset's nondiversifiable risk. If a 1 percent rise in the market tends to result in a 2 percent rise in price of the asset, the beta is 2. If a 1 percent rise in the market tends to result in a 1 percent rise in the price of the asset, the beta is 1. And if a 1 percent rise in the market tends to result in no change in the price of the asset, the beta is zero. As equation (15.6) shows, the larger is beta, the greater is the expected return on the asset, because the greater is the asset's nondiversifiable risk.

Given beta, we can determine the correct discount rate to use in computing an asset's net present value. That discount rate is the expected return on the asset or on another asset with the same risk. It is therefore the risk-free rate plus a risk premium to reflect nondiversifiable risk:

$$\text{Discount rate} = r_f + \beta(r_m - r_f) \tag{15.7}$$

Over the past 60 years, the risk premium on the stock market, $(r_m - r_f)$, has been about 8 percent on average. If the real risk-free rate were 4 percent and beta were 0.5, the correct discount rate would thus be $0.04 + 0.5(0.08) = 0.08$, or 8 percent.

If the asset is a stock, its beta can usually be estimated statistically.[12] When the asset is a new factory, however, determining its beta is more difficult. Many firms therefore use a company cost of capital as a (nominal) discount rate. The company cost of capital is a weighted average of the expected return on the company's stock (which depends on the beta of the stock) and the interest rate it pays for debt. This approach is correct as long as the capital investment in question is typical for the company as a whole. It can be misleading, however, if the capital investment has much more or much less nondiversifiable risk than the company as a whole. In that case it may be better to make a reasoned guess as to how much the revenues from the investment are likely to depend on the overall economy.

EXAMPLE 15.3 CAPITAL INVESTMENT IN THE DISPOSABLE DIAPER INDUSTRY

In Example 13.6, we discussed the disposable diaper industry, which has been dominated by Procter & Gamble, with about a 65 percent market share, and Kimberly-Clark, with another 20 to 25 percent. We explained that their continuing R&D (research and development) expenditures have given these firms a

---

[12]One can estimate beta by running a linear regression of the return on the stock against the excess return on the market, $r_m - r_f$. One would find, for example, that the beta for Digital Equipment is about 1.4, the beta for Eastman Kodak is about 0.8, and the beta for General Motors is about 0.5.

TABLE 15.5 Data for NPV Calculation ($ millions)

	Pre-1990	1990	1991	1992	· · ·	2005
Sales		133.3	266.7	400.0	· · ·	400.0
LESS						
Variable cost		96.7	193.3	290.0	· · ·	290.0
Ongoing R&D		20.0	20.0	20.0	· · ·	20.0
Sales force, ads, and promotion		50.0	50.0	50.0	· · ·	50.0
Operating profit		−33.4	3.4	40.0	· · ·	40.0
LESS						
Construction cost	60.0	60.0	60.0			
Initial R&D	60.0					
NET CASH FLOW	−120.0	−93.4	−56.6	40.0	· · ·	40.0

	Discount Rate:	0.05	0.10	0.15
	NPV:	80.5	−16.9	−75.1

cost advantage that deters entry. Now we'll examine the capital investment decision of a potential entrant.

Suppose you are considering entering this industry. To take advantage of scale economies, both in production and in advertising and distribution, you would need to build three plants at a cost of $60 million each, which, when operating at capacity, would produce 2.5 billion diapers per year. These would be sold at wholesale for about 16 cents per diaper, yielding revenues of about $400 million per year. You can expect your variable production costs to be about $290 million per year, for a net revenue of $110 million per year.

You will have other expenses, however. Using the experience of P&G and Kimberly-Clark as a guide, you can expect to spend about $60 million in R&D before start-up to design an efficient manufacturing process, and another $20 million in R&D during each year of production to maintain and improve that process. Finally, once operating at full capacity, you can expect to spend another $50 million per year for a sales force, advertising, and marketing, for a net operating profit of $40 million per year. The plants will last for 15 years and will then be obsolete.[13]

Is the investment a good idea? To find out, let's calculate its net present value. Table 15.5 shows the relevant numbers. We assume that production begins at 33 percent of capacity in 1990, takes two years to reach full capacity,

[13]These numbers are based on Michael E. Porter, "The Disposable Diaper Industry," Harvard Business School Case 9–380–175, July 1981, the teaching notes that accompany that case, as well as articles from the *New York Times*.

and continues through the year 2005. Given the net cash flows, the NPV is calculated as

$$NPV = -120 - \frac{93.4}{(1 + R)} - \frac{56.6}{(1 + R)^2} + \frac{40}{(1 + R)^3}$$
$$+ \frac{40}{(1 + R)^4} + \cdots + \frac{40}{(1 + R)^{15}}$$

The table shows the NPV for discount rates of 5, 10, and 15 percent.

Note that the NPV is positive for a discount rate of 5 percent, but it is negative for discount rates of 10 or 15 percent. What is the correct discount rate? First, we have ignored inflation, so the discount rate should be in *real* terms. Second, the cash flows are risky—we don't know how efficient our plants will be, how effective our advertising and promotion will be, or even what the future demand for disposable diapers will be. Some of this risk is nondiversifiable.[14] To calculate the risk premium, we will use a beta of 1, which is typical for a producer of consumer products of this sort. Using 4 percent for the real risk-free interest rate and 8 percent for the risk premium on the stock market, our discount rate should be

$$R = 0.04 + 1(0.08) = 0.12$$

At this discount rate, the NPV is clearly negative, so the investment does not make sense. We will not enter the industry; P&G and Kimberly-Clark can breathe a sigh of relief. You should not be surprised, however, that these firms can make money in this market while we cannot. Their experience, years of earlier R&D, and brand name recognition give them a competitive advantage that a new entrant would find hard to overcome. (For example, they would not need to spend $60 million on R&D before building new plants.)

15.6 Investment Decisions by Consumers

We have seen how firms can value future cash flows and thereby decide whether to invest in long-lived capital. Consumers also face decisions of this kind every time they purchase a durable good, such as a car or major appliance. Unlike the decision to purchase food, entertainment, or clothing, buying a durable good involves comparing a flow of *future* benefits with the *current* purchase cost.

---

[14]We could forecast the number of babies that will be born over the next 15 years, but that will be subject to error. Also, consumption of disposable diapers is sensitive to the overall economy. During recessions, some families turn to cloth diapers to save money.

Suppose you are deciding whether to buy a new car. You might plan to keep the car for six or seven years, in which case most of the benefits (and costs of operation) will occur in the future. You must therefore compare the future flow of net benefits from owning the car (the benefit of having transportation less the cost of insurance, maintenance, and gasoline to operate the car) with the purchase price. The same kind of comparison applies to other durable goods. For example, when deciding whether to buy a new air conditioner, you must compare the price of the unit with the present value of the flow of net benefits (the benefit of a cool room less the cost of electricity to operate the unit).

These problems are exactly analogous to the problem of a firm, which must compare a future flow of profits with the current cost of plant and equipment when making a capital investment decision. We can therefore analyze these problems just as we analyzed the firm's investment problem. Let's do this for a consumer's decision to buy a car.

The main benefit from owning a car is the flow of transportation services it provides. The value of those services differs from consumer to consumer (and for any one consumer, it may depend on the particular car—how well it performs, whether it is air conditioned, etc.). Let's assume our consumer values the service at S dollars per year. Let's also assume that the total operating expense (insurance, maintenance, and gasoline) is E dollars per year, that the car costs \$10,000, and that after six years its resale value will be \$2000. The decision to buy the car can then be framed in net present value terms:

$$\text{NPV} = -10{,}000 + (S - E) + \frac{(S - E)}{(1 + R)} + \frac{(S - E)}{(1 + R)^2}$$
$$+ \cdots + \frac{(S - E)}{(1 + R)^6} + \frac{2000}{(1 + R)^6} \tag{15.8}$$

What discount rate R should the consumer use? The consumer should apply the same principle that the firm does—the discount rate is the opportunity cost of money. If the consumer already has \$10,000 and does not need a loan, the correct discount rate is the return that could be earned by investing the money in another asset, say, a savings account or a government bond. On the other hand, if the consumer is in debt, the discount rate would be the borrowing rate that he or she is already paying. This rate is likely to be much higher than the interest rate on a bond or savings account, so the NPV of the investment will be smaller.

EXAMPLE 15.4   CHOOSING AN AIR CONDITIONER

Buying a new air conditioner involves making a trade-off. Some air conditioners cost less, but are less efficient—they consume a lot of electricity relative to their cooling power. Other air conditioners cost more but are also more efficient. Should you buy an inefficient air conditioner that costs less now but will cost more in the future to operate, or an efficient one that costs more now but will cost less to operate?

Let's assume you are comparing air conditioners of equivalent cooling power, so that they yield the same flow of benefits. We can then compare the present discounted values of their costs. Assuming an eight-year lifetime and no resale, the PDV of the costs of buying and operating air conditioner i is

$$PDV = C_i + OC_i + \frac{OC_i}{(1 + R)} + \frac{OC_i}{(1 + R)^2} + \cdots + \frac{OC_i}{(1 + R)^8}$$

where C_i is the purchase price of air conditioner i and OC_i is its average annual operating cost.

Which air conditioner is best depends on your discount rate. If you have little free cash and must borrow, you would probably use a high discount rate. This would make the present value of the future operating costs smaller, so you would probably choose a less expensive but relatively inefficient unit. If you have plenty of free cash, so that your opportunity cost of money (and hence your discount rate) is low, you would probably buy the more expensive unit.

An econometric study of household purchases of air conditioners shows that consumers indeed tend to trade off capital costs and expected future operating costs in just this way, although the discount rates that people use are high—about 20 percent for the population as a whole.[15] (American consumers seem to behave myopically by overdiscounting future savings.) The study also shows that consumers' discount rates vary inversely with their incomes. (For example, people whose 1978 annual income was between $25,000 and $35,000 used discount rates of about 9 percent, while those with incomes under $10,000 used discount rates of 39 percent or more.) We would expect this, because higher-income people are likely to have more free cash available and therefore have a lower opportunity cost of money.

15.7 Intertemporal Production Decisions—Depletable Resources

Firms' production decisions often have *intertemporal* aspects—production today affects sales or costs in the future. The learning curve, which we discussed in Chapter 7, is an example of this. By producing today, the firm gains experience that lowers its future costs. In this case production today is partly an investment in future cost reduction, and the value of this must be taken into account when comparing costs and benefits. Another example is the production of a depletable resource. When the owner of an oil well pumps oil today, less oil is available

[15]See Jerry A. Hausman, "Individual Discount Rates and the Purchase and Utilization of Energy-Using Durables," *Bell Journal of Economics* 10 (Spring 1979): 33–54.

for future production. This must be taken into account when deciding how much to produce.

Production decisions in cases like these involve comparisons between costs and benefits today with costs and benefits in the future. We can make those comparisons using the concept of present discounted value. We'll look in detail at the case of a depletable resource, although the same principles apply to other intertemporal production decisions.

The Production Decision of an Individual Resource Producer

Suppose your rich uncle gave you an oil well. The well contains 1000 barrels of oil that can be produced at a constant average and marginal cost of $10 per barrel. Should you produce all the oil today, or should you save it for the future?[16]

You might think that the answer depends on the profit you can earn if you remove the oil from the ground. After all, why not remove the oil if its price is greater than the cost of extraction? However, this ignores the opportunity cost of using up the oil today so that it is not available for the future.

The correct answer, then, depends not on the current profit level, but on how fast you expect the price of oil to rise. Oil in the ground is like money in the bank, and you should keep it in the ground only if it earns a return at least as high as the market interest rate. So if you expect the price of oil to remain constant or rise very slowly, you would be better off extracting and selling all of it now and investing the proceeds. But if you expect the price of oil to rise rapidly, you should leave it in the ground.

How fast must the price rise for you to keep the oil in the ground? The value of each barrel of oil in your well is equal to the price of oil, less the $10 cost of extracting it. (This is the profit you can obtain by extracting and selling each barrel.) This value must rise at least as fast as the rate of interest for you to keep the oil. Your production decision rule is therefore: *Keep all your oil if you expect its price less its extraction cost to rise faster than the rate of interest. Extract and sell all of it if you expect price less cost to rise at less than the rate of interest.* And what if you expect price less cost to rise at exactly the rate of interest? Then you would be indifferent between extracting the oil and leaving it in the ground. Letting P_t be the price of oil this year, P_{t+1} be the price next year, and c the cost of extraction, we can write this production rule as follows:

$$\text{If } (P_{t+1} - c) > (1 + R)(P_t - c), \text{ keep the oil in the ground.}$$

$$\text{If } (P_{t+1} - c) < (1 + R)(P_t - c), \text{ sell all the oil now.}$$

$$\text{If } (P_{t+1} - c) = (1 + R)(P_t - c), \text{ makes no difference.}$$

---

[16]For most real oil wells, marginal and average cost are not constant, and it would be extremely costly to extract all the oil in a short time. We will ignore this complication.

Given our expectation about the growth rate of oil prices, we can use this rule to determine production. But how fast should we expect the market price of oil to rise?

The Behavior of Market Price

Suppose there were no OPEC cartel, and the oil market consisted of many competitive producers with oil wells like our own. We could then determine how fast oil prices are likely to rise by considering the production decisions of other producers. If other producers want to earn the highest possible return, they will follow the production rule we stated above. This means that *price less marginal cost must rise at exactly the rate of interest.*[17] To see why, suppose price less cost were to rise faster than the rate of interest. Then no one would sell any oil. Inevitably, this would drive the current price of oil up. If, on the other hand, price less cost were to rise at a rate less than the rate of interest, everyone would try to sell all of their oil immediately, which would drive the current price down.

Figure 15.4 illustrates how the market price must rise. The marginal cost of extraction is c, and the price and total quantity produced are initially P_0 and Q_0. Figure 15.4a shows the net price, $P - c$, rising at the rate of interest. Figure 15.4b shows that as price rises, the quantity demanded falls. This continues until time T, when all the oil has been used up, and the price P_T is such that demand is just zero.[18]

User Cost

We saw in Chapter 8 that a competitive firm always produces up to the point where price is equal to marginal cost. However, in a competitive market for an exhaustible resource, price *exceeds* marginal cost (and the difference between price and marginal cost rises over time). Does this conflict with what we learned in Chapter 8?

No, once we recognize that the *total* marginal cost of producing an exhaustible resource is greater than the marginal cost of extracting it from the ground. There

---

[17]This result is called the Hotelling rule for an exhaustible resource, because it was first demonstrated by Harold Hotelling in "The Economics of Exhaustible Resources," *Journal of Political Economy* 39 (April 1931): 137–175.

[18]We have assumed that the market is competitive. If the market were dominated by a cartel or a monopolist, *price would rise more slowly.* The reason is that the monopolist takes into account the value of the *marginal* barrel of oil, because unlike a competitive producer, its marginal revenue from producing and selling that barrel is not equal to the market price. The monopolist will produce at a rate such that *marginal revenue less marginal cost rises at the rate of interest.* (If marginal revenues less marginal cost rise at less than the rate of interest, the monopolist is earning too low a rate of return and should extract the oil faster; if marginal revenue less marginal cost is rising faster than the rate of interest, the monopolist should keep the marginal barrel in the ground.) Since price exceeds marginal revenue, *price* less marginal cost will rise at less than the rate of interest.

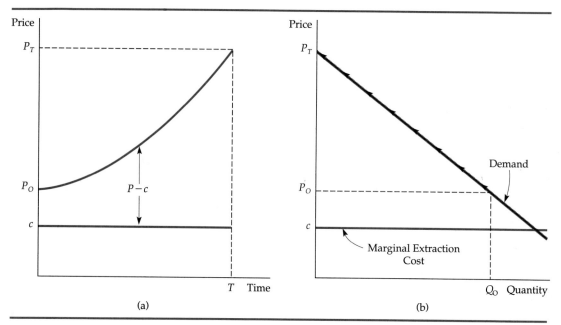

FIGURE 15.4 Price of an Exhaustible Resource. In part (a), the price is shown rising over time. Units of a resource in the ground must earn a return commensurate with that on other assets. Therefore, in a competitive market, price less marginal production cost will rise at the rate of interest. Part (b) shows that over time the price moves up the demand curve.

is an additional opportunity cost because producing and selling a unit today makes it unavailable for production and sale in the future. We call this opportunity cost the *user cost* of production. In Figure 15.4, user cost is the difference between price and marginal production cost. It rises over time because as the resource remaining in the ground becomes scarcer, it becomes more valuable, so that the opportunity cost of depleting another unit becomes higher.

EXAMPLE 15.5 HOW DEPLETABLE ARE DEPLETABLE RESOURCES?

Resources like oil, natural gas, coal, uranium, copper, iron, lead, zinc, nickel, and helium are all depletable—there is a finite amount of each in the earth's crust, so that ultimately the production and consumption of each will cease. Nonetheless, some resources are more depletable than others.

For oil, natural gas, and helium,[19] known and potentially discoverable in-

[19]Almost all helium is a by-product of natural gas.

TABLE 15.6 User Cost as a Fraction of Competitive Price

Resource	User Cost/Competitive Price
Crude oil	.4 to .5
Natural gas	.4 to .5
Uranium	.1 to .2
Copper	.2
Bauxite	.05 to .1
Nickel	.1 to .2

ground reserves are equal to only 50 to 100 years of current consumption. For these resources, the user cost of depletion can be a significant component of the market price. Other resources, however, such as coal and iron, have a proved and potential reserve base equal to several hundred or even thousands of years of current consumption. For these resources, the user cost is very small.

The user cost for a resource can be estimated from geological information about existing and potentially discoverable reserves (i.e., the total amount that can ultimately be produced and consumed) and from knowledge of the demand curve and the rate at which that curve is likely to shift out over time in response to economic growth. Or if the market is competitive, user cost can be determined from the economic rent earned by the owners of resource-bearing lands.

Table 15.6 shows estimates of user cost as a fraction of the competitive price for crude oil, natural gas, uranium, copper, bauxite, and nickel.[20] Note that only for crude oil and natural gas is user cost a substantial component of price. For the other resources, it is small and in some cases almost negligible. Moreover, although most of these resources have experienced sharp price fluctuations, user cost had almost nothing to do with those fluctuations. For example, oil prices changed because of OPEC and political turmoil in the Persion Gulf, natural gas prices because of changes in the government price controls, uranium and bauxite because of cartelization during the 1970s, and copper because of major changes in demand.

Resource depletion, then, has not been very important as a determinant of resource prices over the past few decades. Much more important have been market structure (the extent to which producers collude rather than compete)

[20]Not all resources are sold in competitive markets; the price of crude oil, for example, has since 1974 been largely controlled by OPEC. In this case the competitive price is an estimate based on cost and demand data. The numbers in Table 15.6 are based on R. Pindyck, "Gains to Producers from the Cartelization of Exhaustible Resources," *Review of Economics and Statistics* 60 (1978): 238–251; Kenneth R. Stollery, "Mineral Depletion with Cost as the Extraction Limit: A Model Applied to the Behavior of Prices in the Nickel Industry," *Journal of Environmental Economics and Management* 10 (1983): 151–165; and R. Pindyck, "On Monopoly Power in Extractive Resource Markets," *Journal of Environmental Economics and Management* 14 (1987): 128–142.

and changes in market demand. But the role of depletion should not be ignored. Over the long term it will be the ultimate determinant of resource prices.

15.8 How Are Interest Rates Determined?

We have seen how market interest rates are used to help make capital investment and intertemporal production decisions. But what determines how high interest rates will be and why they fluctuate over time? To answer these questions, remember that an interest rate is a price—the price that borrowers pay lenders to use their funds. Like any market price, interest rates are determined by supply and demand—in this case the supply and demand for loanable funds.

The *supply of loanable funds* comes from households that wish to save part of their incomes in order to consume more in the future (or make bequests to their heirs). For example, some households have high incomes now but expect to earn less in the future after retirement. Saving lets them spread their consumption more evenly over time. Also, because they receive interest on the money they lend, they can consume more in the future in return for consuming less now. As a result, the higher the interest rate, the greater the incentive to save. The supply of loanable funds is therefore an upward-sloping curve, labeled S in Figure 15.5.

The *demand for loanable funds* has two components. First, some households want to consume more than their current incomes, either because their incomes are low now but are expected to grow, or because they want to make a large purchase (e.g., a house, a car, or a college education) that has to be paid for out of future income. These households are willing to pay interest in return for not having to wait to consume. However, the higher the interest rate, the greater the cost of consuming rather than waiting, so the less willing these households will be to borrow. The household demand for loanable funds is therefore a declining function of the interest rate. In Figure 15.5, it is the curve labeled D_H.

The second source of demand for loanable funds is firms that want to make capital investments. Remember that firms will invest in projects with NPV's that are positive, because a positive NPV means that the expected return on the project exceeds the opportunity cost of funds. That opportunity cost—the discount rate used to calculate the NPV—is the interest rate, perhaps adjusted for risk. Often firms borrow to invest because the flow of profits from an investment comes in the future, while the cost of an investment must usually be paid now. Firms' desires to invest are thus an important source of demand for loanable funds.

As we saw earlier, however, the higher the interest rate, the lower the NPV of a project. If interest rates rise, some investment projects that had positive NPVs will now have negative NPVs, and will therefore be cancelled. Overall,

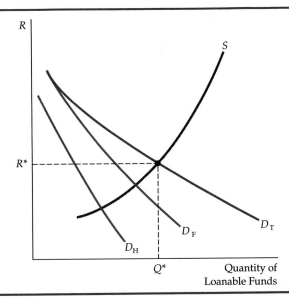

FIGURE 15.5 Supply and Demand for Loanable Funds. Market interest rates are determined by the demand and supply of loanable funds. Households supply funds to consume more in the future; the higher the interest rate, the more they will supply. Households and firms both demand funds, but they demand less the higher the interest rate is. Shifts in the demand or supply curves cause changes in interest rates.

because firms' willingness to invest falls when interest rates rise, their demand for loanable funds also falls. The demand for loanable funds by firms is thus a downward-sloping curve; in Figure 15.5 it is labeled D_F.

The total demand for loanable funds is the sum of the household demand and the firm demand; in Figure 15.5 it is the curve D_T. This total demand curve together with the supply curve determine the equilibrium interest rate. In Figure 15.5, that rate is R^*.

Figure 15.5 can also help us understand why interest rates change. Suppose the economy goes into a recession. Firms will then expect lower sales and lower future profits from new capital investments. The NPVs of projects will fall, and firms' willingness to invest will decline, as will their demand for loanable funds. D_F, and therefore D_T, will shift to the left, and the equilibrium interest rate will fall. Or suppose the federal government spends much more money than it takes through taxes, i.e., runs large deficits, as it did in the 1980s. It will have to borrow to finance these deficits, shifting the total demand for loanable funds D_T to the right, so that R increases. The monetary policies of the Federal Reserve are another important determinant of interest rates. The Federal Reserve can create money, shifting the supply of loanable funds to the right and reducing R.

A Variety of Interest Rates

Figure 15.5 aggregates individual demands and supplies as though there were a single market interest rate. In fact, households, firms, and the government lend and borrow under a variety of terms and conditions. As a result, there is no single "market" interest rate, but rather a wide range of different rates. Here we briefly describe some of the more important interest rates that are quoted in the newspapers, and sometimes used for capital investment decisions.

Treasury Bill Rate   A Treasury bill is a short-term (one year or less) bond issued by the U.S. government. It is a pure *discount bond,* i.e., it makes no coupon payments, but instead is sold at a price less than its redemption value at maturity. For example, a three-month Treasury bill might be sold for $98. In three months it can be redeemed for $100; it thus has an effective three-month yield of about 2 percent and an effective annual yield of about 8 percent.[21] The Treasury bill rate can be viewed as a short-term, risk-free rate.

Treasury Bond Rate   A Treasury bond is a longer-term bond (more than one year, and typically 10 to 30 years) issued by the U.S. government. Rates vary, depending on the maturity of the bond.

Discount Rate   Commercial banks sometimes borrow for short periods from the Federal Reserve. These loans are called *discounts,* and the rate that the Federal Reserve charges on them is the discount rate.

Commercial Paper Rate   Commercial paper refers to short-term (six-months or less) discount bonds issued by high-quality corporate borrowers. Because commercial paper is only slightly riskier than a Treasury bill, the commercial paper rate is usually less than 1 percent higher than the Treasury bill rate.

Prime Rate   This is the rate (sometimes called the *reference rate*) that large banks post as a reference point for short-term loans to their biggest corporate borrowers. Because the banking industry is oligopolistic, this rate does not fluctuate from day to day as other rates do.

Corporate Bond Rate   Newspapers and government publications report the average annual yields on long-term (typically 20-year) corporate bonds in different risk categories (e.g., high-grade bonds, medium-grade bonds, etc.). These average yields indicate how much corporations are paying for long-term debt. However, as we saw in Example 15.2, the yields on corporate bonds can vary

─────────────────

[21]To be exact, the three-month yield is $(100/98) - 1 = 0.0204$, and the annual yield is $(100/98)^4 - 1 = 0.0842$, or 8.42 percent.

considerably depending on the financial strength of the corporation and the time to maturity for the bond.

Summary

1. A firm's holding of capital is measured as a stock, but inputs of labor and raw materials are flows. Its stock of capital enables a firm to earn a flow of profits over time.

2. When a firm makes a capital investment, it spends money now, so that it can earn a flow of profits in the future. To decide whether the investment is worthwhile, the firm must determine the present value of future profits. It does this by discounting those future profits.

3. The present discounted value (PDV) of $1 paid one year from now is $1/(1 + R)$, where R is the interest rate. The PDV of $1 paid n years from now is $1/(1 + R)^n$.

4. A bond is a contract in which a lender agrees to pay the bondholder a stream of money. The value of the bond is the PDV of that stream. The effective yield on a bond is the interest rate that equates that value with the bond's market price. Bond yields differ because of differences in riskiness and time to maturity.

5. Firms can decide whether to undertake a capital investment by applying the Net Present Value (NPV) criterion: Invest if the present value of the expected future cash flows from an investment is larger than the cost of the investment.

6. The discount rate that a firm uses to calculate the NPV for an investment should be the opportunity cost of capital, i.e., the return the firm could earn on a similar investment.

7. When calculating NPVs, if cash flows are in nominal terms, i.e., include inflation, the discount rate should also be nominal, but if cash flows are in real terms, a real discount rate should be used.

8. An adjustment for risk can be made by adding a risk premium to the discount rate. However, the risk premium should reflect only nondiversifiable risk. Using the Capital Asset Pricing Model (CAPM), the risk premium is the "beta" for the project times the risk premium on the stock market as a whole. The "beta" measures the sensitivity of the project's return to movements in the market.

9. Consumers are also faced with investment decisions that require the same kind of analysis as those of firms. When deciding whether to buy a durable good like a car or a major appliance, the consumer must consider the present value of future operating costs.

10. An exhaustible resource in the ground is like money in the bank and must earn a comparable return. Therefore, if the market is competitive, price less marginal extraction cost will grow at the rate of interest. The difference between price and marginal cost is called *user cost*—it is the opportunity cost of depleting a unit of the resource.

11. Market interest rates are determined by the demand and supply of loanable funds. Households supply funds so they can consume more in the future. Households, firms, and the government demand funds. Changes in demand or supply cause changes in interest rates.

Review Questions

1. A firm uses cloth and labor to produce shirts in a factory that it bought for $10 million. Which of its factor inputs are measured as flows and which as stocks? How would your answer change if the firm had leased a factory instead of buying one? Is its output measured as a flow or a stock? Its profit?

2. Suppose the interest rate is 10 percent. If $100 is invested at this rate today, how much will it be worth after one year? After two years? After five years? What is the value today of $100 paid one year from now? Paid two years from now? Paid five years from now?

3. You are offered the choice of two payment streams: (a) $100 paid one year from now and $100 paid two years from now; (b) $80 paid one year from now and $130 paid two years from now. Which payment stream would you prefer if the interest rate is 5 percent? If the interest rate is 15 percent?

4. How does one calculate the present value of a bond? If the interest rate is 5 percent, what is the present value of a perpetuity that pays $1000 per year forever?

5. What is meant by the *effective yield* on a bond? How does one calculate it? Why do some corporate bonds have effective yields that are higher than others?

6. What is the Net Present Value (NPV) criterion for investment decisions? How does one calculate the NPV of an investment project? If all the cash flows for the project are certain, what discount rate should be used to calculate the NPV?

7. What is the difference between a real discount rate and a nominal discount rate? When should a real discount rate be used in an NPV calculation, and when should a nominal rate be used?

8. How is a risk premium used to account for risk in NPV calculations? What is the difference between diversifiable and nondiversifiable risk? Why should only nondiversifiable risk enter into the risk premium?

9. What is meant by the "market return" in the Capital Asset Pricing Model? Why is the market return greater than the risk-free interest rate? What does an asset's "beta" measure in the CAPM? Why should high-beta assets have a higher expected return than low-beta assets?

10. Suppose you are deciding whether to invest $100 million in a steel mill. You know the expected cash flows for the project, but they are risky—steel prices could rise or fall in the future. How would the CAPM help you select a discount rate for an NPV calculation?

11. How does a consumer trade off current and future costs when selecting an air conditioner or other major appliance? How could this selection be aided by an NPV calculation?

12. What is meant by the "user cost" of producing an exhaustible resource? Why does price minus extraction cost rise at the rate of interest in a competitive exhaustible resource market?

13. What determines the supply of loanable funds? The demand for loanable funds? What might cause the supply or demand for loanable funds to shift, and how would that affect interest rates?

Exercises

1. Suppose the interest rate is 10 percent. What is the value of a coupon bond that pays $80 per year for each of the next five years, and then makes a principal repayment of $1000 in the sixth year? Repeat for an interest rate of 15 percent.

2. A bond has two years to mature. It makes a coupon payment of $100 after one year, and both a coupon payment of $100 and a principal repayment of $1000 after two years. The bond is selling for $966. What is its effective yield?

3. Equation (15.5) shows the net present value of an investment in an electric motor factory, where half of the $10 million cost is paid initially and the other half after a year, and where the factory is expected to lose money during its first two years of operation. If the discount rate is 4 percent, what is the NPV? Is the investment worthwhile?

4. Suppose your uncle gave you an oil well like the one described in Section 15.7. (Marginal production cost is constant at $10.) The price of oil is currently $20 but is controlled by a cartel that accounts for a large fraction of total production. Should you produce and sell all your oil now or wait to produce? Explain your answer.

5. *Investing in Wine.* Suppose you are planning to invest in fine wine. Each case costs $100, and you know from experience that the value of a case of wine held for t years is $(100)t^{1/2}$. One hundred cases of wine are available for sale, and the interest rate is 10 percent.
    a. How many cases should you buy, how long should you wait to sell them, and how much money will you receive at the time of their sale?
    b. Suppose that at the time of purchase, someone offers you $130 per case immediately. Should you take the offer?
    c. How would your answers change if the interest rate were only 5 percent?

6. Let's reexamine the capital investment decision in the disposable diaper industry (Example 15.3) from the point of view of an incumbent firm. If P&G or Kimberly-Clark were to expand capacity by building three new plants, they would not need to spend $60 million on R&D before start-up. How does this affect the NPV calculations in Table 15.5? Is the investment profitable at a discount rate of 12 percent?

PART IV

Information, Market Failure, and the Role of Government

Much of that analysis of the first three parts of the book has focused on positive questions—how consumers and firms behave, and how that behavior affects different market structures. Part IV takes a more normative approach—by describing the goal of economic efficiency, and discussing when markets generate efficient outcomes, and when they fail and require government intervention.

Chapter 16 discusses general equilibrium analysis, in which the interactions among related markets are taken into account. This chapter also analyzes the conditions that are required for an economy to be efficient, and shows why a perfectly competitive market is efficient. Chapter 17 examines an important source of market failure, incomplete information. We show that when some economic actors have better information than others, markets may fail to allocate goods efficiently or may not even exist. We also show how sellers of products can avoid problems of asymmetric information by giving potential buyers signals about the quality of their product. Finally, Chapter 18 discusses two additional sources of market failure, externalities and public goods. We then evaluate a number of remedies for these market failures. We show how some failures can be resolved through private bargaining, while others require government intervention.

CHAPTER 16

General Equilibrium and Economic Efficiency

So far in this book we have studied individual markets in isolation. Yet markets are interdependent—conditions in one can affect prices and outputs in others either because one good is an input to the production of another good or because two goods are substitutes or complements. In this chapter we see how a general equilibrium analysis takes these interrelationships into account.

We also expand the concept of economic efficiency that we discussed in Chapter 9, and we discuss the benefits of a competitive market economy. In doing so, we will see the limits to this system: Markets may fail to perform efficiently because one or more of the prerequisites for perfect competition are absent, and because market outcomes may not distribute income appropriately.

We first discuss *general equilibrium analysis* and highlight how one market can affect related markets. Next we analyze economic efficiency, beginning with the exchange of goods among people. We then use this analysis of exchange to discuss whether the outcomes generated by an economy are equitable. To the extent that these outcomes are deemed to be inequitable, government can help redistribute income.

We go on to describe the conditions that an economy must satisfy if it is to produce and distribute goods efficiently. We also explain why a perfectly competitive market system satisfies those conditions. Most markets, however, are not perfectly competitive, and many deviate substantially from that ideal. In the final section of the chapter (as a preview to our detailed discussion of market failure in Chapters 17 and 18), we discuss why markets may fail to work efficiently.

16.1 General Equilibrium Analysis

Most of our discussions of market behavior have involved *partial equilibrium analysis*. In other words, when determining the equilibrium prices and quantities in a market, we presumed that the activity in that market had little or no effect on other markets. For example, in Chapters 2 and 9 we presumed that the wheat market was largely independent of the markets for related products, such as corn and soybeans.

Often a partial equilibrium analysis of this sort is sufficient to understand the behavior and evolution of a market. However, market interrelationships can be important. We saw this in Chapter 2 when we pointed out that a change in the price of one good affects the demand for another if they are complements or substitutes, and in Chapter 8, when we saw that an increase in a firm's input demand can cause both the market price of the input and the product price to rise.

Unlike partial equilibrium analysis, *general equilibrium analysis determines the prices and quantities in all markets simultaneously,* and it explicitly takes feedback effects into account. A *feedback effect* is a price or quantity adjustment in one market caused by price and quantity adjustments in related markets. Suppose, for example, that the U.S. government taxes oil imports. This would immediately shift the supply curve for oil to the left (because less cheap foreign oil is available) and raise the price of oil. But the effect of the tax would not end there. The higher price of oil would increase the demand for and then the price of natural gas. The higher natural gas price would in turn cause oil demand to rise (shift to the right) and increase the oil price even more. The oil and the natural gas markets would continue to interact until eventually an equilibrium would be reached in which the quantity demanded and quantity supplied were equated in both markets.

In practice, we can rarely do a complete general equilibrium analysis. It would be too difficult, for example, to evaluate the effects of a firm's actions on *all* other markets and the corresponding reactions of all the firms in those markets. Instead, we confine ourselves to those markets that are closely related. Two or three markets are often enough. For example, when looking at a tax on oil, we might also look at markets for natural gas, coal, and electricity.

Two Interdependent Markets—Moving to General Equilibrium

To study the interdependence of markets, let's examine the competitive markets for videocassette rentals and movie theater tickets. The two markets are closely related because the widespread ownership of videocassette recorders has given most consumers the option of watching movies at home or at the theater. Changes in pricing or in public policies that affect one market are likely to affect the other market, which in turn causes feedback effects in the first market.

Figures 16.1a and 16.1b show the supply and demand curves for videos and movies. In 16.1a the price of movie tickets is initially $6, and the market is in equilibrium at the intersection of D_M and S_M. In 16.1b, the video market is also in equilibrium with a price of $3.

Now suppose that to raise revenue the government places a tax of $1 on each movie ticket purchased. The effect of the movie tax is determined on a partial

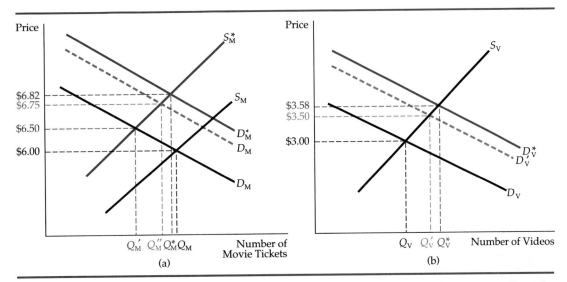

FIGURE 16.1 Two Interdependent Markets: Movie Tickets and Videocassette Rentals.
In a general equilibrium, markets are interdependent, and the prices of all products are simultaneously determined. In this example, a tax on movie tickets causes the supply of movies to shift upward from S_M to S_M^*, shown in part (a). The higher price of movie tickets ($6.50 rather than $6.00) initially increases the demand for videocassettes (from D_V to D_V'), causing the price of videos to rise (from $3.00 to $3.50), shown in part (b). The higher video price feeds back into the movie ticket market, causing demand to increase from D_M to D_M' and the price of movies to increase from $6.50 to $6.75. This interaction among markets continues until a general equilibrium is reached. This is shown as the intersection of D_M^* and S_M^* in part (a), leading to a movie ticket price of $6.82, and by the intersection of D_V^* and S_V in part (b), leading to a video price of $3.85.

equilibrium basis by shifting the supply curve for movies upward by $1, from S_M to S_M^* in Figure 16.1a. Initially, this causes the price of movies to increase to $6.50 and the quantity of movie tickets sold to fall from Q_M to Q_M'. This is as far as a partial equilibrium analysis takes us. But we can go further with a general equilibrium analysis by (1) looking at the effects of the movie tax on the market for videos, and (2) seeing whether there are any feedback effects from the video market to the movie market.

The movie tax affects the market for videos because movies and videos are substitutes. A higher movie price shifts the demand for videos from D_V to D_V' in Figure 16.1b. This, in turn, causes the rental price of videos to increase from $3.00 to $3.50. Note that a tax on one product can affect the prices and sales of other products—something that policymakers should remember when designing tax policies.

What about the market for movies? The original demand curve for movies presumed that the price of videos was unchanged at $3.00. That price is now

$3.50, however, so the demand for movies will shift upward, from D_M to D_M' in Figure 16.1a. The new equilibrium price of movies (at the intersection of S_M^* and D_M') is now $6.75, instead of $6.50, and the quantity of movie tickets purchased has increased from Q_M' to Q_M''. Thus, a partial equilibrium analysis would have underestimated the effect of the tax on the price of movies. The video market is so closely related to the market for movies that to determine the tax's full effect, we need a general equilibrium analysis.

The Attainment of General Equilibrium

This analysis is not yet complete. The change in the market price of movies will generate a feedback effect on the price of videos, which in turn will affect the price of movies, and so on. In the end, we must determine the equilibrium prices and quantities of *both* movies and videos simultaneously. The equilibrium movie price of $6.82 is given in Figure 16.1a by the intersection of the equilibrium supply and demand curves for movie tickets (S_M^* and D_M^*), and the equilibrium video price of $3.58 is given in Figure 16.1b by the intersection of the equilibrium supply and demand curves for videos (S_V^* and D_V^*). These are the correct general equilibrium prices because the video market supply and demand curves have been drawn on the assumption that the price of movie tickets is $6.82, and the movie ticket curves have been drawn on the assumption that the price of videos is $3.58. In other words, both sets of curves are consistent with the prices in related markets, and we have no reason to expect that the supply and demand curves in either market will shift further.[1]

We continue this discussion from a different viewpoint in the next section when we describe situations in which consumers exchange goods among themselves.

EXAMPLE 16.1 THE INTERDEPENDENCE OF INTERNATIONAL MARKETS

Because Brazil and the United States compete in the world soybean market, Brazilian regulation of its own soybean market can significantly affect the U.S. soybeam market, which in turn can have feedback effects on the Brazilian market. This led to unexpected results when Brazil adopted a regulatory policy aimed at increasing short-run domestic supplies and long-run exports of soybeans.[2]

During the late 1960s and early 1970s the Brazilian government limited the export of soybeans. It hoped that making soybeans cheaper in Brazil would

---

[1]To find the general equilibrium prices (and quantities) in practice, we must simultaneously find two prices that equate quantity demanded and quantity supplied in all related markets. For our two markets this would mean solving for the numerical solution to four equations (supply of movie tickets, demand for movie tickets, supply of videos, and demand for videos) in four unknowns.

[2]This example presents a simplified version of the analysis in Gary W. Williams and Robert L. Thompson, "Brazilian Soybean Policy: The International Effects of Intervention," *American Journal of Agricultural Economics* 66 (1984): 488–498.

encourage the domestic sale of soybeans and stimulate the domestic demand for soybean products. Eventually the export controls were to be removed, and it was expected that Brazilian exports would then increase.

This expectation was based on a partial equilibrium analysis of the Brazilian soybean market. However, it would have been more realistic to use a general equilibrium framework that accounts for long-run interactions between the Brazilian and U.S. economies. In reality, lowering of Brazilian exports increased the price and production of soybeans in the United States, making the United States more competitive in the world market. This in turn added to competitive pressures in the Brazilian market, leading in the long run to lower Brazilian soybean production and exports, even after the controls were removed.

Figure 16.2 shows the consequences of the program. The lower two lines show Brazilian soybean exports, and the higher two lines refer to the U.S. In each case, actual exports are shown as a black line, and the estimated level of exports *had the Brazilian government regulations not gone into effect* as a red line.

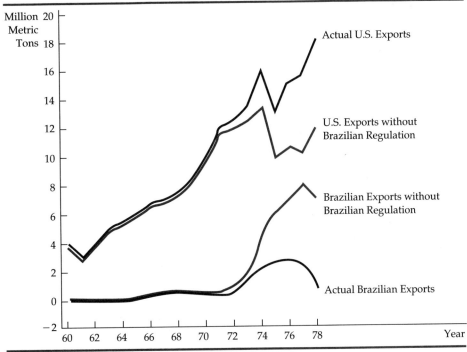

FIGURE 16.2 Soybean Exports—Brazil and the United States. World competition in the soybean market makes the Brazilian and U.S. export markets highly interactive. As a result of the general equilibrium nature of these markets, regulations to stimulate Brazil's domestic economy were counterproductive in the long run. Brazil's actual exports of soybeans were lower (and U.S. exports higher) than they would have been without the regulatory policy.

(The lines diverge from approximately 1970 forward, because the major export controls were put into effect at that time.) The figure shows that soybean exports from Brazil would have been higher, and exports from the United States lower, without the regulatory program. In 1977, for example, Brazilian soybean exports were 73 percent lower than they would have been had the government not intervened. However, between 1973 and 1978, U.S. soybean exports were over 30 percent higher than they would otherwise have been.

Thus, Brazilian regulatory policy hurt Brazil in the long run because policymakers forgot to take fully into account its effect on the U.S. production and export of soybeans.

16.2 Efficiency in Exchange

In Chapter 9 we saw that an unregulated competitive market is efficient because it maximizes consumer and producer surplus. Now let's examine the concept of economic efficiency in more detail, beginning with an *exchange economy*. Here, we analyze the behavior of two consumers who can trade either of two goods between themselves. Suppose the two goods are initially allocated so that both consumers can make themselves better off by trading the goods to each other. This means that the initial allocation of goods is economically *inefficient*. In an *efficient* allocation of goods, no one can be made better off without making someone else worse off. In the subsections that follow, we show why mutually beneficial trades result in an efficient allocation of goods.

The Advantages of Trade

As a general rule, voluntary trade between two people is mutually beneficial.[3] To see how trade makes people better off, let's look at a two-person exchange in detail. Our analysis is based on two important assumptions:
1. Both people have complete information about each other's preferences.
2. Exchanging goods involves no costs, i.e., *transactions costs* are zero.

Suppose James and Karen have 10 units of food and 6 units of clothing between them. Table 16.1 shows that initially James has 7 units of food and 1 unit of clothing, and Karen has 3 units of food and 5 units of clothing. To decide whether a trade between James and Karen would be advantageous, we need to know their preferences for food and clothing. Suppose that because Karen has a lot of clothing and little food, her marginal rate of substitution (MRS) of clothing for food is 3 (to get 3 units of food, she will give up 1 of

---

[3]There are two situations in which trade may not be advantageous. First, limited information may lead people to believe that trade will make them better off when in fact it will not. Second, people may be coerced into making trades, either by physical threats or by the threat of future economic reprisals.

TABLE 16.1 The Advantage of Trade			
Individual	Initial Allocation	Trade	Final Allocation
James	7F, 1C	−1F, +1C	6F, 2C
Karen	3F, 5C	+1F, −1C	4F, 4C

clothing). However, James's MRS of clothing for food is only ½ (he will give up 2 units of clothing to get 1 of food).

There is thus room for mutually advantageous trade, because James values clothing more highly than Karen does, whereas Karen values food more highly than James does. To get another unit of food, James would be willing to trade up to 2 units of clothing. But Karen will give up 1 unit of food for ⅓ unit of clothing. The actual terms of the trade depend on the bargaining process. Among the possible outcomes are a trade of 1 unit of food (by Karen) for anywhere between ⅓ and 2 units of clothing (from James).

Suppose Karen offers James 1 unit of food for 1 unit of clothing, and James agrees. Both will be better off. James will have more food, which he values more than clothing, and Karen will have more clothing, which she values more than food. Whenever two consumers' MRSs are different, there is room for mutually beneficial trade because the allocation of resources is inefficient—trading will make both consumers better off. Conversely, to achieve economic efficiency, the two consumers' MRSs must be equal.

This important result also holds when there are many goods and consumers: *An allocation of goods is efficient only if the goods are distributed so that the marginal rate of substitution between any two pairs of goods is the same for all consumers.*

The Edgeworth Box Diagram

If trade is beneficial, which trades can occur? Which of those trades will allocate goods efficiently among customers, and how much better off will consumers then be? We can answer these questions for our two-person, two-good example by using a diagram called an *Edgeworth Box.*[4]

Figure 16.3 shows an Edgeworth Box in which the horizontal axis describes the number of units of food, and the vertical axis the units of clothing. The length of the box is 10 units of food, the total quantity of food available, and its height is 6 units of clothing, the total quantity of clothing available.

The key to the Edgeworth Box is that each point in the diagram simultaneously describes the market baskets of both consumers. James's holdings are read from the origin at O_J, and Karen's holdings are read in reverse direction

---

[4]The Edgeworth Box is named after political economist F. Y. Edgeworth, who suggested its use in his 1881 book *Mathematical Psychics: An Essay on the Application of Mathematics to the Moral Sciences* (New York: August M. Kelley, 1953).

from the origin at O_K. For example, point A represents the initial allocation of food and clothing. Reading on the horizontal axis from left to right at the bottom of the box, we see that James has 7 units of food, and reading upward along the vertical axis on the left of the diagram, 1 unit of clothing. Thus, for James, A represents 7F and 1C. This leaves 3F and 5C for Karen. Karen's allocation of food (3F) is read from right to left at the top of the box diagram beginning at O_K, and her allocation of clothing (5C) from top to bottom at the right of the box diagram.

We can also see the effect of the trade that Karen and James have made. James gives up 1F in exchange for 1C, moving from A to B. Karen gives up 1C and obtains 1F, also moving from A to B. Point B thus represents the market baskets of both James and Karen after the mutually beneficial trade.

Efficient Allocations

A trade from A to B thus made both Karen and James better off. But is B an efficient allocation? The answer depends on whether James's and Karen's MRSs

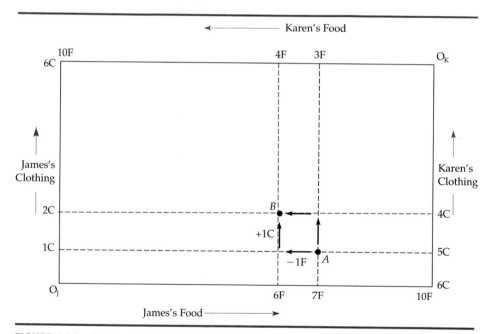

FIGURE 16.3 Exchange in an Edgeworth Box. Each point in the Edgeworth exchange box simultaneously represents James' and Karen's market baskets of food and clothing, under the assumption that there are fixed supplies of both goods. At A, for example, James has 7 units of food and 1 unit of clothing, and Karen has 3 units of food and 5 units of clothing.

are the same at B, which in turn depends on the shape of their indifference curves. Figure 16.4 shows several indifference curves for both James and Karen. James's indifference curves are drawn in the usual way, because his allocations are measured from the origin O_J. But for Karen, we have rotated the indifference curves 180 degrees, so that their origin is at the upper right-hand corner of the box. Karen's indifference curves are convex, just like James's—we simply see them from a different perspective.

Now that we are familiar with the two sets of indifference curves, let's examine which of James's and Karen's curves pass through the initial allocation at A. These curves have been labeled U_J^1 and U_K^1. Both James's and Karen's MRSs give the slope of their indifference curves at A. James's is equal to $\frac{1}{2}$, Karen's to 3. The shaded area between these two indifference curves represents all possible allocations of food and clothing, which would make both James and Karen better off than at A. In other words, it describes all possible mutually beneficial trades.

Starting at A, any trade that moved the allocation of goods outside the shaded area would make one of the two consumers worse off, and therefore it should not occur. We saw that the move from A to B was mutually beneficial. But in

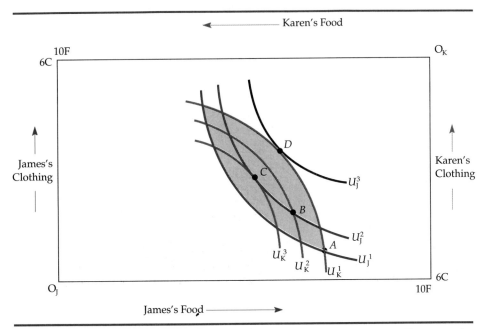

FIGURE 16.4 Efficiency in Exchange. The Edgeworth exchange box illustrates the possibilities for each consumer to increase his or her satisfaction by trading goods. If A gives the initial allocation of resources, the shaded area describes all mutually beneficial trades.

Figure 16.4, B is not an efficient point, because indifference curves U_J^2 and U_K^2 intersect. This means that James's and Karen's MRSs are not the same, and that the allocation is not efficient. This illustrates an important point: *If a trade from an inefficient allocation makes both people better off, the new allocation is not necessarily efficient.*

Suppose that from B an additional trade is made, with James giving up another unit of food to obtain another unit of clothing and Karen giving up a unit of clothing in exchange for a unit of food. Point C in Figure 16.4 gives the new allocation. At C, the MRSs of both people are identical, which is why the indifference curves are tangent there. When the indifference curves are tangent, the MRSs are the same, so that one person cannot be made better off without making the other person worse off. As a result, C represents an efficient allocation.

Of course, C is not the only possible outcome of a bargain between James and Karen. Mutually beneficial trades could move them to any point within the shaded area. If all mutually beneficial trades are made, an efficient allocation will be reached. However, many possible efficient outcomes can be attained. For example, if James is an effective bargainer, a trade might change the allocation of goods from A to D, where indifference curve U_J^3 is tangent to indifference curve U_K^1. This would leave Karen no worse off than she was at A and James much better off. And because no further trade is possible, D is an efficient allocation. But although James prefers D to C, Karen prefers C to D. Both allocations are efficient, and neither is preferred to the other. In general, it is difficult to predict the allocation that will be reached in a bargain because it depends on the bargaining ability of the people involved.

The Contract Curve

We have seen that from an initial allocation many possible efficient allocations can be reached through mutually beneficial trade. Point A was not unique. To find *all possible efficient allocations of food and clothing* between Karen and James, we would look for all points of tangency of one of each of their indifference curves. Figure 16.5 shows the curve drawn through all such efficient allocations; it is called the *contract curve.*

The contract curve shows all allocations from which no mutually beneficial trade can be made. These allocations are sometimes called *Pareto efficient* allocations, after Italian economist Vilfredo Pareto (1848–1923), who developed the concept of efficiency in exchange: *An allocation is Pareto efficient if goods cannot be reallocated to make someone better off without making someone else worse off.* In Figure 16.5 three allocations labeled E, F, and G are Pareto efficient, although each involves a different distribution of food and clothing, because one person could not be made better off without making someone else worse off.

Several properties of the contract curve may help us understand the concept of efficiency in exchange. Once a point on a contract curve, such as E, has been chosen, there is no way to move to another point on the contract curve, say,

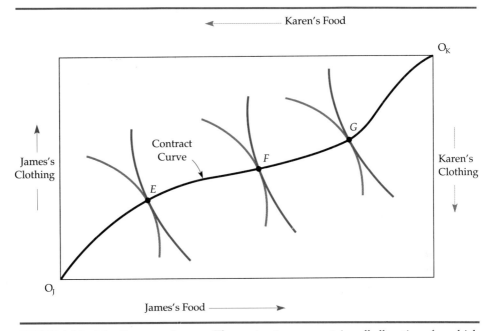

Karen's Food

O_K

James's Clothing

Contract Curve

Karen's Clothing

F

G

E

O_J

James's Food

FIGURE 16.5 The Contract Curve. The contract curve contains all allocations for which consumers' indifference curves are tangent. Every point on the contract curve is efficient because one person cannot be made better off without making the other person worse off.

F, without making one person worse off (in this case, Karen). Without making further comparison between James's and Karen's preferences, we cannot compare allocations *E* and *F*—we simply know that both are efficient. In this sense Pareto efficiency is a modest goal: It says that we should make all mutually beneficial exchanges, but it does not say which exchanges are best. Pareto efficiency can be a powerful concept, however. If a change would improve efficiency, most people would agree that the change is worth making, because it is in everyone's self-interest to support it.

We can frequently improve efficiency even when one aspect of a proposed change makes someone worse off. We need only include a second change in the proposal, so that the *combined* set of changes leaves someone better off and no one worse off than before. Suppose, for example, that we propose to eliminate a quota on automobile imports into the United States. U.S. consumers would then enjoy lower prices and a greater selection of cars, but some U.S. auto workers would lose their jobs. But if eliminating the quota were combined with federal tax breaks and job relocation subsidies for auto workers, so that U.S. consumers would be better off and U.S. auto workers no worse off, the result might increase efficiency.

Consumer Equilibrium in a Competitive Market

In a two-person exchange, the bargaining outcome can depend on circumstances. However, competitive markets have many buyers and sellers, so if people do not like the terms of an exchange, they can look for another seller who offers better terms. As a result, each buyer and seller takes the price of the goods as fixed and decides how much to buy and sell at that price. We can show how competitive markets lead to efficient exchange by using the Edgeworth box diagram to mimic a competitive market. Suppose, for example, that James and Karen each represent an average consumer from a large group of consumers. This allows us to think of them as price takers, even though we are working with only a two-person box diagram.

Figure 16.6 shows the opportunities for trade when we start at the allocation given by point A, and when the prices of both food and clothing are equal to 1. (The actual prices don't matter; what matters is the price of food relative to the price of clothing.) When the price of food and clothing are equal, each unit of food can be exchanged for one unit of clothing. As a result, the price line PP' in the diagram, which has a slope of -1, describes all possible allocations that exchange can achieve.

Suppose each James decides to buy 2 units of clothing and sell 2 units of food in exchange. This would move him from A to C and increase his satisfaction from indifference curve U_J^1 to U_J^2. Meanwhile, each Karen buys 2 units of food and sells 2 units of clothing. This would move her from A to C as well, increasing her satisfaction from indifference curve U_K^1 to U_K^2.

We choose prices for the two goods so that the quantity of food demanded by each Karen is equal to the quantity of food that each James wishes to sell, and the quantity of clothing demanded by each James is equal to the quantity of food that each Karen wishes to sell. As a result, the markets for food and clothing are in competitive equilibrium. A *competitive equilibrium* is a set of prices at which the quantity demanded equals the quantity supplied in every market.

Not all prices are consistent with an equilibrium. For example, if the price of food is 1 and the price of clothing is 3, food must be exchanged for clothing on a 3-to-1 basis. But then James will be unwilling to trade any food to get additional clothing because his MRS of clothing for food is only ½. Karen, on the other hand, would be happy to sell clothing to get more food, but she has no one to trade with. The market is therefore in *disequilibrium*, because the quantity demanded is not equal to the quantity supplied.

Our market is in disequilibrium because we took the prices of food and clothing as given. In a competitive market, prices will *adjust* if there is *excess demand* in some markets, i.e., the quantity demanded of one good is greater than the quantity supplied, and *excess supply* in others, i.e., the quantity supplied is greater than the quantity demanded. In our example, Karen's demand for food is greater than James's willingness to sell it, whereas Karen's willingness to trade clothing is greater than James's demand for it. As a result of this excess demand for food and excess supply of clothing, we would expect the

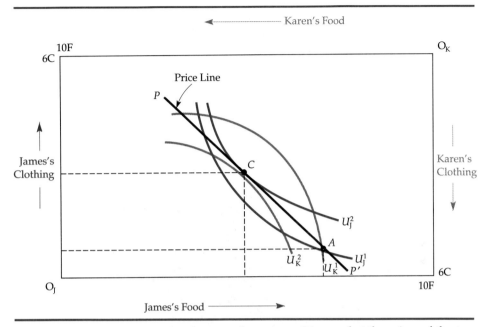

FIGURE 16.6 Competitive Equilibrium. In a competitive market the prices of the two goods determine the terms of exchange among consumers. If *A* is the initial allocation of goods, and the price line *PP'* represents the ratio of prices, the competitive market will lead to an equilibrium at *C*, the point of tangency of both indifference curves. As a result, the competitive equilibrium is efficient.

price of food to increase relative to the price of clothing. And as the price changed, so would the demands of all those in the market. Eventually, the prices would adjust until an equilibrium was reached. In our example, the price of both food and clothing might be 2. We know from the previous analysis that when the price of clothing is equal to the price of food, the market will be in competitive equilibrium. (Recall that only relative prices matter; prices of 2 for clothing and food are equivalent to prices of 1 for each.)

Note the important difference between the exchange situation with two people and the economy with many people (including our two-person economy with many Jameses and many Karens). When only two people are involved, bargaining leaves an indeterminate outcome and rate of exchange. When many people are involved, the prices of the goods are determined by the combined choices of demanders and suppliers of goods. When the market is in disequilibrium, the excess demands and supplies of goods causes prices to adjust until an equilibrium is reached.

We can see from point *C* in Figure 16.6 that *the allocation in a competitive equilibrium is efficient*. Point *C* must occur at the tangency of two indifference curves. If it did not, one of the people would not be maximizing satisfaction. This result holds both in an exchange framework and in a general equilibrium setting in which all markets are perfectly competitive. It is the most direct way of illustrating how Adam Smith's *invisible hand* works. If everyone trades in the marketplace to maximize satisfaction, and all mutually beneficial trades are completed, the resulting equilibrium allocation will be economically efficient.[5]

Let's summarize what we know about a competitive equilibrium from the consumer's perspective. First, because the indifference curves are tangent, all marginal rates of substitution between consumers are equal. Second, because each indifference curve is tangent to the price line, each person's MRS of clothing for food is equal to the ratio of the prices of the two goods. Formally, if P_C and P_F are the two prices

$$MRS_{CF}^J = P_C/P_F = MRS_{CF}^K \tag{16.1}$$

To achieve an efficient allocation when there are many consumers (and many producers) is not easy. It can be done if all markets are perfectly competitive. But efficient outcomes can also be achieved by other means—for example, through a centralized system in which the government allocates all goods and services. The competitive solution is often preferred because it allocates resources with a minimum of information. All consumers must know their own preferences and the prices they face. Consumers do not need to know who is producing what, or what the demands of other consumers are. Other allocation methods need greater information, and as a result they become difficult and cumbersome to manage.

16.3 Equity and Efficiency

We have shown that different efficient allocations of goods are possible, and we have seen how a perfectly competitive economy generates an efficient allocation. But are efficient allocations equitable? Unfortunately, economists and others disagree both about how to define equity and how to quantify it. As a result, no agreement on whether one efficient allocation is preferred to another is possible. Any such view would involve subjective comparisons of utility, and reasonable people could disagree about how to make these comparisons. In this section we discuss this general point and then illustrate it in a particular case by showing that there is no reason to believe that the allocation associated with a competitive equilibrium will be equitable.

---

[5]This result is sometimes called the first theorem of welfare economics. The second theorem of welfare economics states that if individual preferences are convex, then every efficient allocation (every point on the contract curve) is a competitive equilibrium for some initial allocation of goods.

The Utility Possibilities Frontier

For simplicity, we will work with the two-person exchange economy that we analyzed above. Recall that every point on the contract curve shows the levels of utility that James and Karen can achieve. In Figure 16.7 we put the information from the Edgeworth box in a different form. James's utility is measured on the horizontal axis and Karen's on the vertical axis. Any point in the Edgeworth box corresponds to a point in Figure 16.7, because every allocation generates utility for both people. Every movement to the right in Figure 16.7 represents an increase in James's utility, and every upward movement an increase in Karen's.

The *utility possibilities frontier* measures all points in the figure that represent efficient allocations. Point O_J is one extreme in which James has no goods and therefore zero utility, while point O_K is the opposite extreme where Karen has no goods. All other points on the frontier, such as E, F, and G, correspond to points on the contract curve, so that one person cannot be made better off without making the other worse off. Point H, however, represents an inefficient allocation, because any trade within the shaded area makes one or both parties better off. At L both people would be better off, but it is not attainable, because there is not enough of both goods to generate the levels of utility that the point represents.

It might seem reasonable to conclude that an allocation must be efficient to be equitable. Compare point H with F and G. Both F and G are efficient, and

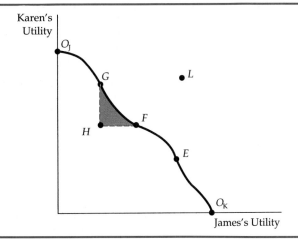

FIGURE 16.7 Utility-Possibilities Frontier. The utility-possibilities frontier shows the levels of satisfaction that each of two people achieve when they have traded to an efficient outcome on the contract curve. Points E, F, and G correspond to points on the contract curve and are efficient. Point H is inefficient because any trade within the shaded area will make both people better off.

(relative to H) each makes one person better off without making the other worse off. We might agree, therefore, that it is inequitable to James or Karen or both for an economy to yield allocation H, as opposed to F or G.

But suppose H and E are the only possible allocations. Is E more equitable than H? Not necessarily. Compared with H, E yields more utility for James and less for Karen. Some people may feel that H is more equitable than E; others may feel the opposite. We can conclude, therefore, that *one inefficient allocation of resources may be more equitable than another, efficient allocation.*

The problem is how to define an equitable allocation. Even if we restrict ourselves to all points on the utility possibilities frontier, which point is the most equitable? *The answer depends on what one thinks equity entails.* One popular view, the *egalitarian*, requires an equal allocation of goods among individuals. Another view, the *utilitarian*, allocates goods and services to maximize the total utility of all members of society. Thus, the utilitarian view supports giving more goods to those who can enjoy them more.[6] (Of course, if all members of society were identical, the utilitarian and egalitarian views would also be identical.)

A third, market-oriented view argues that the outcome of the competitive market process is equitable because it rewards those who are most able and who work the hardest.[7] If E is the competitive equilibrium allocation, for example, E would be deemed to be more equitable than F, even though the goods are less equally allocated.

When more than two people are involved, the meaning of the word equity becomes even more complex. One view of equity emphasizes equality. Realizing, however, that an equal distribution of resources may remove the incentive that most productive people have to work hard (because the wealth they achieve will be taxed away), this view allows inequalities in resources if these inequalities make the least-well-off person in society better off. Then, according to the Rawlsian view,[8] *the most equitable allocation maximizes the utility of the least-well-off person in society.* The Rawlsian view could be consistent with an equal allocation of goods among all members of society, but it need not be. Suppose, for example, that by rewarding more productive people more highly than less productive people, we can get the most productive people to work harder. This hard work could produce more goods and services, some of which could then be reallocated to make the poorest members of society better off.

The four distinct views of equity in Table 16.2 move roughly from most to least egalitarian. The egalitarian explicitly requires equal allocations, while the Rawlsian suggests that a substantial weight will be placed on equality (otherwise some would be much worse off than others). The utilitarian could involve egal-

---

[6]One of the important developers of utilitarian thought was Jeremy Bentham (1748–1832). See *An Introduction to the Principle of Morals and Legislation* (London: Oxford University Press, 1907).

[7]See Robert Nozick, *Anarchy, State, and Utopia* (New York: Basic Books, 1974).

[8]See John Rawls, *A Theory of Justice* (New York: Oxford University Press, 1971).

TABLE 16.2 Four Views of Equity
1. Egalitarian—all members of society receive equal amounts of goods
2. Rawlsian—maximize the utility of the least-well-off person
3. Utilitarian—maximize the total utility of all members of society
4. Market-oriented—the market outcome is the most equitable

itarianism but is more likely to require a substantial difference between the best- and worst-off members of society. Finally, the market-oriented view may lead to substantial inequality in the allocations of goods and services.

Equity and Perfect Competition

A competitive equilibrium leads to a Pareto efficient outcome. But that particular outcome may not be equitable. In fact, a competitive equilibrium could occur at any point on the contract curve, depending on the initial allocation. Imagine, for example, that the initial allocation gave all food and clothing to Karen. This would be at O_K in Figure 16.7, and Karen would have no reason to trade, whatever the price. Point O_K would then be a competitive equilibrium, as would point O_J and all intermediate points on the contract curve.

Because efficient allocations are not necessarily equitable, society must rely to some extent on government to redistribute income or goods among households to achieve equity goals. These goals can be reached through the tax system—a progressive income tax redistributes income from the wealthy to the poor, for example. The government can also provide public services, such as medical aid to the poor (Medicare), or it can transfer funds through programs such as Food Stamps.

Unfortunately, all programs that redistribute income in our society are costly. Taxes may encourage individuals to work less or cause firms to devote resources to avoiding taxes rather than producing output. So as a practical matter, there is a trade-off between the goals of equity and efficiency.[9]

16.4 Efficiency in Production

Earlier in the chapter we described the conditions required to achieve an efficient allocation in the exchange of two goods. Now we consider the efficient use of inputs in the production process. We assume there are fixed total supplies of two inputs, labor and capital, that are needed to produce the same two products, food and clothing. Instead of only two people, however, we now assume

[9]This trade between equity and efficiency is stated clearly by Arthur Oken in his book *Equality and Efficiency: The Big Tradeoff* (Washington, D.C.: The Brookings Institution, 1975).

that many consumers own the inputs to production (including labor) and earn income by selling them. This income, in turn, is allocated between the two goods.

This framework links together the various supply and demand elements of the economy. The two people supply inputs to production and then use the income this brings to demand and consume goods and services. When the price of one input increases, the people who supply a lot of that input earn more income and consume more of one of the two goods. This in turn increases the demand for the inputs needed to produce the good and has a feedback effect on the price of those inputs. Only a general equilibrium analysis can find the prices that equate supply and demand in every market.

Production in the Edgeworth Box

We will continue to use the Edgeworth box diagram, but rather than measure goods on each axis as we did before, now we will measure inputs to the production process. Figure 16.8 shows a box diagram in which labor input is measured along the horizontal axis, and capital input on the vertical axis. Fifty hours of labor and 30 hours of capital are available for the production process. In our earlier analysis of exchange, each origin represented an individual; now each origin represents an output. The food origin is O_F, and O_C is the clothing origin. The only difference between the production analysis and the exchange analysis is that now we measure inputs rather than outputs in the box diagram, and we focus on two outputs rather than two consumers.

Each point in the box diagram represents the labor and capital inputs to the production of food and clothing. For example, A represents the input of 35 hours of labor and 5 hours of capital in the production of food, and the input of 15 hours of labor and 25 hours of capital in the production of clothing. Every way in which labor and capital can be combined to produce the two goods is represented by a point in the box diagram.

A series of production isoquants shows the levels of output produced with the various input combinations. Each isoquant represents the total production of a good that can be obtained, without distinguishing the firm or firms that produced it. We have drawn three food isoquants representing 50, 60, and 80 units of food output. The isoquants for food look just like the isoquants we worked with in Chapter 6, but we have rotated the clothing isoquants by 180 degrees, so that they can be read from the point of view of the origin O_C. For example, the isoquant 50F represents all combinations of labor and capital that combine to produce 50 units of food, while 25C represents all combinations of labor and capital that combine to produce 25 units of clothing.

We have also drawn three clothing isoquants representing 10, 25, and 30

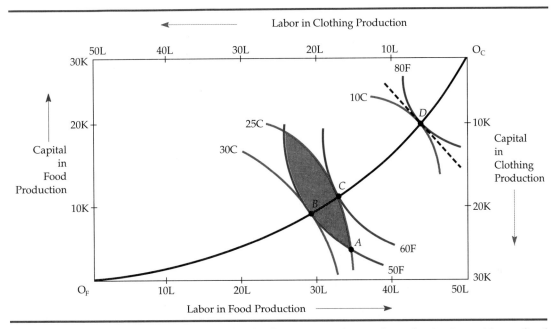

FIGURE 16.8 Efficiency in Production. In an Edgeworth production box with two fixed inputs and two goods, an efficient use of inputs occurs when the isoquants for the two goods are tangent. If production initially uses the inputs described by A, the shaded area shows the region in which more of both outputs can be produced by rearranging input use. Points B, C, and D are on the production contract curve and involve efficient input use.

units of clothing. These isoquants increase in output as we move from upper right to lower left, again because one or both inputs have increased. Now we can see that A simultaneously represents 50 units of food and 25 units of clothing, each associated with a different combination of production inputs.

Input Efficiency

To see how inputs can be combined efficiently, we must find the various combinations of inputs that can be used to produce each of the two outputs. A particular allocation of inputs into the production process is *technically efficient* if the output of one good cannot be increased without decreasing the output of another good. Efficiency in production is not a new concept; in Chapter 6 we saw that a production function represents the maximum output that can be achieved with a given set of inputs. Here we are extending the concept to the production of two goods rather than one. With two goods, efficiency is important because it means that inputs are allocated in the production of both goods, so that production costs are minimized.

Inputs are allocated inefficiently if reallocating them generates more of one or both goods. The box diagram in Figure 16.8 illustrates this. The allocation at A is clearly inefficient because any input combination in the shaded area generates more of both food and clothing. For example, we can move from A to B by switching some labor from the production of food to the production of clothing, and some capital from the production of clothing to the production of food. This generates the same amount of food (50 units), but a larger amount of clothing (from 25 to 30 units).

Points B and C in Figure 16.8 are both efficient allocations. In fact, all points lying on the curve that connects O_F to O_C are efficient. Each of these points is a point of tangency of two isoquants, just as every point on the exchange contract curve represents a point of tangency of two indifference curves. The *production contract curve* represents all technically efficient combinations of inputs. Every point that does not lie on this production contract curve is inefficient because the two isoquants that pass through such a point intersect. When two isoquants intersect, labor and capital can be reallocated to increase the output of at least one of the two goods. Note, for example, that the isoquants intersect at A. From A, we have seen that any allocation within the shaded area increases the production of both goods—so A is technically inefficient.

Producer Equilibrium in a Competitive Input Market

If input markets are competitive, they set the terms of the exchange, and a point of efficient production will be achieved. Let's see why. If the labor and capital markets are perfectly competitive, then the wage rate w will be the same in all industries. Likewise, the rental price of capital r will be the same whether capital is used in the food or clothing industry. We know from Chapter 7 that if producers of food and clothing minimize production costs, they will use combinations of labor and capital, so that the ratio of the marginal products of the two inputs is equal to the ratio of the prices:

$$MP_L/MP_K = w/r$$

But we also showed that the ratio of the marginal products of the two inputs is equal to the marginal rate of technical substitution of labor for capital $MRTS_{LK}$. As a result,

$$MRTS_{LK} = w/r \qquad (16.2)$$

Since the MRTS is the slope of the firm's isoquant, for a competitive equilibrium to occur in the input market, each producer must use labor and capital, so that the slopes of the isoquants are equal to one another and to the ratio of the prices of the two inputs. As a result, the competitive equilibrium must lie on the production contract curve, and the competitive equilibrium is efficient in production.

Where we end up on the production contract curve depends on consumers demands for the two goods. For example, suppose consumers demand much more food than clothing. One possible competitive equilibrium occurs at D in Figure 16.8. Here, the food producer minimizes the cost of producing 80 units of food by employing 43 units of labor and 20 units of capital. The clothing producer generates 10 units of clothing with 7 units of labor and 10 units of capital. The wage rate is equal to the rental price of capital, so the isocost lines have a slope of -1 in the diagram. At these prices neither producer will wish to purchase additional production inputs.

It is easy to check (as we did in Chapter 7) that if we begin at a point off the contract curve, both producers will find it advantageous to hire labor or rent capital so that they can reallocate their inputs to minimize costs. It is also clear from the box diagram that the input market has no unique competitive equilibrium. Efficiency in the use of inputs can involve the production of much food and little clothing, or vice versa.

The Production Possibilities Frontier

The *production possibilities frontier* shows the various combinations of food and clothing that can be produced with fixed inputs of labor and capital. The frontier in Figure 16.9 is derived from the production contract curve in Figure 16.8. Each point on both the contract curve and the production possibilities frontier describes an efficiently produced level of both food and clothing.

We have labeled the points on the frontier to correspond to the points on the production contract curve. Point O_F represents one extreme in which only clothing is produced, and O_C represents the other extreme in which only food is produced. Points B, C, and D are the three other labeled points from the contract curve of Figure 16.8.

The production possibilities frontier is downward-sloping because to produce more food efficiently, one must switch inputs to it from the production of clothing, which in turn lowers the food production level. Because all points lying within the frontier are inefficient, they are off the production contract curve.

The production possibilities frontier is concave (bowed in), i.e., its slope increases in magnitude as more food is produced. To describe this, we define the *marginal rate of transformation of food for clothing* (MRT) as the magnitude of the slope of the frontier at each point. The MRT measures how much clothing must be given up to produce one additional unit of food. For example, at B on the frontier, the MRT is 1, because 1 unit of clothing must be given up to obtain one additional unit of food. At D, however, the MRT is 2,

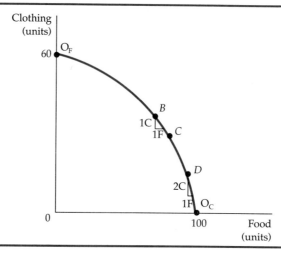

FIGURE 16.9   Production Possibilities Frontier.   The production possibilities frontier shows all efficient combinations of outputs. Points *B*, *C*, and *D* are also taken from comparable points on the production contract curve. The production possibilities frontier is bowed in, because its slope (the marginal rate of transformation) increases as the level of production of food increases.

because 2 units of clothing must be given up to obtain one more unit of food.

Note that as we increase the production of food by moving along the production possibilities frontier, the MRT increases.[10] This happens because the productivity of labor and capital differs depending on whether the inputs are used to produce food or clothing. Suppose we begin at O_F, where only clothing is produced. Now we remove some labor and capital from clothing production, where their marginal products are relatively low, and put them into food production, where their marginal products are high. Then, to obtain the first unit of food, very little clothing production is lost (the MRT is much less than 1). But as we move along the frontier and produce more clothing, the productivities of labor and capital in clothing production fall, and the productivities of labor and capital in food production rise. At *B*, the productivities are equal, and the MRT is 1. Continuing along the frontier, we note that the input productivities in clothing fall more, and the productivities in food increase, so the MRT becomes greater than 1.

We could have described the shape of the production possibilities frontier in

———————————————

[10]The production possibilities frontier need not have a continually increasing MRT. Suppose, for example, that there were strongly decreasing returns to scale in the production of food. Then as inputs were moved from clothing to food production, less food would be produced.

terms of the costs of production. At O_F, where very little clothing output is lost to produce additional food, the marginal cost of producing food is very low (a lot of output is produced with very little input), and the marginal cost of producing clothing is very high (it takes a lot of both inputs to produce another unit of clothing.) Thus, when the MRT is low, so is the ratio of the marginal cost of producing food MC_F to the marginal cost of producing clothing MC_C. In fact, the following condition holds along the production frontier:

$$MRT = MC_F/MC_C \qquad (16.3)$$

This condition is most evident at B, where the MRT is equal to 1. Here, when inputs are switched from clothing to food production, one unit of output is lost and one is gained. If the inputs needed to produce one unit of either product cost $100, the ratio of the marginal costs would be $100/$100, or 1. Equation (16.3) also holds at D (and at every other point on the frontier). Suppose the inputs needed to produce 1 unit of food cost $160. Then, the marginal cost of food would be $160, but the marginal cost of clothing would be only $80 ($160/2 units of clothing). As a result, the ratio of the marginal costs, 2, is equal to the MRT.

Output Efficiency

For an economy to be efficient, it must not only produce goods at minimum cost, *it must also produce goods in combinations that match people's willingness to pay for them*. To understand this, recall from Chapter 3 that the marginal rate of substitution of clothing for food (MRS) measures the consumer's willingness to pay for an additional unit of food in terms of consuming less clothing. But the marginal rate of transformation measures the cost of an additional unit of food in terms of producing less clothing. An economy produces output efficiently only if, for each consumer,

$$MRS = MRT \qquad (16.4)$$

To see why this condition is necessary for efficiency, suppose the MRT equals 1 but the MRS equals 2. Then consumers are willing to give up 2 units of clothing to get 1 unit of food, but the cost of getting the additional food is only 1 unit of lost clothing. Clearly, too little food is being produced. To achieve efficiency, food production must be increased, so that the MRS falls and the MRT increases until the two are equal. The outcome is efficient only when MRS = MRT for all pairs of goods.

Figure 16.10 shows this important efficiency condition graphically. Here, we have superimposed one consumer's indifference curves on the production possibilities frontier from Figure 16.9. Note that C is the only point on the production possibilities frontier that maximizes the consumer's satisfaction. Although all points on the production frontier are technically efficient, they do not all

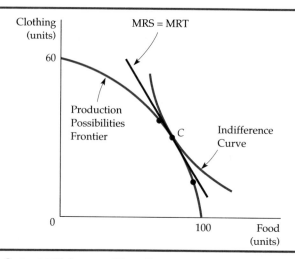

FIGURE 16.10   Output Efficiency.   The efficient combination of outputs is produced when the marginal rate of transformation between the two goods (which measures the cost of producing one good relative to the other) is equal to the consumer's marginal rate of substitution (which measures the marginal benefit of consuming one good relative to the other).

involve the most efficient production of goods from the consumer's perspective. At the point of tangency of the indifference curve and the production frontier, the MRS (the slope of the indifference curve) and the MRT (the slope of the production frontier) are equal.

If you were a planner in charge of managing an economy, you would face a difficult problem. To achieve efficiency you must equate the marginal rate of transformation with the marginal rate of substitution of the consumer. But if different consumers have different preferences for food and clothing, how can you decide what levels of food and clothing to produce and what amount of each to give to every consumer, so that all consumers have the same MRS? The information and logistical costs of doing this are enormous. Fortunately, a well-functioning competitive market system can achieve the same efficient outcome at relatively low cost.

Efficiency in Output Markets

When output markets are perfectly competitive, all consumers allocate their budgets so their marginal rates of substitution between two goods are equal to the price ratio. For our two goods, food and clothing,

$$MRS = P_F/P_C$$

At the same time, each profit-maximizing firm will produce its output up to the point at which price is equal to marginal cost. Again, for our two goods,

$$P_F = MC_F \text{ and } P_C = MC_C$$

Because the marginal rate of transformation is equal to the ratio of the marginal costs of production, it follows that

$$MRT = MC_F/MC_C = P_F/P_C = MRS \tag{16.5}$$

Thus, when both output and input markets are competitive, the production of food and clothing will be efficient in that the MRT is equal to the MRS. This condition is just another version of the marginal benefit–marginal cost rule discussed in Chapter 4 when we described demand curves. There we saw that consumers buy additional units of a good to the point at which the marginal benefit of consumption is equal to the marginal cost. Here the production of food and clothing is chosen so that the marginal benefit of consuming another unit of food is equal to the marginal cost of producing food, and the same is true for the consumption and production of clothing.

Figure 16.11 shows the efficiency of competitive output markets. Suppose the market generates a price ratio of P_F^1/P_C^1. If producers are using inputs efficiently, they will produce food and clothing at A, where the price ratio is equal

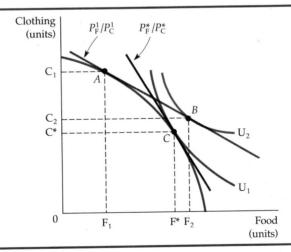

FIGURE 16.11 Competition and Output Efficiency. In a competitive output market, people consume to the point where their marginal rate of substitution is equal to the price ratio. Producers choose outputs, so that the marginal rate of transformation is equal to the price ratio. Because the MRS equals the MRT, the competitive output market is efficient. Any other price ratio will lead to an excess demand for one good and an excess supply of the other.

to the MRT, the slope of the production possibilities frontier. When faced with this budget constraint, however, consumers will consume at B, where they maximize their level of satisfaction (on indifference curve U_2). Because the producer wants to produce F_1 units of food, but consumers want to buy F_2, there will be an excess demand for food. Correspondingly, because consumers wish to buy C_2 units of clothing, but producers wish to sell C_1, there will be an excess supply of clothing. Prices in the market will then adjust—the price of food will rise and that of clothing will fall. As price ratio P_F/P_C increases, the price line will move along the production frontier.

An equilibrium results when the price ratio is P_F^*/P_C^* at C. Here, producers wish to sell F^* units of food and C^* units of clothing, and consumers wish to buy the same amounts. At this equilibrium, the MRT and the MRS are equal, so once again the competitive equilibrium is efficient.

EXAMPLE 16.2 THE EFFECTS OF AUTOMOBILE IMPORT QUOTAS

Governments can use quotas and tariffs to discourage imports and stimulate domestic production. But these devices can restrict or alter consumer choices and thereby generate substantial output inefficiencies. One recent example is the U.S. imposition of quotas on imports of Japanese automobiles.

During the past two decades, the U.S. automobile industry has faced increasing world competition. In 1965, for example, imports were only 6.1 percent of total domestic sales. This percentage increased, however, to 28.8 percent in 1980, when the industry earned a negative profit rate of -9.3 percent on its investment. Part of the industry's difficulty was due to higher quality, lower-priced Japanese cars. To deal with these problems, the automobile industry convinced the government to negotiate a voluntary export restraint (VER) agreement with the Japanese in 1981. The VER limited Japanese exports to the United States to 1.68 million cars per year as compared with the 2.5 million cars imported in 1980. It was argued that the quotas would give U.S. industry time to retool its machines and restructure its union agreements to compete effectively in the world market.

How did these quotas affect the world market? Did they help or hurt American consumers and producers? Answers to these questions require a general equilibrium analysis of the Japanese and U.S. automobile industries, as well as the markets for labor, materials, and other inputs to the production process.

The evidence suggests that the quotas did little to help the industry retool; U.S. manufacturers had already begun to restructure their production toward smaller and more fuel-efficient cars during the late 1970s. (Real investment expenditures increased by 88 percent from 1975–1976 to 1979–1980, for example.) The quotas did encourage the Japanese to sell fewer cars, but Japanese prices rose nearly $1000 per car in 1981–1982 alone, causing a $2 billion increase in revenues. In turn, the higher Japanese prices increased the demand for U.S.

cars, which allowed the U.S. auto industry to increase its prices, wages, and profits. The increased profits were between $900 million and $1.4 billion, substantially less than the Japanese revenue gain. Finally, U.S. consumers were made worse off by the policy, because U.S. automobile prices were approximately $350 to $400 per car higher than they would have been without the export restrictions.[11]

The quotas did, of course, benefit U.S. automobile workers. Without quotas, domestic sales would have been about 500,000 units lower, which translates into about 26,000 jobs. But the higher prices cost consumers well over $4.3 billion dollars, which means that each job that was retained cost approximately $160,000 ($4.3 billion/26,000). The VER was thus an extremely inefficient way to increase domestic employment.

16.5 An Overview—The Efficiency of Competitive Markets

Our analysis of general equilibrium and economic efficiency is now complete. We have shown that a perfectly competitive system of input and output markets will achieve an economically efficient outcome. The competitive system builds on the self-interested goals of consumers and producers, and on the ability of market prices to convey information to both parties. In the next two chapters, we will discuss why markets fail and what government can do about it. First, however, we should sum up the conditions required for economic efficiency and the particular conditions that a perfectly competitive market system satisfies.

1. *Efficiency in Exchange.* All allocations must lie on the exchange contract curve, so that every consumer's marginal rate of substitution of food for clothing is the same:

$$MRS_{FC}^J = MRS_{FC}^K$$

A competitive market achieves this efficient outcome because for consumers the tangency of the budget line and the highest attainable indifference curve assure that

$$MRS_{FC}^J = P_F/P_C = MRS_{FC}^K$$

2. *Efficiency in the Use of Inputs in Production.* All input combinations must lie on the production contract curve, so that every producer's marginal rate of technical substitution of labor for capital is equal in the production of both goods:

$$MRTS_{LK}^F = MRTS_{LK}^C$$

[11]See Robert W. Crandall, "Import Quotas and the Automobile Industry: The Costs of Protectionism," *The Brookings Review* (summer 1984): 8–16.

A competitive market achieves this efficient outcome because each producer maximizes profit by choosing the amount of land and capital inputs to the point at which the ratio of the input prices is equal to the marginal rate of technical substitution in the production process:

$$MRTS_{LK}^{F} = w/r = MRTS_{LK}^{C}$$

3. *Efficiency in the Output Market.* The mix of outputs must be chosen so that the marginal rate of transformation between outputs is equal to consumers' marginal rates of substitution:

$$MRT_{FC} = MRS_{FC} \text{ (for all consumers)}$$

A competitive market achieves this efficient outcome because profit-maximizing producers increase their output to the point at which marginal cost equals price:

$$P_F = MC_F, P_C = MC_C$$

As a result,

$$MRT_{FC} = MC_F/MC_C = P_F/P_C$$

But consumers maximize their satisfaction in competitive markets only if

$$P_F/P_C = MRS_{FC} \text{ (for all consumers)}$$

Therefore,

$$MRS_{FC} = MRT_{FC}$$

and the efficiency conditions are satisfied.

EXAMPLE 16.3   CHINA—THE INEFFICIENCY OF COMMAND AND CONTROL

China has a command economy: Most production decisions are made by planning authorities, who set output levels and prices for most products. As a result, prices do not adjust to market pressures. Central planners thus need to know the relative productive capabilities of each enterprise, individual preferences, and how to coordinate the interdependent production processes to avoid bottlenecks. But to set target levels properly, enterprises must reveal their true capabilities. The problem is that if the information firms give is used to set the minimum target levels, they have an incentive to understate their actual capabilities.

Such inefficiencies have led the Chinese to reexamine their policies, particularly with respect to state management of farms.[12] Before 1978, when efficiency-improving policies were put into effect, central authorities controlled state farms almost completely. The central government (through provincial bureaus) dictated production levels, including the amount of land for each crop.

[12]This section is based on Chung Min Pang and A. John De Boer, "Management Decentralization on China's State Farms," *American Journal of Agricultural Economics* 65 (1983): 658–666.

Farms had virtually no incentive to increase their profitability, and little local discretion in determining the composition and means of production was permitted. Every state farm had to apply to the state for investment expenditure. Wages were based almost exclusively on a common wage scale for all workers, and not on individual performance.

In 1978, the Central Committee of the Chinese Communist Party formalized new policies, known as the Economic Responsibility System, for the agricultural economy. These policies sought to promote agricultural growth and development by increasing efficiency. The rationale was that efficiency could be increased by giving farms and individuals more control and accountability. Under the new wage structure, up to 50 percent of workers' wages is based on individual productivity (as measured by a system of work points) and farm profitability. Farms can also reinvest much of their profit at their own discretion. Finally, prices play a larger role in determining crop production. Although production targets are still set centrally, farms are given less stringent guidelines, such as minimum areas for specific crops. Once targets are met, farms can choose the crop mix that will maximize profit.

We can see how these reforms have affected production by looking at Table 16.3, which shows how farms responded to the change in relative prices between grains and soybeans. To increase the production of soybeans under the pre-1978 stringent target system, central planners would have raised the target level without knowing which farms were best suited for soybean production. As a result, farms that could not produce soybeans efficiently would nonetheless have had to increase soybean output. Under the reform system, central planners let prices change priorities. They know that those farms with a comparative advantage in soybean production will then shift most heavily to this crop. Table 16.3 shows that the relatively rapid increase in the price of soybeans compared with the prices of wheat and rice led to an increased emphasis on soybean production.

TABLE 16.3 Agricultural Production and Prices in China

	Price (yuan/100 jin)				
	1977	1978	1979	1980	1981
Rice	9.81	9.81	11.90	11.97	11.97
Wheat	13.43	13.43	16.38	16.31	16.31
Soybeans	16.30	20.11	23.06	23.06	34.60
Soybean/Rice	1.66	2.05	1.94	1.93	2.89
Soybean/Wheat	1.21	1.05	1.41	1.41	2.12
	Sown Area (as percentage of all crops)				
Grains	63	61	60	61	59
Soybeans	26	30	33	31	33

Note: 1 jin = 500 grams; 1 yuan = $0.53 U.S.

An important benefit of these changes is that more decisions are now being made at the level where information is available. By letting prices convey this information, some of the inefficiencies in the management of Chinese state farms have been overcome.

16.6 Why Markets Fail

We can give two different interpretations to the description of the conditions required for efficiency. The first stresses that competitive markets work, and that we ought to ensure that the prerequisites for competition hold, so that resources can be efficiently allocated. The second stresses that the prerequisites for competition are unlikely to hold, and that we ought to concentrate on how to deal with the failure of competitive markets. Thus far we have focused on the first interpretation. Now, for most of the rest of the book, we concentrate on the second.

Competitive markets fail for four basic reasons: *market power, incomplete information, externalities,* and *public goods.* We will discuss each in turn.

Market Power

We saw in Chapters 10 and 14 that inefficiency arises when a producer or supplier of a factor input has market power. Suppose, for example, that the producer of food in our Edgeworth box diagram has monopoly power. It therefore chooses the output quantity at which marginal revenue (rather than price) is equal to marginal cost, and sells less output at a price higher than in a competitive market. The lower output will mean a lower marginal cost of food production. Meanwhile, the freed-up production inputs will be allocated to produce clothing, whose marginal cost will increase. As a result, the marginal rate of transformation will decrease, because $MRT_{FC} = MC_F/MC_C$. We might end up, for example, at A on the production possibilities frontier in Figure 16.11. Producing too little food and too much clothing is an output inefficiency that arises because firms with market power use a different price in their output decisions than consumers use in their consumption decisions.

A similar argument would apply to market power in an input market. Suppose, for example, that unions gave workers market power over the supply of their labor in the production of food. Too little labor would then be supplied to the food industry at too high a wage (w_F), and too much labor to the clothing industry at too low a wage (w_C). In the clothing industry the input efficiency conditions would be satisfied, because $MRTS_{LK}^C = w_C/r$. But in the food industry, the wage paid would be greater than the wage in the clothing industry.

Therefore, $\text{MRTS}^F_{LK} = w_F/r > w_C/r = \text{MRTS}^C_{LK}$. The result is input inefficiency, because efficiency requires that the marginal rates of technical substitution be equal in the production of all goods.

Incomplete Information

If consumers do not have accurate information about market prices or product quality, the market system will not operate efficiently. This lack of information may give producers an incentive to supply too much of some products and too little of others. In other cases, some consumers may not buy a product even though they would benefit from doing so, while other consumers buy products that leave them worse off. For example, consumers may buy pills that guarantee weight loss, only to find that the pills have no medical value. Finally, a lack of information may prevent some markets from ever developing. It may, for example, be impossible to purchase certain kinds of insurance because suppliers of insurance lack adequate information about who is likely to be at risk.

Each of these informational problems can lead to competitive market inefficiency. We will describe the nature of informational inefficiencies in detail in Chapter 17 and see whether government interventions might cure them.

Externalities

The price system works efficiently because market prices convey information to both producers and consumers. Sometimes, however, market prices do not reflect the activities of either producers or consumers. There is an *externality* when a consumption or production activity has an indirect effect on other consumption or production activities that is not reflected directly in market prices. As we explained in Section 9.2, the word "externality" is used because the effects on others (whether benefits or costs) are external to the market.

Suppose, for example, that a steel plant dumps effluent in a river, which makes a recreation site downstream unsuitable for swimming or fishing. Since there is unlikely to be any market in which the plant manager and the swimmers and fishermen can buy or sell the rights to dump the effluent, an externality exists. This externality understates the cost of waste water in the steel plant and encourages the firm to use too much waste water to produce its steel (recall Example 7.3.) This causes an input inefficiency. If this externality prevails throughout the industry, the price of steel (which is equal to the marginal cost of production) will be lower than if the cost of production reflected the effluent cost. As a result, too much steel will be produced and there will be an output inefficiency.

We will discuss the effects of externalities, and ways to deal with them, in Chapter 18.

Public Goods

The last source of market failure arises when the market fails to supply goods that many consumers value. A *public good* is a good that can be made available cheaply to many consumers, but once the good is provided to some consumers, it is very difficult to prevent others from consuming it. For example, suppose a firm is considering whether to undertake research on a new technology for which it cannot obtain a patent. Once the invention is made public, others can duplicate it. As long as it is difficult to exclude other firms from selling the product, the research will be unprofitable.

Thus, markets undersupply public goods. We will see in Chapter 18 that the government can sometimes resolve this problem either by supplying the good itself or by altering the incentives for private firms to produce it.

Summary

1. Most economic analyses involve partial equilibrium. They study the determination of price and quantity in a market, under the assumption that related markets are unaffected. General equilibrium analyses examine all markets simultaneously, taking into account feedback effects of other markets on the market being studied.

2. An efficient allocation occurs when no one consumer can be made better off by trade without making someone else worse off. When consumers make all mutually advantageous trades, the outcome is efficient and lies on the contract curve.

3. A competitive equilibrium describes a set of prices and quantities, so that when each consumer chooses his or her most preferred allocation, the quantity demanded is equal to the quantity supplied in every market. All competitive equilibrium allocations lie on the exchange contract curve and are Pareto efficient.

4. The utility possibilities frontier measures all efficient allocations (from the exchange contract curve) in terms of the levels of utility that each person achieves. Although both individuals prefer some allocations to an inefficient allocation, not *every* efficient allocation must be so preferred. Thus, an inefficient allocation can be more equitable than an efficient one.

5. Because a competitive equilibrium need not be equitable, the government can help redistribute wealth from rich to poor. Because such redistribution is costly, there is some conflict between equity and efficiency.

6. An allocation of production inputs is technically efficient if the output of one good cannot be increased without decreasing the output of some other good. All points of technical efficiency lie on the production contract curve and represent points of tangency of the isoquants for the two goods.

7. A competitive equilibrium in input markets occurs when the marginal rate of technical substitution between pairs of inputs is equal to the ratio of the prices of the inputs.

8. The production possibilities frontier measures all efficient allocations (from the production contract curve) in terms of the levels of output that can be produced with a given combination of inputs. The frontier is bowed in, because the marginal rate of transformation of food for clothing increases as more food and less clothing are produced. The marginal rate of transformation is equal to the ratio of the marginal cost of producing food to the marginal cost of producing clothing.

9. Efficiency in the allocation of goods to consumers is achieved only when the marginal rate of substitution of one good for another in consumption (which is the same for all consumers) is equal to the marginal rate of transformation of one good for another in production.

10. When input and output markets are perfectly competitive, the marginal rate of substitution (which equals the ratio of the prices of the goods) will equal the marginal rate of transformation (which equals the ratio of the marginal costs of producing the goods).

11. Competitive markets may fail to work efficiently for four reasons. First, firms or consumers may have market power in input or output markets. Second, consumers or producers may have incomplete information and may therefore err in their consumption and production decisions. Third, externalities may be present. Fourth, some public goods may not be produced, even though they could have been produced at low cost and are desired by society.

Questions for Review

1. Why can feedback effects make a general equilibrium analysis substantially different from a partial equilibrium analysis?

2. In the Edgeworth box diagram, explain how one point can simultaneously represent the market baskets owned by two consumers.

3. In the analysis of exchange using the Edgeworth box diagram, explain why both consumers' marginal rates of substitution are equal at every point on the contract curve.

4. "Since all points on a contract curve are efficient, they are all equally desirable from a social point of view." Do you agree with this statement? Explain.

5. How does the utility possibilities frontier relate to the contract curve?

6. In the Edgeworth production box diagram, what conditions must hold for an allocation to be on the production contract curve? Why is a competitive equilibrium on the contract curve?

7. How is the production possibilities frontier related to the production contract curve?

8. What is the marginal rate of transformation (MRT)? Explain why the MRT of one good for another is equal to the ratio of the marginal costs of producing the two goods.

9. Explain why goods will not be distributed efficiently among consumers if the marginal rate of transformation is not equal to the consumers' marginal rate of transformation.

10. What are the four major sources of market failure? In each case, explain briefly why the competitive market does not operate efficiently.

Exercises

1. In the analysis of exchange, suppose both people have identical preferences. Will the contract curve be a straight line? Explain. (Can you think of a counterexample?)

2. Jane has 8 liters of soft drinks and 2 sandwiches. Bob, on the other hand, has 2 liters of soft drinks and 4 sandwiches. With these endowments, Jane's marginal rate of substitution of soft drinks for sandwiches is three, and Bob's MRS is equal to one. Draw an Edgeworth box diagram to show whether this allocation of resources is efficient. If it is, explain why. If it is not, what exchanges will make both parties better off?

3. In the context of our analysis of the Edgeworth production box, suppose a new invention causes a constant-returns-to-scale production process for food to become a sharply-increasing-returns process. How does this change affect the production contract curve?

4. A monopsonist buys labor for less than the competitive wage. What type of inefficiency will this use of monopsony power cause? How would your answer change if the monopsonist in the labor market were also a monopolist in the output market?

5. Under what conditions might the production possibilities frontier not be concave? (An example will suffice.)

6. Suppose gold and silver are substitutes for each other, because both serve as hedges against inflation. Suppose also that the supplies of both are fixed in the short run ($Q_G = 50$, and $Q_S = 200$), and that the demand for gold (G) and the demand for silver (S) are given by the following equations:

$$P_G = 850 - Q_G + 0.5P_S \quad \text{and} \quad P_S = 540 - Q_S + 0.2P_G$$

a. What are the equilibrium prices of gold and silver?
b. Suppose a new discovery of gold increases the quantity supplied by 85 units. How will this discovery affect the prices of both gold and silver?

CHAPTER 17

Markets with Asymmetric Information

For most of this book, we have assumed that consumers and producers have complete information about the economic variables that are relevant for the choices they face. Now we will see what happens when some parties know more than others—i.e., when there is asymmetric information.

Asymmetric information is characteristic of many business situations. Frequently, a seller of a product knows more about its quality than the buyer does. Workers usually know their own skills and abilities better than employers. And business managers know their management capabilities better than owners.

Asymmetric information explains many institutional arrangements in our society. It helps us understand why automobile companies offer warranties on parts and service for new cars; why firms and employees sign contracts that include incentives and rewards; and why the shareholders of corporations need to monitor the behavior of the firm's managers.

We begin by examining a situation in which the sellers of a product have better information about its quality than buyers have. We will see how this kind of asymmetric information can lead to market failure. In the second section we see how sellers can avoid some of the problems associated with asymmetric information by giving potential buyers signals about the quality of their product. Product warranties provide a type of insurance that can be helpful when buyers have less information than sellers. But as the third section shows, the purchase of insurance entails difficulties of its own when buyers have better information than sellers.

In the fourth section we show that managers may pursue goals other than profit maximization when it is costly for the owners of private corporations to monitor the managers' behavior. (In other words, managers have better information than owners.) We also show how firms can give managers an incentive to maximize profits even when monitoring their behavior is costly. Finally, we show that labor markets may operate inefficiently when employees have better information about their productivity than employers have.

17.1 Quality Uncertainty and the Market for "Lemons"

Suppose you bought a new car for $10,000, drove it 100 miles, and then decided you really didn't want it. There was nothing wrong with the car—it performed beautifully and met all your expectations. You simply felt that you could do just as well without it and would be better off saving the money for other things. So you decide to sell the car. How much should you expect to get for it? Probably not more than $8,000—even though the car is brand new, has been driven only 100 miles, and has a warranty that is transferable to a new owner. And it's likely that if you were a prospective buyer, you wouldn't pay much more than $8,000 yourself.

Why does the mere fact that the car is second-hand reduce its value so much? To answer this question, think about your own concerns as a prospective buyer. Why, you would wonder, is this car for sale? Did the owner really change his or her mind about the car just like that, or is there something wrong with it? Perhaps this car is a "lemon."

Used cars sell for much less than new cars because *there is asymmetric information about their quality:* The seller of a used car knows much more about the car than the prospective buyer does. The buyer can hire a mechanic to check the car, but the seller has had experience with it, and will still know more. Furthermore, the very fact that the car is for sale indicates that it may indeed be a "lemon"—why sell a reliable car? As a result, the prospective buyer of a used car will always be suspicious of its quality—and with good reason.

The implications of asymmetric information about product quality were first analyzed by George Akerlof in a classic paper.[1] Akerlof's analysis goes far beyond the market for used cars. The markets for insurance, financial credit, and even employment are also characterized by asymmetric quality information. To understand its implications, we will start with the market for used cars and then see how the same principles apply to other markets.

The Market for Used Cars

Suppose two kinds of used cars are available—high-quality cars and low-quality cars. Also, *suppose that both sellers and buyers can tell which kind of car is which.* There will then be two markets, as illustrated in Figures 17.1a and 17.1b. In Figure 17.1a, S_H is the supply curve for high-quality cars, and D_H is the demand curve. Similarly, S_L and D_L in Figure 17.1b are the supply and demand curves for low-quality cars. Note that S_H is higher than S_L because owners of high-quality cars are more reluctant to part with them and must receive a higher price to do so. Similarly, D_H is higher than D_L because buyers are willing to pay more to get a high-quality car. As the figure shows, the market price for

[1]George A. Akerlof, "The Market for 'Lemons': Quality Uncertainty and the Market Mechanism," *Quarterly Journal of Economics* (August 1970): 488–500.

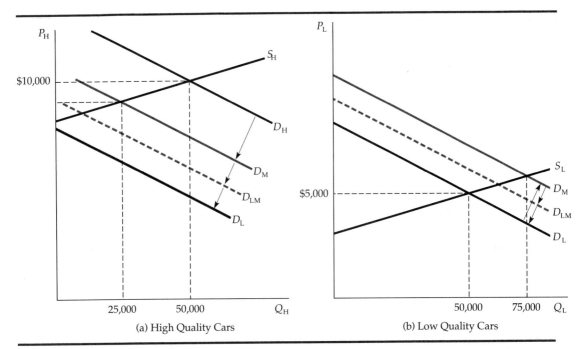

FIGURE 17.1 The Lemons Problem. When sellers of products have better information about product quality than buyers, a lemons market may develop in which low-quality goods drive out high-quality goods. In part (a) the demand curve for high-quality cars shifts from D_H to D_M as buyers lower their expectations about the average quality of cars on the market. Likewise, in part (b) the demand curve for low-quality cars shifts from D_L to D_M. As a result, the quantity of high-quality cars sold falls from 50,000 to 25,000, and the quantity of low-quality cars increases from 50,000 to 75,000.

high-quality cars is $10,000 for low-quality cars $5,000, and 50,000 cars of each type are sold.

In reality, the seller of a used car knows much more about its quality than a buyer does. Consider what happens, then, if sellers know the quality of cars, but buyers do not. (Buyers discover the quality only after they buy a car and drive it for a while.) Initially, buyers might think that the odds are 50-50 that a car they buy will be high quality. (The reason is that when both sellers *and* buyers knew the quality, 50,000 cars of each type were sold.) When making a purchase, buyers would therefore view all cars as being of "medium" quality. (Of course, after buying the car, they will learn its true quality.) The demand for medium-quality cars, denoted by D_M in Figure 17.1, is below D_H but above D_L. As the figure shows, *fewer high-quality cars (25,000) and more low-quality cars (75,000) will now be sold.*

As consumers begin to realize that most cars sold (about three-fourths of the total) are low-quality, their demands shift. As Figure 17.1 shows, the new demand curve might be D_{LM}, which means that on average cars are of low to medium quality. However, the mix of cars then shifts even more heavily to low quality. As a result, the demand curve shifts further to the left, pushing the mix of cars even further to low quality. *This shifting continues until only low-quality cars are sold.* At that point the market price would be too low to bring forth any high-quality cars for sale, so consumers correctly assume that any car they buy will be low quality, and the demand curve will be D_L.

The situation in Figure 17.1 is extreme. The market may come into equilibrium at a price that brings forth at least some high-quality cars. *But the fraction of high-quality cars will be smaller than it would be if consumers could identify quality before making the purchase.* That is why I should expect to sell my brand new car, which *I know* is in perfect condition, for much less than I paid for it. Because of asymmetric information, low-quality goods drive high-quality goods out of the market.

Implications of Asymmetric Information

Our used cars example shows how asymmetric information can result in market failure. In an ideal world of fully functioning markets, consumers would be able to choose between low-quality and high-quality cars. Some would choose the low-quality cars because they cost less, while others would prefer to pay more for high-quality cars. Unfortunately, in the real world, consumers cannot easily determine the quality of a used car until after they purchase it, so the price of used cars falls, and high-quality cars are driven out of the market.

Used cars are just a stylized example to illustrate an important problem that can be found in many markets. Let's look at some other examples of asymmetric information, and then see how the government or private firms might react to it.

Insurance

Why do people over 65 have difficulty buying medical insurance at almost any price? Older people do have a much higher risk of serious illness, but why doesn't the price of insurance rise to reflect that higher risk? The reason is asymmetric information. People who buy insurance know much more about their general health than any insurance company can hope to know, even if it insists on a medical examination. As a result, there is *adverse selection*, much as with used cars. Because unhealthy people are more likely to want insurance, the proportion of unhealthy people in the pool of insured people increases. This forces the price of insurance to rise, so that more healthy people, realizing their low risks, elect not to be insured. This further increases the proportion of unhealthy people, which forces the price of insurance up more, and so on, until nearly all people who want to buy insurance are unhealthy; thus selling insurance becomes unprofitable.

Adverse selection can also make the operation of insurance markets problematic in others ways. For example, suppose an insurance company wants to offer a policy for a particular event, such as an auto accident that results in property damage. It selects a target population—say, men under 25—to whom it wishes to market this policy, and it estimates the frequency of accidents within this group. For some of these people the probability of being in an accident is low, substantially less than .01; for others it is high, substantially more than .01. If the insurance company cannot distinguish between high- and low-risk men, it will base the premium for all men on the average experience, i.e., an accident probability of .01. With better information some people (those with low probabilities of an accident) will choose not to insure, while others (those with high probabilities of an accident) will definitely purchase the insurance. In the extreme only those who are likely to suffer a loss could choose to insure, which would seriously threaten the profitability of the insurance firm.

These kinds of market failure create a role for government. For health insurance, it provides an argument in favor of Medicare or related forms of government health insurance for the elderly. By providing insurance for *all* people over 65, the government eliminates adverse selection.[2]

The Market for Credit

By using a credit card, many of us borrow money without providing any collateral. Most credit cards allow the holder to run a debit of several thousand dollars, and many people hold several credit cards. Credit card companies earn money by charging interest on the debit balance. But how can a credit card company or bank distinguish high-quality borrowers (who pay their debts) from low-quality borrowers (who don't)? Clearly, borrowers know more about whether they will pay than the company does. Again, the "lemons" problem arises. Credit card companies and banks must charge the same interest rate to *all* borrowers, which attracts more low-quality borrowers, which forces the interest rate up, which increases the number of low-quality borrowers, which forces the interest rate up further, and so on.

In fact, credit card companies and banks *can*, at least to some extent, use computerized credit histories, which they often share with one another, to distinguish "low-quality" from "high-quality" borrowers. Many people think that computerized credit histories are an invasion of privacy. Should companies be allowed to keep these credit histories and share them with other companies? We can't answer this question for you, but we can point out that credit histories perform an important function. They eliminate, or at least greatly reduce, the problem of asymmetric information and adverse selection, which might otherwise prevent credit markets from operating. Without these histories, even the creditworthy would find it extremely costly or impossible to borrow money.

---

[2]The same general argument applies to all age groups. That is one reason that insurance companies avoid adverse selection by offering group health insurance policies at places of employment.

The Importance of Reputation and Standardization

Asymmetric information is also present in many other markets. Here are just a few examples: *retail stores* (Will the store repair or allow you to return a defective product? The store knows more about its policy than you do.); *dealers of rare stamps, coins, books, and paintings* (Are the items real or counterfeit? The dealer knows much more about their authenticity than you do.); *roofers, plumbers, and electricians* (When a roofer repairs or renovates the roof of your house, do you climb up to check the quality of the work?); *restaurants* (How often do you go into the kitchen to check if the chef is using fresh ingredients and obeying the health laws?).

In all these cases, the seller knows much more about the quality of the product than the buyer does. Unless sellers can provide information about quality to buyers, low-quality goods and services will drive out the high-quality ones, and there will be market failure. Sellers of high-quality goods and services, therefore, have a big incentive to convince consumers that their quality is indeed high. In the examples cited above, this is done largely by *reputation*. You shop at a particular store because it has a reputation for servicing its products; you hire a particular roofer and plumber because they have a reputation for doing good work; and you go to a particular restaurant because it has a reputation for using fresh ingredients, and nobody you know became sick after eating there.

Sometimes it is impossible for a business to develop a reputation. For example, most of the customers of a diner or a motel on a highway go there only once, or infrequently, while on a trip, so that the business has no opportunity to develop a reputation. How, then, can these diners and motels deal with the "lemons" problem? One way is by *standardization.* In your hometown, you may not prefer to eat regularly at McDonald's. But a McDonald's may look more attractive when you are driving along a highway and want to stop for lunch. The reason is that McDonald's provides a standardized product; the same ingredients are used and the same food is served in every McDonald's anywhere in the country. Who knows? Joe's Diner might serve better food, but you *know* exactly what you will be buying at McDonald's.

EXAMPLE 17.1 LEMONS IN MAJOR LEAGUE BASEBALL

Are there lemons markets in the real world? One way to test for a lemons market is to compare the performance of products that are resold with similar products that are seldom put up for resale. In a lemons market, purchasers of second-hand products will have limited information, and resold products should be lower in quality than products that rarely appear on the market. One such "second-hand" market has been created in recent years by a change in the rules governing contracts in major league baseball.[3]

[3]This example is based on Kenneth Lehn's study of the free agents market. See "Information Asymmetries in Baseball's Free Agent Market," *Economic Inquiry* (1984): 37–44.

TABLE 17.1 Player Disability

	Days Spent on Disabled List per Season		
	Precontract	Postcontract	Percent Change
All players	4.73	12.55	165.4
Renewed players	4.76	9.68	103.4
Free agents	4.67	17.23	268.9

Before 1976, major league baseball teams had the exclusive right to renew their players' contracts. After a 1976 ruling declared this system illegal, a new contracting arrangement was created. After six years of major league service, players can now sign new contracts with their original team or become free agents and sign with new teams. Having many free agents creates a second-hand market in baseball players. The original team can make an offer that will either retain a player or lose him to the free-agent market.

Asymmetric information is prominent in the free-agent market. One potential purchaser, the player's original team, has better information about the player's abilities than other teams have. If we were looking at used cars, we could test for the existence of asymmetric information by comparing their repair records. In baseball we can compare player disability records. If players are working hard and following rigorous conditioning programs, we would expect a low probability of injury and a high probability that they will be able to perform if injured. In other words, more motivated players will spend less time on the bench owing to disabilities. If a lemons market exists, we would expect free agents to have higher disability rates than players who are renewed. Players may also have preexisting physical conditions that their original teams know about that make them less desirable candidates for contract renewal. Because more such players would become free agents, free agents would experience higher disability rates for health reasons.

Table 17.1, which lists the postcontract performance of all players who have signed multiyear contracts, makes two points. First, both free agents and renewed players have increased disability rates after signing contracts. The disabled days per season increase from an average of 4.73 to an average of 12.55. Second, the postcontract disability rates of renewed and not-renewed players are significantly different. On average, renewed players are disabled 9.68 days, free agents 17.23 days.

These two findings suggest a lemons market in free agents that exists because baseball teams know their own players better than the other teams with which they compete.

17.2   Market Signaling

We have seen that asymmetric information can sometimes lead to a "lemons problem": Because sellers know more about the quality of a good than buyers do, buyers may assume that quality is low, so that price falls, and only low-quality goods are sold. We also saw how government intervention (in the market for health insurance, for example) or the development of a reputation (in service industries, for example) can help alleviate this problem. Now we will examine another important mechanism through which sellers and buyers deal with the problem of asymmetric information: *market signaling.* The concept of market signaling was first developed by Michael Spence, who showed that in some markets sellers send buyers *signals* that convey information about a product's quality.[4]

To see how market signaling works, let's look at a *labor market,* which is a good example of a market with asymmetric information. Suppose a firm is thinking about hiring two people. The two workers (the "sellers" of labor) know much more about the quality of the labor they can provide than the firm (the buyer of labor). For example, they know how hard they tend to work, how responsible they are, what their skills are, and so forth. The firm will find these things out only after they have been hired and have been working for some time. At the time they are hired, they look much like any other workers, and the firm knows little about how productive they may turn out to be.

Why don't firms simply hire workers, see how well they work, and then fire those with low productivity? Because this is often very costly. First, in many countries, and in many institutions in the United States, it is very difficult to fire someone who has been working more than a few months. (The firm may have to show just cause or pay severance pay.) Second, in many jobs workers do not become fully productive for at least six months. Considerable on-the-job training may be required into which the firm must invest substantial resources in new employees; therefore it might not learn how good workers are for six months to a year. So firms would be much better off if they knew how productive potential employees are *before* they hire them.

What characteristics can a firm examine to obtain information about people's productivity before it hires them? Can potential employees convey information about their productivity? Dressing well for the job interview might convey some information, but even unproductive people sometimes dress well to get a job. Dressing well is thus a weak signal—it doesn't do much to distinguish high-productivity from low-productivity people. *To be strong, a signal must be easier for high-productivity people to give than for low-productivity people to give, so that high-productivity people are more likely to give it.*

---

[4]The detailed development is in Michael Spence, *Market Signaling* (Cambridge: Harvard University Press, 1974). The basic ideas can also be found in Michael Spence, "Job Market Signaling," *Quarterly Journal of Economics* (1974): 355–374.

For example, *education* is a strong signal in labor markets. A person's educational level can be measured by several things—the number of years of schooling, degrees obtained, the reputation of the university or college that granted the degrees, the person's grade point average, and so on. Of course, education can directly and indirectly improve a person's productivity by providing information, skills, and general knowledge that are helpful in work. But even if education did *not* improve one's productivity, it would still be a useful *signal* of productivity because more productive people will find it easier to attain a high level of education. (Productive people tend to be more intelligent, more motivated, and more energetic and hard-working—characteristics that are also helpful in school.) More productive people are therefore more likely to attain a high level of education *to signal their productivity to firms and thereby obtain better-paying jobs.* And firms are correct in considering education a signal of productivity.

A Simple Model of Job Market Signaling

To understand how signaling works, it will be useful to discuss a simple model.[5] Let's assume there are only low-productivity workers (Group I), whose average and marginal product is 1, and high-productivity workers (Group II), whose average and marginal product is 2. Workers will be employed by competitive firms whose products sell for $10,000, and who expect an average of 10 years of work from each employee. We also assume that half the workers are in Group I and the other half in Group II, so that the *average* productivity of all workers is 1.5, and the expected revenue to be generated from Group I workers is $100,000 ($10,000/year × 10 years) and from Group II workers is $200,000 ($20,000/year × 10 years).

If firms could identify people by their productivity, they would offer all of them a wage equal to their marginal revenue product. Group I people would be paid $10,000 per year, Group II people $20,000. On the other hand, if firms could not identify people's productivity before they hired them, they would pay all workers an annual wage equal to the average productivity (i.e., $15,000). Group I people would then earn more ($15,000 instead of $10,000), at the expense of Group II people (who would earn $15,000 instead of $20,000).

Now let's consider what can happen with signaling via education. Suppose all the attributes of an education (degrees earned, grade point average, etc.) can be summarized by a single index y that represents years of higher education. All education involves a cost, and the higher the educational level y, the higher the cost. This cost includes tuition and books, the opportunity cost of forgone wages, and the psychic cost of having to work hard to obtain high grades. What is important is that *the cost of education is greater for the low-productivity group than for the high-productivity group.* We might expect this for two reasons. First, low-productivity workers may simply be less studious. Second, low-productivity

---

[5]This is essentially the model developed in Spence, *Market Signaling.*

workers may progress more slowly through degree programs in which they enroll. In particular, suppose that for Group I people the cost of attaining educational level y is given by

$$C_I(y) = \$40,000y$$

and for Group II people it is

$$C_{II}(y) = \$20,000y$$

Now suppose (to keep things simple and to dramatize the importance of signaling) that *education does nothing to increase one's productivity; its only value is as a signal.* Let's see if we can find a market equilibrium in which different people obtain different levels of education, and firms look at education as a signal of productivity.

Consider the following possible equilibrium. Suppose firms use this decision rule: *Anyone with an education level of* y^* *or more is a Group II person and is offered a wage of $20,000, and anyone with an education level below* y^* *is a Group I person and is offered a wage of $10,000.* The particular level y^* that the firms choose is arbitrary, but for this decision rule to be part of an equilibrium, firms must have identified people correctly, or else the firms will want to change the rule. Will this rule work?

To answer this, we must determine how much education the people in each group will obtain, *given that firms are using this decision rule.* To do this, remember that education allows one to get a better-paying job. The benefit of education $B(y)$ is the *increase* in the wage associated with each level of education, as shown in Figure 17.2. Observe that $B(y)$ is 0 initially, which represents the $100,000 base 10-year earnings that are earned without any college education. But when the education level reaches y^* or greater, $B(y)$ jumps to $200,000.

How much education should a person obtain? Clearly the choice is between *no* education (i.e., $y = 0$) and an education level of y^*. The reason is that any level of education less than y^* results in the same base earnings of $100,000, so there is no benefit from obtaining an education at a level above 0, but below y^*. Similarly, there is no benefit from obtaining an educational level above y^* because y^* is sufficient to allow one to enjoy the higher total earnings of $200,000.

In deciding how much education to obtain, people compare a benefit of education (the higher earnings) with the cost. People in each group can decide how much education to obtain by making the following cost-benefit calculation: *Obtain the education level* y^* *if the benefit (i.e., the increase in earnings) is at least as large as the cost of this education.* For both groups, the benefit (the increase in earnings) is $100,000. The costs, however, differ for the two groups. For Group I, the cost is $40,000y$, but for Group II the cost is only $20,000y$. Therefore, Group I people will obtain *no* education as long as

$$\$100,000 < \$40,000y^* \text{ or } y^* > 2.5$$

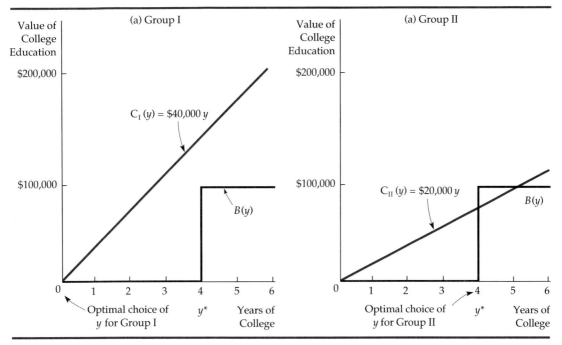

FIGURE 17.2 Signaling. Education can be a useful signal of the high productivity of a group of workers if education is easier to obtain for this group than for the low-productivity group. In part (a) the low-productivity group will choose an education level of $y = 0$ because the cost of education is greater than the increased earnings. However, in part (b), the high-productivity group will choose an education level of $y^* = 4$ because the gain in earnings is greater than the cost.

and Group II people will obtain an education level y^* as long as

$$\$100,000 > \$20,000y^* \text{ or } y^* < 5$$

These results give us an equilibrium *as long as y^* is between 2.5 and 5.* Suppose, for example, that y^* is 4.0, as in Figure 17.2. Then people in Group I will find that education does not pay, and they will not obtain any, whereas people in Group II will find that education does pay, and they will obtain the level $y = 4.0$. Now, when a firm interviews job candidates who have no college education, it correctly assumes they have low productivity and offers them a wage of $10,000. Similarly, when the firm interviews people who have four years of college, it correctly assumes their productivity is high, and their wage should be $20,000. We therefore have an equilibrium; high-productivity people will obtain a college education to signal their productivity, and firms will read this signal and offer them a high wage.

This is a simple, highly stylized model, but it illustrates a significant point: Education can be an important signal that allows firms to sort workers according to productivity. Some workers (those with high productivity) will want to obtain a college education, *even though that education does nothing to increase their productivity.* High-productivity workers simply want to identify themselves as being highly producitve, so they obtain the education to send a signal.

Of course, in the real world, education *does* provide useful knowledge and does increase one's ultimate productivity. (We wouldn't have written this book if we didn't believe that.) But education also serves a signaling function. For example, many firms insist that a prospective manager have an MBA. One reason for this is that MBAs learn economics, finance, and other useful subjects. But there is a second reason—to complete an MBA program takes intelligence, discipline, and hard work, and people with those qualities tend to be very productive.

Guarantees and Warranties

We have stressed the role of signaling in labor markets, but signaling can also play an important role in many other markets in which there is asymmetric information. Consider the markets for such durable goods as televisions, stereos, cameras, and refrigerators. Many firms produce these items, but some of their products are more dependable than others. If consumers could not tell which brands tend to be more dependable, the better brands couldn't be sold for higher prices. Firms that produce a higher-quality, more dependable product would therefore like to make consumers aware of this, but how can they do it in a convincing way? The answer is through *guarantees and warranties.*

Guarantees and warranties effectively signal product quality because an extensive warranty is more costly for the producer of a low-quality item than for the producer of a high-quality item. (The low-quality item is more likely to require servicing under the warranty, which the producer will have to pay for.) As a result, in their own self-interest producers of low-quality items will not offer an extensive warranty. Consumers can therefore correctly view an extensive warranty as a signal of high quality, and they will pay more for products that offer one.

17.3 Moral Hazard

When one party is fully insured and cannot be accurately monitored by an insurance company with limited information, its behavior may change *after* the insurance has been purchased. This is the problem of *moral hazard.* Moral hazard occurs when the party to be insured can affect the probability or magnitude of the event that triggers payment. For example, if I have complete medical insurance coverage, I may visit the doctor more often than I would if my coverage was limited. If the insurance provider can monitor its insurees' behavior, it can charge higher fees for those who make more claims. But if the company cannot monitor behavior, it may find its payments to be larger than expected. With moral hazard, insurance companies may be forced to increase their premiums or even to refuse to sell insurance at all.

Consider, for example, the decisions that both the owners of a warehouse worth $100,000 and their insurance company face. Suppose that if the owners run a $50 fire prevention program for their employees, the probability of a fire is .005. Without this program, the probability of a fire increases to .01. Knowing this, the insurance company faces a dilemma if it cannot monitor whether there will be a fire prevention program. The policy that the insurance company offers cannot include a clause stating that payments will be made only if there is a fire prevention program. If the program were in place, the company could insure the warehouse for a premium equal to the expected loss from a fire, which is $500 (.005 $\times$ $100,000). Once the insurance policy is purchased, however, the owners no longer have an incentive to run the program. If there is a fire, they will be fully compensated for their financial loss. Thus, if the insurance company sold a policy for $500, it will incur losses, because the expected loss from fire will be $1000 (.01 $\times$ $100,000).

The problem of moral hazard arises because people who want insurance can affect the degree of risk involved in an uncertain situation. Unfortunately, moral hazard is not only a problem for insurance companies. It also alters the ability of markets to allocate resources efficiently. Suppose, for example, that D in Figure 17.3 gives the demand for automobile driving in miles-per-week. The demand curve is downward-sloping, because many households switch to alternative transportation as the cost of driving increases. Suppose initially that the cost of transportation includes the insurance cost, and that insurance companies can accurately evaluate accident risks. In this case, there is no moral hazard. Drivers know that more dangerous driving will increase their insurance premium (whether or not an accident occurs) and thereby also increase their total cost of transportation (the cost per mile is assumed to be constant). For example, if the cost of transportation is $1.50 per mile (50 cents of which is insurance cost), the driver will choose to drive 100 miles per week.

Now suppose a moral hazard problem arises because the insurance premium does not depend on individual driving habits. As a result, drivers assume that any additional accident costs that they incur will be spread over a large group, with only a negligible portion accruing to each of them individually. They will now act as if their insurance premium does not vary with the number of miles that they drive. An additional mile of transportation will then cost $1.00, rather than $1.50, and the number of miles driven will increase substantially, from 100 to 140.

This example illustrates a general principle: By lowering the price that people pay for services, moral hazard causes people to demand more than the efficient level of those services.

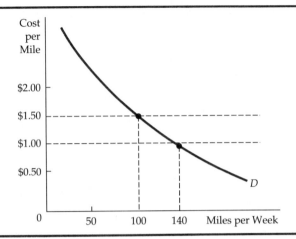

FIGURE 17.3   The Effects of Moral Hazard.   Moral hazard alters the ability of markets to allocate resources efficiently. D gives the demand for automobile driving. With no moral hazard, the cost of transportation is $1.50 per mile, and the driver drives 100 miles, which is the efficient amount with moral hazard. The driver perceives the cost per mile to be $1.00 and drives 140 miles.

EXAMPLE 17.2   REDUCING MORAL HAZARD—WARRANTIES OF ANIMAL HEALTH

Buyers of livestock consider information about the animals' health to be very important.[6] Unhealthy animals gain weight more slowly than healthy animals, and are less likely to reproduce. Because of asymmetric information in the livestock market (sellers know the health of an animal better than buyers do), most states put warranties on the sale of livestock. Under these laws sellers promise (warrant) that their animals are free from hidden diseases and are responsible for all costs arising from any animals that are diseased.

Although warranties solve the problem of the seller's having better information than the buyer, they also create a form of moral hazard. Guaranteeing reimbursement to the buyer for all costs associated with diseased animals means that insurance rates are not tied to the level of care that buyers or their agents take to protect their livestock against disease. As a result of these warranties, livestock buyers tended to avoid early diagnosis of diseased livestock, and losses increased.

---

[6]This example is based on Terence J. Centner and Michael E. Wetzstein, "Reducing Moral Hazard Associated with Implied Warranties of Animal Health," *American Journal of Agricultural Economics* 69 (1987): 143–150.

In response to the moral hazard problem, half the states have modified their warranty laws to require sellers to tell buyers whether livestock are diseased at the time of sale. Some states also require sellers to comply with state and federal animal health regulations. Beyond this, however, warranties that animals are free from hidden disease must be an explicit written or oral guarantee to buyers.

17.4 The Principal-Agent Problem

If information were widely available, and if monitoring the productivity of workers were costless, the owners of a business could ensure that their managers and workers were working effectively. In most firms, however, owners can't monitor everything that employees do—employees have better information than owners. This information asymmetry creates a *principal-agent* problem.

An *agency relationship* exists whenever there is an employment relationship in which one person's welfare depends on what another person does.[7] The *agent* is the person who acts, and the *principal* is the party whom the action affects. In our business example, the manager and the workers are agents, and the owner is the principal. The principal-agent problem is that managers may pursue their own goals, even at the cost of obtaining lower profits for the owners.

Agency relationships are widespread in our society. For example, doctors serve as agents for hospitals, and as such, may select patients and do procedures consistent with their personal preferences, but not with the objectives of the hospital. Similarly, managers of housing properties, who serve as agents for property owners, may not maintain the property the way that the owners prefer.

How does incomplete information and costly monitoring affect how agents act? And what mechanisms can give managers the incentive to operate in the owner's interest? These questions are central to any principal-agent analysis. In this section we study the principal-agent problem from several perspectives. First, we look at the owner-manager problem within private and public enterprises. Second, we discuss how owners can use contractual relationships with their employees to deal with the principal-agent problems.

---

[7]For more discussion of agency costs, see Jensen and Meckling, "Theory of the Firm: Managerial Behavior, Agency Costs, and Ownership Structure," *Journal of Financial Economics* 11 (1976): 305–360; and Fama, "Agency Problems and the Theory of the Firm," *Journal of Political Economy* 88 (1980): 288–307. See also Oliver Williamson, *The Economic Institutions of Capitalism* (New York: Free Press, 1985).

The Principal-Agent Problem in Private Enterprises

An individual family or financial institution owns more than 10 percent of the shares of only 16 of the 100 largest industrial corporations.[8] Clearly, most large firms are controlled by management. The fact that most stockholders have only a small percentage of the firm's total equity makes it difficult for them to obtain information about how well the firm's managers are performing. One function of owners (or their representatives) is to monitor the behavior of managers. But monitoring is costly, and information is expensive to gather and use, at least for an individual.[9]

Managers of private enterprises can thus pursue their own objectives. But what are these objectives? One view is that managers are more concerned with growth than with profit per se; more rapid growth and larger market share provide more cash flow, which in turn allows managers to enjoy more perks.[10] Another view deemphasizes growth per se but does emphasize the utility that managers get from their jobs, not only from profit but also from the respect of their peers, the power to control the corporation, the fringe benefits and other perks, and a long tenure on the job.[11]

However, there are some important limitations to managers' ability to deviate from the objectives of owners. First, stockholders can complain loudly when they feel that managers are behaving improperly, and in exceptional cases they can oust the current management (perhaps with the help of the board of directors of the corporation, whose job it is to monitor managerial behavior). Second, a vigorous market for corporate control can develop. If a takeover bid becomes more likely when the firm is poorly managed, managers will have a strong incentive to pursue the goal of profit maximization. Third, there can be a highly developed market for managers. If managers who maximize profit are in great

---

[8]See Merritt B. Fox, *Finance and Industrial Performance in a Dynamic Economy* (New York: Columbia University Press, 1987).

[9]If I as a stockholder devote substantial energy and resources to obtain information about the management of a corporation, that information would be quite valuable to other investors. Yet there is no obvious way in which I could be reimbursed for my expenses. Essentially, there are economies of scale in gathering information of this sort, and no obvious way in which the information can be sold. These characteristics make information a *public good,* about which we will have more to say in the next chapter. For the moment, we can see that because there is no reason to expect a competitive market for information to develop, managers can pursue objectives that are different from profit maximization without losing their jobs.

[10]See for example, William Baumol, *Business Behavior, Value, and Growth,* rev. ed. (New York: Harcourt, Brace, 1967); and Robin Marris, *The Economic Theory of Managerial Capitalism* (London: Macmillan, 1967).

[11]See, for example, Oliver Williamson, *Corporate Control and Business Behavior* (Englewood Cliffs, N.J.: Prentice-Hall, 1964). These differing views about managerial objectives do not reject the view that business people optimize; rather they suggest alternative optimizing goals. But one might argue that limited information precludes optimizing behavior by firms, as, for example, in Richard R. Nelson and Sidney G. Winter, *An Evolutionary Theory of Economic Change* (Cambridge, Mass.: Harvard University Press, 1982).

demand, they will earn high wages, which in turn will give other managers an incentive to pursue the same goal.

Unfortunately, the means by which stockholders control managers' behavior are limited and imperfect. Corporate takeovers may be motivated by personal and economic power, for example, instead of economic efficiency. The managers' labor market may also not work perfectly, given that top managers are frequently near retirement and have long-term contracts. As a result, it is important to look for solutions to the principal-agent problem in which owners alter the incentives that managers face, without resort to government intervention. We consider some of these solutions in the next section.

EXAMPLE 17.3 BANK MANAGERS AS AGENTS

In a competitive environment where firms that do not profit-maximize are subject to takeovers, both manager-controlled and owner-controlled firms demand the efficient level of inputs, and managers are not able to favor their own personal expenditure items. In a noncompetitive environment, however, two influences affect the input demands of firms, depending on their owner status. First, all firms in such a market have market power, which leads to lower output levels and, therefore, a lower demand for inputs. Yet, second, when managers control firms, they might spend more on such inputs as staff size, office furnishings, and other luxuries.

A study of the banking industry in Pennsylvania helps to evaluate the second point.[12] The study uses data on 365 banks for 1970 and estimates total bank expenditures in three categories: wages and salaries, furniture and equipment, and general occupancy. The results show little difference between manager-controlled and owner-controlled banks with respect to wages and salary. The major difference was in expenses for furniture and equipment and general occupancy. Here manager-controlled banks with market power spent approximately 6 percent more on both these items than owner-controlled banks.

The sample of banks was too large for this result to be due to chance. Therefore, the study supports the view that manager-controlled firms in noncompetitive industries prefer certain expense items, even at the cost of failure to maximize the firm's profit. In short, there is a principal-agent problem.

The Principal-Agent Problem in Public Enterprises

The principal-agent framework can also help us study the behavior of the managers of public organizations. There managers may be interested in power and

[12]This section relies on Timothy H. Hannan and Ferdinand Mavinga, "Expense Preference and Managerial Control: the Case of the Banking Firm," *Bell Journal* 11 (autumn 1980): 671–682.

perquisites, both of which can be obtained by expanding their organization beyond its "efficient" level. Because it is also costly to monitor the behavior of public managers, there are no guarantees that they will produce the efficient output. Legislative checks on a government agency are not likely to be effective as long as the agency has better information about its costs than the legislature has.

Although the public sector lacks some of the market forces that keep private managers in line, government agencies can still be effectively monitored. First, managers of government agencies care about more than just the size of their agency. Indeed, many choose lower-paying public jobs because they are concerned about the "public interest." Second, public managers are subject to the rigors of the managerial job market, much the way private managers are. If public managers are perceived to be pursuing improper objectives, their ability to obtain high salaries in the future might be impaired. Third, the legislature and other government agencies perform an oversight function. For example, the Government Accounting Office and the Office of Management and Budget spend much of their energy monitoring other agencies.

At the local rather than the federal level, public managers are subject to even more checks. Suppose, for example, that a city transit agency has expanded bus service beyond the efficient level. Then, the citizens can vote the transit managers out of office, or, if all else fails, use alternative transportation or even move. And competition among agencies can be as effective as competition among private firms in constraining the nonprofit-maximizing behavior of managers.

EXAMPLE 17.4 THE MANAGERS OF NONPROFIT HOSPITALS AS AGENTS

The same questions that apply to public enterprises that governments run also apply to nonprofit enterprises that governments regulate. Are the goals of the managers of nonprofit organizations different from the goals of for-profit organizations? Are nonprofit organizations more or less efficient than for-profit firms? One area where this debate can be evaluated is in the provision of health care, because both nonprofit and for-profit hospitals are numerous in the United States. A study of 725 hospitals, from 14 major hospital chains, was aimed at exactly this issue.[13] The return on investment and average costs of the two types of hospitals were compared to determine if they performed differently.

The study found that for 1977 and 1981 the rate of returns between the two types of hospitals did indeed differ. For example, in 1977 for-profits earned an 11.6 percent return, while nonprofits earned 8.8 percent. In 1981, for-profits earned 12.7 percent and nonprofits only 7.4 percent. A straight comparison of returns and costs of these hospitals is not appropriate, however, because the

[13]Regina E. Herzlinger and William S. Krasker, "Who Profits from Nonprofits?," *Harvard Business Review* 65 (Jan.-Feb. 1987): 93–106.

hospitals perform different functions. For example, 24 percent of the nonprofit hospitals provide medical residency programs as compared with only 6 percent of the for-profit hospitals. Similar differences can be found in the provision of speciality care, where 10 percent of the nonprofits have open-heart units as compared with 5 percent of the for-profits. In addition, 43 percent of nonprofits had premature infant units, while only 29 percent of the for-profits had the equivalent units.

Fortunately, through a statistical regression analysis, in which we control for the differences in the services performed, we can determine whether differences in services account for the higher costs. The study found that after adjusting for services performed, the average cost of a patient day in nonprofit hospitals was 8 percent higher than in for-profit hospitals. This implies that the profit status of the hospital affects its performance in the way theory might predict: Without the competitive forces faced by for-profit hospitals, nonprofit hospitals may not be cost-conscious.

Of course, we cannot conclude from these results that nonprofit hospitals serve no useful function. Bear in mind that they provide services that society may wish to subsidize. However, the added cost of running a nonprofit hospital should be considered when determining whether it should be granted tax-exempt status.

Incentives in the Principal-Agent Framework

We have seen why managers' and owners' objectives are likely to differ within the principal-agent framework. How, therefore, can owners design reward systems so that managers and workers can come as close as possible to meeting the owners' goals? To answer this question, let's study a specific problem.[14]

A small manufacturer uses labor and machinery to produce watches. The owners want to maximize their profit. They must rely on a machine repairperson whose effort will influence the likelihood that the machines break down, and thus affect the firm's level of profit. Profit also depends on other random factors, such as the quality of parts and the reliability of other labor. As a result of high monitoring costs, the owners can neither measure the effort of the repairperson directly nor be sure that the same effort will always generate the same profit level. Table 17.2 describes these circumstances.

The table shows that the repairperson can make either a low or high amount of effort. Low effort generates either $10,000 or $20,000 profit (with equal probability), depending on the random factors that we mentioned. We've labeled the lower of the two profit levels "poor luck," and the higher profit level "good luck." When the repairperson makes a high effort, the profit will be either

---

[14]This discussion is motivated in part by Bengt Holmstrom, "Moral Hazard and Observability," *Bell Journal of Economics* 10 (1979): 74–91.

TABLE 17.2 The Profit from Making Watches

	Poor Luck	Good Luck
Low effort ($a = 0$)	$10,000	$20,000
High effort ($a = 1$)	$20,000	$40,000

$20,000 (when there is poor luck) or $40,000 (when there is good luck). These numbers highlight the problem of incomplete information, because the owners cannot know whether the repairperson has made a low or high effort when the firm's profit is $20,000.[15]

Now suppose the repairperson's goal is to maximize the wage payment that he receives, net of the cost of lost leisure and unpleasant work time associated with any effort that he makes. To simplify, we'll suppose that the cost of effort is 0 for low effort and $10,000 for high effort. (Formally, $c = \$10,000a$.)

Now we can state the principal-agent problem from the owners' perspective. The owners' goal is to maximize expected profit, given the uncertainty of outcomes and given that the repairperson's behavior cannot be monitored. The owners can contract to pay the repairperson for his work, but the payment scheme must be based entirely on the measurable output (profit) of the manufacturing process, not on the repairperson's effort. To signify this link, we describe the payment scheme as $w(\pi)$, stressing that payments can depend only on measured profit.

What is the best payment scheme? And can that scheme be as effective as one based on effort rather than output? We can only begin to study the answers here. The best payment scheme depends on the nature of production, the degree of uncertainty, and the objectives of both owners and managers. The arrangement will not always be as effective as an ideal scheme that is directly tied to effort. A lack of information can lower economic efficiency, because both the owners' profit and the repairperson's payment may fall at the same time.

Let's see how to design a payment scheme when the repairperson wishes to maximize his payment received net of the cost of effort made.[16] Suppose first that the owners offer a fixed wage payment to the repairperson. Any wage will do, but we can see things most clearly if we assume that the wage is 0. (You might presume that 0 represents that this wage is no higher than the wage rate paid in other comparable jobs.) Facing a wage of 0, the repairperson has no incentive to make a high level of effort. The reason is simple: The repairperson does not share in any of the gains that the owners enjoy from the increased

---

[15]That the profit will be exactly $20,000 in both cases makes our analysis striking, but the point of the analysis applies quite generally.

[16]Our assumption that the repairperson wishes to maximize payments implicitly assumes that he is risk neutral. In general, when the agent is risk neutral, no efficiency is lost. If, however, the repairperson were risk averse, the problem would be more difficult, and efficiency would be lost.

effort. It follows, therefore, that a fixed payment will lead to an inefficient outcome. When $a = 0$, and $w = 0$, the owner will earn an expected profit of $15,000, and the repairperson a net wage of 0.

Both the owners and the repairperson will be better off under a payment scheme that rewards the repairperson for his productive effort. Suppose, for example, that the owners offer the repairperson the following payment scheme:

$$\text{If } \pi = \$10,000 \text{ or } \$20,000, \, w = 0$$
$$\text{If } \pi = \$40,000, \, w = \$24,000 \tag{17.1}$$

Under this bonus arrangement, the repairperson knows that a low effort generates no payment. A high effort, however, generates an expected payment of $12,000, and a payment net of the cost of effort of $2,000. Clearly, the repairperson will choose to make a high level of effort. This makes the owners better off than before, because they are assured of an expected profit of $30,000, and a net profit of $18,000.

This isn't the only payment scheme that will work for the owners, however. Suppose they contract to have the worker participate in a profit-sharing arrangement when profits are greater than $15,000:

$$w = 0.8(\pi - \$15,000) \tag{17.2}$$

If the repairperson offers low effort, he receives an expected payment of 0. But if he offers a high level of effort, his expected payment is $12,000, and his expected payment net of the cost of effort is $2,000. (The principal's net profit is $18,000 as before.)

Thus, in our example, a profit-sharing payment arrangement achieves the identical outcome as a bonus payment system. In more complex situations, the incentive effects of the two types of arrangements will differ. However, the principle that this example illustrates applies to all principal-agent problems. When it is impossible to measure effort directly, an incentive structure that rewards the outcome of high levels of effort can induce agents to aim for the goals that the owners set.

17.5 Asymmetric Information in Labor Markets: Efficiency Wage Theory

When the labor market is competitive, all who wish to work will find jobs for a wage equal to their marginal product. Yet most countries have substantial unemployment even though many people are aggressively seeking work. Many of the unemployed would presumably work even for a lower wage rate than that being received by employed people. Why don't we see firms cutting wage rates, increasing employment levels, and thereby increasing their profit? Can our models of competitive equilibrium explain persistent unemployment?

In this section we show how the *efficiency wage theory* can explain the presence of unemployment and wage discrimination.[17] Efficiency wage theory makes two important extensions to the simple competitive labor market theory that we already presented. The first concerns the influence of wages on labor productivity. We have thus far determined labor productivity according to workers' abilities and firms' investment in capital. Efficiency wage models recognize that labor productivity also depends on what wage rate is paid.[18]

There are various explanations for this relationship. In developing countries, economists have suggested that the productivity of workers depends on the wage rate for nutritional reasons. Better-paid workers can afford to buy more and better food and are therefore healthier and can work harder. Although this may explain the wage/productivity link in the Third World, it does not seem to make sense for countries like the United States.

A more appropriate explanation for the United States is found in the more recent theoretical models, such as the *shirking models*. Because monitoring workers is costly or impossible, firms in these models have imperfect information about worker productivity and there is a principal-agent problem. In its simplest form the shirking model assumes perfectly competitive markets, so all workers are equally productive and earn the same wage. Once hired, workers can either work productively or slack off (shirk). But because information about their performance is limited, workers may not get fired for shirking.

The model works as follows. If a firm pays its workers the market clearing wage w^*, they have an incentive to shirk. Even if they get caught and are fired (and they might not be), they can immediately get hired somewhere else for the same wage. In this situation, the threat of being fired does not impose a cost on workers, so they have no incentive to be productive. As an incentive not to shirk, a firm must offer workers a higher wage. At this higher wage, workers who are fired for shirking will have to face a decrease in wages if they get hired by another firm at w^*. If the difference in wages is large enough, workers will be induced to be productive, and this firm will not have a problem with shirking. The wage at which no shirking occurs is the *efficiency wage*.

Up to this point, we have looked at only one firm. But all firms face the problem of shirking. This means that all firms will offer wages greater than the market clearing wage w^*, say, w_e (efficiency wage). Does this remove the incentive for workers not to shirk, because they will be hired at the higher wage by other firms if they get fired? No, because all firms are offering wages greater than w^*, the demand for labor is less than the market-clearing quantity, and there is unemployment. This means that workers fired for shirking will face a spell of unemployment before earning w_e at another firm.

[17]The general discussion builds on Janet L. Yellen, "Efficiency Wage Models of Unemployment," *American Economic Review*, 74 (May 1984): 200–205. The graphical analysis relies on Joseph E. Stiglitz, "The Causes and Consequences of the Dependence of Quality on Price," *Journal of Economic Literature* 25 (March 1987): 1–48.

[18]This linkage between productivity and wages has been discussed by economists before the development of efficiency wage theory, most notably by Karl Marx.

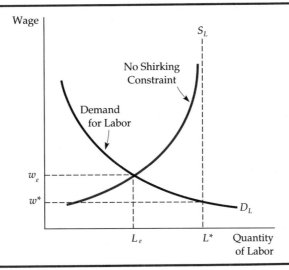

FIGURE 17.4 Unemployment in a Shirking Model. Unemployment can arise in otherwise competitive labor markets when employers cannot accurately monitor workers. In the figure the "no shirking constraint" gives the wage necessary to keep workers from shirking on the job. The firm hires L_e workers (at a higher than competitive efficiency wage w_e), creating $L^* - L_e$ of unemployment.

Figure 17.4 shows shirking in the labor market. The demand for labor D_L is downward-sloping for the traditional reasons. If there were no shirking, the intersection of D_L with the supply of labor (S_L) would set the market wage at w^* and full employment would result (L^*). With shirking, however, individual firms are unwilling to pay w^*. Rather, for every level of unemployment in the labor market, firms need to pay some wage greater than w^* to induce workers to be productive. This wage is shown as the no shirking constraint (NSC) curve. This curve shows the minimum wage workers need earn in order not to shirk, for each level of unemployment. Note that the greater the level of unemployment, the smaller the difference between the efficiency wage and w^*. This is because with high levels of unemployment, people who shirk risk long periods of unemployment and therefore don't need much inducement to be productive.

In Figure 17.4, the equilibrium wage will be at the intersection of the NSC curve and D_L curves, with L_e workers earning w_e. This is because the NSC curve gives the lowest wage that firms can pay and still avoid shirking. Firms do not need to pay more than this to get the number of workers they need, and they will not pay less than this because of shirking. Note that the NSC curve never crosses the labor supply curve. This means that there will always be some unemployment in equilibrium.

EXAMPLE 17.5 **EFFICIENCY WAGES AT FORD MOTOR COMPANY**

One of the early examples of the payment of efficiency wages can be found in the history of Ford, one of America's major automobile producers.[19] Before 1913 automobile production had depended heavily on skilled workers. But the introduction of the assembly line drastically changed the workplace. Now jobs demanded much less skill, and production depended more and more on maintaining the assembly line equipment. As the automobile plants changed, workers became increasingly disenchanted. In 1913, turnover at Ford was 380 percent. The following year, it rose to 1000 percent, and profit margins fell sharply.

Ford needed to maintain a stable work force, and Henry Ford (and his business partner James Couzens) provided it. In 1914, when the going wage for a day's work in industry averaged between $2.00 and $3.00, Ford Motor Company introduced a pay policy of $5.00 a day for its workers. Improved labor efficiency (not generosity) was behind this policy. The goal was to attract better workers who would stay with their jobs, and eventually to increase profits.

Although Henry Ford was attacked for it, this policy succeeded. The work force did become more stable, and the publicity helped Ford's sales. And because Henry Ford had his pick of workers, he could hire a group that was on average more productive. Ford stated that the wage increase did in fact increase the loyalty and personal efficiency of his workers, and quantitative estimates support his statements. According to calculations by Ford's chief of labor relations, productivity increased by 51 percent. Another study concluded that absenteeism had been halved, and discharges for cause had declined sharply. So the efficiency increase more than offset the increase in wages. As a result, Ford's profitability rose substantially: from $30 million in 1914 to $60 million in 1916.

Summary

1. The seller of a product often has better information about its quality than the buyer. Asymmetric information of this type creates a market failure in which bad products tend to drive good products out of the market. The market failure can be eliminated if sellers offer standardized products, provide guarantees or warranties, or find other ways to maintain a good reputation for their product.

2. Insurance markets frequently involve asymmetric information because the insuring party has better information about the risk involved than the insurance company. This can

[19]See J. R. Lee, "So-called profit sharing system in the Ford plant," *Annals of the American Academy of Political and Social Science* (May, 1915): 297–310; and David Halberstam, *The Reckoning* (New York: William Morrow, 1986), 91–92.

lead to adverse selection, in which the poorer risks choose to insure, and good risks do not. Another problem for insurance markets is moral hazard, in which the insuring party takes less care to avoid losses after insuring than before.

3. Sellers can deal with the problem of asymmetric information by sending buyers signals about the quality of their product. For example, workers can signal their high productivity by obtaining a high level of education.

4. Asymmetric information may make it costly for the owners of firms (the principal) to monitor accurately the behavior of the firm's manager (the agent). Managers may seek higher fringe benefits for themselves, or a goal of sales maximization, even though the shareholders would prefer to maximize profit.

5. Owners can avoid some of the principal-agent problems by designing contracts that give their agents the incentive to perform productively.

6. Asymmetric information can explain why labor markets have substantial unemployment when some workers are actively seeking work. According to efficiency wage theory, a wage higher than the competitive wage (the efficiency wage) increases worker productivity by discouraging workers from shirking on the job.

Questions for Review

1. Explain why asymmetric information between buyers and sellers can lead to a market failure when a market is otherwise perfectly competitive.

2. If the used car market is a "lemons" market, how would you expect the repair record of used cars that are sold to compare with the repair record of those not sold?

3. Explain the difference between adverse selection and moral hazard in insurance markets. Can one exist without the other?

4. Describe several ways in which sellers can convince buyers that their products are of high quality. Which methods apply in the following cases: the sale of Maytag washing machines, the sale of Burger King hamburgers, the sale of large diamonds?

5. Why might a seller find it advantageous to signal the quality of her product? How are guarantees and warranties a form of market signaling?

6. Explain why managers of firms might be able to achieve objectives other than profit maximization, the goal of the firm's shareholders.

7. Explain how the principal-agent model can be used to explain why public enterprises, such as post offices, might pursue goals other than profit maximization.

8. Explain why bonus and profit-sharing payment schemes are likely to resolve principal-agent problems, whereas a fixed wage payment will not.

9. What is an efficiency wage? Explain why it is profitable for the firm to pay an efficiency wage when workers have better information about their productivity than firms do.

Exercises

1. Faced with a reputation for producing automobiles with poor repair records, a number of American automobile companies have offered an extensive set of guarantees to car purchasers (e.g., a seven-year warranty on all parts and labor associated with mechanical problems).

a. In light of your knowledge of the lemons market, explain why this is a reasonable policy.

b. Is the policy likely to create a moral hazard problem? Explain.

2. An insurance company is considering issuing three types of fire insurance policies: (i) complete insurance coverage, (ii) complete coverage above and beyond a $10,000 deductible, and (iii) 90 percent coverage of all losses. Compare these policies in terms of the extent to which they are likely to create moral hazard problems.

3. To promote competition and consumer welfare, the Federal Trade Commission requires firms to advertise truthfully. How does truth in advertising promote competition? Why would a market be any less competitive if firms advertised deceptively?

4. Many consumers view a well-known brand name as a signal of quality and are willing to pay more for a brand name product (e.g., Bayer aspirin instead of generic aspirin, Birds Eye frozen vegetables instead of the supermarket's own brand, etc.). Can a brand name provide a useful signal of quality? Explain why or why not?

5. Eugene Savas in an article titled "Municipal Monopoly" has argued that "the inefficiency of municipal services is not due to bad commissioners, mayors, managers, workers, unions, or labor leaders; it is a natural consequence of a monopoly system." Use one or two public services as an example to evaluate this argument. Then, comment on each of the two following proposals for dealing with the problem of local monopoly:

a. Open the service to competitive bidding from both private and public agencies.

b. Require public services to be provided on a smaller scale at the neighborhood rather than at the community level.

CHAPTER 18

Externalities and Public Goods

In this chapter we study *externalities*—the effects of production and consumption activities not directly reflected in the market—and *public goods*—goods that benefit all consumers but that the market either undersupplies or does not supply at all. Externalities and public goods are important sources of market failure and thus raise serious public policy questions. For example, how much effluent, if any, should firms be allowed to dump into rivers and streams? How strict should automobile emission standards be? How much money should the government spend on national defense? education? basic research? public television?

When externalities are present, the price of a good need not reflect its social value. As a result, firms may produce too much or too little, so that the market outcome is inefficient. We begin by describing externalities and showing exactly how they create market inefficiencies. We then evaluate some of the possible remedies for dealing with them. Some alternatives involve government regulation, while others rely primarily on bargaining among individuals or on the legal right of those adversely affected to sue those who create the externality.

Next, we analyze public goods. The marginal cost of providing a public good to an additional consumer is zero, and people cannot be excluded from consuming it. We distinguish between goods that are difficult to provide privately and publicly provided goods that could have been provided by the market. We conclude by describing the problem policymakers face when trying to decide how much of a public good to provide.

18.1 Externalities

Externalities can arise between producers, between customers, or between consumers and producers. Externalities can be *negative*—when the action of one party imposes costs on another party—or *positive*—when the action of one party benefits another party.

A negative externality occurs, for example, when a steel plant dumps its waste in a river that fishermen downstream depend on for their daily catch. The more waste the steel plant dumps in the river, the fewer fish it will support. The negative externality arises because the steel firm has no incentive to account for the external costs that it imposes on fishermen when making its production decision. A positive externality would occur when a homeowner repaints her house and plants an attractive garden. All the neighbors benefit from this activity, yet the decision to repaint and landscape probably did not take these benefits for the neighbors into account. The benefits are thus a positive externality.

Negative Externalities and Inefficiency

Because externalities are not reflected in market prices, they can be a source of economic inefficiency. To see why, let's take our example of a steel plant dumping waste in a river. Figure 18.1a shows the production decision of the steel plant in a competitive market, and part (b) shows the market demand and supply curves, assuming that all steel plants generate similar externalities. We

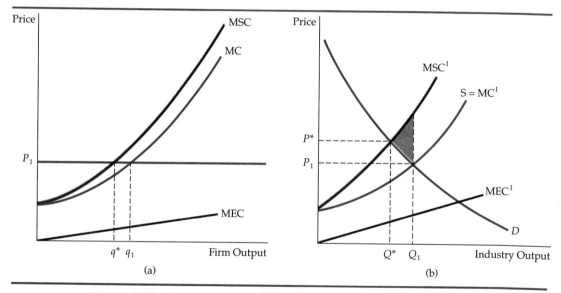

FIGURE 18.1 External Costs. When there are negative externalities, marginal social costs MSC are higher than marginal private costs MC. The difference is the marginal external cost MEC. In part (a), a profit-maximizing firm produces at q_1, where price is equal to MC. The efficient output is q^*, at which price equals MSC. In part (b), the industry competitive output is Q_1, at the intersection of industry supply MC^I and demand D. However, the efficient output Q^* is lower, at the intersection of demand and marginal social cost MSC^I.

assume that the firm has a fixed proportions production function, and that therefore it cannot alter its input combinations; effluent can be reduced only by lowering output. We will analyze the nature of the externality in two steps: first when only one steel plant pollutes, and then when all steel plants pollute in the same way.

The price of steel is P_1, at the intersection of the demand and supply curves in Figure 18.1b. The MC curve in part (a) gives a typical steel firm's marginal cost of production. The firm maximizes profit by producing output q_1, at which marginal cost is equal to price (which equals marginal revenue, because the firm takes price as given). As the firm's output changes, however, the external cost imposed on fishermen downstream also changes. This external cost is given by the *marginal external cost (MEC) curve* in Figure 18.1a. The curve is upward-sloping for most forms of pollution because as the firm produces additional output and dumps additional effluent in the river, the incremental harm to the fish industry increases.

From a social point of view, the firm produces too much output. The efficient output is the level at which the price of the product is equal to the *marginal social cost* of production. This marginal social cost is the marginal cost of production *plus* the marginal external cost of dumping effluent. In Figure 18.1a, the marginal social cost curve is obtained by adding marginal cost and marginal external cost for each level of output (i.e., MSC = MC + MEC). The marginal social cost curve MSC intersects the price line at the output q^*. Because only one plant is dumping effluent into the river in this case, the market price of the product is unchanged. However, the firm is producing too much output (q_1 instead of q^*) and generating too much effluent.

Now consider what happens when all steel plants dump their effluent into rivers. In Figure 18.1b the MC^I curve is the industry supply curve. The marginal external cost associated with the industry output, MEC^I, is obtained by summing the marginal cost of every person harmed at each level of output. The MSC^I curve represents the sum of the marginal cost of production and the marginal external cost *for all steel firms*. As a result, $MSC^I = MC^I + MEC^I$.

Is industry output efficient when there are externalities? As Figure 18.1b shows, the efficient industry output level is the one at which the marginal benefit of an additional unit of output is equal to the marginal social cost. Because the demand curve measures the marginal benefit to consumers, the efficient output is given at Q^*, at the intersection of the marginal social cost MSC^I and demand D curves. The competitive industry output, however, is at Q_1, the intersection of the demand curve and the supply curve, MC^I. Clearly, industry output is too high.

In our example, each unit of output results in some effluent being dumped. Therefore, whether we are looking at one firm's pollution or the entire industry's, the economic efficiency is the excess production that causes too much effluent to be dumped in the river. But the source of the inefficiency is the incorrect pricing of the product. The market price P_1 in Figure 18.1b is too low—

it reflects the firms' marginal private cost of production, but not the marginal *social* cost. Only at the higher price P^* will steel firms produce the efficient level of output.

What is the cost to society of this inefficiency? For any output greater than Q^*, the social cost is given by the difference between the social marginal cost and the marginal benefit (which is given by the demand curve). As a result, the aggregate social cost can be determined by summing the difference between MSC^I and D for all units of production that exceed the efficient level. In Figure 18.1b this social cost is shown as the shaded area that represents the difference between the MSC and the D curves, measured from output level Q^* to output Q_1.

Externalities generate long-run as well as short-run inefficiencies. In Chapter 8 we saw that firms enter a competitive industry whenever the price of the product is above the *average cost* of production, and exit whenever price is below average cost. In long-run equilibrium, price is equal to (long-run) average cost. When there are negative externalities, the average private cost of production is less than the average social cost. As a result, some firms remain in the industry even when it would be efficient for them to leave. Thus, negative externalities encourage too many firms to remain in the industry.

Positive Externalities and Inefficiency

Externalities can also result in too little production, as the example of a home-owner repairing and landscaping her house shows. In Figure 18.2 the horizontal axis measures the homeowner's investment (in dollars) in repairs and land-scaping. The marginal cost curve for home repair shows the cost of repairs as more work is done on the house; it is horizontal because this cost is unaffected by the amount of repairs that any one person undertakes. The demand curve D measures the marginal private benefit of the repairs to the homeowner. The homeowner will choose to invest q_1 in repairs, at the intersection of her demand and marginal cost curves. But repairs generate external benefits to the neighbors, as the *marginal external benefit* curve, MEB, shows. This curve is downward-sloping in this example because the marginal benefit is large for a small amount of repair but falls as the repair work becomes extensive.

The marginal social benefit curve MSB is calculated by adding the marginal private benefit and the marginal external benefit at every level of output. In short, $MSB = D + MEB$. The efficient level of output q^* is the level of output at which the marginal social benefit of additional repairs is equal to the marginal cost of those repairs. This is found at the intersection of the MSB and MC curves. The inefficiency arises because the homeowner doesn't capture all the benefits of her investment in repairs and landscaping. As a result, the price P_1 is too high to encourage her to invest in the socially desirable level of house repair.

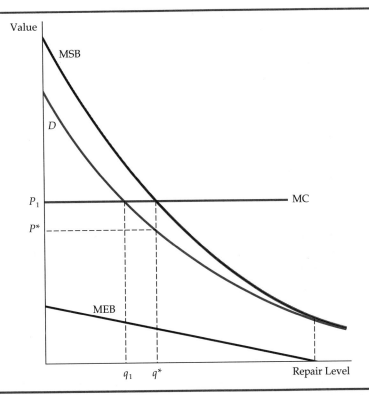

FIGURE 18.2 External Benefits.   When there are positive externalities, marginal social benefits MSB are higher than marginal benefits D. The difference is the marginal external benefit MEB. A self-interested homeowner invests q_1 in repairs, determined by the intersection of the marginal benefit curve D and the marginal cost curve MC. The efficient level of repair q^* is higher, and is given by the intersection of the marginal social benefit and marginal cost curves.

A lower price P^* is required to encourage the efficient level of supply. As Figure 18.2 shows, at P^* the homeowner will choose the level of repairs given by q^*.

Another example of a positive externality is the money that firms spend on research and development (R&D). Often the innovations resulting from the research cannot be protected from other firms. Suppose, for example, that one firm's research effort leads to a new design for a product. If that design can be patented, the firm can earn substantial profit by manufacturing and marketing the new product. If the new design can legally be adopted (or closely imitated) by other firms, however, those firms can manufacture and market similar products, thereby competing away some of the developing firm's profit. There is then little reward for doing R&D, and the market is likely to underfund it.

18.2   Ways of Correcting Market Failure

How can the inefficiency resulting from an externality be remedied? If the firm that generates the externality has a fixed-proportions production technology, the externality can be reduced only by encouraging the firm to produce less. This can be achieved through an output tax, as we saw in Chapter 8. Fortunately, most firms can substitute among inputs in the production process by altering their choice of technology. For example, a manufacturer can add a scrubber to its smokestack to reduce its emissions of pollutants. As a result of the change in technology, firms can reduce the externalities that they generate without reducing output as much as they would if the technology were fixed.

Consider a firm that sells its output in a competitive market. The firm emits pollutants that damage the air quality in the neighborhood. The firm can reduce the amount of pollution, but only at a cost. Figure 18.3 illustrates this. The horizontal axis represents the level of factory emissions. An emissions level of 26 units corresponds to the firm's profit-maximizing output. The curve labeled MSC represents the *marginal social cost of emissions*. This social cost curve represents the increased harm to the neighborhood associated with the emissions

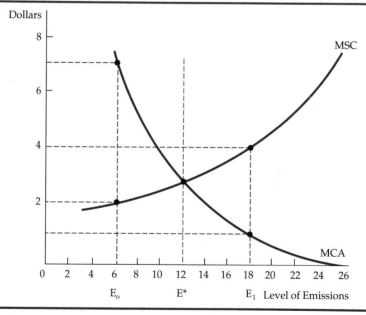

FIGURE 18.3   The Efficient Level of Emissions.   The efficient level of factory emissions is the level that equates the marginal social cost of emissions MSC to the benefit associated with lower abatement costs MCA. The efficient level of 12 units is given at E* in the figure.

of the factory, and it is therefore equivalent to the MEC curve described earlier. The MSC curve slopes upward because the *marginal* cost of the externality is higher the more extensive it is. (Evidence from studies of the effects of air and water pollution suggests that small levels of pollutants generate little harm. However, the harm increases substantially as the levels of pollutants increase.)

The curve labeled MCA is the *marginal cost of abating emissions*. It measures the additional cost to the firm of installing pollution control equipment. The MCA curve is downward-sloping because the marginal cost of reducing emissions is low when the reduction has been slight, and high when it has been substantial. (A slight reduction is inexpensive—the firm can reschedule production so the greatest emissions occur at night, when few people are outside—but substantial reductions require costly changes in the production process.)

The efficient level of emissions, 12 units, is at point E^*, where the marginal social cost of emissions, \$3, is equal to the marginal cost of abatement. At E^*, the sum of the firm's abatement costs and of the external cost to the neighborhood is minimized.[1] Note that if emissions are lower than E^*, say, E_0, the marginal benefit of emissions, \$7, is greater than the marginal social cost, \$2, so emissions are too low. However, if the level of emissions is E_1, the marginal social cost, \$4, is greater than the marginal benefit, \$1, so emissions are too high.

We can encourage the firm to reduce emissions to E^* in three ways: emissions standards, emissions fees, and transferable emission permits. Let's look at each method.

An Emissions Standard

An *emissions standard* is a legal limit on how much pollutant a firm can emit. If the firm exceeds the limit, it can face substantial monetary and even criminal penalties. In Figure 18.4, the efficient emission standard is 12 units, at point E^*. The firm will be heavily penalized for emissions greater than this.

The standard assures that the firm produces efficiently. The firm meets the standard by installing pollution abatement equipment. The increased abatement expenditure will cause the firm's average cost curve to rise (by the average cost of abatement). Firms will find its profitable to enter the industry only if the price of the product is greater than the average cost of production and abatement—the efficient condition for the industry.[2]

An Emissions Fee

An *emissions fee* is a charge levied on each unit of a firm's emissions. A \$3 emissions fee will generate efficient behavior by our factory, as Figure 18.4

---

[1] This analysis presumes that no consumer surplus is lost if less of the product is produced.

[2] This assumes that the social costs of emissions do not change over time. If they do, the efficient standard will change as well.

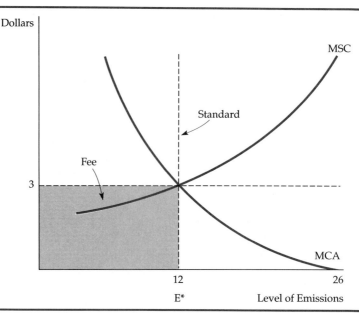

FIGURE 18.4   Standards and Fees.   The efficient level of emissions at E* can be achieved either through an emissions fee or an emissions standard. Facing a fee of $3 per unit of emissions, a firm reduces emissions up to the point at which the fee is equal to the marginal benefit. The same level of emissions reduction can be achieved with a standard that limits emissions to 12 units.

shows. With this fee, the firm minimizes its costs by reducing emissions from 26 to 12 units. To see why, note that the first unit of emissions can be reduced (from 26 to 25 units of emissions) at very little cost (the marginal cost of additional abatement is close to zero). Therefore, for very little cost the firm can avoid paying the $3 per unit fee. In fact, for all levels of emission above 12 units, the marginal cost of abatement is less than the emissions fee, so it pays to reduce emissions. Below 12 units, however, the marginal cost of abatement is greater than the fee, so the firm will prefer to pay the fee rather than reduce emissions further. The firm will therefore pay a total fee given by the dark shaded rectangle and will incur a total abatement cost shown by the lightly shaded triangle. This cost is less than the fee the firm would pay if it did not reduce its emissions at all.

Standards versus Fees

In the United States and some other countries, governments have historically relied on standards rather than fees to regulate emissions. However, some countries, for example, West Germany, have used fees successfully. Is there any reason to prefer one method to the other?

The answer is that there are important differences between standards and fees when the policymaker has incomplete information and when it is costly to regulate firms' emissions. To understand these differences, let's suppose that because of administrative costs the agency that regulates emissions must charge the same fee or set the same standard for all firms.

First, let's examine the case for fees. Consider two firms that are near each other, so that the marginal social cost of emissions is the same no matter which firm reduces its emissions. Because the firms have different production processes and different abatement costs, however, their marginal cost of abatement curves are not the same. Figure 18.5 shows why emissions fees are preferable to standards in this case. MCA_1 and MCA_2 represent the marginal cost of abatement curves for the two firms. Each firm initially generates 14 units of emissions. Suppose we want to reduce total emissions by 14 units. Figure 18.5 shows that the cheapest way to do this is to have Firm 1 reduce emissions by 6 units and Firm 2 reduce emissions by 8 units. With these reductions, both firms have marginal costs of abatement of $3. But consider what happens if the regulatory agency asks both firms to reduce their emissions by 7 units. Then

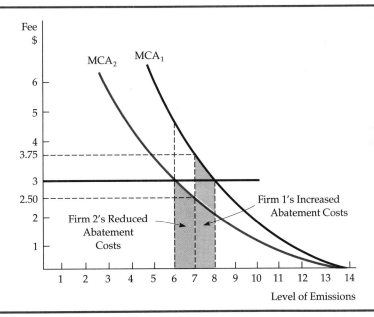

FIGURE 18.5 Cost Minimization with an Emissions Fee. With limited information, a policymaker may be faced with the choice of either a single emissions fee or a single emissions standard for all firms. The emissions fee of $3 achieves an emissions level of 14 units more cheaply than a 7-unit-per-firm emissions standard. With the emissions fee, the firm with a lower abatement cost curve (Firm 2) reduces emissions more than the firm with a higher marginal cost (Firm 1).

the marginal cost of abatement of Firm 1 increases from $3 to $3.75, and the marginal cost of abatement of Firm 2 decreases from $3 to $2.50. This cannot be cost-minimizing, because the second firm can reduce emissions more cheaply than the first. Only when the marginal cost of abatement is equal for both firms will emissions be reduced by 14 units at minimum cost.

Now we can see why an emissions fee ($3) might be preferable to an emissions standard (7 units). With a $3 emissions fee, Firm 1 will reduce emissions by 6 units and Firm 2 by 8 units, the efficient outcome. By contrast, with the emissions standard Firm 1 incurs additional abatement costs given by the shaded area between 7 and 8 units of emission. But Firm 2 enjoys reduced abatement costs given by the shaded area between 6 and 7 units of emission. Clearly, the added abatement costs to Firm 1 are larger than the reduced costs to Firm 2. The emissions fee thus achieves the same level of emissions at a lower cost than the equal per-firm emissions standard.

In general, fees can be preferable to standards for several reasons. First, when standards must be assessed equally for all firms, fees achieve the same emissions reduction at a lower cost. Second, fees give a firm a strong incentive to install new equipment that would allow it to reduce emissions *even further*. Suppose the standard requires that each firm reduce its emission by 6 units, from 14 to 8. Firm 1 is considering installing new emissions devices that would lower its marginal cost of abatement from MCA_1 to MCA_2. If the equipment is relatively inexpensive, the firm will install it because this equipment would lower the cost of meeting the standard. However, a $3 emission fee would provide a greater incentive for the firm to reduce emissions. With the fee, not only will the firm's cost of abatement be lower on the first 6 units of reduction, it will also be cheaper to reduce emissions by 2 more units (because the emissions fee is greater than the marginal abatement cost for emissions levels between 6 and 8).

Now let's examine the case for standards by looking at Figure 18.6. The marginal social cost curve is very steep, while the marginal benefit curve is relatively flat. The efficient emissions fee is $8. But suppose because of limited information, a lower fee of $7 is charged (this amounts to a ⅛ or 12.5 percent reduction). Because the MCA curve is flat, the firm's emissions will be increased from 8 to 11 units. This lowers the firm's abatement costs somewhat, but because the MSC curve is steep, there will be substantial additional social costs. The increase in social costs, less the savings in abatement costs, is given by the entire shaded (light and dark) triangle ABC.

What happens if a comparable error is made in setting the standard? The efficient standard is 8 units of emissions. But suppose the standard is relaxed by 12.5 percent, from 8 to 9 units. This will lead to an increase in social costs and a decrease in abatement costs as before. But the net increase in social costs, given by the darkly shaded triangle ADE, is substantially smaller than before.

This example illustrates the difference between standards and fees. When the marginal social cost curve is relatively steep and the marginal cost of abatement curve relatively flat, the cost of not reducing emissions sufficiently is high,

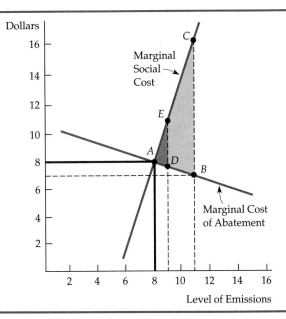

FIGURE 18.6 A Standard May be Preferable to a Fee. When the government has limited information about the costs and benefits of pollution abatement, either a standard or a fee may be preferable. The standard is preferable when the marginal social cost curve is steep and the marginal cost curve is relatively flat. Here a 12.5 percent error in setting the standard leads to extra social costs given by triangle *ADE*. The same percentage error in setting a fee would result in excess costs given by triangle *ABC*.

and a standard is preferable to a fee. With incomplete information, standards offer more certainty about emissions levels but leave the costs of abatement uncertain. Fees, on the other hand, offer certainty about the costs of abatement but leave the reduction of emissions levels uncertain. Which policy is preferable depends, therefore, on the nature of uncertainty and on the shapes of the cost curves.

Transferable Emissions Permits

Suppose we want to reduce emissions substantially, but because of uncertainty we can't rely entirely on an emissions fee. We also want to avoid imposing high costs on the firms that reduce their emissions the most. We can reach our goals by introducing *transferable emissions permits*—each firm must have a permit to generate emissions. Permits are allocated among firms, with the total number of permits equal to the total desired level of emissions. The permits are marketable—they can be bought and sold.

Such a system gives firms an incentive to trade permits. Suppose the two firms in Figure 18.5 were given permits to emit up to 7 units. Firm 1, facing a relatively high marginal cost of abatement, would pay up to $3.75 to buy a permit for one unit of emissions, but the value of that permit is only $2.50 to Firm 2. Firm 1 should therefore sell its permit to Firm 2 for a price between $2.50 and $3.75.

If there are enough firms and enough permits, a competitive market for the permits will develop. In market equilibrium, the price of a permit equals the marginal cost of abatement for all firms; otherwise a firm will find it advantageous to buy more permits. The total level of emissions will then be the level chosen by an administration agency. The emissions will also be reduced at minimum cost. Those firms with relatively low marginal cost of abatement curves will be reducing emissions the most, and those firms with relatively high marginal cost of abatement curves will be buying more permits and reducing emissions the least.

Marketable emissions permits create a market for externalities. This market approach is appealing because it combines some of the advantageous features of a system of standards with the cost advantages of a fee system. The agency that administers the system determines the total number of permits and therefore the total amount of emissions, just as a system of standards would do. But the marketability of the permits allows pollution abatement to be achieved at minimum cost, just as a system of fees would do.[3]

EXAMPLE 18.1   THE COSTS AND BENEFITS OF REDUCED SULFUR DIOXIDE EMISSIONS

In 1968 Philadelphia imposed air quality regulations that limited the maximum allowable sulfur content in fuel oil to 1.0 percent or less. This regulation decreased sulfur dioxide levels in the air substantially—from 0.10 parts per million in 1968 to a level below 0.025 parts per million in 1973. This increased air quality led to better human health, less damage to materials, and higher property values. But these improvements had a cost: Industrial, manufacturing, commercial, and residential fuel users had to alter their fuel choices and to install pollution-control equipment to abate the pollution. Was the benefit—the reduction in social cost due to the abatement—worth the additional abatement cost? A cost-benefit study of reductions in sulfur dioxide emissions provides some answers.[4]

---

[3]With limited information and costly monitoring, a marketable permit system is not always ideal. For example, if the total number of permits is chosen incorrectly and the marginal cost of abatement rises sharply for some firms, a permit system could drive those firms out of business by imposing high abatement costs. (This would be a problem for fees as well.) For further discussion of fees, standards, and transferable pollution permits see William J. Baumol and Wallace E. Oates, *Economics, Environmental Policy, and the Quality of Life* (Englewood Cliffs, N.J.: Prentice-Hall, 1979).

[4]The study is by Thomas R. Irvin, "A Cost-Benefit analysis of Sulfur Dioxide Abatement Regulations in Philadelphia," *Business Economics* (Sept. 1977): 12–20.

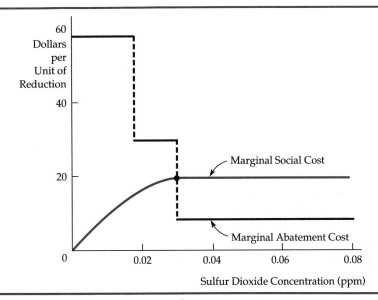

FIGURE 18.7   Sulfur Dioxide Emissions Reductions.   The efficient sulfur dioxide concentration equates the marginal abatement cost to the marginal social cost. Here the marginal abatement cost curve is a series of steps, each representing the use of a different abatement technology.

In Philadelphia the emissions reductions necessitated increased costs of converting from coal and oil to gas to comply with the air quality regulation. Emissions control equipment also had to be added to manufacturing processes to ensure that fuels were used efficiently. Figure 18.7 shows the marginal social cost of reductions in emissions and the marginal cost to the firm of reducing emissions. Note that the marginal abatement cost is not a smooth, continuous curve. The jumps occur whenever new capital-intensive pollution control equipment is needed to improve fuel efficiency.

The benefits of reduced sulfur dioxide emissions can be divided into three parts: (1) reductions in illness and death from diseases like cancer, bronchitis, pneumonia, emphysema, asthma, and the common cold; (2) reductions in materials costs caused by corrosion of metals, stone, and paint; and (3) improvements in visibility and other aesthetic values.

Because benefits are the negative of social costs, we can obtain information about the marginal social cost curve by asking how each of these three types of benefits decreases in value when sulfur dioxide concentrations are increased. For very low concentrations, evidence suggests little health, material, or aesthetic effects. But for moderate concentrations of sulfur dioxide, studies of respiratory diseases, corrosion of materials, and lost visibility suggest that marginal social costs are positive and relatively constant. Thus, the marginal social cost curve is shown to rise initially and then become horizontal.

The efficient level of reduced sulfur dioxide emissions is given by the number of parts per million of sulfur dioxide at which the marginal cost of reduced emissions is equal to the marginal social cost. We can see from Figure 18.7 that this level is approximately 0.0275 parts per million. The marginal social cost and marginal abatement cost curves intersect at a point where the marginal abatement cost curve is sharply decreasing owing to the introduction of expensive desulfurization equipment. Because 0.0275 parts per million is slightly below the emissions level achieved in 1973 by the regulation, we can conclude that the regulation improved economic efficiency. In fact, given that sulfur dioxide levels were above 0.0275 parts per million for most of the period, it appears that the regulations were not stringent enough to achieve the most efficient outcome.

18.3 Externalities and Property Rights

We have seen how government regulation can deal with the inefficiencies that arise from externalities. Emissions fees and transferable emissions permits work because they change a firm's incentives—forcing it to take into account the external costs that it imposes. But government regulation is not the only way to deal with externalities. In this section we show that in some circumstances inefficiencies can be eliminated through private bargaining among the affected parties, or by a legal system in which parties can sue to recover the damages they suffer.

Property Rights

The concept of property rights underlies our entire discussion of externalities. *Property rights* are the legal rules that describe what people or firms may do with their property. When people have property rights to land, for example, they may build on it or sell it. They are also protected from interference with their use of those rights.

To see why property rights are important, let's return to our example of the firm that dumps effluent into the river. We assumed that it had a property right to use the river to dispose of its waste, and that the fishermen did not have a property right to "effluent-free" water in which to fish. As a result, the firm had no incentive to include the cost of effluent in its production calculations. In other words, the firm externalized the costs generated by the effluent. Suppose the fishermen owned the river, i.e., had a property right to clean water.

They could then demand that the firm pay them for the right to dump effluent. The firm would either cease production or pay the costs associated with the effluent. These costs would be internalized (they would no longer be external to the firm), and an efficient allocation of resources could be achieved.

Bargaining and Economic Efficiency

Economic efficiency can be achieved without government intervention when the externality affects relatively few parties and when property rights are well specified. To see how this might arise, let's consider a numerical version of the effluent example. Suppose the steel factory's effluent reduces the fishermen's profit. As Table 18.1 shows, the factory can install a filter system to reduce its effluent, or the fishermen can pay for the installation of a water treatment plant.[5]

TABLE 18.1 Profits under Alternative Emissions Choices (daily)

	Factory Profit	Fishermen's Profit	Total Profit
No filter, no treatment plant	$500	$100	$600
Filter, no treatment plant	$300	$500	$800
No filter, treatment plant	$500	$200	$700
Filter, treatment plant	$300	$300	$600

The efficient solution maximizes the joint profit of the factory and the fishermen. This occurs when the factory installs a filter and the fishermen do not build a treatment plant. Let's see how alternative property rights lead to these two parties to negotiate different solutions.

Suppose the factory has the property right to dump effluent into the river. Initially, the fishermen's profit is $100 and the factory's is $500. By installing a treatment plant, the fishermen can increase their profit to $200, so that the joint profit without cooperation is $700 ($500 + $200). Moreover, the fishermen are willing to pay the factory up to $300 to install a filter ($300 is the difference between the $500 profit with a filter and the $200 profit without cooperation). Because the factory loses only $200 in profit by installing a filter, it will be willing to do so if it is more than compensated for its loss. The gain to both parties by cooperating is equal to $100 in this case (the $300 gain to the fishermen less the $200 cost of a filter).

Suppose the factory and the fishermen agree to split this gain equally by having the fishermen pay the factory $250 to install the filter. As Table 18.2

---

[5]For a more extensive discussion of a variant of this example and of the bargaining that follows, see Robert Cooter and Thomas Ulen, *Law and Economics* (Glenview, Ill.: Scott-Foresman, 1987), chapter 4.

TABLE 18.2 Bargaining with Alternative Property Rights		
	Right to Dump	Right to Clean Water
No cooperation		
Profit of factory	$500	$300
Profit of fishermen	$200	$500
Cooperation		
Profit of factory	$550	$300
Profit of fishermen	$250	$500

shows, this bargaining solution achieves the efficient outcome. Under the column "Right to Dump," we see that without cooperation the fishermen earn a profit of $200 and the factory $500. With cooperation, the profit of both increases by $50.

Now suppose the fishermen are given the property right to clean water, which requires the factory to install the filter. The factory earns a profit of $300 and the fishermen $500. Because neither party can be made better off by bargaining, the initial outcome is efficient.

This analysis applies to all situations in which property rights are well specified. *When parties can bargain without cost and to their mutual advantage, the resulting outcome will be efficient, regardless of how the property rights are specified.* However, the allocation of profit between the two parties will depend on the assignment of property rights. The underlined proposition is called the *Coase Theorem*, in honor of Ronald Coase, who did much to develop it.[6]

Costly Bargaining—The Role of Strategic Behavior

Bargaining can be time-consuming and costly, especially when property rights are not clearly specified. Then neither party is sure how hard to bargain before the other party will agree to a settlement. In our example, both parties knew that the bargaining process had to settle on a payment between $200 and $300. If the parties were unsure of the property rights, however, the fishermen might be willing to pay only $100, and the bargaining process would break down.

Bargaining can also break down even when communication and monitoring are costless, if both parties believe they can and should obtain larger gains. One party makes a demand for a large share and refuses to bargain, assuming incorrectly that the other party will eventually concede. This *strategic behavior* can lead to an inefficient, noncooperative outcome. Suppose the factory has the right to emit effluent and claims that it will not install a filter unless it receives $300, and its offer is final. The fishermen offer to pay at most $250, however,

[6]See Ronald Coase, "The Problem of Social Cost," *Journal of Law and Economics* 3 (1960): 1–44.

believing that eventually the factory will agree to the "fair" solution. In this situation, an agreement may never be reached, especially if one or both parties want to earn a reputation for tough bargaining.[7]

A Legal Solution—Suing for Damages

In many situations involving externalities, a party that is harmed (the victim) by another has the legal right to bring suit. If successful, the victim can recover monetary damages equal to the harm it has been caused. A suit for damages is different from an emissions or effluent fee, because the victim, not the government, is paid.

To see how the potential for a lawsuit can lead to an efficient outcome, let's reexamine our fishermen–factory example. Suppose first that the fishermen are given the right to clean water (meaning that the factory is responsible for harm to the fishermen *if* the factory does not install a filter). The harm to the fishermen in this case is $400 (the difference between the profit that the fishermen make when there is no effluent [$500] and their profit when there is effluent [$100]). The factory has the following options:

1. Do not install filter, pay damages: Profit = $100 ($500 − $400)

2. Install filter, avoid damages: Profit = $300 ($500 − $200)

The factory will find it advantageous to install a filter, which is substantially cheaper than paying damages, and the efficient outcome will be achieved.

An efficient outcome (with a different division of profits) will also be achieved if the factory is given the property right to emit effluent. Under the law, the fishermen would have the legal right to require the factory to install the filter, but they would have to pay the factory for its $200 lost profit (not for the cost of the filter). This leaves the fishermen three options:

1. Put in a treatment plant: Profit = $200

2. Have factory put in a filter, but pay damages: Profit = $300 ($500 − $200).

3. Do not put in treatment plant or require a filter: Profit = $100

The fishermen earn the highest profit if they take the second option; they will require the factory to put in a filter but compensate the factory $200 for its lost profit. Just as in the situation in which the fishermen had the right to clean

---

[7]The importance of strategic behavior and the possible breakdown of bargaining due to threatening actions was emphasized in the seventeenth century by Thomas Hobbes. Hobbes believed people would rarely agree on an appropriate division of the gains from bargaining, even when there were few costs to the bargaining process. The Hobbesian view of the world is contrasted with Coase's view in Robert Cooter, "The Cost of Coase," *Journal of Legal Studies* 11 (1982): 1–34.

water, this outcome is efficient, because the filter has been installed. Note, however, that the $300 profit is substantially less than the $500 profit that the fishermen get when they have a right to clean water.

This example shows that a suit for damages eliminates the need for bargaining because it specifies the consequences of the choices that the parties have to make. Giving the party that is harmed the right to recover damages from the injuring party ensures an efficient outcome.[8]

EXAMPLE 18.2 THE COASE THEOREM AT WORK

The Coase Theorem applies to governments as well as to people. Witness a September 1987 cooperative agreement between New York City and New Jersey.

For many years garbage spilling from waterfront trash facilities from New York harbor had adversely affected the quality of water along the New Jersey shore and occasionally littered the beaches there as well. The greatest publicity occurred on August 13–15, 1987, when more than 200 tons of garbage, including syringes and crack-cocaine vials, formed a 50-mile-long slick off the New Jersey shore.

The property rights are reasonably clear in this situation. New Jersey has the right to clean beaches, and can sue New York City to recover damages associated with garbage spills. New Jersey can also ask the court to grant an injunction that would require New York City to stop using its trash facilities until the problem is removed.

But New Jersey wanted cleaner beaches, not simply the recovery of damages. And New York wanted to be able to operate its trash facility. As a result, there was room for mutually beneficial exchange. After two weeks of negotiations, New York and New Jersey reached a settlement.

New Jersey agreed not to bring a lawsuit against the city. New York City agreed to use special boats and other floatation devices to contain spills that might arise on Staten Island and Brooklyn. It also agreed to create a monitoring team to survey all trash facilities and shut down those that failed to comply. At the same time, New Jersey officials were allowed unlimited access to New York City's trash facilities to check the effectiveness of the program.

---

[8]This analysis assumes that the parties have perfect information. When information is imperfect, suing for damages may lead to inefficient outcomes.

18.4   Common Property Resources

Occasionally externalities arise when resources can be used without payment. *Common property resources* are those to which anyone has free access. Air and water are the two most common examples of these resources. Other examples include fish and animal populations and mineral exploration and extraction. Let's look at some of the inefficiencies that can occur when resources are common property rather than privately owned.

Consider a large lake with trout, to which an unlimited number of fishermen have access. Each fisherman fishes up to the point at which the revenue from fishing (or the marginal value, if fishing is for sport instead of profit) is equal to the cost. But his private cost understates the true cost to society because it fails to account for the fact that more fishing reduces the stock of fish, making less available for others. The lake is a common property resource, and no fisherman has the incentive to take into account how his fishing affects the opportunities of others. This leads to an inefficiency—too much fishing.

Figure 18.8 illustrates this. Suppose someone controlled the fishing in the lake and could determine how many fishermen had access to it. The efficient level Q^* is determined at the point at which the marginal benefit of fishing is equal to the marginal social cost. The marginal benefit is given by the demand

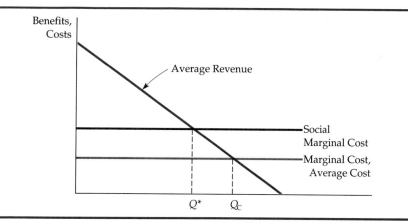

FIGURE 18.8   Common Property Resources.   When a common property resource, such as a fishery, is accessible to all, the resource is used up to the point Q_C at which the private cost is equal to the additional revenue generated. This usage exceeds the efficient level Q^* at which the marginal social cost of using the resource is equal to the marginal benefit (as given by the demand curve).

or average revenue curve. The marginal social cost is shown in the diagram to include not only the private operating costs but also the social cost of depleting the stock of fish.

Now compare the efficient outcome with what happens when the lake is common property. Then, the marginal external costs are not taken into account, and each fisherman fishes until there is no longer any profit to be made. When only Q^* fishing effort is made, the revenue from fishing is greater than the cost, and there is a profit to be earned by fishing more. Entry into the fishing business occurs until the point at which the average revenue is equal to the average cost, point Q_C in our diagram. With a fishing effort of Q_C, too much effort will have been made to catch too few fish.

There is a relatively simple solution to the common property resource problem—let a single owner manage the resource. The owner will set a fee for use of the resource that is equal to the marginal cost of depleting the stock of fish. Facing the payment of this fee, fishermen in the aggregate will no longer find it profitable to catch more than Q^* fish. Unfortunately, most common property resources are vast, and single ownership may not be practical. In this case, government ownership or direct government regulation may be more appropriate.

EXAMPLE 18.3 CRAWFISH FISHING IN LOUISIANA

In recent years, crawfish has become a popular restaurant item. In 1950, for example, the annual crawfish harvest in the Atchafalaya river basin in Louisiana was just over 1 million pounds. By 1981 it had grown to 28.1 million pounds. Because most crawfish grow in ponds to which fishermen have unlimited access, a common property resource problem has arisen—too many crawfish have been trapped, causing the crawfish population to fall far below the efficient level.

How serious is the problem? Specifically, what is the social cost of unlimited access to fishermen? The answer can be found by estimating the private cost of trapping crawfish, the marginal social cost, and the demand for crawfish (which represents the revenue to fishermen and the marginal benefit to society).

Figure 18.9 shows portions of the relevant curves.[9] Both curves are upward-sloping because as the catch increases, so does the additional effort that must be made to obtain it. The demand curve is downward-sloping but elastic, because other shellfish are close substitutes for crawfish.

We can find the efficient crawfish catch graphically or algebraically. To do so, let F represent the catch of crawfish in millions of pounds per year (shown on the horizontal axis), and let C represent costs in dollars per pound (shown

---

[9]This example was based on Frederick W. Bell, "Mitigating the Tragedy of the Commons," *Southern Economic Journal* 52 (1986): 653–664.

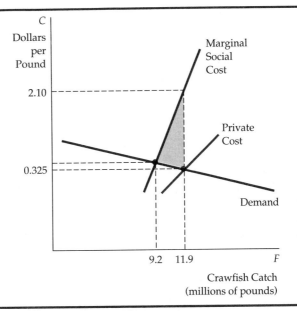

FIGURE 18.9 Crawfish as a Common Property Resource. Because crawfish are reared in ponds to which fishermen have unlimited access, they are a common property resource. The efficient level of fishing occurs when the marginal benefit is equal to the marginal social cost. However, the actual level of fishing occurs at the point at which the demand for crawfish is equal to the private cost of fishing. The shaded area represents the social cost of the common property resource.

on the vertical axis). In the region where the various curves intersect, the three curves in the graph are as follows:

Demand: $C = 0.401 - 0.0064\,F$

Marginal Social Cost: $C = -5.645 + 0.6509\,F$

Private Cost: $C = -0.357 + 0.0573\,F$

The efficient crawfish catch of 9.2 million pounds is determined by equating demand to marginal social cost and is shown graphically as the intersection of the two curves. The actual catch, 11.9 million pounds, is determined by equating demand to private cost and is shown graphically as the intersection of those two curves. The shaded area in the figure measures the social cost of free access. This represents the excess of social cost above private cost of fishing summed from the efficient level (where marginal benefit is equal to marginal social cost) to the actual level (where demand is equal to private cost). In this case, the social cost is the area of a triangle with a base of 2.7 million pounds (11.9 − 9.2), and a height of $1.785 ($2.10 − $0.325), or $2,410,000.

18.5 Public Goods

We have seen that externalities, including common property resources, create market inefficiencies that sometimes warrant government regulation. When, if ever, should governments replace private firms as the producer of goods and services? In this section we describe a set of conditions under which the private market either may not provide a good at all or may not price it properly once it is available.

Public goods have two characteristics: They are nonrival and nonexclusive. A good is *nonrival* if for any given level of production, the marginal cost of providing it to an additional consumer is zero. For most goods that are provided privately, the marginal cost of producing more of the good is positive. But for some goods, additional consumers do not add to cost. Consider the use of a highway during a period of low traffic volume. Because the highway already exists and there is no congestion, the additional cost of driving on it is zero. Or consider the use of a lighthouse by a ship. Once the lighthouse is built and functioning, its use by an additional ship adds nothing to it running costs.

Of course, most goods are rival in consumption. For example, when you buy furniture, you have ruled out the possibility that someone else can buy it—thus, the furniture is a rival good. Goods that are rival must be allocated among individuals. Goods that are nonrival can be made available to everyone without affecting any individual's opportunity for consuming them.

A good is *nonexclusive* if people cannot be excluded from consuming it. As a consequence, it is difficult or impossible to charge people for using nonexclusive goods—the goods can be enjoyed without direct payment. One example of a nonexclusive good is national defense. Once a nation has provided for its national defense, all citizens enjoy its benefits.

Nonexclusive goods need not be national in character. If a state or city eradicates an agricultural pest, all farmers and consumers benefit. It would be virtually impossible to exclude a particular farmer from the benefits of the program. Of course, most goods are exclusive. Automobiles are exclusive (as well as rival). If a store sells a new car to one consumer, then the store has excluded other individuals from buying the car.

Some goods are exclusive but nonrival. For example, in periods of low traffic, travel on the bridge is nonrival, because an additional car on the bridge does not lower the speed of other cars. But bridge travel is exclusive because bridge authorities can keep people from using it. A television signal is another example. Once a signal is broadcast, the marginal cost of making the broadcast available to another user is zero, so the good is nonrival. But broadcast signals are exclusive, because by scrambling the signal and charging for the code that allows it to be unscrambled, a company can exclude certain users.

Some goods are nonexclusive but rival. Air is nonexclusive but can be rival if the emissions of one firm adversely affect the quality of the air and the ability of others to enjoy it. An ocean or large lake is nonexclusive, but fishing is rival, because it imposes costs on others—the more fish caught, the fewer fish available to others.

Public goods, which are both nonrival and nonexclusive, provide benefits to people at zero marginal cost—no one can be excluded from enjoying them. The classic example of a public good is national defense. Defense is nonexclusive, as we have seen, but it is also nonrival, because the marginal cost of providing defense to an additional person is zero. The lighthouse mentioned earlier is also a public good, because it is nonrival and nonexclusive, i.e., it would be difficult to charge ships for the benefits they receive from it.[10]

The list of public goods is much smaller than the list of goods that governments provide. Many publicly provided goods are either rival in consumption, exclusive, or both. For example, high school education is rival in consumption. There is a positive marginal cost of providing education to one more child, because other children get less attention as class sizes increase. Likewise, charging tuition can exclude some children from enjoying education. Public education is provided by local government because it entails positive externalities, not because it is a public good.

Finally, consider the management of a national park. The public can be excluded from using the park (i.e., from consuming) by raising entrance and camping fees. Use of the park is also rival—because of crowded conditions, the entrance of an additional car into a park can reduce the benefits that others receive from it.

Efficiency and Public Goods

The efficient level of provision of a private good is determined by comparing the marginal benefit of an additional unit to the marginal cost of producing the unit. Efficiency is achieved when the marginal benefit and the marginal cost are equal. The same principle applies to public goods, but the analysis is different. With private goods, the marginal benefit is measured by the benefit the consumer receives. With a public good, we must ask how much each person values an additional unit of output. The marginal benefit is obtained by adding these values for all people who enjoy the good. Then to determine the efficient level of provision of a public good, we must equate the sum of these marginal benefits to the marginal cost of production.

Figure 18.10 illustrates the efficient level of producing a public good. D_1 represents the demand for the public good by one consumer, and D_2 the demand by a second consumer. Each demand curve tells us the marginal benefit that the consumer gets from consuming every level of output. For example, when there are 2 units of the public good, the first consumer is willing to pay

---

[10]Lighthouses need not be provided by the government. See Ronald Coase, "The Lighthouse in Economics," *Journal of Law and Economics* 17 (1974): 357–376, for a description of how lighthouses were privately provided in England during the nineteenth century.

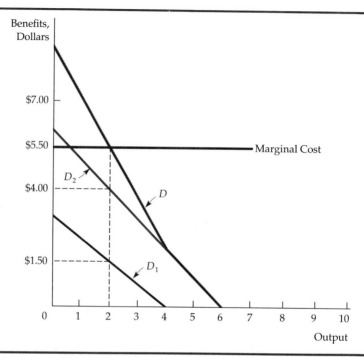

FIGURE 18.10 Efficient Public Good Provision. When a good is nonrival, the social marginal benefit of consumption, given by the demand curve D, is determined by vertically summing the individual demand curve for the good, D_1 and D_2. The efficient level of provision is given by the output at which the demand curve and the marginal cost curve intersect.

$1.50 for the good, and $1.50 is the marginal benefit. Similarly, the second consumer has a marginal benefit of $4.00.

To calculate the sum of the marginal benefits to both people, we must add each of the demand curves *vertically*. For example, when the output is 2 units, we add the marginal benefit of $1.50 to the marginal benefit of $4.00 to obtain a marginal social benefit of $5.50. When this is calculated for every level of public output, we obtain the aggregate demand curve for the public good D.

The efficient amount of output is the one at which the marginal benefit to society is equal to the marginal cost. This occurs at the intersection of the demand and the marginal cost curves. In our example, the marginal cost of production is $5.50, so 2 is the efficient output level.

To see why 2 is efficient, note what happens if only 1 unit of output is provided: The marginal cost remains at $5.50, but the marginal benefit is approximately $7.00. Because the marginal benefit is greater than the marginal cost, too little of the good has been provided. Similarly, suppose 3 units of the public good have been produced. Now the marginal benefit of approximately $4.00 is less than the marginal cost of $5.50, and too much of the good has again been provided. Only when the marginal social benefit is equal to the marginal cost is the public good provided efficiently.[11]

Public Goods and Market Failure

Suppose you are an entrepreneur who is considering providing a mosquito abatement program for your community. You know that the program is worth more to the community than the $50,000 it will cost. Can you make a profit by providing the program privately? You would break even if you assessed a $5 fee to each of the 10,000 households in your community. But you cannot force them to pay the fee, let alone devise a system in which those households that value mosquito abatement the most pay the highest fees.

The problem is that mosquito abatement is nonexclusive—there is no way to provide the service without benefiting everyone. As a result, households do not have the incentive to pay what the program really is worth to them. People act as *free riders*, understating the value of the program so that they can enjoy its benefit without paying for it.

With public goods, the presence of free riders makes it difficult or impossible for markets to provide goods efficiently. Perhaps if a few people were involved and the program were relatively inexpensive, all households might agree voluntarily to share its costs. However, when many households are involved, voluntary private arrangements are usually ineffective, and the public good must be subsidized or provided by governments if it is to be produced efficiently.

EXAMPLE 18.4 THE DEMAND FOR CLEAN AIR

In Example 4.4 we used the demand curve for clean air to calculate the benefits of a cleaner environment. Now let's examine the public good characteristics of clean air. Many factors, including the weather, driving patterns, and industrial emissions determine air quality in a region. Any effort to clean up the air will generally improve air quality throughout the region. As a result, clean air is nonexclusive—it is difficult to stop any one person from enjoying it. Clean air is also nonrival—my enjoyment does not inhibit yours.

Because clean air is a public good, it is difficult to estimate people's demands for it. There is no explicit market for clean air, and thus no directly observable market prices can be interpreted as the rate at which people are willing to trade clean air for other commodities. However, we can obtain estimates by indirect

---

[11]We have shown that nonexclusive, nonrival goods are inefficiently provided. A similar argument would apply to nonrival but exclusive goods.

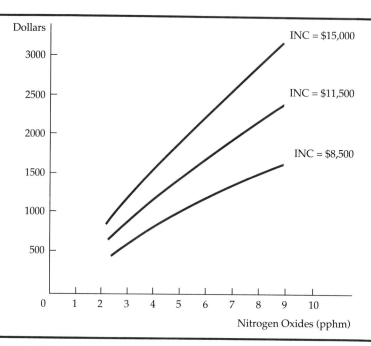

FIGURE 18.11 The Demand for Clean Air. The three curves describe the willingness to pay for clean air (a reduction in the level of nitrogen oxides) for each of three different households (low income, middle income, and high income). In general, higher-income households have greater demands for clean air than lower-income households. Each household is less willing to pay for clean air as the level of air quality increases.

means. One approach infers people's willingness to pay for clean air from the housing market on the grounds that households will pay more for a home located in an area with good air quality than for an otherwise identical home in an area with poor air quality.

Let's look at the estimates of the demand for clean air obtained from a statistical analysis of housing data for the Boston metropolitan area.[12] The statistical analysis correlates housing prices with the quality of air and other characteristics of the houses and the neighborhoods in which they are located. It then isolates and estimates the extent to which housing price differences are due only to air quality differences. These housing price differences vary by neighborhood and therefore by the income of the people who live in those neighborhoods. For example, we would expect people in higher-income neighborhoods to value an improvement in air quality more than people in lower-income neighborhoods.

[12]See David Harrison, Jr., and Daniel L. Rubinfeld, "Hedonic Housing Prices and the Demand for Clean Air," *Journal of Environmental Economics and Management* 5 (1978): 81–102.

More generally, people's demands for clean air, like their demands for most public goods, vary depending on the amount of clean air available and on their tastes. Figure 18.11 shows three such demand curves in which the value that people put on clean air depends on the level of nitrogen oxides and on their income.

The horizontal axis measures the level of air pollution in terms of parts per hundred million (pphm) of nitrogen oxides in the air, and the vertical axis measures each household's willingness to pay for a one-part-per-million reduction in the nitrogen oxide level. (The presumption is that a decrease in nitrogen oxides in the air corresponds to an improvement in air quality.) Each of the three demand curves is associated with a different income: the first with $8,500, the second with $11,500, and the third with $15,000. All apply to Boston in 1970.

The demand curves are upward-sloping because we are measuring pollution rather than clean air on the horizontal axis. As we would expect, the cleaner the air, the lower the willingness to pay for more of the good. These differences in the willingness to pay for clean air vary substantially. In Boston, for example, nitrogen oxide levels ranged from 3 to 9 pphm. A middle-income household earning $11,500 per year would be willing to pay roughly $800 for a 1 pphm reduction in nitrogen oxide levels, but the willingness-to-pay figure would jump to approximately $2,200 for a 1 pphm reduction when the level is 9 pphm.

Note also that the demand for clean air increases (shifts upward) with income. Higher-income households are willing to pay substantially more to obtain a small improvement in air quality than lower-income households. At low nitrogen oxide levels (3 pphm), the differential between low- and middle-income households is only $200, but at high levels (9 pphm), the differential increases to about $700.

With the quantitative information about the demand for clean air and separate estimates of the costs of improving air quality, we can determine whether the benefits of environmental regulations outweigh the costs. A study by the National Academy of Sciences of the regulations on automobile emissions did just this. The study found that automobile emissions controls would lower the level of pollutants such as nitrogen oxides by approximately 10 percent. The benefit to all residents of the United States of this 10 percent improvement in air quality was calculated to be approximately $2 billion. The study also estimated that it would cost somewhat less than $2 billion to install pollution control equipment in automobiles to meet the automobile emissions standards. The study concluded, therefore, that the benefits of the regulations did outweigh the costs.[13]

---

[13]See U.S. Senate, Committee on Public Works, *Air Quality and Automobile Emission Control*, Vol. 4 (Washington, D.C.: U.S. Government Printing Office, Sept. 1974).

18.6   Private Preferences for Public Goods

Government production of a public good is advantageous because the government has the power to assess taxes or fees to pay for it. But how can government determine how much of a public good to provide when the free rider problem gives people the incentive to misrepresent their preferences? In this section we discuss one mechanism for determining private preferences for goods that the government produces.

Voting is commonly used to decide allocation questions. For example, people vote directly on some local budget issues and elect legislators who vote on others. Many state and local referenda are based on *majority rule voting:* Each person has one vote, and the candidate or the issue that receives more than 50 percent of the votes wins. Let's see how majority rule voting determines the provision of public education. Figure 18.12 describes the preferences for spending on education (on a per pupil basis) of three citizens who are representative of three similar groups of people in the school district.

Curve W_1 gives the first citizen's willingness to pay for education, net of any required tax payments. The willingness to pay for each spending level is the maximum amount of money the citizen will pay to enjoy that spending level

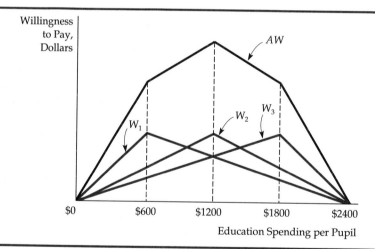

FIGURE 18.12   Determining the Level of Educational Spending.   The efficient level of educational spending is determined by summing the willingness to pay for education (net of tax payments) of each of three citizens. Curves W_1, W_2, and W_3 represent their willingness to pay, and curve AW represents the aggregate willingness to pay. The efficient level of spending is $1200 per pupil. The level of spending actually provided is the level demanded by the median voter. In this particular case, the median voter's preference (given by the peak of the W_2 curve) is also the efficient level.

rather than no spending at all.[14] In general, the benefit from increased spending on education increases as spending increases. But the tax payments required to pay for that education increase as well. The willingness-to-pay curve, which represents the net benefit of educational spending, initially slopes upward because the citizen places great value on relatively low spending levels. When spending increases beyond $600 per pupil, however, the value that the household puts on education increases at a diminishing rate, so the net benefit actually declines. Eventually, the spending level becomes so great (at $2400 per pupil) that the citizen is indifferent between this level of spending and no spending at all.

Curve W_2, which represents the second citizen's willingness to pay (net of taxes) is similarly shaped but reaches its maximum at a spending level of $1200 per pupil. Finally, W_3, the willingness to pay of the third citizen, peaks at $1800 per pupil.

The solid line labeled AW represents the aggregate willingness to pay for education—the vertical summation of the W_1, W_2, and W_3 curves. The AW curve provides a measure of the maximum amount that all three citizens are willing to pay to enjoy each spending level. As Figure 18.12 shows, the aggregate willingness to pay is maximized when $1200 per pupil is spent. Because the AW curve measures the benefit of spending net of the tax payments required to pay for that spending, the maximum point, $1200 per pupil, also represents the efficient level of spending.

Will majority rule voting achieve the efficient outcome in this case? Suppose the public must vote whether to spend $1200 or $600 per pupil. The first citizen will vote for $600, but the other two citizens will vote for $1200, which will then have been chosen by majority rule. In fact, $1200 per pupil will beat any other alternative in a majority rule vote. Thus, $1200 represents the most preferred alternative of the *median voter*, the citizen with the median or middle preference. (The first citizen prefers $600 and the third $1800.) *Under majority rule voting, the preferred spending level of the median voter will always win an election against any other alternative.*

But will the preference of the median voter be the efficient level of spending? The answer in this case is yes, because $1200 is efficient. But the preference of the median voter is often *not* the efficient spending level. Suppose the third citizen's preferences were the same as the second's. Then, the median voter's choice would still be $1200 per pupil, but the efficient level of spending would be less than $1200 (because the efficient level involves an average of the preferences of all three citizens). In this case, majority rule would lead to too much spending on education. And if we reversed the example so that the first and second citizens' preferences were identical, majority rule would generate too little educational spending.

---

[14]In other words, the willingness to pay measures the consumer surplus that the citizen enjoys when a particular level of spending is chosen.

Thus, majority rule voting allows the preferences of the median voter to determine referenda outcomes, but these outcomes need not be economically efficient. Majority rule is inefficient because it weighs each citizen's preference equally—the efficient outcome weighs each citizen's vote by his or her strength of preference.

Summary

1. There is an externality when a producer or a consumer affects the production or consumption activities of others in a manner that is not directly reflected in the market. Externalities cause market inefficiencies because they inhibit the ability of market prices to convey accurate information about how much to produce and how much to buy.

2. Pollution is a common example of an externality that leads to market failure. It can be corrected by emissions standards, emissions fees, or marketable emissions permits. When there is uncertainty about costs and benefits, any of these mechanisms can be preferable, depending on the shapes of the marginal social cost and marginal benefit curves.

3. Inefficiencies due to market failure may be eliminated through private bargaining among the affected parties. According to the Coase Theorem, the bargaining solution will be efficient when property rights are clearly specified, when transactions costs are zero, and when there is no strategic behavior. But bargaining is unlikely to generate an efficient outcome because parties frequently behave strategically.

4. Common property resources are not controlled by a single person and can be used without a price being paid. As a result of the free usage, an externality is created in which the current overuse of the resource harms those who might use it in the future.

5. Goods that private markets are not likely to produce efficiently are either nonrival or nonexclusive. Public goods are both. A good is nonrival if for any given level of production, the marginal cost of providing it to an additional consumer is zero. A good is nonexclusive if it is expensive or impossible to exclude people from consuming it.

6. A public good is provided efficiently when the vertical sum of the individual demands for the public good is equal to the marginal cost of producing it.

7. Majority rule voting is one way for citizens to voice their preference for public goods. Under majority rule, the level of spending provided will be that preferred by the median voter. This need not be the efficient outcome, however.

Questions for Review

1. Which of the following describes an externality and which does not? Explain the difference.

   a. A policy of restricted coffee exports in Brazil causes the U.S. price of coffee to rise, which in turn also causes the price of tea to increase.

   b. An advertising blimp distracts a motorist who then hits a telephone pole.

2. Compare and contrast the following three mechanisms for treating pollution externalities when the costs and benefits of abatement are uncertain: (a) an emissions fee, (b) an emissions standard, and (c) a system of transferable emissions permits.

3. When do externalities require government intervention, and when is such intervention unlikely to be necessary?

4. An emissions fee is paid to the government, whereas an injurer that is sued and is held liable pays damages directly to the party harmed by an externality. What differences in the behavior of victims might you expect to arise under these two arrangements?

5. Explain why free access to a common property resource generates an inefficient outcome.

6. Public goods are both nonrival and nonexclusive. Explain each of these terms and state clearly how they differ from each other.

7. Public television is funded in part by private donations, even though it can be watched for free by anyone with a television set. Can you explain this phenomenon in light of the free rider problem?

8. Explain why the median voter outcome need not be efficient when majority rule voting determines the level of public spending.

Exercises

1. Assume there are three groups in a community. Their demand curves for public television in hours of programming per hour, T, are given respectively by

$$W_1 = \$150 - T, \quad W_2 = \$200 - 2T, \quad W_3 = \$250 - T.$$

Suppose public television is a pure public good that can be produced at a constant marginal cost of $200 per hour.
   a. What is the efficient number of hours of public television?
   b. How much public television would a competitive private market provide?

2. Reconsider the common resource problem as given by Example 18.3. Suppose that crawfish popularity continues to increase, and that the demand curve shifts from $C = 0.401 - 0.0064 \, F$ to $C = 0.50 - 0.0064 \, F$. How does this shift in demand affect the actual crawfish catch, the efficient catch, and the social cost of common access? (Hint: Use the Marginal Social Cost and Private Cost curves given in the example.)

3. A beekeeper lives adjacent to an apple orchard. The orchard owner benefits from the bees because each hive pollinates about 1 acre of apple trees. The orchard owner pays nothing for this service, however, because the bees come to the orchard without his having to do anything. There are not enough bees to pollinate the entire orchard, and the orchard owner must complete the pollination by artificial means, at a cost of $10 per acre of trees.

Beekeeping has a marginal cost $MC = 10 + 2Q$, where Q is the number of beehives. Each hive yields $20 worth of honey.
   a. How many beehives will the beekeeper maintain?

b. Is this the economically efficient number of hives?

c. What changes would lead to the more efficient operation?

4. A number of firms have located in the western portion of town, after single-family residences took up the eastern portion. Each firm produces the same product and in the process emits noxious fumes, which adversely affect the residents of the community.

a. Explain why there is an externality created by the firms.

b. Do you think that private bargaining can resolve the problem with the externality? Explain.

c. How might the community determine the efficient level of air quality?

5. Four firms located at different points on a river dump various quantities of effluent into it. The effluent adversely affects the quality of swimming for homeowners who live downstream. These people can build swimming pools to avoid swimming in the river, and the firms can purchase filters that eliminate harmful chemicals in the material that is dumped in the river. As a policy adviser for a regional planning organization, how would you compare and contrast the following options for dealing with the harmful effect of the effluent:

a. An equal rate effluent fee on firms located on the river.

b. An equal standard per firm on the level of effluent to be dumped by each firm.

c. A transferable effluent permit system, in which the aggregate level of effluent is fixed and all firms receive identical permits.

6. The Georges Bank, a highly productive fishing area off New England, can be divided into two zones in terms of fish population. Zone A has the higher population per square mile but is subject to severe diminishing returns to fishing effort. The daily fish catch (in tons) in Zone A is

$$F_1 = 200(X_1) - 2(X_1)^2$$

where X_1 is the number of boats fishing there. Zone B has fewer fish per acre but is larger, and diminishing returns are less of a problem. Its daily fish catch is

$$F_2 = 100(X_2) - (X_2)^2$$

where X_2 is the number of boats fishing in Zone B. The marginal fish catch MFC in each zone can be represented as

$$MFC_1 = 200 - 4(X_1)$$

$$MFC_2 = 100 - 2(X_2)$$

There are 100 boats now licensed by the U.S. government to fish in these two zones. The fish are sold at $100 per ton. The total cost (capital and operating) per boat is constant at $1000 per day. Answer the following questions about this situation.

a. If the boats are allowed to fish where they want, with no government restriction, how many will fish in each zone? What will be the gross value of the catch?

b. If the U.S. government can restrict the boats, how many should be allocated to each zone? What will the gross value of the catch be? Assume the total number of boats remains at 100.

c. If additional fishermen want to buy boats and join the fishing fleet, should a government wishing to maximize the net value of the fish catch grant them licenses to do so? Why or why not?

The Basics of Regression

This appendix explains the basics of multiple regression analysis, using an example to illustrate its application in economics.[1] Multiple regression is a means of fitting economic relationships to data. It lets us quantify economic relationships and test hypotheses about them.

In a *linear regression*, the relationships that we fit to the data are of the following form:

$$Y = b_0 + b_1X_1 + b_2X_2 + \cdots + b_kX_k + e \qquad (A.1)$$

Equation (A.1) relates a *dependent* variable Y to several *independent* (or *explanatory*) variables, X_1, X_2, ... For example, in an equation with two independent variables, Y might be the demand for a good, X_1 its price, and X_2 income. The equation also includes an *error term e* that represents the collective influence of any omitted variables that may also affect Y (for example, prices of other goods, the weather, unexplainable shifts in consumers' tastes, etc.). Data are available for Y and the Xs, but the error term is assumed to be unobservable.

Note that Equation (A.1) must be linear in the *parameters*, but it need not be linear in the variables. For example, if Equation (A.1) represented a demand function, Y might be the *logarithm* of quantity (log Q), X the logarithm of price (log P), and Z the logarithm of income (log I):

$$\log Q = b_0 + b_1 \log P + b_2 \log I + e \qquad (A.2)$$

Our objective is to obtain *estimates* of the parameters b_0, b_1, . . . , b_k that provide a "best fit" to the data. We explain how this is done below.

An Example

Suppose we wish to explain and then forecast quarterly automobile sales in the United States. Let's start with a simplified case in which sales (in billions of dollars) S is the dependent variable that will be explained, and the only explanatory variable is the price of new automobiles P (measured by a new car price index scaled so that 1967 = 100). We could write this simple model as

$$S = b_0 + b_1P + e \qquad (A.3)$$

[1] For a textbook treatment of applied econometrics, see R. S. Pindyck and D. L. Rubinfeld, *Econometric Models and Economic Forecasts*, 2nd ed. (New York: McGraw-Hill, 1981).

In Equation (A.3), b_0 and b_1 are the parameters to be determined from the data, and e is the random error term. The parameter b_0 is the intercept, while b_1 is the slope—it measures the effect of a change in the new car price index on automobile sales.

Were no error term present, the relationship between S and P would be a straight line that describes the systematic relationship between the two variables. However, not all the actual observations fall on the line, so the error term e is required to account for omitted factors.

Estimation

Some criterion for a "best fit" is needed to choose values for the regression parameters. The criterion most often used is to *minimize the sum of squared residuals* between the actual values of Y and the fitted (or "predicted") values for Y obtained after equation (A.1) has been estimated. This is called the *least-squares* criterion. If we denote the estimated parameters (or *coefficients*) for the model in (A.1) by $\hat{b}_0, \hat{b}_1, \ldots, \hat{b}_k$, then the *predicted* or *fitted* values for Y are given by

$$\hat{Y} = \hat{b}_0 + \hat{b}_1 X_1 + \cdots + \hat{b}_k X_k \tag{A.4}$$

Figure A.1 illustrates this for our example in which there is a single independent variable. The data are shown as a scatter of points with sales on the vertical axis and price on the horizontal. The fitted regression line is drawn through the data points. The fitted value for sales associated with any particular value for the price values P_i is given by $\hat{S}_i = b_0 + \hat{b}_1 P_i$ (at point B).

For each data point, the regression *residual* is the difference between the actual and fitted value of the dependent variable. The residual $\hat{e}_i$, associated with data point A in the figure, is given by $\hat{e}_i = S_i - \hat{S}_i$. The parameter values are chosen so that when all the residuals are squared and then summed, the resulting sum is minimized. In this way positive errors and negative errors are treated symmetrically, and large errors are given a more-than-proportional weight. This criterion lets us do some simple statistical tests to help interpret the regression, as we will see shortly.

As an example of estimation, let's return to the two-variable model of auto sales given by equation (A.3). The result of fitting this equation to the data using the least-squares criterion is

$$\hat{S} = -25.5 + 0.57P \tag{A.5}$$

In equation (A.5), the intercept -25.5 indicates that if the price index were zero, sales would be -25.5 billion. The slope parameter indicates that a 1-unit increase in the price index for new cars leads to a \$0.57 billion increase in auto sales. This rather surprising result—an upward-sloping demand curve—is inconsistent with economic theory and should make us question the validity of

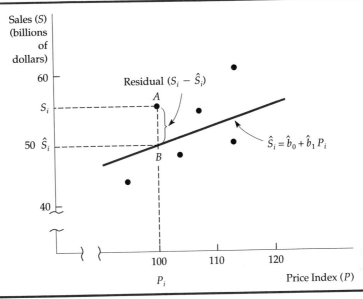

FIGURE A.1   Least-Squares.   The regression line is chosen to minimize the sum of squared residuals. The residual associated with price P_i is given by line AB.

our model. As we will see, we got this result because important determinants of sales were omitted from the model.

Let's expand the model to consider the possible effects of two additional explanatory variables, personal income I (in billions of dollars) and the rate of interest R (the three-month Treasury bill rate). The estimated regression when there are three explanatory variables is

$$\hat{S} = 51.1 - 0.42P + 0.046I - 0.84R \qquad (A.6)$$

The importance of including all important variables in the model is suggested by the change in the regression results after the income and interest rate variables are added. Note that the coefficient of the P variable has changed substantially, from 0.57 to -0.42. The coefficient -0.42 measures the effect of an increase in price on sales, *with the effect of interest rates and income held constant*. The negative price coefficient is consistent with a downward-sloping demand curve. Clearly the failure to control for interest rates and income leads to the false conclusion that sales and price are positively related.

The income coefficient, 0.046, tells us that for every \$1 billion increase in personal income in the United States, automobile sales are likely to increase by \$46 million (or \$0.046 billion). The interest rate coefficient reflects that for every one percentage point increase in the rate of interest, automobile sales are likely to fall by $840 million. Clearly, automobile sales are very sensitive to the cost of borrowing.

Statistical Tests

Our estimates of the true (but unknown) parameters are numbers that depend on the set of observations that we started with, that is, with our *sample*. With a different sample we would obtain different estimates.[2] If we continue to collect more and more samples and generate additional estimates, the estimates of each parameter will follow a probability distribution. This can be summarized by a *mean* and a measure of dispersion around that mean, a standard deviation that we refer to as the *standard error of the coefficient*.

For any particular sample, the least-squares estimates provide "best guesses" of the true underlying parameters. In fact, least-squares has several desirable properties. First, least-squares estimates are *unbiased*. Intuitively, this means that if we could run our regression over and over again with different samples, the average of the many estimates we obtained for each coefficient would be the true parameter. Second, least-squares are *consistent*, i.e., if our sample was very large, we would obtain estimates that came very close to the true parameters.

Once we have information about the probability distribution for each of the coefficients that we are estimating, we can make statistical statements about our knowledge of the true parameters. In econometric work we usually assume that the error term is normally distributed, from which it follows that the estimated parameters will also be normally distributed. The normal distribution has the property that the area within 1.96 standard errors of its mean is equal to 95 percent of the total area. With this information, we can ask the following question: Given that our parameter estimate is, say, the number $\hat{b}$, can we construct an interval around $\hat{b}$ such that there is a 95 percent probability that the true parameter lies within that interval? The answer is yes, and this 95 percent *confidence interval* is given by

$$\hat{b} \pm 1.96 \text{ (standard error of } \hat{b}) \tag{A.7}$$

Thus when working with an estimated regression equation, we must not only look at the *point* estimates, but also examine the standard errors of the coefficients to determine bounds for the true parameters.[3]

If a 95 percent confidence interval contains 0, then the true parameter b may actually be zero (even if our estimate $\hat{b}$ is not), which implies that the corre-

---

[2]The least-squares formula that generates these estimates is called the least-squares *estimator,* and its values vary from sample to sample.

[3]When there are fewer than 100 observations, we multiply the standard error by a number somewhat larger than 1.96.

sponding independent variable may *not* really affect the dependent variable, even if we thought it does and it seems to do so in our particular sample. We can test the hypothesis that a true parameter is actually equal to 0 by looking at its t-*statistic,* which is defined as

$$t = \frac{\hat{b}}{\text{standard error of } \hat{b}} \tag{A.8}$$

If the *t*-statistic is less than 1.96 in magnitude, the 95 percent confidence interval around $\hat{b}$ must include 0, and therefore there is at least a 5 percent chance that *b* equals 0. Because this means that we cannot reject the hypothesis that *b* equals 0, we therefore say that our estimate, whatever it may be, is *not statistically significant.* Conversely, if the *t*-statistic is greater than 1.96 in absolute value, we conclude the true value of *b* is unlikely to be 0 (intuitively: $\hat{b}$ is "too far" from 0 to be consistent with the true *b* being 0). In this case we reject the hypothesis that *b* = 0 and call our estimate *statistically significant.*

Equation (A.9) shows the multiple regression for our auto sales model (equation A.5) with a set of standard errors and *t*-statistics added:

$$\hat{S} = 51.1 \quad -0.42P \quad +0.046I \quad -0.84R$$
$$(9.4) \quad (0.13) \quad (0.006) \quad (0.32) \tag{A.9}$$
$$t = 5.44 \quad -3.23 \quad \quad 8.23 \quad \quad 2.63$$

The standard error of each estimated parameter is given in parentheses just below the parameter, and the corresponding *t*-statistics appear below that.

Let's begin by considering the price variable. The standard error of 0.13 is small relative to the coefficient -0.42. In fact, we can be 95 percent certain that the *true* value of the price coefficient is -0.42 plus or minus 1.96 standard deviations (i.e., -0.42 plus or minus $[1.96][0.13] = -0.42 \pm 0.26$). This puts the true value of the coefficient between -0.16 and -0.68. Because this range does not include zero, the effect of price is both significantly different from zero and negative. We can also see this from the *t*-statistic. The *t* of -3.23 reported in equation (A.9) for the price variable is equal to -0.42 divided by 0.13. Because this *t*-statistic exceeds 1.96 in absolute value, we can conclude that price is a significant determinant of auto sales.

Note that the income and interest rate variables are also significantly different from zero. The regression results tell us that an increase in income is likely to have a statistically significant positive effect on auto sales, whereas an increase in interest rates will have a significant negative effect.

Goodness of Fit

Reported regression results usually contain not only the point estimates of the parameters and their standard errors or *t*-statistics but also other information that tells us how closely the regression line fits the data. One statistic, the *standard error of the regression*, SER, is an estimate of the standard deviation of the regression error term e. A zero SER occurs whenever all the data points lie exactly on the regression line. Other things being equal, the larger the standard error of the regression, the poorer the fit of the data to the model will be. To decide whether the SER is large or small, we compare it in magnitude with the mean of the dependent variable. This comparison provides a measure of the *relative* size of the SER, a more meaningful statistic than its absolute size.

R-*squared* (R^2) is a statistic that measures the percentage of the variation in the dependent variable that is accounted for by all the explanatory variables.[4] Thus R^2 provides a measure of the overall goodness-of-fit of the multiple regression equation.[5] Its value ranges from 0 to 1. An R^2 of 0 means that the independent variables explain none of the variation of the dependent variable, while an R^2 of 1 means that the independent variables explain the variation in the dependent variable perfectly. The R-squared for the sales equation (A.9) is 0.94. This tells us that the three independent variables explain 94 percent of the variation in sales.

Note that a high R^2 does not by itself mean that the variables actually included in the model are the appropriate ones. First, the R^2 varies with the types of data being studied. Time series data with substantial upward growth usually generate much higher R^2s than do cross-section data. Second, the underlying economic theory provides a vital check. If a regression of auto sales on the price of wheat happened to yield a high R^2, we would question the model's reliability.

The overall reliability of a regression result depends on the formulation of the model. When studying an estimated regression we should consider things that might make the reported results suspicious. First, have variables that should appear in the relationship been omitted? That is, is the *specification* of the equation wrong? Second, is the functional form of the equation correct? For instance, should variables be in logarithms? Third, is there another relationship that relates one of the explanatory variables (say, X) to the dependent variable Y? If so, X and Y are jointly determined, and one must deal with a two-equation model, not one with a single equation. Finally, does adding or removing one or two data points result in a major change in the estimated coefficients i.e., is the equation *robust*? If not, one should be very careful not to overstate the importance or reliability of the results.

Economic Forecasting

A forecast is a prediction about the values of the dependent variable, given information about the explanatory variables. Often, we use regressions models to generate *ex ante* forecasts, in which we predict values of the dependent var-

---

[4]The variation in Y is the sum of the squared deviations of Y from its mean.

[5]R^2 and SER provide similar information about goodness of fit, because $R^2 = 1 - SER^2/Variance\ (Y)$.

iable beyond the time period over which the model has been estimated. (If we know the values of the explanatory variables, the forecast is *unconditional*; if they must be predicted as well, the forecast is *conditional* on these predictions.) Sometimes *ex post* forecasts, in which we predict what the value of the dependent variable would have been had the values of the independent variables been different, can be useful. An *ex post* forecast has a forecast period such that all values of the dependent and explanatory variables are known. Thus, *ex post* forecasts can be checked against existing data and provide a direct means of evaluating a model.

For example, reconsider the auto sales regression discussed above. In general, the forecasted value for auto sales is given by

$$\hat{S} = \hat{b}_0 + \hat{b}_1 P + \hat{b}_2 Y + \hat{b}_3 R + \hat{e} \tag{A.10}$$

where $\hat{e}$ is our prediction for the error term. Without additional information, we usually take $\hat{e}$ to be zero.

Then, to calculate the forecast we use the estimated sales equation:

$$\hat{S} = 51.1 - 0.42P + 0.046Y - 0.84R \tag{A.11}$$

We can use (A.11) to predict sales when, for example, $P = 100$, $Y = \$1$ trillion, and $R = 8$ percent. Then,

$$\hat{S} = 51.1 - 0.42(100) + 0.046(1000 \text{ billion}) - 0.84(8) = \$48.4 \text{ billion}.$$

Note that $48.4 billion is an *ex post* forecast for a time when $P = 100$, $Y = \$1$ trillion, and $R = 8$ percent.

Can one tell how reliable such a forecast is? The answer is yes for both *ex ante* and *ex post* forecasts, and the means is a statistic called the *standard error of forecast* (SEF). The SEF measures the standard deviation of the forecast error that is made within a sample in which the explanatory variables are known with certainty. Two sources of error are implicit in the SEF. The first source is the error term itself, because $\hat{e}$ may not equal 0 in the forecast period. The second source arises because the estimated parameters of the regression model may not be exactly equal to the true regression parameters (e.g., $\hat{b}_1 \neq b_1$).

The SEF can be used to determine how reliable a given forecast is. In equation (A.11), the SEF is $7.0 billion. If the sample size is large enough, the probability is roughly 95 percent that the predicted sales will be within 1.96 standard errors of the forecasted value. In this case, the 95 percent confidence interval is $48.4 billion ± $14.0 billion, i.e., from $34.4 billion to $62.4 billion.

Now suppose we wish to calculate an *ex ante* forecast for automobile sales, i.e., we wish to forecast sales at some date in the future, such as 1992. To do so, the forecast must be conditional, because we need to predict the values for the independent variables before calculating our forecast for automobile sales. Assume, for example, that our predictions of these variables are as follows: $\hat{P} = 200$, $\hat{Y} = \$5$ trillion, and $\hat{R} = 10$ percent. Then, our forecast is given by $\hat{P} = 51.1 - 0.42(200) + 0.046(5000 \text{ billion}) - 0.84(10) = \$190.8$ billion. Here $190.8 billion is an *ex ante* conditional forecast.

Because we are predicting the future, and the explanatory variables do not lie close to the means of the variables throughout our period of study, the SEF is equal to $8.2 billion, which is somewhat greater than the SEF that we calculated previously.[6] The 95 percent confidence interval associated with our forecast is the interval from $174.4 billion to $207.2 billion.

EXAMPLE A.1 THE DEMAND FOR COAL

Suppose we want to estimate the demand for bituminous coal (given by sales in tons per year, COAL), and then use the relationship to forecast future coal sales. We would expect the quantity demanded to depend on the price of coal (given by the Producer Price Index for coal, PCOAL) and on the price of a close substitute for coal (given by the Producer Price Index for natural gas, PGAS). Because coal is used to produce steel and electricity, we would also expect the level of steel production (given by the Federal Reserve Board Index of iron and steel production, FIS), and electricity production (given by the Federal Reserve Board Index of electric utility production, FEU) to be important demand determinants.

Our model of coal demand is therefore given by the following equation:

$$\text{COAL} = b_0 + b_1\,\text{PCOAL} + b_2\,\text{PGAS} + b_3\,\text{FIS} + b_4\,\text{FEU} + e$$

From our theory, we would expect the parameter b_1 to be negative, because the demand curve for coal is downward-sloping. We would also expect b_2 to be positive, because a higher price of natural gas should lead industrial consumers of energy to substitute coal for natural gas. Finally, we would expect both b_3 and b_4 to be positive, because the greater the production of steel and electricity, the greater the demand for coal.

This model was estimated by applying the least-squares criterion to monthly time-series data covering eight years. The estimated model (with t-statistics in parentheses) is as follows:

$$\text{COAL} = 12{,}262 + 92.34\,\text{FIS} + 118.57\,\text{FEU} - 48.90\,\text{PCOAL} + 118.91\,\text{PGAS}$$
$$\quad\quad (3.51)\quad (6.46)\quad\quad (7.14)\quad\quad\quad (-3.82)\quad\quad\quad (3.18)$$

$$R^2 = 0.692 \quad\quad \text{SER} = 120{,}000$$

Note that all the estimated coefficients have the signs that econometric theory would predict. Each coefficient is also statistically significantly different from zero, because the t-statistics are all greater than 1.96 in absolute value. The R^2 of 0.692 says that the model explains more than two-thirds of the variation in coal sales. The standard error of the regression SER is equal to 120,000 tons of

---

[6]Calculating the SEF is beyond the scope of this appendix. For details, see Pindyck and Rubinfeld, *Econometric Models and Economic Forecasts*, chapter 6.

TABLE A.1 Forecasting Coal Demand

	Forecast	Confidence Interval
1-month forecast (tons)	5.2 million	4.9 − 5.5 million
6-month forecast (tons)	4.7 million	4.4 − 5.0 million
12-month forecast (tons)	5.0 million	4.7 − 5.3 million

coal. Because the mean level of coal production was 3.9 million tons, SER represents approximately 3 percent of the mean value of the dependent variable. This suggests a reasonably good model fit.

Now suppose we want to use the estimated coal demand equation to forecast coal sales up to one year into the future. To do so, we substitute values for each of the explanatory values for the 12-month forecasting period into the estimated equation. We also estimate the standard error of forecast (the estimate is 0.17 million tons) and use it to calculate 95 percent confidence intervals for the forecasted values of coal demand. Some representative forecasts and confidence intervals are given in Table A.1 above.

Summary

1. Multiple regression is a means of fitting economic relationships to data.

2. The linear regression model, which relates one dependent variable to one or more independent variables, is usually estimated by choosing the intercept and slope parameters that minimize the sum of the squared residuals between the actual and predicted values of the dependent variable.

3. In a multiple-regression model, each slope coefficient measures the effect on the dependent variable of a change in the corresponding independent variable, holding the effects of all other interdependent variables constant.

4. A t-test can be used to test the hypothesis that a particular slope coefficient is different from zero.

5. The overall fit of the regression equation can be evaluated using the standard error of the regression (a value close to zero means a good fit), or R^2-squared (a value close to one means a good fit).

6. Regression models can be used to forecast future values of the dependent variable. The standard error of forecast (SEF) measures accuracy of the forecast.

Index